Beyond Me

Dissecting Ego To Find The Innate Love At Humanity's Core

A New Psychology As Philosophy

Robert Spencer Knotts

Beyond Me

Socrates, Emerson & Co.

Copyright 2018 - © - Robert Spencer Knotts

All rights reserved, including the right to reproduce this book or portions thereof in any form whatsoever.

Formatting: Wild Seas Formatting
(http://www.WildSeasFormatting.com)
Author photo: Keith Spencer
Cover design: Molly Seabrook

First edition: April 2019

For information:

Socrates, Emerson & Co.
604 NE 2nd Street, Suite 331,
Dania Beach, FL 33004

Library of Congress Control Number: TXu 2-118-846
ISBN: 978-1-7339127-0-9

Contents

Preface   Writing for a different reader. A broad overview of Beyond Me.   1

Chapter 1: Me, Until I'm More A search for individual identity. Profound self-obsession, profound self-doubt. Identity Failure introduced, an unrecognized human illness. Identity poses introduced. The new philosophy of Rational Faith offers one cure for Identity Failure. Identity Failure in bullet points.   7

Chapter 2: Untying The Knotts An author's experience steeped in the self. Learning to explore within. "Why Method." Dialogue, me with me. Testing the observations. A powerful introspection: "intrasentience."   21

Chapter 3: The Microscopic Me Websites of the mind. Nexes introduced, five categories of emotional strength. Vericepts introduced, "truth concepts." Quancepts introduced, particles of mind. Small things making big things within the mind as elsewhere in nature.   47

Chapter 4: Fundamentally, Me Psychogravity introduced, a gravity of the mind. Connection with quancepts, vericepts, nexes. Emotions through numerical values. Tigertails introduced, the refusal to let go of pain. Most Immediate Emotional Necessity. A Fundamental Law of Mind. Will to live.   73

Chapter 5: Deeply Determined Deepwanting introduced, a profound motivator. The difference between what we say we want and what we truly want. Dominance of the necessary. The 1 – 1,000 scale of emotional strength. The Free Will Paradox.   109

Chapter 6: To Me Or Not To Me Identity Failure and the Fundamental Law of Mind. Identity Failure defined in detail. Self-confusion. Identity Failure as "normal."   145

Chapter 7: A Fitting Experience The Grand Trio introduced. Identity poses explained. Irrational fixed identities based on realities. Origin of identity poses. Pose-weakeners and pose-strengtheners introduced, making psychological compromises. Identity Failure as a cause of repressed emotions   173

Chapter 8: All Too Normal Tick-tock, Identity Failure explained through a unique minute by minute drama and the use of numerical values.   243

Chapter 9: The Why Within You Identity Failure in others, observed and analyzed. Voices of the mind as Identity Failure. Identity Failure in you: a test. Will to die. The Fundamental Question, introduced. A thought experiment: the mud hut and you. Questions for you.   305

Chapter 10: A World Of Me Identity Failure as a new lens to understand our world. The lust for money and lust for power. Hitler and history's despots. Of terrorists, gangsters and thrill killers. Of slavery and racism. Dr. King and the "drum major instinct." Of patriotism, war and soldiers. Of sexism, abuse, addiction and self-harm. The new distractions. 345

Chapter 11: The Other Half Isolation and Identity Failure. Romance and romanticism, holdovers from the past. Being "unforgettable." Romance as addiction. Of sex and Identity Failure. Of gender roles and sexual identities. Extra challenges for the LGBTQ community. The romantic view of life. Primary emotions. Finding the innate love within each individual. The desire to be. 403

Chapter 12: A Bitter Pill The mindbody. Dr. John E. Sarno's great insights. Repressed Emotion Transfer introduced. The physical response to rage. Illness as the mind's misguided effort to help the individual. 447

Chapter 13: Physics Of The Mind Insights from within. Psychophysics 101. The details explained, combining the psychological concepts of Beyond Me into a unified theory. Chain of consciousness explored in detail. A logic of the mind. Of conditioning, coincidence and chance. A summary. An equation of human value. 483

PreScript The science as philosophy. A Fundamental Value. Rational Faith explained, its system and tenets. Beyond romanticism. Implications for childrearing. A new faith, defined. Seven Articles of Rational Faith. 553

Glossary 587

About The Author 593

Dedication

This book is dedicated to

Ralph Waldo Emerson

Dr. Jacob Bronowski

Dr. John E. Sarno

Each man hugely influenced my life and work in different ways. I am deeply grateful to all three.

"When good is near you, when you have life in yourself, it is not by any known or accustomed way; you shall not discern the footprints of any other; you shall not see the face of man; you shall not hear any name; the way, the thought, the good, shall be wholly strange and new."
Ralph Waldo Emerson

Preface

"What I am looking for is not out there, it is in me."
Helen Keller

A Different Read

You won't like this book.

Take my advice and close the cover if you're holding it now. Or click out of these pages if you're reading or listening with electronics of some sort. My intent is to be entirely truthful with you about everything that I set down here, from the first-page quotation mark to the final-page period. And that unsanded honesty begins now, at the beginning.

So I must preface all that follows with this caution: You're simply not going to feel any interest in what I have to tell you. You will much prefer some other book.

If you're most people, that is.

Obviously the chances suggest it's highly likely that you are most people. Your tastes probably place you among the vast swath of many, the wide mass of humanity. And nothing wrong with this, of course. You and all those fellow folks are part of an enormous psychological majority. This means that I may not know you personally but still can guess a few stray ends and odd pieces about your preferences.

First, you are uncomfortable thinking in concepts. And if that very sentence feels foreign to you, my point is quickly proven. Reflection about ideas isn't something you do. This is absolutely fine. Most people hate exploring ideas, intangible things such as human values and ethics, logic and rationality. If that's you, please understand that you perhaps should find something else to occupy your valuable time. Beyond Me is all about concepts, especially an expansive collection of new psychological concepts with crisply coined words to express them. My readers also will encounter some unique perspectives on familiar concepts. On the ageless debate of free will versus determinism, with discussions starting in Chapter 5 about what I call the Free Will Paradox. On romance and sexuality in Chapter 11, with a proposed redefinition of love that replaces sentimentality with something even more deeply human, a force dynamic and intrinsic to every psyche. On health as influenced by self-image, which you'll find in Chapter 12 ... And so on and so on. Each chapter offers fresh ideas about our humanity based almost entirely on more than four decades of direct carefully documented personal experience. You'll see what I mean.

Second, you prefer to rely on expert opinion about complex subjects rather than to weigh complicated facts for yourself. Again, no worries there. You stand firmly alongside the great preponderance of individuals when they are given challenging information. For most people, truth is a multiple choice test. They read or hear or somehow learn about this or that viewpoint on a difficult issue, then come across another viewpoint on the same issue and perhaps stumble into one or two more viewpoints still – and finally they pick which of those opinions seems best. That's how many persons think. They don't, really. They simply choose which outside idea to believe. A, B, C or D. Even experts love expert opinion. Life seems easier when choices are limited for you, all collectively tilted to favor the most impressive available authority. To the average person big titles carry big influence. If you're one of them, this book isn't for you.

Still here, still with me? Good for you. But wait ... there's more. Don't settle in quite yet for a long read.

Because Beyond Me is a long long read. Of necessity. I've tried to waste not a word, to leave no repetitious paragraph or superfluous page in the finished book. But the major themes of Beyond Me all require a meticulous construction, idea by idea, atop an unshakable foundation. That foundation is directly observed experience. To comprehend the most significant later psychological and philosophical concepts, then, my readers first must grasp fully the more basic earlier ideas, each explained in sufficient detail to understand them. So yes, my third point is this: You probably won't like my book because you prefer shorter books, simpler books. Or books shorter and simpler than Beyond Me anyway. To read and understand Beyond Me demands an emotional commitment – one that most people are unlikely to make.

Then there's this, the fourth and most important point of all: If you're most people, you don't seek a deep self-knowledge. Actually, you run from it. You change the subject of casual conversations that veer near genuine emotional insights. You prefer not to explore your more hidden feelings about yourself. Or anyone else. Chats that delve too seriously into human motivation feel particularly unwelcome so you work at keeping the discussions closer to the surface, focused on the obvious rather than the profound. Because, really, who knows why anyone does anything? Who cares? We are what we are so let's just deal with it and move on. If this is your approach to everyday life, my friend, believe me when I insist that Beyond Me is beyond you, far outside the parameters of your personality. The wise thing for you is just to put it down now, no harm done. And no hard feelings in the least by this author.

I understand. I have many friends and family members who feel exactly the same as you.

No, if you're most people, you won't just dislike this book. You'll hate it.

But maybe you're different. Maybe.

At its core Beyond Me probes for the intersection between psychology and philosophy based entirely on the empirical. Chapter by chapter it lays out a highly detailed personal experience intended to reveal some unrecognized facets of the human psyche, many hiding in plain sight. They've been there before us all along awaiting our closer observation.

For instance, students of the mind have long noted that our thoughts shape our individual existence. Beyond Me gives a detailed new account of human consciousness that says something else is going on. Something that shapes our lives a fraction of a moment before the thoughts ever happen. You'll read about that starting in Chapter 3, a topic that's further developed throughout the remainder of the book. Beyond Me posits new concepts to express the process by which we acquire our beliefs, how those beliefs affect our behavior and why this happens. It offers a precisely worded psychological law, explains key elements of human motivation through the use of numbers and presents an equation of three letters and two mathematical symbols that I believe expresses a profound truth of our humanity.

If this sounds intriguing to you then do press on, dear reader. Maybe you are different afterall.

A Different Reader

As a lifelong writer now in my mid-60s, I have learned that a project of this kind requires me to keep my readers in mind in a different way than any other book, play, poem, essay or article has demanded of me. I am devoting several years of my life to assembling observations that I firmly believe uncover something quite new about me, about you, about all human beings – why we live as we do and how we can live more fully. Beyond Me builds a step by step case aimed at proving that individuals must learn to transcend our self-obsessed egos. And providing a specific new method to do that. It's an intensely optimistic perspective on our humanity, every concept grounded in precisely dissected experience.

And at its end sits a new philosophy that was shaped entirely by these empirical observations. I call it Rational Faith. This philosophy offers concrete articles of faith based not on superstition or tradition but on observable human experience. Its ideas can be challenged, tested and proven. Or disproven. The last chapter of this book twines together those various threads. It also previews one additional and final volume of Beyond Me, now being written, which will explain the philosophical concepts in much greater detail. Nonetheless, the present work brings this discussion to a satisfying conclusion even as it sets up what will follow.

You could skip to that last chapter now to see for yourself, of course, or to any of the other chapters mentioned in this preface. I can sympathize with your curiosity. But you won't understand them yet, not really, not without first absorbing the foundational concepts and the empirical observations that justify them all along the pathway to Rational Faith. It is a patient process for any reader, necessarily so.

Yet in the early 21st Century, we live very impatient lives. Instant electronic communication has reprogrammed our nervous systems to anticipate a near constant stream of gratifications. Shallow gratifications, surely, but without them most of us quickly gravitate toward an anxious restlessness. We want the next pleasant emotional jolt. As a result, everything is shorter, brighter – even many of our books. Reality is compacted into 150 small pages, with large text spread out to make the content appear longer and weightier. For this, no one can be blamed. Authors want someone to read their work, understandably. As do publishers. Understandably. So now bookbuyers can grab it at lunch, read it after dinner, finish it before bed. Then grab the next book tomorrow.

Since first conceiving Beyond Me I've had to grapple with the unsettling realization that no one may want to read this book despite all my labors over such a long time. As I've explained, most people simply will not feel engaged by these discussions. And many other people will react to my claims in this preface with high skepticism. They won't recognize my name, won't consider my credentials sufficiently impressive to take me seriously. They will decide they're too busy, or perhaps too impatient, to find out for themselves if I'm telling the truth.

That's the probable reaction anyway. It's what I expect – at first.

I believe Beyond Me is the type of book that will find its audience over time. One person will tell the next. The ideas all make sense, examining everyday experience with new insights methodically explained. These chapters can help individuals better understand themselves and others by peering at our common problems through a clearer lens. And they also present solutions to those problems – solutions that really do work as they teach individuals to transcend a self-centered life in exchange for an existence that fulfills as it focuses on helping others. All of it experience-based, all of it welcoming critical examination. Beyond Me persuasively demonstrates that human beings are psychologically constructed to function fully by helping other human beings in meaningful ways. And the book argues that there is no other method for an individual to function fully.

You'll see what I mean.

To better cope with the emotional demands of writing Beyond Me I've drawn inspiration from James Joyce, who arguably created two of the most challenging books in human history. It seems Joyce held in mind one perfect reader for his works, someone who eagerly would summon the patience and interest to plow into the massive complexities of Ulysses or Finnegans Wake. So each day before writing I too imagined one reader, someone who surely exists not only in my imagination but also in the very real world. Someone who would stumble upon my book soon after publication. This reader is a genuine intellectual who firmly believes in empirical knowledge. My reader loves learning about psychology but does not yet possess any of the ideas I put forward in Beyond Me. And this reader judges my work entirely by the quality of the evidence, not by virtue of impressive degrees or prestigious affiliations.

This is a person of a more profound intellect. Of great curiosity combined with openmindedness. It is someone with a passion for thought, for new ideas, for self-knowledge. I trust this person to eagerly summon the patience and interest to plow into the considerable complexities of Beyond Me. They are unlike those of Ulysses or Finnegans Wake, no verbal puzzles to solve or literary techniques to decipher. Rather I've tried my hardest to make these observations, these ideas and theories, as clear and comprehensible as possible for me to do.

I am highly confident of my work. I want you to understand it. I want it to help you and in time to help others too.

I truly believe that it will. In time …

But I need your help for that. So if by now you feel emboldened to make this psychological sojourn, I can only extend my sincere thanks and wish you well as you depart. And I also ask you to recount for others all that you find revealed there. Without exaggeration or immodesty, I believe you will discover a book unlike any other you have read.

And if you like it, you are just the reader I've been writing for all these long years.

Chapter 1: Me, Until I'm More

"What a man thinks of himself, that is what determines his fate."
　　　　　　　　　Henry David Thoreau

Me Seeking Me

Who am I? Really?

And what?

For a long time, anyone's guess seemed every ounce as weighty as my own.

Weightier in some ways. Folks could tell the who and what somehow, they just knew by looking at me. And I knew how much they knew – indeed, I often simply accepted that others knew me much better than I knew me. These insightful people around me everywhere could discern whether I was a good person or a bad man. A nice guy or a meanhearted egomaniac. Intelligent or stupid. Funny or silly. Genuinely gifted or just barely mediocre.

Sometimes their judgments of my value were written down or spoken out, perhaps coming from a teacher when I was a child or from a girlfriend in adolescence or from an employer during my adulthood. But usually their opinions were more implied than overt, conveyed through expressions and behavior rather than with words. And I understood what they meant, all those expressions and all that behavior pointed toward me daily. I could interpret the significance.

Oddly enough, other people's notions about me shifted sharply from one day to the next, sometimes hour by hour. They might reveal that I was meanhearted on Monday but nice once more as Wednesday unfolded. I could recognize my intelligence reflected in one man's enthusiasm toward me by morning but see only my stupidity in another man's afternoon indifference.

What was wrong with me?

Something, clearly.

Why else would these outside judgments of Bob so often differ drastically from my judgments of Bob? I felt sure that I really was a good person, a nice guy, intelligent and funny and perhaps even gifted. This was the me I knew, the human being I'd lived with all my life. But I couldn't relax into these identities as the true Bob. Not when so many other people saw someone else entirely in gazing my way. They spotted the flaws that I couldn't. They uncovered the weaknesses and the shortcomings that I was unable to identify from within.

So I continued to search for the real Bob in their eyes, in their words and their expressions and their behavior. Sometimes my flaws alone glared back at me. But often I detected approval of me in these outside opinions, some fashion of appreciation in their words or expressions or behavior. And I felt validated as a human being. Because another human being had found in Bob some important quality of the human being I believed Bob should be.

That experience always intoxicated me. And no other experience could ever quite equal it.

I craved this sensation constantly. Craved appreciation, approval, validation from parents and siblings, from teachers and bosses, from friends and from lovers and from spouses. From readers and editors and publishers. For some reason I needed other people to perceive significant aspects of my personality exactly as I perceived them. The closer that these other ideas of me came to my ideas of me, the happier my life. I felt important, I felt valuable. My existence seemed good.

But whenever the outer and inner opinions of Bob drifted too far apart, I became miserable. Other people perceived significant aspects of my personality differently than I perceived them. Maybe I really wasn't so important, maybe I was worth far less than I'd imagined. My existence might not be much good at all.

And whenever this happened, my profound self-doubts carried me right back to those same three questions.

Who am I? Really?

And what?

That was life as me, more or less, as I had known it for some half century before starting work on this book. I think I was about 10 years old when it began: the painful self-awareness, the worrying, the confusion about my identity. From then on I strained and tussled with the world daily to attract validation of Bob anywhere I could find it. In any form – words or expressions or behavior. Even outside events could make me feel more valuable as a human being if they went my way, or less if they turned against my interests. There seemed a mad, contradictory, absurdly neurotic character to this effort at finding exterior confirmation of my life's value.

But I accepted that my continual quest for appreciation was just human nature. Afterall, everyone else appeared to want the approval of others too, with some folks needing less than me and some requiring much more of it. Each member of the human race seemed irrationally angered by even the slightest criticism, irrationally joyful over even the faintest praise. Experience had well taught me the results of the right word or expression or behavior directed at someone – and the consequences of the wrong word or expression or behavior.

Why? What was going on … really?

Day in and day out all our lives, we were like addicts scrounging for another fix of the one thing that made our existence feel bearable.

We craved the next injection of me.

All Me & More

That's how things were.

My needs, my wants, my tastes, my preferences. Particularly the appreciation of anything me by anyone other than me. I might care about the people who weren't Bob – and I surely did. I always had tried hard to be kind, generous, loving. A nice guy, a good person. But somehow out in the world every day among all the non-Bobs, I found that Bob usually advanced to the foreground of my immediate interests no matter how well-meaning my treatment of others.

No question that this perpetual search for me had infected my life with anxiety, but there was nothing to be done. Anxiety and terrible fears, as you will soon read. Seething angers as well and that gnawing sense of something fundamentally flawed about me. My addiction to outside appreciation had awarded me with these unwanted prizes of my humanity, the trophies of a commonplace psychological dilemma: Like almost everybody else, I needed others to validate my understanding of myself, to agree with me about me. But others often didn't agree, and never completely so. No one got me as I got me, though I kept grasping in both my professional life and my personal life for someone who could.

I remained puzzled and pained. Who was I really? And what was I?

Over the years I noticed that my self-doubts caused me many many many problems in the world. You will read about some of those too. Unhealthy relationships, destructive reactions, irrational judgments that bubbled up from my relentless confusions about Bob, the who and the what of me. I also observed that my problems frequently twisted themselves into problems for other people, from family to friends to colleagues to strangers. Things I said or didn't say to them, things I did or didn't do. My obsession with me created most of the damage that I inflicted upon both myself and my fellow human beings. The older I got, the clearer this became to me.

And over the years I noticed that you suffered precisely the same misery, whoever you were. The details didn't matter much. As best I could surmise after travels on six continents, every other you on the planet also suffered from it. In this way you each were pretty much like me. Meaning it was all "me" nearly all the time for everyone of us. The daily pursuit of immediate self-interest, the anxieties and fears and angers that emerged from our individual doubts, the desperation for outside appreciation, the harm to ourselves and others when the appreciation didn't come. Every individual at the center of their personal universe.

Oh yes, I concluded, this is human nature. Clearly just the way we are.

Except that it isn't.

Identities, Failed

Year by year by year during my life's meandering journey, the dark confusions about me very slowly crystallized into a revelation: My worst struggles weren't the necessary result of my basic nature as a human being. They were an affliction, a malady of mind.

I needed more than 40 years of introspection and reflection to discover that my battles over self-concept are understood best as the result of a wondrously complex psychological phenomenon I've named "Identity Failure." Or "I.F." for brevity. Here is the broadbrush outline of that mental process as I observe it: I am forever attempting to validate an array of self-images that I've accumulated during my life as accurate representations of me. They exist only in my head. I call these "identity poses." Bob-the-writer, Bob-the-nice-guy, Bob-the-deep-thinker and so on, every one of them a distortion of reality. Each identity pose is an inflexible and irrational concept of Bob, though a large part of me firmly feels they are real. But I also was raised to believe that I need confirmation by other people in order to fully accept these self-images as true components of my personality. I may see myself as Bob-the-nice-guy … until someone else suggests I'm not so nice. Then the doubts return. Unfortunately for many reasons I'll explain later, I never can confirm these self-images to my satisfaction for long, if at all. This causes the repeated collapse of my inner sense of individual identity to varying degrees. My belief in Bob's best qualities begins to fail – Identity Failure.

Put more simply, my mind has stored a diverse group of identities that I feel represent Bob. However I've learned to trust other people's opinions of Bob as the required validation for my own beliefs about me. When their opinions differ from my opinions, I'm prone to a self-doubt so profound that it amounts to a condition more ominous than the word "doubt" suggests. It is self-confusion, a frighteningly deep mental uncertainty about who and what I am. This is the partial failure of some portion of my self-concept, of my identity as I believe it to be. At these times there's the me I know from within and the me I accept from the opinions of others.

As I have experienced this, I. F. can give me the worst feelings I ever have. At its most severe, a sense of worthlessness, hopelessness, a crushing anxiety and terror of the future. So my mind automatically attempts anything and everything to avoid an awareness of Identity Failure. I try to pretend the conflict doesn't exist.

And yet somehow I frequently gravitate toward feeling bad about myself, even though rationally that's the last thing I want.

For most of my life I have suffered from this acquired corruption of my psyche, an illness learned by living. I mean those words literally.

Identity Failure is an illness. But that's an idea much more easily written than completely accepted by me. I've endured more miseries than I can express in my decades-long efforts to thoroughly understand this process – and to fully believe that it's true.

I believe it now. Fully and completely. Yes, I believe that Identity Failure is a genuine psychological disease.

But even this difficult level of self-confidence came to me with less emotional resistance than believing in the unavoidable extension of my personal condition. Because I could not escape the logical conclusion that almost every other human being must suffer from the same psychological disease. We each are struggling to confirm through the judgments of the outside world a broad collection of individual self-images that are entirely irrational. When we can't do it, we each become sick. Year by year by year, sick at heart, sick of mind. We constantly look for our true selves in the eyes of others, but the truth isn't there.

At last after great struggle, then, I have come to accept that many of humanity's worst problems are the problems of Identity Failure.

Most of Beyond Me is devoted to firmly grounding my audacious claim in directly observed personal experience, carefully explaining each new chunk of observation before laying it down as a foundation for the next piece. Should you take time to read all these chunks and pieces just as carefully, I believe, you are likely to end up agreeing with many of my conclusions.

Perhaps you've even noticed this tendency toward destructive self-doubt in your own life. Perhaps you've observed it in others. Possibly you have witnessed some of the extensive damage that accompanies Identity Failure in any of its many forms – consequences you will find clearly explained throughout this book. The condition goes by many everyday names. "Insecurity" is among the most common. Or maybe "shyness" or "lack of confidence" or "social anxiety." Or on the other end of the same spectrum, "arrogance," "egotism," sometimes "megalomania." The malady masks itself inside many of our fears and angers, within our betrayals and hostilities and aggressions.

If that concept of a pervasive unrecognized psychological illness seems exceptionally troubling to you, allow me to offer reassurances.

I think instead my theory is supremely hopeful. It means that humanity is not permanently anchored to many of our most selfish individual tendencies and the serious problems they produce in society: Our need for feelings of importance in the eyes of others, to prove our value through any means available, to establish supremacy whether among individuals, groups or nations, in large ways and small. The unending bickering and petty envy, the tribal mentality that foments the distrust and dislike and diminishment of people considered rivals, violence in the name of virtue. Prejudice, racism, even war. Read on, please. You will see what I mean.

Identity Failure also is hopeful precisely because it is learned – and can be unlearned. Children can be raised with innovative methods that avoid this psychological infection. Adults can discover new emotional resources and fresh ways of seeing reality that lessen or eliminate our me-first approach to living, the emotional driver of Identity Failure. That's the underlying problem in a nutshell: Too much me. So much "me" that we each become ill with it. The new philosophy of Rational Faith outlined in this volume offers individuals one way out. It's a solution to me-first that is not idealistic but rather highly practical, rooted entirely in the psyche's natural soils.

Rational Faith is a cure for Identity Failure.

I eventually concluded that Identity Failure is a genuine illness for a variety of reasons. First, it is both abnormal and harmful, like any other disease of the mind or body. I have observed directly that Identity Failure is a corruption of the intrinsic elements of my makeup, those functions that appear to be most naturally and fundamentally me. I now recognize that from my earliest moments of life onward I was taught the lessons of I.F. by my parents, then by the rest of my family and their friends, then by almost everyone else I ever met. The need for outside appreciation isn't basic to me ... or to you. It's an idea embedded in our minds over time, warping who we really are.

Second, the characteristics of Identity Failure are the same in you as in me as in all of us. And they become obvious once clearly identified. The basic causes are identical, the basic symptoms are identical, with variations only in specifics and intensity as in many diseases. Maybe my mother and brother most influenced the formation of damaging self-images in my early childhood, but it was a father and sister for you, to simplify the point. My need for outside validation may be more frequent and crippling than yours, perhaps, but the underlying psychological dynamics are the same.

Third, identifying this disease as what it is helps us to more accurately map its boundaries. We can view the condition with less confusion by encompassing the vast complexities of Identity Failure within the concept of illness. Initially this will make attacks on my theory simpler too – no doubt at first many will scoff at the notion of a nearly universal human sickness fueling many of our troubles as the species Homo sapiens. Ultimately, though, I feel confident this concept will gain a wide acceptance. After you understand the details, it simply makes sense.

The self-caused problems of humanity are very real. So is Identity Failure.

A Damaged Architecture

When I observe the complicated processes of I.F. at work within my head, I see my interaction with outside forces constantly weakening a fundamentally sound psychological structure. Basically, a mind corrupted through contact with the world. In one sense my mind is like a solidly constructed building with plumbing systems that quickly rust out from polluted city water. Overall most things are just fine, thank you – but some serious damage is causing leaks.

This is an important point. It means most things about my psyche are just fine, thank you. The damage isn't structural but rather something that can be reached and repaired. I know this because for more than 45 years to date I've closely observed and teased out and examined many other of my psychological components, the forces that I now understand exist in complex interplay with Identity Failure. In the next chapter you'll read about the how and why of all this observing and teasing and examining. That work has engaged a massive amount of my time during the whole of my adult life. A highly detailed, rationally defensible knowledge of my basic nature, and yours to the extent possible, has been my obsession since the age of 20.

At this writing, I am 66-years-old.

And as I've observed the mental processes at work in my own head, one unifying experience became apparent: All of them in some form or fashion clearly are connected to my concept of myself. More specifically, to my belief in my individual value. Each time I explore an element of my psyche deeply enough, I bump into this same truth. My life essentially revolves around the way I view me, just as Thoreau suggested: "What a man thinks of himself, that is what determines his fate." Every interior waterway leads me back to that same home port, no matter how hard I've looked for other harbors during my prolonged psychological voyages. I've found no escape from this circuit, no alternative route. I exist in a perpetual search for the value of my own existence.

Even more significantly, this search appears to be a basic psychological function. It is built-in – intrinsic, automatic, necessary. I have come to regard it as a fundamental mechanism of my mind, a process at the core of many other subtly interconnected processes that together determine my thoughts and feelings and actions. It is me at the deepest level. It's how I work.

That is what I watch happening daily within my mind.

These may strike you as startling statements. They even strike me that way if I imagine coming across them for the first time. Believe me, I entirely understand how surprising my assertions might seem to a person without any similar experiences. And how skeptical some readers may feel at the beginning of my narrative. I can't blame you one bit. I'll make a pitch for my authenticity shortly. For now, though, let me offer a few facts that may be somewhat reassuring: I am a fully functioning longtime professional writer with a background in serious investigative journalism. So I'm accustomed to sorting through complicated information to find meaningful patterns just as I've done with my psychological observations. I've written 24 published books and five plays. I'm also the founder of an empirically based 501(c)3 nonprofit group, the Humanity Project, which provides free youth and parental programs sponsored by well-known national and regional organizations. I have conceived each of those programs, creating them from scratch either entirely alone or with partial assistance from students. I might add that there's no history of insanity in my family. I hope this helps a little.

I also should mention that I've stumbled into writings and quotes that bolstered my confidence in the validity of my evolving ideas. The observation by Henry David Thoreau is among dozens of examples, many of which I'll include in Beyond Me. Some are centuries old, others more current. Some have seemed to confirm that I was on the right track, others have offered invaluable guidance as I groped for the proper direction. The writings of Ralph Waldo Emerson, especially his profound essay "Self-Reliance," have been hugely important to my own explorations over the past 20 years or so. To me, his insights into human behavior even today remain too little understood. And in Chapter 10, you'll find Dr. Martin Luther King Jr. quoted at length about what he called "the drum major instinct," a psychological urge for superiority that all people must learn to control. In part Dr. King said, "And think of what has happened in history as a result of this perverted use of the drum major instinct. It has led to the most tragic prejudice, the most tragic expressions of man's inhumanity to man." I believe that Dr. King's drum major instinct is Identity Failure by yet another name.

Still, I have tried throughout this book to keep in mind my focus on personal experience above all else. In recent years I came across another grand quote, this one attributed to Buddha. I think of it often: "Believe nothing just because a so-called wise person said it. Believe nothing just because a belief is generally held. Believe nothing just because it is said in ancient books. Believe nothing just because it is said to be of divine origin. Believe nothing just because someone else believes it. Believe only what you yourself test and judge to be true."

Whether Buddha really said this or not, I couldn't express the idea better. Or agree with it more – after I myself tested it and judged it to be true, of course. For me now, experience is god, the only reliable path toward truth.

More Than Me

As this self-reliant attitude in me matured I finally have been emboldened to write an unlikely book, a first-hand account of one human being's long and probing explorations within his mind as well as the equally lengthy effort to make sense of them. I've accumulated a large volume of empirical evidence to back up my findings, many thousands of meticulously examined observations. Beyond Me will present that case for whatever it may be worth.

If nothing else this book offers an extraordinarily detailed examination of one psyche's fundamental functions as viewed from within. I don't believe another psychological journey has been carried out in just this way over such an expanse of time, with a clearly written record left behind. This alone surely has some value.

To comprehend with an open attitude what I saw for myself inside me, I was forced to create many new concepts expressed by many new names. Those "crisply coined words" mentioned in my preface. You will encounter vericepts and quancepts among them, discrete basic units of interpreted experience that appear integral to the psychological function that leads to our thoughts. You'll also read about deepwanting and psychogravity, tigertails and pose-strengtheners, primary emotions and chain of consciousness and psychophysics among others.

But quite honestly I would not have written Beyond Me if I believed it an account of one man's mind only, no matter how accurate the facts. That was never the point. My need to better understand me was equaled by my need to better understand you. And to help you understand us. I can't explore inside the mind of anyone else. But I can transfer my understanding of me to my interpretations of the people around me. What I've discovered is that these psychological insights work much better than anything I'd believed in the past. Folks simply make a lot more sense to me now. And this realization enables me to interact more effectively with others by seeing them as perpetually locked in identity struggles of their own, every fellow human being reflected back to me by the light of my self-knowledge. I don't claim to know all about you. I claim only to know a lot about me, as far as I can determine anyhow. Since I operate under the assumption that you and I share many fundamental similarities, far more than differences, I also can't avoid the notion that my self-knowledge must tell me something meaningful about you.

That's the reason Beyond Me exists. Because I passionately believe that my knowledge of me helps greatly to comprehend you. Whoever you are. And because I believe just as passionately that the information in this book also can help you to more fully comprehend you – and everyone else. All of it with the ultimate aim of backlighting

Identity Failure as a central human problem, throwing this psychological dynamic into sharp relief. And then discovering ways in which individuals may transcend Identity Failure, fulfilling more of our humanity. To me, no lesser purpose would have seemed worth the trouble.

Behavior that once bewildered me bewilders me no more, disturbing as that behavior nonetheless may still be. Things large and small around me have come into clearer focus. People who talk ceaselessly and others who talk almost never. Exercisers who obsessively pump barbells and eaters who can't pass by a candy machine. Smartphone users who never look up and homeless men who shout obscenities toward the top of skyscrapers. Poor villagers who endure war because they won't stop hating other poor villagers who live across some invisible national boundary. Suicide bombers and petty demanding bosses and aggressive drivers. Dictators who provoke military confrontations to grab new territories and profit-obsessed CEOs who value money above everything else. Good things too, the creators and doers and helpers and inspirers among us – it all seems more understandable. My list is endless and I see examples everywhere. It's how I view our world based on my four and a half decades of intensive introspection.

A very personal knowledge has metamorphosed for me into what seems a more universal insight.

The me portion of this knowledge can be boiled down to several main points:

- I believe that psychological conflicts about my identity were learned, Identity Failure as a byproduct of my upbringing and other experiences.
- I believe that Identity Failure caused many of my problems and the problems I created for others, the source of my destructive tendencies.
- I believe that I could have been raised in ways that would have avoided Identity Failure and the damage it caused.
- I believe that I can unlearn Identity Failure, improving life as an adult for me and those around me.
- Finally, and most significantly, I believe that unlearning Identity Failure frees an intrinsic human drive to be, to exist,

and to focus this drive on helping other people overcome their problems.

By delving deeply into me, I connected in the end with us. That's the most profound lesson I've learned. A me-first lifestyle isn't in my true self-interest and doesn't work. By unlearning Identity Failure, I rise above my self-obsessed ego to recognize something more basic to my nature: a need for self-expression that only can be deeply fulfilled by service to my fellow human beings. So much me ultimately becomes more than me.

The wider applications of this personal knowledge also can be boiled down to several main points:

- I believe that many of humanity's serious personal and social problems result from individual struggles with identity. Society's troubles often are an extension of Identity Failure as continually played out by struggling individuals forced to interact.
- I believe that children can be raised in ways that will avoid Identity Failure and the damage it causes.
- I believe this innovative childrearing slowly will improve society at the individual level, one person at a time.
- I believe that adults can unlearn Identity Failure, improving life for themselves and those around them.
- I believe that unlearning Identity Failure will free their intrinsic human drive to be, allowing them to focus this drive on helping other people overcome their problems.

You and I and everyone else are psychologically constructed to fulfill our individual humanity by helping others. Helping not in superficial ways but in purposeful ways that express those individual qualities we value most in ourselves. We each must find the best that's in us and discover how to use it to improve life for other human beings. I hope to establish that this form of sharing isn't a selfless act carried out by do-gooders. It's in our own deepest self-interest, always. In every situation. And that's why more individuals may want to do it as part of their daily lives.

Yes, I know. More of those startling statements, aren't they? I entirely agree with you. But the goal of Beyond Me is to express my ideas as clearly as possible – and then to back them all up with carefully detailed empirical evidence. The evidence for those bullet points takes up the remainder of this book.

Right, wrong or somewhere in the middle, I will be entirely truthful with you about everything just as promised in the preface. Why would I waste my time on anything else? I had battled against myself for two decades to keep all of these observations and concepts and theories private. I felt certain no one would believe me. Then I wrestled with myself for two decades more to find the confidence to express them. The process has been excruciating. Today, though, I recognize that creating Beyond Me is a central part of living my own philosophy of Rational Faith, a life focused on sharing my experience to help other people. In the end, I am a writer. What else could I have done? I can't say for certain how my book will aid other people, of course, but I have my hopes.

At this point you well may ask yourself, "Who is this guy to offer such sweeping conclusions?" Who indeed? And what? I had asked the same questions with a fearful impact too often during my long resistance to this full accounting of my experiences. But now it is time to write everything down, setting aside my doubts. Instead I take some comfort in a comment by Albert Einstein: "It's not that I'm so smart, it's just that I stay with problems longer." Without implying comparisons between his insights and mine, I nonetheless find in this instance that I can borrow Einstein's sentiments fairly.

I have stayed with this problem: Who am I? Really? And what?

I have stayed with it for a long time, for a very long time.

Chapter 2: Untying The Knotts

"Everyone thinks of changing the world but no one thinks of changing himself."
Leo Tolstoy

Finding My Way

No doubt you have doubts.

Doubts about Beyond Me, perhaps a few, perhaps many. And I suppose that's as it should be in the early going. My surprising theories require much solid evidence I've so far had no opportunity to present. Assuming you're coming at this book without any knowledge of my earlier work, I'm probably safe with one assumption more: You're not sure what to make of me either. Not yet.

Before the extensive empirical evidence that backs up my ideas, then, you need some better sense of the author. How could I possibly know what I claim to know? Have I really experienced all I say I've experienced, observed directly all the psychological forces I insist I've seen for myself?

In short, you likely harbor some version of those same three questions I'd asked myself for so long. You well may wonder, with justification: "Who is this man? Really? And what?"

So in this chapter, let me tell you.

In the pages immediately ahead you'll come across several brief accounts of youthful experiences that will require you to judge whether I've offered accurate descriptions of my past. I can assure you that I have, here just as everywhere else in Beyond Me. But you decide for yourself. Ask if the detail and specificity feel real to you. Do the separate events hang together as a credible whole? Do they make sense based on your own experience? On the other hand, the short professional history I'll provide is mostly factual material that you can verify easily in our Internet world. If you don't believe that I've done what I say I've done, by all means check things out for yourself.

There's no reason to wonder about any of it.

But to begin our sojourn into me and beyond, I should go back some distance. A long distance.

Since at least my teenage years, I've always felt there must be some "right" way to live my life. Some approach that would allow me to do well by other individuals as I also enjoyed my days – and most importantly, developed whatever talents I could share with the world. Some system or technique of human fulfillment that worked for me in every situation, a key that never failed to unlock the best of Bob. Yet I could never find it.

During an abbreviated college career, I was an English major who took psychology and philosophy classes each semester in the hope of discovering some answers. I tried to fit into the pre-made clothes of existentialism, Freudianism, behaviorism, egoism, pragmatism. But the ideas I gleaned from the theories of other people in time all failed to work in my own life. They didn't make sense to me in some way or other. Nonetheless I believed that any genuine solution must be found at the basic level of human nature somehow, a philosophy or psychology that had been created as an extension of the mind's most profound functions, both the rational and the irrational. The best part of each individual would only emerge by exploring the deepest part of each individual.

This notion still seems inescapable. How can someone possibly understand what anything should do without first knowing what it can do? How it is made, how it works at a fundamental level... For me, any other approach would seem like trying to drive a car without learning the basic functions of the brakes and accelerator and tires and the engine's need for gasoline. With no meaningful knowledge of what a car really is, I can't understand its limitations or its possibilities. I can't make an informed decision about what it can do. And what it should do.

Around that point, at age 20, an intense emotional crisis catapulted me on an interior search for Bob that has lasted until this moment more than four and a half decades later. I'll tell you more about that trauma shortly. But I realized then that no matter how long was needed I would have to dig by myself for the foundation of who and what I am, for a highly detailed rational understanding of the things that make me me. There was nothing noble about this journey, believe me. It appeared the only possible route toward the "right" way to live my life. I felt obsessed to know how I worked – and why. Which in turn would help me to determine what I could do and should do. My personal ethics would be assembled piece by piece from a science I would carry out with my own methods, using introspection to acquire self-knowledge.

I insert the word "science" in this context somewhat hesitantly and only after years of reflection and doubt about its accuracy. Is it really science in some fashion that I've been doing? It always has seemed so to me. And I believe that it is science in this sense: My conclusions were formed largely from extensive direct observations that were analyzed critically over many years, then molded slowly into hypotheses that I tested and re-tested at length in all the ways I could find. As I'll explain later in the book, I also believe that at least some of these hypotheses lend themselves to experiment and confirmation by others who might wish to challenge them. The word "science" just means knowledge, yes, but science as our society uses the word involves a process of outside verification. I would welcome wholeheartedly any effort that subjects my theories to rigorous tests. If you're interested after reading this book, please test away and let me know what you learn.

Observation and experimentation aimed at uncovering truth appear built into my nature in some manner just as investigative reporting came naturally. I say that without pretension or pride but rather as a simple fact about who I seem to be. Whenever something feels very important to me, I experience a visceral need to analyze it independent of any source of information outside me. I have to figure things out for myself until the major parts seem to fit together comfortably. Until I can feel that it makes sense. This compulsion has caused me a great deal of misery, as you might imagine. But it's one important reason that Beyond Me exists.

By now I have watched my psyche's mechanisms so often and at such length that I'm certain I can see in great detail how they operate. It's like looking many times daily through some interior microscope. I have never read of someone doing something similar over such a prolonged period, but who knows? Perhaps thousands have done so. In any case I'm often reminded of William Beaumont, the 19th Century physician who for years could directly peer into a gunshot victim's open digestive system to watch its functions firsthand. I often enjoy what may be a similar sense of discovery when observing the functions of my mind. There is no visible gurgle and pulse of these psychological processes, of course, but I can feel them happening inside me all the same.

Baby Steps

Because genuine introspection is so unfamiliar to most people I know, I probably should define the term as I mean it.

For me, introspection is the in-depth observation of my many emotions, feelings, thoughts, beliefs and other elements that seem to appear in my mind from nowhere, followed by efforts to understand them and so better understand the whole of me. It has taken much practice to see myself in any depth through my own eyes, not those of my family or friends or colleagues. And to learn how to sensitively detect, isolate and analyze the complex interwoven processes I find there. Introspection goes much deeper than the kind of pondering I do when deciding whether to move into a new apartment or take another job or whatever the choice. I sense that's what my friends mean if they talk about introspection: reflection that includes taking one's feelings into account, basically. But to me introspection involves looking far, far inward, then focusing on the things I find through feeling them.

As Gloucester says in King Lear, "I see it feelingly." That's how introspection is for me.

I believe that many folks vastly underestimate the capabilities of our mind. Our capacity for profound and insightful introspection is one of the areas where we sell ourselves short, in my judgment.

But why? Afterall, even a small child can tell if she's happy or sad, angry or frightened, amused or surprised. How does she know? How do any of us? We feel it, that's all. We are able to know what we feel and articulate it. That's the beginning of introspection, those moments when the little girl says, "I hit you because I was angry because you took away my book." She looked inside, observed how she felt, why she felt it and how the feeling made her react, then accurately reported her psychological experience.

Surely one of our great gifts as humans is not just self-awareness, the knowledge of our own existence, but also self-observation, the knowledge of what we're feeling, thinking, believing, experiencing at any given moment. To say we have this ability is not pop psychology or New Age speculation. It's experienced fact.

Most great athletes learn a related skill. They call it "listening to their bodies." They teach themselves how to feel physical sensations many of us would overlook, to understand why they're feeling those things and what it all means. That slight tingling in the elbow might suggest that they've started to throw the baseball too hard. That hint of a sore spot on their toe could indicate that they've been running on the wrong part of their foot. They have simply refined something we all do without thinking about it, like our ability to feel a sensation in our stomach and know we have eaten too much buttered popcorn. We all listen to our bodies. Some people are simply much better at this than others.

In a similar way I've worked hard to refine the ability to listen to my mind. It starts with that same skill we all have. Like the little girl, anyone can tell what surface emotion they're feeling if they try for a moment. If they observe their inner world a bit longer, they probably can explain more or less why they're feeling what they are. At least they can offer one or two of the most obvious reasons.

But in a more sophisticated form, introspection involves feeling that surface emotion, then peeling it back to reveal deeper and deeper layers of emotions as well as the memories, thoughts, beliefs and other mental elements that we uncover along the way. Then, if we want, we can separate those elements, examining each in detail. In time, we can learn to observe the interplay of these elements, even exploring how and why they function as they do.

As I've labored at this within myself, I have employed a meticulous observation that "sees" by feeling my way cautiously through the complicated psychological mechanisms. This introspective process usually is slow, often painfully slow, skeptical and repetitious and tedious. But it provides me with direct interior observations that over many years have led to meaningful insights about my mind. I then test and re-test these insights in myriad ways as I challenge them from every angle I can imagine during day to day living over many more years.

I believe that introspection is both an innate and a learned ability. How much we learn depends on how much we develop this very human talent.

Inward Turned

It is hard enough to be honest with myself. About anything. It is hardest of all to be honest with myself about myself. The strength of my most thoroughly buried feelings about Bob can seem overwhelming when first experienced. But through determined and repeated attempts over the long decades I have learned to work my way past this barrier. Even today this sometimes requires an exhausting amount of emotional effort, a kind of intense willpower to break the instinctive resistance. For the most part, though, I manage to crack down through the surface pretty well much of the time.

I suspect that introspective tendencies fairly early became ingrained in my personality. I grew up essentially as an only child, my brother and sister 13 and 10 years older respectively, and I wasn't popular with other kids until high school. I usually got good grades and on many evenings I poured through the encyclopedia for hours, skipping around from article to article as various topics tugged my interest. As a boy, I was sensitive and alone and lonely. I turned inward.

A bit later I could sense a growing attraction to the hippie subculture. The self-examining music, the free-your-mind Eastern-tinted philosophy, the camaraderie with anyone who wore long hair, eventually some of the "mind-expanding" drugs, though mostly just pot. It appealed to me intensely. The attitudes of the 60s and early 70s that inspired me to grow my own hair past shoulder-length held out the hope of a better world by being better individuals. That's how I saw the movement anyway. As one of my favorite songs of the era told us, "You hold the key to love and fear, all in your trembling hand. Just one key unlocks them both. It's there at your command." I believed it then. I believe it now. The difference is that now I can explain why this seems true and what that means. Those lyrics no longer represent to me merely some sweet sentiment about a hopeful future but rather a lovely poetic expression of a reality I've experienced.

Very soon, though, none of that would matter to me as much for a while. I wasn't sure I would survive to be part of any world, better or not.

Examining Hellfire

By this time in my life, I was living with a girlfriend. I was far too young for that responsibility, barely 18 when we moved in together. She was a very pretty, artistic and gentle young woman named Lydia. During our time together, as we prepared to leave college and move to Switzerland, I suffered a massive anxiety attack one morning while cramming for an abnormal psychology exam. The room suddenly swirled and then briefly faded to black before things at last cleared into focus, accompanied by a terror I'd never felt.

At 20, I was sure I was losing my mind.

I discovered myself consigned to some form of psychological inferno, a nearly constant searing fear so hellish I wouldn't have imagined it possible before the experience. I endured some rounds of talk therapy without success. But my torments only worsened as I dwelled on my fear throughout each day and deep into many nights. Eventually I concluded that my only hope of relief was to engineer some escape for myself. I'd always trusted my intellect – it would have to rescue me now.

I was fiercely motivated. We've all had the experience of being somewhere we desperately wanted to leave, whether in a hospital room or a jail cell or an unhappy marital bed or some other prison. I felt that I was in a place much much worse than any of those. And my determination to leave was total. I believed my one chance of living any worthwhile existence must be hidden inside me already, awaiting discovery: Somewhere within my psyche, something was terribly wrong with Bob. And I had to find and fix it.

So after Lydia and I parted ways the following year, I began to sit alone for hours nearly every evening trying to look into my head. Slowly, very slowly over many months, I taught myself to directly observe the complexities and subtleties of my own thoughts and emotions. To feel them, to see them. I learned the language of my mind.

Seeing What's What Within

I first began to explore my psyche more deeply by asking the same question endlessly. "Why?" I would isolate one tiny area of my feelings or thoughts, or examine one possible specific source of my misery, probing for the "why" about it from every perspective I could imagine, each time attempting to answer that question as honestly as possible. If I wasn't satisfied with my response, if my answer felt too easy or simplistic or phony in any way, I'd try again. And again. Over and over and over, examining a subject for hours and days and weeks. And months, when necessary.

This may sound extreme but that's what I did. It seemed the best approach I could find and I sometimes still use it to this day. I named this process back then, simply if unpoetically, my "why method."

I feel it may be valuable to offer a detailed concrete example of how that method works for me. This true particular is given at some length for one reason: It helps to show one of the ways I learned introspection. This incident wasn't my initial introspective attempt by any means. I'm not sure exactly what issue I tackled first but I know that it pre-dated this example. I also should note that this happened more than 40 years ago. Honestly, it is difficult to remember all the specifics with the certainty I'd like, though the longer I try to recall them the more things come back to me. But I believe the following is a fair approximation of how sometime around 1975 I examined one particular issue related to my consuming anxiety.

Preparing To Ask Why

As suggested, I had sought advice from several therapists before plunging into my problems head-on alone. One of these psychologists decided that I could be suffering from "a conflict of values." Her vague comment didn't help at the time but did stay with me. And many months later, this is one of the areas I began to explore with my inward investigative method.

I recall sitting cross-legged in my usual spot one evening, on top of my blue sleeping bag in the frigid rundown apartment I rented for $95 a month in Burlington, Vermont. The place was infested with cockroaches and my sleeping bag was stretched out on a thin lounge chair pad that served as my mattress. And in that usual spot I was doing the usual thing, wondering what on earth was wrong with me. Why did I feel so overcome with anxiety all the time? I already had devoted long, long thought to many different aspects of my personality and my life. I believed I was making slow progress. I was feeling less afraid, bit by bit. Then I recalled the therapist's remark, as I often had before now. This time, though, I began to give it serious reflection.

What could she have meant? Maybe I did have a problem with my values somehow. I certainly didn't believe in all of the same values as my parents. She was right about that much anyway. Could this really cause all my anxious distress?

So I picked an entry point from among my experience and stepped in to see for myself. First, what did I view as my parents' key values? I created a long mental list, which included things I agreed with such as honesty, integrity, kindness. But the list included other values such as their strong disapproval of alcohol and profanity and an apparent total disinterest in sexuality. Then I made my own list of values, especially those that I felt differed from my parents. My list at the time included an appreciation for alcohol and marijuana, an enjoyment of profanity and a powerful lusty sexuality. Well, so what? What about all of that?

As I thought about these issues, I could feel the tense tangle of emotions they knotted inside me. I believed that this indicated I might be on to something of importance. I was, indeed, resisting my efforts to examine these questions. I didn't want to look any further.

So I dug in more firmly. I would try to ignore that tension as much as possible to re-focus on the subject at hand. What, if any, role in producing my anxiety was played by the partial disagreement with my parents' values? I hadn't discussed any of this with my folks, ever. I had kept my differences with them to myself. Why should it bother me?

I remember feeling skeptical that this conflict alone could create all my emotional agonies but I suspected it might be part of a very complex problem. To understand the large problem, I felt certain, I would have to explore and fully understand each of its component parts. Including this one, the conflict of values.

Digging Deeper

I started to ask myself about these different values of mine. How did I feel about my recreational drinking and pot smoking? About using swear words when my parents never breathed a profanity? About my sexuality when sex didn't seem to exist in our home, when I never even saw my parents kiss or hold hands?

It was quickly obvious that the sexual issue was much more significant to me than the others. I could feel this, could sense the strength of emotion generated by thinking about sex in the context of my parents. I probably did feel guilty at times about the smoking and drinking, maybe even about cursing so freely around friends. And as best I can remember, I spent a serious number of hours examining over and over whether I might be hiding from some deeper truth about my feelings in these areas.

Eventually I decided that sex was likely the main culprit when it came to values. By then I had asked myself countless times: How did I really feel about sex? Was I hiding from any conflicts? Did I harbor some concealed negative attitudes toward sexuality?

On the surface I seemed very much a proponent of the free-love, let-it-all-hang-out ethos of the era. I had not only lived with a girlfriend but I also had enjoyed a few other partners by age 22. Sex was healthy and brought people together. It was a positive force in the world. That's always what I had told myself and my friends. But I wondered now: Were some very different feelings about sexuality somewhere below my openminded exterior?

I kept probing. After long evenings given to this kind of introspection I finally understood that there was more to my sexuality, something tucked well beneath my superficial joie de vivre. I did have some problem feeling comfortable with sex, it now appeared.

But how? And why?

Dialogue, Me With Me

So I just dug in again.

Question to myself: All right now, think! What do you really feel about sex? Look deeper.

Answer: "As best I can tell, I genuinely love it. Really! I can feel that's the truth."

Question: Anything else, though? Look again! Deeper.

Answer: "Too often I want it and can't get it. I think about it a lot. I need it. Very much. It's important to me."

I don't recall how many hours or rounds of this type of self-analysis were necessary before I finally came up with a new answer: "I feel obsessed with sex sometimes."

I found this response very interesting. It was true. But I hadn't recognized it until that instant. I didn't know where all this was leading but that realization seemed significant.

More questions and answers then, me to me.

Why? Why do you feel obsessed?

"I think about it all the time. I am intensely attracted to dozens of women every day of my life. I wish I could have sex with all of them. I want to try unconventional sex, such as a ménage a trois and other group sexual stuff. That seems excessive!"

Why?

"No one else I know seems to feel that way. I guess I feel kind of weird about these feelings. Yes. Yes, that's true. I do, I can feel that now. I feel weird about it."

Why?

"I don't know. It just feels strange."

Once more, I don't remember how long or how many times I had to press myself for something deeper. I do know that in my earlier days of introspection I often had to ask myself the same specific question dozens of times over many evenings. Even now I occasionally must do the same thing before scraping down to the bedrock bottom level of my feelings. But when I reach that place, I recognize it absolutely.

Dialogue, Part Two

And so I continued to confront myself about my values: Why? Why does your sexual attitude seem strange to you? Look again!

"Because it doesn't seem normal!"

But why? You must know this answer somewhere inside you. Just keep looking!

"Because it's not something I feel people should want to do, I guess. Part of me feels it's fine. I don't have any problem with other people doing it, if I knew any people who were. But I don't know any. And part of me doesn't feel it's fine. Not for me."

Why? Why do you feel it isn't OK for you?

"Like I said, it's kind of weird somehow."

But why, why do you feel that way?

"I don't … Maybe. It's like there's something wrong with me or something. I think that's kind of how it makes me feel. Yeah, I think so. Being so obsessed with sex makes me feel like I've got something wrong with me somehow, I think."

Why?

"Like I said, because no one else is this way."

No one? How do you know what is in people's heads?

"Well, sure, I've read magazine articles about people who feel like me. Some of them do have sex with lots of different partners, I suppose. I'm all for that. I've believed in the idea of free love since high school. But … "

But … what?

"I don't feel like I should want that. Not me."

Why?

"It's weird, it's excessive in some way. Part of me feels that."

But you just said you think it's OK.

"But I feel … I don't know. I guess I feel like I'm weird and excessive and strange for wanting it. I don't know a single person who seems to have the obsession with sex that I do. So it's not so much that the sex itself is weird. For others anyway. It's that I'm terrible for wanting it so much."

You can see where this is going, layer by layer cutting around the issue, each time a little deeper. Again, I don't know how long and how many levels of "why" were needed to arrive at that point but I know this is a much-compressed version of what actually happened. However lengthy the analysis, though, I realized at last what looks obvious now. That I felt more than just terrible. I felt as if there was something really wrong with me because I constantly was interested in sex – and as a young adult, interested in some untraditional styles of sex at that. In this way, I was fundamentally flawed as a human being.

In other words, yes, a conflict of values in some sense. I grew up in a Beaver Cleaver suburbia where people supposedly lived their lives of simple motivations and innocent actions. Everyone around me as a boy appeared that way, my family and my family's friends and my friends' families. Sexuality didn't exist there. And sex wasn't shown on TV or in the movies that I saw. Kids told dirty jokes about it. Which was exactly how we thought of them – "dirty" jokes. But no one I knew in real life seemed to truly crave sex as I did. Certainly not my parents in any way, shape or form. Most certainly not with multiple partners. How awful, how strange of me! Only a flawed person would want that, clearly.

Without ever being aware of it, I'd compared the superficial behavior of people in my youth with the complicated, surging human feelings inside me. I then had formed the conclusion that I was deeply weird. Something was wrong with me for feeling as I did about sex. By the time I was 22-years-old that sense of strangeness was very intense. And it was directly in conflict with my genuine beliefs about the great value of sexuality, which even at that age was something I'd considered at length.

Observing The Observer

This was not the ultimate source of my anxiety, as things turned out. But it relates directly to what I uncovered at the bottom of it all, the much deeper and broader problem of Identity Failure that I'll fully explain later. The example here provided merely offers a specific glimpse into my early introspective process. The conclusions about my sexual conflict were important to me but, in retrospect, hardly uncommon or unexpected.

I do feel I should touch for now on one point I'd passed over quickly before this – the idea of testing and re-testing introspective insights.

I'm acutely aware that the act of observation changes what is being observed. But that's true in subatomic physics as well as in psychological experiments or field research into orangutans or anything else. With introspection, the distortions tend to coalesce around seeing what I want to see instead of seeing what's there. I recognize the endless possibilities for self-deception and misinterpretation when looking within my own mind. So before launching into any form of self-analysis, I try everything possible to diminish that problem. I begin by aggressively looking for any indicators of emotional resistance to the topic, telltale symptoms of tension that might betray hiding something from myself or other warnings of potential inaccuracy. Do I have trouble focusing on the issue? Does my eye twitch or my heart rate jump? Do I feel afraid or anxious when I begin to examine the subject? And so on …

Once I'm satisfied that I want to find the truth without undue emotional aversion, I begin to look persistently for answers. I've always formed my conclusions slowly, cautiously and with great skepticism. And then I try to check the answers with that same slow, cautious, skeptical approach. I often would not accept the validity of what seemed like important insights about my mind until I had experienced, questioned, challenged, re-experienced and tested them repeatedly, hundreds or even thousands of times over many years. I mean that literally. I didn't tally these numbers back then, obviously. But I know how obsessively I looked for the truth inside me and for how long. It's not hard to do a very broad calculation now.

I've found that I seem to be able to discover the truth in myself if I honestly want to find it and persist for whatever period is needed. That may sound too simple. But it's what I've experienced. The validity of my observations about me has played out over time in my daily life as well as through insights that eventually assembled themselves into a coherent vision of my humanity and the humanity of others. By which I mean this book, Beyond Me. In the end, my introspective conclusions over the past 45 years have worked. That may be the most meaningful test of all.

But along that path I've also created many specific methods to confirm or disprove my interior observations. Briefly for the moment, I'll describe one technique that I often use. It requires considerable imagination, mentally projecting myself into a variety of different scenarios to experience my reactions. I probably drew on this technique to begin checking the insights into my sexual conflict. I don't know that I did so exactly as I'm about to describe it, but I feel sure that I carried out a very similar process. This is how it works.

How I Would Feel ... If

In that sexual conflict, I felt there was something flawed about me partly because no one seemed to share my intense sexuality. To challenge and test my conclusion, I would imagine a hypothetical situation designed to uncover ways I might be wrong about it. A type of thought experiment, really.

I might ask myself this question: What if a person I had long respected suddenly told me they felt about sex just as I did? Would I view my sexual attitudes differently? Would it make any difference? I then imagined a specific person and created all the details necessary for me to react emotionally to their sexual admission, to feel as naturally as possible what I would feel in real life. Then I would note whether my own sexuality felt detectably less strange to me as a result. Did the tension I observed inside me earlier when I explored my deeper sexual feelings begin to diminish or increase or stay the same after listening to this imaginary admission? I would continue the process by asking myself other questions to experience the scene as vividly as possible, looking at my inner responses from a variety of angles.

Then I might try a different scenario: What if my parents had behaved in ways that seemed to agree with my sexual values? How would that feel to me? Once more I imagined the particulars in sufficient detail to experience a significant portion of any feelings that would surface if that situation were true. Enough genuine feelings, I'm convinced, that the method offered me one valuable approach to self-verification. Actors routinely draw deep emotions from themselves by reacting genuinely to fictional scenarios. I seem able to do the same thing.

If my internal responses to these scenarios time after time consistently appeared to verify my conclusion about a sexual conflict, I accepted this as one small piece of evidence that my interpretation could be correct. I may have learned that, yes, I'd have felt more "normal" about my sexuality if my parents had held similar attitudes. The difference between the reality and the imaginary was revealing: In truth my folks saw sex one way, I saw it another. And I had reacted by feeling flawed as a human being. But the minute their attitudes and mine agreed, I felt much less flawed. This altered response would suggest that my real-life disagreement with my parents was important to me, creating part of the confusion over my values. And at least part of my anxiety.

That's only one of the ways I would start to question my conclusions about this sexual conflict, of course. And not necessarily the best or most reliable method. But it serves for the moment as a quick example of how I often began to test my introspective insights.

A Connoisseur Of Mind

Learning to understand the nuances of mind is very much like developing any other highly refined powers of observation, as I noted earlier. And one analogy keeps popping into my head – the appreciation of fine wines.

Naturally I'm not suggesting that one activity is as significant as the other or that learning to understand the complex flavors of wine is nearly as challenging as learning to understand complex psychological motivations. It's just that in recent years I've come to a somewhat more sophisticated enjoyment of wines. And as I gain, sip by sip, a greater analytical insight into wine's subtleties, I am seeing some clear analogies with the process of gaining introspective insight.

Back when I first sampled wine, in my late teens, I knew nothing.

Remember, my parents didn't drink. All wine tasted odd and musty somehow. About this same time I learned that most decent wine was either red or white and each color had a different kind of flavor. The reds seemed richer, the whites lighter in taste.

As I occasionally tasted a few different brands heading into my early 20s, I acquired a bit more knowledge. Wine could have what people called a "dry" quality, which struck me as a peculiar term for a liquid. Or it could be "sweet," which apparently was the opposite characteristic of dry. Wine wasn't my beverage of choice then. So my experience over the next 10 years or so was extremely limited. And I don't recall that my appreciation of wines during this time developed much beyond what I've described.

Refining The Palate

In my 30s and 40s I started to travel overseas more often, sampling a wider variety of foods. This broadened my exposure to good wines and I began to like them a lot. I learned that cabernet sauvignon was my favorite variety, as it still is. My palate began to distinguish somewhat finer differences, for example the distinction between a cab and a pinot. But I still couldn't really describe what I was tasting in any meaningful way.

Many years later this began to change. I had started attending wine tastings on a semi-regular basis, sitting among people much more knowledgeable about wine than I ever will be. I listened to them, discussed and debated with them, as we compared some 16 wines in an evening. Each time I felt myself learning more about how to understand what's what in wines, much as I have learned to understand what's what in my mind. I also made sure to go with a designated driver.

One of the skills I'm still gaining is the ability to isolate a specific aroma or taste. For some reason this hasn't been easy for me. People around me talk about the wine's "cinnamon nose" or "blackberry finish" and I know what they mean. But I often can't place the scent or flavor clearly enough to agree or disagree. I've reached a level where I may recognize an aroma in the wine similar to a smell I know, but I still can't identify what had produced that scent in the past. I can't put a name to it. Was that really cinnamon, or was it nutmeg?

Blackberry or strawberry? Earth or leather?

This process especially reminds me of the step-by-step learning that took place in developing my introspective skills. For example, I had to teach myself to tease out specific emotions among the complex blend of general feelings. What am I really sensing within me? Is that anger or jealousy? Fear or self-contempt? Genuine affection for someone or only a desire to be loved by them?

Just as with wine, we can acquire the ability to compare the present with the past and to distinguish the dominant from the subtle, the significant from the minor. And in time, to understand a great deal more about what goes on inside us. The proof of this hopeful notion is there within your own mind. You need only look for it yourself.

"Intrasentience"

All of this introspective work on my part has brought me to another of my immodest conclusions. I've realized that I need a better word than "introspection" to describe what I experience. Being a professional writer, I'm more than happy to take the liberty of inventing a word that works better: "intrasentience." The adjective, of course, would be "intrasentient."

For me the term "introspection" is tainted with too many associations, connotations and meanings to really express the idea I have in mind. As I'd pointed out before, "introspection" often involves a relatively shallow form of self-reflection. On the other hand, "intrasentience" captures the spirit of my experiences within. It suggests to me an inner type of perception, a consciousness of psychological events based on feeling. And that's precisely how this phenomenon seems to me – like another sense. Throughout my adulthood, I've had the impression of seeing inside myself.

Not that I ever intended to tell anyone about my psychological observations. Quite the opposite. They were my most tightly guarded secret.

So for about the first 20 years of serious intrasentience, I mentioned my inner explorations to no one. Not even a vague reference during conversation. Not to my first wife, not to my family, not to my friends. I was sure nobody would believe me. But I found that my self-knowledge was enormously useful in everyday life as well as in my journalism career. It provided important insights about myself and often helped me more accurately penetrate the motivations of others. I knew what to ask people because I understood something of their emotions.

From early 1980 until December 1994 I worked as a reporter without any thought of ever revealing my private psychological theories. I'd had no formal journalistic training other than as a columnist at my high school newspaper. I clambered my way into a full-time daily reporting job by 1983 at the age of 30, one freelance story at a time to build my experience and refine my talents. My employers found that I had a distinct flair for probing deeply and accurately into a broad range of stories that included exposing the misdeeds of international con artists, local politicians, school bus drivers, auto safety experts and big-time developers. I saw these articles as my effort to change the world in whatever small ways I could. As both a broadcast and print reporter, I grabbed for every opportunity to spend weeks or months investigating an issue as thoroughly as possible. I'm proud to say that I never was asked to issue a retraction or correction of any kind in all those years. I took accuracy seriously. Eventually I wrote a series of exposes for the South Florida Sun Sentinel that resulted in the arrest and conviction of a notorious British con man who preyed on AIDS and cancer patients, a frighteningly convincing criminal known in England as "King Con." This lengthy investigation provided the basis of my novel, Hard News. And I spent nearly a year investigating air bag injuries a full half-decade before the federal government acknowledged any problems with the technology, a series of reports widely picked up by news media around the United States. I loved my work and I still feel profound respect for talented, persistent journalists.

After my escape from the corporate meddling that afflicted daily journalism by then, I began to write many articles for national publications that included Sports Illustrated, Reader's Digest, USA Weekend, Family Circle, The New York Times and Travel & Leisure, among others. I also formed a relationship with the then-fledgling Arthur Frommer's Budget Travel, ultimately being named as a contributing editor who worked mainly on enterprise stories for the popular magazine. At the same time I authored children's books –

nonfiction on topics that varied as widely as the Olympics, Florida history and Native peoples, fiction in thriller tales with positive messages about self-trust and overcoming fear. Between 1995 and 2002 I wrote 24 published books, 23 of these for young readers.

In 2000, I was commissioned by the distinguished regional theater, Coconut Grove Playhouse, to create a play with music about teen suicide. It had a very successful run, mostly in South Florida schools where guidance counselors told us the intense drama may have saved lives. The play apparently opened up some students to conversations about their suicidal feelings, talks initiated by the counselors who had recorded the names of kids crying during the production.

That same year, after welcoming the Millennium with my second wife in Athens at the foot of the Acropolis, I began to sense a shift in my outlook. I now viewed myself more as a serious writer, less as a journalist. Writers write what they know and what they are. How could I avoid my own psychological story, which even then seemed to me a darned good tale? And as my writing matured, I started to accept the inevitability of putting all this down on paper. As a freelance writer I also had much more time for reflection and examination of my inner world than any time since my 20s. By around 1997, I looked on these interior explorations no longer as fueled only by my private need for emotional health and a psychology based system of personal ethics. I wanted to understand my unique journey much more fully – and to get all the key details right.

I searched for holes in my knowledge of me, gaps that needed filling in the tale before I could write. Of course there were many, very many. And so my decades-old need to know myself deeply was augmented by an investigator's quest for accurate answers. Answers based on experience, answers that would stand up to critical examination. I had no idea precisely what I would do with those answers or whether anyone would want to read them. Or how long finding them would require. But I could feel this was where the reporting of my personal story should take me.

I was influenced and aided greatly by many thinkers whose work I still massively admire. In later chapters I'll explain these influences more fully for reasons that will become apparent. But for now I should acknowledge a deep debt to people who include the previously mentioned Ralph Waldo Emerson and Henry David Thoreau as well as Mohandas K. Gandhi, all of whose portraits hang over my desk. And to Dr. Jacob Bronowski and Dr. John Sarno. And Socrates and Shakespeare and Leonardo too as well as Buddha and some of his more insightful latter-day followers. Among many others.

But it was a simple quotation I stumbled across in 2004 that most helped my psychological experience to gel over the following ten years leading up to Beyond Me – and my discovery of Identity Failure. One day at a Barnes and Noble bookstore in Fort Lauderdale, I somewhat sheepishly pulled down a volume that intrigued me: "How to Win Friends and Influence People" by Dale Carnegie. I did this sheepishly because I'd been afflicted throughout my life with an excessive fear of outside opinions about me. What if someone saw me reading this book? Surely I'd look like some sort of loser. So I stood among the stacks and browsed passages quickly, scanning this chapter and that chapter. I found Carnegie's book insightful. Then in Chapter 2, I read the quote that instantly connected with so much of my experience over the previous 30 years. It was by William James, the great psychologist and philosopher, who wrote: "The deepest principle in human nature is the craving to be appreciated." Sigmund Freud and John Dewey were among those who recognized the same need, Carnegie noted, calling it "the desire to be great" and "the desire to be important," respectively. Wow.

I read the whole book a year later. But the quote by James obsessed me from that first moment on. By this time I had come to recognize that I was overwhelmingly my own worst enemy. I was probably too aware of my deepest insecurities and of my continual struggle for, yes, appreciation. Dewey's use of the word "importance" felt even closer to the mark for me. Like nearly all of us, I wanted others to "get" me. My importance, my value. And when my wife or family, friends or colleagues didn't get me at all, I doubted myself. Was I really who and what I so strongly believed myself to be?

I'd also clearly seen that my problems resulted in large part from this profound insecurity – and so did the problems I caused other people. My insecurities often were reflected in my behavior. Through careful observation of my wife and others, through remembering and through reading and through any other method I could gather reliable information, I slowly started to believe that the same thing likely was true for many if not most human beings. We each appeared deeply torn about ourselves as individuals, about the who and what of our identities. It seemed mostly just a matter of degree, this person struggling more obviously with ego than that person. Two plays, some poems and various writings by me explored my growing conviction that the world's troubles often were an extension of this reality, social turmoil as a result of individual turmoil. That's how the world looked to me.

The insights by James, Freud and Dewey had allowed me to detect a common thread among all this chaos. The more basic problem, it seemed, was my struggle for recognition from others as a powerful fundamental force within my psyche. And apparently this same problem also drove the behavior of every person.

It began to make sense. And the more I observed, the more I found that this fundamental force appeared to be a huge part of everything I did. And everything others did as best I could glean from their actions and words.

Person By Person

During the next ten years, I turned my investigator's eye toward that specific subject for countless hours. I did this primarily through intrasentience and the rigorous inner testing process I briefly discussed earlier in this chapter. By now I was able to see only one truly sensible course to change society in a broad, meaningful way. Marie Curie outlined this idea: "You cannot hope to build a better world without improving the individuals. To that end each of us must work for his own improvement, and at the same time share a general responsibility for all humanity, our particular duty being to aid those to whom we think we can be most useful." To truly change the world, we would have to change individuals, one at a time. Or so it seemed to me then.

And still seems now.

In 2005 I founded the Humanity Project, a 501c3 nonprofit organization with a literary and educational mission. My goal was to create practical but innovative programs expressed through artistic methods, all to help change society by changing individuals. A daunting task, for sure. To date we have three major programs grounded in the belief that every person desires a feeling of their individual value more than anything – and that almost everyone looks to other people to help gain this feeling. We think any program intended to motivate human beings must take this reality into full account to be most effective. If we can make kids feel better about themselves by strengthening their feelings of importance, they're more likely to change in the ways we hope for them. All Humanity Project programs are empirically based and empirically tested for results as best we can. The testing shows they work. And our impressive sponsors and other partners prove we have earned significant community support.

Antibullying Through The Arts has been around the longest, since 2008, and has been acclaimed by educators and media for teaching elementary school children that, "Bullying hurts everyone in this school ... and it takes everyone to stop it!" It works by helping the bullied and especially the bystanders to feel better about themselves through cooperative efforts to curtail school bullying. We don't tell the kids that this is how it works, naturally, but that's what really is going on. Our Humanity Club program brings together handpicked all-girl student leaders to promote gender equality, with our training focused on the concepts of respect, diversity and self-worth – the stated core values of the Humanity Project. These young leaders then help us to create, deliver and reinforce an original presentation for all students at their school about these same values, working toward schoolwide participation in the Humanity Club. And our I Care driver safety program for teens and parents discourages distracted disrespectful driving by focusing on friendship and family love. Program participants modify bad habits by sharing materials and pledges among close friends and family, with engaging lessons that emphasize safeguarding these key relationships through attentive driving. We also held what turned out to be the nation's first mass antibullying march for children on November 16, 2008, the Thousand Youth March for Humanity. It attracted more than 2,100 marchers, grades K-12, to downtown Fort Lauderdale on a sunny Sunday morning.

As I began to write this book in mid-2014, nearly nine years had passed since I founded the Humanity Project. During that entire period I repeatedly told my family and friends as well as some supporters and sponsors and colleagues that I planned to write a book that would fully explain the personal experiences behind this organization. I was painfully aware that I never could describe in conversation my true hopes for the Humanity Project – and the substantial psychological insight that underpins each program. Only the book could do that. This situation often surfaced as a source of intense frustration and many times of deep embarrassment too. I was forever asking everyone to trust me, to believe that the Humanity Project's programs and materials really were based on decades of personal observation and thought.

The voluminous details of that experience needed complete airing. Without them, no one could remotely understand the weight of critically examined evidence that lay beneath the organization's efforts. But I felt myself prepared insufficiently to write the book until now, something that was more instinctive sense than logical decision. Experience has taught me to trust that insistent sensation of instinct, an idea first offered me by Emerson: "Trust the instinct to the end, though you can render no reason." His quote also hangs above my desk.

During my journalism years, I'd learned when I had gathered enough information to write my stories and when I hadn't. I could feel when I needed to continue reporting and when I was ready to detail the information for the public. With this book, I similarly sensed that I was in a prolonged but essential reporting phase of the work. Decades of factfinding about me and about us. Only at this point does my instinct tell me that most of the heavy reporting is complete. It's time to write at last.

A Fair Reading

I accept that my book well may prompt dismissive chuckles among some casual readers who happen across it. Identity Failure? Psychophysics? Deepwanting? Intrasentience?

Indeed ...

Our culture doesn't embrace inward observation as a source of real knowledge – meticulous, detailed, verifiable insight into our own humanity. Anyone today who wants to follow the Ancient Greek precept inscribed above the Oracle of Delphi to "Know Thyself" seems likely to be dismissed as a naive New Ager with too much time on their hands.

I disagree.

I love science in the deepest sense as our imperfect human quest to unfold a greater understanding of nature, little by little by little. Including human nature. As my background may suggest, I believe in the empirical. And I require much sensible evidence to support my core beliefs and values. Science is in my nature, seemingly. When I was a child of only seven-years-old, I fancied myself a great surgeon in the making. Several frogs sadly paid the ultimate price for my surgical training. My mother liked to tell the story about my detailed second grade paper on the function of the spleen. Even then I was drawn toward scientific knowledge. And though my career goals have changed, my fundamental approach to life hasn't.

So this book most distinctly is no exercise in navel-gazing. You are welcome to chuckle with the others, of course. But I hope for a reader who may approach the following pages with some fairminded appraisal of the observations and ideas that have resulted from four and a half decades of labored reflection. With more clarity and confidence than in anything else I've ever believed, I know what I have experienced within.

That story begins with an exploration of some fundamental psychological functions that I believe significantly shape my behavior … and yours. They are the building bricks of consciousness, a key to understanding our undiagnosed struggles with Identity Failure.

As you will soon see I've watched this process take place many times, all observed directly with my own intrasentient eyes.

Chapter 3: The Microscopic Me

"…My conclusions were arrived at as a result of simple and plain experience, which is the true mistress."
Leonardo da Vinci

The Layers Peeled

First I needed to accept that my mind is an onion. Metaphorically speaking, of course.

This concept of a layered consciousness has remained central to my personal psychological explorations and I've come to believe that it was an essential foundation. Until I recognized that I could peel back my psyche, descending through level after level after level, I was unable to make any real headway in understanding me. Now the concept seems both fundamental and obvious.

Obvious it was not when I began unpeeling myself.

I learned the process in those endless Vermont evenings, sitting crosslegged on my thin blue cotton sleeping bag. My "why method" cleared away the debris little by little for a descent through the many layers that had concealed my true problem, the source of my anxiety: I felt there was something profoundly wrong with me, as if some intrinsic elements of myself were not good enough by the standards of humanity.

One evening especially stands out for me. It was the night I realized my mother had played a huge role in forming my self-critical feelings. She had developed an uncanny skill, I understood then – a talent for disapproval and belittling without taking responsibility for it. This was a form of passive aggression common in her. Mom could make me feel bad about myself for … whatever it might be. Perhaps some interest of mine that she deemed inappropriate or unworthy such as my love for the music of The Beatles. One example. Then she would make me feel bad about myself all over again for pointing out that her disapproval upset me, as if I were imagining it all. This is not a recipe for self-trust in a child. That night sitting alone in Vermont I could tell instantly that at last I'd shoveled far down to a bedrock conflict inside me – my mother often was subtly critical of me in ways that encouraged feeling fundamentally flawed as a human being. Without knowing it, without intending it, she had instilled a strong sense that something was wrong with me.

I sobbed uncontrollably for a time.

I was 23-years-old.

Me 101: A Primer

I am now convinced that on this night I had for the first time in my life cracked well inside what Freud would have deemed my unconscious.

My conflicted feelings about my mother and their influence on my self-image weren't the only profound confusions concealed deeply within. But they were among the most profound and the deepest. I've confirmed this assessment of my psyche more times than I could estimate over the decades since that epiphany in Vermont. And to this day I view that moment of insight as the true beginning of my self-knowledge, my base camp for all the psychological explorations that would follow.

Because I have become such a frequent visitor to these most hidden regions of my mind, I often can descend rapidly through many inner levels to experience frightening feelings and troubling clashes among my concepts. I can peel back the onion's layers until I put my fingers around the tightly compressed bud at the center, the core of my problem. Many times this bud is only partly exposed when I first come upon it. That's when a more exhausting work begins, still often a struggle to keep peeling deeper.

But experience has taught me the value of this difficult effort. The answer I'm looking for is always tucked away somewhere among the secret folds of my psyche. I sometimes must even go so far as to unfold those folds, discovering not only the hidden problem but the materials that hide it.

It's been that way from age 23 on, when I needed to know more than the personal source of conflict, looking beyond the individual specifics like my feelings about Mom. I experienced something like a compulsion to dissect the basic psychological mechanisms at work during my emotional battles as best I could – much as I dissected those unlucky frogs in my youth.

What really made the whole thing tick?

As the result of doing this for more than 40 years, I have accumulated uncountable observations of my mind in action that finally now make sense to me. I required decades to sort through these, puzzle out the pieces and push them into place so that a coherent picture emerged. When I finally could see the whole more clearly, though, I understood that I had identified key components of my consciousness. And yours too, I believe.

Those fundamentals are integral to the story of Identity Failure, our nearly universal affliction of self-doubt, self-criticism, self-sabotage. Later chapters will show precisely how the various components interact to produce our symptoms: what's happening at a basic emotional level, how we feel when that's happening. But to comprehend I. F., we first must examine the raw materials of consciousness itself.

What really makes the whole thing tick?

I've found that the best starting points are things I've named nexes, vericepts and quancepts.

Websites Of The Mind

It's easiest to begin with the easiest to understand.

And the largest of the elements.

Nexes.

Most simply put, these are collections of each individual's experiences as stored in the mind and arranged by topic. Nothing new in that. Psychology has long understood that the psyche absorbs information, then categorizes and cross-references it in highly complex ways. Let's say I visit a foreign city for the first time. Perhaps Rome. My mind gathers information about Rome based on existing experiences with other cities, other people, myself and the world as a whole. Some very broad examples: Are the Romans as friendly as

Venetians? Is Rome's food as good as in Paris? Do the monuments impress as much as those of Athens? I draw on earlier experiences to form a new nexus about Rome, a collection of my many interpretations about this delightful Italian city. Some of these interpretations will be specific to Rome alone, such as the design of Trevi Fountain. But even at Trevi Fountain, other interpretations will add to existing experiences already stored in my head – connected with my previous interpretations related to fountains, waterworks, sculptures, Italian art, the Renaissance, beauty, romance and many more subjects. And my experiences at Trevi Fountain also will be influenced by my earlier experiences with other fountains, waterworks, sculptures and so forth. If I've always enjoyed fountains, I'm more likely to enjoy Trevi Fountain too.

This means some of my experiences at Trevi Fountain as elsewhere in Rome will feel brand new to me. Others will remind me somehow of previous experiences. And some previous experiences will help determine how I feel about Trevi Fountain.

That's the general idea at its most basic. Think of nexes for now as something akin to individual websites inside your mind's Internet, groupings of information about everything that you ever experience. Everything. Politics and dandruff, paintings and dessert. Shoelaces and puppies and thunderstorms and smartphones. Beethoven's symphonies and honesty and racial diversity and mathematics. Everything in your experience – and everyone in your experience. Each of these groupings is made of many many individual interpretations about that thing or person.

I define "interpretations" as the judgments you make about each characteristic of every thing or every person – all that you believe to be real about it. We make thousands of such interpretations daily. Some are deliberate: "Do I like this wine? Is that aroma in my wine glass more like cinnamon or nutmeg?" But most are automatic, formed without any awareness by us. We see a face in the crowd, then peer more closely to interpret if this is the familiar smile of our friend, Keith. Or we wake up, glance out the window and instantly judge if we are pleased by today's sunshine. Or we listen to a new pop song and within seconds may scurry to download it to our phone – or to click over to a rap song we like much better.

Every interpretation such as these is possible only because of previous interpretations we've made about the subject and the many things related to it. Just as with Trevi Fountain. Or that dandruff. I may notice a scattering of white skinflakes on the shoulder of my black jacket, brushing it off with annoyance. But my feeling about dandruff at that moment comes partly from seeing it on myself and others in the past. At those times I made lots of automatic judgments about its size, consistency, appearance, source, cause, what clothing most reveals flakes, what clothing most hides flakes, how other people react to dandruff, etc. I also was hugely influenced by advertising and what I regarded as the prevailing opinion in society about dandruff, forming many more judgments in response. Each of those instant judgments was an interpretation that added to my nexus about dandruff. You too probably have some modest-sized website about dandruff in your mind, prosaic as this sounds. Each automatic interpretation you've made about dandruff is like a page of information within that psychological site.

This is a highly simplistic description of nexes as I define the word. But it's a start. Because you will find throughout Beyond Me that nexes are crucial to comprehending both the dynamics of Identity Failure as well as some fundamental workings of the mind as I attempt to explain them in these pages.

I've studied these collections of interpretations for many years within me. And I have called them "nexes" simply as my own shortened plural for "nexus" because I find "nexuses" unwieldy. Obviously the word "nexus" is common, used in many different contexts. But to me it seems the best noun to combine with other words for my purposes, as you will soon read. Inside each mind, then, a nexus is a cluster of stored interpretations, the combination of many discrete units of experience into larger units of experience.

Judgment Plus

To extend the website analogy a bit further, remember that each nexus is linked to other nexes. As a good website will include links to outside websites about related topics, so our mental nexes link to other information associated with each subject in our mind. My new Trevi Fountain nexus would include all those links mentioned and a great many others – fountains, waterworks, Italian art and the rest along with tourists, photographs, coins, superstitions and historic sites among a large number of psychological connections. My dandruff nexus would link with nexes about such things as health, hair, physical appearance, clothing, social status, friends, strangers and a large array of other topics that in any way related to dandruff in my experience.

But here is where the website comparison breaks down. Now that you've learned it, I'd ask that you push this analogy to the back of your mind.

Because to deepen your understanding of nexes, you must add a critical characteristic that profoundly alters the concept. And to do that, you must allow yourself to think differently. I'm not aware of anything in everyday experience that functions in a manner comparable to nexes, including websites. And here's why: Nexes are more than simply a collection of information about various topics. More than just interpretations, stored experiences. Nexes also include the emotions your mind has connected with each separate experience.

The interpretations and emotions become one. Indivisible.

I can't sufficiently emphasize the importance of this notion.

So let me try to clarify, first by noting what a nexus isn't. A nexus most definitely isn't a collection of information that creates emotions after that information is recalled. The emotion is not a response, like feeling sad after watching an online documentary about poverty. No, not at all.

Rather each separate interpretation and the emotions connected with it combine to make the two parts of a single psychological entity. The banana peel and the fruit inside it. The emotion becomes permanently attached at the time the interpretation is formed in the mind.

It happens in one psychic gulp: Interpretation+Emotion.

Idea+Energy, all of a piece. You cannot separate the two at this basic psychological level. Once the concept is active in the mind, so are the emotions attached to that concept.

Shortly I'll describe how I believe this process takes place and its enormous significance in my overall understanding of the psyche. And Identity Failure. I'm not aware of any previous account that sorts through this complex psychological mechanism as it is described in this chapter and beyond.

But what's most important to grasp right now is this: Each nexus is charged with emotion, sometimes a little, sometimes a lot. More than the information, more than the individual interpretations that make up each nexus, those emotions are essential to the psychological importance of the nexus. It's the combination, conflict and release of emotions among nexes that is crucial.

Nexes are not created equal. They vary greatly in size from one another and include emotions of greatly varying strengths. Reflect for a moment on your own life. Some topics stir hardly any feeling. Others can swarm you with emotions, maybe an overwhelming fear or an irresistible desire. What you're experiencing are nexes in their vast variety. The nexus about my mother is massive, containing extremely powerful emotions. My nexus about Trevi Fountain is relatively small, with emotions of only a modest intensity.

The size of a nexus refers to the number of individual interpretations within it. The strength of a nexus refers to the power of the emotions within it, which relates to its size. The more interpretations, the more emotions attached to those interpretations. The emotions are released automatically when our mind accesses the information – our interpretations of ourselves and the world activated as needed during daily living along with the emotions connected with those interpretations.

Our nexes are the aggregate of us each. They are everything we believe real and everything we feel about that reality.

Sizing It Up

For probably at least 20 years or so at this writing, I've felt highly attuned to the way in which my mind collects and separates information into categories, very small categories and very large categories as well as everything in between. I could sense their relative emotional strength or weakness in my psyche, I was aware when related categories of information combined forces to sway my thoughts and feelings.

Nexes are one of the gates to understanding myself.

So it has made sense for me to create broad classifications of nexes based on their size and strength. I've divided them into just five categories, from smallest to largest. I wouldn't even begin to speculate on how many separate interpretations comprise each of my five nexus categories. But the number would be astronomical for the larger categories, no doubt.

These are my working definitions for each of those categories: micronexes, mininexes, midnexes, macronexes and supernexes:

- Micronexes: The simplest, most basic clusters of my interpreted experience. I have only the vaguest sense of just how basic this kind of basic really is. There's been no compelling reason for me to define any nexus in excruciating detail. For me, a micronexus is a fundamental clump of interpreted experience with very little emotion attached to it.
- Mininexes: A somewhat greater amount of information with somewhat greater emotion attached to that information but nothing of any substantial significance. Essentially, a small grouping of information without any strong emotion attached.
- Midnexes: To me, these are meaningful collections of interpreted experience. They include significant information with significant emotion, though in varying amounts – which is the way I see all of these five categories, by the way. They're extremely broad definitions and, as such, each has room for variations. I view midnexes as complex bunches of information and emotion that don't include topics connected with deeply powerful values, beliefs and so on. What matters to me in thinking about the category is this: A midnexus has emotional significance without involving those interpretations of my experience that carry great emotional importance to me.
- Macronexes: These are greatly significant clusters of interpreted experience. They include vast amounts of information and vast amounts of emotion. When something in daily life activates a macronexus, that something feels very important to me.
- Supernexes: I classify these as the largest, strongest clusters of interpreted experience. They would include my deepest values, my most powerful beliefs, my most meaningful attachments to people such as close family members. These

clusters generate enormous amounts of emotion, fed by countless interpretations made over a very long time.

Broad as these five categories are, I hope they may clarify my main point: To me, nexes are clusters of interpreted experience, each separate interpretation bundled and stored as one with the emotions that originally accompanied it. These nexes are grouped in a wide variety of configurations and strengths. What's significant about them in my life is their relative power, their emotional force – the amount of energy emitted within me by any nexus. This point will become very clear in the coming chapters.

I also think the existence of nexes helps explain one of the more puzzling situations that's recurred throughout my life. How can I have such diametrically opposed feelings at once? Love and hate for the same person at the same moment, as an obvious example. Or perhaps I intensely want a new job but I also genuinely want to keep the one I have. Or I savor living where I am … and I feel a deep desire to move. This sort of dilemma is a common reality for me, sometimes in conflicts of minor importance but sometimes in clashes among major elements of my personality. In his brilliant book of the same name about psychosomatic illness, Dr. John Sarno calls this "the divided mind." Based on my experience, Dr. Sarno's phrase is very accurate.

But how does this happen?

It's perfectly understandable when I think how nexes function within me. Each nexus contains its own collection of interpretations with attached emotions, though of course a nexus typically is linked with many other nexes in complex ways as I've suggested. But in every mind a staggering variety of very different nexes exists at the same time. Many of these are not linked to each other, formed independently during separate moments of our lives. As a child I loved milk chocolate candy, today I don't much care for it. I prefer dark chocolate. So I have conflicting interpretations floating around my head about these two types of chocolate. One set of these interpretations, one nexus, reflects my true feelings as a youth. The other nexus is valid now. Not a big deal for me – I just go with the dark chocolate.

But what if separate and distinct nexes about much more substantive issues conflict? And what if that conflict isn't so easily resolved?

Let's imagine I'm growing uncomfortable in a marriage, increasingly restless and dissatisfied. But I have a deeper problem to resolve. My psyche includes a macronexus that involves my need for emotional security, with terrible fears of abandonment and isolation. This macronexus generates feelings of strong attachment to my wife. At the same time my mind harbors a supernexus all about my need for emotional freedom, with even fiercer fears of stifling constraint and destructive commitment. This generates feelings of intense rage toward my wife. Both nexes are highly active as I fret over what to do.

It's easy to see why I would experience a very troubling combination of thoughts and feelings, all at once. Which do I really want, marriage or divorce? Security or freedom? The problem is that I honestly want both, even if present reality makes that impossible. Independently over my lifetime, my interpretations-with-emotion have created forceful feelings about the importance of emotional security and other interpretations-with-emotion have created forceful feelings about the importance of emotional freedom. As I consider divorce, the macronexus and the supernexus each will fill me with intense amounts of emotional energy directly in conflict with the other. I know that kind of inner battle too well.

But even this is hugely oversimplified. In any emotional conflict of that scope, great arrays of other nexes also will be activated, linked to one side of the conflict or the other. The macronexus or the supernexus. Perhaps even to both at the same time.

Still the oversimplified point is plain enough. Nexes cause our psychological conflicts, sometimes over what kind of chocolate to buy. Sometimes over something as disturbing as whether to file for divorce.

They're also the source of Identity Failure. You will see what I mean.

But first we should closely examine a more fundamental component of the psyche to better comprehend the structure, function and behavior of nexes in our everyday lives. This will help explain a lot.

Allow me to introduce you to the vericept.

Truth Concept

If a nexus is just many separate small bundles of interpretation-with-emotion, what psychological process creates those bundles? How does the mind absorb our raw experiences moment to moment, then judge what to make of each distinct moment?

I believe I know.

Because I have observed this process for myself, in myself. I've felt it transforming my experiences into my feelings. Each transformation produces a permanent but minute element of my psyche that I've named "vericepts." The word means, "truth concepts." To my knowledge, neither this term nor this idea exists in any other context. I've also refined my theory a bit further by dividing vericepts into two distinct types: "ravericepts," or "rational vericepts" and "irvericepts," or "irrational vericepts."

A tiny splash of bathwater requires longer to rise and fall than the time it takes to form a vericept in my mind.

The discovery of the vericept has seemed enormously useful in making sense of my basic psychological functions. I didn't begin to understand it as I do now, in some detail, until probably early 2011. My brief notes on vericepts go back at least as far as that year and I didn't start notetaking on the topic for quite a while. Before this, I had explored the concept carefully for perhaps two years or so. But it wasn't until 2014 that I felt fully confident of their actual existence. Vericepts are especially tricky to examine within me because by their very nature they cannot be directly observed. Instead I have learned to detect their afterglow, as it were. And through experience I also have come to understand their pivotal role in my life.

Vericepts are my interpretations of myself and the world around me. Not conscious deliberate interpretations. Vericepts are automatic, subliminal and virtually instantaneous – and each is fused to the emotion of that instant. Again, the interpretation and the emotion become one thing. Together they give me a feeling about that moment in time. Vericepts are the basic materials of my consciousness. Every day, I estimate, I add thousands more vericepts to the existing contents of my mind, where they are integrated with all my earlier interpretations of life and living.

On March 26, 2012, I made this note, "Vericept: the conversion of interpreted experience into accepted reality." I still think that's a good general definition, though I would insert one word for additional clarity: "the automatic conversion of interpreted experience into accepted reality." My mind must interpret what's happening as I make my way through the day, automatically decide what to believe in every quick-passing situation and then retain that slice of information for the future. That's precisely what the vericept does.

Vericepts often occur in rapid succession – now and again now and again now. Then yet again, all perhaps in the space of five or six or seven seconds. Or longer. Or shorter. As best I can tell, vericepts do not form at regular intervals but rather as the mind determines the need to assess the instant. Those assessments feel as brief and natural to me as drawing a breath. Or blinking my eyes. I think that's roughly how fast they happen too, about the flick of an eyelid.

But here's a major point that's taken me much effort to sort through: A vericept can be crammed with information, all absorbed in a single instant. It is my whole experience of one moment as I interpret that moment. Everything is accepted together, one piece, and retained as a microscopic bit of reality no matter how rational or irrational my interpretation actually may be. This means that bodily sensations as well as associations and memories connected with that moment's experience may be taken in as part of the vericept. And the feelings active in the moment will be stored too. Then all this information and feeling comes together as one overall judgment of that moment, all the details and emotions still part of the single vericept but all of them summed up into an essence. One interpretation made of many parts.

That's the way we live at a more observable level of the everyday. We meet someone new and notice a collection of characteristics: his appearance and manner, his smile, his handshake, the way he treats us and others. Then at the end of the evening, we may sum it all up with one conscious judgment: "I like him. He's very pleasant and enjoyable to be around." One interpretation made of many parts.

The vericept works much the same in me – except the vericept's interpretation happens instantly and without deliberate thought. We couldn't function if we needed to sort through everything consciously before each judgment. The mind requires a mechanism that does this for us immediately based on our prior interpretations. Based on our experience.

Let's say I'm having a picnic on a hot and humid afternoon with a very close friend, Cynthia. We're sitting on a wool blanket that she brought along and flies are pestering us as we try to eat. When yet another fly lands on my potato salad, I swat at it – and form a vericept about my experience. My mind subliminally interprets what's happening at that moment:

"Feeling hot now and getting too hot to stand this much more but I think I can last a while longer but I'm already very uncomfortable. This wool blanket is scratchy and makes this moment much worse and I blame Cynthia for bringing it on a hot day because this is the kind of misjudgment she often makes, doing things without thinking them through. I'm getting angry at her again as I do sometimes and I feel bad about it and it's probably my fault because I get angry too easily. I'm a bad person sometimes and it makes me angry when people put me in that position so I feel bad about myself. This moment with Cynthia is not fun! I want to go home!"

Along with my suppressed anger toward Cynthia, my feelings at that instant might well include my deeper affection for her and my desire to keep her as a friend, perhaps along with an unspoken sexual attraction for her. Add in my reactions to any repressed emotions that are active in this instant's experience: For instance, I could feel strong anxiety and suffer from a throbbing pain in my neck as responses to a forceful repressed rage generated by Cynthia's picnic.

Then imagine all of this is absorbed in a fleeting instant, in a fractional second. Every bit of it automatically accepted by my psyche as an accurate representation of the moment's reality. That interpretation-with-emotion forms a single discrete bite of information about my picnic experience. One vericept. And I swallow it whole, like an oyster. The vericept's details and emotions are the elements of one interpretation that will be summed up in my mind by an overall feeling: "This moment with Cynthia is not fun! I want to go home!" That's what it all means to me, the significance of this moment as permanently stored in my head.

One interpretation made of many parts.

Other vericepts very soon will join with this one, doubtless also interpreting my outing as unpleasant and increasing my uncomfortable feelings – and my desire to go home.

As the vericepts accumulate I will become more aware of my growing discomfort, which will ratchet higher and higher in what may seem like a series of intensifying bursts. New vericepts will take this escalating misery into account as part of future interpretations: The awareness of the awareness of my unhappiness, as it were, further contributes to my unhappiness.

Energetic Bits

Emotion is the psychological form of energy. Literally energy, as in physics. Just as fusion is the energy generated by a star.

Emotion = energy.

That's how I think about it. The psychological energy that motivates each individual is emotion.

As with nexes, then, the most important characteristic of vericepts is the emotion they contain. By fusing interpretation and emotion into a single psychological entity, interpretation-with-emotion, a vericept stores energy. And when a vericept is activated by the mind, it releases this energy. And when this energy is released, it contributes to motivation. A vericept also contains information – that instantaneous and automatic interpretation of one moment, like my picnic vericept just described. This information becomes active in the mind along with the energy.

Together they help push me toward something. Maybe toward my next thought or feeling or action. Or even toward inaction, as when I refrain from offering some comment or freeze up with fear. A vericept's emotion provides that forward push, a vericept's interpretation determines the direction of the push.

So you can see the significance of vericepts. One by one they build an individual's reality, what's believed and what's felt. This is why I am spending so much time explaining the psyche's basic components as I have identified them in myself, including nexes and vericepts. And why these components are central forces in my Identity Failure. And yours. They contribute hugely toward creating the distorted beliefs and irrational emotions that so frequently diminish our lives and damage the people around us. They construct our warped self-images and the urgent need to validate them in the outside world.

Whether grounded in the irrational or the rational, though, vericepts and nexes always are big players in the mind. When vericepts related to some common topic combine into a nexus, they become more powerful. No longer merely a small bit of interpretation-with-emotion as a motivator, but many bits working as one. Whenever vast numbers of vericepts join together, the resulting nexus can exert massive energy to drive my behavior. A supernexus holds a frightening influence over my life.

Remember that nexes often continue to gain this influence with time, adding more and more vericepts as my experiences pile up. My psyche generates an almost constant river of new vericepts. As best I can determine, each vericept is instantly classified by topic or, more often, topics – plural. It joins existing nexes on those topics, just as my picnic vericept surely would contribute additional information and feeling to any future experiences with Cynthia as well as with picnics and wool blankets and flies and eating al fresco and hot days and a broad range of other subjects that exist in my mind – including my self-concepts. My sense of being a good or bad friend, selfish or giving, intolerant or laid-back, weak or strong and much more. All will be influenced later by the vericepts generated now during my outing. The picnic isn't likely to make me feel any better about myself, connecting with deeper existing feelings of self-confusion. Part of me will blame me for the unpleasantness. In other words this experience will intensify my Identity Failure, a major reason for my misery during this meetup with a valued friend.

But there's another important characteristic of the vericept, a function that makes this entity even more significant in the psyche. Because a new vericept doesn't only add a fresh interpretation with its attached emotion to my existing nexes. A new vericept also activates the nexes it joins. And when this takes place, those nexes release some or all of that stored information and emotion into the mind.

The vericept has more than one duty to perform within every human being. It automatically judges what's real and what isn't at a specific instant, then this information along with the emotions that were present at that instant are transmitted for classification and storage in the mind. It becomes a new chunk of reality as accepted by the individual. While all this happens, the vericept also releases into consciousness at least part of the previously retained information and emotions on those topics.

In one sense, the vericept might be compared to the arrival of a highly prized party guest: The new partygoer contributes her intelligence and wit to the celebration for everyone to enjoy as she inspires a more sparkling conversation among the earlier guests. This charming latecomer adds something important to the occasion at the same time her presence frees something important that's already there.

Like that convivial woman, the mind's newly arrived vericept at once both adds and frees.

That's how I observe vericepts operating in my mind.

As with nexes, various vericepts vary. They possess differing amounts of information and energy. And as I've stressed, they assemble themselves into combinations of widely different sizes as well, coalescing in greater or smaller numbers as nexes around everything in my mind's experience: micronexes, mininexes, midnexes, macronexes and supernexes. On topics both major and minor. I view this psychological process exactly as I understand nature to work in other ways. Small things combine to make big things. Protons in a specific number combine to make an element. Gas and dust within a nebula combine to make a cosmic cloud, which forms rocks that combine to make boulders that eventually combine to make planets. Raindrops combine into puddles that combine into creeks that combine into rivers.

That's the fundamental method of nature as I understand it. And though I didn't set out to look for this same process inside myself, that's what I've found there too.

Again, for clarity, I should stress this important point about my picnic vericept: All that information would not enter my head as some stream of consciousness in any form. You might be forgiven for thinking of vericepts in that manner because of the lengthy description of a single moment in time. But that's mistaken. This entire string of information is captured at once, much as if I were taking a snapshot of my thoughts and memories and sensory experiences and other elements related to that moment as I interpret it. And my emotions at that moment are absorbed with the rest, attached to the information as one unit. Everything soaked in, classified and permanently stored in my mind – summed up as an overall feeling. "This moment with Cynthia is not fun! I want to go home!" That's one reason vericepts seem to me so significant in understanding consciousness. As noted before, they are automatic, subliminal and virtually instantaneous, the building bricks of the things we each believe, think and feel. Their concealment from our awareness makes knowledge of their presence that much more necessary.

When examining my vericepts, I've found it helpful to use those two categories I mentioned: "ravericepts," or "rational vericepts" and "irvericepts," or "irrational vericepts." I define ravericepts as rational because they are interpretations of experience based on my deeper values and beliefs, genuine preferences, clear-eyed judgments and so forth. And I consider irvericepts to be irrational for the opposite reasons. They are interpretations of experience based on distorted values and beliefs, superficial preferences, emotional judgments, etc.

I would classify the picnic vericept as an irvericept for this reason. Though I may indeed have been uncomfortably hot and fly-pestered in ways I genuinely dislike, the vericept was formed irrationally from all the other elements that entered into it. My feelings about Cynthia and her poor judgment, for example, as well as my irrational perceptions about myself among others.

I can test out this irrationality with a very simple thought experiment: Let's assume I was sexually attracted to my close friend, Cynthia, as I'd suggested. And let's imagine that she felt the same and, for the first time, confessed her attraction during our outdoor adventure. Whether or not we acted on all this affection just then, my feelings about the picnic very likely would have changed dramatically after listening to Cynthia's expression of desire. And if we'd had sex, chances are good I wouldn't even have noticed that I was lying on a scratchy blanket. So it wasn't the temperature or fabric that determined how I felt about that single moment in the vericept I described. My interpretation of the picnic was shaped by a soup of conflicting emotions rather than judgment that would stand up to critical analysis. On the other hand if my vericept had been limited to a rational interpretation of that instant of heat and insect nuisances, I would classify it as a ravericept. I honestly don't enjoy eating outside in sweltering heat and humidity among flies. That's a genuine preference based on my personality, not an irrational reaction formed mainly by feelings unrelated to heat and humidity and flies.

As you might expect, I believe the vast majority of my vericepts are irvericepts. Irrational interpretations of myself and the world. As you also might expect, this is a problem. A big problem. I'll get into the specifics of that in a later chapter, showing how it can smear my perceptions of myself and the world. And cause me and the people around me no end of troubles.

Comets Of The Mind

I have pointed out that I cannot directly examine my vericepts – and you may wonder how I know they exist since I base my concepts on observed personal experience. Good question. I've found that if I wait for a vericept to happen and watch for it, my mind instead is engaged in the waiting and watching. I can't follow the flight of a vericept through consciousness.

To understand what was happening, I had to assemble information in true investigative fashion. I couldn't witness the act but I could see the results. And more. Eventually I was able to estimate duration because I could sense when I wasn't experiencing a vericept, then feel a sudden shift in my psychological landscape and immediately recognize that something inside me had happened very quickly. I've even learned to retroactively analyze some of a vericept's content simply by way of my altered feelings. It's as if I can re-visit a portion of the new information and emotion, like following a rope that extends outside a cave to discover part of what's hidden within the hollowed rock. I can sense some elements of the fresh interpretation-with-emotion right after it's absorbed by my psyche.

I began to suspect something like vericepts were real for this reason: My sensitivity to psychological variations grew so acute that I became aware of what appeared to be frequent ultra-brief pauses in the flow of consciousness – and as I looked for these, I formed the theory that my mind might be recording instants of my life. Something like mental snapshots. For a long while I believed that, if this really was taking place, those snapshots likely all were trying to answer one question: "How am I right now?" Perhaps their purpose was to function as guardians of my well-being, the mind's frequent automatic efforts to discern if I was OK in the present moment.

But I no longer believe that's true. Instead vericepts seem much more as I have described them: "The automatic conversion of interpreted experience into accepted reality." Vericepts can be about anything in my orbit, inside me or outside me. They are not the safekeeping angels of the mind but rather the creators of all I believe true.

Another of the ways I confirmed the presence of vericepts to my satisfaction emerged from something odd that I've noticed often all my life. Let's go back to the picnic again as a for-instance. I experienced this as an increasingly unpleasant event where I grew more and more uncomfortable and anxious and angry. But how did the moodshifts happen? Nothing really was changing about my situation except that I'd lost a few more drops of sweat and swatted several more flies. The mounting anger seemed completely out of proportion to the reality. When I add vericepts into the equation, my reaction is understandable. Each new unit of information and emotion that I absorbed as a vericept intensified my feelings during the picnic. It contributed more unpleasant information and emotion, it activated more of my existing unpleasant information and emotion. Unhappy quickly turned into unhappier, which just as quickly turned into a kind of suppressed fury as the unpleasant vericepts piled up, one after another after another.

Vericepts also help explain emotions that swiftly jump from this to that without any obvious spark. For example, I might be going through an unusually anxious period of my life, as I did from 2014 to 2018 when writing the early drafts of Beyond Me. I struggled almost daily with fearful thoughts and difficult emotions as I tried to summon the courage to record my experiences at last. But naturally I had some relaxed hours among the recurring pain. Occasionally these hours were spent alone at home watching baseball games on TV with popcorn. At those times, living seemed relatively enjoyable – briefly.

Yet if something, anything, generated just the wrong irvericept at just the wrong moment, I might well feel an enormous change of mood in two seconds or less. Something, almost anything really, could trigger this when my feelings were so often in such turmoil. Even the seemingly insignificant at that wrong moment, perhaps an inconsistent relief pitcher brought into the game by my baseball team when we held only a one-run lead. "Why is this manager so stupid? And why can't people learn to think more clearly? No one likes to use their brain! And why am I writing a book nobody will really try to comprehend anyway? No one ever appreciates my best work!" That last sentence sums up the overall feeling this vericept would leave with me: "No one ever appreciates my best work!" Such a vericept might begin to propel me from a sense of ease to great anxiety, leaving me to wonder why I suffered this madly altered state of mind during a pleasant televised ball game.

What on earth had happened?

Until I remember vericepts, which allows me to process that sudden troubling feeling. And perhaps challenge my irrational reaction.

Vericepts help make sense of everyday experience. I gravitate toward joy or despair, contentment or anxiety as a direct result of my vericepts and the nexes they join. Just as I gravitated toward anger at the picnic. And my thoughts, then, trail this stream of vericepts – another reflection of vericept existence. Vericepts can explain the seemingly wild and random and erratic nature of conscious thought.

Because vericepts precede thoughts.

It's often been said that our thoughts create our lives. I believe that vericepts create our lives. And trigger our thoughts in turn. I am certain that thoughts follow my vericepts. I've observed this, felt this, made mental notes of this countless times.

I view vericepts as something like psychological comets with thoughts as their tails, all that I think merely the discernible traces trailing through my psyche in the dark.

Particles Of Mind

Throughout the rest of this book I will expand on my theory about nexes and vericepts. You'll more clearly understand what they are, how they work, where precisely they fit into consciousness. And their crucial impact on our lives, including their influence on what I believe is humanity's widespread infection with Identity Failure.

But first I must lay a more solid conceptual foundation, introducing other important new psychological mechanisms I've identified in me that function alongside nexes and vericepts.

One of those mechanisms is the quancept. For "quantum concept."

Obviously I coin that term to make a point about the invisible, fleeting and microscopic nature of this entity. For these very reasons, quancepts have proven incredibly difficult to study. I can't seem to observe them in any fashion, unlike vericepts that I've learned to glimpse immediately after they're absorbed into my mind. The quancept is something I strongly suspect is true based on other evidence, even though never seen for myself. To me, this situation is somewhat similar to our belief in atoms long before Einstein verified their existence. The concept works, likely has some validity but could easily be erroneous in certain respects.

For now I will offer only a summary of the quancept to round out our initial examination of three key basic elements of the psyche as I understand them. A more complete explanation of the quancept will come later, after that solid conceptual foundation is fully poured and hardened.

With those caveats, let me explain what I believe is happening.

Quancepts are extraordinarily brief automatic self-observations made with enormous frequency by the mind. They differ from vericepts, which form judgments about the present moment and store these interpretations-with-emotion for future use. Quancepts don't interpret our experience as vericepts do. Rather quancepts function as something like psychological sorting mechanisms. Filters of the mind. They each pull together a quantity of information that appears significant to me right now, presenting it to the psyche for possible inclusion within the next vericept.

In essence a quancept says to the mind, "Here, this is what you need to know in this moment as a basis for the next interpretation of reality." That is, in order to form the next vericept, the next lightning concept that converts my experience into my understanding of truth.

The quancept gives me the facts of this moment as determined automatically by the mind, the vericept automatically decides which facts are worth believing at this moment. The mind really is a kind of machine, as has been said many times by others. But nature has designed it as an elegantly swift and subtle and sweeping device indeed, far more automatic than commonly believed.

A quancept seems to pause the flow of feelings for a semi-instant to assess which among the many active feelings are most important now, meaning most strongly engaged and emitting the most forceful emotions. The quancept is why I had detected those ultra-brief pauses during my awareness of consciousness, not the vericept. The quancept processes the feelings, basically, giving priority to the most immediately powerful. At that same semi-instant the mind assesses a vast amount of other information also available just then about the individual and the world. The psyche seeks out key relevant details that can be exploited to help a person cope in the moment.

Then the quancept somehow offers up this information for consideration, everything done in an instant far briefer than a camera flash. That's the quancept, that tiny subliminal assessment.

The quancept's precise nature remains a mystery to me. It could be an unknown variety of concept as the word suggests, some strange collection of observations rolled together in the mind's equivalent of a subatomic particle. Or it really may be more a filtering or sorting process of some kind. I just can't tell with any of my methods. And what happens after the quancept's appearance is only an educated guess. Educated, I emphasize, but still a guess. I suspect that quancepts trigger nexes. The mind activates nexes related to this moment's most useful information, giving these topics more psychological significance. More immediate emotional force, thereby creating a new feeling. This is the point when another vericept forms, cementing to my memory a fresh interpretation of this moment in this world.

Science has long known about the power of subliminal suggestions, the mind's ability to absorb and react to information we're not conscious of ever receiving. The subliminal popcorn suggestion at the movie theater is a classic example from the past. Dr. Sarno's work also shows clearly that our psyche must recognize many physical and emotional conditions that lie outside our conscious awareness. They are detected subconsciously, then exploited as needed by the psyche. More on this phenomenon later in the book as part of my discussion about Identity Failure and our health. But to me, these psychological realities support the notion of the quancept.

So does a personal observation I've made many times, mentioned just above. It's that miniscule pause in my chain of consciousness. This appears as a stutter in the flow of feelings. That sensation is what launched me on my original pursuit of vericepts, some powerful sense that my mind was stopping for mini-assessments of my changing situation moment after moment. Something akin to mental snapshots, the wandering psyche halting repeatedly for photo ops.

I puzzled over this unexpected sensation. I doubted its existence. Yet I felt for it over and over within me and even spoke to a few friends to learn if they'd also experienced these mental stutters. They hadn't. But I had and continued to do so – on so many occasions that in time I was convinced they were real after years of uncertainty.

Vericepts are real. I'm sure of it. Quancepts, or something like them, also appear real. I can directly feel the vericept's new interpretation of experience. I sometimes can directly feel that pause I attribute to the quancept. I needed years more to understand they were two psychological mechanisms, not one.

Within my chain of consciousness, the action comes subtle and quick in the extreme. And observations of this process are always challenging.

A Chaos Of Experience

So the quancept sets up the vericept. The quancept makes the vericept possible by identifying the most relevant information, including strong feelings, and sending it all for the mind's subsequent consideration.

Then the vericept judges reality and sends this small interpretation of truth to join many other interpretations. Each vericept merges with the earlier interpretations of truth stored in one or more related nexes.

Small things making big things, a chain of consciousness as suggested by my crude drawing:

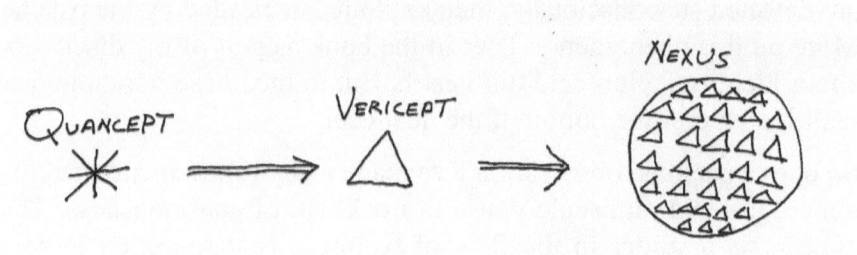

If you stop to mull your own daily existence, imagine the vast amounts of information that your mind must sift through, isolate, judge and dismiss or accept. That's happening many times during every waking minute. Both within and without the psyche, experience continually washes over you. It is a chaos of sensations and feelings and thoughts. Some are very important to you, perhaps even to your survival in the next moment. Others are irrelevant right now. Very clearly, the mind must have some almost-instantaneous system for interpreting things based on your previous experience. Such a mechanism surely would be an evolutionary advance necessary for the functional existence of an organism like you.

I believe the basic components of that mechanism are the quancept, the vericept and the nexus. As I've indicated, there's a great deal more to say on this topic – all part of my exploration of the cause and cure for Identity Failure. And all of it a basis for the new philosophy of Rational Faith.

The mind sorts through our chaotic experience, decides what to believe is true, then classifies and stores these truths and their accompanying feelings to tap whenever needed. Information in the form of automatic interpretations, motivation in the form of attached emotion.

But that's only the beginning of the complicated process that makes you into you and me into me. And generates our destructive self-obsession, our desperate need for approval by other people.

Now's the point in this story when the psyche's action becomes enormously interesting: the combination and interplay of nexes and their interaction with other fundamental forces of mind. Forces that coalesce to form a single psychological focal point in the life of each individual. Forces that determine our behavior and our personalities.

See what you think after reading a bit more. You may be surprised. Everything up to now was merely the groundwork for everything else to follow.

Here's where the good stuff begins.

Chapter 4: Fundamentally, Me

"Your vision will only become clear when you look into your own heart. Who looks outside, dreams. Who looks inside, awakens."
Carl Jung

An Energy Of Me

My emotions seek satisfaction.

That's how I've thought of it since at least the age of 22. That's how I've experienced my emotions consistently for more than 44 years.

During that entire time I could feel what this meant in my daily life, could sense how profoundly this phenomenon determined my thoughts and feelings and actions. It's as if my emotions require me to exist in some specific way that seems most likely to relieve them. As a great thirst demands a drink, as a great itch demands a scratch, so great emotion demands its own form of satisfaction. Or so it always has seemed within me.

I recall a moment when that idea became painfully clear. I was living in San Francisco, where I had moved with Lydia in January 1974 and had broken off our relationship later that year. This was yet several months before I'd packed up for Vermont in hopes that the state's natural beauty and more grounded lifestyle might help to clear my head from that persistent intense anxiety, the emotional hellfire that tormented me still. For a while after our breakup Lydia and I continued to see each other often, enjoying our sexual relationship as in the past. Until she began to see someone else. One night I phoned her at home very late and got no answer. Suddenly I found myself sprinting through the city over three long blocks to her apartment so I could peer up at her second floor window for a light. Was she home or was she with him?

Of course I had no real answer after all that running. As I recall, her light was off but what did that mean? I remember the forlorn walk back to my apartment on Jones Street – and the observation that already fascinated me: I had felt robotic, loping over the sidewalk automatically without any intent to do this. It was as if I'd been possessed. My legs had churned energetically with no deliberate desire to make them churn. But possessed by what? Just exactly what had happened to me when I'd felt compelled to race toward Lydia's Powell Street window? As I reflected on this experience, I eventually understood that my powerful emotions about her had demanded this action as a way of satisfying themselves. Like that thirst or that itch, my emotions clearly required me to satisfy them in whatever manner felt most necessary at that moment.

Once aware of it, I continued to see this same dynamic played out in small ways and large during everyday living, if usually with much less dramatic responses. I felt things and those things sought some path toward satisfaction.

Following my move from San Francisco, I'd viewed emotional satisfaction for many years in that same broad, simple but useful way: I felt things and those things sought some path toward satisfaction. The more intensely I felt them, the more intense their need for satisfaction. Just like my mindless sprint to Lydia's place. My dictionary defines satisfaction as "the fulfillment or gratification of a desire, a need or an appetite." I saw emotional satisfaction as the fulfillment or gratification of my feelings. I didn't require any concept more involved than this in order to apply it to my life. Not until later years, that is, when I began to flesh out my empirically based theories into a more coherent system that could better help me and might be explained to others sensibly.

That's the challenging bit, the explaining. Because to me, everything I'm describing in Beyond Me is part of one integrated concept of mind, inseparable from the other elements. Part A doesn't really exist in isolation from Parts B, C and D or any other element right on through Part Z. They're all combined into that single everything. This is where my earlier analogy about exploring the functions of an automobile breaks down completely. An engine can operate by itself, without the brakes and tires. But it's not that way in my head. Emotional satisfaction is bound up with my idea of nexes and vericepts and quancepts. And so on, as you'll soon read. One can't function without the others.

Nonetheless, I can only tell this story by teasing out the major components of me to explain them as best I can. That's simply a limitation of the narrative form. So I'm trying to work us through these components, step by step, hopeful that in the end you may come to see them as I do – indeed as one integrated concept of mind that outlines who I am, why I do what I do and how I can live a more constructive life as a direct result of this knowledge.

And, I believe, who you are and why you do what you do and how you can live a more constructive life too. As a direct result of this knowledge.

As I've long observed them, those major components of our psyche appear neutral: They can combine in ways that aid the individual or damage the individual. Identity Failure exists in you and in me and in nearly everybody else precisely because some of those significant psychological components interact in highly destructive combinations. We were raised to feel some intense emotional need for outside validation, the approval and appreciation of other people. An irrational need that never can be fully satisfied. The specific interaction of those interior components creates that feeling in us, that irrational need. And that equally irrational dissatisfaction.

This is Identity Failure.

To recognize the interplay of our mind's key components at the deepest levels is to comprehend the scope of Identity Failure – its complexity and power as a profoundly damaging force on individuals and on society.

But this very same recognition also creates a psychological blueprint for our escape from Identity Failure. The cure is concealed among the cause.

That's the reason we must explore those components with fresh eyes, reaching new conclusions about what's at work within us if we'll only look more carefully. I've learned that I cannot understand Identity Failure unless I first grasp the fundamental dynamics that create the identity as well as the failure. Nexes, vericepts and quancepts are only a basic but necessary beginning – the groundwork for the rest of this psychological narrative, and in a real sense the most esoteric portion of it.

From here the story connects more recognizably with our daily experience even as it becomes more elaborately involved, a tale both more familiar and more fantastic.

A Satisfying Conclusion

The process I've called emotional satisfaction merits a closer examination as a base for exploring several other psychological mechanisms in this chapter.

On the surface the concept appears ordinary. Emotion seeks an outlet. Of course it does.

But whenever I watch emotional satisfaction within me, I observe a complex psychological action that I can describe simply: My emotions are satisfied when they are replaced with other emotions – but in a highly specific way that I'll get into shortly. Basically my emotion is satisfied by going away, with different emotions flowing into place instead. In this case my earlier analogies hold up. A thirst is satisfied by ending, an itch is satisfied by stopping. My emotions are satisfied by ending too, though of course really giving way to new emotions. Again, though, only a certain kind of emotions will work as replacements at any given moment. It depends on the situation.

Imagine that you feel enraged right now. If your mind works anything like mine, you would feel dangerously in the grip of this irrational emotion, as if you might harm someone physically. I'm not talking annoyance or anger. I mean rage. But the instant something satisfies that emotion by replacing it with another powerful emotion of a particular type, the rage is gone. It is satisfied. Let's say you punch a hole in the drywall and suddenly you feel alarmed at your violence and embarrassed by the damage. Your rage well may disappear. Or you yell insults at the person who has infuriated you. After a time, the fury probably dissipates. Or perhaps that same person quickly apologizes in a way that feels genuine. Chances are good that you may no longer feel enraged after the apology.

I can put this in a more helpful context with another moment from my own life. It happened sometime around 1999, as I remember. I was sitting on our patio with my then-wife, Jill, as we sipped vodka martinis after a tiring, stressful day of work for us both. Across the street from our home an old man pulled up to a neighbor's house in his weathered pickup truck and then turned on the loudest pest chemical sprayer we'd ever heard. He began to hose down our neighbor's lawn to kill ants, the sprayer's awful belching endless and deafening. Jill and I fumed to ourselves for quite a while until, finally, I shouted at the man to turn the damned thing off. He did and immediately walked toward me across our lawn. I pushed open the screen door and marched out to greet him, eager for a heated argument. But the old man instead offered two words that instantly satisfied my anger by eliminating it: "You're right!" he said with a warm smile. Then he added, "I have to do something about that old thing. It's a noisy mess and I'm sorry!" I soon ended up apologizing to him, sincerely, for my outburst. Later Jill and I even hired him to maintain our own grass. I remember now that his name was Woody. So Woody the pest control man had helped me to feel utterly justified in my fury at him as well as sympathetic toward his economic situation, which presumably had forced him to continue using that ancient machine.

I clearly recall the feeling after those first two words from Woody, as if someone had let out my emotion much as an untied balloon deflates.

All that rage simply vanished into the air.

A Gravity Of Mind

Closely related to my notion of emotional satisfaction is the concept of psychogravity.

In physics, we understand gravity as a warping of space-time that pushes an object toward another. Gravity isn't a pull but rather a push. Looking within, I see my psyche warped in ways that appear to me as a human equivalent. Over the decades I gradually have learned to observe forces of mind that push my inner life powerfully in a definite direction, with my thoughts only the most obvious evidence of that push. I am so familiar with this emotional coercion that I've needed to give it a name. I simply call it psychogravity.

Like the other psychological forces I've watched, psychogravity is neither good nor bad, constructive nor destructive. It just is.

Gravity can drive together stars in an explosive cataclysm or guide earth through life-giving orbit. Psychogravity can alter my existence in ways that I find highly desirable at times and highly undesirable at others. Or something in between.

Essentially, I view psychogravity as a psychological process that propels me toward a connected set of quancepts, vericepts, thoughts, feelings and actions. By "connected set" I mean they are linked somehow within my mind, each set sharing some theme in common. Joy or sadness would be very general examples. Or the theme might be something very specific, like the desire to travel to Rome or eat a chocolate cupcake or have sex with the person across the room or anything else that draws me to it powerfully. That cupcake would have to represent much more to me than a mere cupcake to influence my psychogravity, though – maybe as an easy way to break a diet that I hate following.

Psychogravity is the force that bends my inner universe toward something I deeply want, sometimes briefly before an even more desirable thing suddenly alters my mind's course, sometimes with long-sustained power. A shifting gravity of the mind. Under psychogravity's sway, my consciousness warps toward that connected set of quancepts, vericepts, thoughts, feelings and actions. That is, consciousness itself changes as determined by whatever I truly want right now. My vericepts, those instant interpretations of experience, will vary enormously depending on whether psychogravity pushes me toward joy or sadness, Rome or a cupcake or sex. I automatically will interpret reality differently, moment to moment. Naturally, my thoughts and feelings and actions will be different too. Automatically, usually without my awareness.

At a more concealed level of mind, my quancepts also will change with shifts of psychogravity. Quancepts –those frequent, fleeting and automatic assessments of my mind's most relevant information at the present moment. Quancepts draw on this instant's prevailing feelings and the immediate situation to filter out what's important for the vericepts that follow. Vericepts are very different based on psychogravitational push because the quancepts are very different first.

Psychogravity reveals the true strength of my deeper needs and wants in this moment. And under its influence those feelings of joy or sadness expand, my desire for the trip or the cupcake or the person intensify.

Emotional satisfaction is the end my mind automatically seeks when in that gravitational grip. My psyche tries to find a way to relieve the pressure of the building emotion by replacing it with other emotions that I find comfortable and satisfying to me at that moment. This releases the emotional energy, new emotions taking over to seek their own form of satisfaction and release.

I'm sure these descriptions may feel a bit vague and confusing. I'll pull them together much more specifically soon as I sort through those psychological components I mentioned, part by part.

Let's start by wrapping together all the explanations about psychogravity with a precise definition: Psychogravity is the increasing emotional strength of a connected set of interpretations. These can be interpretations I've made about anything, gaining energy in the form of stronger emotion. This strengthening then pushes me toward satisfying the emotions connected with those interpretations – emotions that seek satisfaction through thoughts and feelings and actions. And through new vericepts too.

In more everyday terms, let me take sadness as a good for-instance. Gravitating toward sadness is an experience I know well. Though this example is hypothetical, it mirrors a reality I've gone through in various forms countless times during my life. I may wake up feeling out of sorts somehow. But I don't know why. I notice it's cloudy outside and the weather strikes me as a harsh start to my day – we might have rain and, at the least, it will be gloomy. Where's the sunshine when I need it? I sit down with my morning paper and coffee but the news all seems dark, menacing and unsettling. Now I feel myself drifting toward a funk, automatically and without any intention of heading in that direction. As when I ran to Lydia's apartment, I am on autopilot.

Moody thoughts begin to crowd in on me. I watch a leaf fall from a tree and think of death. I begin to ruminate on the brevity of life and the struggles in my own existence, especially old wounds that I feel were caused by people. A line from Macbeth pops to mind now: "Out,

out, brief candle. Life's but a walking shadow ..." I notice myself sinking further, as though against my will, but can't seem to stop the slide. I feel a walk outside might be helpful but instead I lie on my couch after putting on mournful classical music in the background. I reflect on my dead parents, feeling alone and abandoned. A tragic car crash from today's newspaper floats through my brain then, more proof of the heartache so prevalent in our world. Why is life so often tragic? Why do we have to suffer so much needless misery? What is wrong with us?

And on and on and on it goes. Maybe for an hour, maybe all day. Maybe this starts a longer descent into the morose, where for weeks or months I often feel irrationally angry and sad and bitter and frustrated and afraid. All of this feeds my anxiety and sometimes depression too. I am caught in the furious clutch of psychogravity that pushes me over and over toward a mental place that is very unhealthy – and only getting unhealthier by the minute. This place feeds irrational information to my quancepts, in turn distorting my vericepts as I automatically interpret moment-to-moment experience through a darkened lens. As a result of these new vericepts, my thoughts and my feelings and my actions are darkened too, all carrying me down. That is psychogravity at work.

But why? What's really happening here?

I will want to return to that example later in this chapter to dissect part of it more carefully. But to answer those questions, we first need to go back to something else. Nexes.

You'll recall that I broadly defined these as clusters of vericepts – those discrete units of experience, or vericepts, combining into larger units of experience, or nexes, around some type of topic. Vericepts create nexes. And remember that I see my nexes existing in massively varied sizes and strengths, from micronexes to supernexes. I have nexes of one kind or another stored in my head about an uncountable array of topics. On turnips and chewing gum, on morality and on Shakespeare and on Papua New Guinea. On the Humanity Project and my sister, on telephones and wasps and picnics and stray hairs in my bathroom sink. Uncountable because they include every experience in my life. Everything classified, clusters of smaller nexes that combine to become large nexes on important subjects such as Shakespeare and telephones and very large nexes on very important subjects such as my sister and morality and the Humanity Project.

Each nexus emits its own energy in the form of emotions attached to that nexus. A grouping of related large, powerful nexes carries enormous emotion.

Nexes, then, are blocks of my interpretations of everything, all the things I believe real outside me and within me. And all classified by topic as well as connected to other nexes on related topics. I believe my intentional analytical thoughts basically are a way of controlling the creation of vericepts as they are formed and classified in my mind. Essentially I am influencing the content of the vericepts by deliberate thinking. Those vericepts then join all the others wherever they best fit into my view of reality just like those that form without deliberate thought.

As I examine nexes, what matters most to me is their relative strength. Which ones have the greatest amount of emotion attached to them when they are activated inside me. Because that's what determines the process of psychogravity and the automatic psychological effort to satisfy emotions that emanate from a connected set of interpretations, like those associated with my growing sadness.

You may wonder how my nexes are activated, by which I mean triggered. Turned on, in essence. It's as if I have all these blocks of experience-and-emotion related to sadness laying relatively dormant within me, more or less switched off for the time being as other things dominate my consciousness. How then are those sadness nexes switched on?

They're switched on by quancepts and vericepts.

Perhaps it's something I see such as the rain or the falling leaf. Or it could be something I hear like a song, or something I smell such as a perfume. A sensory experience of any sort. Maybe it's a casual comment by someone or a phrase I read on a sign. Whatever it may be, my automatic mental sorting process and my automatic interpretation of that moment click the nexus on-button. Quancepts and vericepts. I'm sure we all know the sense of some strong set of thoughts and feelings taking over our heads, abruptly and without warning. When that happens inside me, I've learned, forceful nexes have been turned on by my mind's mechanisms that decide what's real and what isn't.

Quancepts and vericepts.

I've also long recognized the huge role of conditioning in my life. Very often I discover nexes have been activated as a direct result of this psychological phenomenon: I experience strong feelings from a relatively insignificant stimulus now because that stimulus was linked coincidentally with those strong feelings in the past. No doubt you already understand the way conditioning works. But here again, quancepts and vericepts are key. In the above sadness example, my reactions to both the rain and the falling leaf would have resulted from conditioning, significantly but not solely. I had felt sad during many previous rainstorms and many previous autumns of falling leaves, over time associating feelings of sadness with these unrelated natural events. So today's rainshower or tumbling leaf may create new quancepts and vericepts that activate some of my nexes connected with sadness. And with them, perhaps, some very strong emotions.

That won't happen every time I see rain or a falling leaf, of course. My response will depend on my prevailing mood and other experiences affecting me at this moment. Quancepts, vericepts, thoughts, feelings and actions are molded automatically in accordance with the mind's direction. Psychogravity will greatly influence what I make of that rain and that leaf.

My interpretations align with my mood.

A Force Of Mind

As I interpret experience instant by instant through my vericepts, each new vericept both joins and activates an existing nexus. More than one, usually. My vericept about rain, which I interpreted as sad, gave more size and strength to various sadness nexes by adding my interpretations of that rainy moment along with its attached emotion. And that new rain-sadness vericept activated those nexes at the same time.

I strongly suspect that I have very many nexes of very many sizes that focus on sadness in some way, though I have not tried to specifically identify or tally them. I believe the smaller nexes then combined into what I would call a macronexus about sadness: a greatly significant cluster of interpreted experience, with vast amounts of information and emotion. No doubt this macronexus connects with other large nexes that store sadness interpretations and feelings. For instance, a supernexus about my parents would include interpretations of sad moments that involved them, including their deaths.

But here's the main point I'm trying to make just now. In the hypothetical sadness anecdote, my relatively dormant sadness nexes were awakened and powered up, in effect, by a series of quancepts and vericepts. The sadness nexes then emitted a strong force in my psyche. And they began to exert a greater and greater psychogravitational push within me, coloring new quancepts and vericepts as well as the thoughts and feelings and actions that followed. I was gravitating toward sadness. I could sense myself being overcome by my sorrows. The activation of sadness nexes by quancepts and vericepts is part of the reason why that happened.

But remember that fresh vericepts join my psyche at a very rapid pace, sometimes every couple of seconds or so. And in all likelihood, at least some of the vericepts entering my mind are unrelated to this sadness. Quancepts are detecting other relevant information to pass along based on what's happening at that moment. These quancepts and vericepts are activating nexes connected with whatever their unrelated subject may be – perhaps baseball if I happen to be reading the newspaper sports page.

And here's where all that interior action starts to get even more fascinating. As unrelated quancepts and vericepts enter my mind, they activate unrelated feelings. This creates a psychological contest for supremacy based on the relative strength of those unrelated feelings, the kind of emotional conflict that happens inside each of us all day long. Psychogravity favors the winner of these contests. In this situation, psychogravity will help determine whether I remain sad or not – and in other situations to help decide whether I suffer a worsening episode of Identity Failure or not.

For simplicity at this point let me focus on only those two topics as if they existed in isolation inside my head, absent interactions with quancepts and vericepts and nexes about other things. Sadness and sports. My psychogravitational push before I open the sports section is strongly toward sadness. But what happens when my experience with baseball is now also awakened and powered up by reading the newspaper? It depends, essentially, on how strongly it is powered. That is, my response will be determined by how much emotional energy is attached to the particular nexes activated by my reading.

I happen to be a lifelong fan of the Detroit Tigers, my hometown team as a child. My baseball idol is Al Kaline. If a news account surprises me with word of a key trade that brings the Tigers brilliant new pitching talent, I probably will feel a sharp shift in the psychogravitational push. The sadness nexes exert less influence because they suddenly are counteracted in part by my enthusiasm for the Tigers.

I feel better, more optimistic, more alive. Depending on the force of that baseball enthusiasm, this emotional shift may only last momentarily before I lapse back into a descent toward thickening sadness: "Ah whatever, who cares! Today's Tigers always find a way to lose without taking another World Series title!" Or the news could change my outlook entirely, lifting me out of the sadness: "This is exactly the trade the Tigers need! Now they'll be sure to win another World Series title!" It's all about how much emotion is generated by my sadness right now versus how much emotion is generated now by my love of baseball and especially the Detroit Tigers.

Again, vericepts add energy to my psyche in the form of emotions but also release emotional energy from the nexes they activate on any given subject. If that subject is something I care about a lot, then lots of emotion will be stored with the information I've retained about it. In this case, the Detroit Tigers. Because of my experience with life, however, sadness also has great emotional weight in my mind – very much more emotion than I have for the Tigers, unfortunately. That means I probably will experience some strange combination of sadness-emotion and baseball-emotion as a kind of alternating psychogravitational push. First in this direction, then in that. I'm feeling sad and then sadder, until I read the sports news. Then I'm feeling more cheerful until I see the leaf fall, which causes me to feel sadder again until I go back to finish the sports story, which makes me feel somewhat optimistic. Etcetera.

Which nexes will win the battle by gaining the greater

psychogravitational influence, sadness or baseball? It depends entirely on which nexes exert more emotion at that time. If I'd recently been having a hard go in daily life, many nexes related to my miseries would be relatively active. And so I'm primed for the sadness nexes to seize control of me. On the other hand if I was, say, a rabid Tigers season ticketholder who lived and died with the team's fortunes, this important news about the pitching staff might feel much more important than my non-baseball troubles. And I would gravitate toward a more hopeful outlook.

That explanation reminds me of a traditional Cherokee story that I heard from a close friend, Gabriela Pinto. This is my re-telling, apropos of psychogravity as I see it functioning within me: An old Cherokee chief was talking to his grandson. "There are two wolves inside every human being," he told the boy. "One of them is angry, uncertain, fearful, violent. The other is loving, confident, courageous and helpful. These two wolves are always in a battle with each other to see which will win!" The amazed youngster looked up at his grandfather and asked, "So which wolf will win this battle inside me, Grandfather?" The Cherokee chief replied with a question: "Which wolf do you feed?"

It's a great tale with very real meaning in my life. Far too often I've fed the sick wolf rather than the healthy wolf, as I think of them. I'm learning to change that. But the story also makes a valuable point about how I see my mind working: Whichever nexes exert the greater emotional force during any period will win. If my sadness feels more important, I'll continue growing sad. If my Tigers feel more important, I'll come out of my sadness with a renewed cheerfulness. And when something else replaces the sadness or Tigers because it feels more important right then, I'll gravitate toward those nexes.

All Mixed Up

I often view this process in terms of physics. That's exactly how it seems to me, actually, as though at the fundamental level my mind is all about energy. Observable energy within my psyche is emotion, a psychological force rather than a cosmic force.

Believe me, I don't use the word "energy" in any remotely spiritual or New Age sense. I mean it literally with emotion as one human equivalent of energy as understood in physics: a source of usable power. Like a calorie.

After watching my mind so closely for so long, I'm also convinced that the processes and functions I see operating within me could be expressed in mathematical equations. Immediately below you'll find some very simple numbers that make a straightforward point. Later chapters employ numerical values in a more sophisticated way to demonstrate important concepts about emotions and Identity Failure – and later still in Beyond Me I will offer a new equation that I believe represents something profound about the human mind and human life. But sadly I lack the math background to seriously attempt more than this, translating my verbal descriptions of psychological processes into figures. Still, I can feel the dynamics inside me, the creation and conflict and release of internal forces in ways that seem to suggest the interplay of energy within the larger universe. There must be some way to convert these phenomena into precise equations. Or so it appears to me as a non-physicist.

This much is certain, though: I am in a constant psychogravitational flow, a natural process much more complex and subtle than the example of sadness versus baseball that I used for illustration purposes. I have countless nexes inside of me – all sizes, all levels of energy, representing all the experiences that ever have passed into my head. I accumulate more vericepts each day by the thousands, which join and activate some of these nexes. As this particular midnexus is turned on followed by that macronexus and another macronexus followed by a supernexus and a mininexus, my psychogravity is continually altered. That goes on without interruption.

It's also why I nearly always experience life as a complex soup of feelings rather than pure feeling of any kind.

Consider this somewhat more realistic example. Say some experience activates in my mind a nexus about a musical instrument. The violin. I've been a musician since childhood, now playing several instruments and performing with many bands since age 12. I'm a former classical music radio program host as well as a past classical concert critic for two newspapers in Vermont. These days I compose my own music. Lots of experience with music, then, but I don't play the violin. So I'm guessing here that if I could fully analyze my "violin nexus" I'd classify it as a midnexus, a nexus with significant information and emotion. Now we'll go one step further by giving this nexus a number to represent its relative strength at this moment on a scale of 1-100, with 100 being the strongest possible emotional energy. The violin midnexus might be 25, let's guess, with essentially positive feelings. I like violin music and I've heard a great deal of it.

Now we can imagine that a macronexus about Beethoven is activated next, with much stronger emotion. I tend to view Beethoven reverently and still hold on to many romantic associations with him and his extraordinary music. He's my favorite composer. So the vast majority of my feelings connected with him are positive: a sense of optimism, courage, hope, admiration of highly original artistic achievement and much more. Let me give the Beethoven macronexus a 45 out of 100.

Then another macronexus about the sorrows of being a great artist is activated, a topic related to Beethoven. I feel very strongly about this subject for many reasons. I hold in my memory a large collection of biographical accounts and anecdotes and quotes about struggling artists, many troubled creative histories stored for recall. This nexus would include a broad spread of related interpretations. Feelings of anger at the world for undervaluing art; frustration that profound achievement so often goes so long unrecognized; memories of my now-deceased friend, Hal Schaefer, who I regard as a genuine if largely unrecognized jazz great; the many occasions when I felt my own best artistic work was ignored. And so much more. The feelings contained within this macronexus are mainly negative – and strong. I'd give it a 55 out of 100, perhaps even more.

Now a supernexus is activated, related to Beethoven and artists specifically and all of us generally: Information and emotion connected with my belief in the importance of every individual contributing our best work to society. My mind stores a massive amount of energy on that topic, much of it positive, some of it negative. This would include feelings of inspiration that I've drawn from my knowledge of important artists and scientists and philosophers and leaders, among others. It would include personal struggles to contribute what I regard as my most valuable creations. And it would include examples of folks I've known with large talents that went undeveloped, their achievements lost – a genuine tragedy that evokes strong emotions in me. Many other associated topics as well, with their combined energy level at perhaps something like 80.

Finally, a mininexus is suddenly activated about an entirely unrelated subject. I see a new neighbor walk past me. We've not yet met and I have few experiences connected with him. Little information, little emotion. But somehow I've drawn the conclusion that he seems like "a nice guy," falling back on that all-purpose American cliché about people. The mininexus has a value of only eight.

All right then. Just think about these diverse feelings coming alive in this way within my psyche during the same period of time. Maybe all activated to their full strength within ten minutes. How am I feeling overall at that moment? Happy? Sad? Troubled? Excited? There's a great deal of emotion that exerts a psychogravitational push toward a more positive mindset, but also a great deal of emotional energy pushing me toward the negative. Forceful feelings of varying power at once.

When this energy is combined and competing, I might find myself with a somewhat stronger sense of positive rather than negative feeling. Inspired and motivated to write my book perhaps but at the same time discouraged and frustrated by society's widespread indifference to anything truly new. Even the small and weak "nice guy nexus" involving my new neighbor would exert some bit of influence on my prevailing mood, likely activating vaguely hopeful feelings about my relationship with other human beings.

This is another of my vast oversimplifications, of course. In reality, it's almost certain that only some parts of my Beethoven nexus or social-contribution nexus or any of the others would be activated during this period. Beethoven, then, might account for just a 30 or so on my energy scale in the real world over those ten minutes. And the strength of his nexus would wax and wane rather than remain constant during the experience. But I hope the simplified details make the point. Psychogravity as I see it functioning within me is a continual flow of energy that pushes me in complicated ways toward broader states of being. In this case, toward a generally positive frame of mind with undertones of negative feelings.

That frame of mind will last only briefly as my interior experience is reshaped by new quancepts and vericepts activating other nexes. The psychogravitational push will change direction.

As a quick aside, I might add that I see this complexity of feeling described here as the reason classical music is uniquely enriching.

Honestly, I adore nearly every genre of music. If you looked at my collection you would find much jazz and rock and blues along with world music of many types, from Chinese to Greek to Norwegian to Indian to Moroccan to Hawaiian and more. And I'm a lifelong obsessive Beatles fan. But to me, great classical compositions offer a depth and power that no other music matches. I believe that's because it expresses so many different feelings at the same time, much as we experience life. The first violins may sound hopeful while the French horns play a somber tune at the same instant that the insistent timpani offer courage and the bassoons are playful.

That mix of feelings mirrors our deeper emotional lives. Classical music feels to us more like life feels to us.

Tiger By The Tail

Putting music to one side, I want to bring back something I discussed earlier in this chapter. Emotional satisfaction. You'll recall I noted that my emotions are satisfied when they are replaced with other emotions in a specific manner. This emotion or set of emotions goes away, replaced by that flow of different emotions. The emotions that disappear have been satisfied, in my terminology, much as a thirst or an itch.

Now in the specific example just above, I'd decided I would experience a somewhat greater force of positive rather than negative feelings after the activation of those various competing nexes. I would feel a sense of inspiration and motivation as well as some lesser sense of discouragement and frustration, with a little hope mixed in. But how would I experience that peculiar emotional combination in real life during those ten minutes? What overarching feeling would I have? Are only the positive emotions seeking satisfaction during that time because they're strongest – meaning that I'd feel pretty good overall?

The overarching feeling probably would seem rather uncomfortable.

And no, not only positive emotions would seek satisfaction. They all would.

As I understand this process within me, both these broad strains of feeling simultaneously would seek emotional satisfaction during the ten minutes, the positive set of feelings and the negative set of feelings together. They would compete for supremacy in me, like the wolves in that Cherokee tale. All the mainly positive emotions connected with the violin and Beethoven, all the negative emotions connected with artistic suffering. The intense emotions from the supernexus about contributions to the world and all the other active emotions from the other nexes too. These specifically would include joy from the violin and Beethoven, anger and fear from the artistic-suffering nexus, more anger from the supernexus but also lots of love for individuals and humanity in general … and much much more too.

Each charge of emotional energy from each active nexus would seek satisfaction at the same time. Obviously they can't all be satisfied, though. The emotions would conflict, with powerful psychological energies demanding satisfaction in very different forms. Because I couldn't possibly meet that demand my psyche automatically would find whatever felt like the best compromise, a path of least resistance that would be expressed through the quancepts, vericepts, thoughts, feelings and actions that followed the activation of all these nexes. My mind would do its best to satisfy all the emotions, hopeless as the task really would be. The more powerful emotions would demand the most attention but every one of those emotions is part of the mix gravitating toward what seems the best available form of satisfaction overall at that time.

At an everyday level, this might have felt as though I were in an odd mood. If asked how I was feeling I would have told you, "I feel all right, basically, I want to get some work done. But I don't know … I guess something's bothering me in some weird way. I can't really tell you why. I just don't feel quite as good today as I'd like." The emotions seeking satisfaction would be in a battle, making me feel that a relatively enjoyable day was marred by some sort of mild depression. Until something else happened that could rearrange things in my head, of course.

Emotional satisfaction is further complicated in my life by the existence of another psychological phenomenon that I've named, "tigertails." And no, the term is not related to the Detroit Tigers in any way, despite my team's coincidental role in this chapter and despite my great affection for them. Baseball and psychology do mix in my world, but not in this case.

Tigertails are something well known to me. They involve powerful, persistent efforts at emotional satisfaction, holding enormous sway over my interior life despite anything else that may happen unrelated to them. A tigertail feels very, very important to me. There is, in other words, great emotion coming from the nexes of a tigertail. A tigertail bends my psychogravity strongly towards it. But it also seems always to be irrational – and destructive to me.

More specifically, and clearly, this is what I call a tigertail: A past experience that feels so significant to me that I refuse to let go of it emotionally, though my insistence on holding fast only damages me now. This might happen in the turbulent wake following a serious loss, disappointment, failure, illness, misery of one kind or another. Or it could focus on a previous period of life that felt glorious, heroic – like being the long-ago star of a championship college hockey team. As with so many other psychological forces, tigertails come in varying strengths. It just depends how much emotion is attached to the specific nexes activated by the tigertail.

A small example from my experience would be individual rejections I've received as a writer from editors and publishers. In some cases, I viewed these for many years as personal affronts – and I remained angry about them. A major example from my life would be something I alluded to earlier: a feeling that my best creative work remains largely unknown and unappreciated. I required decades of effort, and a deeper understanding of myself as explained in this book, to overcome that bitterness and that rage. I would not let go of those feelings, adding poison to my daily existence for a long time.

So why did I, why do any of us, so often cling to the worst torments? This very different example may help to better make the point.

A classic tigertail would be a mother who will not let go of profound grief for a dead son. Her mourning becomes her entire life, with thoughts related to this child occupying much of her psychological world year after year after year. We've all heard stories of similar obsessions. Clearly, a very intense form of tigertail – and it seems to defy our attempts to make sense of the mother's response. Grief is destroying this woman's daily living, essentially adding her destruction to the tragedy of her son. Why?

If the mother's tigertail resembles my own, this psychic grasping results from a complex of psychological forces that can be simply summarized: the experience appears too frightening to respond in any other way. That's why I've named it a tigertail – it feels like something that will devour me if I let go of it, like holding on to a fierce tiger's tail. In truth, though, holding on to that psychological tiger only keeps it close enough to continue clawing at me over and over. If I let it go, the tiger runs away.

But letting go emotionally isn't easy. Sometimes it can feel impossible.

The process involves allowing yourself to feel the past experience that's so painful, which means fully accepting both the pain and the reality of the experience. I have to really feel that it simply is part of my life now. And that I can do nothing to change it. I also have to free myself of an overwhelming sense that my self-image requires clasping tight to that experience. For me, for that mother, holding the tigertail feels necessary at some deep and hidden levels of the psyche. Many of them. For instance, my tigertail allowed me to maintain a self-image as a profoundly misunderstood creator whose true worth will some day be widely acknowledged. That felt very important to me. The mother's tigertail helped her maintain a self-image as deeply devoted to her son, in death no less than in life. That felt very important to her.

When your identity feeds off such concepts to any large extent, letting go can resist even the most determined attempts.

I've found this idea of tigertails very helpful to me because it's so connected to emotional satisfaction and psychogravity. A strong tigertail like the one about my creative work massively influences my inner universe. The tigertail's extraordinarily powerful emotions insist on satisfaction, warping my life through their psychogravitational push. They can alter my moment-to-moment interpretations of almost everything, a great many of my quancepts and vericepts each day, shading them blackly with rage and fear as well as confusion about my value. These vericepts then form highly forceful nexes and also change for the worse many other nexes they join. My thoughts, my feelings, my actions often bend toward that tigertail. Yet I still refuse to let go.

Once again, I am in the grip of psychogravity … and now feel I can't escape.

A Fundamental Law Of Me

All of this leads me at last to one of the central topics of this book. And to one of the most remarkably immodest statements I plan to make. I believe I have discovered a fundamental law of my human nature, a basic principle of me. I think that both emotional satisfaction and psychogravity behave in a very specific way as a result of this fundamental law. I have found that this law forms an underlying cause for everything I do, from the smallest things to the largest things. It shapes my quancepts, my vericepts, my nexes, my thoughts, my feelings and my actions every moment of every day.

I have for many years felt utterly convinced that I am governed by natural laws, just like everything else in the universe. I can only assume this is true of all people but of course can speak with total confidence about myself alone. I did, though, scribble a quick note on 6/18/12 that says, "Human beings are governed by natural laws, like stars or trees or eagles. Only by understanding those natural laws can we then create governments, social structures, organizations, programs, social reforms, relationships, etc. that sensibly reflect those natural laws – i.e. reflect human nature at a deep level."

I'd formed that conviction long before then and it's still what I believe. I am certain these natural laws are the keys to understanding who and what I am and how I can best live my life. Let me tell you what I've seen at work within.

I began with a more general principle that I called by the acronym, "MIEN," all in capital letters to distinguish it from the word with an identical spelling but very different meaning. But I pronounce it the same. In my personal system of psychology, MIEN stands for this:

"Most Immediate Emotional Necessity." For a time I believed the MIEN might represent my mind's deepest aim, instant by instant. In April 2010, I wrote another note that read, "It's not 'survival of the fittest' – it's 'dominance of the necessary.'" I'd forgotten about that observation until I stumbled across it when pawing through a file, but I still like the sentence. And though my theory has been significantly developed beyond the concept of the MIEN, as you'll read shortly, I believe this 2010 statement stands up. My mind seeks whatever feels most emotionally necessary right now. The perceived necessity dominates.

That's what MIEN means. My psyche continually gravitates toward anything that feels as if it can do the best job of satisfying my emotions overall. My actions and other behavior gravitate in this way as well as my interpretations of the world and of myself, whether through automatic quancepts and vericepts or conscious thought. My emotions and feelings and all the things I say out loud. They're determined by what seems to my mind the most immediate emotional necessity at that moment.

Remember the paragraph above? "Each charge of emotional energy from each active nexus would seek satisfaction. Obviously they can't all be satisfied, though. The emotions would conflict, with powerful psychological energies demanding satisfaction in very different ways. Because I couldn't possibly meet that demand, my psyche automatically would find whatever felt like the best compromise, a path of least resistance that would be expressed through the quancepts, vericepts, thoughts, feelings and actions that followed the activation of all these nexes. My mind would do its best to satisfy all the emotions, hopeless as the task really would be. The more powerful emotions would demand the most attention but every one of those emotions is part of the mix gravitating toward what seems the best available form of satisfaction overall at that time."

We can view this best available form of satisfaction as the MIEN. My psyche makes something feel more essential to me than anything else right then, no matter how rational or irrational, wise or just plain crazy it really may be.

I see this as highly important because it tells me that my life is determined by my emotions. And it tells me that this happens because some of those emotions seem more important than others at any given minute. Further it tells me that this is an uninterrupted psychological process in which the satisfaction of some emotions seems so urgent that it feels immediately necessary to my psyche. My mind gravitates toward the MIEN.

In a sense ...

But obviously this leaves the central issue unanswered: What exactly is the MIEN? Why does one thing ever feel more emotionally necessary at a given moment than any other thing?

Though my family wasn't poor, I recall stealing record albums from several shops as a 16-year-old boy – so what about this theft had felt so immediately important to me? And why would starting to write an unusually complicated book with little popular appeal feel necessary to a 61-year-old author? Then and now and in between, my behavior often has seemed to make absolutely no practical sense. But it did make sense. And the reason was the same for both the 16-year-old boy and the 61-year-old man.

It's because the MEIN is governed by a much deeper natural law of my mind. I now view this law as a fundamental psychological process.

This is what it says: I interpret experience to create the weakest possible emotional resistance to the strongest possible feelings that my existence is valuable to me at this moment in this world.

I've tested countless formulations of that idea for several years now. I believe this phrase comes closest to the reality taking place in my mind. It's my best approximation through written language – and naturally, requires detailed explanation. But I feel highly confident that it's accurate.

I interpret experience to create the weakest possible emotional resistance to the strongest possible feelings that my existence is valuable to me at this moment in this world.

The Fundamentals, Closeup

I will break down that sentence into its component parts for a closer look at each major concept within it, first briefly then with more substance.

"I interpret experience" means that my mind processes the raw experience of life as a series of frequent interpretations of that experience, beliefs about reality stored as usable information with attached emotion. Information-and-emotion, or vericepts. These interpretations happen automatically, usually without any deliberate thought, and form according to the demands of this fundamental psychological law. And they lead to responses such as thoughts, feelings, actions that are expressions of this same law.

"To create the weakest possible emotional resistance" means that I interpret experience in whatever way seems to best avoid conflicts with the most emotionally satisfying feelings moment to moment. My mind attempts to minimize the presence of any information-and-emotion that would resist other information-and-emotion that feels most satisfying just then, weakening the psychological clash as much as possible.

"To the strongest possible feelings" means that I interpret experience in whatever way seems to best offer the most emotionally satisfying information-and-emotion moment to moment. My mind attempts to maximize the strength of these feelings.

"That my existence is valuable to me ..." means that the most emotionally satisfying information-and-emotion moment to moment is whatever maximizes my feelings that living matters, that my existence has value to me.

"At this moment" means that only the present really matters to my psyche, the value of my existence as it seems at this instant – which often may include the remembered past and anticipated future.

"In this world" means that my mind automatically places me in the context of the world as perceived in that instant. My interpretation of everything that isn't me directly influences my sense of self-value.

This fundamental law means that my mind automatically latches on to the interpretation of reality that feels most emotionally comfortable to me at that moment, no matter how painful or self-destructive it actually may be. And with that interpretation, my mind creates the subsequent thoughts, feelings, words and actions that also feel most comfortable in that same way. They are the most comfortable because they seem most emotionally satisfying, not necessarily the most pleasant. They create the least inner conflict with the most satisfaction right now.

You'll recall again that my emotions are satisfied when they're replaced with other emotions, different emotions taking over. Those new emotions will be caused by my mind's automatic effort to create the weakest possible emotional resistance to the strongest possible feelings that my existence is valuable to me at this moment in this world. And the psychogravitational push within me will be toward whatever seems best able to give me those feelings, no matter what it is. Training for an Olympic marathon or starting a heroin addiction, volunteering with a homeless shelter or joining a racist cult, learning yoga or allowing depression to overwhelm my days. Even my own suicide would be explained by this same dynamic. I'll get into that peculiar notion further on in the book.

This concept of a fundamental law governing my psyche has taken me a very long time to understand. More than 40 years. I approach it with humility, believe me, but also with confidence.

For many of those years I thought that my life was determined by whether I felt like a worthy human being, meaning that I had to feel valuable *to the world*. I had to feel like a somebody rather than an anybody or a nobody in society, somehow some way. I had to feel important, as Dewey concluded. Originally I formulated my fundamental law with the words "to the world." Now I see the idea more precisely. Because I don't need to feel that the outside world values me – that anyone else needs me or loves me or wants me or appreciates me or even likes me. I've learned that I need to feel valuable to myself *in this world*. That small preposition gave me fits: In or to? It makes a huge difference. Ultimately I realized that I had been mistaken in my initial "to the world" conception mostly because my own self-worth was so tightly bound up with how others saw me. In my mind, it appeared as if I had to feel valuable to the world when I really didn't. Something deeper was going on.

Fundamentally, I'm in a perpetual existential battle. I need to believe that my life is valuable to me alone but in the context of the larger world. Basically then, I'm forever trying to help myself feel that my life as I view it right now is worth living. Is my existence valuable enough to carry on … or not? That's a very scary notion to confront.

I grasped my "to the world" error through the same experience that has led me toward many of my self-discoveries. Abject terror. Not too long before I wrote this chapter's first draft in December 2014 I began suffering middle-of-the-night episodes of heart palpitations and trembling so extreme I sometimes seriously feared I was about to die. I understood these were triggered in large part by emotional conflicts related to my work.

But I couldn't seem to stop the episodes. Beginning in the summer and autumn of 2014, I felt desperate.

I was profoundly afraid in a way I'd never before experienced, fearful of immediate death. In real ways this was even more disturbing than my youthful anxiety attack, which at least didn't appear life-threatening. So once again, at 61 as back when I was 23, I weeded through my feelings during long black hours over many nights. Though, fortunately, not nearly as many nights. I concluded that my physical reactions indeed all stemmed from severe anxiety. No enormous surprise there, really, with lesser physical symptoms long a commonplace expression of my emotions. But now I recognized that my ambitious new professional efforts, both writing this book and guiding the Humanity Project's evolution, had stirred up a thick residue of uncertainty from my earlier years. Uncertainty about who I was, uncertainty about me.

It was Identity Failure, in the severe. And I would require my own new philosophy of Rational Faith for a meaningful cure, as this book will explain.

But something good came from my horrific sense of impending death, oddly enough: I learned with great clarity that I don't need to feel valuable to the world but rather in the world. That precise wording is significant. And I directly experienced the difference. Because during those attacks I had wanted to live, very much so, whether or not I could accomplish all I felt capable of doing. No matter who appreciated or understood my work. Or loved me personally. "I want to live!" – I repeated this plea over and over alone in tears on more than one night as I watched for signs of a heart attack or stroke that might overtake me on the spot. I had wanted Bob Knotts to survive because staying alive mattered to me and only to me right then, for Bob Knotts. This much was frighteningly clear at those moments.

I could feel a surging will to live even in our difficult world and even if my life should appear entirely without value to everyone else in our world. In those instants of hovering doom, I was very well aware that I cared most of all about enduring until another dawn.

"My existence … at this moment in this world." That's just another way of saying I need to feel my life has value in the circumstances of this moment, in the immediate situation. It's what my mind continually assesses through quancepts and vericepts, interpreting my experience to best meet my continual emotional need.

Think how much information can get packed into a vericept during an instant's interpretation, remembering my example back at the picnic with Cynthia. My mind can absorb a lot in the sub-second interval required to form and accept a vericept as reality. All that information is altered automatically to make it as emotionally satisfying as possible in that situation. Emotionally satisfying because it seems the best compromise consistent with the fundamental law of my mind.

At the deepest level as well as at every other level of my life, I behave according to my mind's natural law.

Surely No Picnic

Sometimes it's almost hard for me to believe how extraordinarily self-absorbed one human being can be.

On the day of the fictional picnic, I would have viewed that difficult alfresco experience as an extension of my life. I'd have taken it all personally. Like many of us, I suspect, I have had a tendency to do that with everything that happened. It was as if I were the center of our vast universe and each thing occurring anywhere was intended to help or hinder me. That's how it has felt in the past far far too often. So those outside things were included in my mind's assessments about the value of my existence … in this world.

That's what I really mean by those three words. The situation I'm in at this moment in this world contributes enormously to the sense of my life's value to me – information typically included in some measure as part of my quancepts and vericepts. Whether I feel fulfilled or bored by my circumstances right now, financially rewarded or struggling, sexually satisfied or frustrated. And any other situation that my mind deems caused by something outside me. Some will seem more important at times, others at other times. But these life circumstances are significant parts of my mental equation about the value of living at all.

Until, that is, my life appears genuinely threatened. As I so painfully learned. That's when I recognize the intrinsic value to me of staying alive, apart from anything else. I've also now seen that Rational Faith promotes an unconditional self-value by diminishing or eliminating Identity Failure. It helps me feel my life is worth living. This is among the more important strengths of the new philosophy.

I surely could have used a sharper sense of my life's unconditional value at the picnic with Cynthia. My situation seemed very personal – it was all about me. The heat, the blanket, the flies, Cynthia's bad planning. Despite their trivial significance rationally, those circumstances at the time felt urgent. Perhaps, very briefly, more important than almost anything else. Life was making me miserable. I badly wanted life to treat me better.

But how to change things at that moment?

Yelling angrily at Cynthia would have made me feel irrational, out of control and probably a bit crazy. An outburst would have offended a friend, possibly costing me her friendship. I would have lost any chance at a sexual relationship with her. I would have violated my own sense of ethical behavior toward others. And so on, a long list. Any kind of attack on her would have created emotional resistance to my feelings of self-value – that is, would have formed emotional conflicts in me. So I avoided yelling and other displays of anger as best I could, my mind creating the weakest possible emotional resistance in that awkward situation.

At the other end of the emotional scale, I felt personally offended that Cynthia didn't show more concern for my feelings. I was angry that she put me in a situation so unpleasant. Worse, I was growing very uncomfortable with myself as Identity Failure strengthened: I should be more forgiving of people, I should not take minor problems so seriously, I should not get so angry, etc. etc. There was something wrong with me for feeling as I did – and Cynthia's picnic made me feel this way. My value was under assault by my fear. In response I was becoming enraged, vericept by vericept. These feelings demanded emotional satisfaction as well. Though the situation I experienced at the picnic was inconsequential and very temporary, I couldn't step back to view it rationally. Instead my sense of self-value felt directly threatened because life was treating me poorly at that moment.

So my psyche reacted automatically, without a deliberate thought from me. My mind found a compromise that created the strongest possible feelings that my existence was valuable to me at that moment in that world: I simply clammed up. When I insert myself in this imaginary situation, that's how I feel sure I would have responded. I suffered mostly in silence, probably with some mildly irked facial expressions and comments mixed in to ease my emotional pressure without risking an obvious attack on Cynthia. I muddled through, as I often have felt forced to do around others in unhappy real life moments. My psyche's automatic solution at the picnic was to endure, flare off a few sarcastic remarks offered as humor and just end the outing as soon as possible. Then I would hurry home and fume to myself the rest of the day – and probably behave strangely the next time Cynthia called me.

She would have no idea why I sounded so rushed and curt on the phone. But I would know.

I still felt very angry about that insufferable picnic.

Will To Live

Self-absorbed indeed.

Could something so insignificant as a rotten picnic actually manufacture doubt about whether my very existence feels valuable to me at a given moment? Is everything really all about Bob to that extent?

On the surface, that seems like a far-fetched idea. But I am sure now this dynamic is exactly what's happening all the time whenever I am afflicted with Identity Failure. It is part and parcel of the me-obsessed life that flows from this malady of mind. Me, at the center of the universe.

Without Identity Failure, my psyche continues to seek the strongest possible feelings of my value just the same. Constantly, in all I am and all I do. The fundamental law still reigns supreme, precisely as before. But as you will learn, I find this sense of my value in entirely different ways once Identity Failure is eliminated. I no longer feel the universe is about me. Instead my attention becomes focused on sharing my best with others, on helping people meaningfully whenever I can.

Still, that fundamental law means my feelings about Bob fuel my whole life. With or without Identity Failure. It doesn't matter if I gain those feelings from outside sources because of I.F. or from inner resources as a healthy man.

My mind is constructed so that I must believe my own existence is valuable to me here and now. Always. That's the ultimate psychological purpose of the fundamental law. It creates this feeling of individual value.

That mechanism makes great sense as the driving dynamic of my mind. Pull back a bit to view it from a farther distance, from an almost evolutionary vantage point: What better preoccupation for my psyche than continually striving to generate greater motivation to live? To keep up the moment by moment fight, fueled by a constant flow of emotional energy? That's how my mind functions in every situation all the time. That's what it is attempting to do.

In the early months of writing Beyond Me I stumbled across something that I found especially encouraging. The German philosopher Arthur Schopenhauer, who lived from 1788 to 1860, wrote about the "will to live." I confess a general ignorance of Schopenhauer and my stumble did little to thrust me into serious study of his work. But Schopenhauer's phrase seems to sum up, in broad-outline fashion, the very psychological mechanism I'm talking about. My mind is always attempting to give me a more powerful will to live. This is what the fundamental law says: I interpret experience to create the weakest possible emotional resistance to the strongest possible feelings that my existence is valuable to me at this moment in this world.

I'm forever trying to make my life feel more worth living.

Though unrelated to my skimpy knowledge of Schopenhauer, I might add parenthetically that since college I've deliberately been very selective about my readings in both philosophy and psychology. I began to explore these two subjects seriously each semester during my 1½-year university stint, which ended when Lydia and I moved briefly to Switzerland. I never went back to school but began much independent studying for a long time as I worked at my writing career. The basics about philosophy and psychology that I gained in college were the foundation for all my later thinking on these topics. I have, though, tried to avoid learning much about very contemporary trends in philosophy or psychology so that I could understand my own experience without excessive outside influence. Naturally, I've read some current ideas in these fields. But this has been infrequent and superficial. I didn't want to know what others had found because I was trying hard to find it for myself based on direct experience. Keeping my vision as unaffected as possible seemed wise.

In any case, I should clarify an important point connected with this discussion about a fundamental law of my mind. That foundational principle of motivation means that the greater psychological force with the least psychological resistance relative to that force will win any emotional conflict. And that greater force, again, is whatever creates the strongest possible feelings that my existence is valuable to me at this moment in this world. Anything my mind believes best meets that most immediate emotional necessity carries the day with me, whether in quancept or vericept, in thought, word or deed.

It's all a matter of energy, of relative strength, just as anywhere else in nature. The stronger force prevails, whether that natural force is brute energy as in geology or adaptability as in natural selection. As I noted earlier, when I'm looking within my psyche it's not survival of the fittest. It's dominance of the necessary.

And what feels necessary to me at this moment depends on what's been happening in the moments beforehand. On which particular nexes are most active right now. Which wolf have I been feeding, the healthy wolf or the sick wolf? Which nexes now exert the greatest emotional force?

A Gravitational Sadness, Revisited

Those more active nexes alter my interpretation of this moment by shaping the new quancept and the new vericept, as I've explained.

And that new vericept will add fresh emotional strength to the more active nexes as it also activates more of the energy in those nexes.

Let me go back to the sadness example from early in this chapter. Though hypothetical, it may give a bit more clarity to this notion of a fundamental law of my psyche. You'll recall that for whatever reason, I woke up feeling out of sorts. I often wonder if this happens because of my dreams, perhaps my mood on awakening influenced by lingering feelings from nightmares of some kind as my mind worked through powerful emotional conflicts. I'm not sure but that's how it seems. In any case my morning began badly on this day. I felt uncomfortable, irritable. And now let's also imagine that in the period leading up to this morning I had been wrestling with some tough financial problems. Nexes charged with negative emotions already were active. And sadness beckoned.

It could have been otherwise, obviously.

If I'd had a good night's sleep and awakened thoroughly refreshed, despite my money struggles, I might have viewed the cloudy weather through another lens. For example, it all could have appeared relaxing and cozy for writing at home all day. Or if life had been treating me well, maybe with a lucrative new sponsor for the Humanity Project, I'd have shrugged off the weather with hardly a thought. "It's cloudy and may rain today. No big deal, I've plenty to do inside." Whatever is going on in my head at this moment sets me up for what will happen next. That's why it's so hard for me to escape strong moods, overcome powerful destructive emotions, wrestle with tigertails. One thing leads to the next thing inside me.

On this particular imaginary morning, I felt the weather harsh and gloomy. So why would that depressed feeling satisfy the most immediate emotional necessity? Why would it create the weakest possible emotional resistance to the strongest possible feelings that my existence is valuable to me at this moment in this world? I believe that could have happened for many, many reasons. But let me pick the one that would be most likely for me at such a time: My sad interpretation of the weather allowed me to feel more comfortable with my out-of-sorts mood as well as the financial troubles that happened before the morning.

Without the slightest deliberate effort on my part, my mind automatically helped me justify my negative feelings with no guilt, without reproaching myself in any way for them. "I feel blue because the world is such a sad place. Just look around at things..." That would be the general sense, though I probably wouldn't think those words. It's simply how the world would feel to me right then, an automatic interpretation that I accepted as reality. A vericept.

This interpretation would minimize the emotional resistance at the same time it would maximize the feelings that my existence was valuable to me at that moment in this world. And it would launch an ongoing string of vericepts in a similar morose vein. But why?

The morning funk was preceded by recent negative feelings about the world and about myself. Perhaps from the day before, perhaps longer. But my sadness didn't appear from nowhere. There was a cause. So we'll assume my money shortages recently had left me feeling professionally unappreciated once more: "No one remotely gets what I'm trying to do. No wonder I'm broke!" My emotions already would have been weighed down with intense anger at a conscious level plus a repressed rage beneath the surface. This, along with rekindled fears that I might be wrong about who and what I am – all mingled with self-pity and bitterness and a raft of irrational feelings that would have added up to one nasty mindset.

Then came my out-of-sorts awakening to a cloudy world. How convenient for me. The existing negative emotions that had remained relatively active inside me that morning would have seemed validated by what I saw outside me, first in the weather, then through the newspaper and the fallen leaf and the rest of it. These emotions probably would have been further satisfied by a rash of new vericepts connected with old wounds. The sorrowed interpretations would pile on: About my rage over artistic talent ignored by society through the ages, my fury over perceived injustices against my own work, my terror that those who rejected my writings could be right ... and vericepts created by many other negative feelings as well. All those feelings would have exerted a strong gravitational energy in me.

My morning sadness allowed them to flow more freely, with less conflict from rational thought – one sad thought or feeling replaced by the next even sadder thought or feeling. The mournful classical music would have felt good, felt comfortable to me. Memories of my dead parents were welcomed in a way. At some psychological level, I actually would have been enjoying myself because I experienced a sense of vindication over my most active feelings about life at the time.

The sadness minimized the emotional resistance by helping to suppress any activation of more rational nexes that would have conflicted with my negative feelings about life. And the sadness maximized the feelings that my existence was valuable to me at that moment in this world by assuring me that the problem wasn't me, the problem was them. "I'm OK, they're terrible – those people out there, in society, especially the people in charge of things. I'm doing my best but life's unfair. What can I do when that's just how it is?" I would have felt relieved of responsibility at the moment and could have luxuriated in my misery with a fairly clear conscience. Sadness would have taken over easily at this point, with little resistance.

That's how it all happens inside me, whether my prevailing emotions are positive or negative or some middling mix. The fundamental law of me determines how I react to everything. It causes the effects that are my life: I interpret experience to create the weakest possible emotional resistance to the strongest possible feelings that my existence is valuable to me at this moment in this world.

Mind Over Me

Which leads me to a confession of sorts. I never intended to permanently identify that psychological law by the name I've been using. "Fundamental law of me." It was merely a stopgap phrase until I could reach the proper point in my story to come clean.

This is the point.

The name I really want to attach to that profound inner mechanism is this: "Fundamental Law of Mind." I feel certain there are other fundamental laws that govern the psyche – but I don't know what they are. If I did, I would call this the First Fundamental Law of Mind. For now, I'll have to leave off the first.

I delayed revealing the proper name because I felt the concept might be easier to accept initially in the limited context of my own psyche. Its discovery, afterall, resulted from my direct personal experience. And I wanted to tell you more about the notion before offering the admittedly bold assertion that I'm convinced it is a universal human truth. But yes, I firmly believe this basic law determines much about all our lives. Why we do what we do, how we go about doing it.

The Fundamental Law of Mind.

In finished form, here is what it says: "Individuals interpret experience to create the weakest possible emotional resistance to the strongest possible feelings that their existence is valuable to them at this moment in this world."

It's what makes us each tick at the most fundamental level of our psyche. We are in a perpetual struggle to feel that our own existence is valuable to us right now, right here.

To Want Or Not To Want

But I've found there's still another layer in the exploration of my deepest motivation. Something else that helps explain why I do what I do, why I am as I am.

I hinted at it just above when I said, "At some psychological level, I actually would have been enjoying myself because I experienced a sense of vindication over my most active feelings about life at the time." I believe this means that, in reality, I truly wanted to feel sad. I wasn't aware of it, and I would have denied it if asked. But that's what was happening.

I've found, then, that all of this psychological complexity appears to boil down to something very simple at its bottom: What do I deeply want? Not what do I think I want, mind you, but what do I genuinely want at the cellar-floor level of my humanity, that place dominated by powerful preferences often concealed from my view.

I believe it's a subject significant enough to give over nearly a whole chapter to it.

That's what you'll find next, a key part of my story about Identity Failure and Rational Faith certainly. Because I've learned that I generally seem to get what I really want from my life, day to day. The trouble is that what I think I want and what I really want often are very different things.

Even when I am sure they're not.

Chapter 5: Deeply Determined

"Human behavior flows from three main sources: desire, emotion and knowledge."
                                    Plato

Desire, Much Wanted

I agree with Plato's quote. He would, no doubt, be gratified.

Or perhaps he would feel something entirely different based on his knowledge as well as his immediate emotions and desires. If I had the chance to speak with Plato I actually would suggest one small change to his observation based on my experience: I would substitute the word "information" for "knowledge." I suspect that's really what he meant. Because it's not only knowledge that shapes my behavior, it's any interpretation of myself or the world that I believe true. It's everything that I regard as meaningful information, all the moments I distill into my view of reality no matter how ludicrous this may be if critically examined. It's not what I know, it's what I believe I know.

I like to think Plato would approve of that minor revision. The alteration allows me to plug his idea very snugly into my theories about human motivation. So far I've been talking about information and emotion to explain why I do what I do. I've discussed quancepts and vericepts and nexes, emotional satisfaction and tigertails, the MIEN or Most Immediate Emotional Necessity – and what I call the Fundamental Law of Mind. Together, these elements are the information and emotion that combine to help make me who and what I am. And they result in something I termed psychogravity, the increasing emotional strength of a connected set of interpretations. Psychogravity pushes me toward specific quancepts and vericepts and thoughts and feelings and actions in ways that remind me of physical gravity pushing a baseball toward the earth or a comet toward the sun.

Which brings me to my personal experience with Plato's desire.

What is it that I truly want while these things are happening inside my head? Am I simply a victim pushed around by automatic psychogravitational thrusts, coerced this way and that by the interaction of information and emotion inside me without the ability to change direction? Is it possible for me to want constructive behavior, to desire it wholly without serious reservations, but still be driven by psychogravity into living destructively? Or can my free will overcome these forces?

What is the role of desire among the great philosopher's trio of psychological forces?

To me, Plato's desire is the crux of the matter.

My earlier discussions offered relevant key psychological details as I see them at work within my head. The MIEN, for instance, seems a useful general concept about my motivations. The Fundamental Law of Mind is a precise and, I feel sure, accurate description of how my psyche works at its core. I believe this law profoundly shapes everything I do. It is my mind's most basic mechanism.

But even these ideas still leave out the question of whether I have to do what I do. And at another level, how I feel about what I do. Let me frame the matter with a familiar metaphor: the lost seaman. In everyday living, am I in the position of a sailor adrift at sea, genuinely hoping my lifeboat will catch a current that brings me ashore but entirely at the mercy of wave and wind? My desire plays no part in my fate. Or does my boat come equipped with oars that offer me the opportunity to save myself? My desire, then, may be a critical part of the outcome.

During my daily life, this issue of what I truly want helps me to bring the theoretical into the realm of the practical. How do I honestly feel about my behavior, including my thoughts and emotions? Do I want what's happening now or something else? If I don't want it, why am I doing it? And too often the follow up query, me to me: Why do I keep doing this same thing I don't want, again and again and again?

These are thoughts that return me to basic motivation as I've understood it since childhood – very simply, what do I want? At the same time, they point me toward a single dominant psychological force within me that expresses the end result of all those other mechanisms of mind: "Deepwanting," I have named it.

The meaning is as obvious as it sounds. Deepwanting causes me to do what I deeply want to do. Always. And I can do nothing else until I change what I deeply want.

Wanting The Bad Stuff

I create my own reality in a sense.

I make things happen, inside me and outside me as I navigate the world. Very often, these are things I can't imagine ever wanting. Why would I want to lose a job or alienate a friend? Why would I want to struggle for money? Why would I want to get sick? But I've learned that I have wanted all of those things and much worse for myself. As well as wanting many very good things too, of course.

This idea is so important in my life because it helps me better control my thoughts, feelings and actions. And the vericepts that precede them.

Whenever I find myself bobbing helplessly on chaotic psychological currents, I usually can't spot a sensible way out of my situation by relying on complex concepts about nexes and the Fundamental Law of Mind and so forth. These theories often feel too complicated to apply when I'm already deep in the grasp of powerful emotions and shifting circumstances. With some notable exceptions, many of my ideas have provided me only limited help in the midst of such intense confusions. Great help at other times, but limited during periods of turmoil.

An understanding of deepwanting is easier to hang on to during emotional crisis – I'm doing whatever I'm doing because it's precisely what I want. With that notion in hand I can challenge my vericepts, my thoughts and my feelings, finally assembling a more rational and constructive interpretation of my problem. And this typically leads me to some solution, some way out.

Let's imagine I repeatedly do self-destructive things on the job whenever I'm around my boss, making critical remarks about her decisions and showing up late for work despite her warnings. Knowing that I'm motivated by complicated arrays of vericepts and nexes isn't likely to change the predictable result – getting fired. The same is true even if I recognize that my behavior somehow reflects the Fundamental Law of Mind: My comments and tardiness stem from interpreting experience to create the weakest possible emotional resistance to the strongest possible feelings that my existence is valuable to me at this moment in this world. That's what is happening within me, but it's hard to synthesize this concept into usable knowledge when I'm under relentless pressure.

But once I understand that I'm forever tweaking my boss's nose because that's what I really want to do, I have a chance to take more control. It makes sense suddenly. I can find the handles on those oars I just mentioned, rowing myself toward some shoreline. And I can do this because the circumstances feel familiar. I know what it means for me to want something. And I have learned that I can change what I want through a conscious process of critical reflection. Do I want to get fired? Why? Can I afford to lose my job right now? Is there a more sensible strategy to change jobs? Etcetera.

If I actually will spend the time and energy to sort through such questions, I can alter my deeper motivations. This deliberate effort may activate constructive nexes about financial responsibility and wise transitions in life, for instance. At the same time, nexes that harbor anger about my boss would weaken. In turn, this permits me to become a better employee until I'm sensibly prepared to quit the job that I quite clearly detest.

Sick At Heart

Deepwanting.

I may not have called it by that name for a long time. But I have been intensely aware of this psychological reality in my life for many years.

Let me give you an example that may help to clarify the concept. I've been keeping notebooks off and on since I lived in San Francisco in the mid-1970s. I have hundreds of notes to myself about everything from political candidates to my psychological observations, from classical music to my parents, from innovative golf swings of the future to the Big Bang Theory. One of those notes in one of those notebooks dates from summer 1998. Unusually for me, I forgot to record the specific day for this entry but the preceding note was dated 7/16/98 and the entry afterwards was dated 8/8/98.

Including ampersands and punctuation as I had these in the notebook, here is what I wrote in my typical semi-legible longhand scrawl:

"I have been fascinated for more than 20 years by the interaction between mind & body & how this influences our illnesses. Just last night & today I had another lesson – I felt exhausted from all the recent stress with the house & career & everything going on, especially all the house & money problems. In the middle of the night, I awoke with what felt like the start of a cold. But by drinking several glasses of water, using my steam inhaler & taking some vitamins I took some active steps to head it off.

"However, I know that the most important thing I did was to consciously remind myself why I didn't want to get sick.

"I long ago realized that people often bring on or at least allow illnesses that they could prevent. They very rarely do this consciously. But at an emotional level, they see things about the illness as a way of finding some emotional relief, a 'satisfaction' of emotional needs.

"For example, I understood that I 'wanted' to get sick at some level for several reasons: to escape responsibility for dealing with any more problems ('I'd fix it but I'm sick'); to show Jill how stressed I've been so she'll offer the understanding of my feelings I crave; to force myself to slow down physically & mentally in order to get the break & rest I feel that I need; to reinforce for myself that I can't allow myself in the future to get as depressed as I did briefly on Saturday without suffering physical consequences; to avoid outside responsibilities such as doing a planned interview with a former Castro prisoner in Miami, making dinner plans with a friend in Miami, etc. (again, I can honestly tell them, 'Sorry but I was sick.'). This is an incomplete list but the point is clear: People often unknowingly will their own illnesses or at least don't fight them when those illnesses try to take hold. It's critical to not allow any belief that makes illness any type of solution in one's life. If you believe at any level that illness in any way is helpful or beneficial or a relief for problems, you open the door for illness to step inside. You must consciously reinforce the belief that illness is always a waste of time & energy, a needless cause of suffering & not a solution for anything.

"You must also be honest enough with yourself & self-aware enough to recognize when you need to slow down, need some understanding & so on. Then take constructive steps to meet those needs: e.g. take a 'mental health day;' talk to your spouse or friends about your feelings to get the understanding & sympathy you need, etc.

"Illness is often used as a cure. It is not a cure for anything – it causes its own problems &, though it can satisfy some emotional needs, there are more constructive ways to accomplish the same emotional goals, without suffering through illness & without making yourself into a person who increasingly sees illness as a solution to trouble & stress."

I can't tell you how many times I've pulled out this passage to re-read it during turbulent periods when I feel myself gravitating toward symptoms of some kind or other. It always, always helps me a lot.

I no longer see the same need for glasses of water or extra vitamins – or the steam inhaler, which I ditched some 20 years ago as I write this. But more strongly now than then, I recognize how crucial it is for me to want health.

Dr. John E. Sarno of the New York University School of Medicine has carried out decades of pioneering work on mindbody medicine, enormously important research I learned about in 2000. My debt to him personally and professionally is greater than I can express, though I'll do my best in a later chapter about health as it relates to Identity Failure. Through Dr. Sarno's writings, I've learned that my mind and body are indivisible in ways I hadn't guessed when recording that notebook entry in 1998.

The notebook passage, though, offers a perfect example of what I'm talking about here. Deepwanting.

I remember that night very well. I could sense myself being drawn toward sickness, though I have always detested being ill. It's not too much to say I despise sickness, a feeling that appears stronger in me than I've detected in other people. Illness offends me in some intense and personal way. But there I was anyhow, gravitating inexorably toward days or weeks of feeling rotten.

Why so?

I deepwanted to get sick because I could see no other path to satisfy those feelings I wrote about in the notebook. Not until I analyzed my feelings at least. Large amounts of emotional energy were active inside me, energy so painful that I felt myself being overwhelmed by it. Just imagine how much emotion came attached to the things I discussed. My wife, Jill, and my urgent desire for her understanding. Bitter disappointments in my writing career. Intractable struggles to afford a house that Jill wanted but I never did. Big stuff, all that. And little, if any, of it quick or easy to correct. Many major problems all were working against me at once, as I perceived my situation that night. Other smaller responsibilities loomed that I also wanted to escape.

At a deeper level, I felt significant doubts about myself. Identity Failure. Maybe I wasn't a good writer afterall. Maybe there was something wrong with me to dislike owning a house. Maybe I was a bad husband to Jill. Maybe I was a failure for not making more money to support a costlier lifestyle. Maybe the universe was punishing me for some reason I didn't understand. Maybe, maybe, maybe. This deep self-confusion then activated powerful fears and equally powerful rage about the overall situation. Rage that I didn't know how to cope with effectively, meaning that I repressed most of it.

All told, this was one grand recipe for illness.

Sickness felt like the best compromise solution to all these problems. Sickness looked like the Most Immediate Emotional Necessity. Sickness appeared the best available opportunity to interpret experience to create the weakest possible emotional resistance to the strongest possible feelings that my existence was valuable to me at that moment in that world. To endure my difficult circumstances, sickness is what I wanted.

Deepwanted, that is.

Fortunately, I was able to find an alternative that night, doubtless motivated powerfully by my hatred of illness. By recognizing that at a deeper psychological level I actually wanted to get sick, I could think through the problems enough to realize that sickness wasn't what I wanted at all. There was another way.

A Most Forceful Force

Deepwanting is as real as the everyday wanting I've known since childhood.

When I hunger for an ice cream cone, I want it. This general feeling emanates from a huge number of earlier interpretations made during my experiences with ice cream. These have gathered together into large groups of interpretations with their attached emotion – vericepts about ice cream becoming nexes about ice cream. I happen to love ice cream. I'm sure I have sizable nexes about ice cream. To this day, I happily add to those nexes any chance I get.

Since I first tasted ice cream as a very young boy, I've been storing lots of information and emotion about that surprising dessert. Those ice cream-related nexes have been activated whenever I desire an ice cream cone today. This is the underlying psychological reality at such moments as I would explain it. But as I actually experience these moments, I simply want to eat some ice cream. That's how I felt at six-years-old when the Good Humor truck rolled by my family's home and that's how I feel now whenever I come within a mile of a Ben & Jerry's ice cream shop. New York Super Fudge Chunk for me, please.

To want in that way feels like a power at work inside me. And so it is. It's how I experience all that information and emotion about ice cream, a genuine psychological force. Desire, in Plato's word.

The same is true for deepwanting.

No matter how many complex processes are happening in my psyche, I experience a very forceful force indeed – something I can recognize for myself. I wanted the ice cream cone, I deepwanted to get sick.

The difference is that what I want typically is apparent, but what I deepwant isn't.

I know when I crave licking my way through Ben & Jerry's ice cream or catching a good movie or drifting asleep or making love. Or conversely when I don't want to meet with someone, don't want to go somewhere, don't want to do something. Or whatever else. I believe even such everyday actions or inactions actually do reflect what I deepwant, as you will see. Yet at the time I'm not aware of this more profound subtext. I am in touch only with the more obvious feeling of wanting or not wanting something. The surface desire. I could tell you about any of these desires easily and I'm more than pleased to do so.

I am, though, mostly oblivious to the things I deepwant. I can uncover this force within, yes, but often not without considerable energy to unpeel many layers of mind. Deepwanting's motivations arise from enormously powerful nexes that interact to drive me toward psychological goals that feel very important in my life. I deepwant the things that matter most to me at the moment, even if from the outside they may appear trivial or destructive. From the inside, they feel necessary.

Deepwanting, then, always involves the interplay of astronomical numbers of vericepts in massive nexes that cause my desires at the deepest levels of my psyche. Deepwanting is the overwhelming need to satisfy my most powerful, most thoroughly ingrained nexes in whatever way appears the best possible at the time. It's an expression of my very core. The deep, foundational, insistent desire.

No matter how inexplicable it may seem.

Like all other aspects of my psychological experience, deepwanting is governed by the Fundamental Law of Mind. This is true for both deepwanting's origins in my head as well as its function in my everyday life.

Deepwanting began when my core values along with core concepts about myself and the world formed from early childhood on according to the dictates of the Fundamental Law of Mind. Smaller nexes involving these values and concepts collected to make large nexes. Large nexes collected to make larger nexes and so on, just as I've outlined in previous chapters. Small things combine to make big things in nature – and in me. This growth happened as part of creating the weakest possible emotional resistance to the strongest possible feelings that my existence was valuable to me at those moments in that world. I was interpreting experiences with my family, with friends, with everyone and everything in ways that made me feel as good about myself as seemed possible. This included adopting some of their values and beliefs as my own. Bob, as I wanted to be, was taking shape.

Those core values and core concepts also assert themselves today according to that same fundamental law. Anything contrary to them creates emotional resistance, anything consistent with them creates feelings that my existence is valuable to me. This means my core values and core concepts greatly influence the formation of new quancepts and vericepts and nexes. And so naturally such core values and core concepts also affect my thoughts and words and actions enormously every day. To a very significant degree, they determine how I interpret experience. They influence the exact manner in which my mind automatically creates the weakest possible emotional resistance to the strongest possible feelings that my existence is valuable to me at this moment in this world.

Essentially, those core values and core concepts mold my psyche in their image.

Let me give a brief example that may help clear up this point. We'll return to my near-infirmity described in the 1998 notebook entry. As I'd just noted about this night, "To endure my difficult circumstances of the moment, sickness is what I wanted."

But why?

Here's part of that cause. At a very young age I already cared deeply about other people. I wanted to make folks feel good, not bad. I have distinct memories of this sensibility from at least seven-years-old if not before. All my caring exerted a powerful force that strongly influenced my nascent psyche. It altered my vericepts, it shaped my nexes. It built small nexes into large nexes. As a result, some of my deepest core values and core concepts materialized around my desire to make folks feel good, not bad.

Those youthful caring nexes helped to determine the MIEN for me at any given moment. They became important psychological elements that the Fundamental Law of Mind had to take into account throughout each day. This was a huge force in my life back then.

And now. And it was one of the significant reasons I deepwanted sickness during my 1998 episode. I didn't really want to get sick. What I wanted was to escape a situation in the world that felt otherwise inescapable if I was to maintain my self-image as a highly responsible and capable person who treats others with honesty and with consideration. I still deeply wanted to make folks feel good, not bad. So sickness felt like the best available compromise until I reasoned through the problems.

Deepwanting is the insistent overall craving for something that feels profoundly significant to me, my truest and deepest desire underlying all the other desires about that thing. In a meaningful sense, deepwanting is the sum of my psyche's parts at a given moment. It demands that I hold fiercely on to those values that I feel make me me – and to keep holding on no matter what.

In life, there's what I claim to want and there's what I deepwant.

Deceptive Desires

I suspect many folks may understand the difference between what they say they want and what they truly want. I've certainly often caught people talking in similar terms.

Think of examples you may have heard about serious confusion of this sort. Maybe the guy who believed he wanted to be a doctor like his dad, graduated from medical school and practiced for years before suddenly recognizing he didn't like medicine at all. Or the woman who remained in a lengthy marriage, telling everyone for decades that she was happy before realizing at last that she had never enjoyed life with her husband. Or the criminal who finally gained his long-sought freedom from a prison term but almost immediately committed another crime that he knew would soon return him to his cell.

We can easily imagine some of the more superficial motivations behind their self-deceptions. But I believe each individual really would have been driven by much deeper values. What they deepwanted was to maintain their feeling of commitment to these core personal values. Perhaps the doctor felt an insistent need to repay good parents for his upbringing as well as to honor family tradition, deepwanting especially to please his father. The woman may have valued adhering to traditional female roles, needing others to see her as a loving wife. The convict may have been a thief who valued his record of nonviolent crime but feared he now might harm someone without constant supervision. Or whatever the specifics may be. Values such as those could be strong enough to cause deepwanting, I suspect, though they probably would reflect even more basic values of some kind. Maybe the thief needed to see himself as fundamentally kindhearted despite his crimes. Possibly the wife needed marriage to feel she was a worthy human being. And the doctor might have required paternal approval to gain feelings of individual value.

We frequently act against our own interests because it's what we really want to do at some level. The examples are countless and, I believe, the continual stuff of the everyday.

That's surely true in my own life. As I see it, I am perpetually doing what I deepwant to do and nothing else.

Sometimes there's no conflict between what I believe I want and what I deepwant. Writing this book, for instance. Sometimes there is a conflict in me between the two forms of wanting but they involve no great issue at the time. I think I want a second martini but really don't. Minor as that situation sounds, I have found even small decisions connect with deeper values in me. Everything does. For instance, I may order the unwanted martini because my psyche insists on strengthening my self-image as a nice guy: My friend ordered another drink at the bar and I didn't want her to feel abandoned by her companion for the evening. My concern about this activated a very deep need to avoid harming people in any way, even insignificant ways whenever possible. So I drank another cocktail I didn't enjoy because that felt comfortable to me.

I didn't want the martini. But I deepwanted the martini.

At other times, though, the conflict between what I want and what I deepwant is important. One major area of my life where this has become obvious to me is money.

Basically, I've never had any – and at some point, I was forced to admit to myself that's because I never wanted any real money. Naturally, I have hated worrying all the time about income and expenses. I've found it debilitating, exhausting and enraging, just as during the period recounted in my notebook passage. Money troubles make me miserable. So why was I forever struggling just to survive financially? Why did I keep doing this same thing I didn't want, again and again and again?

Because I deepwanted it. Or more specifically, I deepwanted to focus on things in life I felt more important than money rather than to devote the attention to my income that would have eased my fiscal problems. Since becoming financially independent of my parents at age 21, and even well before, I've felt very afraid of the corrupting influence of money. As a 17-year-old hippie, I dismissed as shallow materialists everyone who cared much about money. I still felt that way when I lived in San Francisco. And all my time as an adult in Vermont. And I've felt more or less that same way during my nearly 30 years to date in South Florida. I have been terrified of possessing real money, no matter whether I did something to get it or the dollars somehow dropped into my hands.

What would money do to me? Would it diminish my motivation to pursue creative achievement? Would it make me callous to the needs of others? Would it warp my values? I didn't know what it was to exist without money worries – and like the ex-con who quickly returned to prison, I've kept going back to my confinement because it feels familiar. Miserable, restrictive … and comfortable.

After realizing this truth several years ago, I've slowly come around to a more helpful attitude. That's happened by thinking through the issue more carefully and critically, exactly as I did on the night I wanted to get a cold. For one thing, I've understood that my parents seem to have shared a similar attitude about money. The dad I adored was always complaining about how unlucky he was with finances compared to some of his more well-heeled friends. But to me now, it looks very much like he lived with a deep reluctance to do the things needed to acquire all that cash he supposedly so wanted.

I suspect my father deepwanted to live pretty much the lifestyle we had – low-to-mid middle class Midwestern, with money a frequent concern. It was what he knew. It was comfortable.

I'm sure my parents' behavior greatly affected my attitudes about money, combining with my own interests and sensibilities as a boy. Artistic, creative, people-centered from the start along with an intense attraction to science and knowledge. Things weren't that important to me, ever, with the major exceptions of my World Book Encyclopedia as well as my first full-size drum set when I was 11-years-old. I remember that my grandmother had to loan my parents the money for those drums, an act of generosity that Dad proudly announced to me during dinner one night in Ohio. I still recall this moment with great affection.

Over the years of my childhood and then into adulthood until recently, those interests and sensibilities together with my experiences created huge conflicts in me about money.

I knew I needed it, obviously, and I wanted it at some level for the freedom that money could buy. But more deeply, my large complex of misconceptions and fears overpowered the desire for anything much beyond a subsistence income. Only yesterday, in fact, I found myself briefly musing about what my life would feel like without any money worries ever again – and part of me rebelled at the idea. It still scared me. I could feel the old questions coming around once more: "What would money do to me? Would it diminish my motivation to pursue creative achievement? Would it make me callous to the needs of others? Would it warp my values?"

This time, though, I was soon able to push those fears away, reminding myself why I do now want at least a comfortable living without any more financial miseries if possible. I believe I even could handle an impressive chunk of funds today with no undue anguish. I surely am willing to try getting used to it.

That said, I must confess that I continue to dance the rim of the economic inferno.

I have no savings at all. I have fairly major credit card debt. Any massive expense that I couldn't charge to one of those cards would put me quickly into bankruptcy in my mid-60s. That frightens me, as you would expect.

But the prospect of refocusing my attitudes and values sufficiently to truly eliminate that risk frightens me more. To this day, I continue to deepwant the lifestyle I have – low-to-mid middle class South Floridian, with money a frequent concern.

Like father, like son.

Dominance Of The Necessary

There's something shocking about discovering that I often want things that are bad for me. I want to feel things that harm me, believe things that diminish me, do things that sabotage me. I want to be in ways that are destructive to my own best interests, painfully and repeatedly punishing me. There's nothing fun about being broke.

Perhaps a more specific, detailed explanation is needed to make the issue entirely understandable.

You'll recall that, in Chapter Four, I wrote this: "That foundational principle of motivation (the Fundamental Law of Mind) means that the greater psychological force with the least psychological resistance relative to that force will win any emotional conflict. And that greater force, again, is whatever creates the strongest possible feelings that my existence is valuable to me at this moment in this world. Anything my mind believes best meets that most immediate emotional necessity carries the day with me, whether in quancept or vericept, in thought, word or deed. It's all a matter of energy, of relative strength, just as anywhere else in nature. The stronger force prevails, whether that natural force is brute energy as in geology or adaptability as in natural selection. As I noted earlier, when I'm looking within my psyche it's not survival of the fittest. It's dominance of the necessary."

That's precisely how it works with deepwanting too.

I deepwant whatever feels most necessary at the time. So how could fiscal insecurity feel necessary to me? I can broadly illustrate by choosing just a few key elements among the large number of nexes that make up this complex inside me. And as I also did in the previous chapter, I'll assign a number value to these elements. This time around, though, I'm going to use a larger scale – one that I think works better for self-reported feelings. Rather than a 1-100 scale I'll demonstrate with a 1-1,000 scale, which seems to me big enough to reflect finer emotional distinctions but small enough to be easily comprehensible. Most of us know what a thousand is.

An additional word of explanation about my numerical system: The top end of the scale represents the strongest possible force from any single nexus. It does not suggest the strongest possible emotion that I can have overall as a human being. I'm not sure there is a maximum of any kind. And if there is, I'd have no clue what that might be. I mention this to clarify that nexes can combine to reach emotional levels far in excess of 1,000. That's how I see things working inside me. Emotions from this combine with emotions from that to gain strength.

Remember also, these numbers stand for the strength of my emotions specifically connected with my beliefs about money, fiscal security and similar topics. But the emotions would be attached to my interpretations in a wide variety of nexes, including many nexes focused on topics other than fiscal issues. In my mind, lots of subjects somehow connect with my relationship to money. Some of these carry information-and-emotion that can push me toward a stronger desire for money – maybe my notions about old age in American society, which brings poverty to many people. Other relatively unrelated nexes carry information-and-emotion that can push me away from the desire for money – possibly my ideas about pretension, a frequent affliction of monied folks I've met. So for this example I'm saying some of the vericepts, some of the interpretations-with-emotion, in each of these nexes described below are connected with my beliefs about money. The numbers, then, show the relative power of those money-related vericepts that are active at some moment when I am making financial decisions. And all this is intended only to illustrate deepwanting something that's bad for me.

With the higher numbers representing stronger emotional energy, I'll begin with a core value that carries great force in my life. It's a supernexus that I'd mentioned before: My belief in the importance of every individual contributing our best work to society. As I said then, there's a massive amount of energy here – and some of that energy figures heavily into my feelings about money. This nexus would include both accurate and romanticized tales of great persons who struggled with poverty to fulfill their talents. It would include many troubling instances of people who exchanged their true gifts in return for higher incomes, examples drawn from both history and my experience around others. It would include my lifelong attitudes about greedy individuals and greedy companies that sacrificed a greater good for cash. It would include experiences with little or no payment for much of my own most serious writing, my need to feel a strong sense of personal integrity in my professional life and a lot more too. These are among the money-related vericepts within this supernexus. All together, these money-related vericepts exert a powerful psychogravitational push in me toward doing what I consider my best work without much regard for the income it produces. I'll assign that supernexus an anti-money force of 900 for this example.

A related supernexus involves my passionate need to live a full life of meaning and purpose. To me, this goal has appeared largely unrelated to money except for the opportunities money may purchase to focus on more important things such as my serious writing. Yet I've usually found some way to focus on more important things anyhow, despite a lack of money. And again, I fear the corrupting power that great amounts of funds might exert on me, partly concerned that wealth could over-activate hedonistic tendencies I've long seen in myself. Though this supernexus also includes positive interpretations about money's contributions to a purposeful life, the vast weight of its money-related vericepts run contrary to that: Money often saps meaning and purpose from life. It is a threat. I'd give this supernexus an anti-money emotional strength of 925.

As I've suggested, a vast number of nexes would play a role in my negative attitudes about money. Many more of them than I know. Another would involve the deep value I attach to helping people, something that until recent years didn't much recognize money's potential for good. Without elaborating on the components of this third supernexus unnecessarily, I simply will give it an emotional energy rating of 975 in my life. It's a big value for me, obviously, pushing me toward living without serious reflection about finances.

For this very broad example, I'm ignoring significant nuances of these nexes as I did before. It's unlikely that any supernexus would be fully activated at once and the strength of these nexes each would wax and wane rather than being constant. But this makes my point, I hope.

So with three hugely forceful core values already identified on the anti-money side of things, let me move on briefly to some elements on the other half of my psyche's money equation. That is, nexes that sometimes can push me toward pursuing money. Of course these would include a nexus with information-and-emotion about the many benefits that money offers the individual, a topic I would guess to have formed a midnexus in me – you'll recall that a midnexus sits appropriately in the middle on my nexus scale, below a supernexus and macronexus but above a micronexus and mininexus in size and power. This midnexus would contain information-and-emotion about the importance of money for living an acceptably comfortable life, for instance. And about the fun that money can give, everything from some of those hedonistic pleasures I alluded to, such as good food and beverage, to the cultural enrichments of travel and concertgoing. Etcetera. I'll number this midnexus with a pro-money emotional force of only 450 in me. Writing down that modest number surprises even me, and explains a lot. But this is how I honestly would estimate its importance in this example.

Other nexes that exert mainly pro-money energy in my life include one about my genuine enjoyment of five-star luxury, something I've been fortunate enough to experience many times. Obviously, this nearly always has happened at no cost to me through invitations to very expensive black tie galas and especially through opportunities to write about extended ultra-luxury foreign cruises. I savor the high life when it's available, from attentive personal service to top quality champagne and rich truffles. I'd give my luxury nexus roughly a 200 rating, perhaps less.

Another positive-money nexus would revolve around opportunities I've had to be generous, whether toward a charity or a homeless person or to friends or family. Money's potential for good, as I said. I love the feeling although I've never had a large enough bank account to do this regularly. But as I age, the chances for financial generosity have increased somewhat and I have liked this. I would assign the moneygiver nexus a 250.

It's clear enough where all this is heading without further prolonging the explanation. The amount of emotional energy attached to my non-material core values is greatly stronger than the amount of energy connected with my pro-money concepts. My deepest sense of who and what I am is tied up in fundamental beliefs that essentially dismiss money as a nuisance. And often view it as a danger. Until and unless that changes somehow, I probably won't truly alter my approach to money – and my financial condition likely won't improve much either. I'll stay a low-to-mid middle class South Floridian, with money a frequent concern. It's still what makes me most comfortable. It's what I really want.

It's what I deepwant.

The example also more plainly reveals the difference between wanting and deepwanting. Do I want money? Of course. I'm an American male in 2019, with many idle wishes and hopes and desires that require money. If a quiz show host were to question me on the topic, I'd naturally reply, "Sure, I'd like the chance to win a million dollars!" I'd feel and I'd appear just as greedy as the next American male – or female. That's the surface desire I talked about.

But as we've seen, it's not my true desire. My deep self doesn't much want money at all.

A Quick Aside

An unusually analytical reader at this point may feel a question surfacing: What's the difference between deepwanting, psychogravity and tigertails?

(Please don't feel badly if this hasn't occurred to you yet. It would have. If you've stuck with Beyond Me this far, you surely are the different reader mentioned in my preface. You're unusually curious. And unusually smart. And I believe you'll find that the coming chapters offer you increasingly significant rewards to repay your curiosity and intelligence. And your patience ... The best of this book is yet to come.)

So, then, to the question. Very briefly for now.

- Deepwanting is a state of mind that expresses our most emotionally powerful values. We deepwant what we most care about.
- Psychogravity is a process that supports what we deepwant. It increases the emotional strength of a connected set of interpretations that help us move toward whatever we deepwant in any situation.
- Tigertail is the intense desire to satisfy some deepwanted values that feel profoundly threatened by circumstances. The fear of violating these values fuels self-destructive repetition, such as the woman who clings to motherhood despite her son's death.

The Fundamental Law of Mind governs all of these and every other aspect of the psyche's function. Deepwanting, psychogravity and tigertails all help individuals interpret experience to create the weakest possible emotional resistance to the strongest possible feelings that their existence is valuable to them at this moment in this world.

As our story progresses, these concepts will come into sharper focus. Each is integral to a full understanding of Identity Failure, both the problem and the solution.

Too Much, But Not Enough

I've learned that deepwanting brings many peculiarities to the lives of human beings.

Because it's not only possible to truly want something that's very bad for me. I also can want excessively something that's very good for me.

It is an odd and unexpected twist. I know what it's like to want something too much. You probably do as well. I've heard a fair number of people make this point over the years, including athletes who admitted they probably wanted to win the Super Bowl or an Olympic gold medal too intensely – and lost as a direct result.

I think the notion is worth mentioning in light of my insistence that I usually get what I most deeply want in life. And that this appears true for others too. On the surface, there seems a contradiction here: How can I want something so deeply that my desire is self-defeating?

In my own experience, the problem is semantics more than psychological paradox. Semantics ... and misunderstanding my own true intent. Because when I want something in a way that appears excessive, I'm deepwanting other things rather than the one thing I'm so focused on outwardly. And unbeknownst to me, the heated pursuit of those other things is what becomes self-defeating.

Another personal for-instance is called for here. One telling example from my life involves intensely wanting a romantic relationship soon after meeting an appealing woman. I made this same mistake repeatedly starting in adolescence. I would chat with someone who seemed lovely and intelligent, then find myself fantasizing about how wonderful our time together could be for years to come. She is fun and funny, she is gorgeous, she is smart as a whip. Most of all, she seems caring and warm and emotionally healthy. Wow, what a combo. Somewhere around this juncture I would begin to want the relationship with her too strongly. Far too strongly. In a few cases, I'm sure that I scared off women who actually might have become friends with me – and perhaps could have become more than that. In some other cases, I put myself in awkward positions only to find out this person was nothing like the female I'd so feverishly imagined. Perhaps I'd arranged a full day's outing together after a brief first meeting, which resulted in a long and unpleasant date for us both. Most often I simply obsessed about this remarkable being to the point of distraction, sometimes actually making myself briefly ill. Or I would find myself so overcome with twitchy jitters when we next met that my nerves interfered with getting to know each other comfortably. Until, inevitably, most of these relationships soon vanished and I felt furious with myself for indulging in such foolish fantasy. At first blush, my excess enthusiasm looks like I wanted a romance with these women too much. Extreme deepwanting.

Except that's not what happened.

Instead, they each became a focal point for other issues in my life. Even before adulthood, I suffered from a profoundly sentimental delusion – the sense that I could in some way merge with a woman emotionally, establishing the deepest possible connection with her as a human being. A "soul mate" in common terms, though I hate the phrase. I have believed so intensely in this kind of psychological connection that I've tried to make it happen in each long-term relationship of my life. And, as explained, in many briefer relationships as well. I now believe that such a desire is both impossible to fulfill and extraordinarily unhealthy for me as well as for any other person involved. My rational view of relationships has changed dramatically over the years, a much-needed fresh perspective that grew out of my understanding of Identity Failure. I've devoted Chapter 11 entirely to these new ideas about romance.

Today I can see that I wasn't deepwanting any woman at all during these episodes. Not really.

My passion didn't swell to extremes simply because I so wanted to be around her. I deepwanted her in order to meet other emotional needs that I felt could be filled with such a soulful mating. I deepwanted to feel that I was very highly valuable in the eyes of a person I valued very highly, an extraordinary kind of mutual admiration society that would play out through our everyday behavior. I would help her without being asked, she would help me without being asked. In particular, we would reflect our best qualities back to each other continually, like mirrors that revealed only the most beautiful parts of our bodies. My feelings of inadequacy, of struggling with some built-in flaw as a human, would be eased enormously by this woman – and I would diminish her feelings of being inadequate and flawed.

She would be the answer to all my daily battles with myself. In turn, I would be her answer. At many levels in me, this relationship would help me achieve major psychological goals. These would include my need to help others, my need to love deeply and feel loved deeply, my need to live a full existence of meaning and purpose. Not the total fulfillment in all these areas, naturally, but a satisfaction of those and other needs in my private life anyway.

Basically, I've deepwanted to escape the realities of life as an individual human through forging a deep relationship with another individual human. I was looking for an easier way to deal with Identity Failure.

Misled by romantic songs and movies and sentimental friends and family, encouraged by a culture that still celebrates soulmating as an attainable state of being, I exerted great amounts of energy in pursuit of this refuge from the world. When I appeared to want a new woman too much, I really deepwanted to convert this new woman into my savior. And to become her savior as well. These were heady emotions and they often pushed me toward self-defeating thoughts and words and actions – and feelings, especially those obsessive feelings.

I suspect something similar goes on inside the heads of the athletes I mentioned and others who seem to want something too much. They're not wanting simply the Super Bowl title or the Olympic gold medal. Like me, they are each at cross-purposes, viewing these achievements as ways to obtain something else they deepwant. That confused pursuit prevents them from meeting those genuine deeper wants. Or from rearranging their understanding of life enough to deepwant something more constructive for themselves than, say, gaining feelings of individual value through fame. That true need in such an instance, the need for public adoration, can become inflamed to the extent that it overwhelms their athletic desire for a victory. And guarantees defeat.

Unfreely Free

If I or anyone sincerely deepwants something constructive, we're likely to get it in some form. The intense, persistent desire generally brings about a good result. So yes, then, I'm saying I believe that I can deliberately shape my future – and I believe others can as well.

This same opinion has been commonly voiced for centuries, of course, and expressed much better by others before me, including these lovely examples:

- "The greatest discovery of my generation is that a human being can alter his life by altering his attitudes." William James
- "I know of no more encouraging fact than the unquestionable ability of man to elevate his life by a conscious endeavor." Henry David Thoreau

That's been my experience too. Consciously altering my attitudes can give me the ability to elevate my life. That's what I meant just a moment ago when I talked about "rearranging their understanding of life enough to deepwant something more constructive for themselves..." Those athletes would have to think through their beliefs and values so they could form healthier attitudes, much as I did the night I deepwanted to get sick. We can change what's about to happen through a conscious endeavor, as Professor James and Mister Thoreau suggest. We can teach ourselves to desire, to deepwant, something better.

But I often find this an imposing case of much easier said than accomplished. I know it's possible. I've done it. Many times. But under powerful emotional pressure, I can feel utterly helpless – a victim of life's forces outside my control. I'm unable to consciously alter my attitudes enough to elevate my life or anything else for that matter. I can't change what I'm deepwanting. I am overwhelmed and floundering, adrift on those psychological currents.

What's happening here? It's a question I've wrestled with for more hours than I care to guess. Probably some thousands of hours. Honestly. And I think it relates directly to the subject of deepwanting: Why do I want what I want and can I intentionally change it to turn my life in a constructive direction? Is my profoundest desire caused or can I deliberately instill that desire in myself?

I view this as the classic philosophical question about free will versus determinism. I've both enjoyed and endured a fierce fascination with the issue since I first learned about it in an Eastern Michigan University ethics class in 1973. The concept of determinism never had occurred to me before then, the idea that our lives may be entirely cause-and-effect. We have no genuine control.

Or are we free in some real way?

It's what I was getting at toward the beginning of this chapter: "Am I simply a victim pushed around by automatic psychogravitational thrusts, coerced this way and that by the interaction of information and emotion inside me without the ability to change direction? Is it possible for me to want constructive behavior, to desire it wholly without serious reservations, but still be driven by psychogravity into living destructively? Or can my free will overcome these forces?"

When still in college, I soon adopted the belief that everything is determined. Somewhat later in my 20s, as I remember, I found it necessary to shift my position because free will seemed so central to living a healthy life. After this I more or less vacillated back and forth for many years, often agonizing at great length over the issue … until I reached a conclusion that surprised me.

Both things are true, simultaneously. That's still what I believe. Of course this seems a paradox, the ideas appearing mutually exclusive. Things are caused or they're not. We have some measure of control over life or we don't.

For a long while I felt that the apparent paradox literally existed. Both free will and determinism were realities of human life. The dividing line I saw was time, whether we looked backwards at events that already happened or ahead at events that hadn't happened.

These days I hold a similar but more subtle notion based on my personal experience. I believe that all things are the result of enormous complexes of cause-and-effect, including who I am, what I am and all the quancepts and vericepts and thoughts and emotions and feelings and words and deeds that pass through me. My life is determined.

But …

Free will exists as well. Anyone who has felt this surge of power and confidence would know what I mean – and it's not sensible for me to deny free will's existence in my life. I've experienced it. So determinism and free will do indeed coexist, in my judgment. Here's where the subtler side of my notion comes, as I see it. Within me free will is a feeling, a psychological reality. It seems a vitally important state of mind for my well-being as I try to take my life where I want it to go. But I believe this state of mind itself is caused. And its presence simply causes healthier, more desirable effects than feeling like a hopeless victim.

I view free will and its benefits, then, as among the more helpful results of nature's causes and effects, including all those psychological causes I've detailed so far in this book. That's how I experience the free will versus determinism question. Free will's an illusion in a real sense, but an essential one to maintain. And to do that, I must believe sincerely that it exists.

I call this the Free Will Paradox.

The very instant I truly adopt a belief that free will is real, my whole attitude changes and most definitely elevates my life. I have taken responsibility for where I am at this moment and where I will go in the moments to follow. That sense of responsibility does many things. I feel powerful and effective. I feel confident and hopeful. I see new and realistic opportunities to create change, convinced I can make them happen. The fundamental feelings of individual value that I so incessantly seek are strengthened greatly. I view life as more manageable, diminishing the rage that constantly thrums through my psyche. Free will sustains me as I move forward, bolstering the persistence that's crucial to any significant accomplishment or worthwhile change.

All these benefits along with the other pluses of free will usually cause a better outcome for me. Free will means I can create a good life if I try.

Making Freedom Ring

Not that any of this comes easily for me most of the time. I frequently struggle to fully accept responsibility for my future. I'm better at holding on to some sense that I exercise control over many major parts of my life in the long term. But far too often I still feel the victim of immediate events. Naturally enough, this tends to happen when things outside me aren't going well, when life is tough. It's a lot easier to feel I've got the world on a string, to quote the old song, when the world's not trying to tug the string from my clenched knuckles.

To apply free will in everyday living, I first must understand the concept thoroughly. In essence, I must have built up my free will nexes to sufficient strength with large amounts of information and emotion about that idea: what free will really means in my life, how to make it happen, readings about free will, examples of my own successful efforts to implement free will and so on. Free will must be an important active presence in my psyche so the notion exerts adequate psychological energy to overcome other inner forces that make me feel victimized and powerless.

Then to tap into this reservoir of experience, my head must be in the right place. I have to feel ready to change things. Because if events have swamped my sense of free will, I won't do anything except passively give into my difficult situation. I may hope for better. I may pray. But I can't take action that will make anything good happen. I'll only feel lost.

Change must appear so necessary that I deepwant something different than what exists now.

If I can recover the feeling of my power as an individual, find again some belief that I can improve my situation despite the world's obstacles, I may be able to grasp the handle that begins to cause change. The lifeboat oar is visibly near my hands, ready for rowing.

I wish it was easier for me to grab free will. And to hold on, despite modern life's ferocious distractions. It isn't, though I've learned that transcending my ego offers great help.

Identity Failure drains my belief in free will. Overcoming I.F. bolsters my belief, as I'll further explain later in the book.

Self-value gained from within rather than from without gives me a sense of potency as a person.

Living The Paradox

But even during those times when I lack a strong sense of control over my future, the Free Will Paradox is useful in the everyday. It influences my view of myself, my life, every other person and everything that happens. Fairly useful indeed, all of that.

At a practical level, the paradox of responsibility as I understand it shakes out to this way of looking at things: Everything that has happened up to this instant had to happen. It was caused, determined. But the future can be changed through effort. It is subject to human will. In this way determinism and free will are reconciled for me, sharing a sensible, constructive coexistence. I find that this concept reflects the reality of my world as I know it, both my interior world and the world around me.

The Free Will Paradox works.

It doesn't matter that I really believe the future also is determined.

Information and emotion will combine to form desire, or deepwanting, that will cause all the effects that emanate from me. This will happen according to the psychological forces I've been laying out, such things as quancepts and vericepts and nexes and the MIEN and the Fundamental Law of Mind. Many things will flow together in incomprehensibly complex configurations to cause other things: in my mind, in my behavior, in my life.

I believe the same is true of every other person – all that they will be and all that they will do, entirely caused. And I believe everything in nature happens in similar ways, resulting from the wondrously complicated interaction of many preceding causes and effects. It is a viewpoint I have gained from a lifetime's passion for science. Things are caused. As a matter of possible small curiosity, let me add parenthetically that I share Einstein's views on this. I also don't believe God plays dice with the world, even at the sub-atomic level. Everything is cause and effect. And I would bet that some day Einstein will be proven right about this.

Everything may well be determined, including me. But to believe I have no control doesn't work in practice, no matter how true this may be in reality. That's because more important realities necessitate that

I assume responsibility for the future: the realities of my mind. To live productively and healthfully, I must feel my own power to cause change.

I have to believe in free will.

And free will is real. It is real because it's an experienced state of mind, as I outlined above, a feeling that causes healthier, more desirable effects than feeling like a hopeless victim. It's a discernible reality of the human psyche. I am very aware when it's there and equally aware when it's not. I suspect you are too. Doubtless, each of us knows what it's like to feel in control or out of control.

If I'd not believed in my power to cause change, I wouldn't have been able to prevent my illness back in 1998 – and countless times since then. A sense of victimhood causes certain things to happen to me, a sense of free will causes very different things to take place.

Free will is real. So is determinism. Or so I choose to believe.

Causing The Right Effects

You still may wonder just what the heck I'm talking about here. If free will is real, then this must be some innate human ability as most folks probably think of it. God or nature somehow infused us with the gift of choice and the capacity to make those choices happen. Our decisions are, well, free.

That's not how it works for me, as best I can tell. There's no moment when I'm detached from the effects of all my preceding experience. This experience determines how I think and feel and act. And it's impossible for me to think or feel or act otherwise.

Remember the earlier example about my attitudes toward money. Though it was highly simplified, the explanation perhaps provided enough detail to demonstrate that those attitudes clearly were caused by all of the interpretations related to money that I'd accepted as truth and all the forceful emotion attached to that information. As a result of those attitudes, my behavior with money flowed as a necessary consequence.

That's always how it appears in my life. To change, I need either to activate or create a sufficient strength of different interpretations and emotion, causing me to deepwant something else.

For instance, what if the frustration at my relative poverty became so great that I began to rethink some of my core values? And I then seized responsibility for improving my fiscal condition through what I considered to be the use of my free will ... My new reflections on finances might emphasize things like the importance of money in living a life of meaning and purpose, focusing on my ability to help those in dire financial need. I could consciously redefine "meaning and purpose" in this way, making the concept much less about fulfillment of talent and much more about monetary conditions for myself and others. As long as I genuinely accepted this reinterpretation, my pro-money nexes would gain great emotional force in my life and my anti-money nexes would lose some large amount of power to influence my behavior. Or I might even begin to see my efforts to contribute my best work to society from new perspectives. I would remember the examples of great entrepreneurs past and present, drawing inspiration for an altered take on wealth from folks like Gates and Buffett and Carnegie. They proved having money can bring positives to the world. I also well could decide that I had struggled long enough and deserved an easier existence at this point in my life, allowing pro-money nexes such as those related to luxury to acquire more psychological force – perhaps rating a 650 now instead of 200 or less.

If I thought long enough and deeply enough about all of this, motivated by sufficient emotional energy, I indeed would change some of my mind's nexus ratings about money and related subjects such as social contribution as well. I would interpret money differently and therefore feel differently about it throughout each day. And my subsequent quancepts and vericepts and thoughts and actions would follow as a necessary consequence. Probably I then would acquire more money, perhaps a lot of it.

This chain of events would have been set in motion by the intense frustration about my poor fiscal health. In other words, it would have been caused by the combination of all my preceding quancepts and vericepts and thoughts and feelings about money. And an existing belief in free will. Without a very strong conviction that I could elevate my life by a conscious endeavor, to paraphrase Thoreau, I never would have succeeded.

I was able to assert my free will because life caused me to do this. My situation made free will feel necessary. My deliberate efforts and their moneygaining results were necessitated by the processes happening in my psyche. Naturally I suffered some unpleasant sense of battling with myself along the way, fighting against my past to form new ideas and values. The emotional effort felt exhausting, with great psychological strength and persistence required over a long period before I finally changed my ways. But the dynamics taking place within my mind made it impossible to quit, no matter how it seemed to me at the time. I had significantly rewritten the psychological equations involving all-things-money. The stronger emotional force now was on the other side.

Recall what I wrote earlier about this issue in my life: "The amount of emotional energy attached to my non-material core values is greatly stronger than the amount of energy connected with my pro-money concepts. My deepest sense of who and what I am is tied up in fundamental beliefs that essentially dismiss money as a nuisance. And often view it as a danger. Until and unless that changes somehow, I probably won't truly alter my approach to money – and my financial condition likely won't improve much either."

That's just what I did in this example. Propelled by some overwhelming sense of monetary frustration, I changed my fundamental beliefs about money. This change of beliefs was caused. And in turn that caused a significant change in my finances.

Free will really is determined like everything else.

My effort was deliberate every step of the way. But no matter how free I felt, each step was caused by the ones before it.

Don't Touch!

Or take just one more brief example, something much simpler still for added clarity.

When I was a child, I somehow learned that stove burners were bad things to touch. I'm not sure if I fingered a hot one or simply built the concept around parental warnings as well as my own observations about intimidating gas flames and heat so strong I could feel it warm my face. This hot burner thing is a commonly used specific intended to show how kids learn.

But think about what's actually happening inside me today. I have never intentionally touched a hot burner since childhood, a result that was caused by that early lesson. At this moment, I couldn't touch one. I have lots of information and emotion related to heat and burns and hot stoves, all floating forcefully through my brain. Much emotional energy coming from strong nexes filled with my experience. I cannot act contrary to that information and emotion now. It has created an intense desire to avoid burns, no doubt drawing emotional power from even larger nexes about things such as health and self-harm that would make me deepwant to remain unburned. I can only overcome that desire by some furious countervailing motivation.

Information and emotion have caused an effect. Knowledge and emotion, in Plato's words. They've combined to create desire.

I can't do anything else given everything that's come before in my life. To put my hand on a hot burner, true, I can use free will. Through sheer gut-twisting willpower I can decide to burn my flesh. But though this surely is an act of will, it isn't an act that's free in any meaningful sense. The will to overpower my fear of the burner would have to come from somewhere first. It would have to be caused by great emotions that forced me to prove something to myself or others for purposes that appeared necessary to me at the moment – perhaps I would need to demonstrate toughness in some extreme if unlikely situation. It would, then, have to feel more important to burn myself than not to burn myself.

I would have the feeling of making a choice. I could bask in a sense of freedom: "I can choose to put my hand on the burner or put it safely back in my pocket!" But the quancepts and vericepts and thoughts and feelings that finally led me to an action, one way or the other, together would combine to determine that choice. As with rewiring my attitudes about money, I would do what I had to do.

Freedom's Cause

This means that I can summon free will in my life only because I learned the idea somewhere. And learned how it helps me.

I didn't necessarily have to pick up the concept from a philosophy class. Or from any book or any person. But in some form or fashion, I must have come into contact with the belief that I can make things happen by choosing to make them happen – and then I must have discovered by experience that I was right. I somehow understood what free will is. And I saw that free will brings more desirable effects. Then experience after experience with free will gave me confidence in it, adding strength to my belief.

Again, I also must keep stirring the emotional pot as it were, thinking thoughts that activate my free will nexes to release helpful emotion. "Yes, I can seize hold of my situation now. No, I don't need to allow myself to be shoved around by the world's forces. Yes, yes, I have to assume responsibility for what will take place going forward."

An abiding conviction in free will's reality alters deepwanting in my mind. Feeling more powerful and effective and confident and hopeful, seeing new and realistic opportunities to create change, strengthening my fundamental feelings of individual value and all the other advantages of free will – together they rewrite those psychological equations, changing the emotional numbers so that I truly desire something more constructive than I had desired before.

I alter the physics of my psyche.

To remember the existence of free will as I've come to understand it helps me regain a sense of more control despite the world's abuses. But I must cause myself to feel free through repeated refreshers drawn from experience.

Best Of Both Worlds

At the same time I must constantly remind myself that everything from now backwards in time was caused. Everything, in my view. All that I've done, all that others have done, all that has happened in the universe. It was determined by the collision of unimaginable numbers of variables.

This makes for a most peculiar intellectual balancing act. The Free Will Paradox at first feels like a bizarre notion.

But the virtue of my concept of free will and determinism is that it does two things simultaneously, both helpful in my daily life: First, it empowers me to make efforts that typically cause a better outcome in the future; second, it relieves me of guilt, blame, shame and other destructive feelings about everything that's occurred in the past. Free will exists for me going forward, determinism in the past and present. I'm responsible only for what hasn't happened yet, but in no way responsible for what already has happened right up to this very instant.

This wonderfully useful state of mind is only useful, or wonderful for that matter, when I can adopt it completely. That's not easy ... but it's possible. Doing it requires a total faith in my own experience, allowing me to bend my mind in this unorthodox manner. I can shape my future, I had no hand in the shape of my past.

When I manage to get myself comfortable with that strange notion, I can more easily let go of rage and bitterness about things. Everything had to happen exactly as it happened. And I can more easily feel confidence as I move through the day. I will cope with the world because I possess powerful traits that I can assert at will to influence events.

I accept this as a necessary paradox of daily living: one view looking ahead on the highway, another in the rearview mirror. As long as I can hold to that odd vision I'm able to help myself accept things I can't change and change things I can, much as expressed in an old prayer. It's not a perfect system in that way, mind you, but it works.

And it's the truth as I see it – my truth, created as the necessary outcome of my experience.

Poisonous Praise

Of course, there's another side to all this. To commit myself completely to that world view, I must accept that I have no responsibility for the praiseworthy components of my life either. If the bad things I do were caused, so were the good things. I can't have it both ways.

The same is true for good things that happen to me or good things done by others or good things that happen to them. All determined, as seen through the philosophy of Rational Faith.

That's an especially challenging concept for me because I've been so hooked into praise all my life as a source of self-value, mainlining it like a narcotic every chance I've spotted. From the earliest childhood moments I can recall until my early 60s, I was addicted to outside approval in order to gain some psychological equilibrium. I often wonder whether I literally have been addicted to this kind of appreciation, something that would show up like any other addiction if activated during brain scans.

I don't know for sure. I would guess the answer is yes.

I do know that I can't allow myself the addiction any longer, and for reasons that go well beyond philosophical consistency. The Free Will Paradox is helpful in this way too, pushing me away from a need for emotional rewards gained from without. Because my perspective on free will and determinism means I must accept that everything I've done was caused – and therefore never legitimately praiseworthy by others. It's not as if I had a choice. I'm not responsible for creating the Humanity Project. Or for helping kids to stop bullying or find feelings of their individual worth. I'm not responsible for my books and plays and poems and stories and other writings, no matter how fine anyone may think they are. I'm not even responsible for being a writer at all. It was caused, determined by that same collision of unimaginable numbers of variables.

I'm reminded here of a great line from my favorite movie, a film I have named in print as my choice for the finest ever made. "Lawrence of Arabia," directed by the brilliant Sir David Lean. At one point in the story, Lawrence remarks that a man can do what he wants: "But he can't want what he wants." To me, that's insightful. I can choose to write this particular book … or not. It doesn't matter in this case that I believe my choice was determined. The option is within the scope of my authority over my own life. But I can't choose to be a mathematician instead of a writer, at least not if I hope to make my fullest contribution to the world. A wise person learns what they already are, then develops and shares it.

I find that there's no problem in feeling pride and appreciation for my efforts when those feelings come from within, my own awareness of my own achievement. It may have been determined, but I still am the owner of that accomplishment. I am the conduit to bring it into the world. Recognizing that for myself is important to my mental health.

But there's a distinct problem in feeling pride and appreciation that comes from praise by others. It is destructive in the extreme, I've learned, feeding the Identity Failure I regard as my worst problem. Every instant that I absorb vericepts interpreting my life as more valuable based on someone's opinion, I increase the strength of I.F. in my psychological universe. My nexes related to the need for other people to understand and appreciate me, to view me as important, rise on the 1-1,000 rating scale of emotional force. And so psychogravity pushes me more powerfully toward further seeking outside praise.

The addiction worsens.

As a friend of mine wisely noted on the Internet: "Praise is like poison – harmless unless you swallow it." I agree with him entirely.

Teaching myself to dismiss feelings of gratification from outside praise has pushed me one significant step away from Identity Failure. If I don't let myself feel good from praise, then I automatically tend to reject feeling bad from criticism. And I become less plugged into people's opinions about me. In that way I learn to be more psychologically self-reliant, the opposite of Identity Failure.

It may come as no surprise that initially this is a hard thing to do. But it's well worthwhile. As with other aspects of the Free Will Paradox, a psychological forcefield against outside praise helps repel the miseries of an existence centered mostly around me. My wants, my feelings, my needs, my pain, my pleasure. Me.

All Bob, all the time. It's a horrible way to live.

I can rise above that self-obsession, though. The Free Will Paradox assists this effort.

Responsibility for the future engages my fullest resources and focuses them on the task at hand. An acceptance of determinism in the present and past helps to liberate me from clinging to so much rage and bitterness at the world, at life. I immediately feel relieved by the Free Will Paradox. The world appears challenging but exquisite in its complexity – and manageable for me if I try.

I can influence what will be in ways that I choose. I had no choice about anything that already is. Neither did anyone else.

That's the attitude I try to cultivate throughout each day.

Battling Toward Beyond

Without a constant search for outside approval, I'm freed to connect much more intensely with my deeper self-interest, the core values that often become so buried under the tonnage of the world's opinion of Bob. I can draw energy from the grand forces that are the best of me: my need to help people and to express my love and to contribute all I can to society's improvement. To avoid harming people whenever possible. To live a full life of meaning and purpose. To experience life's better offerings as intensely and completely as I can. These are the things I truly deepwant.

I understand now that my lifelong goal has been to find a way to be this kind of person. To live it more or less consistently. It's why I have explored my mind so thoroughly and so meticulously for so long. Who am I? What am I, really? And how can I use that knowledge to be the man I want to be?

The system that evolved from these decades of effort works. At least it works for me. Rational Faith, which importantly includes the concepts of deepwanting and the Free Will Paradox. I believe strongly my new philosophy will work just as well for others.

Desire, emotion and information taught me brutal lessons about the urgency for this transcension of my ego. Over and over again, Identity Failure damaged my existence at the profoundest levels. And many times nearly destroyed me, quite literally. If you read the next chapter you'll understand.

Oh yes, living for myself wasn't simply a failure for me. It was a disaster.

Chapter 6: To Me Or Not To Me

"If I have lost confidence in myself, I have the universe against me."
                    Ralph Waldo Emerson

Limited Vision

It always felt like the only way.

I had to help me. I had to get what I needed now – and with any luck, get what I wanted too.

I needed many things. Yes, I needed more money and I needed a newer car and I needed a nicer apartment. I needed sponsors for my nonprofit group. I needed time to write this book. Beyond all else, though, I needed recognition, understanding, praise. Appreciation. As often as I could find it and from as many people as possible.

I also wanted things I knew I didn't really need. I wanted a television with a bigger screen. I wanted to dine in restaurants more often. I wanted another travel writing trip overseas.

Oh yes, and I needed more than this and, yes, I wanted more than this. Much more than this. The catalogue of my personal needs and personal wants could not be filled, could not be satisfied. It was limitless in scale, reaching into even the most trivial parts of my life. I deserved smooth-flowing highway traffic on my drive to a meeting, with as many green lights on the city streets as possible. I deserved my Detroit Tigers to win most ball games they played this season and, preferably, the World Series championship. I deserved to open the daily newspaper to find stories that lifted my hopes.

There was a lot that I needed. There was a lot more that I wanted. I deserved it all. Getting it from the world was my real job, all day every day of my existence. Without harming others if at all possible, true enough, preferably even helping some people along the way if I could. That made me feel better about it. "Giving back," as they say. Though I'm not a parent, I do realize that I might easily have put my children's needs ahead of mine if I were. I also recognize that I would view my children as an extension of me – my needs satisfied through taking care of their needs. My kids as me.

In the end my psyche gravitated much of the time toward taking care of me, first and foremost in whatever form felt most significant. This isn't how I thought of things then, nor did I appear selfish. Most folks likely would have judged quite the opposite. I really listened, I genuinely cared, I honestly tried to help. But no, I'm talking a much deeper level of psyche here well below the obvious. In that place I alone was the center of my universe. Indeed to me I was the center of the universe itself if I'm honest about it. Nothing else appeared to me so central as my needs, my wants. What I deserved. Nothing else ever mattered quite so much.

Surely, this is just human nature. What other way was there for me to live? For any of us? We are constructed to look out for ourselves above all.

Aren't we?

Unfortunately, it doesn't work. I've learned that self-obsession of this sort is profoundly counterproductive. And I've observed directly within my own mind that it's profoundly counterproductive for a very good reason: A self-obsessed life doesn't conform to the laws of human nature, it violates them. It gums up the psychological mechanisms that determine who and what I am. I am not built to live for me alone – or for me through my children either.

I am built to share my experience with others in ways that are meaningful to me and helpful to them, which in turn helps me more than anything else. And all of this helps society. It's what I call shared value, the core of my philosophy of Rational Faith. That lifestyle is consistent with the realities of my mind, the most basic mechanisms as best I've been able to identify them over the past four and a half decades – the many elements I've written about so far, including quancepts and vericepts and nexes, psychogravity and the Fundamental Law of Mind and deepwanting. Those psychological forces function much more smoothly when my attention is focused on helping others rather than helping myself. The new approach works.

But that is not how I've lived most of my years on this planet. Me and more me and my needs and my wants and me me me, that's how it was. Even when I wrote yet another draft of this chapter as late as summer 2018, I still was battling to fully conquer that same problem. Those many needs and many wants of mine too often remained at the forefront of my mind, all safely concealed from the notice of others.

Why? What motivates this self-destructive way of being?

It is the psychological condition I've named Identity Failure, or I.F. for short. Overwhelmingly it has been the worst problem in my life, as I'll try to demonstrate very clearly in this chapter and the two following.

Then I'll make the case that Identity Failure is the worst problem in your life too.

Fundamentally Me

To understand how I.F. works in me, I must always remember the Fundamental Law of Mind. It's the key to Identity Failure. I am highly confident that this psychological law operates quite precisely as I've written it: Individuals interpret experience to create the weakest possible emotional resistance to the strongest possible feelings that their existence is valuable to them at this moment in this world. I am forever trying to make myself feel that my life right now is worth it. That I'm OK as an individual and life as I live it in this moment is OK.

Essentially, I'm engaged in a perpetual existential battle within my mind, instant by instant automatically searching out justifications for being alive. I know that sounds exaggerated at first blush, perhaps overly dramatic. But it's not – read on, please. In Darwin's Origin of Species, the third chapter is titled, "Struggle for Existence." The phrase is apt if applied to my life too: That's what is happening continually in my head. At the deepest and most hidden levels, my mind is locked in a psychological struggle to justify my existence to myself.

I mean that literally. It's a different version of Schopenhauer's will to live. That's what I seek at bottom. I'm looking to strengthen my will to live, all the time, every moment of the day and night. So my mind automatically interprets the world in whatever ways best meet this psychological need given the immediate internal and external conditions, moment to moment. That's what the Fundamental Law of Mind is saying.

I've learned about all that firsthand, through tortured experience. I now see that I have endured years of my life when my will to live was forced to contend in frightening ways with some increasing desire for non-existence. Part of me didn't want to go on, to cope with the world's frustrations and disappointments and sufferings. I was in worsening emotional pain. And I was growing tired. Only some parts of me, mind you, but enough of me for several years starting in 2013 that my mind created extremely destructive distractions to avoid most awareness of my fatigue with life. That fatigue horrified me so much that I wasn't even conscious of it for a very long time. I didn't want to know.

But after surviving far too many of those anguished endless nights I mentioned earlier in the book, I understood a vital lesson. I do want to live, very much. I want to live more than I want any other thing. The problem was that I'd tied my feelings of self-value to the world's treatment of me. I'd come to believe intensely that I needed to be certain things, personally and professionally, to make my life worth living. And that I needed the world to confirm I was those things so I could comfortably accept them as really me. Yet the world wasn't confirming these qualities of mine, at least not in any form I found satisfying emotionally. So over the years, I started to doubt myself at some level profoundly and darkly.

Oddly enough, at another level I enjoyed a fierce new confidence, making me a man in desperate inner conflict. I wasn't sure what to believe about my value in this world. Sometimes I felt one way about me, sometimes quite the opposite.

Frequently the doubts controlled my life. And the fatigue took deeper root. Maybe I truly wasn't the things I needed to be for my life to have value to me. Maybe there was something wrong with me. The whole world couldn't be wrong and me right. Or maybe that's exactly how things were – I was living a worthwhile existence in a society that constantly wronged me by ignoring my best work. In either case, that society was beginning to feel unlivable for me. And eventually I became aware of this fatigue. Still my mind worked hard to hide the feeling from my attention as much as possible. My psyche conjured up nearly continual anxiety of extraordinary intensity, along with a wide array of physical and emotional symptoms. In reaction to the fatigue and the anxiety and the symptoms, a furious anger often flushed through me. Anger at other people, at myself, at the world. I was fearful too, more deeply afraid than I'd felt since the period after my anxiety attack when I was 20-years-old.

This was Identity Failure in the extreme. My ego was crashing around me, in the process causing me suffering of a kind I'd never experienced before. As months of this torment turned into more than five years of repeated miseries, a portion of my intense will to live began to flag. And that terrified me above everything, only adding to my suffering as I tried to run from these feelings. Today I know that during this time I genuinely feared that I might commit suicide.

I feel sure that the only reason I didn't fall apart completely was my self-knowledge, gained with so much labor over so many decades. In the blackest and longest and loneliest nights, I remembered what I had learned about my mind – and trusted it. There was nothing else for me to do. Outwardly I appeared to function normally, writing this book and advancing the programs of the Humanity Project. Within, I often felt as if I was barely managing to cope.

But those nights and those years informed my insights into Identity Failure, lending new depth and new certainty. I already had understood the problem with reasonable accuracy by then, having struggled with it for so long. I even had named the condition well before my meltdown. Now, though, I had lived it to the pit of my soul, some of the worst that Identity Failure could offer me.

And it came like an epiphany.

Identity Failure Defined

I find Identity Failure a funny thing. Not funny haha, as we say in 21st Century America, meaning that it's not amusing. Hardly. I'm using the word "funny" here as in peculiar. It's peculiar to me as a professional writer because I now recognize that the psychological phenomenon is uniquely hard to describe. Different from anything I've come across in a writing career that began for me in high school.

In essence I.F. is a very simple condition. It should be simple to explain. But Identity Failure has so many facets, so many angles and surfaces, that a full account is highly challenging. I think of this like trying to describe a diamond. Superficially, that's easy. But a richer and more meaningful description is tough. As I reflected on this chapter for several months before starting to write it, I've found myself more than once spontaneously uttering the word, "Wow!" I've felt astonished at the complexity and breadth of the topic even after closely observing it daily for many many years. Piece by piece over that time, I'd constructed my understanding of Identity Failure. But until I was forced to sort through the main details to explain them, I hadn't fully realized how elaborately complicated the concept really is. Diamond-like, the subtleties appear endless.

So let me begin with the most basic possible description, a starter lesson in I.F. as I observe it within my mind. Identity Failure 101. When I am in Identity Failure's grasp, here is what takes place:

- I believe that specific qualities of myself give my life its value. (Being "very smart," let's say, or "a nice guy." Together, these many specific qualities create my overall idea of "me" and a feeling of my life's value to me.)
- I feel that only outside opinion can truly confirm that I possess those specific qualities. (I require the opinion of others to prove to myself that I'm very smart or a nice guy, etc.)
- Outside opinion doesn't confirm those specific qualities in ways that I find convincing. (The opinion of others doesn't seem to verify that I'm very smart or a nice guy, etc.)
- Without this confirmation, I become confused about some portion of my identity. (I question whether I'm very smart or a nice guy, etc.)
- I begin to fear that I'm not who and what I need to be. (I feel there may be something deeply wrong with me.)
- I begin to fear my life may be losing some portion of its value to me. (I start to feel unsure whether living is worthwhile if there's really something so deeply wrong with me.)
- I seek outside opinion that will confirm those specific qualities in ways I find convincing. (I feel desperate for others to verify there's not something deeply wrong with me by confirming I'm very smart or a nice guy, etc.)

- Still lacking that outside opinion, I react in ways intended to preserve the strongest possible feelings that my life is valuable to me without confirmation from others. (I think, feel and do whatever seems to make me feel better about myself right now.)

In essence, that's it. But there's so much more to it.

Technically, the final two bullet points aren't Identity Failure so much as they are the result of Identity Failure. I seek outside confirmation as a consequence of feeling I.F., that deep uncertainty about myself and the value of my life. If I don't get confirmation, I react in whatever way seems to best preserve some sense of my identity and my life's value. But I included those concepts among the bullet points for simplicity and clarity.

For greater clarity, if perhaps not simplicity, let me also give a more psychologically accurate definition of Identity Failure. This is how I would explain I.F. if speaking to a therapist, a more precise description that necessarily is based on my definition of the Fundamental Law of Mind: Identity Failure results from significant emotional resistance to a self-image that contributes significantly to my feelings that my existence is valuable to me at this moment in this world.

Identity Failure happens when I begin to seriously doubt I can be something that I feel I need to be to fit into the world – some self-image so important to me that it helps make my life seem worth living. Those doubts create emotional resistance to this self-image, by which I mean they cause new and deeper self-doubts, fears and other feelings that make it harder for me to accept this self-image as reality. Emotional conflict, in other words.

These negative feelings emit emotional energy that flows counter to the positive self-image I need, like a powerful air current that pushes away a weaker one. And so this emotional resistance weakens my sense of the value of my life, creating some level of uncertainty about my will to live. I grow afraid because I'm not feeling the desire to be alive with quite the same conviction.

If this continues for long enough, my will to live itself will start to fade. Part of me will want to die.

The Damage Done

In this way, I.F. had trapped me inside a cell of my very own construction. A mental prison. My value as a human being appeared bound up with specific qualities I believed that I possessed, qualities I required the world to validate as my proof of ownership. When the world didn't do this, I felt bad about both myself and the world. And I looked even more desperately for the world's appreciation. It was like a lockup of the mind, with the jail-door key held by everyone else but me.

As you would expect, this confinement caused me no end of serious trouble. I could easily fill the next several pages of this book with a list of problems created by Identity Failure – and even that list would be incomplete. No doubt I've suffered from I.F. in some ways I've not yet even identified. But I have compiled a pretty good inventory so far, offered here briefly.

Intense chronic anxiety with intermittent bouts of anxiety attacks as well as episodes of minor to moderate depression. Phobias, in later years particularly – fears of things I knew I wasn't truly afraid of. Later on I'll explain why I believe many physical pains, symptoms and illnesses also resulted from my Identity Failure. I include these troubles in my long personal accounting.

I.F. played a large part in my two marriages and two divorces, significantly driving my need to be with someone and then to get away from that very person. It undermined friendships and other relationships, even some with close family members. Identity Failure fueled a strong need to prove many qualities to myself such as my assertiveness, my sexuality and my intelligence. My superiority to others in some ways. When I had been boastful and arrogant, it was mainly from Identity Failure. Also when I had felt withdrawn and complacent. And I.F. had made me jealous, insanely at certain moments in the past, and it had made me angry toward jealous lovers at other moments. It caused speeding tickets and car accidents, including a frightening crash when I was a teenager. Identity Failure, the lot of it.

As noted, the list is long, so sadly long.

I.F. made me vastly less able to help others – it was all about my needs much of the time. Identity Failure even could have seriously damaged the quality of my work if I hadn't been acutely vigilant about defending against that. When my behavior was thoughtless, rude, crass, shallow, hostile, timid, deceitful or plain stupid, Identity Failure almost always was the source. The same with offering superficial friendliness or insincere compliments, trying to seem like that "nice guy," making a public point of my generosity. On and on the list continues, my very human roll of flaws and faults, mistakes and miscalculations. In my life, these flowed quite naturally from I.F.

There were exceptions, no doubt, flaws and faults with other causes. But I can't think of any offhand. Or even after careful reflection. When I examine my weaknesses, my shortcomings, my psychological issues, I reliably trace them back to the same spot in my psyche: Identity Failure and its consequences.

That's been an astonishing thing for me to learn. One problem causing almost all my other problems.

You may well wonder, How is that even possible? On the surface, this sounds beyond simplistic. But there's nothing remotely simplistic about Identity Failure as you'll see for yourself.

I.F. is a massive, complex and highly subtle psychological condition. And it was so pervasive and so influential in my psyche because it resulted directly from the Fundamental Law of Mind: that endless quest to feel that my own life is valuable to me, right now. Identity Failure was tightly bolted to this fundamental psychological process, both of them grinding on moment to moment during my daily existence. Basically I.F. was the consequence of my misguided attempts to satisfy the Fundamental Law of Mind. Some of these attempts came through seeking outside appreciation, some came through my responses to a lack of outside appreciation.

Let me explain it another way: I experienced deeply unsettling self-doubts on a routine basis, "insecurities" most folks would call these. Some were obvious to me, others so subtle or so unsettling that I was unaware of them. But collectively they helped motivate much of my behavior. That's because they constantly pushed me to seek outside appreciation in some form to prove that my self-doubts were wrong. My will to live required repeated helpings of appreciation by other people. If I didn't feel this appreciation in ways that I found satisfying, I did what I could to create a sense of my individual value in the absence of external support. I found it somewhere else as best I was able.

This way of living was from the outside in – my inner life dependent on the outer world. Which made the quality of my entire life dependent on the world's treatment of me.

Self-confusion

For most of my years, Identity Failure was unknown to me. It just felt like being Bob.

It felt like uncertainty or it felt like anxiety, but really was Identity Failure. It felt like anger or felt like jealousy, felt like an urgent need for someone's approval, but really was Identity Failure. It felt like a desire to prove myself smart or sexy to someone else. It felt like a wish to be viewed as a decent person. When I wanted to get married, it felt like a need to formalize an intimate relationship with a person I believed was uniquely admirable. When I wanted to get divorced, it felt like a need to break free of a person who now seemed uniquely unsuitable for me. Identity Failure sometimes felt like an urge to be envied by peers, to show off. It felt like a desire to prove my courage. It felt like insisting on respect from others or finding solitude away from the judgment of others, felt like justifiable anger or understandable fear. It felt like annoyance with the world's stupidity or fury at the world's injustice. It felt like discomfort with crowds and fear of strangers. But the feelings all came from Identity Failure, in whole or in significant part. I see that now.

When much later I tried to get in touch with my Identity Failure as directly as I could, below many many layers of other emotions, the condition mostly felt like a horrendous confusion. An insecurity so insecure that it was more than insecurity. More than just doubt.

It was a profound confusion about some significant aspect of who and what I am, with one or more personal qualities called into question. I now think of that feeling as "self-confusion." And I believe it's one of the very worst feelings I can have as a human being. It can create massive emotional pain. As I'll explain in the next chapter, this state of mind sets off a chain reaction of negative emotions. But that sense of deep uncertainty, the self-confusion, also has another more apparent consequence. It makes me feel almost constantly as if there's something wrong with me, as if I'm somehow deeply and intrinsically flawed as an individual. That feeling results from Identity Failure too.

When this feeling became very strong I desperately sought out someone else, or even something else, to make me feel better – to convince me that I wasn't so flawed. More often than not, I didn't find it. Not enough of it anyway. Then my reactions to this lack of support kicked in. I tried to lessen my self-confusion, my feelings of being flawed, through whatever means seemed the best available under the immediate circumstances.

That was when I.F. caused my most serious problems. I felt myself in a situation where I was fiercely in need of something I couldn't get, much like a drug addict without access to his drug. Like the addict, my needs had to be met somehow. I was going after that sense of my own value, the feeling that my life as an individual was valuable. I usually didn't know this is what I wanted, though. I only knew I felt bad about things for some reason and I wanted to feel better.

My psyche did what it could to help out. The anger and the jealousy and the divorces. The rudeness and shallowness, the illnesses and the crazy driving. Proving my courage and insisting on respect and finding solitude away from the judgment of others. I've discovered that a great deal of my inner and outer life was motivated by my efforts to compensate for Identity Failure – anything to dilute the self-confusion, to minimize the feeling that there was something deeply wrong with me. To pump up my ego, in conventional terms. That includes my thoughts and feelings, attitudes and opinions along with many things I did. Or didn't do.

This is another big reason I.F. was such a central force in my daily existence. Identity Failure didn't only push me to search for praise and understanding and appreciation. It forced me to search for anything that I could accept at the moment as the best available alternative to praise and understanding and appreciation. Until I fully embraced the philosophy of Rational Faith, that was a greatly important truth of the everyday for me.

All Me, All The Time

I.F. was the major reason I viewed life as all about Bob. My needs, my wants. Me as the center of the universe.

Because I was in a continuous quest for validation of my identity, I always was trying to satisfy my immediate emotions above all else. I needed the world to show me how great I was so I could believe it. When it didn't, my mind exploited other ways to feel that I was valuable as an individual. Everything was about me, my identity, my value. Me, me and more me every instant. As for my deep feelings of caring about others, my need to help people – these of course were part of my psychological mix as well. But they too often were buried under the more pressing layers of me. Or these deeper feelings emerged as efforts to prove to others how kind or generous or loving I could be. The feelings were genuine but quickly became corrupted by Identity Failure's demands.

That me-centered attitude was exacerbated by another reality of my psyche: My irrational nature. At bottom my mind functions irrationally almost all the time, only latching on to some semblance of the rational through experience and training. Even today I still too frequently view myself and other people and the world-as-a-whole through muddied spectacles, though I'm perfectly capable of seeing quite clearly quite often. But my moment-to-moment existence easily becomes detached from the most meaningful lessons of my experience. And so I frequently can react to things initially based on emotion.

In the past this type of irrationality tinted daily living with concerns over one main issue: the way I felt at the moment. My life's value at deep levels appeared intimately connected with my immediate self-interest, especially my immediate feelings of well-being and happiness.

Recall my picnic with Cynthia, all the heat and the bugs. Yes, I believe my life itself would have begun to feel less than OK somehow during that miserable outing … in part because I didn't see the experience rationally while living through it. Identity Failure creates intense doubt about myself in this very moment and in this very place. So at the picnic I felt trapped by the emotions of the instant, including deeper feelings about myself as a friend and as a human being in that situation.

"Right now" was the only thing that seemed relevant to me during that picnic and during most minutes of most days of my life until more recently. If "right now" was awful in ways that felt significant, my existence started to feel awful as well until the experience ended. At the picnic I wanted to get out, now. And because I couldn't do this consistent with my self-image, I felt irrationally confined by circumstances that caused bad feelings about myself. And because I felt so irrationally confined by those circumstances, some tiny corner of me began to feel less certain about the value of my life.

Again, it's a very subtle process. But it's real. I'm not suggesting I'd have felt suicidal over a miserable picnic, of course, only that at some thoroughly hidden emotional level I would have feared that my life was becoming just a tad less valuable to me.

When it comes to the value of my life, just a tad less can feel unnerving.

Majorly Mundane

That's precisely what I have seen at work in daily living. The minor and the mundane can feel major because they have touched a far deeper nerve than I realized at the moment they were happening.

I've felt personally insulted when stopped by too many red traffic lights while driving a car. I've felt personally disappointed over the loss of a baseball game by my Detroit Tigers. I've felt personally wounded by reading a newspaper story about some sad event in Egypt or China or wherever else. I'm not talking about rational sentiments here, keep in mind. I wasn't reacting sensibly to being late for a meeting or watching a failure by favorite athletes, I wasn't simply feeling compassion for someone far way who was suffering. Each of these three experiences and countless others of personal insignificance made me strongly feel something about me ... and about my very existence. Each felt extremely personal at the time. Irrationally personal. I was personally angry or depressed or distraught in ways that defied reason.

You may wonder, so what if I was ticked off by some red lights?

What's the difference if I was upset by a baseball score or a news story? True enough. In and of themselves, my feelings during those times weren't especially important, not really. My responses were telling, though, revealing something below the surface of my mind that was important indeed. Each of them resulted from Identity Failure. They show how I.F. infected so many aspects of daily life, even in the smallest ways. They indicate how invasive Identity Failure had become for me.

When I experienced I.F. the slightest annoyances could assume greater meaning than even I could believe then. They took on an absurd importance. I mean, really, red traffic lights? Why did this happen?

It happened in large part because my identity was so deeply dependent on the world around me: how the world saw me, how the world treated me. Or rather it was dependent on how I felt the world saw and treated me. If I didn't perceive enough validation from other people, I began to doubt myself. Their appreciation or lack of appreciation hugely influenced how I felt about me. And over time it also influenced how I felt about other people in general – and about society and about life.

If other people mistreated me in ways that felt significant over a long period, the world started to feel like a bad place to me. I had no rational perspective on the situation. Eventually I found evidence to support those irrational feelings more and more often, nearly everywhere I looked. Yes, everything became personal. The traffic lights and the ball game and the Egyptian news. Bob really was the center of the universe.

Automatically, my mind gravitated toward disturbing interpretations of many things happening around me. This helped me to feel a little better about my own disappointments and frustrations. Temporarily better, very temporarily. It was just one more reaction to Identity Failure. Because the world felt increasingly like a bad place for Bob, the world felt increasingly like a bad place. Period. It wasn't me, it was them.

But at those moments I also clearly recognized how the world could become a much better place. A better place for Bob, a better place period.

All it would take is a little more appreciation. Appreciation, that is, of Bob.

Very Human Craving

Let me ask you to think back to what I wrote in Chapter 2. You'll recall that in 2004 I came across a justly famous Dale Carnegie book that included this quote by William James: "The deepest principle in human nature is the craving to be appreciated."

When I first read this, I didn't question the statement. Not the part of it, anyway, about the craving for appreciation. That much seemed obvious to me. I soon found the complete thought profoundly insightful, an accurate observation about every human being. Certainly it squared with my own experience, personally as well as what I saw in others. Something within us at the deepest level fueled our need for recognition, approval, praise, appreciation. Importance, as I came to think of it after John Dewey's characterization of the same inner drive.

I believe that James' wise perception of people helped introduce me to the notion that such a fundamental principle of human psychology could be identified. I had long before this accepted that human beings are governed by natural laws, like everything else in the universe. The laws of human nature. Why wouldn't that be true? But as I pursued my own definition of a fundamental law of my mind, I came to realize over time that I disagreed with Dr. James in an important way. I still find his idea profoundly insightful. But now I view craving appreciation as a telling symptom of the deepest principle rather than an expression of the core principle itself. It's the result of trying to satisfy the Fundamental Law of Mind through outside opinion.

When I'm trying to maintain my emotional equilibrium based on the reactions of others, my existence in some real way feels in a state of constant peril. I have given them the authority to pronounce my life worthwhile or not rather than claiming that judgment for myself only. Their approval, their understanding of me, their appreciation becomes central to my own assessment of my individual value at this moment in this world.

I begin to feel uncertain, insecure.

What happens to me if I don't get the approval I require? My life starts to feel less valuable to me – a terrifying feeling indeed. So I crave anything and everything that can restore a sense of my life's value. And it's this need, I believe, that creates the craving to be appreciated that William James recognized.

A Subtle Strength

Obviously, I.F. comes in many colors and many tones. Like any mental state, the intensity varies widely. Something could prick open a couple of minor doubts about a couple of specific qualities that gave my life some of its value. My emotional reaction to the slight wound was barely noticeable to me. (For example, I liked to think of myself as a safe and courteous motorist. It was a small but real part of the way I saw me in the past, under Identity Failure's influence. When I sometimes failed to be safe and courteous, I could start to feel a little bad about my character.)

Or I could be assaulted by many major doubts about many specific qualities that gave my life much of its value. My emotional reaction to this attack was deeply troubling to me. (For instance, I wanted to think of myself as making important contributions to society, especially through excellence as a writer and thinker. This desire connected with many key parts of my identity. If something deeply rattled those feelings about myself, I could feel intensely uncertain about my value as a human being. As indeed I sometimes did ...)

Or I.F. can arrive with a strength somewhere in between the extremes.

It was the same with any of those very deeply hidden fears that my life might be losing some of its value to me. They could be vague and weak among all the elements of my mind, or they could be strong and intimidating. Or in between. Of course, I wouldn't be aware of any of these feelings about the value of my life – not unless they became so chronic and so forceful that they intruded in some manner into my consciousness, as happened to me in my early 60s.

During everyday life with I.F. in the past I usually was in one of those in-between places, both with the self-doubts and with the fears about life's value. That was my normal existence in general. I experienced some doubts about myself but found ways to offset them so I could feel somewhat OK about me much of the time. Those self-doubts in turn raised some lesser levels of fear about the value of my life, though again these fears mostly didn't register in my consciousness. They were unconscious, as the therapists would note. Being the more self-aware type, I was often in touch with at least some sense of my doubts about me. Frequently, these self-doubts simply made me feel anxious and uneasy for reasons that weren't immediately clear.

Returning to my 1-1,000 scale for self-reported feelings, let me offer a rough estimate that may help show the relative strength of the self-doubt and the fear about life's value as they typically existed in my psyche. I'll use one set of numbers to reflect the intensity of my doubts about me and another set of numbers to express the intensity of my fear about the value of my life. Remember that 1 is the weakest feeling on this scale, 1,000 the strongest I could have.

First, the strength of my self-doubts. On what I would consider a typical day during most of my adult life, I might have awakened with almost no reading, perhaps just a 50 or 60 out of a possible 1,000 for the power of my self-doubts. That increased quickly as I began to move through my morning, up to maybe 250 or 300 or more. It all depended on how I slept, what was going on that day and what happened the day before, among other factors. But I'd started to feel anxious. The self-doubts easily could intensify during the morning to, oh say, 400 or so then might drop as I began to work. And so on … This brief example may get across the notion that my self-doubts strengthened and weakened, usually without increasing to massive levels. Caused by Identity Failure, they were a presence but more or less under control.

Next, the strength of my fear that my life could be losing some value. This is a somewhat more speculative reading for reasons already offered: Most of that action happened far below my psychic surface, also caused by Identity Failure. Still, I feel I've had enough direct experience with this now to give some general numbers that may make the point.

On that very same morning, I would estimate that my degree of such fear would vary from almost undetectable when I awoke to well under 100 as my day really got going. By the time my self-doubts peaked at the 400 level, this type of fear also would have peaked at perhaps somewhere in the 150-200 range. That's my best fairly educated guess – and nothing more than that.

But I offered these numerical details for a reason. They may further clarify the subtlety of this psychological process. I needed more than 40 years of intense self-scrutiny to fully recognize Identity Failure. What it is, how it works. Especially I required all that time to understand the inextricable connection to my most fundamental psychological processes, though I had suspected for a long while that something like this might be happening. These are tough threads to isolate and identify accurately among the fabric of my psyche.

Without question I recognize now that I.F. is a reality. It has been a hugely important element of my mind, but never the only element. Identity Failure always existed in a contest with other aspects of my psyche. I've learned, for example, that I always possessed a deep self-trust independent of outside opinion as well as a great passion to help others. Even if partially buried, those feelings and all the other positive parts of me created countervailing forces to Identity Failure.

Together they were ingredients in a continually changing psychological soup, positive and negative elements alike. There's a lot bubbling around up there.

I.F. has massively influenced my existence, likely from infancy on. Through my upbringing as well as through both community and culture, I had learned that I need you so that I could be me.

Believing that lesson was a very very very big mistake.

A Normal Life

All my life, praise-seeking was the stuff of the everyday. That's how I grew up, with two parents who savored attention and appreciation. The opinions of others also seemed to weigh heavily in the lives of my siblings. Then I came along, nearly 13 years younger than my brother and more than ten years younger than my sister. I was born into a family of mostly kindhearted, soft-spoken approval lovers.

My father was witty and watched for the reaction to his humor, like all comics amateur or pro. And when Dad got the response he wanted, his face swirled into a charming expression of satisfied success. He was a salesman for a large part of his life, with our family's livelihood dependent on customer opinions of him far more than of his products. Connecting with people in that way was in his nature and he was good at it, very good, both professionally and personally. He genuinely loved people and it showed. But he also loved being loved by people. And it showed.

My mother had been abandoned early in childhood, never knowing her real parents. Evidently she was born out of wedlock, a huge humiliation at the time of her birth in 1917. Mom bounced around some before ending up with adopted parents who included a well-intentioned but undemonstrative mother. No doubt at least partly due to all this, she became obsessed with others' opinions of her. By the time I was born my mother was overweight for a short woman and seemed to talk constantly about dieting, though she rarely had any success with it – I recall that just weeks before her death at almost 95-years-old, Mom spoke to me during a phone conversation about her need to lose some weight.

The anecdotes are endless about her concern for social appearances. One good example: When I was ten, Dad took Mom and me on a six-week business trip with him around the western United States, driving from Ohio all the way to California and back. Though I have visited 53 countries so far, I think of that journey as one of the most magical travel experiences of my life. I remember that we pulled into a lovely luxury hotel in Long Beach, California, accommodations of a kind I'd never seen before. In the lobby I openly marveled at all the splendor as kids will, saying something like, "Wow, isn't this great?" Mom looked down, very gently and quietly shushing me: "We don't want them to think we're rubes!" she muttered. That was my mother until the day she passed away. What people thought of her and Dad and my brother and sister and me mattered enormously to Mom.

My brother, Bill, was a personable and goodhearted fellow who always had appeared to focus on the importance of outside opinions about him as well as other folks' feelings about his wife and children and grandchildren. Like our parents, he was a people pleaser – or so it seemed to me in my limited time with him before his death in 2018. We were never close. I clearly remember his efforts to correct my behavior when I was young, all with an emphasis on how people saw me. For instance, I recall his brief scolding one afternoon when I was about seven-years-old for casually boasting to my friends about something. "No one's going to like you if you keep bragging like that!" he warned. And this was the message about life I generally picked up from Bill: We should always behave in ways that others will like.

My sister, Sondra, is an acutely sensitive and loving soul. I adore her. All her life, Sondra has worked hard to make people happy – especially me and other members of our family, including her husband, three kids and four grandkids. With friends and acquaintances too, even strangers, my sister wants everyone to feel good. And if for any reason it seems someone doesn't feel good around her, this troubles Sondra. Should that person also criticize her somehow, my sister usually reacts with hurt feelings. It's a common trait in highly sensitive folks and I shared it myself for most of my life.

In a nutshell, that's my family. But obviously, I didn't encounter praise-seeking and approval-loving only from them. I saw it everywhere I went, among everyone I knew. Other than the degree of my mother's obsession with outside opinion, I'm not sure we were all that much different from most families then. Or now.

The children I knew appeared to live for ways to show off their superiority in order to earn approval. Especially their athletic superiority, which nearly always seemed vastly superior to mine. They looked for that approval from peers, from coaches and teachers, from parents and relatives, from the friends of those parents and the friends of those relatives. Their families also seemed to seek appreciation in their own fashion. Like the Knotts family, they worried what people thought. Like us, they were sensitive to criticism. Like us, they fed off impressing other human beings.

I saw similar behavior permeating my culture. From characters on television shows, from professional athletes, from movie stars and from famous musicians. From everyone, as far as I could tell. To me, this was the way things were in the world. Normal. Necessary for each individual – and certainly very necessary for me.

That's how it all looked for decades. I estimate the process of weaning myself away from outside approval required some 20 years and maybe more. Phase by phase, I had begun during my 40s by understanding that I needed some version of Emerson's self-reliance in daily life. Until at last I recognized that a complete freedom was essential: to live entirely absent outside psychological support. For a long time, I wouldn't have believed that it was possible for me or anyone else.

It is possible.

Still, I sometimes even yet feel like that drug addict who craves a needle. I know very well how bad it is for me but I want it anyway. Again, the solution for me has been Rational Faith. As I've applied these ideas more and more effectively, my desire for outside understanding and approval has faded.

In My Life

I talked briefly about my family, their approval-seeking tendencies. Let me talk at some greater length about my own while growing up.

I remember feeling like a happy child until about age ten. These days in my Humanity Project work inside the schools, I've noticed that this seems about the period when many kids become interested in pleasing the crowd. They grow self-conscious in ways they hadn't been earlier. And they crave appreciation from peers. That was my experience too. Before that age I felt mostly focused on pleasing my parents.

But by ten, I wanted the other kids to like me too. By then I already was feeling some uneasiness in school when my family moved, again – this time to a small Cleveland, Ohio suburb called Aurora. I think the population was something like 2,000, if memory serves. We had moved several times because my dad kept earning promotions and transfers as he segued from salesman to sales manager to vice president of sales. I was in three schools in three states in third grade. Not easy for any child. When my folks built a new home in Aurora, I was closing in on 11-years-old. My first experience with neighbor boys set the tone for the rest of my tortured existence there, a moment entirely a product of my youthful Identity Failure. My "insecurity" if you will.

During a family visit to the house as it was under construction, I met two brothers from the home next door and, yes, I began to brag to them about my toughness. Bill surely was right about that tendency in me, if perhaps less than sensitive in the way he tried to help me overcome it. I know now that I bragged because of that strong insecurity, of course. It was I.F., childhood version: I wasn't sure people would like me unless I impressed them with some skill or knowledge I possessed. I needed to be something that would amaze the other kids, even if I had to invent it. So I told the new-neighborhood brothers that I'd been trained in karate and judo though at the time I'd taken exactly zero lessons. The brothers said I would be welcomed into the tight-knit housing development, with its little clique of boys our age. I clearly had all the powers needed to put the local bully, Tim, in his proper place.

Naturally, Tim showed up soon after this backyard chat. And naturally I felt compelled to prove myself to the brothers by challenging this athletic kid to a fight, repeatedly.

I was throwing baseball pitches for him to hit, answering his complaints about my throws three times with a robust, "Wanna make something out of it?" Twice, the answer was, "No." The third time, though, he'd had enough. "Yeah," he said, tossing aside the bat. We knotted ourselves into the typical boyish wrestlefest, arms and legs flailing amid pushes and shoves. No punches thrown. I remember vividly the point when I'd managed to force Tim under me on the ground as I sat on him. Basically, it seemed that I'd won our scuffle – but I didn't have any idea what to do next. I wasn't willing to hammer him with my fist. I didn't really want to hurt Tim at all. What's a kid to do? Being much stronger than me, he soon took advantage of my indecision, rolling me over until he was on top. Tim knew what to do next all right. He pushed his elbow into my eye hard, pressing it around the socket until I yelled that I would give up. I walked back to my parents' car, covered in dust and crying.

Welcome to Aurora.

For the next five years, I was bullied and humiliated and harassed intermittently, right up until we moved back to the Detroit area in autumn 1968. (The same year my Detroit Tigers won the World Series, by the way ...) I was tormented not only by Tim but by his two brothers as well as the two brothers who asked me to rescue the neighborhood and a couple of other boys too. It was one of the most horrible periods of my life, leaving scars that still flare up painfully as an adult.

I took all the bullying very seriously. And I was utterly mystified about why they hated me so much. What did I keep doing to inspire their contempt? What was wrong with me? I just couldn't understand.

I badly wanted to be liked by them, by everybody. I liked them, afterall, and tried hard to say and do the things they would like in return. As you'd expect, it didn't work. If anything, my people-pleasing and sensitivity only made me into a more tempting target, someone who would react as they wanted when the kids ganged up to abuse me. I also stood out from them in many ways. Smarter, artsy, better in school, more imaginative. Less athletic, less physically fit, less likely to blend into a group, less able to brush off criticism.

Perhaps most confusing to me was the inconsistency of this bullying. One day we all were pals. The following day they made fun of me at the bus stop. We played on the same Little League baseball and freshman football teams, rooting each other on. Then the next thing I knew, a guy from our gang would inform me that Tim wanted to fight me again. It went on this way for the whole five years pretty much.

Worst of all, one of my parents was supportive of me, the other wasn't. My dad offered his usual unconditional love and encouragement, often expressing anger about the neighborhood boys when I was having troubles. My mom – she kept wondering what I'd done to cause the bullying. Exactly as I wondered myself, her doubts significantly intensifying my own confusion. What was wrong with me? Even Mom wanted to know.

This also was the time in my life when I learned the difference between being alone with someone and being with them in a group. I can't remember a single incident of true bullying when I was one-on-one with any of those kids. Just the contrary, really. Tim often came over to spend the night with me, watching TV shows together as I cooked up hamburgers for us. My only homosexual experiences happened with Tim – nothing too serious, just the common sexual experimenting of pubescence. On at least two different nights when we were probably 12 or 13-years-old, we kissed each other. More than a peck, mind you, we got into several seconds of adolescent making out. But whenever Tim or another friend joined other kids, things around me often turned tense. Again, I was deeply confused by the change. What was I doing wrong?

These were my early lessons in crowd dynamics. To this day I'm more comfortable one-on-one than in groups. I find that most individuals are delightful if alone and relaxed. Add just one person to the mix and the chemistry is never the same.

At least now I know why: I.F., Identity Failure, is the culprit here.

I've seen it in myself many times, I've seen it in others many times. For my part, I understand what sometimes happened when I was with someone only to watch our twosome grow into a threesome or foursome or more. That was when I suddenly became aware of what others thought about me in a heightened way, often wrestling with some desire to focus extra attention on new members of our gathering if they seemed more interesting or important to me somehow.

These days, not really true anymore. I'm learning. But that was my tendency and the same appears to happen with most human beings I know. The reaction of either the majority or the perceived group leader assumes undue significance.

Their approval becomes the psychological center of gravity.

Significant Opinions

By this time, I.F. had me full in its maw.

I recall feeling very bad about myself sometimes in Aurora, very good at other times. Generally, it depended on who I was with. At school or out in the neighborhood I normally felt anxious, except when I was in the classroom with a teacher. At home I felt more at ease. My feelings about myself already depended heavily on outside opinion.

I recognize that I was forming huge nexes about me, some of them starting in those Aurora years. The world was shaping my understanding of who I was – and wasn't.

I was a weird person sometimes. I could become awkward easily around people my age, saying or doing the wrong thing. Lots of kids didn't like me for some mysterious reason. I wasn't good at sports. I wasn't good at games that required hand-eye coordination. I was highly sexual, masturbating often and pouring through the sexy pages of my mother's department store catalogues – I didn't see this as a bad thing, really, though I remember feeling vaguely embarrassed by my secret habits. The pile of my negative or questionable traits felt imposing, each one built from large numbers of vericepts as I misinterpreted the things that happened within me and around me.

The list of positive traits grew too. I was very smart, with a natural analytical bent that drew me toward science. I was highly musical and a fine drummer, playing gigs as a 12-year-old in an adult semi-pro jazz band. I was a talented young writer who loved to read non-fiction, especially the encyclopedia. I was a champion speller and competed at a district spelling bee after winning my school contest. I was a warm and kindhearted child. I was polite, always a gentleman to women in particular and often using "sir" and "ma'am" around grownups. And I was comfortable and personable around those adults. I felt close to my family and they to me. And so on.

I was forming self-images that I would build on during my adulthood, all constructed out of my experience. These were the raw materials for the psychological concepts ahead. Though I didn't know it, I was carving the masks of my own identity.

Powerful People-Pleasing

My people-pleasing took many forms in the years leading up to my twenties.

I had always enjoyed meeting the expectations of teachers I respected, befriending some of them outside the classroom in high school and college. I worried constantly about how others saw me, peers and adults alike. I hated the feeling of disappointing my parents, particularly my father, even as I grew more and more rebellious away from home. Around them I tried to appear as much the good boy of my youth as I could muster, but I also wanted to fit in with kids who smoked cigarettes and marijuana and dropped psychedelic drugs. I strained to impress fellow teens, at times by my crazy-fast driving – a dangerous habit resulting in that serious accident when I was 16. No one hurt, thankfully. I fell into the hippie clique at high school, smoking pot daily by my senior year. I lied to close friends about sexual exploits that never happened and engaged in real sexual adventures that sometimes were thoughtless toward the girls involved.

This may seem like fairly normal teenage behavior in many ways. Yes, it was. Yes, it is.

Today's teens likely would recognize themselves in at least some parts of that description. My youthful search for outside approval seemed very normal then and seems very normal now. But it also was very destructive. And it was entirely unnecessary.

This quest for validation wasn't an integral part of my humanity, it was something learned – craving appreciation as a destructive expression of a more fundamental principle of my psyche. I needed the world to make me feel important. It was I.F., Identity Failure, confusion about who and what I was at my deepest levels. That's the underlying cause behind each of those youthful experiences. Every one was an effort to get others to confirm some self-identity, some way of me seeing me.

As I look back on my life today, I can spot a broad variety of identities that I accepted as me from my late adolescence until my mid-60s. Oddly enough, many of them seem like diametrical opposites. I loved to show off my abilities in public; I feared disapproval and often preferred being alone with my thoughts. I was a devil-may-care who tempted danger with risky activities such as auto racing and shark diving; I felt petrified of incapacitating injury and valued my health more than almost anything. I hungered for a profound soulmate relationship with one extraordinary woman; I lusted after sexual relationships with many women.

Each of these mindsets reflected my own view of me – at times. Now this type of person, then that type of person, depending on the circumstances. And I perceived each of these identities as a positive thing, some perspective on Bob that allowed me to fit comfortably into the world moment to moment. The fear of injury was part of a self-image representing my commendable focus on healthful living, for example. That preference for being alone seemed a way of being smart.

Together, with countless other self-images, they made up my overall understanding of me for most of my life.

It was pure hell.

Warped Images

The problem here wasn't that I felt conflicting emotions or harbored conflicting goals. That truly is an integral part of my humanity, as far as I can tell. Conflict is inherent in nature – and in human nature. It's clearly built into my nature. My feelings, desires, wants, needs are at cross-purposes all the time. Daily living is about reconciling them the best I can under the prevailing circumstances.

The problem was that these emotions and goals were part of hardened attitudes about myself. They were rigid, simplistic self-concepts. Each of them was an inflexible interpretation of self, each a great complex of vericepts fused into a great complex of nexes that comprised one aspect of my identity as I saw it. Taken together at the time, all those huge nexes collectively represented "me."

But those identities were not realistic. They were by their very nature distortions, meaning that it was impossible to live up to those expectations effectively for long. And on top of that, I was looking for the world to confirm that the identities were accurate representations of me. Other people became the arbiter of my value. I got by when self-images of great significance to me felt supported by the world. I struggled terribly when such self-images felt threatened by the world. That's when I looked for other ways to feel that I was OK.

The experience taught me that I'd been mistaken about many many things for much of my life. Here's one of the key things: I had always viewed self-doubt and uncertainty as symptoms of another problem in myself. Some deeply ingrained psychological issue of my past. But I discovered that doubt of this sort wasn't a symptom of another problem at all. Doubt was the problem. There was nothing wrong with me. Except a persistent feeling that something was wrong with me, which stemmed from that deep active self-confusion.

Identity Failure made me feel this way.

Those feelings simply seemed part and parcel of everyday life, the regrettable but unavoidable psychological result of being normal. I lived in a way that I thought I was supposed to live, the way everyone else lived as best I could tell. I craved appreciation. And the feelings I felt and the conflicts I suffered and the damage I inflicted on myself and others and society, they appeared to be a necessary evil. People are what they are.

Except they aren't.

The great discovery of my life is that Identity Failure isn't necessary at all. It's not a normal condition of my humanity, it is a problem caused by what I'd believed normal.

More than that, Identity Failure is a disease. And whenever I suffer from it, I am sick.

Chapter 7: A Fitting Experience

"Not in the shouts and plaudits of the throng, but in ourselves, are triumph and defeat."
   Henry Wadsworth Longfellow

The Grand Trio

I am real. Or so I like to think anyway.

To twist Gertrude Stein's phrase, there is a there there. Not only the obvious things anyone can see but also the concealed elements of the organism that exists as Bob Knotts – thoughts and emotions, judgments and feelings, memories and talents and tastes as they each have formed in me. Like you, like each of us, I am unlike any other human being past, present or future. An unrepeated and unrepeatable combination of characteristics both physically and psychologically.

I am unique.

At the same time, of course, there is a world out there, something that isn't me. There's most definitely a there there too. The nebulas and black holes aren't me and the ice-rings of Saturn aren't me. The seawaves and the mountain caps, the whales and the tigers, the pineapples and pistachios and potatoes aren't me. The one-way streets and the suspension bridges and the highrise condos aren't me either. All the people on earth but one aren't me. You're not me. I may simply call it the world, as I usually do, or society or the universe. However broad the concept, all of it in one form or another is what's out there beyond me. I am a solitary minute creation in a universe whose vastness continues to expand for us under the persistent explorations of science, Bob as a staggering insignificance. Among all the sentences in all the books in all the libraries that ever have existed, I am a single period.

Both the universe and I appear real, entirely independent of my awareness of our existence – leaving aside here the fascinating intricacies of knowledge theories offered by physicists and philosophers. From my everyday point of view, there is a there there and there is a there here. That's how I see things. There's the world and there's me.

And there is one important thing more floating continually through my mind: How the world and I fit together. I feel the need for us to mesh comfortably, the world and me, like the teeth that connect the two parts of a motorized gear. This is my relationship not *to* the world, but *with* the world, meaning that my mind views the world and me as two separate dynamic parts that I somehow must connect with each other. I feel good whenever that seems to happen. I experience a calmer sense of my place in the larger scheme. And when it seems not to happen, I feel bad. Very bad indeed. And that badness often has left me wondering, Is it the world or is it me? Who's wrong here?

Typically, I ended up mostly blaming me.

All the information in my head, I believe, can be divided among just three basic categories: My interpretations of the world, my interpretations of me, my interpretations of the way the world and I fit together. A grand psychological trio. Astronomically numerous discrete units of information, my vericepts, have formed together to make massive networks of information, my nexes, each involving one of these three things.

My interpretation of the world and my interpretation of me determine my understanding of their connection. They interact to create my interpretation of how the world and I fit together. For instance, when I view the world as essentially welcoming to me as a writer and at the same time I see my writing as valuable, I feel relatively comfortable with my role in society. I fit in. The world, the universe seem good. When I view the world as essentially hostile to my writing and I also question my work's value, I feel highly uncomfortable with my role in society. I don't fit in. The world, the universe seem bad. Those are only two general examples of the kind of thing I'm talking about. The specifics vary wildly, endless combinations of my feelings about the broad universe outside me together with my feelings about the solitary universe within me.

A rough diagram illustrates the point here – very rough, as you see. But I wanted to make my book's few drawings by myself for some reason. Pride of ownership perhaps or something, despite a painfully obvious lack of illustration skills. My version of the classic overlapping circles. You'll notice the two main circles that represent most of my interpretations of my experience, either about the outside world or about me. Then there's that smaller shaded area in the middle where they combine to create my interpretations of how the world and I fit together. All the concepts that enter my head fall into one of those three categories.

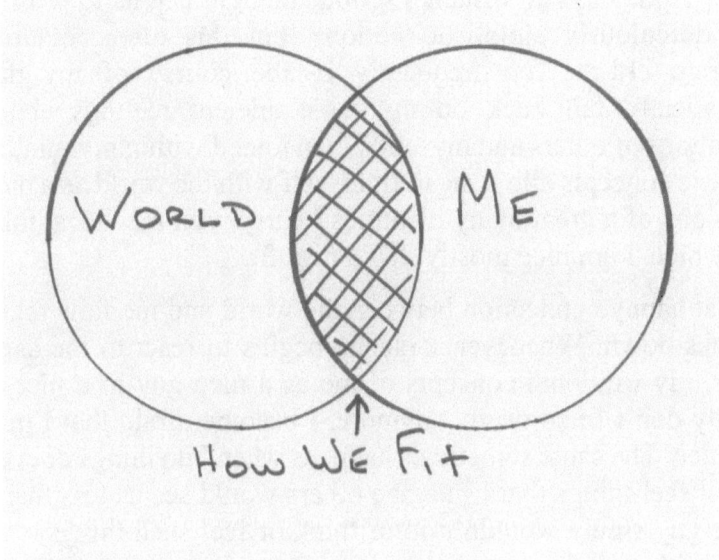

Sad to say, vastly more of all those concepts are irrational rather than rational, both my understandings of the world and of me. And so, naturally, my interpretations of my relationship with the world are just as irrational. As I wrote in the last chapter, "At bottom my mind functions irrationally almost all the time, only latching on to some semblance of the rational through experience and training. Even today I still too frequently view myself and other people and the world-as-a-whole through muddied spectacles, though I'm perfectly capable of seeing quite clearly quite often. But my moment-to-moment existence easily becomes detached from the most meaningful lessons of my experience. And so I frequently can react to things initially based on emotion."

Like all of us, I am fundamentally an irrational creature.

As a result I've spent much of my life trying to fit together an unrealistic concept of the world with an unrealistic concept of myself, struggling to make those gears mesh. One of my most insistent beliefs offers a brief glimpse for now at an aspect of this conflict: Lingering strongly from my childhood, some portion of my psyche often still perceives most people as nice. And another even more powerful portion of my head sees myself in the same way. As a nice guy. Whatever nice really means ... Not much, to my way of viewing reality. These days an instant's serious thought begins to brush away these ridiculously simplistic notions, but this often requires my deliberate effort. Too frequently in the course of my days, I automatically fall back on my most ancient feelings about the motivations of others and myself. When joined within my mind, these two basic concepts allow me to fit myself with the world as a nice guy – only one of a great many identities I carry with me. Most folks are mostly nice, I am nice mostly. It's a neat fit.

But that happy connection between the world and me fails regularly. It breaks down. Whenever someone begins to react to me as if I'm unnice, my irrational concepts of me as a nice guy in a nice world abruptly don't fit so neatly anymore. I become afraid that I may not be so nice. The same sometimes happens when I do things or even just think or feel things that I imagine others would see as less than nice. A nice guy surely wouldn't do or think or feel such things – what's wrong with me?

I have suffered miserably from that uncertainty about myself. I hated feeling as if I had hurt other people, or might hurt them. And I hated feeling that other people saw me as someone who was harmful or angry or insensitive or uncaring, or might see me that way. This troubled me deeply.

Sometimes in the past I challenged these feelings, relaxing as I reasoned them through to more sensible thoughts. Usually, though, I gravitated back eventually in daily life to seeing the world in the same childlike way. Most folks are mostly nice, I am nice mostly. It never worked for long. Force them together however I would, the beliefs always wound up grinding against each other in a noisy psychological clash.

It was the clang of Identity Failure.

A Warped Perspective

Recall how I defined Identity Failure, or I.F., in the previous chapter:

"Identity Failure results from significant emotional resistance to a self-image that contributes significantly to my feelings that my existence is valuable to me at this moment in the world. Identity Failure happens when I begin to seriously doubt I can be something that I feel I need to be to fit into the world – some self-image so important to me that it helps make my life seem worth living. Those doubts create emotional resistance to this self-image, by which I mean they cause new and deeper self-doubts, fears and other feelings that make it harder for me to accept this self-image as reality. Emotional conflict, in other words. These negative feelings emit emotional energy that flows counter to the positive self-image I need, like a powerful air current that pushes away a weaker one. And so this emotional resistance weakens my sense of the value of my life, creating some level of uncertainty about my will to live. I grow afraid because I'm not feeling the desire to be alive with quite the same conviction. If this continues for long enough, my will to live itself will start to fade. Part of me will want to die."

I also think it's worth looking once more at those bulleted basics about Identity Failure's process. Here they are again as spelled out in Chapter 6:

- I believe that specific qualities of myself give my life its value. (Being "very smart," let's say, or "a nice guy." Together, these many specific qualities create my overall idea of "me" and a feeling of my life's value to me.)
- I feel that only outside opinion can truly confirm that I possess those specific qualities. (I require the opinion of others to prove to myself that I'm very smart or a nice guy, etc.)
- Outside opinion doesn't confirm those specific qualities in ways that I find convincing. (The opinion of others doesn't seem to verify that I'm very smart or a nice guy, etc.)
- Without this confirmation, I become confused about some portion of my identity. (I question whether I'm very smart or a nice guy, etc.)
- I begin to fear that I'm not who and what I need to be. (I feel there may be something deeply wrong with me.)

- I begin to fear my life may be losing some portion of its value to me. (I start to feel unsure whether living is worthwhile if there's really something so deeply wrong with me.)
- I seek outside opinion that will confirm those specific qualities in ways I find convincing. (I feel desperate for others to verify there's not something deeply wrong with me by confirming I'm very smart or a nice guy, etc.)
- Still lacking that outside opinion, I react in ways intended to preserve the strongest possible feelings that my life is valuable to me without confirmation from others. (I think, feel and do whatever seems to make me feel better about myself right now.)

As mentioned then, those last two bullet points really aren't Identity Failure but rather the result of Identity Failure: "I seek outside confirmation as a consequence of feeling I.F., that deep uncertainty about myself and the value of my life. If I don't get confirmation, I react in whatever way seems to best preserve some sense of my identity and my life's value."

Please keep in mind that this entire process is irrational. I.F. is an illness, literally. And every element of it is part of the disease. That includes everything about the first bullet point, my belief that specific qualities of Bob give my life its value. Profoundly irrational. As are the specific qualities themselves – like seeing myself as Mr. Nice Guy. Examined critically, those qualities of Bob are absurd. All of them, every single one whatever it may be. "Nice guy," "very smart," or perhaps "adventurous," "health-conscious," "highly sexed" and the rest, each concept warped beyond rational recognition into a caricature of a human being. But they are how I have perceived myself for most of my days until recently.

The way I view outside opinions about those specific qualities also is profoundly irrational. In other words, my perception of what others think about me is nonsense. Whether I feel others do, or would, see me as good or smart or whatever – or whether I feel they don't or wouldn't. As I'll explain shortly, this process is much less about anything happening to me from the outside world than it is about things happening to me from the inside world. In my mind. It's not really what's said or done to me by others that matters, it's how I interpret what others say or do to me.

Curiously enough, this is even true when no one has said anything to me at all.

An Awkward Fit

Here's how it works in my head, the deeper psychological mechanisms as I have long watched them causing my Identity Failure. Those irrational self-images are one of the keys to understanding this process.

My psyche automatically attempts to mesh the world and me in ways that feel most emotionally satisfying, most comfortable to me. To do this, it draws on the massive numbers of vericepts and nexes that collectively comprise all my concepts about the world and about me. Every interpretation of the things that aren't me and every interpretation of the things that are me: My mind looks for the best opportunity to line up the gears. It creates connections, finding ways to link the world-stuff such as social values and cultural tastes and economic opportunities with the me-stuff such as my values and interests and talents. It opens a spot in the universe for Bob.

The most interesting psychological action, and the problems, arise from those automatic efforts to make the two sides fit together – the shaded area in my illustration.

The first step in this extraordinarily complicated process was my psyche's creation of many distinct and separate self-images. I can only assume this began in earliest infancy and I know it continued into my 60s. Though I've worked hard to see myself more rationally in later years, I sometimes still tussle with the self-images of my past. Every self-image is a psychologically complex construction and at the same time entirely unrealistic. Irrational, as I've noted. They are rigid, simplistic images of myself. Each of them is an inflexible interpretation of me, each a great complex of vericepts fused into a great complex of nexes that has become one aspect of my identity as I have seen it. Nice guy, very smart, adventurous and so on.

Every self-image represents some way I felt the world and I connected. That's their psychological purpose.

I have named these self-images "identity poses." My dictionary defines a pose as a bodily attitude or position, as if for a portrait. My identity poses are a psychological version of this. They are the ways I have presented myself to the world in order to fit in as I felt best possible for me at any given moment. Much more significantly, they are the ways I have presented myself to myself, my own posing for my own appreciation. They are the self-images that seemed to make my life feel most valuable. And for most of my life, I believed they were accurate representations of who and what I was.

Identity poses simply are the ways I saw me. But at a more profound level far below my awareness, I felt as if these poses best helped me live with the continual demands of the Fundamental Law of Mind: They allowed me to interpret experience to create the weakest possible emotional resistance to the strongest possible feelings that my existence was valuable to me at any given moment in this world. That was their deepest function. Without knowing it, I created a vast array of identities aimed at making me comfortable in my own skin. Lots of different, often contradictory, identity poses to prove my value to me in this world. Most often they helped me fit with the world by feeling more important in a situation. Sometimes they helped me fit with the world by feeling less important in a situation, which at the time preserved some other more valued identity pose I felt might otherwise be threatened. You'll see what I mean.

In either case, my identity poses laid the foundation for my Identity Failure.

De-Posed

An irrational, inflexible self-image is an identity pose. Each identity pose is made up of some huge number of concepts that have combined into one larger concept, a whole identity that I see as me in some situations. All of these separate identities, or identity poses, together have created my overall concept of Bob for most of my life – now this one, now that one as needed.

Some of these identity poses are larger and more significant to me than others. That is, some involve major aspects of me as I view myself. Others are about relatively minor personality traits. Major identity poses would include things such as my self-images as nice guy, very smart, highly creative, helpful to others and so on. Minor identity poses would include such self-images as being a good driver, being well-read and being knowledgeable about the natural world among many others. If a major identity pose feels threatened, I'll almost certainly react angrily whether I show it or not. If a minor identity pose comes under fire, I won't care nearly so much.

This means some identity poses have been extremely important to my feelings about my life's value, others a bit less so, still others of even less importance and on down the line of emotional significance. The biggest identity poses are those composed of the largest number of concepts, thereby feeling most important to my sense of self-value. And vice versa: The smallest identity poses contain the fewest concepts and are least important to my self-value.

More specifically, all these identity poses are constructed from two basic psychological elements as I've defined them: Vericepts and nexes. Again, vericepts are my automatic, instantaneous and very frequent interpretations of the world, of me and of the way the world and I fit together. Each is a mental snapshot of a moment as I understand it now. And nexes are the collections of those same automatic interpretations assembled into my larger beliefs about the world, me and the way the world and I fit together. Each is a psychological photo album of past moments as I viewed them at the time, arranged by subject.

You'll remember that vericepts carry a chunk of information that I accept as reality in one psychological gulp without any awareness of it. That chunk of information may be relatively small and insignificant. Or it may be relatively large and complex, as in the vericept I described for my unpleasant picnic with Cynthia. They indeed are like mental photographs I click off, an unending rapid series of images that record not only what I see with my eyes but the overall interpretations of my experience. Each vericept enters my head with emotion attached to it, a key part of the process to remember. Vericepts also can be rational or irrational. Ravericepts are rational vericepts with information that would withstand logical scrutiny. Irvericepts are irrational vericepts that would not stand up to critical thinking. Overwhelmingly, most of my vericepts are irrational.

Also you'll recall that nexes come in vastly different sizes and strengths, from micronexus to supernexus in my terminology. A supernexus is a massive combination of smaller nexes all somehow related to one subject, carrying with it an extremely significant amount of emotional energy. Because each vericept within each nexus contains its own attached emotion, that's a huge force of emotion at the supernexus level. Supernexes are about the most important things in my life, always stirring up very powerful feelings.

So then you might imagine the influence of my largest identity poses, which can grow to supernexus strength. They have been a dominant presence in my life.

It is critical to understand that an identity pose isn't some deliberate conscious pretense. It's not acting. Not at all. Like so many of my psychological functions, it's an automatic response to my immediate circumstances – and like all my psychological functions, it is my mind's best attempt at fulfilling the demands of the Fundamental Law of Mind. I'm trying to make my life feel as valuable to me as possible at this moment in this world. Identity poses are my psyche's effort to fit the world and me together, satisfying my emotions in the way that seems to work best right now.

It's also important to know that identity poses are not something I feel only in public. Quite the contrary. Well into my 60s, I lived with my identity poses nearly all the time, night and day, around other people or all alone. Identity poses didn't form in my head for me to impress others. They formed to impress me. They're an attempt to make me feel good about me. As often as not, though, this effort boomerangs – and accomplishes exactly the reverse. They make me feel bad about me.

So far, so useful, this background information. All of it needed to understand the central psychological significance of identity poses in determining the quality of my life until recently. And to recognize later how Rational Faith helped me move beyond this destructive me-centered way of living, finding something deeper and much more constructive that also may benefit you. My long self-analysis of identity poses, Identity Failure and related issues is what allowed me finally to become Bob so fully that I became more – and I hope to outline a path for others to do the same for themselves, contributing to a healthier and more rational society in the process. That's the larger goal. For now, I ask for your patience. Read on, please.

To better observe how identity poses function, let's look closely at my "nice guy" identity pose. Since as long ago as I can recall, all the way up until the past few years, I've generally felt most comfortable in daily life by seeing myself as that nice guy I mentioned earlier. I remember an incident when I worked briefly as a ski department manager in a New Jersey sporting good shop that was run by a wonderfully decent man named Jim Taylor. Lydia and I had just returned from our brief venture to Europe, living with my parents while we saved money for the move to San Francisco. I was 20-years-old. One day Mr. Taylor and I were opening boxes of new ski equipment with a few other young guys who worked under us. For whatever reason during our conversation, I tried to act tough by muttering some sort of profanity. I'll never forget my boss's immediate response. Looking up at me with a smile, Mr. Taylor said, "Bob, no matter how hard you try, you'll always be a nice guy." It stuck with me. And as he predicted, the nice guy self-image also has stuck with me for most of my life.

Looked at in one way, Bob as a "nice guy" actually makes some sense. But the truth is much more complex, subtle and nuanced than the nice guy identity pose. I do hold a strong genuine belief in kindness and sensitivity toward others and I'm often willing to sacrifice something I want for something that someone else seems to want more. Bob can seem "nice" to folks in part because I'm aware of my deep need to help people – and the value to myself of helping them. I also was brought up to be polite and soft-spoken, contributing to the niceness impression. Etcetera. But here's where I must disagree with my cheerful former employer: Seen rationally, this behavior isn't "nice" in the way the word usually is meant. And certainly not in the way Mr. Taylor meant it. When I break free of my identity poses, I live with a clear recognition of my personality's inconsistencies and contradictions, the facets of Bob that on the surface seem like paradoxes. I can sense the variations of feelings and values that arise during my dealings with others. And I understand that no matter how it appears from the outside, I'm not really being nice. I'm simply behaving based on my entirely rational concepts of the world, of myself and of how the world and I fit together. I try to help people because I have learned rationally that helping people is good for me as well as for them as well as for the society in general. That's not nice, it's wisdom gained through experience.

My identity pose as a nice guy is something very different. The above beliefs are founded on ravericepts, or rational interpretations of experience. Bob-the-nice-guy is rooted in irvericepts, or irrational interpretations of experience about things such as kindness and sensitivity toward others – huge amounts of baseless concepts that congealed into an identity both simplistic and destructive.

So what are some of the many personality traits I have accepted as key qualities for being a nice guy? How do I feel about myself when I assume that irrational nice guy self-image?

I feel that I am a basically gentle person, for one thing. I feel that I am extremely sensitive to other people's feelings, trying my best to avoid hurting their egos. I feel that I'm open and friendly, hoping for the same in return. When I wave hello at someone, I expect a return wave; when I smile at someone, I expect a smile to come back at me. When it doesn't, I feel puzzled and at least vaguely hurt, sometimes offended – though I try to avoid expressing my reaction to that person. These are just a few elements of my nice guy identity pose.

I also want other people to do well, celebrating their successes and victories. When others don't offer me the same kind of enthusiasm, yes I'm usually upset but I try hard to understand and forgive.

I speak courteously, liberally peppering my conversation with the words "please" and "thank you." In my manner too I am a gentleman, especially toward the women I often have tended to idealize. I would never take advantage of another person sexually, I would rarely take advantage of anyone for any reason unless I viewed this somehow as justifiable payback for serious offenses against me. I smile around other people, though it often is the wan smile of the nice guy, something Emerson called "the forced smile which we put on in company where we do not feel at ease, in answer to conversation which does not interest us." How true … I know that feeling well. I am self-consciously hygienic in my personal habits and dress. I offer compliments readily, sincerely in most cases but not in every instance. I believe it's OK to lie if needed to make people feel good about themselves, despite my preference for honesty. I think that I'm respectful of others' rights and opinions publicly, if frequently critical of their ideas in private. Basically, I regard myself as a considerate and compassionate and acutely sensitive human being.

Always.

Bob-the-nice-guy.

Unreally Nice

What's so terrible about that, right? I'm sure after reading this highly incomplete list, you're thinking, "Gosh, he really is a nice guy!" Yep, that's me.

And no, it's not me at all.

It's the me I needed to believe so I could feel more valuable as a human being. Or rather, it's the me I believed I needed to believe. And what's wrong with it is this: The self-image is entirely a fantasy. A "nice guy" of that sort doesn't exist in nature. Nor does a "nice girl" for that matter. Accepting it as an important part of my basic personality only fits the world and me together in ways that don't really work very well.

Here's what I mean.

My psyche has squeezed the life out of all those self-concepts that collectively formed my nice guy identity pose. Bob as gentle and sensitive, open and friendly and so forth. As bound up in my nice guy identity pose, those qualities lack the depth and complexity that is a truer reflection of my humanity. Each separate quality has rigidified into the type of personality trait I might recognize in a simplistic television character. Every aspect of my niceness is flat, two-dimensional, lacking shadows. There is no there there.

Like that bit about me as a basically gentle person.

Nonsense. I am not gentle, not when I escape Identity Failure's talons. Whenever I see Bob more rationally, I suddenly feel myself more than anything else as a dynamic being. I am naturally enthusiastic, playful, opinionated, talkative. I love to make jokes and, like my father, bad puns. I sense a great surging lifeforce in me. I am intensely creative and I'm passionate to express this in many ways. I want to do things and accomplish them quickly and well, moving on to the next thing. I enjoy being a bit provocative in conversation, embracing an intelligent argument with someone who is equally informed and confident. Yes, I do care about the feelings of others – and through creating the philosophy of Rational Faith I have built a philosophical and psychological system that allows me to more carefully manage my interactions with others than in the past. Rational Faith helps people feel good around me rather than threatened by my energy. But I also am much less inclined to agonize about my impact on the folks nearby when I'm essentially free of my identity poses. Which of course means also essentially free of Identity Failure. I do the best I can with others and move on. By my definition, that's not a "basically gentle person."

Without question there are gentle elements to me when I am more fully and rationally myself. Many of them, actually, with each available when I feel it's appropriate. No doubt my mind contains much information and emotion involving Bob's gentleness, both rational and irrational information and emotion. But no, I'm not a "basically gentle person."

Like every part of that nice guy identity pose, Bob-the-gentle-person is a stereotyped concept. It is shallow, it is superficial, it is unrealistic, it is inflexible. A closer examination of Bob-the-gentle-person may help explain why that's true – and why this means the nice guy and all my identity poses are just as shallow and superficial and unrealistic and inflexible.

And destructive to me and others.

Gentle On My Mind

The information and emotion that coalesced into my Bob-the-gentle-person concept have formed a nexus, one component of the much larger nice guy nexus. I would estimate that Bob-the-gentle-person is a midnexus, a meaningful collection of interpreted experience containing significant amounts of information and emotion. I'd categorize the nice guy identity pose as a macronexus with greatly significant clusters of interpreted experience – vast amounts of information and emotion.

When the macronexus that's my nice guy identity pose is activated, Bob-the-gentle-person midnexus often kicks in as part of it. And at those times, these are among the personality characteristics I must maintain to view myself as a "basically gentle person": My words, facial expressions, gestures and other actions must always be non-threatening, always intended to soothe and reassure. I should always strive for the opposite of intimidation. And I must always care about the well-being of others, even when no one is around. Harboring anger, resentment, bitterness, animosity, dislike, these are never acceptable feelings for a nice guy like me. Never.

As a gentle person, I must forever battle against these feelings when they surface, striving for compassion and caring and, hopefully, love toward others. My sexuality should be part of this caring and love, not simply male lust. I should always believe in peace at the local, national and international levels, detesting war and violence in all forms except when absolutely necessary for self-defense. I must still hold dear many of the ideals from my hippie period, proudly adapting the peace-and-love message to my adult existence. In my personal life, I must treat friends as affectionately and tenderly as possible. I must without fail be able to view myself as fundamentally decent, even when my irrational emotions may cause temporary lapses. Because I am a gentle person, I should feel bad about these lapses. I must always want the best for everyone and should almost always put my own needs second to theirs. I also should smile as often as I can to convey my gentleness to the world.

As I suggested, it's only a very partial listing of the characteristics I demand as part of Bob's basic gentleness. The gentleness in turn is only one of the very many irrational and inflexible components of my nice guy identity pose. My nice guy identity pose is only one of many identity poses my mind has created to somehow fit together the world and me.

Pieces of Peace

I hope my detailed descriptions may get across one of the central points about identity poses. Their irrationality, as I keep stressing over and over. I fret about clarity around this notion for a good reason: In the end, the difference between a rational self-image and an irrational self-image boils down to their levels of depth and complexity, the sophistication of the concepts. I could use the same words to describe both a true characteristic of my personality and a distorted characteristic. But I can distinctly feel the difference emotionally. And the difference is enormous.

Take my belief in peace as a brief example of this idea, breaking down the nice guy identity pose still further. Remember that in my psyche as anywhere else in nature, big things are made from many small things. We've already looked at some major components of my overall nice guy identity pose, then focused in on only one of those components. Bob-the-gentle-person. Now we can delve just a bit into a smaller concept that helps make up my Bob-the-gentle-person self-image – my love of peace. But of course it's only love of peace as that exists irrationally in my mind.

There's a very real, rational part of my value system that believes in peace. It is a significant part of me. I can explain that rational value clearly and sensibly. This is a genuine portion of my genuine self, which is never fixed and rigid but continually evolving. Bob – always becoming something else. In rational moments, I can feel this value's rightful place in my broader belief system, a rich and complex component of a rich and complex set of concepts.

But in irrational periods, under the sway of my nice guy identity pose, my belief in peace loses that rich complexity. It becomes a penstroke in a dashed-off caricature. Bob loves peace because Bob is gentle. Peace-and-love, peace-and-love, all shallow and simplistic. I see myself much as I did during my hippie years, sweet and loving and tender and unwilling even to harm an insect if avoidable. The rich and complex qualities of my deep belief in peace are lost, replaced with Bob-the-peaceful-person.

The difference between these rational and irrational self-images as peaceful is the difference between a sophisticated concept and a stereotype. They feel very different, they are very different. There's a huge distinction between feeling that I possess some personality trait as one important part of my complicated being or feeling that the same trait defines me. If I feel, "I'm often capable of being very smart" this recognizes that my capacity for being very smart is only one small portion of me. And it's a flexible idea: Sometimes I'm not very smart. But if I feel, "I'm a very smart person" I have become locked into a caricature of me, one key trait that is dominant and inflexible. Bob simply *is* very smart.

I can embrace reality's multi-layered depths or I can believe that only a single simplistic layer of reality exists at this moment. The personality traits within my identity poses are all single layers. Bob-the-gentle-person, Bob-the-sensitive-person, Bob-the-peaceful-person, etc. There are no multi-layered depths. Each small element that makes a larger element that makes a still larger element – all absurdly simplistic. And this makes the identity poses themselves absurdly simplistic.

It's absolutely necessary to understand this when thinking about identity poses.

As they are simplistically shallow, so they also are simplistically rigid, both the personality characteristics within identity poses and the complete identity poses. The elements and the whole. That's another hallmark. Each separate characteristic and each separate identity pose is fixed in my mind, each viewed in the moment as if a permanent part of who and what I am. This is how it feels to me when an identity pose is activated, when I assume that particular identity. There's no leeway, no room for fluctuation. I can't see myself as reasonably nice. It's not enough to feel I'm gentle when the time is right for gentleness. I can't tolerate the feeling that I'm not so peaceful sometimes. No layers. No changes allowed except to possess even more of the identity's defining characteristics, never less of these. The nice guy can become nicer, the gentle guy gentler. But not nastier, not tougher.

An identity pose is a stick-figure sketch that I accept as an accurate portrait of the essential me, with every broad exaggerated line needed to justify my own value as a human being. They all seem to make up a vital part of Bob's identity. This is why I react so forcefully if an important identity pose such as Mr. Nice Guy feels under threat from the world in some way. It's really a threat to my sense of my life's value. In the psychological struggle for existence, my right to exist feels under attack.

An additional hallmark of identity poses is my harsh enforcement of them. I can't cut myself any slack. When I'm busy being a nice guy, I must always be gentle and sensitive and all the other things, peaceful and open and friendly and on and on. In public or in private, it makes no difference to my psyche. My mind will launch an often-fierce attack on my self-value whenever I deviate much from this requirement. This is who I am, this is who I must be always. Or else.

Always, at least, until my mind assumes a different identity pose in a new situation. During my years as a reporter, for instance, Bob-the-nice-guy sometimes didn't fit very well with my workaday world in the newsroom – so somewhere along the line my psyche formed Bob-the-tough-reporter. I often would shift from the nice guy identity pose to this much more forceful identity: The tough, driven, truthseeking journalist. It's another of the many Bobs I've carried around in my head. Bob-the-tough-reporter, coexisting with Bob-the-nice-guy and all the others. Each in turn equally inflexible about what I need to be at a particular moment, a rigid simplistic identity constructed out of rigid simplistic personality traits. Because the process is so fundamentally irrational I rarely need to reconcile these identity poses, no necessity to account sensibly for being so many different types of people. Whether nice or truthseeking or something else, the identity simply feels like me right then.

Or maybe it isn't me at all. And that's where I've run into trouble when dealing with the world.

A Puzzling Fit

As long as I feel the world and I fit each other with reasonable ease, I'm all right. Again, that's the purpose of the nice guy and all other identity poses. They're my mind's attempts to join the two. There are my interpretations of the world, there are my interpretations of me – the identity poses try fitting them together like the pieces of a puzzle.

My nice guy identity pose accomplishes this in many, many ways.

Perhaps the most effective approach to illustrate this is with a simple chart. The left side represents a few of my irrational interpretations of the world, the right side offers a few of the ways my irrational nice guy identity pose fits those elements of the world together with me. In other words, the right side represents the overlap, the shaded area of the earlier diagram. None of my interpretations of Bob are included here because they were explained at some length above – my ways of seeing me as a nice guy, which otherwise would be another column in this chart.

Of course the chart is only to serve as the shortest of shorthand versions of the reality. On the left, each world-interpretation really would be a sizable nexus made of many smaller irrational interpretations of the world. On the right, each way of fitting together the world and me would exist in my mind as a sizable nexus made of many smaller irrational interpretations about how to best connect the outside universe with the inside Bob. I suspect my psyche would have gathered up enough material for a midnexus on each point on both sides of the below chart.

Some of my World-interpretations	How Nice Guy Identity Pose Connects World and Me
Most people are basically nice in some way, with many personality variations.	Being a nice guy places me in the mainstream of humanity.
My family members all are nice people.	Being nice allows me to feel a closer kinship with my family.
Most people like others to be nice.	Being nice helps me get along with people.
Nice people are admirable, always caring about the welfare of others.	Being nice means I am admirable, always caring about the welfare of others.
Nice people are more comfortable to be around.	Most people feel more comfortable around me when I'm a nice guy.
Most people are easily hurt, with fragile egos. Sometimes they respond aggressively or even violently.	Being a nice guy makes people less likely to become easily angered with me and so less likely to attack me verbally or physically.
The world is full of violence, hostility, rudeness as well as over-competitiveness, laziness, stupidity, ignorance and more.	Being a nice guy helps me to mask my intense fury at other individuals and at the world, a template for self-control and social acceptability.

Remember, this is a hugely incomplete list. These brief summaries only hint at the complex realities underlying each of those interpretations on both left and right sides. The psychological mechanisms that created those interpretations are elaborately complicated and the size and strength of the interpretations are great, even if each concept is simplistic when contrasted with reality. Still, I hope the list provides some meaningful explanation for the moment.

Again, the right side list would be part of the shaded area in the middle of my tragically hand-drawn intersecting circles. As I said then, that's where the psychological action really is.

Because those are the concepts that help me to feel my existence is worth something to me.

Value Conscious

It's not so much the identity poses themselves that give me a sense of my value in this world. It's what those identity poses mean to me, the ways they connect the world and me.

Being a nice guy in itself doesn't provide that feeling I crave. But seeing myself as part of humanity's mainstream and sharing a closer kinship with my family, oh, these most certainly do offer that sense of my importance. My value. The same with all the other right-hand column characteristics – they each create some portion of my self-justification for being alive. They help make me feel my life at this moment in this world is valuable.

Within the nice guy identity pose, as with all identity poses, some of those right-hand column characteristics may feel more important to my self-value than others at any particular moment, depending on the situation externally and internally. That is, some elements of an identity pose can take psychological precedence over other elements according to my circumstances. If I'm in a business meeting, an ability to get along with people and make them comfortable may feel like the most valuable part of being a nice guy just then. If I'm very unsure of myself in that same meeting, an ability to lessen the likelihood of angering colleagues may feel like one of the most important aspects of my nice guy identity pose. If the meeting is with another nonprofit group leader, I may find more self-worth because Bob-the-nice-guy means being an admirable person who always cares about the welfare of my fellow human beings. And so forth. My mind automatically latches on to those characteristics of an identity pose that create the strongest feelings of my value right now. I don't plan it that way, I'm usually not aware of the process at all. But that's how it works.

And it works that way not only with the characteristics within every identity pose but with each identity pose itself. My mind selects whichever identity pose feels best suited to the situation. From Bob-the-nice-guy to Bob-the-tough-reporter to Bob-the-something-else. My mind gravitates toward the most comfortable fit with the world at this moment.

For most of my years, my mind required many different identity poses to cope with the world. I've never felt any need to attempt cataloguing these so I can't give an accurate count of how many identity poses have accumulated in my mind. But I conservatively estimate there must be dozens of them. Together they made my overall self-image, my concept of Bob. Those I've identified are all over the psychological map, lots of personalities ready to go when needed during everyday living. Personalities that are massively varied and sometimes mutually exclusive.

There's Bob-the-mature-and-experienced-man and Bob-the-exuberant-manchild, for instance. Bob-the-deep-thinker and Bob-the-crude-jokester. Bob-the-sophisticate, Bob-the-earthy-guy, Bob-the-unpretentious-person.

Bob-the-world-traveler, Bob-the-sexual-stud, Bob-the-artist, Bob-the-gifted-musician, Bob-the-romantic-male, Bob-the-playful-funster, Bob-the-wild-partier, Bob-the-rebel, Bob-the-bookworm, Bob-the-anxious-intellectual, Bob-the-tortured-genius, Bob-the-confident-adult, Bob-the-concerned-friend, Bob-the-social-activist, Bob-the-misunderstood-loner, Bob-the-decent-athlete, Bob-the-total-klutz. There's Bob-the-daring-driver and Bob-the-safe-driver too. There's Bob-the-patient-listener and Bob-the-passionate-talker. There's even Bob-the-good-person, which is related to the nice guy identity pose but even more sweeping and more powerful. Dozens and dozens, as I suggested. Just how many dozens, I have no sensible idea.

Each one is a whole separate identity that my mind accepts as Bob when this feels necessary to my sense of self-value. Some larger and stronger than others. Some more important to me than others. Some more often used than others. But every identity pose is made of massive groupings of one of the most basic mechanisms of my psyche: Vericepts, each taken in during a single eyeblink of time. The vericepts eventually gathered into larger concepts and then still larger concepts and then concepts larger still, from micronexes to supernexes size and strength, like cosmic dust forming itself bit by bit into rocks and meteors and planets. Every identity pose represents a specific set of personality traits that feels most valuable to me in certain situations, the best way for me to be what I need to be at the time. When I'm a nice guy I feel like one sort of person, when I'm a tough reporter I feel like another sort of person, when I'm a deep thinker I feel like a person who's much unlike either the nice guy or tough reporter.

I've named this phenomenon "identity poses" because the metaphor better jibes with related aspects of Identity Failure that I'll describe later in this chapter. Originally, though, I thought of my identity poses as "identity masks" – that's how they still seem to me in some ways. They're like distinct masks I pull from my psychic wall to don and doff as needed. Probably that notion appeals to me partly because I own a wonderful collection of real masks that I've picked up on trips to such places as Papua New Guinea and Thailand, Russia and Italy, Indonesia and Malaysia and Korea and Haiti and Greece. I love them. But I've most definitely come to unlove the psychological versions, whether I dub these identity masks or identity poses. They have been central to the presence of my life's most intense, most persistent and most damaging problem.

Identity Failure.

The continual psychological struggle for existence that's a fundamental part of my nature had acquired a primary aim: To maintain a belief in my identity poses. As long as Identity Failure had hold of me, I wanted more than anything to feel this solidly confident belief in my identity poses. In my terminology, I deepwanted it.

Some of those identity poses I deepwanted more than life itself.

In recent years I've learned that I was entirely prepared to die if death seemed required to maintain some highly significant self-images. Under I.F., my most important identity poses are basic to my concept of Bob and so to my concept of Bob's value. I have many times felt as if my unrelenting pursuit of self-knowledge, my theories, Rational Faith might be killing me quite literally – the sense of horrible isolation that grew from these efforts, the overwhelming anxiety and rage that erupted from the isolation, the psychological and physical symptoms that utterly assaulted my life day in and day out for some five years as a result. I wasn't sure for a long time if I was greatly shortening my lifespan from all this. Still am not sure as I write this chapter's final draft in February 2019. I am hopeful now that it needn't be the case, that it's not too late for my health to recover as I have transitioned to a much more rational approach to my life. But the work was so thoroughly integrated into my deepest feelings of self-value that any damage to my health ultimately didn't matter to me. Or not enough to quit anyway. I had no intention of stopping, no matter what happened to me.

I suffered in this way because of my identity poses, pure and simple. Because of Identity Failure. A more rational attitude about my work from the start would have diminished or eliminated the identity poses, creating much less psychological conflict and much less misery, emotional and physical. I wouldn't have endured the torturous results of feeling so misunderstood and so alone for so long, which happened because I couldn't get outside confirmation for some key identity poses. Without I.F., premature death wouldn't have seemed like an issue.

But my absolute persistence despite what felt like the real possibility of early and even imminent death says a lot about both my identity poses and Identity Failure. That's how important some of my identity poses were to me. More important than living because without them my life felt worthless.

When afflicted with Identity Failure, I would rather die than give up the most important ways I see myself.

Elements Of Truth

Irrational as they are, though, identity poses are something else as well. They are based on reality.

At least they're based on something about myself that I believe to be real. I've learned there is some element of perceived truth to each identity pose.

I wondered about this for a while. Consider my childhood incident in the new neighborhood, that way-back moment when I bragged to the kids about my martial arts skills. Skills I didn't have. Was that an identity pose that I'd made up from whole cloth?

No, it wasn't. It was a lie, pure and simple. I knew I was lying at the moment I uttered the first brag. I was fibbing quite deliberately to impress some boys who I very much hoped would admire me. And that's been the case whenever I later lied about me – my accomplishments, my skills, my travels or whatever felt necessary at those times. I wasn't creating an identity pose. I was just lying.

To qualify as an identity pose, I must believe it's true. Otherwise it doesn't make me feel valuable for long. And to believe it's true, any identity pose must draw on at least some truths about me as I see them.

I can't very well believe myself a great mathematician. I hated math in school and have used little but arithmetic since, to my regret in more recent years. No one ever has noted any outstanding math ability in me. There's no pool of evidence about my math prowess to siphon off for an identity pose as Bob-the-great-mathematician.

But my writing, that's a different tale. I've all along had a clear sense of my talent as a writer, often supplemented with outside confirmation of one sort or another. Early on from teachers and parents, then from teachers and peers when I gained attention as a controversial high school columnist on the political issues of 1970 and 1971. I felt I was a good writer. The world seemed to confirm it. A bit later I saw myself as the equivalent of a young Ernest Hemingway, whose short stories I was busy gobbling by my senior high school year. I believed that I was blossoming as a literary whizkid, just like Ernest. I even had some outside support to bolster this identity pose, including enthusiasm from my girlfriend, Lydia, and some teachers in high school and college. But the larger world of literary magazine editors almost entirely disagreed, rejecting nearly all my stories and also my poems. And of course they were right. I wasn't blossoming as a literary whizkid. My development took a long time as an extremely hard-working adult writer. It was pained and gradual, not sudden and fullblown.

Still, I knew for sure that I could write. So I built a succession of Bob-the-writer identity poses founded simultaneously on my achievements and my feelings about where those achievements could next lead me. Each identity pose far exceeded any image of me the world appeared to have at the time, but each felt justified by some earlier outside appreciation of me as a writer. And justified too by experiences such as my fulfillment of potential in other areas of my life, those moments when I'd observed how time and effort could bring about real improvement. I also was keenly aware of past struggles by great writers who were underestimated in their era, another boost for a writer who believed in his future importance. Most of all I sensed what

I could become and I then formed identity poses from these feelings of potential, supported by confidence drawn from my earlier writing experiences in the world. In each identity pose, some portion of truth was lodged within the concept.

I created the identity pose, then tried to prove my new self-image was right. At 27 I worked at the University of Vermont library but saw myself really as a newspaper freelance writer, based partly on my high school journalism success. That same year while still at the library I worked myself into a part-time freelance gig handling feature and hard news assignments for Vermont newspapers. But very soon I saw that Bob really was a full-time reporter, based in part on my freelance scoops missed by full-time competitors. There was some element of truth to my full-time reporter identity pose even before I was hired full-time by Vermont's major radio news station. It's who I felt I truly was, needing only the world's confirmation. After several years as a radio and then television reporter, I understood that Bob really was a newspaper investigative journalist. I had broken many significant investigative stories by then and at age 36 I transferred my investigative skills from broadcast to print journalism after landing a job at one of Florida's major regional newspapers.

It went on like this, right up into my early 60s.

Based partly on my journalism experience, I believed in my ability to become a national magazine writer and book author. After writing national magazine stories and books for a few years, I felt my strong writing qualified me as a developing playwright and poet. Then I thought my plays and poems offered some basis to see myself as the author of multi-media literary works expressing philosophical ideas through my own nonprofit organization. And then I decided a lifetime's work as a highly introspective writer qualified me as the creator of a psychology-based original philosophy of life called Rational Faith, a self-image that existed for a time as an identity pose – though now of course viewed by me in a more rational light.

And no, this little section of my book isn't intended as bragging. Despite my past tendencies, that's not my goal here. My encapsulated work history is offered only to demonstrate something. It all helps make my point about the elements of truth within an identity pose. Each Bob-the-writer identity pose has been based on some elements drawn from real world success.

Not a single Bob-the-writer identity pose in my head was rational. Every one of them was absurd in its one-dimensional rigidity. A caricature of a real human, as I've said. However, each of those identity poses was built on experiences that allowed me to accept it as the truth of me even if the world didn't agree at the time. The experiences provided some sensible rationale to believe in the caricature.

Identity poses aren't complete nonsense. They are grotesque distortions of reality: Caricatures, stick figures. Call them what you like. Or perhaps we might think of them as funhouse mirrors that make me look skinny or fat. The self-images reflected back to me by my identity poses are as ridiculous as the images bouncing off those mirrors. They seem like me, but aren't. Obviously, though, they are partly me.

That's precisely why I have learned to feel so strongly about them. They really seem to be Bob. They seem to be the reason for Bob's value in the outside world.

And as it happens, the outside world is precisely where each of my identity poses originated.

Me, Ready-made

I recognize that my identity poses weren't created simply from the material of my imagination, like characters I would invent when writing a novel. Not at all. Actually they were formed as my mind drew from sources everywhere around me, including the imaginations of other writers.

I can see now that identity poses first entered my mind ready-made from the world, a huge repertoire of guises that supposedly represented real-life people. Television, movies, books and other cultural influences offered me images of one-dimensional identities I was able to absorb or reject as part of my own identity. I learned about being a nice guy from television characters especially, but also from films. Television and film also showed me different ways of being human in the world. I learned there were committed and selfless professionals working to save others, in particular doctors who always knew what to do and when to do it. I learned there were folks defined by their intelligence such as scientists and there were other folks who lived through their creativity such as musicians. As a boy I felt something in common with all these types, though I wasn't sure just what it was. I learned as well about many other kinds of people who were nothing like me. Natural athletes. And tough insensitive men, some of them violent but others who worked as police to protect us. There were loners and invalids and some people with no sense of humor. Still others were naturally funny. No, I wasn't like any of them.

I remember very clearly in my early 20s becoming aware of the toxic influence that the actor John Wayne cast over my perception of what manhood should be, then consciously working to separate my identity from the gung-ho super-macho character he always played. Until that time I had simply accepted that he represented something true about ideal manliness. His public image was only one of many that afflicted me. My culture fed pre-made identities to me, ready for my psyche to swallow. Silly personality types, really, that my mind exploited to fit together the world and me. These identities offered me ways of being Bob in the world – Bob as I wanted to see myself. Bob as I wanted others to see me. Each with some basis in the reality of me as I understood it.

Even more importantly, I soaked up similar lessons from people in real life. Everyone on earth appeared to fall into easily identifiable categories: "He's a nice guy," my father would say. Or sometimes, "He's not nice." Or Dad would pull out the many other adjectives still commonly used to characterize human beings. "Funny," "nasty," "stupid," "pleasant," "awful," "charming" and many many more too. My entire family normally referred to people this way, summing up the living and the dead and the fictional in a couple of words. And of course I saw each of my family members as nice. It was clear to me that being nice was one highly important quality for living in the world. I suspect that quite early in my childhood I'd constructed a well-developed nexus about being a nice guy.

Everyone else talked about everyone else just as my family did. Adults and kids alike used the same descriptions, my teachers and my coaches and the friends of my parents along with all the children I knew. Even those who appeared as themselves on television – talk show hosts and newscasters and game show contestants. Based on what I heard, everybody recognized that our planet was peopled by distinct types. The very types my family discussed, the very types I saw among television and movie characters. That's simply how it was in this world of ours.

And some of those types helped Bob understand himself. Nice guy, very smart and the others. Combined, those types would become me. They were my collection of identity poses, with verification of some sort coming from the outside world. People treated me like a nice guy more often than not, especially adults. Most people treated me like I was smart, even kids who resented my intelligence. Yes, I really was a nice guy, really was smart. These identities surely were accurate reflections of Bob.

Naturally enough, I acquired new identity poses and shed other identity poses over the years. I was about 17 before Bob-the-sexual-stud made himself known to me. Much earlier identity poses such as Bob-the-sweet-boy disappeared.

And as with Bob-the-writer, some of my identity poses evolved as I grew up. When I was a child, Bob-the-nice-guy included immature qualities like an unquestioning enthusiasm for all family activities and a close attention to the emotional needs of my parents. Later, Bob-the-nice-guy included new qualities like courtesy when driving a car and respectful behavior toward women I dated. Still simplistic, still rigid, still absurdly irrational. But yes, many identity poses in time became different. Somewhat.

And this capacity for identity poses to change is worth emphasis. With little deliberate effort my mind selected some of the world's personality types as more or less suitable for Bob, then shaped and shaded them, adding new caricature lines and erasing other lines to better represent me. I've made Bob-the-nice-guy into my personal version of the nice guy type, Bob-the-tough-reporter into my personal version of the tough journalist type, altering every identity pose as needed by my psyche. Adding some characteristics to the identity pose, subtracting other characteristics. I adapted each identity pose to make a better fit, like tailoring an off-the-rack business suit.

Did all of my identity poses come to me ready-made? Or did I invent some in the beginning for myself? I'm not absolutely sure about all of them, of course, because I can't go back to experience their origins directly. But I've tried to reconstruct some of my identity poses as best my memory allows, attempting to relive the feelings and examine what may have been happening to me. And recently I found myself trying to build a brand new identity pose without knowing it at first, giving me the opportunity to directly observe how my mind was going about it.

This is my best educated guess about the formation of my identity poses: Self-images began to form in my earliest days after birth as I reacted to my treatment by the world, my parents especially. As I progressed through infancy, people behaved in ways that continued shaping my idea of me – they loved me or didn't, they paid attention to me or didn't and so forth. And some of those people also told me that I exuded specific qualities as part of being Bob. "You're such a good boy!" "You're so smart!" or whatever it may have been. Likely at least some of those qualities reflected attributes that I possessed genetically at the start. From the world around me, I must have begun to identify very simple personality types as I grew up, including examples from television and movies and books as well as people I knew. Perhaps types such as a "brave" person, a "nice" person, a "kind" person, a "selfish" person, a "mean" person. These all influenced my self-image as I started to recognize some as identities appropriate for myself. Each new identity served as an outlet for a portion of my existing emotional needs.

And once my mind had settled on this outlet, the budding identity pose continued to develop through automatic psychological efforts: Squeezing my thoughts, feelings, words and actions into the identity pose as much as possible; learning more about the identity pose from other people I viewed as admirable examples; trying to emulate those examples; looking for outside validation to prove my identity pose was Bob; coping with lack of outside validation in whatever ways seemed best at the moment. And on it went from there, an interplay of those elements over and over.

Every identity pose appears to bear great similarities to simplistic personality types I've seen somewhere, either in the real world as I understood this or as portrayed in stories. And as best I can tell, every identity pose indeed first requires an outside example as a template. I distinctly remember feeling like a talented writer long before my Bob-the-writer identity pose existed. The thought of writing professionally never seriously entered my consciousness until my 11th grade journalism class – thank you, Mr. Doug Johnson. He was an inspiring teacher and a mentor who greatly influenced my life through nurturing my enthusiasm for writing and reporting. But I recall feeling long before this that writing was among my talents. Sometimes my teachers even called on me to read my work to the class. I was aware of my ability with words and I was aware others were aware of the same thing in me. Yet at that point my writing talent seemed simply one part of Bob-the-good-student, not an independent identity. From 11th grade on, though, Bob-the-writer appeared and became an ever-expanding identity pose.

To me, this history suggests that I couldn't draw together the threads of my writing talent into an identity pose until a rigid and simplistic concept presented itself to me through Mr. Johnson's journalism class – I could write professionally as a journalist. That was an idea I found both appealing and potentially suitable for me. Suddenly Bob-the-writer offered fresh opportunities to satisfy my emotions, to do some of the things I felt were important for me. These included expressing my intellect creatively, making some positive impact on society and helping other people to understand important information about the world. It was a new way to be Bob. Those feelings were at least partly rational, but the self-image I manufactured to satisfy them was not. Bob-the-writer was an identity pose from the beginning, based on elements of the man I genuinely saw myself to be.

Thinking back, I was most definitely one of those kids who always longed to grow into some adult identity. I hated childhood, honestly, and looked forward eagerly to achieving meaningful social goals. No later than five-years-old I focused this passion on being a doctor. My great-grandfather had been a well-known doctor in Illinois and other family members on my father's side also had been medical men – doubtless serving as early encouragement for me to focus on medicine. Bob-the-future-doctor continued until at least age 12 or so, then went through a series of what I saw as possible adult Bobs: lawyer, physicist, professional snow skier believe it or not ... Each one seemed like it might be the real me. Then journalism turned up and from that moment I was heading off along my writing career. On the way, non-professional identities also came and went. I distinctly remember when I adopted the hippie persona at about 16 or maybe 17-years-old. I can retrace that identity pose's evolution with a fair degree of confidence, so strong are the memories. My concept of a hippie was growing and changing at the same time that my self-image was growing and changing. The hippie concept and the self-image were coming closer together starting when I was about 14. Increasingly I was drawn toward the hippie ideal of a non-violent world revolution whose goal was peace and love. The rebellion of hippiedom matched my own desire to escape my family's traditional values. The open sexuality and experimentation with drugs intrigued me. After so many years of being bullied, I also sought some meaningful way to feel that I belonged to a group of people. Informally joining a tribe of loving and deeply insightful peers felt irresistible – though I quickly learned the reality didn't always live up to the image.

As with Bob-the-writer, evidently, Bob-the-hippie formed as a result of a template handed to me by the world, a pre-made identity that I merged with my existing interests and talents and personality. At 17 and 18, I felt much like other hippies I saw around me, but also a bit different. An individual. I was Bob-the-hippie, unique in some fashion. But in many particulars I also wanted to be seen as a hippie like all the others.

My very recent attempt to create a new identity pose was something I recognized while first writing this very section of this chapter in January 2016. That experience provided me with a direct close-up perspective on the process, at least as it happened this time around. I understood one morning that my mind was working hard to form a fresh self-image of Bob. Yes, Bob as a moral leader, as someone who carries ethical ideas to people through public speaking as well as through writings. As with the other identity poses, I initially borrowed that self-image. In this case, from my view of moral leaders past and present. And as with the others, there was some reasonable basis for it.

The urge for this identity pose seemed to emerge from a variety of emotional needs searching for some outlet at the time. A desire to help others in person, which I had come to see as a more effective method than writing to reach some people. Especially young people. A need to feel comfortable teaching ideas in the messy face-to-face setting, where progress is so hard to measure. Other motivations for my moral leader identity pose included a very strong emotional need for a greater number of significant human interactions than I'd had in recent years, freeing myself from an isolation that resulted in large part from my struggles with Identity Failure. For lots of different but related reasons, my psyche was pushing me toward some self-image that accommodated a new way of being Bob: leadership about ethics, taking my deepest-held ideas on morality to adults and kids alike in much more intimate forms than I ever had before. Strangers and I, sitting across from each other in a room as I led serious discussions about things like self-value.

In the Humanity Project's first ten years, I had done a fair amount of public speaking and presentations, as required. But it all felt like something I had to do rather than a real aspect of my real work. And other than during our antibullying programs for young kids, I didn't enjoy it either. On top of this, powerful new anxieties about social interactions had surfaced from my bout of heightened Identity Failure. I often felt intensely nervous around people.

Now, though, I recognized a necessity to speak with strangers of all ages often, comfortably and confidently. How could I reconcile the conflict?

My mind looked for answers and at last latched on to the concept of a moral leader, as I understood the idea. I accepted that moral leaders often needed to take their work to the public in person after creating that work in solitude, as I did. I saw moral leaders as human beings with beliefs of depth and originality, very much as I saw my beliefs. I felt moral leaders were humanistic and substantive, mostly true intellectuals driven by the genuine purpose of helping others. I could live with Bob-the-moral-leader. This concept just might work to better fit the world and me together.

And that's the moment when I realized what I was doing. I was forming a new identity pose. I immediately took down notes as I explored the burgeoning self-image, including those psychological elements I could examine directly and other elements that I believed were likely to emerge later in the process. This required speculation in the last four points below, then, but speculation informed by my previous experience with Identity Failure.

This is what I wrote in bullet points on January 25, 2016:

- I need to speak in public about moral/intellectual issues – deepwanting to satisfy specific emotions.
- A "moral leader" does that (identity pose).
- These are qualities of a moral leader.
- I have some qualities (x y & z) that allow me to become that.
- I have other qualities (A B & C) I can develop to become that.
- I can imagine the type of moral leader Bob could become – adapted to my situation & needs.
- I want to become a moral leader.
- I work to develop qualities & tap into existing qualities & focus on my effort to become a moral leader.
- I see progress as I do this, allowing me to begin seeing myself as a moral leader.
- I look for outside validation that I'm a moral leader.
- Without it I look for ways to justify my moral leader identity pose without outside validation.

All of this seems to confirm what I'd already believed: An identity pose bundles together a variety of my related pre-existing emotional needs, which find an outlet through a simplistic personality type I see in the outside world.

An identity pose gives me a clearly defined, simple-to-understand connection with that world. And it offers an additional way to find my value according to the Fundamental Law of Mind. In this instance I felt a strong need to speak about my philosophical ideas in public for many reasons. I then recognized a moral leader as someone who does just this in a manner that seemed a comfortable fit with my personality and beliefs. I knew that I already possessed some qualities of moral leadership and felt I could develop other needed qualities. This combination of new interpretations about my situation allowed me to deepwant to become a moral leader – to want this new identity without any serious emotional conflict. That deepwanting already was gaining strength when I became aware of the nascent Bob-the-moral-leader identity. Based on experience, I believed other things almost surely would have followed if I hadn't recognized what was happening: I would have worked in the world to justify that identity pose and in time achieved enough success in my view to qualify. I then would have added Bob-the-moral-leader to my repertoire of self-images, a brand new identity pose contributing feelings of my life's value.

Bob-the-moral-leader would have allowed me to satisfy some of my emotional needs as it further developed my abilities by offering a clear concept about what I "should" be in the world. But I would end up seeing myself only as a caricature of a true moral leader. And I would expect me to live up to that irrational self-image or else.

That's what would have taken place if I hadn't learned by then to distance myself from all identity poses as much as possible. And I would have suffered in time as a result.

One thing I know for sure. However they were created in my head during childhood and beyond, my identity poses became the most immediately important concern of my life.

Opinions Outside

Think back to those bullet points about Identity Failure for a moment, please.

This was the first of them:

- I believe that specific qualities of myself give my life its value. (Being "very smart," let's say, or "a nice guy." Together, these many specific qualities create my overall idea of "me" and a feeling of my life's value to me.)

That was a very broad description of my identity poses. The identity poses and the characteristics that make up each identity pose seem to give my life its value.

Here was the second bullet point:

- I feel that only outside opinion can truly confirm that I possess those specific qualities. (I require the opinion of others to prove to myself that I'm very smart or a nice guy, etc.)

That's been true my entire life until I created Rational Faith. Why?

The quick and simple answer is this: I was taught to believe it. From the moment I was born until the moment I began to question this idea, I utterly accepted that other people helped to determine my worth. I'm not certain exactly when that questioning moment first came to me, but Emerson, Buddha and other thinkers nudged me toward psychological self-reliance at least by my early 50s, perhaps some years before. At that point I felt there was something to this independent mindset but wasn't able to seriously attempt living that way until my early 60s.

Before that time, family and friends and total strangers and everyone in between served as the arbiters of my value as a human being. And as a writer, as a journalist, as a thinker, as a musician. As a friend, as a brother, as a son, as a colleague. As everything. Everything I'd ever believed myself to be, all of it perpetually awaiting the confirmation of others.

I was raised from my first instant of breath onward to accept my dependency on other people. Physical dependency soon turned into psychological dependency. My mother and father decided if I was a good boy or not. Honest or not. Loving or not. Was I brave, was I kind, was I selfish, was I mean? Was I smart? Was I nice? My parents told me. My brother and sister as well, then other relatives and family friends and playmates and teachers. Everyone had a say about my self-image – and my self-value. Was I this or was I that? I couldn't know with confidence for myself. But they seemed to know.

In this sense I believe that my upbringing was little different from that of nearly every child on earth: I learned that my self-value legitimately rested significantly with other people. Not me but them. As far as I can tell after visiting six continents, whatever the culture, whatever the customs and beliefs, most of us are taught to take the opinions of others to heart. Outside reactions validate who we are, what we should and shouldn't be, what we can and can't do.

I surely was taught this.

In many respects, this dependency on outside opinion for my feelings of self-value is at the core of my Identity Failure. It's the fulcrum on which Identity Failure balances.

In Chapter 6 I talked about my family as people-pleasers, their obsession with external judgments about them. And my own obsession with the same thing, my complete and total acceptance that others understood vitally important things about me that I couldn't understand without their opinions. These folks knew me in some key ways better than I ever could know me.

As the bullet point says, I felt that only outside opinion could truly confirm that I possessed those specific qualities that gave my life its value. I required the opinion of others to prove to myself that I was very smart or a nice guy or whatever.

This attitude set me up for what I was to endure day in and day out until age 65.

A Forceful Weakening

The third bullet point accurately outlines the next step in the complicated psychological process of Identity Failure. Kind of.

This is what it said:

- Outside opinion doesn't confirm those specific qualities in ways that I find convincing. (The opinion of others doesn't seem to verify that I'm very smart or a nice guy, etc.)

That's accurate because it reflects the problem I've run into constantly by depending on other people for my self-value. But it's only kind of accurate because other people aren't the genuine problem at all. I'm the problem.

The lack of confirmation really comes from within, not without. It only seems to begin outside me.

Many times in my life, for example, my mother muttered some comment that made me doubt whether I was a nice guy just then. Or sometimes it was her expression or something she said merely through saying nothing. Except that's wrong. It wasn't her comment or expression or even her silence that disturbed me. It was the way I interpreted her comment or expression or silence – and the resulting internal commentary that followed immediately.

Those inner voices caused the trouble back then. And today too whenever I suffer Identity Failure. It's not anything anyone says or does, or doesn't say or doesn't do to me. It's what my mind makes of their comment or action, it's the way my psyche reacts in order to preserve the strongest possible feelings of my value with the least possible emotional resistance.

I've found over more than four decades of intrasentient observation that this conflict feels like it comes from the world. But really doesn't. As if from the comments and reactions of other people, the chaotic flow of events in society around me. That's how it seems.

Actually, though, it comes from *imagined* criticisms of me, assaults on myself generated for specific purposes by my own mind. These attacks may arrive in the subtle form of vericepts that I inhale automatically like breaths of air without my awareness. Or they may charge at me through thoughts and feelings of which I'm painfully aware, imaginary voices that insistently spew out the many things I'm afraid may be wrong with me.

I've named these self-criticisms "pose-weakeners." It's as though I carry some version of the world inside my head, a whole panel of critics and naysayers and cynics, an inner jury whose sole job is to remind me of the negative and the destructive, the inadequate and the faulty, the insufficient and the excessive characteristics of me. They work as an untiring team to weaken the identity poses that become their targets. As such they are my pose-weakeners and the psychological effect they cause is something I predictably call pose-weakening.

For most of my life pose-weakeners created pose-weakening in my mind countless times every day. This means that some of my identity poses were assaulted to varying degrees by me, degrading their overall emotional strength in my life. They were weakened, as still happens when I experience Identity Failure. The things that I feel make me me, the identities that connect the world and me – some of these are ridiculed, diminished, laughed at, derided, undermined, questioned and viciously attacked by my own mind. They are battered by relentless bullying of me, by me. These bullies are my pose-weakeners and, no, I don't have them simply because I was bullied as a child. They're an integral part of my psyche. Pose-weakeners stir up a terrible uncertainty about myself. Pose-weakeners create self-confusion, the profound doubt about who I am and about my value in this world. It's an automatic psychological process that happens when

I depend on outside opinion to confirm my value.

For many many years I knew nothing about pose-weakeners or pose-weakening. I only knew I frequently felt very bad about myself.

Pose-weakeners often come in the form of vericepts that feed me irrational interpretations of my experience at that moment, taken in all at once as a single concept. Perhaps something like, "That was a terrible thing to say to your mother and you really might be a terrible person" as a simple for instance. Or they may come to me as feelings or thoughts that seem to bubble up from nowhere, one after another. "You said something awful to your mother. That hurt her feelings. What kind of person are you to do that? You really might be a terrible person!" Again, a simplified for instance. Often pose-weakeners feel like actual voices, though of course they're not. There's nothing delusional or hallucinatory about them. But in my mind, pose-weakeners have become connected with real outside criticism I've experienced so they now can create much the same feeling as actually hearing someone attack me. It's as if I'm listening to harsh voices saying nasty things. I sometimes literally put my fingers in my ears to quiet them, though I'm fully aware there's no actual sound to muffle. I may even yell softly to myself, "Shut up!" Odd as this may appear, it actually helps though usually not for very long.

Pose-weakeners happen for several reasons. First, because I've collected a great many negative irrational notions about myself over my lifetime. In my terminology, these notions are negative irvericepts like the one just above involving my mother, some with much more information included within a single moment's interpretation – my irvericept about the unpleasant picnic with Cynthia, for example. I can swallow a lot of ideas about myself and the world and my connection with the world all at once, whole. These negative irvericepts cluster together by subject to form nexes. So just as I have a very large nice-guy nexus, for instance, I also have a big terrible-guy nexus, all the things related to seeing myself as a terrible-guy. Not an identity pose in this case because identity poses are always something I view as positive self-images in some way. Obviously this big irrational terrible-guy nexus is composed of huge numbers of smaller nexes about somehow seeing myself as a terrible person. And just as I have a large very-smart-guy nexus about my intellectual abilities, I have a sizable very-dumb-guy nexus that pulls together experiences that made me feel small intellectually. And so on and so on, groupings of experiences about my good and my bad and all that falls between.

That's the broad point here. But it's helpful to understand the main details.

At the deepest psychological levels, pose-weakeners are the consequence of powerful negative nexes that have been activated in my mind by something. Sometimes, it seems, by almost anything. These particular nexes cause pose-weakening because they're made of many negative irvericepts about me like those involving my mother or the picnic with Cynthia. Upsetting concepts about Bob. Each of the negative vericepts, and so each of the negative nexes, has emotion attached to it as part of its psychological construction. The emotions are bound up with the concepts, fused together as one. So when the negative nexes are activated, they emit significant amounts of their emotional energy. Think of each nexus as a little like an engine that sits inert until started, when it gives off its energy. But the energy emitted from these negative nexes is a negative emotional energy, basically meaning forms of fear and anger. Like an engine that belches a choking black exhaust. Those negative nexes generate brand new negative irvericepts that add to these and other negative nexes. The new negative irvericepts also activate other negative nexes in a kind of chain reaction: Vericept, nexus, vericept, nexus, vericept, nexus. Naturally all of this increases the negative emotional energy in my mind, with the destructive elements gaining power. More irvericepts and more activated negative nexes mean more negative emotion. These emotions cause a range of feelings that are destructive to me and to others around me.

This is psychogravity in action: The increasing emotional strength of a connected set of interpretations about anything. The negative nexes are gaining energy in the form of more emotion. As a result, I'm feeling and thinking more and more bad things about myself, the world and my connection with the world. It all snowballs.

Pose-weakeners are among these bad things. The attacking voices in my head get louder. Some of Bob's cherished identity poses are under assault by Bob himself.

Trading Targets

But why?

Why on earth would my own mind besiege anything that matters so much to me? What causes the psychological self-destruction?

It's taken me a long time to figure this out. But the answer makes sense, completely consistent with the Fundamental Law of Mind.

It's a compromise. A psychological compromise.

Pose-weakeners attack identity poses that feel less vulnerable than other cherished identity poses to complete collapse. Again, this is an automatic process, not a choice, not a deliberate effort in any form or fashion. My mind gravitates toward generating criticisms of this identity pose in order to fend off even more terrifying criticisms of that identity pose. The phenomenon is a diversionary tactic, a defense mechanism.

For me it's more emotionally comfortable to repel furious self-attacks against Bob as an artist than to cope with equally strident batterings against Bob as a nice guy. I'm much more sure of my creative and artistic abilities than I am about my own humanity. My deepest fear, I think, is that there's something intrinsically wrong with me as a human being. That's one big part of the reason I needed to understand myself as thoroughly as I have, using that experience to discover some rational way for me to exist in the world: I am trying to feel confident that I'm basically OK. I'm in a war with my own Identity Failure, my repeated feelings that I may somehow be fundamentally flawed.

To better understand how pose-weakeners work, let's look back one more time on the last chapter's definition of Identity Failure and the explanation that followed:

"Identity Failure results from significant emotional resistance to a self-image that contributes significantly to my feelings that my existence is valuable to me at this moment in the world. Identity Failure happens when I begin to seriously doubt I can be something that I feel I need to be to fit into the world – some self-image so important to me that it helps make my life seem worth living. Those doubts create emotional resistance to this self-image, by which I mean they cause new and deeper self-doubts, fears and other feelings that make it harder for me to accept this self-image as reality. Emotional conflict, in other words. These negative feelings emit emotional energy that flows counter to the positive self-image I need, like a powerful air current that pushes away a weaker one. And so this emotional resistance weakens my sense of the value of my life, creating some level of uncertainty about my will to live. I grow afraid because I'm not feeling the desire to be alive with quite the same conviction."

So Identity Failure happens when an identity pose comes under attack. This attack comes in the form of pose-weakeners. The purpose of those pose-weakeners is to preserve feelings of self-value attached to some highly important identity pose by attacking another identity pose of sufficient psychological importance to satisfy my emotions at that moment.

I've built up many doubts over my lifetime about some extremely important self-images such as Bob-the-nice-guy. I feel unsure about this identity pose based on experiences that include my not-so-nice thoughts, feelings and actions – things I believed I shouldn't have thought or felt or done. Lots of negative reactions to me by other people contributed as well. Of course these outside responses especially cut because I've learned to depend on the world to confirm Bob-the-nice-guy for me. But just now, at this moment, the world isn't giving me sufficient confirmation of Bob-the-nice-guy, which increases my existing self-doubts about this.

I react to that self-doubt with very strong negative emotions. At a profound level, I'm terrified by the possibility I may not be a nice guy afterall. I'm intensely uncertain about it. I'm so afraid that I can't allow any of those negative emotions to reach me – my nice guy identity pose is too important to my feelings of self-value. My mind then protects itself from this uncertainty about being a nice guy, repressing those terrifying feelings so I'm unaware of them.

But I still have all those highly charged negative emotions floating around inside me. And I must satisfy them somehow. My psyche does this by generating vericepts, feelings and thoughts that feel something like outside voices criticizing me. Except that this stream of interior criticism focuses on some other uncertainty about myself that I can better handle emotionally. It targets one or more identity poses I care about sufficiently to accomplish that psychological trade-off. My psyche tries to retain as much feeling of self-value as possible by attacking me for something other than not being nice ... perhaps instead making me intensely doubt my creative and artistic abilities.

In this way my mind maintains an emotional comfort level to the extent it deems feasible. It strikes a psychological compromise to manage my powerful doubts about being a nice guy by exploiting some lesser but still highly significant level of uncertainty about being an artist.

And it does this according to the Fundamental Law of Mind. My mind continually interprets my experience to create the weakest possible emotional resistance to the strongest possible feelings that my existence is valuable to me at this moment in this world. By providing a strengthening force of emotional energy to attack Bob-the-artist, my pose-weakeners create less emotional resistance to Bob-the-nice-guy. I'm not so troubled by my conflicts about being a nice guy, in other words. Overall my psyche has weakened resistance and preserved feelings of self-value in what seems the best available manner under the present circumstances.

It has traded one greatly vulnerable psychological target for another target that feels slightly less vulnerable. I've now recognized that until recent years this sort of psychological compromise was the constant stuff of the everyday for me.

It's a simple exchange in the end, giving up one intolerable emotional agony in return for a misery that feels only a bit more bearable.

A For B & C

Identity poses are part of a remarkably complex process that includes pose-weakeners. To further explain identity poses, I must emphasize one more key point as background.

Not only is each of them irrational, as I've said repeatedly, but all identity poses exist in a condition of perpetual uncertainty. I can never feel fully relaxed, fully confident of any identity pose precisely because they are irrational, because they do not and cannot exist in nature. There is no organism that is a nice guy, or an artist or anything else in the way that I imagine myself to be those things when they are my identity poses. In one sense, it's as if I'm trying to feel that I'm really a unicorn. Like it or not, I can't escape the repeated awareness that I'm not. Also, I depend on the world to verify each identity pose. The world doesn't do this for me with anything like the frequency or credibility I need to completely believe in any identity pose.

Insecurity is built into each identity pose.

This means every identity pose is open to attack via pose-weakeners. To some extent or other, every identity pose is vulnerable.

That's important to keep in mind when understanding Identity Failure. My psyche automatically exploits the built-in uncertainty about whichever identity pose seems the most suitable target at this moment. I'm not creating doubt about some identity pose of which I am genuinely confident. I already feel unsure about the identity pose that comes under attack, an assault that's merely compensating for deep doubts about another more important identity pose. This is why pose-weakening works so well from the standpoint of maintaining psychic equilibrium. My mind has a vast range of identity poses available for its task, typically combining assaults on more than one identity pose to serve the purpose.

The issue is only of degree. Degrees of an identity pose's emotional significance to me – in this case, how strongly I value Bob-the-nice-guy versus Bob-the-artist. In the past, the psychological balancing act among all my identity poses resulted in an almost perpetual state of Identity Failure as my psyche made compromise after compromise to maintain as much feeling of self-value as it could.

Let me clarify all this with my 1 - 1,000 scale of emotional strength. Again, 1 represents the weakest feelings and 1,000 the strongest feelings possible. The numbers can better illustrate the purpose of my pose-weakeners, my psychological compromisers. Figures demonstrate how pose-weakeners help me to preserve feelings of self-value attached to highly significant identity poses by blasting other identity poses of lesser but sufficient significance to satisfy my emotions at the present moment.

For simplicity, I'll assign a numerical strength to the emotions connected with three different identity poses: Bob-the-nice-guy, with an emotional strength of 800; Bob-the-artist, with an emotional strength of 600; Bob-the-rebel, with an emotional strength of 150. I include the third and least significant of these identity poses to help make the point. As before, the numbers represent very simplified and constant expressions of complex psychological states that continuously change, in real life varying in strength and importance depending on my situation at that time. I offer them here as more or less accurate measures that suggest the relative significance of three different identity poses that I've identified in myself.

So how does pose-weakening happen?

Let's say I'm working on a new poem. I've written many poems and love creating poetry. On this hypothetical afternoon, I'm in the midst of an intense and productive poetry-writing session, making headway on a difficult passage that I feel breaks fresh poetic ground for me in some way. I'm buoyed by a gratifying sense of creative power and originality as my Bob-the-artist identity pose seems confirmed for the moment. But I've forgotten to silence my phone and a close friend now calls to discuss a problem I consider minor – and irritating. We've scheduled a social get-together the next night and he's having second thoughts about our dinner reservations. Maybe we should pick a different place to eat.

At this instant, I couldn't care less about eating anything, especially tomorrow's dinner. I only want to write my poem. My mind now is flooded with irrevicepts, then with irrational feelings and thoughts about my friend: "Why are you bothering me in the middle of a work day with something so trivial?" "Who cares what we eat for dinner?" "I wish you weren't so neurotic that you let such small things bother you so often!" Among many others.

Until these soon are joined by irrevicepts and irrational feelings and thoughts about something else: "I should be more patient with people!" "I can be such a jerk sometimes!" "Why am I so angry about nothing?" Among many many others.

The phone call lasts just six minutes. But it's been enough.

Because yesterday I had a short run-in with an angry person who wanted my parking spot at the gym. And I didn't call my sister as I'd promised. And for some reason I had been dreading this dinner with my close friend, possibly anticipating his angst about our restaurant choice. These slight experiences and multitudes of others like them of varying importance in the recent past already had pushed me toward significant discomfort about Bob-the-nice-guy. Maybe I'm really not.

Until this trivial phone call from my friend I had managed to dismiss many of these upset feelings, rationalizing yesterday's experiences in various ways. But my angry thoughts and feelings during today's call suddenly knocked me over the ledge. I'm abruptly seized by Identity Failure about Bob-the-nice-guy, one of my most valued identity poses.

Now my mind threatens to kick up negative feelings about myself over an identity pose that carries a terrifying 800 emotional force. My psyche could respond with an endless number of reactions, depending on the specific circumstances inside my head and outside in the world. My mind will select the reaction that it deems best suited to create the weakest possible emotional resistance to the strongest possible feelings that my existence is valuable to me at this moment in this world.

The best apparent solution at this particular moment involves diverting my attention to something at hand – my poetry. My mind automatically looks for the easiest, most available weakness in my Bob-the-artist identity pose right now, working on that with a sudden and unexpected fury. "This passage probably isn't so great!" "Nobody reads my poetry anyway so why bother?" "No one ever has seriously called you a poet!" These and similar pose-weakeners exploit the existing uncertainty about my Bob-the-artist identity pose, whose emotional force is strong but much less than Bob-the-nice-guy: 600 emotional strength rather than 800.

The attacking irvericepts and all the powerful emotions and feelings and thoughts that follow about me as an artist – they are terrifying as well but still psychologically preferable to allowing myself to seriously doubt Bob-the-nice-guy under these circumstances. The nice guy identity pose would cause an uncertainty that bites too deeply after all that's happened. So my mind chooses to endure the onslaught about myself as an artist, sensing its relative emotional strength. And sensing something else too: At bottom I'm extremely sure of my creative and literary abilities. The pose-weakeners can bash me all they want but in the end I'll elbow them away from my thoughts and continue the poem. My mind knows this about me.

If the uncertainty about Bob-the-nice-guy is profound enough or lasting enough, my mind may also attack other identity poses such as Bob-the-rebel, with an emotional strength of 150. "You always think you're so original but poetry like this has been done before!" "What's so wonderful about this passage?" "Who do you think you are anyway, some genius?" Even combined with the 600 emotional force of Bob-the-artist, my psyche still is ahead of the game. It's coping with a 750 strength psychologically rather than an 800 strength. And my mind is aware that I'm also reasonably confident at a deeper level about my originality and independent creativity. With both Bob-the-rebel and Bob-the-artist, I may sometimes seriously rattle my feelings of self-value through a barrage of pose-weakeners, those inner critical voices. But pose-weakeners are unlikely to cause any major failure of either of those identity poses.

My intellect makes a safer target than my soul. I've always felt much better able to maintain confidence in achievements I can compare to those of other people than in complicated feelings and thoughts and values I'm unable to hold up for comparison. That's been yet another important motivation for me to create a rational system of values that I can justify intellectually, another need for Rational Faith. There's no necessity for comparisons. These ideas stand on their own.

Accentuate The Positive

Pose-weakeners have a flip side, psychologically. As you might expect, I call these pose-strengtheners.

They achieve a similar purpose in my head, preserving self-value by focusing on this identity pose rather than that identity pose. But pose-strengtheners accomplish their task in precisely the opposite manner.

Like pose-weakeners, pose-strengtheners come to me through vericepts, thoughts and feelings. Like pose-weakeners, pose-strengtheners often make themselves known to me through those inner voices, the inaudible judgmental commentaries that can feel so persistent and real. But the commentaries offered by pose-strengtheners are all about positive judgments of myself.

Well, in a way…

This is how it works in me. Basically, my mind automatically hones in on one major identity pose, something I find significant to my sense of self-value. Perhaps it is Bob-the-artist. Then my mind inflates this identity pose, building it into my main identity. To me, Bob-the-artist starts to represent almost all of Bob, the truly valuable part of Bob. My mind exaggerates the importance of this Bob-the-artist identity pose in part through vericepts, thoughts and feelings that continuously praise my artistic abilities and accomplishments. These are pose-strengtheners and they can include the inner voices. But now they are voices that bolster my self-image in this specific way rather than attacking my self-image as pose-weakeners do.

My psyche's goal is to turn one identity pose as much as possible into me. Me, as I think of me and want the world to think of me. That one identity pose usually seems to fold other related if less significant identity poses into this psychological effort too, my mind also emphasizing maybe Bob-the-rebel and Bob-the-deep-thinker as support for Bob-the-artist. The process is fluid and complex, of course, but the purpose of pose-strengtheners is straightforward.

Pose-strengtheners create stronger feelings of self-value by exaggerating the significance of an identity pose I can more easily accept as me. Bob-the-artist in this case. And thereby pose-strengtheners lessen the significance to me of other important identity poses that I more deeply doubt. Perhaps Bob-the-nice-guy.

Those more deeply doubted identity poses might be more central to my feelings of self-value than those I'm exaggerating, as Bob-the-nice-guy is more key to me than Bob-the-artist. But my pose-strengtheners blow out of proportion a significant identity pose I can more comfortably accept as real – and then try to build my sense of self-value based mainly around this exaggerated identity pose and others related to it. To a large extent, Bob-the-artist takes over my identity. It becomes my justification for existence.

My mind does all this by focusing much attention on that identity pose throughout each day. This attention is through a stream of vericepts, thoughts and feelings. (Though other related identity poses are involved, let me write about the process just now in the singular for clarity and simplicity. I'll talk here only about Bob-the-artist.)

The exaggerated identity pose may be based on some of my qualities that had attracted past outside appreciation. As mentioned, I've been told since childhood how creative I am, especially in my writing and musical abilities. In more recent times, some of my artistic works such as plays and music also earned outside admiration, if only from a limited audience. There's a basis from the world for my belief in Bob-the-artist. I have real experiences with others to help me buy into the notion. But as with all identity poses, I'm still insecure about whether it's really me – just not as insecure as with some other highly significant identity poses. To pump up my belief in Bob-the-artist I seek repeated appreciation, not only publications and productions but also recognition from colleagues, media, friends, family. Anyone. Everyone if possible. If I get that appreciation in forms I find credible and satisfying, I feel good for a while. For a while, for a while. If I don't, I have to find other ways to keep believing in Bob-the-artist, alternative methods to maintain this identity pose.

That's not only a good example. It actually happened as Bob-the-artist gained more and more importance to me over the years. When I failed to get sufficient outside acclaim to fully confirm this self-image, my mind automatically reacted by attacking a world that seemed determined to ignore my best work. I grew very, very angry, hiding it from others as much as possible but expressing my rage constantly through a stream of vericepts, thoughts and feelings. "Society always dismisses real artists at first!" "The average person is incapable of understanding originality!" "They're all idiots, everybody!" These notions helped me to hang on to Bob-the-artist in the face of rejection and indifference. And allowed me to retain an identity that felt valuable enough to justify my existence when I had become so uncertain about other highly significant identity poses.

Pose-strengtheners also can fill a smaller psychological hole. I may "hear" these interior voices of praise briefly in some uncomfortable situation that stirs up self-doubt – falling back on the value of Bob-the-artist at a moment when Bob-the-nice-guy feels under direct attack, for example. My pose-strengtheners aren't always part of a long-term massive effort at ego inflation. This process can happen occasionally or regularly, depending on the circumstances in my life. It can be fairly subtle. Or it can be overt, loud and plain obnoxious. Pose-strengtheners account for my tendency toward bragging as a youth and even much later as an adult. It's the classic compensation that psychologists talk about. I am making up for self-doubts in other areas of my life.

But my pose-strengtheners go deeper than simply compensating for my self-perceived deficiencies. They are an integral part of the psychic process of creating and maintaining identity poses. My mind automatically accentuates the positive self-image, some identity pose that makes me feel important even if I can't live up to other more significant identity poses. I may not be a nice guy afterall but, hey, I'm an original artist – the world will just have to deal with my eccentricities in order to benefit from my work. That's the psychological equation, the calculus used by pose-strengtheners to maintain my emotional equilibrium.

Pose-strengtheners contribute to Identity Failure in many ways, converting one self-image into my reason for being. If I make myself believe Bob-the-artist is my only real value and then that identity pose abruptly comes under serious attack from without and within, I am in deep trouble. It even could be a formula for suicide. Pose-strengtheners also set me up for suffering a plague of frequent self-doubt about my value in other ways. True, they help me to minimize the psychological significance of some identities that are important to me such as Bob-the-nice-guy. But only to minimize their importance, not eliminate it. Under the sway of I.F., I'm unlikely ever to overcome the feeling that I should be a nice guy, no matter how much outside acclaim I might achieve as an artist. Such feelings will continue to haunt me without my understanding why I'm so troubled.

Often, though, pose-strengtheners can push away many of those feelings for a time with constant reminders about my value as Bob-the-artist. Or whatever identity it may be.

My pose-strengtheners try to make me happy for being one thing because I can't be another thing. They are compensation for my disappointment in me.

Building Energy

As ever in my psyche, all mechanisms and processes appear to boil down to a matter of true energy. Energy in the same sense as the word is defined in physics, meaning usable power or the capacity to do work. In the functions of my mind, energy is emotion and more emotion creates more energy. When the issue is psychological force versus psychological force, the greater force will win. And the greater psychological force is whatever releases the most emotion.

Pose-strengtheners help me build energy for some key identity poses. For some of my important self-images, that is. And over time pose-strengtheners can help diminish some of the energy released by other key identity poses that I have more trouble accepting as me. By dwelling on more plausible identity poses, I add information and emotion to nexes about self-images such as Bob-the-artist through a constant stream of vericepts. More emotion means more energy. If I keep stressing these positives all the time, my mind can diminish the amount of active emotion from other key identity poses it feels are less plausible such as Bob-the-nice-guy.

With my 1 – 1,000 scale of emotional force, then, let's go back to my poetry writing session but with a twist. Several twists.

Perhaps I've been writing many poems in recent months. One of them was accepted for publication by a prestigious literary magazine. I feel each poem is better than the poem before it – and I believe that I'm breaking new ground not only for me but for poetry. I'm doing something genuinely new and valuable as an artist. Through these and other circumstances, I've been able to begin seeing myself as an artistic genius. For me, Bob-the-genius has even greater emotional force than Bob-the-artist because it means making a major contribution to humanity in whatever field of endeavor. The concept connects with many other significant nexes including those related to my belief in the importance of every individual contributing our best work to society. I would estimate that at moments when I've more fully believed myself a true genius of some sort, the emotional force from that belief might be in the range of 850 or more. It's long been a compelling, if yes, irrational identity pose for me.

Now let's say I'm writing that same poem as earlier. I've also had exactly the same experiences the day before, the parking lot run-in and the like. But I've more comfortably dismissed all those as trivial things – because, well, I'm a genius. The world has to make allowances for me when necessary for my work. During an intense poetry-writing session I've forgotten to silence my phone as before, my close friend calls with his frets over dinner plans. And my head is flooded with those annoyed vericepts, feelings and thoughts: "Why are you bothering me in the middle of a work day with something so trivial?" "Who cares what we eat for dinner?" "I wish you weren't so neurotic that you let such small things bother you so often!"

This time, however, the ending differs.

For months I've been strengthening my Bob-the-genius identity pose, bolstering the concept to its full 850 emotional force. And beyond. As I've dwelled on the pending poetry publication and the quality of my recent work, I have greatly increased the number of vericepts in my mind about Bob-the-genius as well as the size and strength of nexes built from these and related vericepts. The concept now is gaining emotional force. And over and over my psyche automatically has used this growing identity pose to shoulder aside concerns about other important identities, including Bob-the-nice-guy. Every time I begin to worry I'm not so nice, my mind automatically responds with a pose-strengthener about Bob-the-genius. It doesn't matter so much anymore if I'm nice. Genius is what matters. That's what an expanding number of vericepts, thoughts and feelings keep reminding me.

I suspect, without being entirely sure, that Bob-the-nice-guy in this example still would carry the same emotional force in me as before – I think that emotions probably don't go away. But now more of those emotions are inactive or repressed. Bob-the-nice-guy is being buried as my mind convinces itself this identity pose is less significant than once believed. That would mean Bob-the-nice-guy has been reduced to, say, a 750 active force in my daily life. Over time it can be reduced further, possibly to something in the 500ish range, I imagine.

This difference in Bob-the-nice-guy's effective emotional strength relative to the force of Bob-the-genius is the critical point here. Without Bob-the-genius in the earlier poetry writing example, I began to feel bad about my angry reaction to the friend's phone call. Then pose-weakeners kicked in to maintain a better sense of emotional balance, to manage all the energy from my Bob-the-nice-guy identity pose. Not now. No. Now at the moment I would have felt bad about my anger, my mind summons the energy from Bob-the-genius to dismiss those self-critical vericepts, thoughts and feelings. They're not important, my mind reminds itself. But my work is very important. I can almost literally hear those inner voices, the pose-strengtheners in full choir:

"You can't put up with this nonsense! You have valuable work to do!"

"If he wants to be my friend from now on, he needs to understand how important my writing really is!"

"I'm a genius! I shouldn't be dealing with trivia when I'm working!"

So I may snap irritably at my friend, "Call me tomorrow morning! I'm busy writing, for Pete's sake! Why are you bothering me with this now?" Almost certainly, my response will be harsh in some way – and it will hurt my friend's feelings unnecessarily.

The change was a matter of the mind's physics. Psychophysics, I call it. Psychic force vs. psychic force. The emotional energy from Bob-the-nice-guy was overwhelmed in the second example by the energy emitted from Bob-the-genius. And those altered dynamics also altered my behavior dramatically.

This is deepwanting in action. You will recall how I defined that new term in Chapter 5: "Deepwanting is the insistent overall craving for something that feels profoundly significant to me, my truest and deepest desire underlying all the other desires about that thing."

No need this time around to pummel myself as an artist or poet or rebel or anything else because of my friend's interruption. My sense of self-value was preserved sufficiently by the rising power of Bob-the-genius. It held more sway over my emotional life at the time than Bob-the-nice-guy.

Bob-the-genius is what I deepwanted.

Mixed Feelings

Not all my pose-strengtheners offer me undiluted praise. Most certainly not.

I've discovered that pose-strengtheners make the most of what's available at the moment. All my psychological mechanisms and processes appear to do this. My mind assesses the situation at this instant and finds the best way to minimize emotional conflict and maximize feelings of self-value, according to the Fundamental Law of Mind. But in the case of pose-strengtheners, this means that my psyche may turn the unflattering or unpleasant into something valuable about me, transforming negatives into positives to bolster some key identity pose.

One for instance may serve here: Physical symptoms. Pains, maladies, illnesses, sufferings of the body. Normally these things diminish my sense of self-value, increasing the feeling that something is wrong with Bob. Bob is flawed and here's more proof, that persistent cough. But sometimes my mind will change up the way it views physical symptoms. Sometimes I may take that cough as evidence of sufferings caused me by the world, unfairly. I am a victim, a martyr for my cause.

That cough, in other words, becomes yet another symbol of Bob-the-artist or even Bob-the-genius. Only now it's the suffering-artist or tortured-genius. I cough and my psyche immediately absorbs information about that physical response along with other information it deems significant as part of a new vericept – it forms an instant interpretation of my experience that includes details about the cough along with my sense of being ignored as an artist or unrecognized as a genius. All that information becomes intertwined now, balled up in one. By doing this, my mind creates a new interpretation of my present circumstances using the cough to make me feel better about myself. It can work the same way for many other identity poses including Bob-the-nice-guy. I might for instance feel like a nice guy who's been driven to a troubling persistent cough by my conflicts with a brutal society.

"See what everyone has done to you now? A nice person treated so badly that you're sick!"

The world's innocent victim – through pose-strengtheners this concept is easily included within a broad range of identity poses to build self-value rather than undermine it. Martyrdom helps make a miserable situation a whole lot less miserable.

High On Me

That craving to be appreciated identified by the great William James is the craving for pose-strengtheners. In my psyche, the addiction to outside praise and recognition and gratitude really is an addiction to my inner voices – the inner voices that sing of their appreciation for Bob.

I do believe this has been a true addiction for me. Loosely expressed, I was addicted to identity poses. Specifically, I was addicted to pose-strengtheners. But it's not a physical addiction. It was a psychological addiction, like being hooked on gambling or sex. Indeed if I were addicted to those things they would have been part of my addiction to pose-strengtheners in some peculiar manner, I believe. I would have sought the high of self-value that gambling or sex briefly provided me, the interior voice telling me for the instant that I'd won something valuable and so I was valuable too.

But no, for me it was always other things. I felt high when someone whose intellect I respected spoke with strong admiration of my writing, or perhaps of my music or a Humanity Project program I created. I first had to believe that this person got, really got, what I was trying to do. And for that to happen, I had to see in this person the experience that would have allowed her or him to get it. I wanted to be understood profoundly for qualities I had long felt are among my best: creativity, insight, imagination, innovativeness. When someone else capable of understanding had discovered those characteristics in my work, and therefore in Bob, I felt much much better than cocaine ever made me feel during a few experimentations in my 30s. There's no other intoxication to equal the overwhelming self-approval that can come from meaningful outside appreciation.

But my addiction wasn't only to appreciation that made me feel good about my work. I also was hooked on appreciation of my other identity poses. I wanted others to get Bob in those ways too, depending on circumstances: who I was with, what I wanted from them, how I wanted them to see me and how I wanted to see myself in their presence. If I was playing a concert with a band, I wanted the performers and audience to get Bob-the-gifted-musician. If I was at a black tie gala, I was hoping for appreciation of Bob-the-sophisticate. If I'd made love with a beautiful woman, I wanted her to get Bob-the-sexual-stud. I didn't particularly care at the time if that beautiful woman greatly admired my intellect. I just wanted her to see me as a hot lover.

You grasp the idea, no doubt. My psyche sought fixes of self-value from others based on my situation at the moment. The specifics varied based on the circumstances at that instant – yet the need was the same. I wanted people to get me, deeply, in the same way I got myself. Naturally it never really happened and for a very good reason. I understand now it's not possible. Never was. It seems possible and many times I believed it was happening. Our culture is filled with the idea of soulmates in one form or another. But it never did happen. No one ever could get Bob as I got Bob.

No one ever can get anyone as they get themselves. That is the human condition.

My true high didn't come from them anyway, no matter what they did or said. It came from me. It was caused by my interpretation of their actions or comments according to the Fundamental Law of Mind, a rush of self-value that resulted from finding a significant if temporary fit between society and Bob. A rush when they got that I'm musically gifted. A rush when they got that I know my way around social settings. A rush when she got that I'm sexually unquenchable. The behavior of other people allowed me to justify a firmer belief that my existence was valuable to me at that moment in this world. Their actions or words greatly weakened my emotional resistance to such a belief, took away much of the psychic conflict over the self-image I wanted to accept. And greatly strengthened my feelings of self-value right then.

But those other people didn't truly give me the addictive buzz. They only made it easier for me to give it to myself. I administered my own injections of pose-strengtheners. And it's the pose-strengtheners I craved. Even since creating Rational Faith, I sometimes still do. Addictions of any sort are tough to overcome.

As with pose-weakeners, pose-strengtheners don't require having people around. I can simply remember something that was said, or maybe recall some approving gesture or expression. Or something that wasn't said, the praise of silence that some reserved types know how to convey. If the memory is made of someone's words, those comments may come back to me note-for-note precisely as uttered or they may be gross distortions that reflect what I want to remember.

Very often in the past I merely imagined what someone might do or say to me, whether a real person such as my mother or father or some unspecified human beings such as "editors" or "writers." Or people of the future, the discerning readers or listeners of many decades hence who would more fully appreciate my accomplishments. Even fantasies about what folks in earlier periods of history surely would have felt about me or my work, most definitely I could imagine those for a fix of pose-strengtheners: "They would have understood me much better back in the 1920s!" All or any of these could be among the sources of my pose-strengtheners.

Pose-strengtheners are just my mind talking to itself in praise of me rather than the much more frequent imagined condemnations of Bob. For a pose-strengthener to give me an emotional boost, I must accept it as real in some way, an accurate reflection of outside opinion in a form that justifies my belief in an identity pose. That's why actual outside appreciation is so compelling. Easier to accept. If a magazine editor enthusiastically tells me my new article is great, I have little trouble using her comments to bolster my Bob-the-writer identity pose: "See? I've still got the touch as a national magazine writer!" I can replay her compliment over and over as needed, for many years if I attach enough importance to it. But if this editor only pays my fee without commenting on the article's quality, I have a tougher time feeling as good about my writing abilities. My imagination in this situation isn't quite so powerful as my memory: To simply conclude the editor liked my article because she bought it for publication doesn't feed my ego as effectively as remembering her direct praise.

In the end, pose-strengtheners have been the drug I took to feel my life was valuable. They permitted me to justify my existence to myself. That need for pose-strengtheners, that craving, was my addiction.

And like any addict, I could find the world a terrible place without the fixes I required.

Turning The Thermostat

Ah yes, the world …

That's what all this has been about, you'll recall. Identity poses help me find some way conceptually to fit the world and me together. For most of my life, identity poses have served as the active link in the shaded area of my diagram, the oval in my psychic spheres overlapping Bob and the universe. Identity poses allow me to feel my existence is valuable right now and right here, at this moment and in this world of ours as I see it.

When that happens I conjure the mental images of Bob that seem to offer me the strongest feelings of self-value. Simplistic, irrational and inflexible mental images. Then I try to get the outside world to agree with me. I look for confirmation of my identity poses.

I won't get it, not enough of it anyway. My ego requires frequent feedings. That's when Identity Failure sets in. To varying degrees depending on circumstances in my world and in my mind, I will doubt myself profoundly. I will feel self-confusion, a deeply unsettling uncertainty about the value of my own existence.

That's because at such times I need the identity poses to feel I'm me. They are Bob, those silly identities, as far as I'm concerned then. They create my value in this world.

Pose-weakeners and pose-strengtheners are my psyche's automatic efforts to give me the strongest feelings of self-value that appear possible in that immediate situation. Now attacking this self-image, next pumping up that self-image. Weakening Pose A and Pose B to protect the more powerful Pose C. Strengthening Pose D to levels forceful enough to overcome Pose C. It's a continual flow of emotional activity to cope with an ever-changing, unpredictable and often chaotic world.

In a sense, an identity pose is my psychological thermostat, a mechanism for keeping my feelings of self-value as comfortable as possible in the world. Pose-weakeners and pose-strengtheners are the hands that adjust the thermostat's temperature up and down as needed.

Failing Miserably

When pose-weakeners threaten my identity poses, I experience I. F. and the endless problems it causes me. All the miseries I described in the previous chapter, Identity Failure as I have experienced it day to day until more recently.

And more, a great deal more misery too.

From mid-2013 to mid-2018 I suffered massively almost daily in many ways from emotions so intense that I mostly refused to even acknowledge some of the most terrifying of these were part of my psyche. I did understand that my torments were caused by Identity Failure.

As the last chapter focused on how it feels to live with Identity Failure, this chapter is intended to explain as precisely as possible just how and why Identity Failure happens. Everything in this chapter up to here was needed as background to grasp the underlying mechanics of Identity Failure. But there's more.

Returning to the bullet points of Chapter 6, we've already seen that the first three points involve identity poses and pose-weakeners. Now let's skip for a moment to the final two bullet points in that list, which are about the response to Identity Failure:

- I seek outside opinion that will confirm those specific qualities in ways I find convincing. (I feel desperate for others to verify there's not something deeply wrong with me by confirming I'm very smart or a nice guy, etc.)
- Still lacking that outside opinion, I react in ways intended to preserve the strongest possible feelings that my life is valuable to me without confirmation from others. (I think, feel and do whatever seems to make me feel better about myself right now.)

These two points involve the search for pose-strengtheners. I look for other people to provide me convincing proof that I am who I feel I am, justification for boosting my ego through pose-strengtheners. When I can't find that proof in all the ways I need, I create alternative means to give myself pose-strengtheners as best I can under the circumstances, moment to moment. I may feel like a terrible human being at this instant, but I remind myself that I'm an artist who recently completed a great poem. I can hear the future calling out accolades to me as a literary innovator. In this way, my psyche does its foremost to maintain emotional equilibrium.

But the psychological system is hugely imperfect at its most efficient.

I may feel better about myself because I'm an artist but at some deep levels I still feel awful as the terrible person I can't help believing Bob to be.

Feeling awful is Identity Failure, accounting for the remaining three bullet points:

- Without this confirmation, I become confused about some portion of my identity. (I question whether I'm very smart or a nice guy, etc.)
- I begin to fear that I'm not who and what I need to be. (I feel there may be something deeply wrong with me.)
- I begin to fear my life may be losing some portion of its value to me. (I start to feel unsure whether living is worthwhile if there's really something so deeply wrong with me.)

Identity Failure. The self-doubt so profound it's more than self-doubt. It's self-confusion. And the terror that results from this soul-splintering confusion.

Nearly continuous during most periods of my life, the experience at its most intense is horrifying. Even the most garden variety I.F. is distinctly upsetting – and something else as well.

It is infuriating beyond words.

All The Rage

Identity Failure creates rage. Rage that can feel so shockingly forceful that my mind automatically pushes it from my awareness. It's one of those profoundly disturbing emotions just mentioned, feelings so intense that I mostly refuse to even acknowledge they're part of my psyche.

In the language of psychology, of course, these are repressed emotions. Freud and others recognized them as a significant reality of our psyches long ago. Often our minds stir up feelings that don't fit with the person we feel we should be: "Bob's a nice guy," my head may decide, "and he's not supposed to feel furious with his best friend over nothing." That sort of thing.

So my head just represses it, pushes those feelings far below the psychic surface. But as I've observed firsthand, the emotions are still there in some form – and they find highly creative and highly destructive ways to make themselves known to me.

I had learned about repression in school, my first college semester's psych class as I recall. Psychology 101 at Eastern Michigan University. But it wasn't until I had the great fortune in 2000 to come across the work of Dr. John Sarno on mindbody medicine that I began to understand just how pervasive and influential all that repression was in my life.

I've referred to Dr. Sarno before in this book. In Chapter 12, I will explain in much more detail exactly why his pioneering research and discoveries seem relevant to my new philosophy of Rational Faith. But I bring him up in this context because his books on health and medicine were critical to my recognition of repression's huge role in the everyday existence of Bob. And everyone else.

My mind generates rage repeatedly, many times about nothing truly important. That's also what Dr. Sarno describes and what Freud identified. The difference is that I now know all that rage in Bob comes as the direct result of all that Identity Failure in Bob.

More than this, I actually believe that Identity Failure well may be my only psychological function with enough force to create emotions requiring repression. Through Dr. Sarno's long experience I've learned that repression has caused physical health issues for me, major and minor. And it also was responsible for my strong anxiety and mild-to-moderate depressions and intermittent phobias, all topics I'll come back to in that later chapter. I've seen up close how repression has damaged relationships of many sorts, including my business relationships. It has molded distinctly destructive attitudes too as buried emotions have manifested their presence over the years through a vast range of uncharitable feelings about other people. And the raft of other problems I outlined briefly in Chapter 6, my need to prove my authority, sexuality, intelligence, being boastful and arrogant at times and all the rest.

Caused in part by repression. Which is caused by Identity Failure.

Repression is not the only big problem created by I. F., though. During my long addiction to identity poses, my Identity Failure enormously shaped and hugely limited my understanding of myself, other human beings and the world at large. The universe, really. Identity Failure caused pose-weakeners that delivered an almost constant barrage of self-criticism of all kinds. Identity Failure diminished my interactions with society, personally and professionally, hindering my development and my contributions to the well-being of others. Identity Failure caused pose-strengtheners that overcompensated for my imagined shortcomings – and locked me into accepting those shortcomings.

But repressed emotions have been among the most damaging byproducts of Identity Failure. As it turns out, my Identity Failure caused my repressed emotions and my repressed emotions contributed to my Identity Failure. It was an ongoing and very complicated interaction as I watched it within. And because I still occasionally suffer brief bouts of I.F. despite my Rational Faith, I continue to struggle sometimes with these powerful concealed emotions. No philosophy, no system for living, is perfection. Rational Faith has allowed me to rise beyond my self-centered life of identity poses and outside validation – but as I noted, addictions of any sort are tough to overcome.

So then, what I am really saying? Just this: That Identity Failure has been the scourge of my lifetime, bringing me the endless troubles that resulted from identity poses, pose-weakeners, pose-strengtheners.

And repression.

Let me tell you about the repression.

Violent Reactions

Identity Failure causes repressed emotions for a simple reason: because Identity Failure causes the kind of emotions my mind feels it needs to automatically repress. Yes, I know – a circular logic. But hear me out.

It seems to begin with a sense of my soul unsettled, something about my self-image that suddenly feels much in doubt. At very deep levels of my mind, I am confused about me and about my value in this world and so about the value of my life. Part of me is questioning the worth of being alive.

There are massive amounts of emotion attached to my sense of self-value. Those emotions are deeply disturbing whenever my self-value looks uncertain. I.F. activates lots of negative emotions about things that seem greatly significant to my sense of self-value at the moment, even if they're not significant at all. As we've seen, a red traffic light at the wrong time can fire up my Identity Failure. Or a bad picnic. When the whole world seems like it's about me, meaningless events can feel like a personal affront. Bob at the center of the universe again. My needs, my wants, my feelings.

Identity Failure upsets me so profoundly that it brings into doubt whether the world and I really can fit together any longer. Maybe there's something deeply wrong with me somehow. Whenever that profound uncertainty surfaces, my psyche typically responds by burying it. This is the self-doubt so strong that it's more than self-doubt and it's also usually too much for me to handle during daily life. Self-confusion, as I call it, the feeling that accompanies Identity Failure.

My identity poses, pose-weakeners and pose-strengtheners have combined to set up the conditions for this self-confusion. Together, they've driven me to deepwant outside validation of my significant self-images. The self-confusion surfaces when I don't get that validation.

So now the self-confusion about those self-images, those identity poses, is repressed.

Step 1.

Step 2 is my mind's automatic reaction to this repressed self-confusion. Terror. That's the next emotional link in the psychological chain here. An emotion far beyond mere fear, a terror so intense and so abject that my psyche doesn't want to know anything about it. Even the fact that it exists.

I have seen that I.F. terrifies me more than nearly any other feeling I can have. And I repress this terror automatically and instantly whenever it tries to enter my consciousness. I am terrified of me at such moments, meaning that I'm terrified there's something really wrong with me. Which could mean there may be something really wrong with my life – I'm already feeling enormously uncertain, afterall, so how can I tell for sure? Which perhaps could mean my life isn't as valuable as I need to feel that it is. Which then calls into question whether my existence is worthy of continuing. I may lose my psychological struggle for existence.

To me the word I used above, "soul," is a poetic term for a very real force in my life. I pull out this word whenever I want to express something about the fullest and deepest part of my being, without speculating about whether it may exist or not. I don't know about that. I do know that my soul suggests the essence of me – and I recognize it is my soul that's terrified by I.F.

These two psychological forces, the self-confusion and terror, are profoundly repressed in me. It's taken me many years to better understand their dynamics … and I recognize there is a great deal I still don't know about them. But I've observed repeatedly over those years that they are the beginning elements in Identity Failure's destructive cycle of repression.

Now, Step 3. The chain of emotions from I.F. continues to grow next by the onset of rage that appears to be the automatic result of feeling terror so intensely. I've long realized that anger and its much stronger version, rage, are my psychological responses to powerful fear. If I become afraid to any degree, I normally soon become angry. If I'm terrified, I can grow enraged. I've spotted similar reactions in others during real life and even in fictional films, where the script writer understands that a character hopelessly trapped by a killer can cope believably with imminent death by letting out a furious yell. Rage can overwhelm terror even if there's a gun barrel pointed at your head, assuming those writers have it right. I suspect they do.

Like my terror, my rage is automatically and instantly repressed. It's a psychological reality that Dr. Sarno discusses at great length in order to explain strategies for curing the illnesses that erupt from this hidden rage, something he's observed closely over decades of experience with thousands of patients through the New York University School of Medicine. He writes about "the reservoir of rage" in each of us. In me, rage is a consequence of Identity Failure. Rage in all its forms, including repressed rage of which I'm not directly aware, suppressed rage that I sense but smother and also the rage that I may at times express through words or actions. I understand now that if I hammer my fist into a cupboard door, I'm experiencing I.F.

Since I was lucky enough to find Dr. Sarno's work, I have explored this side of myself with the same persistence I've focused on other elements of my psyche. And I have reached my own conclusions about repression as it occurs in me. I believe that I've been able to trace my struggles with repression first to I.F., then to terror and then to rage. And to observe that the rage serves as an ultimate psychological fuel for many of my physical and psychological miseries, exactly as Dr. Sarno has so wonderfully described. Rage is a powerful source of human energy. When repression diverts my rage away from the true target of that hostility, this emotion can create huge problems.

But I also have seen that my rage itself goes through stages, with an early form of rage generating later forms of rage. This happens as a type of psychological protection, just as terror replaces self-confusion and then rage replaces terror. Each emotional state feels more satisfying to my psyche than the one before it, feels more acceptable somehow and more comfortable. That's the ultimate purpose of my repression, I've learned, to keep my emotions in balance according to the Fundamental Law of Mind. Repression helps me maintain my identity poses.

When I suffer rage as a response to the terrors of I.F., it always feels like rage at the world in some way. At the beginning. How long the world remains the focus of my rage appears to vary a lot, as best I can determine. But when I dig down into these concealed emotions, my most basic rage is directed at other people or at some portion of society or both. I am blaming others for causing my problems at the moment, as I tried to blame Cynthia initially for the picnic debacle. She stirred up very very uncomfortable conflicts in me. As a result, I was enraged at some level with her.

But for me this rage at the world soon ignites rage at myself. At some point I begin to blame me as well as the world – and later, I blame mainly me. Naturally, these feelings blend into each other as I go through everyday life, rage at the world and rage at me all part of my overall rage. These two types of rage, though, appear entirely distinguishable from each other, with clearly different targets. I start by accusing the world, then turn the accusations against myself. A sustained fury at Bob can feel more tolerable than a burning fury at the world.

Finally, I seem to blame something more general. I blame life. If my inner torment continues for any great length, I turn from rage at the world to rage at myself and then to a rage at life. This last form of rage took me a very long time to notice – I suspect it's more deeply repressed than the others because it's more terrifying to me. Hating life can feel like hating to be alive. And that edges me closer to suicidal feelings. However I'm quite sure that it's real, bubbling up as needed when things appear to conspire against me for too long. Again, I want to stress that I don't see one form of rage disappearing as the next comes into play. They seem to blend together but with discernible dividing lines so that it makes sense to differentiate among them.

As you might expect by now, I've felt the need to name these different forms of rage. First is what I'm calling "world-rage," followed by "self-rage" and then "life-rage." The words as I employ them help me clarify and understand the feelings I have experienced.

The three forms of rage are almost completely repressed in me. Due to my familiarity with my mind's functions, I'm often able to tap into the margins of these emotions. I can feel a bit of them directly, sometimes much more than a bit. On occasion when necessary, I've experienced them to the point that I erupted in tears when first feeling these deeper levels of my repressed emotions. I also frequently can sense something of their vast scope and fearful force in my life. To call them powerful is an understatement.

Life-rage especially is fascinating to me. All of my repressed emotions fascinate, certainly, but life-rage feels particularly intriguing. I think it might be termed "universal-rage" or even "god-rage" as easily as "life-rage." Leaving aside the issue of god for now, and my own beliefs as they relate to Rational Faith, I nonetheless experience this emotion as a type of outrage at some power beyond me. At the universe, yes, but at life too. At fate, at god. It's the sort of feeling that could prompt me to fling my arms skyward with the words, "Why have you done this to me?" Life-rage is rage at feeling myself the victim of a situation I find almost unbearable.

I've very often observed as well that these repressed emotions typically launch a cycle of repression, another topic I'll get into later with more specifics. For now it's enough to know that my rage often causes more Identity Failure, which causes more terror, which causes more world-rage and more self-rage and more life-rage ... and on and on. It's the vicious cycle. Or more accurately it's yet one more complex psychological interaction, not necessarily happening in the same order all the time. World-rage, for instance, can create more Identity Failure. So can self-rage. Life-rage can cause more self-rage. Etc., etc. They seem to bounce around in a cascade of reactions to one another as determined by the Fundamental Law of Mind.

The rage may help me deal with my terror but rage also is greatly unsettling to my sense of identity, which is why it's repressed in the first place. It doesn't fit with the ways I see me, isn't consistent with any of my identity poses. Nice guys aren't supposed to become enraged over red traffic lights. So my rage scares the devil out of me – and only ends up causing more Identity Failure.

And the chain reaction continues.

Stuff Of The Everyday

As extreme as these emotions may seem to be, they were not uncommon. Quite the opposite, sorry to say. For much of my lifetime Identity Failure and its accompanying palette of repressed emotions were normal problems for me, recurring so frequently throughout each day that I would be hard-pressed to tally the incidents during any typical 24-hour period if I tried. In the hundreds, I would guess.

Before Rational Faith, I was continually attempting to be who I thought I should be at some moment rather than who I was, trying to fit the world and me together in whatever manner felt most workable. I was, in other words, forever shoe-horning Bob into some identity pose and then making every effort to verify it through something or someone outside me. My perpetual search for external validation affected virtually everything I felt and thought and did all day every day, casting a pall over my existence. Because of this search, I often doubted myself in broadly significant ways. Because of this search, I frequently felt there was something intrinsically flawed about me. Because of this search, I looked for solutions to my emotional distress in everyone I knew or met. And because I didn't find the solutions, my mind created other forms of validation as best it could. Often these were destructive to me.

I normally had no idea any of this was going on. Instant to instant in my everyday world I simply lived what seemed a normal life. As I

described in the last chapter, I.F. just felt like me being me. Just Bob suffering through Bob's usual problems.

But it wasn't. It wasn't me at all – it was me being twisted by a psychological force constructed of misunderstanding and ignorance and emotion. It was me being sick. Psychologically, emotionally ill. Identity Failure was not a built-in component of my personality. It was a disease acquired over time, learned day by day. Until, day by day, Identity Failure finally wound around my personality like the branches of a strangler fig tree that takes over a healthy neighboring tree, overwhelming it.

For most of my life, Bob Knotts was overwhelmed by Identity Failure.

And because of all my experience with Identity Failure, based on all my years of miserable firsthand learning about it, I am as certain as I possibly can be that you have been overwhelmed by Identity Failure too. Nearly everyone has.

I've suggested as much before this, of course, even stated the idea quite plainly. But after reading so many details about this affliction, you perhaps may rightly find the assertion about your life a bit shocking. It's still a bit shocking to me – and I've been aware of this problem for a long long while. Yes, I'm saying that you also endure the torments of Identity Failure. You also grapple with the troubles caused by identity poses, pose-weakeners, pose-strengtheners, repressed emotions.

What seems like just You suffering through Your usual problems, isn't.

The troubles you so often endure aren't a necessary part of being human, merely your unavoidable struggles and sufferings. Much of your life really is you experiencing Identity Failure.

Beginning in Chapter 9, I'll begin to lay out my reasons for believing that Identity Failure is an almost universal condition among human beings and that I.F. also is responsible for a vast amount of human suffering throughout history. Now there's a shocking statement for you. I believe with great confidence that the evidence will back me up and I'll do my best to lay out enough of it to convince you as well.

I've spent so much time explaining Identity Failure precisely because I believe that it's such a widespread affliction. My hope is that you will begin to see yourself and others very differently, each person's image freshly detailed under Identity Failure's glare. I want you to recognize everyone through what you're reading about me. My problem is your problem and it is their problem.

It is our problem.

And I hope you'll then go on to read about a new idea that offers one rational solution to this problem: The philosophy of Rational Faith. It was needed to save me from the worst confusions and miseries caused by Identity Failure and I believe it may help you and others too.

But before I get to Chapter 9, I will have to write Chapter 8. And Chapter 8 will serve one more grand helping of Identity Failure as lived by Bob, though in a fresh dramatic format that demonstrates competing psychological forces through dialogue as well as with interior narratives that draw on mathematical values. You'll find it quite different from anything else you've read so far. Again, all of this is provided for important background when I later broaden the discussion to include us all.

In Chapter 6, the experience of Identity Failure: how it feels for me to live with it. In Chapter 7, the underlying psychological mechanics of Identity Failure: how it actually works in my mind.

In Chapter 8, a combination of the two previous chapters wrapped up as an extended example drawn from my life: how the psychological mechanics of Identity Failure caused me to feel what I felt and do what I did when the disorder had a tight hold on me. A case history of Bob, as it were, told in a way that may help you better see how all the dynamics flow during everyday living.

This can wind together some of the various fibers, I think. It can reveal I.F. as the true force of nature that it is – a grand power propelled by the psychological demands of the Fundamental Law of Mind and deepwanting.

As with all forces of nature, Identity Failure is mesmerizing to observe closely. And as with all forces of nature, it is neither good nor bad. It simply is. The bad of Identity Failure is like the bad of a typhoon or tidal wave, bad not in its existence but in its destructive impact on my life.

And yours.

Chapter 8: All Too Normal

> "He then learns that in going down into the secrets of his own mind he has descended into the secrets of all minds."
> Ralph Waldo Emerson

Tick-Tock

It is 5:48 p.m.

Actually, 5:48 and 16 seconds to more precisely observe the moment, a Friday after-work escape into springtime South Florida. And every instant will matter.

You sit patiently somewhere observing as this short human drama opens, a playlet of Identity Failure acted out as you look on with interest. Many big things will happen quickly now. You need only remain where you are – and watch. Watch it all closely, closely. Watch it closely.

You see as Bob hurries in his car toward some seaside café in Fort Lauderdale, glancing at the dashboard clock with an anxious irritation. He sits stuck behind what feels an endless red traffic light. You also somehow understand that he's running slightly late for a meetup with an old colleague, someone Bob had mostly enjoyed back in the long past newspaper days of payphone dictations and pagination copydesks, of pressrun deadlines and photographer pockets stuffed with canisters of film. It is an era two decades gone, by 2016 already feeling as dry and curled as old newsprint.

They had been newsroom co-workers and little more, Bob and Gary, often exchanging first-of-morning pleasantries and sometimes end-of-afternoon complaints about dull editing by dullard editors. All reporters share a visceral attraction to such complaints, which oddly bond them as colleagues. Still Bob and Gary had lost touch during those 20-plus years before spotting each other recently across a local coffee shop, swapping cellphone numbers along with agreement on the need for a good catch-up.

Bob relished each opportunity to rehash those years with his former newsmates, savoring again the kind of camaraderie he still missed since going solo as a writer. In Bob's eyes, Gary had been a solid journeyman journalist – accurate, with passable writing skills. By contrast Bob had been one of his newspaper's top writers and reporters as evidenced by his page-one investigations as well as feature story datelines from such places as Hawaii and France. Bob since had moved on to write national magazine articles and then many books and even some plays and poems, also founding a nonprofit group at one point. Gary had remained in the same Fort Lauderdale newsroom, writing much the same local articles as back in the day.

Before leaving for the café, Bob had decided to avoid talking too much about his latter accomplishments. Especially knowing as he did that Gary always had overestimated his own skills and resented the newsroom success of others – sometimes even poking small but pointed barbs at Bob's investigations and other front page pieces. For this reason Bob would only briefly mention that just today he'd completed a new fable, something he thought exceptionally bright and inventive and witty. Bob enjoyed a buoyant self-satisfaction about the piece, which he'd quickly judged among his best writing to date. This additional flush of confidence was especially welcome now, coming only two days after a disappointing rejection of his play "In Mordant Whispers" by a Miami theater director. Bob had been dwelling on this latest slight over a drama that he felt worthy of the top theaters anywhere. And dwelling as well on this latest reminder of the world's unfairness toward what he insisted were his most original and powerful works. It seemed no one ever got Bob. Or Bob's finest writing. A feeling of intellectual isolation often tortured him.

But now it is 5:48:16 p.m. on a lovely tropical Friday, oceanside in South Florida. Nearly there, Bob now is exactly three minutes and sixteen seconds beyond their agreed Happy Hour hour. He will arrive shortly.

So yes, please do watch it all quite closely as Bob and Gary meet again. Because a pleasant springtime escape is about to go very wrong.

Ordinary World

It all seems so normal. It all is so normal.

The normal and the everyday of Identity Failure, as you will soon see. Keep watching our brief scene.

It is the drama within the mundane, the extraordinary core of ordinary life.

I've experienced scenes just like this many times in times now well-past, whether with old colleagues or new acquaintances, with neighbors or with friends or even with relatives. The situation is familiar to me. It is taken from my real world.

But to effectively recreate the truth of that situation, I must employ the dramatist's fictional technique. This is the approach so brilliantly rendered in my favorite play by an American author, "Long Day's Journey Into Night" by Eugene O'Neill. In that remarkable drama, O'Neill draws from his agonizing family history to transform the reality of many decades into a revealing single day. Rather than attempt some literal transcription of events, he condensed the conflicts of Family O'Neill within a more comprehensible retelling as Family Tyrone.

Striving toward my own deeper accuracies, then, I felt Identity Failure could be viewed more clearly through a similar synthesis of actual events. This means the specifics of my scene are imagined but drawn from genuine experiences. That method seemed particularly appropriate because the underlying psychological dynamics necessarily require this sort of dramatization. I can't possibly know exactly what was happening in the depths of my mind during a social outing with a former colleague or anyone else – I was otherwise occupied, obviously. But I can and do know what happens in the depths of my mind at other times, whether with or without someone else there. That's what I've been writing about at some length in this book of course. This knowledge gained from direct experience allows me to assemble a highly realistic scene about I.F., crafted carefully to convey what really happens to me as a result of this illness. And why.

So that is what you'll find here: A very normal scenario played out over a period of exactly 13 minutes and 27 seconds.

Reading through our scene the first time, you'll see everything take place without interruption or explanation. It should feel something like looking over a movie script, which I hope may help you visualize the situation as though it were happening in front of your eyes.

But the second time through these same events – well, that's where I'll do my best to portray the fundamental psychological mechanisms that drive the observable behavior. The psychophysics below the action's surface, as it were, broken down second by second. Identity Failure as a profoundly human theater piece.

Toward that end I also must offer my usual disclaimer when describing my psyche's complexities. I can't emphasize enough that such descriptions can never provide a full and complete accounting of things going on inside my head. Far from it, indeed.

I've taken great pains to explain how key elements of my mind function as best I can tell after decades of observation. And to break these key elements down into the detail I felt needed in order to be as clear and understandable as sensibly required for this book. Every one of those elements plays a central role in the overall tale of Rational Faith, each a main character in the storyline. They're necessary to the psychological narrative that may reveal something about who I am at the deepest level. And who I believe you are too. And what all of that means about how we live our lives today and how we may be able to live them more constructively in the future. For ourselves, for others and for society as a whole.

That's the point of writing a book about Rational Faith in the first place. It is a philosophy of living based on direct empirical experience minutely observed and analyzed over some 45 years.

But I don't for an instant believe these are all the psychological forces of consequence in my mind. I know for a fact that they're not – because I've seen firsthand many other forces at play.

What I've been describing through these first several chapters are only the most significant of those many psychic forces, at least as I see them within me. They form the fundamental physics of my mind, the dynamics that make me me.

Yet when I describe some expression of these dynamics such as identity poses, I'm limited in the way of every storyteller. To make the narrative engaging and clear, I must leave out a lot of important details and keep only those absolutely needed to advance the tale. Because a sound grasp of the underlying psychological mechanisms is so central to Rational Faith, I do attempt to include perhaps more of those details than the most effective storytelling might otherwise dictate. Basically, I include whatever I think any interested reader really should know now to make their own judgment about this philosophy later.

But I fear you'd recoil at the monotonous descriptions if I tried to spell out every exception, every qualification, every simultaneous event, every possible variation of these psychological mechanisms. Instead I try to relate some sense of the complexities I observe within me when this seems helpful.

Here as previously I'll also rely on my 1 - 1,000 system for representing emotional force. I'm using this approach to represent the relative emotional strength generated by identity poses, as I'd done in Chapter 7. And now also the relative emotional resistance to each identity pose as well as the force of repressed rage. It will all become quite clear to you. Like nexes, identity poses can combine forces to reach levels greatly more powerful than 1,000 on the scale of emotional energy.

All of this long-winded explanation is intended to answer some questions that may have lingered in your thoughts up until now. And to point out that the psychological forces described in this scene are like the scene itself: Taken from my real-life experiences but recreated dramatically to illustrate how Identity Failure works in the ordinary world.

The dialogue and action among characters are as normal and everyday as it gets.

And very sadly, so is the psychological action below the surface.

Surprise, Surprise

The scene opens at a small but pretty outdoor café along oceanside's State Road A1A in Fort Lauderdale. It is April 2016. We see a crowded restaurant and then notice one table off to the café's left side farthest from views of the Atlantic Ocean. A somewhat pudgy, balding late-middle-aged man sits talking with an older gray-haired woman. In the distance over the woman's shoulder, we spot another late-middle-aged man walking hurriedly toward the café. We recognize that it is Bob.

Bob hates being late – to anything. And almost as much, he hates when anyone else is late for anything. Despite this lifelong punctuality, Bob found that seasonal traffic and South Florida's maddeningly prolonged traffic lights had conspired against his best intentions. He snatches yet another quick glimpse at his watch now, takes a few last steps across the sidewalk in a kind of jog, then forces himself into a friendly smile as he looks around the packed café for Gary.

For an instant the smile fades before Bob recovers it, with effort. There is someone else at the table with Gary. The additional guest is completely unexpected by Bob. And just as completely unknown. He wonders who she is and why she is here when he had hoped to spend all their time reminiscing about the newsroom days.

Oh well. Bob keeps smiling anyway … and steps over to Gary's table, shaking hands with him and looking toward the woman with as much feigned delight as he can muster. But he's never been very good at faking emotions.

It is 5:51:09 p.m.

>Gary
(Smiling as he shakes hands)
Hey, here he is! I was almost gonna text you in another minute. Not like you to be the last one here.
>(Looking at the woman)
Bob's, like, *never* late. Well … *almost* never!

>Bob
(Apologetically)
Yeah, I know. Sorry, sorry! Traffic was painful tonight. Really … sorry! And then I hit enough of those idiotic endless red lights around here …
>(Checking his irritation with a forced smile, then looking directly at the woman)
You know? You just sit at some of these red lights so long that you could get out, then wash and wax your car before the light turns green!

They all laugh politely. Gary realizes the situation.

Gary

Oh, yeah, Karen meet Bob. Bob – Karen. She's a neighbor of mine at the condo. We bumped into each other when I was leaving to come here. I asked her if she wanted to come along.

Karen
(Looking away from Bob as she speaks)
I hope that's not any problem. I don't want to intrude.

Bob

Nope. No problem for me at all, of course. The more the merrier!
(Shaking hands with Karen)
Nice to meet you, Karen.

Karen smiles vaguely at Bob without making eye contact. There's a brief but slightly awkward silence.

It is 5:51:57 p.m.

Bob
(Noticing their drinks as he sits at their table)
And wow, you've already got cocktails. You must have gotten here early, eh? I'm not *that* late!
(He forces a snorted chuckle)

Gary

Yeah, she rode with me. Got here, what? I guess about five minutes early or so, right? We had no problem with traffic at all.

Karen nods in agreement, looking past the crowd toward the ocean.

Gary

I'm usually the guy who's late for everything. I remember that really pissed you off at all those newsroom lunches. "Where the hell is Gary?!" Right?

Bob
(With a forced laugh)
Really? I guess I don't remember. We did have some fun back then, didn't we? The whole newsroom gang, those huge group lunches at Creolina's and wherever else. Remember?

(Warming to the memory)
All of us grabbing for those blistering hot sauces, right? Too funny!
(To Karen, with a smile)
A bunch of us reporters would go for lunch to this tiny Cajun place called Creolina's near downtown. And we'd get all macho, pouring their hottest most-blistering hot sauces all over our food. Almost seems kinda crazy when I look back now, ya know? But it was fun!

Karen

Oh, Lord! That does sound a bit crazy to me, honestly. I don't care much for hot spicy foods.

Gary

Even I don't eat food too spicy anymore. Bothers my stomach and then I don't get any sleep. Gettin' old, I guess, hey dude?

Bob

Well, I still eat some pretty darned spicy food sometimes. Even at my decrepit age!
(Laughs with some effort)
Anyway I guess I'm kind of a believer in the "age is all in your head" theory, really. That's how I see it anyhow. I think people can stay more youthful with the right attitude. It's almost like we shape our own aging process in some way, maybe.

Gary
(Smiling uncomfortably)
Well, I don't know about your head. But I'm pretty sure my age is in my stomach! I just can't eat the hot stuff anymore. And I pay a price if I try!

Karen
(Coolly)
I think it's easy to say "everything's in your head" if you don't happen to have the same problem. I don't really buy that argument.
(Changing the subject abruptly)
Where's the menu? I'm about ready to order. Some lovely seafood sounds good. Maybe mahi, something mild would be nice for me.
(Looking up and smiling a genuine smile for the first time. Waving at someone)
Oh good! Here she is. Over here!

Another woman makes her way through the crowded café toward their table. With a broad smile, she waves at Karen. This woman is an attractive 30-something, stylishly dressed, with long curled hair of vibrant brown. She notices Gary now, offering him a brief but enthusiastic wave as well. She does not seem to notice Bob at all. The young woman immediately kisses Karen on both cheeks, European style, makes smiling eye contact with Gary again and sits at their table.

                    Karen
I'm so glad you could make it! I'm dying to hear how everything all went today!

                    Gary
This is Karen's daughter. She used to live at the same condo building – they were both my neighbors for years.
          (Handling introductions perfunctorily)
Allison – Bob. Bob – Allison.

It is 5:53:54 p.m.

                    Bob
    (Shaking hands with Allison, with a grin intended to seem charming)
Hi Allison. Very nice to meet you. We've been having a nice chat with your mom. I used to work with Gary. I'm a writer too.

                    Allison
    (Pleasantly. Making eye contact as they finish shaking hands)
Hi Bob. It's good to meet you. Sorry I'm so late.

                    Bob
Oh, you're not that late! I haven't even ordered a drink yet.

Gary glances toward Bob, surprised at his eagerness to overlook Allison's tardiness.

                    Karen
                 (To Allison)
What would you like, honey? A glass of wine?

                    Bob
        (Looking around, suddenly helpful)
Let me see if I can grab a waiter for us.

Gary
I've known Allison since she was just this high – not even tall enough to see over this table. Now look at her!

Bob
(Admiringly)
Yes, she's certainly grown into a beautiful young woman.
(Waving one hand, without success)
Waiter! Excuse me! Didn't see me …

Allison
Thank you, Bob. That's always a nice thing to hear. So you're a reporter at Gary's newspaper?

Bob
(With poorly feigned modesty)
Used to be – long time ago! I'm a writer. Just finished a new piece today, actually, a new fictional story that deals with human values. I'm writing a series of them for my nonprofit group. And I've written a bunch of books and plays and things.
(Pausing a beat for Allison's reaction. Hearing nothing, he quickly plunges forward with his story anyway)
I was a contributing editor at a national travel magazine for a few years. And I've also done quite a bit of sports writing since leaving the paper – you know, for magazines like USA Weekend and Sports Illustrated. What about you?

Allison
Oh, how interesting. I love the theater! Would I know any of your plays?

Gary
(Dismissively but with a smile)
I don't think his work has quite made it to Broadway yet. Unless I missed something …

It is 5:55:02 p.m.

Bob
(Ignoring Gary)
You might have seen something by me. I wrote a play about teen suicide that was commissioned by Coconut Grove Playhouse. And I composed the music for it too. That was a tough subject to write about but it was the job I was given and, well …

Karen
(Changing the subject quickly when Bob pauses)
Speaking of jobs, Allison just started a new job yesterday, didn't you?

Allison
I did! I'm a paralegal at a law firm in Miami.

Karen
(Proudly)
She wants to be a lawyer! How did it go today?

Gary
(Sounding a bit too interested in this news)
You did? A new job? I didn't know that! Good for you, kiddo! That's a big deal for you.

Allison
It's going great so far. Everyone's been really nice. A couple of the big bosses even took me to lunch today as a kind of welcoming gift, I guess. I thought it was sweet.

Karen
How could they not love you already? This will be a brand new start, Ali! Just the thing you needed.

It is 5:55:41 p.m.

Gary
Absolutely! You're gonna do amazing down there!

Bob
(Rubbing his shoulder briefly as if it has become suddenly stiff)
That's terrific. Congratulations. Sounds like a wonderful opportunity.

Gary
At least you were smart enough to stay away from working at a newspaper!

Bob
(Seeing an opening to shift the discussion from Allison's job. To Gary)
And how are things in the newsroom these days anyhow? They still cutting back on everything?
(To Allison)
That's part of the reason I left daily journalism so many years ago. The publisher was chopping our news budget and focusing on soft-news stories so much that I couldn't really do my job anymore. I'd been doing a lot of investigative reporting back then.

Gary
You wouldn't be doing those pieces today, I can promise you. Though to tell you the truth, I could never understand how you managed to snag that kind of time from the editors. Six months or more for some of those stories. Amazing!
(With a laugh)
It made me wonder which editors you were blackmailing!

Bob
(Defensively)
Because they were good stories, Gary. They weren't giving me six months to work on investigations for absolutely no reason. I worked for a year on a couple of projects.

Gary
Well OK, whatever! We saw things differently. But yeah, believe me, they're a lot more careful now with newsroom resources. They'd never let somebody work for months on the kind of stuff you were doing back then.

Bob
(Trying vainly to appear lighthearted)
Yeah, you're right, it was pretty lame stuff. Looking into airbag injuries five years before the Feds even admitted they had a dangerous problem. Or putting Basil Wainwright in federal prison for illegal treatments to AIDS and cancer patients. Or my investi—
(Stopping himself. With a forced chuckle)
Oh, anyway, whatever, right? Glad to hear the newspaper's not bothering with stuff like that anymore, Gary. They were all total time-wasters for sure.

Allison
(Pause. Then changing the subject to ease the tension)
I don't understand how newspapers stay in business at all. No one my age reads a newspaper. I don't know one friend who even reads a newspaper online.

It is 5:56:56 p.m.

Bob
Unfortunately, that's sad but true. Young people don't follow the news anymore.

Allison
No, we follow the news. You're wrong. But newspapers seem so totally old-school now.

Karen
I haven't had the newspaper delivered in years. I just don't like to read much anymore. And the newspaper's too depressing for me. I feel bad when I read it.

Gary
(Laughing)
I feel bad when I write it!

Karen and Allison laugh heartily with Gary. Bob forces himself to chuckle again. He fiddles with the napkin sitting nearest him on the table, foot bouncing nervously. He squirms a bit in his chair and looks out past the crowd toward the ocean as Karen had done earlier. A vague smile has settled across his lips.

Karen has said something that makes Allison laugh again but Bob didn't hear it. Nor does he hear Allison's reply or Gary's remark after that. Bob looks around for a waiter, waves again but without the waiter taking notice.

Bob
(Rising from his chair. With a weak smile)
Excuse me a moment – I have to hit the restroom. Gary, if we ever see a waiter would you order me a beer? Anything's fine. Sam Adams if they have it.

                    Gary
Will do. Want a burger or something to go with that? We're all going to eat something, I think.

                   Allison
Definitely, I'm starved! That lunch they bought for me was a long time ago. Do we have a menu?

                    Karen
I have to eat something. And yes, Ali, I want to hear more about your new job today.

                     Bob
Nothing for me, thanks. Just a quick beer. I can't stay too long anyway.

It is 5:57:48 p.m.

We watch Bob walk briskly across the café, abruptly stop the first waiter he sees and point toward Gary's table.

                     Bob
             (With sharp irritation)
Excuse me. I wonder is there anyone waiting on that table over there in the corner? We've been sitting here forever and no one's even looked our way.

                    Waiter
        (Curtly, pointing toward the crowd)
We're very very busy, sir! You can see for yourself ... I'll get someone over there as soon as we can.

                     Bob
This just seems ridiculous. You folks really need to hire more wait staff if you can't handle the business!

Bob shakes his head as he walks quickly to the bathroom. He looks around after the bathroom door closes behind him, glancing beneath the three stalls for telltale feet. After confirming that he is alone, Bob stares at the mirror, peering deep into his own eyes. Then he notices that dark reddened blotches had broken out on his face, a common reaction by him to stress in social situations. He rubs and then stretches his shoulder, as if trying to ease a sharp pain.

>
> Bob
> (Very angrily but in a carefully controlled whisper)
> God damn it! Damn, damn! Try to have a pleasant evening with people and … Always turns into a pain in the ass!

He paces a bit in the bathroom, glancing briefly toward the mirror a few more times. Bob pulls out a paper towel and holds it now.

>
> Bob
> (With intense frustration but in the same whisper)
> Unbelievable!

Bob aggressively crumples the paper towel and tosses it furiously into the waste basket.

>
> Bob
> Unbelievable! God damn it anyway!

Bob calmly washes his hands, throws the wet paper towel into the waste basket gently and walks as slowly as possible back to Gary's table. Allison is talking.

It is 6:02 p.m. exactly.

>
> Allison
> …and really feeling good now. Thanks, Gary. I really am. I'm loving my new job and my new apartment. Things are so much better.

>
> Gary
> (To Bob)
> Allison's been kind of sick for a while. But she's doing a lot better now. Oh, I ordered you a Sam Adams.

>
> Bob
> (So softly that he is barely audible)
> Thanks.

Allison
(To Bob)
I was bulimic for a long time. Since I was a kid really, when I was just starting middle school.

Bob
I'm sorry to hear that. Oh good – here's that beer. Finally.

A waiter delivers a glass of red wine to Allison and then a Samuel Adams beer to Bob, who immediately begins to drink it from the bottle.

Karen
(Proudly)
Yes, Ali's definitely doing a lot better now. She's starting a brand new life. Things are going your way at last, honey.

Allison
I hope so, Mom. I … I think so too. It feels good to get out like this and have a good job and just feel normal, you know?

Bob
(With feigned interest between swigs of beer)
It certainly sounds like you have a good job. You said the law firm's in … uh, was it Fort Lauderdale?

Karen
Miami! It's a huge firm. They have offices in three states. Who knows where this kind of opportunity could lead.

Allison
(Suddenly embarrassed)
I'm only a paralegal, Mom. I'm not a lawyer.

Karen
You will be.

Gary
(To Bob as the waiter approaches again. Irritably)
We're gonna order now. You're not eating anything? At all? I thought we were having some dinner tonight or whatever.

Bob
Nothing for me, thanks. I need to finish this beer and head out, unfortunately. We'll do dinner another time.

It is 6:03:28 p.m.

Gary, Karen and Allison order their dinners now. Bob gazes out past the crowd toward the ocean once more, sipping his beer almost continuously. Under the table, out of sight, Bob's right knee bounces rapidly up and down. He listens to their meal orders and feels his stomach rumble. He is getting hungry.

Bob examines the beer bottle to determine how much he has left to drink, then looks toward Allison as she speaks. But Bob has no idea what she's talking about now. He wonders what time it is and how much longer he needs to linger to avoid appearing rude. A vague smile again has settled across his mouth as Gary and Karen say something to each other.

It is 6:04:36 p.m.

Rewind

The scene opens at a small but pretty outdoor café along oceanside's State Road A1A in Fort Lauderdale. It is April 2016. We see a crowded restaurant and then notice one table off to the café's left side farthest from views of the Atlantic Ocean. A somewhat pudgy, balding late-middle-aged man sits talking with an older gray-haired woman. In the distance over the woman's shoulder, we spot another late-middle-aged man walking hurriedly toward the café. We recognize that it is Bob.

But something is different now.

Somehow we can observe not only the outer but also the inner man, occasional glimpses of Bob's psyche unfolding before us to reveal the several personas inside the single person at this brief April moment in this small café world. Somehow we see them all quite clearly ... And more, as we will see.

Yes, because we understand now that it is Bob-the-nice-guy who glances anxiously at his watch yet again. And that he is closely accompanied by one of his many frequent partners, Bob-the-reliable-person, who urges Bob to break into a kind of jog across the last few steps of the sidewalk. Joining them is Bob-the-artist, who had just that afternoon proudly completed a short work of fiction and so wants only to dwell on this achievement tonight. Bob-the-anxious-intellectual also is there, nervous at leaving his safe writer's lair for an uncertain social outing with someone who often had proven prickly to be around. It has been a long long time since the last real chat with Gary. Bob-the-anxious-intellectual doesn't feel much like smiling at the prospect.

But as ever, looming in the background is another Bob of even greater presence: Bob-the-good-person. Only rarely do any other Bob-the-somethings rise to the fore without Bob-the-good-person showing up soon after to review and supervise the thoughts, feelings and actions. When Bob is under the influence of Identity Failure, mostly all day mostly every day, Bob-the-good-person comes and goes frequently to maintain Bob's feeling of his underlying human decency. Bob-the-good-person is among the most central of all the many Bobs that exist inside him.

Other Bobs will join this uncomfortably diverse group soon. But after a quick prompting from Bob-the-good-person, Bob-the-nice-guy of course carries the moment as so often happens, forcing Bob into a friendly smile when stepping into the cafe.

Vericept after vericept after vericept materialize as if formed from the air around Bob, a succession of instantaneous interpretations of his experience automatically created by his psyche now and again now and now once more, each inhaled without his slightest awareness – breaths of information heavily scented with emotion. Every vericept renders Bob's understanding of reality as it is happening. And concealed from his consciousness, every vericept locks that understanding permanently in place. They all join the uncountable others in his mind, each a record of a moment in his life, a clump of information and emotion inextricably commingled to form a single psychological building block that fits together with the blocks already there.

After the forced smile, Bob-the-nice-guy tussles for an instant with three of the other Bobs: They are not happy after noticing an unwelcome stranger at Gary's table. In a spray of new vericepts, each of the three offers his assessment of this unexpected situation with a stunning swiftness: Bob-the-reliable-person notes that Gary always was unpredictable and cannot be depended on even to meet one-on-one as planned. Bob-the-artist points out that a third person will make turning the dinner conversation to the new fable much more difficult, decreasing the prospects of any prolonged ego-boosting talk about Bob's writing. Bob-the-anxious-intellectual decides the get-together will be even more unpleasant than he'd imagined during the drive over.

All of this happens without Bob knowing all of this happens. And all of this makes Bob momentarily feel miserable now.

But Bob-the-nice-guy summons enough energy to regain the smile, easing the misery. Then together with Bob-the-good-person, he wonders who this strange woman is and why she is here when he had hoped to spend all their time reminiscing about the newsroom days. That would have been ... better, much better. Oh well, Bob-the-nice-guy decides, before he steps over to the table and shakes hands with Gary and looks toward the woman with as much feigned delight as he can muster.

It is 5:51:09 p.m.

The psychophysics:

Identity Failure was settling in for Bob-the-nice-guy. The emotional resistance to this identity pose came in the form of rapid streams of vericepts absorbed into his psyche, each activating powerful nexes about what's required of a nice guy at this moment in this world. The vericepts in part insisted over and over that nice guys don't keep a friend waiting alone in a restaurant and nice guys allow extra time to navigate traffic tie-ups during South Florida's high tourist season. These two concepts were integral elements of many new vericepts entering Bob's head on the hurried walk toward the cafe. They helped form Bob's overall interpretation of his arrival, in turn activating nexes about other nice guy qualities he may lack. As Bob glanced at his watch, then, all these nexes collectively emitted a negative counterforce at a 390 level of emotional energy, significant resistance that challenged Bob's 775-level positive feelings of being a nice guy at this moment. And with each second's watchtick, the resistance within him grew. From 390 to 400. From 400 to 415 ...

You have watched it all happening before you ... and you will see much more as the internal drama continues: Simply put, Bob's positive feelings at the café express the strength of his belief in an identity pose – positive emotional energy. The level of confidence in that identity pose, basically. His negative feelings, or resistance, express the strength of his confusion about an identity pose – negative emotional energy. The level of his doubt about an identity pose. This clash of psychological forces is a constant and a continual in Bob's life, as it is in nearly every human life. And as with other people, the dominant emotional forces that are active moment to moment in Bob's mind will overpower the weaker emotions. Dominance of the necessary.

At this very moment, Bob needed the appreciative behavior and opinions of others to prove to himself that he was still a nice guy. Bob-the-nice-guy contributed strongly to Bob's overall sense of the value of his own existence in this situation. But validation of Bob-the-nice-guy must come from someone else – the quicker, the better.

In similar fashion, Bob-the-reliable-person was under assault. Vericepts about such notions as the importance of punctuality in a reliable person also were part of Bob's interior life now, activating other nexes about punctuality and reliability and subjects related. Combined, the nexes emitted a negative emotional energy of 235 that threatened his Bob-the-reliable-person identity pose, which had its own positive emotional energy of 450 at the moment.

Taken all together this meant the negative emotional energy that conflicted with Bob-the-nice-guy and Bob-the-reliable-person came to 625 and mounting – with the positive emotional energy from these two identity poses idling relatively constant for the moment around 1225. That situation offered Bob a significant psychological force in opposition to his self-images as a perpetually nice guy and an unfailingly reliable person. And the result was that Bob overall felt very uncomfortable, anxious in the extreme, embarrassed at his lateness, intensely focused on getting to Gary's table sooner than soon. That unpleasant feeling impulsively launched his body into a kind of jog to arrive an instant before he would otherwise.

As we observed all this action at the deepest levels of Bob's psyche, something else became strikingly clear. His psychological self-flagellation served a vital purpose: to protect Bob-the-good-person.

At this moment, in this situation, Bob-the-good-person felt greatly vulnerable as he does frequently during daily life. That happens because Bob-the-good-person has set himself very very very high ethical standards of human goodness to uphold more or less continually – and these standards often are impossible for Bob to meet. Right now and commonly, Bob-the-good-person carried a massive positive emotional force of 920. But this identity pose also is highly sensitive to outside opinion, real or perceived. Even vague suggestions of doubt by others about Bob-the-good-person can quickly intensify emotional resistance to this identity pose. Even vaguely imagined suggestions of possible doubt by others about Bob-the-good-person can do the same. And any significant emotional resistance to Bob-the-good-person feels terrifying because that resistance generates vericepts and thoughts and feelings that are always deeply unsettling, easily challenging Bob's basic sense of his own humanity: "Maybe there's something wrong with me as a human being." "Maybe I'm not a good person." "Maybe I'm deeply flawed in some way that's really built into my personality." Arriving late to meet an old friend threatened to begin a powerful chain of such vericepts and thoughts and feelings, raising the real potential of extremely forceful levels of emotional resistance to Bob-the-good-person.

Whenever that had happened in the past, the disturbance was profoundly disruptive to Bob's psyche and to his life for some days or longer. Much longer, sometimes. Bob needs almost always to feel that Bob-the-good-person is alive and well.

To prevent Identity Failure over Bob-the-good-person now, pose-weakeners automatically, repeatedly and furiously attacked Bob-the-nice-guy and Bob-the-reliable-person. By forcing these two identity poses into a much more heightened state of Identity Failure than was usual during everyday living, Bob's mind had insulated Bob-the-good-person from serious challenge. Any significant doubts about Bob-the-good-person were repressed immediately. This repressed energy helped to fuel the attack. The rising insecurity about Bob-the-

nice-guy and Bob-the-reliable person also guarded Bob-the-good-person in another way, emphasizing Bob's good-person guilt, embarrassment and regret over the late arrival. A good person feels bad about hurting others in any way. Feeling bad about hurting Gary made Bob feel good in this situation. Or at least, made Bob feel better because this feeling must mean he really is a good person.

Bob's psychological struggle for existence continued in other ways too, the unending fight to feel that his life is valuable to him at this moment in this world – the constant necessity to satisfy the Fundamental Law of Mind.

And this was where Bob-the-artist nicely helped satisfy some of the psychological needs at hand. That familiar identity pose provided Bob another tool to maintain his emotional equilibrium as he rushed to the cafe. Work and writing were Bob's intended topics of the evening with Gary in any case, subjects that felt most appropriate for an extended chat with a former newsroom colleague. But after completing his new fable and believing in its artistic importance, Bob had created another psychic opportunity for increasing self-value at this café get-together. Yes, Bob-the-artist would serve quite well under these circumstances, with pose-strengtheners elevating its emotional force.

As Bob entered the café, Bob-the-artist already was fluctuating somewhere between 535 and 720 positive emotional levels, reducing the psychological significance of Bob-the-nice-guy and Bob-the-reliable-person while helping to relieve his attention from any issues about Bob-the-good-person. At the instant of Bob's arrival, emotional resistance to Bob-the-artist was very weak, hovering near a force of 90 or less.

Without even the remotest awareness of it, Bob's mind was generally gravitating toward Bob-the-artist as he looked around the restaurant for Gary. He was increasing the level of emotional energy produced by Bob-the-artist by focusing on this identity pose over and over. Each new vericept about his latest literary accomplishment activated more nexes involving Bob's writing prowess, his creative gifts, his growing significance as a man of letters. Bob-the-artist also smoothed the way for Bob-the-anxious-intellectual to romanticize Bob's anxiety over the meeting with Gary, justifying this unease as the understandable consequence of life as a creative deep thinker. Just now Bob-the-

anxious-intellectual exerted a positive force of roughly 200 against a slightly varying negative emotional level of 85.

And so, bottom line at this moment: Bob-the-good-person was holding somewhere around 920, protected by repression from significant conflicting negative emotional energy. That repressed negative emotional energy was at 605, systematically exploring Bob's psyche for focal points that could best satisfy it in this situation. Bob-the-nice-guy and Bob-the-reliable-person were wavering around a combined 600 positive emotional energy after subtracting negative emotional forces, but they were faltering as emotional resistance increased. Some of this resistance came from a re-direction of Bob-the-good-person's repressed negative energy. Bob-the-artist together with the related Bob-the-anxious-intellectual were varying from a 560 up to a 745 positive emotional level after accounting for the negative emotions arrayed against them – with Bob-the-artist becoming the dominant identity pose.

If asked at this instant to envision the evening ahead, Bob would have told you that he only wanted to relive the newsroom years and discuss the decline of American journalism with an old colleague. But Bob would have been deceiving himself. Because what Bob deepwanted, what his psyche craved, was the chance to impress Gary, to eke from him at least some grudging admiration and respect for Bob's writing talents. This would help to counteract the Identity Failure he was experiencing over Bob-the-nice-guy and Bob-the-reliable-person. This would further insulate Bob-the-good-person from Bob's persistent self-doubts. And it would dilute worries about Bob-the-artist lingering from the Miami theater rejection two days earlier.

Bob-the-artist would help Bob to justify his own existence.

But after spotting the unknown and uninvited guest with Gary, Bob felt troubled far more than he knew. And his Identity Failure flared. For a fraction of a moment, Bob-the-good-person again came under threat of psychological attack before the feeling was immediately repressed: A good person would welcome anyone and everyone, at any time – or so he was reminded by a vericept until that interpretation of experience evaporated among a welter of other vericepts that felt more acceptable to him. And so Bob-the-reliable-person, Bob-the-artist and Bob-the-anxious-intellectual each weighed in with new vericepts by rapid turns, all ultimately focused on further boosting the power of Bob-the-artist as the preferred identity pose. In this situation, Bob-the-artist felt most comfortable to Bob. But only very briefly, very very briefly.

Because now confronted with the reality of another human being seated at Gary's table, Bob's most immediate emotional necessity changed yet again: to show goodness toward this stranger, niceness in coping with an unexpected guest. Anything else felt ... not good. And not nice. And so it happened that Bob-the-good-person helped Bob-the-nice-guy push aside Bob-the-artist ... for a time. Bob-the-artist and Bob-the-anxious-intellectual together fell to 570. The deliberate effort to smile, to walk eagerly to Gary's table, to shake hands and express delight at the stranger's presence – these actions weakened the emotional resistance to Bob-the-nice-guy as they also presented the real possibility of earning Bob-the-nice-guy some much-needed outside appreciation to prove Bob indeed was still a nice guy afterall.

It is 5:51:09 p.m.

                          Gary
              (Smiling as he shakes hands)
Hey, here he is! I was almost gonna text you in another minute. Not like you to be the last one here.
                 (Looking at the woman)
Bob's, like, *never* late. Well ... *almost* never!

                          Bob
                    (Apologetically)
Yeah, I know. Sorry, sorry! Traffic was painful tonight. Really ... sorry! And then I hit enough of those idiotic endless red lights around here ...
(Checking his irritation with a forced smile, then looking directly at the woman)
    You know? You just sit at some of these red lights so long that you could
    get out, then wash and wax your car before the light turns green!

They all laugh politely. Gary realizes the situation.

                          Gary
Oh, yeah, Karen meet Bob. Bob – Karen. She's a neighbor of mine at the condo. We bumped into each other when I was leaving to come here. I asked her if she wanted to come along.

Karen
(Looking away from Bob as she speaks)
I hope that's not any problem. I don't want to intrude.

Bob
Nope. No problem for me at all, of course. The more the merrier!
(Shaking hands with Karen)
Nice to meet you, Karen.

Karen smiles vaguely at Bob without making eye contact. There's a brief but slightly awkward silence.

It is 5:51:57 p.m.

Who's Where Within

We can recognize at this instant that Bob-the-nice-guy and Bob-the-reliable-person are busily grappling for dominance over Bob-the-artist and Bob-the-anxious-intellectual. Bob-the-good-person sits protected far in the shadows, still the looming if precariously balanced psychological presence.

Because we understand that Bob-the-nice-guy and Bob-the-reliable-person had just been feeling better, rather more comfortable as they'd settled into the café arrival with strong apologies and sensible explanations. Only a little understanding along with a bit of reassurance from Gary and the stranger, oh yes, these kindnesses would have gone some ways toward easing the arrival tensions suffered by Bob-the-nice-guy and Bob-the-reliable-person. Yes, two amiable Bobs who then would have joined Gary and the stranger for a reasonably pleasant dinner, with Bob-the-nice-guy and Bob-the-reliable-person as the main companions seated on Bob's side of the table.

Instead there was something else: Disturbing information that this stranger had intruded on the dinner merely by whim. A chance meeting between neighbors, a thoughtless invitation despite prior plans … How typically Gary it all seemed suddenly, this awkward situation!

And so Bob-the-artist and Bob-the-anxious-intellectual were pressed to step forward again.

Because it is much harder for Bob-the-nice-guy to care about niceness when others with him aren't nice as well. Because it is much harder for Bob-the-reliable-person to care about reliability when others with him aren't reliable as well. The importance of these two identity poses to Bob was fading.

All of this allowed Bob-the-artist and Bob-the-anxious-intellectual both to feel themselves justifiably angry. Because anger is sometimes in their nature, these two, the artist and the intellectual, sometimes needed to defend the pursuit of the art and the intellect. Or so they believe. To them an anger that is artistic and intellectual can seem perfectly acceptable in this world at times. At times, at times. At the café, such anger was something well-suited for repeated attempts to elbow aside Bob-the-nice-guy and Bob-the-reliable-person. By now, Bob-the-reliable-person already had begun slowly to leave the café in any case. He was no longer needed.

Ah, but Bob-the-nice-guy is rarely so easily dismissed, not with Bob-the-good-person nearly always somewhere in the background. And so suddenly, despite it all, a resurgent Bob-the-nice-guy appeared. And from him came the forced handshake with this stranger accompanied by welcoming words mostly intended as friendly. Both Bob-the-good-person and Bob-the-nice-guy had seen to that.

But the handshake and the words somehow had seemed insincere. Both Bob-the-artist and Bob-the-anxious-intellectual had seen to that. And so we understand that the busy grappling among the Bobs would continue …

The psychophysics:

For a moment, for several moments really, things were looking up for Bob at the deepest levels of mind.

Apologies and explanations upon greeting Gary and the stranger had diminished emotional resistance to Bob-the-nice-guy and Bob-the-reliable-person. From a negative force that had topped out at 635, resistance to these two identity poses combined had fallen to 500 and well on its way to lower levels.

This negative force stood in opposition to the stronger positive emotional energy, Bob-the-nice-guy and Bob-the-reliable-person together remaining about 1225 or so. Bob was feeling more like a nice guy and a reliable person as he offered up his mea culpas. Only outside validation was needed for further strengthening – and a psychogravitational push generally toward Bob-the-nice-guy.

But suddenly Bob-the-nice-guy and Bob-the-reliable-person were less important identities for Bob to maintain in this situation. And for an instant, there was a serious psychological danger. Feeling blindsided and mistreated by Gary's impulsive dinner invitation to his neighbor, Bob's instantly rising anger momentarily threatened Bob-the-good-person. Good people should never get truly angry at other people. But this new opening for potentially significant Identity Failure was quickly repressed as Bob-the-artist and Bob-the-anxious-intellectual indignantly emerged with renewed vigor. Their anger was forceful enough to push aside the possible bout of a highly destructive form of Identity Failure, aiding in the successful repression.

This unending emotional flow, this continual strengthening and weakening and replacing of one emotion by another, of many emotions by many other emotions, these feelings that build and dissipate and give way to different feelings ... this perpetual shifting within, the forces that warp and bend the fabric of a psyche to create psychogravitational push in first this direction and then that ...they are the physics of the mind. As with the dynamics of the universe, everything here is energy. It is energy generated and energy transferred, it is energy created and energy released and energy in conflict with other energy.

And as ever anywhere in nature, the stronger forces of energy overcome the weaker forces of energy.

And in Bob's mind, in any mind, energy is emotion.

Like the pirouette ballet of stars and planets, then, like the valleyed warping of spacetime, the movements of mind obey the natural laws established within their own human universe – the universe within.

And the universe within functions with a fundamental goal. To create the weakest possible emotional resistance to the strongest possible feelings that one's existence is valuable at this moment in this world. At the deepest psychological levels, this is what is happening moment to moment, every moment of every day.

So now at the café, as during every now of his life, Bob was propelled automatically and irresistibly toward vericepts and thoughts and feelings, toward words and actions that felt best able to satisfy this constant need. And he was pushed away from those that didn't. Together this created a profound effect that shaped Bob's life at the moment, as during all moments of Bob's life – it decided what he deepwanted right then.

All these inner realities had combined themselves in a way that determined how Bob reacted to the news about this unexpected dinner guest. Which is to say, not well.

As Bob stood at the table after Gary's introduction, the force of anger from Bob-the-artist and Bob-the-anxious-intellectual had further increased, strengthening the importance of these two identity poses while diminishing the emotional power of Bob-the-nice-guy and Bob-the-reliable-person. With relatively slight emotional resistance, Bob-the-artist and Bob-the-anxious-intellectual had rebounded to an effective 745 and rising, including 210 from their anger alone – still a level of anger that felt sensible under the circumstances. It had been absorbed quite easily within Bob-the-artist and Bob-the-anxious-intellectual. Together they allowed Bob to feel superior to Gary and his dinner guest now, much smarter and more individually valuable to society, much wiser with more refined sensibilities. And very justifiably angered by the situation.

What Bob deepwanted at this point was to exploit Bob-the-artist to prove his rarefied significance in the world, perhaps enlisting assistance from Bob-the-deep-thinker and even Bob-the-genius. Working as one psychological team, these and related identity poses would extract from Gary and the stranger some of the needed admiration and respect, the appreciation and confirmation of Bob's superiority.

Still Bob-the-artist and Bob-the-anxious-intellectual remained now a team of two with no open and easy path to dominance. They were unable to overwhelm Bob-the-nice-guy even as Bob-the-reliable-person faded yet farther from importance as a result of Gary's too-obvious lack of reliability. For Bob just then, his own reliability no *longer seemed an issue. His niceness was. And as almost always, his goodness as well.*

To avoid potentially strong feelings of Identity Failure over Bob-the-nice-guy, to avoid altogether any feelings of Identity Failure over Bob-the-good-person, Bob summoned more of the combined positive emotional energy from those two identity poses in order to fuel a friendly comment and handshake. But this friendly effort met resistance from Bob-the-artist and Bob-the-anxious-intellectual, with their substantial energy levels coercing a less than enthusiastic tone of voice, facial expression and handshake.

That lack of enthusiasm immediately concerned Bob-the-good-person, offering yet another potential challenge to Bob's overall sense of goodness. Good people are always good to other people, which includes a friendly enthusiasm. So Bob's failed enthusiasm had struck an extremely sensitive psychic nerve. Because Bob had said and done things now, actually spoken words and committed actions in the real world, that might be seen as un-good – words and actions a good person wouldn't say or do. Yes, unenthusiastic words and unenthusiastic actions that might be seen by others as un-good. And therefore they had become words and actions that generated strong new emotional resistance to Bob-the-good-person, a significant unsettling of this highly significant identity pose.

Bob was feeling less sure of his own goodness than usual by a factor of more than two. And for an instant, he was aware of this horrible feeling. Maybe something really was wrong with him.

A 650 level of negative emotional energy abruptly had opposed the roughly 920 level of positive emotional energy from Bob-the-good-person. An opposing and significantly unsettling negative emotional energy that was, however, entirely and thoroughly and very effectively repressed very quickly indeed.

After that first instant, Bob no longer was aware of his Identity Failure over Bob-the-good-person, no longer feeling that sense of self-confusion. This negative emotional energy remained an active psychological force, though, as repressed emotion does – always becoming a negative emotional energy that is simply channeled somewhere else.

In this case, channeled ultimately into rage.

In a vericept, Bob's mind instantly and automatically had interpreted Bob's lack of enthusiasm as a real threat to Bob-the-good-person. In turn this had created deeply disturbing self-confusion and an accompanying terror that were repressed. These diminished the positive emotional energy of Bob-the-good-person, ignited more negative emotional energy about other identity poses such as Bob-the-nice guy. And touched off rage, nothing like his mere anger earlier.

Yes, this rage had resulted from a perceived serious challenge to Bob-the-good-person. This rage was intense: Climbing in an instant to 590 and on the rise. A huge, blistering rage toward Gary and the stranger for making Bob feel bad about Bob – and for again raising doubts about Bob's right to exist. For making Bob feel something might be wrong with him as a person.

It was a huge, blistering rage of which Bob was entirely unaware.

Because such rage is completely unacceptable to Bob-the-nice-guy and naturally also to Bob-the-good-person, among other Bobs. And whenever Identity Failure fuels such intense rage, Bob's mind automatically makes Bob unaware of the rage ... something that happens much more often than even Bob would suspect, something that happens over some smallthing-or-other sometimes many times nearly every day. Sometimes more.

At a deep level of mind, Bob often responds to the world by feeling something may be wrong with Bob. At a deep, deep, very deep level.

And so, yes, the rage was immediately repressed along with those other terrifying and unacceptable emotions. And so, yes, this repressed negative emotional energy of rage was simply channeled somewhere else. At 590, then 595, then 598 and climbing still, the energy of this rage was re-directed into Bob's body, a common outlet for his repressed emotion. So that Bob's latent small patches of facial seborrhea began to turn a more apparent red now and so that a fatigued shoulder muscle from yesterday's workout now began to sharply ache.

Within Bob's mind, then, these are the most active and influential forces at this café moment:

Bob-the-good-person – Positive: 920. Negative: 650 (repressed) = 270 positive emotional energy.

Bob-the-nice-guy – Positive: 560. Negative: 295 = 265 positive emotional energy.

Bob-the-reliable-person – Positive: 120. Negative: 50 = 70 positive emotional energy.

Bob-the-artist – Positive: 735. Negative: 135 = 600 positive emotional energy.

Bob-the-anxious-intellectual – Positive: 450. Negative: 220 = 230 positive emotional energy.

Rage (repressed) – 615 negative emotional energy.

Bob's net positive emotional energy = 820 combined from the most active forces.

This 820 is well below a level of comfort for Bob. Typically his positive emotional energy hovers closer to 1,500 or higher – much much more when he feels truly good about himself and the world.

Bob now can sense his mind in forceful conflict with itself, the sufferings of an anxious soul. The negative forces in opposition to the positive forces. The destructive in him busily wrestling with the constructive in him. He doesn't know the details of his identity poses and energy levels right now, of course, but Bob can feel their results all too well.

Yes, Bob feels increasingly miserable before the evening even has begun. He struggles at this moment to maintain psychological equilibrium, to rescue his individual value from the threats to that individual value by an unappreciative society. He still needs to prove himself a nice guy – and simultaneously prove himself better than others.

His rage isn't truly rage at Gary and Karen.

Bob's rage is a long-long-festering rage at the universe, an unfair universe he's forced to endure now once again. Bob's rage is with a universe that so often makes Bob feel bad about Bob.

It is 5:51:57 p.m.

> **Bob**
> (Noticing their drinks as he sits at their table)
> And wow, you've already got cocktails. You must have gotten here early, eh? I'm not *that* late!
> (He forces a snorted chuckle)

> **Gary**
> Yeah, she rode with me. Got here, what? I guess about five minutes early or so, right? We had no problem with traffic at all.

Karen nods in agreement, looking past the crowd toward the ocean.

> **Gary**
> I'm usually the guy who's late for everything. I remember that really pissed you off at all those newsroom lunches. "Where the hell is Gary?!" Right?

> **Bob**
> (With a forced laugh)
> Really? I guess I don't remember. We did have some fun back then, didn't we? The whole newsroom gang, those huge group lunches at Creolina's and wherever else. Remember?
> (Warming to the memory)
> All of us grabbing for those blistering hot sauces, right? Too funny!
> (To Karen, with a smile)
> A bunch of us reporters would go for lunch to this tiny Cajun place called Creolina's near downtown. And we'd get all macho, pouring their hottest most-blistering hot sauces all over our food. Almost seems kinda crazy when I look back now, ya know? But it was fun!

> **Karen**
> Oh, Lord! That does sound a bit crazy to me, honestly. I don't care much for hot spicy foods.

> **Gary**
> Even I don't eat food too spicy anymore. Bothers my stomach and then I don't get any sleep. Gettin' old, I guess, hey dude?

Bob
Well, I still eat some pretty darned spicy food sometimes. Even at my decrepit age!
(Laughs with some effort)
Anyway I guess I'm kind of a believer in the "age is all in your head" theory, really. That's how I see it anyhow. I think people can stay more youthful with the right attitude. It's almost like we shape our own aging process in some way, maybe.

Gary
(Smiling uncomfortably)
Well, I don't know about your head. But I'm pretty sure my age is in my stomach! I just can't eat the hot stuff anymore. And I pay a price if I try!

Karen
(Coolly)
I think it's easy to say "everything's in your head" if you don't happen to have the same problem. I don't really buy that argument.
(Changing the subject abruptly)
Where's the menu? I'm about ready to order. Some lovely seafood sounds good. Maybe mahi, something mild would be nice for me.
(Looking up and smiling a genuine smile for the first time. Waving at someone)
Oh good! Here she is. Over here!

Another woman makes her way through the crowded café toward their table. With a broad smile, she waves at Karen. This woman is an attractive 30-something, stylishly dressed, with long curled hair of vibrant brown. She notices Gary now, offering him a brief but enthusiastic wave as well. She does not seem to notice Bob at all. The young woman immediately kisses Karen on both cheeks, European style, makes smiling eye contact with Gary again and sits at their table.

Karen
I'm so glad you could make it! I'm dying to hear how everything all went today!

Gary
This is Karen's daughter. She used to live at the same condo building – they were both my neighbors for years.
(Handling introductions perfunctorily)
Allison – Bob. Bob – Allison.

It is 5:53:54 p.m.

Who's Where Within: Part 2

It was, of course, Bob-the-artist who had addressed Gary and Karen first now. This much was obvious from the slightly irritated comment kept in check with some difficulty, restrained mainly by Bob-the-nice-guy. Supervised as usual by Bob-the-good-person.

Bob-the-artist had been teetering on a fine edge for an instant, threatening to emerge with far too much superiority and condescension for comfort. For the comfort, that is, of the nice guy and good person identities that are often so very powerful in Bob.

Yet there was something else too: Somehow in that unwelcome situation Bob-the-nice-guy felt like an unacceptably weak reaction for this identity pose to dominate again. A more assertive alternative was needed just about the time that Gary had mentioned their group lunches outside the newsroom. It was perfect.

Enter Bob-the-tough-reporter accompanied by Bob-the-unpretentious-person. Bob's warm newspaper memories had come from them both, with Bob-the-tough-reporter's macho bravado softened by Bob-the-unpretentious-person's straightforward reportage of some lively but entirely humble meals.

But the reaction to his comment was an unwelcome surprise – Karen's suggestion that a taste for spicy food in some way is foolish, Gary's agreement based on an aging digestive system. Perhaps Bob's palate was unsophisticated. Perhaps Bob was trying to act younger than his years should allow. Perhaps …

Mellowed by Bob-the-nice-guy, Bob-the-tough-reporter offered his brief no-nonsense retort. Followed immediately by a visit from Bob-the-deep-thinker with Bob-the-unpretentious-person very near his side. No, Bob wasn't about to put up with silliness about spicy foods and age. But his response would be sensible, without over-reaction. It would be intelligent and thoughtful, without condescension.

Bob was pleased with this response. For a moment or two.

Until the response to the response, that annoying so-elderly reply by Gary and that stupid so-offensive reply by Karen, all of it ending abruptly by her change of subject. Then there was the arrival of yet another uninvited and unwanted guest, one more person to divert attention from the engaging conversation that otherwise would have happened.

Bob-the-good-person was watching over everything carefully as this unfolded. Bob-the-good-person made sure Bob-the-nice-guy said and did nothing at all.

But Bob-the-artist was making a comeback just then, joined by Bob-the-writer. They were looking for the first available opportunity to jointly say hello to Gary and Karen and Allison.

The psychophysics:

The artist's ascendance within Bob's mind had given way quickly to the tough reporter.

Yes, the good person was there as almost always. Yes, the nice guy was there as required by nearly every social gathering of any kind with Bob. Each of these Bobs was still strong, of course of course.

But Gary's reference to their newsroom days instantly had awakened Bob-the-tough-reporter – and strengthened him too. Strengthened Bob-the-tough-reporter so much and so quickly that this force of emotion required immediate weakening for Bob to feel comfortable with it, reducing the possibility that Bob would suddenly seem too tough, too blunt, too boastful. Bob-the-unpretentious-person had served that purpose quite well, softening any likely tough reporter sting.

Bob-the-tough-reporter had lingered and listened then, listened to Karen and listened to Gary, again gaining tough reporter emotional energy. Yes, gaining so much emotional energy that Bob-the-nice-guy was needed now, hurriedly called back with sufficient force to reduce the even greater possibility Bob would suddenly seem too tough, too blunt, too boastful. And angry.

Bob was getting angry again. Angrier at his two tablemates than before and aware of this as it was happening, though absorbing the feeling within his Bob-the-tough-reporter identity pose as justifiable anger.

And this was where Bob-the-deep-thinker had worked so well for Bob, with an intellect made less threatening to Gary and Karen by the deep thinker's nearby unpretentious mate. Bob's response had felt just right, felt so comfortable, meeting the immediate approval of Bob-the-nice-guy and Bob-the-good-person. If the situation had allowed, they both would have rewarded Bob with a big smile.

Until the response to the response.

And then the rage flared again, repressed as before. Redirected as before. Climbing this time to 620, 623, 625 and beyond. So that Bob's latent small patches of facial seborrhea were feeling noticeably warm and discomforting to him as the red intensified now and so that the sharp ache of his fatigued shoulder muscle felt suddenly more troublesome.

Then yet another intruding dinner guest had arrived – and the repressed rage jumped: 645, 649, 650. And onward ...

Bob once more could sense his deepening emotional conflict, his worsening struggle to maintain psychological equilibrium. All this was more or less apparent to him, but it was the result of something that was far from apparent. Well below his awareness, the feelings were assaulting Bob intensely and repeatedly. Perhaps there was something deeply wrong with Bob as a human being. Perhaps Bob wasn't a good person afterall. All, all, all of these, all were feelings repressed, instantly repressed.

The universe was making Bob feel bad about Bob. Again. He was more in doubt about the value of his own existence at this moment in this world. All, all, all fuel for that rage, a rage repressed.

And this forced on him an abrupt strengthening of Bob-the-good-person and Bob-the-nice-guy, who together held Bob motionless and silent as Allison had arrived. They made sure an acceptable minimum level of goodness and niceness was maintained. But even this powerful pair, even Bob-the-good-person and Bob-the-nice-guy, could not push aside another building force of emotion. No, they could not fully resist the strengthening emotional energy of Bob-the-artist and Bob-the-writer. Bob-the-artist had weakened in the face of Bob-the-tough-reporter but was back now, joined by Bob-the-writer – an identity pose that represented Bob's self-image as a polished pro who could write anything well at any time. To free these two together, to express them, to draw validation for them by others, ah, this is what Bob deepwanted now. Despite continuing resistance from Bob-the-good-person and Bob-the-nice-guy ... because superiority and boasting are neither good nor nice.

But that was less important now. Bob-the-artist and Bob-the-writer had joined the table together at this moment with the intent of holding court.

Within Bob's mind, then, these are the most active and influential forces at this café moment:

Bob-the-good-person – Positive: 895. Negative: 665 (repressed) = 230 positive emotional energy.

Bob-the-nice-guy – Positive: 535. Negative: 240 = 295 positive emotional energy.

Bob-the-artist – Positive: 705. Negative: 200 = 505 positive emotional energy.

Bob-the-writer – Positive: 585. Negative: 155 = 430 positive emotional energy.

Rage (repressed) – 665 negative emotional energy.

*****

Bob's net positive emotional energy = 795 combined from the most active forces.

Yes, yes... There really might be something wrong, deeply and intrinsically wrong, with Bob as a human being. Bob-the-artist and Bob-the-writer were badly needed to rescue Bob from what could become a very bad night. Or maybe even worse than that.

It is 5:53:54 p.m.

Bob
(Shaking hands with Allison, with a grin intended to seem charming)
Hi Allison. Very nice to meet you. We've been having a nice chat with your mom. I used to work with Gary. I'm a writer too.

Allison
(Pleasantly. Making eye contact as they finish shaking hands)
Hi Bob. It's good to meet you. Sorry I'm so late.

Bob
Oh, you're not that late! I haven't even ordered a drink yet.

Gary glances toward Bob, surprised at his eagerness to overlook Allison's tardiness.

Karen
(To Allison)
What would you like, honey? A glass of wine?

Bob
(Looking around, suddenly helpful)
Let me see if I can grab a waiter for us.

Gary
I've known Allison since she was just this high – not even tall enough to see over this table. Now look at her!

Bob
(Admiringly)
Yes, she's certainly grown into a beautiful young woman.
(Waving one hand, without success)
Waiter! Excuse me! Didn't see me ...

Allison
Thank you, Bob. That's always a nice thing to hear. So you're a reporter at Gary's newspaper?

Bob
(With poorly feigned modesty)
Used to be – long time ago! I'm a writer. Just finished a new piece today, actually, a new fictional story that deals with human values. I'm writing a series of them for my nonprofit group. And I've written a bunch of books and plays and things.
(Pausing a beat for Allison's reaction. Hearing nothing, he quickly plunges forward with his story anyway)
I was a contributing editor at a national travel magazine for a few years. And I've also done quite a bit of sports writing since leaving the paper – you know, for magazines like USA Weekend and Sports Illustrated. What about you?

Allison
Oh, how interesting. I love the theater! Would I know any of your plays?

Gary
(Dismissively but with a smile)
I don't think his work has quite made it to Broadway yet. Unless I missed something ...

It is 5:55:02 p.m.

Who's Where Within: Part 3

Bob-the-writer was the first who was pleased to make Allison's acquaintance. Just over his shoulder: Bob-the-artist, sitting closely behind as an observer for the moment and waiting for his turn to speak.

Then as so often happens in Bob's daily life, other new and unexpected visitors had arrived. From within. Yes, two other new and unexpected Bobs as so often happens. Unexpected but not unwelcome, this pair, almost never unwelcome to Bob.

Bob-the-romantic-male had entered the room and the conversation – encouraged by an eager Bob-the-sexual-stud.

They were among Bob's personal favorites, this pair, nearly always arriving in tandem but not always both remaining for long. Sometimes one or the other would leave the room. Now, though, they were together and looking for some strong assistance from Bob-the-writer and soon Bob-the-artist as well.

Yes, for it was Bob-the-romantic-male who so quickly forgave Allison's lateness. And it was Bob-the-romantic-male who so helpfully sought out the attention of a waiter. These were the least efforts that a romantic male could make under the circumstances.

Of course Bob-the-anxious-intellectual had returned briefly when the waiter had failed to notice Bob, thereby preserving Bob's dignity in an otherwise awkward moment. But Bob-the-anxious-intellectual had come and gone away almost before Bob had felt his presence at all.

Because it was at this moment that Bob-the-romantic-male had introduced Allison to Bob-the-writer, who had wasted little time in his chatty efforts to catch the attention of an attractive young woman at the table. Although it must be noted that Bob-the-writer had some help in shaping the tone and substance of his opening pitch to Allison, an assist from his wingmen Bob-the-unpretentious-person and Bob-the-nice-guy.

With Bob-the-good-person naturally still looming somewhere behind them all. Through their combined efforts, Bob had barely noticed Gary's slight – a dismissive comment about Bob's success that at another moment might well have infuriated Bob. But no, this collection of Bobs couldn't have cared less just then.

The Psychophysics:

Within Bob's mind, then, these are the most active and influential forces at this café moment:

Bob-the-good-person – Positive: 905. Negative: 625 (repressed) = 280 positive emotional energy.

Bob-the-nice-guy – Positive: 560. Negative: 200 = 360 positive emotional energy.

Bob-the-romantic-male – Positive: 680. Negative: 240 = 440 positive emotional energy.

Bob-the-sexual-stud – Positive: 595. Negative: 165 = 430 positive emotional energy.

Bob-the-unpretentious-person – Positive: 100. Negative: 40 = 60 positive emotional energy.

Bob-the-artist – Positive: 320. Negative: 90 = 230 positive emotional energy.

Bob-the-writer – Positive: 240. Negative: 145 = 95 positive emotional energy.

Rage (repressed) – 660 negative emotional energy.

*****

Bob's net positive emotional energy = 1235 combined from the most active forces.

Such a sudden positive spike was something common at the deepest levels of Bob's mind – common when Bob was around an attractive woman. Especially so when that attractive woman's attractiveness was enhanced by a warm and welcoming personality. Intelligence was another grand bonus.

True, there was always some psychological resistance to Bob-the-romantic-male, always more than some resistance to Bob-the-sexual-stud. Because to Bob-the-nice-guy and even more for Bob-the-good-person, romance and sexuality in the beginning often carried with them the possibility of manipulation, perhaps seducing someone to do something that someone might not really want to do. This concern brought out negative emotional energy. At a more intellectual level, Bob believed romance probably was a flawed unhealthy notion handed down from humanity's past and he feared the inherent irrational nature of sexuality. From all these and many other causes, Bob-the-romantic-male, and Bob-the-sexual-stud particularly, were often forced to tread quite cautiously at first.

But their arrival on any scene nearly always eased Bob's sense of something wrong with Bob. Sometimes greatly reducing the feeling, sometimes lessening it by a little. And thereby strengthening the feelings that his existence was valuable to him at this moment in this world.

With good psychological reason. In the presence of a woman who seemed both interesting and interested in any way, both Bob-the-romantic-male and Bob-the-sexual-stud created additional forms of validation by others. That's because this male duo of romance-and-sexuality often attracted some variety of approval from the woman or women in their company: So just a smile could confirm Bob's sense of power as a person, merely a handtouch could establish Bob's sense of appeal as a man.

Yes, any interesting and interested woman could instantly diminish Bob's Identity Failure. Positive emotional energy climbed, negative emotional energy dipped. The world, the universe seemed a much more welcoming place for Bob. For the moment anyway, the world, the universe were smiling and touching his hand.

Allison's interest in Bob's work had shifted his psychogravitational push somewhat, altering its path: The positive emotional energy from

Bob-the-romantic-male and Bob-the-sexual-stud were driving Bob toward seeking outside appreciation for Bob-the-writer and Bob-the-artist more as means to an end now rather than ends in themselves. Bob-the-writer and Bob-the-artist suddenly offered ways to attract a more serious interest from Allison, despite the significant difference in age between her and Bob. Yes, it was Bob-the-romantic-male and Bob-the-sexual-stud who had become most in need of satisfaction now.

With a little help from their two literary friends.

It is 5:55:02 p.m.

                    Bob
               (Ignoring Gary)
You might have seen something by me. I wrote a play about teen suicide that was commissioned by Coconut Grove Playhouse. And I composed the music for it too. That was a tough subject to write about but it was the job I was given and, well …

                   Karen
     (Changing the subject quickly when Bob pauses)
Speaking of jobs, Allison just started a new job yesterday, didn't you?

                  Allison
I did! I'm a paralegal at a law firm in Miami.

                  Karen
               (Proudly)
She wants to be a lawyer! How did it go today?

                  Gary
    (Sounding a bit too interested in this news)
You did? A new job? I didn't know that! Good for you, kiddo! That's a big deal for you.

                  Allison
It's going great so far. Everyone's been really nice. A couple of the big bosses even took me to lunch today as a kind of welcoming gift, I guess. I thought it was sweet.

Karen
How could they not love you already? This will be a brand new start, Ali! Just the thing you needed.

It is 5:55:41 p.m.

Who's Where Within: Part 4

Uh-oh.

Every Bob-the-something, any Bob-the-anything, oh yes, they all harbor the same pet peeves in this world. More than pet peeves, really.

Because some things simply aren't said or done to Bob-the-something or Bob-the-anything, sins in the form of insults, deeply personal affronts. Some things should never be said or done to Bob.

Karen had just committed one of these sins.

Karen had just changed the subject when the subject was Bob. With all-too-obvious intent, with an eagerness that Bob felt had skated close to a public rudeness, Karen had turned the conversation away from Bob to someone else – with the cheerful assistance of that someone else.

Uh-oh.

Neither Bob-the-romantic-male nor Bob-the-sexual-stud was amused. The same for Bob-the-writer and Bob-the-artist, no, not entertained by this at all. Clearly Gary had been almost as enthusiastic as Karen and Allison about their new dinnertime topic. Clearly. Clearly no one was interested in Bob at all.

No one ever got Bob.

Now Bob-the-anxious-intellectual instantly returned to this peculiar party, remembering Gary's slight about Bob's plays with a familiar sense of misery: Why bother to bother with anyone? They're all so dense! And Bob-the-writer and Bob-the-artist were working themselves toward a kind of suppressed fury, a feeling they deemed more or less justifiable under the circumstances, a feeling they would feel beneath an outer veneer of niceness and goodness.

And Bob-the-romantic-male and Bob-the-sexual-stud? They

disappeared now as suddenly as they'd arrived, first stepping into the café within a period of seconds, then stepping away from the café within seconds more. Both gone and already almost entirely out of sight.

In precisely 39 seconds, the Bobs had been reshuffled dramatically. Between 5:55:02 p.m. and 5:55:41 p.m., some Bobs had left. Some Bobs had arrived.

Although Karen and Allison and Gary didn't know it, they had just welcomed to their table Bob-the-misunderstood-loner.

The psychophysics:

The energy from Bob-the-romantic-male and Bob-the-sexual-stud had been instantly siphoned from the café, with almost all the emotional force that had animated this pair now vanished. There was no strong desire to satisfy the needs of romance and sexuality any longer. Anger and rage had taken their place.

And fear.

Under the careful supervision of Bob-the-good-person, of course, Bob-the-writer and Bob-the-artist were wallowing in their suppressed anger through an onslaught of vericepts and thoughts and feelings. Bob-the-nice-guy might usually have been expected to raise objections, but not so much this time. Karen had violated the rules of civil conversation, attacking Bob's value with a skillfully indirect but unmistakable intent. Bob-the-nice-guy couldn't offer Karen a vigorous defense. Even Bob-the-good-person didn't seem to much mind the anger, his emotional force fading sharply along with some of the repressed resistance to his force.

So with an anger considered justifiable indeed now, Bob-the-writer and Bob-the-artist gained emotional strength to a level just shy of a conscious fury. With relatively limited resistance. Yes, a fairly weak level of resistance that came from nexes about the importance of promoting tolerance and respect and peacefulness through Bob's writing and Bob's daily life. But tolerance and respect and peacefulness didn't feel like central issues at the moment. At the same time, Bob-the-writer and Bob-the-artist acquired additional emotional force from powerful nexes about the social value of literature and art and some such: Obviously, Bob-the-writer and Bob-the-artist offered greater value to society than anyone at the table. As a result of all this and more, Bob-the-writer had jumped to a 715 level and Bob-the-artist to an emotional energy of 790 without major interference from opposing emotions.

The repressed rage was spiking once more too.

In 39 seconds, the world had become an inhospitable place for Bob again.

This occurred because small everyday moments often felt more significant to Bob than they rightly were. Things that happened to him now routinely seemed like fresh examples of painful things that had happened to him long before – but really weren't the same at all. And this occurred because highly forceful negative emotions constantly pushed for some form of satisfaction within Bob's psyche, distorting his understanding of the present through streaming irvericepts. Irrational interpretations of his experience, moment to moment.

Bob carried many many nexes of much much painful emotion throughout each day, tigertails of misery he was afraid to let go of. Painful rejections by editors and artistic directors and agents. Infuriating misunderstandings and indifferences by both colleagues and laymen toward his best writing. The draining financial struggles that had resulted. All of this had long ago created a growing sense in him of self-confusion. He believed in the quality of his work – and the value of his existence based on that work. Why couldn't anyone else truly see it too? He craved validation, craved appreciation, some form of outside confirmation for all the greatness he saw within himself.

Who was he, afterall? A great writer? Or not?

Over the months and years, this Identity Failure had enormously strengthened Bob's feelings that something might be deeply wrong with him. How could everyone else be mistaken? It must be him, or was it? Was he crazy? Was the world? Was he a genius? Was he suffering delusions of grandeur? How could he know for sure without at least one deeply respected someone to assure him that, yes, Bob was right about Bob?

Such powerful feelings added more power to already powerful negative nexes about the world and Bob and their connection to each other, about the relationship of Bob and the world. Countless nexes had already filled to brimming with misinterpretations and irrational negative emotions involving the world's unfairness or everyone's stupidity or Bob's bad professional luck or all the things that might be wrong with Bob. And on and on...

And all of it had worked on Bob over the months and years, like long months and endless years of some psychological limbo that had for some reason been forced on him, a worsening purgatory of tormented confusion about himself and the world. Could the world and Bob any longer co-exist so that Bob's life felt valuable to Bob? It was a profound question. And as a larger part of him wondered if the answer might be no, a larger part of him also was slowly starting to lose his psychological struggle to exist. Some portion of Bob had started to hate life because life so often felt like such prolonged unendurable pain.

These negative nexes with negative emotions created negative feelings, including a great rage deeply repressed. A great rage at the world and himself and the universe: world-rage, self-rage, life-rage. It was those feelings that had been re-called to action in Bob's mind through the café situation.

Bob-the-misunderstood-loner was one of Bob's answers to all this, an identity pose that always was an effort to salvage feelings of self-value from the purgatorial furies. Bob-the-misunderstood-loner was gaining strength now along with Bob-the-writer and Bob-the-artist as the conversation droned on among Karen and Allison and Gary.

Within Bob's mind, then, these are the most active and influential forces at this café moment:

Bob-the-good-person – Positive: 545. Negative: 430 (repressed) = 115 positive emotional energy.

Bob-the-artist – Positive: 790. Negative: 165 = 625 positive emotional energy.

Bob-the-writer – Positive: 715. Negative: 115 = 600 positive emotional energy.

Bob-the-misunderstood-loner – Positive: 420. Negative: 290 = 130 positive emotional energy.

Rage (repressed) – 800 negative emotional energy.

*****

Bob's net positive emotional energy = 670 combined from the most active forces.

Bob was feeling worse still about the value of Bob's existence.

It is 5:55:41 p.m.

                    Gary
Absolutely! You're gonna do amazing down there!

                    Bob
(Rubbing his shoulder briefly as if it has become suddenly stiff)
That's terrific. Congratulations. Sounds like a wonderful opportunity.

                    Gary
At least you were smart enough to stay away from working at a newspaper!

                    Bob
(Seeing an opening to shift the discussion from Allison's job. To Gary)
And how are things in the newsroom these days anyhow? They still cutting back on everything?
                (To Allison)
That's part of the reason I left daily journalism so many years ago. The publisher was chopping our news budget and focusing on soft-news stories so much that I couldn't really do my job anymore. I'd been doing a lot of investigative reporting back then.

                    Gary
You wouldn't be doing those pieces today, I can promise you. Though to tell you the truth, I could never understand how you managed to snag that kind of time from the editors. Six months or more for some of those stories. Amazing!
                (With a laugh)
It made me wonder which editors you were blackmailing!

                    Bob
                (Defensively)
Because they were good stories, Gary. They weren't giving me six months to work on investigations for absolutely no reason. I worked for

a year on a couple of projects.

>Gary
Well OK, whatever! We saw things differently. But yeah, believe me, they're a lot more careful now with newsroom resources. They'd never let somebody work for months on the kind of stuff you were doing back then.

>Bob
>(Trying vainly to appear lighthearted)
Yeah, you're right, it was pretty lame stuff. Looking into airbag injuries five years before the Feds even admitted they had a dangerous problem. Or putting Basil Wainwright in federal prison for illegal treatments to AIDS and cancer patients. Or my investi—
>(Stopping himself. With a forced chuckle)
Oh, anyway, whatever, right? Glad to hear the newspaper's not bothering with stuff like that anymore, Gary. They were all total time-wasters for sure.

>Allison
>(Pause. Then changing the subject to ease the tension)
I don't understand how newspapers stay in business at all. No one my age reads a newspaper. I don't know one friend who even reads a newspaper online.

It is 5:56:56 p.m.

Who's Where Within: Part 5

In just that brief time, Bob-the-good-person had come to feel uncomfortable. In just 75 seconds, very uncomfortable with a positive emotional energy from Bob-the-good-person that was far too weak to sustain for long – Bob had to feel good about being good. And so Bob-the-good-person had insisted that Bob-the-nice-guy make his return to the table, sore shoulder and all. Together they had offered Allison a few kind words with enough enthusiasm to sound more or less sincere.

Until unexpectedly, an opportunity... An opening appeared for Bob-the-writer, who was joined almost instantly by Bob-the-tough-reporter even as Bob-the-artist beat a rapid retreat. Bob-the-artist wasn't needed at the moment.

Along with Bob-the-misunderstood-loner, the four other Bobs in the café now all tussled among themselves to aid the defense of Bob: Bob-the-good-person, Bob-the-nice-guy, Bob-the-writer, Bob-the-tough-reporter, each teaming up and taking his turn in whatever way worked best for Bob.

The psychophysics:

Within Bob's mind, then, these are the most active and influential forces at this café moment:

Bob-the-good-person – Positive: 765. Negative: 535 (repressed) = 230 positive emotional energy.

Bob-the-nice-guy – Positive: 585. Negative: 330 = 255 positive emotional energy.

Bob-the-writer – Positive: 590. Negative: 115 = 475 positive emotional energy.

Bob-the-tough-reporter –Positive: 620. Negative: 175 = 445 positive emotional energy.

Bob-the-misunderstood-loner – Positive: 380. Negative: 245 = 135 positive emotional energy.

Rage (repressed) – 745 negative emotional energy.

* * * * *

Bob's net positive emotional energy = 795 combined from the most active forces.

It is 5:56:56 p.m.

Bob
Unfortunately, that's sad but true. Young people don't follow the news anymore.

Allison
No, we follow the news. You're wrong. But newspapers seem so totally old-school now.

Karen
I haven't had the newspaper delivered in years. I just don't like to read

much anymore. And the newspaper's too depressing for me. I feel bad when I read it.

>   Gary
>   (Laughing)
> I feel bad when I write it!

Karen and Allison laugh heartily with Gary. Bob forces himself to chuckle again. He fiddles with the napkin sitting nearest him on the table, foot bouncing nervously. He squirms a bit in his chair and looks out past the crowd toward the ocean as Karen had done earlier. A vague smile has settled across his lips.

Karen has said something that makes Allison laugh again but Bob didn't hear it. Nor does he hear Allison's reply or Gary's remark after that. Bob looks around for a waiter, waves again but without the waiter taking notice.

>   Bob
>   (Rising from his chair. With a weak smile)
> Excuse me a moment – I have to hit the restroom. Gary, if we ever see a waiter would you order me a beer? Anything's fine. Sam Adams if they have it.

>   Gary
> Will do. Want a burger or something to go with that? We're all going to eat something, I think.

>   Allison
> Definitely, I'm starved! That lunch they bought for me was a long time ago. Do we have a menu?

>   Karen
> I have to eat something. And yes, Ali, I want to hear more about your new job today.

>   Bob
> Nothing for me, thanks. Just a quick beer. I can't stay too long anyway.

It is 5:57:48 p.m.

Who's Where Within: Part 6

Less than a single minute. Tick-tock. Less than 60 seconds passed before Bob-the-tough-reporter had given up. As had his close companion Bob-the-writer. Yes, both Bobs had abandoned any hope of meaningful conversation on this night in this café with these people.

Bob-the-misunderstood-loner was hardly surprised. Together with Bob-the-anxious-intellectual – well, it was just what they had expected. Because no one ever got Bob. People are idiots.

And precisely at the moment that Karen and Allison and Gary had laughed at Gary's joke, precisely as Bob-the-good-person had forced Bob-the-nice-guy to chuckle along at what seemed a silly joke ... yes, at this precise moment Bob-the-artist had joined the table once more. Bob-the-artist would help Bob to feel above it all, oh, far above all the shallow chit-chat, all the juvenile humor, all the petty insults.

Bob-the-artist was superior to such nonsense, a feeling reinforced by Bob-the-misunderstood-loner and Bob-the-anxious-intellectual. A feeling tempered by Bob-the-good-person and Bob-the-nice-guy, who couldn't find any remotely graceful way to leave the café so soon without staying for a quick drink.

Then working almost as one, this whole group of Bobs had decided a bathroom break away from the shallow chit-chat and juvenile humor and petty insults might help Bob a lot.

The psychophysics:

Within Bob's mind, then, these are the most active and influential forces at this café moment:

Bob-the-good-person – Positive: 725. Negative: 550 (repressed) = 175 positive emotional energy.

Bob-the-nice-guy – Positive: 560. Negative: 355 = 205 positive emotional energy.

Bob-the-artist – Positive: 645. Negative: 105 = 540 positive emotional energy.

Bob-the-anxious-intellectual – Positive: 490. Negative: 175 = 315 positive emotional energy.

Bob-the-misunderstood-loner – Positive:440. Negative: 185 = 255 positive emotional energy.

Rage (repressed) – 795 negative emotional energy.

*****

Bob's net positive emotional energy = 695 combined from the most active forces.

The shifts of emotional energy now formed a new psychogravitational push, a relentless effort to satisfy the combined forces of Bob-the-artist and Bob-the-anxious-intellectual and Bob-the-misunderstood-loner. Together with the repressed rage, these identity poses had driven Bob toward fulfilling his evening of misery.

Vericept by vericept, thought by thought, feeling by feeling, Bob was drifting toward a vortex of negative emotional energy. Anger and rage, fear and terror, self-confusion and self-contempt. Identity Failure was in full control of Bob.

It is 5:57:48 p.m.

We watch Bob walk briskly across the café, abruptly stop the first waiter he sees and point toward Gary's table.

Bob
(With sharp irritation)

Excuse me. I wonder is there anyone waiting on that table over there in the corner? We've been sitting here forever and no one's even looked our way.

Waiter
(Curtly, pointing toward the crowd)

We're very very busy, sir! You can see for yourself ... I'll get someone over there as soon as we can.

Bob

This just seems ridiculous. You folks really need to hire more wait staff if you can't handle the business!

Bob shakes his head as he walks quickly to the bathroom. He looks around after the bathroom door closes behind him, glancing beneath the three stalls for telltale feet. After confirming that he is alone, Bob stares at the mirror, peering deep into his own eyes. Then he notices that dark reddened blotches had broken out on his face, a common reaction by him to stress in social situations. He rubs and then stretches his shoulder, as if trying to ease a sharp pain.

Bob
(Very angrily but in a carefully controlled whisper)
God damn it! Damn, damn! Try to have a pleasant evening with people and ... Always turns into a pain in the ass!

He paces a bit in the bathroom, glancing briefly toward the mirror a few more times. Bob pulls out a paper towel and holds it now.

Bob
(With intense frustration but in the same whisper)
Unbelievable!

Bob aggressively crumples the paper towel and tosses it furiously into the waste basket.

Bob
Unbelievable! God damn it anyway!

Bob calmly washes his hands, throws the wet paper towel into the waste basket gently and walks as slowly as possible back to Gary's table. Allison is talking.

It is 6:02 p.m. exactly.

Who's Where Within: Part 7

A new Bob had been called to service briefly on the way to the bathroom. Yes, Bob-the-world-traveler had been trotted out along with Bob-the-anxious-intellectual to speak with the waiter. Because, yes, Bob-the-world-traveler knew a thing or two or three about restaurants, fine restaurants and fine service all over the planet. Standing nearby but unrequired: Bob-the-sophisticate, ready if needed to stand up tall to a lowly waiter in a small and ordinary cafe.

Into the bathroom had walked Bob-the-anxious-intellectual with Bob-the-misunderstood-loner and Bob-the-artist. With no necessity for

Bob-the-nice-guy now, Bob-the-good-person had only to enforce a whispered tone that prevented overhearing by anyone who otherwise could be within earshot of an angry voice. Oh, and he also had pulled out a paper towel to hold, should anyone walk in without warning to wonder what Bob was doing. For the moment, this would have to be enough goodness for Bob.

So then Bob-the-anxious-intellectual and Bob-the-misunderstood-loner and Bob-the-artist, these were the primary players in the bathroom tirade. And not one of them was feeling very sure of himself at this moment in this world. Not sure at all.

The psychophysics:

The resistance was strengthening, greatly strengthening vericept by vericept, thought by thought, feeling by feeling. Bob now actually wondered for some moments to himself if something was wrong with Bob.

Oh, surely, surely Bob-the-anxious-intellectual and Bob-the-misunderstood-loner and Bob-the-artist did their best to rally him from this self-confusion. What else was to be expected of the world by such an intellectual and loner and artist as he? Hardly the first intellectual and loner and artist to find the company of ordinary society distasteful in the extreme. All three identity poses had gained emotional force as the pose-strengtheners had kicked in.

But, no, the resistance continued strengthening too. As earlier, exactly as earlier, these negative nexes with negative emotions created negative feelings, including a great rage deeply repressed. A great rage at the world and himself and the universe: world-rage, self-rage, life-rage. It was these feelings that had been brought to action once more in Bob's mind through the café situation.

And they had intensified.

Maybe Bob wasn't really an intellectual or loner or artist in the way he imagined himself. Maybe Bob was a fraud. Maybe Bob was a confused individual or perhaps truly strange somehow. Maybe Bob was crazy.

Yes, maybe Bob wasn't a nice guy, not even that. Hidden far away from view, Bob also felt terrified that Bob might not be a good person either. All hidden, this terror ... far away from view.

Within Bob's mind, then, these are the most active and influential forces at this café moment:

Bob-the-good-person – Positive: 715. Negative: 570 (repressed) = 145 positive emotional energy.

Bob-the-artist – Positive: 735. Negative: 205 = 530 positive emotional energy.

Bob-the-anxious-intellectual – Positive: 580. Negative: 230 = 350 positive emotional energy.

Bob-the-misunderstood-loner – Positive:590. Negative: 220 = 370 positive emotional energy.

Rage (repressed) – 805 negative emotional energy.

*****

Bob's net positive emotional energy = 590 combined from the most active forces.

It is 6:02 p.m. exactly.

Allison

...and really feeling good now. Thanks, Gary. I really am. I'm loving my new job and my new apartment. Things are so much better.

Gary
(To Bob)

Allison's been kind of sick for a while. But she's doing a lot better now. Oh, I ordered you a Sam Adams.

Bob
(So softly that he is barely audible)

Thanks.

Allison
(To Bob)

I was bulimic for a long time. Since I was a kid really, when I was just starting middle school.

Bob
I'm sorry to hear that. Oh good – here's that beer. Finally.

A waiter delivers a glass of red wine to Allison and then a Samuel Adams beer to Bob, who immediately begins to drink it from the bottle.

Karen
(Proudly)
Yes, Ali's definitely doing a lot better now. She's starting a brand new life. Things are going your way at last, honey.

Allison
I hope so, Mom. I ... I think so too. It feels good to get out like this and have a good job and just feel normal, you know?

Bob
(With feigned interest between swigs of beer)
It certainly sounds like you have a good job. You said the law firm's in ... uh, was it Fort Lauderdale?

Karen
Miami! It's a huge firm. They have offices in three states. Who knows where this kind of opportunity could lead.

Allison
(Suddenly embarrassed)
I'm only a paralegal, Mom. I'm not a lawyer.

Karen
You will be.

Gary
(To Bob as the waiter approaches again. Irritably)
We're gonna order now. You're not eating anything? At all? I thought we were having some dinner tonight or whatever.

Bob
Nothing for me, thanks. I need to finish this beer and head out, unfortunately. We'll do dinner another time.

It is 6:03:28 p.m.

Who's Where Within: Part 8

Oh, there had been moments within this one minute and 28 seconds. Moments inside the span of 88 seconds when Bob-the-romantic-male and even Bob-the-deep-thinker had almost rallied and roused Bob from a miserable lethargy. A moment when Allison had talked directly to Bob, yes this had certainly attracted his attention. For an instant only. A moment too of hearing about her deeply personal battle with illness – and perhaps another moment or two too.

Moments when one or the other of these two Bobs had tried to see beyond the emotions of earlier moments, to care about something other than Bob's immediate emotional needs.

But it was too late.

Instead we had noticed Bob-the-good-person hanging on now as best he could, drawing support from time to time from Bob-the-nice-guy. Working together, this pair had been able to summon for Allison only a half-hearted sympathy and forced interest. A sympathy and interest further diluted by Bob-the-anxious-intellectual and Bob-the-misunderstood-loner and Bob-the-artist.

Yes, the unhappy gang still was all there. And growing unhappier still.

The psychophysics:

The psychogravitational push had quickened, a building force of negative emotional energy that had demanded satisfaction now. And now again and again now.

Pose-weakeners attacked Bob-the-artist. Pose-weakeners attacked Bob-the-anxious-intellectual. Pose-weakeners attacked Bob-the-misunderstood-loner. Even Bob-the-nice-guy suffered from this assault, with negative emotional energy emitted from negative nexes about his many failures as a nice guy. Bob didn't feel like such a nice guy now.

And all of this, of course, was to construct a wall of protection around Bob-the-good-person, guarding Bob's sense of fundamental human decency. If not entirely successfully now.

Within Bob's mind, then, these are the most active and influential forces at this café moment:

Bob-the-good-person – Positive: 690. Negative: 585 (repressed) = 105 positive emotional energy.

Bob-the-nice-guy – Positive: 475. Negative: 320 = 155 positive emotional energy.

Bob-the-artist – Positive: 695. Negative: 235 = 460 positive emotional energy.

Bob-the-anxious-intellectual – Positive: 570. Negative: 250 = 320 positive emotional energy.

Bob-the-misunderstood-loner – Positive:555. Negative: 240 = 315 positive emotional energy.

Rage (repressed) – 820 negative emotional energy.

*****

Bob's net positive emotional energy = 535 combined from the most active forces.

It is 6:03:28 p.m.

Gary, Karen and Allison order their dinners now. Bob gazes out past the crowd toward the ocean once more, sipping his beer almost continuously. Under the table, out of sight, Bob's right knee bounces rapidly up and down. He listens to their meal orders and feels his stomach rumble. He is getting hungry.

Bob examines the beer bottle to determine how much he has left to drink, then looks toward Allison as she speaks. But Bob has no idea what she's talking about now. He wonders what time it is and how much longer he needs to linger to avoid appearing rude. A vague smile again has settled across his mouth as Gary and Karen say something to each other.

It is 6:04:36 p.m.

Curtain Call: The Cast Of Characters

At the café while sitting in his own chair, Bob was far from alone – as we have seen. Many Bobs sat with him. But Bob was not alone in being far from alone while sitting in a single chair on this evening at this cafe. Without his awareness, Bob had been joined by many more table guests than he'd ever suspected. Each chair had been occupied by several.

Yes, more than two dozen other personas had taken their seats beside Bob without so much as a single introduction. This had been a large-cast production indeed.

Unbeknownst to him, Bob hadn't simply shaken hands with Gary, his old newsroom comrade. No, Bob had shaken hands with Gary-the-jovial-socializer, who'd been joined at that moment by Gary-the-sharpwitted-man. And he had not merely greeted Karen, a neighbor of Gary's. No, Bob first had said hello to Karen-the-sensitive-female, who had felt instantly troubled by Bob's lack of enthusiasm over her presence. This was the same Karen who had avoided eye contact and then gazed out toward the ocean shortly after, along with Karen-the-self-respecting-adult who had offered her some emotional support by ignoring Bob in what felt like a mature and dignified manner.

So you can imagine how many Garys and how many Karens had been part of this crowded party. Gary-the-reporter among them and Gary-the-plainspoken-realist too. And Karen-the-polite-neighbor and Karen-the-blunt-truthteller. These among many many others.

And then Karen-the-loving-mother had come to the table just as Allison-the-urban-professional had entered our drama. Along with Allison-the-considerate-stranger and Allison-the-arts-lover and Allison-the-recovering-bulimic and Allison-the-beautiful-woman. Among many others.

Yes, they all had made their appearances during that brief 13 minutes and 27 seconds of our playlet – and during the following 16 minutes and 44 seconds before four of the Bobs finally had agreed on a suitable moment to exit the scene.

Many Garys, many Karens, many Allisons. Many Bobs.

All of them sitting together. Although neither Gary nor Karen nor Allison nor Bob had noticed any of these other characters. To them, the situation had seemed like nothing more than a simple exchange of words among four people having drinks. Whatever.

But it had been something more than that. Yes, this had been a dance of sorts not unlike the pirouette ballet of stars and planets in some sense. At the very deepest levels of four individual psyches, grand emotional forces had erupted and subsided and combined their energies throughout that 13 minutes and 27 seconds. And the 16 minutes and 44 seconds that followed. The relative strength and weakness of those emotional forces had determined the evening's events, creating that exchange of words through psychological necessity.

Not one of those four people could have said or done or thought or felt anything other than they did, not without acquiring a knowledge about themselves that would have allowed change. Everything that happened to them at the café had been caused by everything that happened to them before the café – or more precisely, by everything they had believed about their pre-café experiences.

Like nearly all human interaction, it was all reaction, all emotion, all irrational.

And the common denominator had been Identity Failure.

Go back and re-read the original scene without descriptions now, if you care to. You'll see. No less for Gary and Karen and Allison than for Bob, the unrelenting demands of the Fundamental Law of Mind had formed every one of their reactions. The same even was true for the curt waiter confronted by Bob. For each of them, the evening was all about me.

Just like nearly every other evening and nearly every other moment of their lives.

Without a more protracted demonstration of the psychic elements at work here, you nonetheless may sense the depth and force of emotion at that table. In the most mundane of situations among the most everyday conversation. The insecurities behind the subtle comments, the hurt feelings beneath the small actions. The goal of each person had been to defend their own ego and, in any way that seemed possible, to attract some form of appreciation. Somehow, from someone.

But now imagine this scene happening in a real café with real people, with you the eavesdropper. Ask yourself if you would have suspected the underlying psychological drama taking place. Would you have believed that these four individuals each had been suffering from powerful old conflicts and desperate unhealed wounds during their very ordinary conversation?

We are not accustomed to viewing daily life in that way, as a continual struggle for feelings of value within our individual existence. But I believe passionately that we should begin to see human behavior through this lens.

Not necessarily dwelling on the complexities of identity poses during our dealings with others, of course, or trying to analyze the relative strengths of emotional energy fields as we go through our day. Yet I do think we require a clear understanding that each of us suffers from the same illness: Identity Failure. And that this illness and the underlying psychological dynamics don't merely influence our lives – they create our lives.

Obviously, this leaves aside the impact of outside forces such as poverty, lack of education, natural disasters, repressive governments, destructive customs and the like. As well as the role of genetics in shaping our individual futures. No matter our genes, though, our minds are governed by the same basic laws. Rich or poor, educated or ignorant, we each are locked in a perpetual struggle to feel that our individual existence is valuable to us at this moment in this world. And we each thrive or wither based on our interpretations of that struggle.

At the beginning of this book I quoted Henry David Thoreau, among the great minds who long ago recognized a fundamental truth of our humanity: "What a man thinks of himself, that is what determines his fate." If this truth now creates great troubles for nearly all individuals, as I believe, then it also offers great opportunities for significant change, individually and as a society. We can learn to see ourselves and others very differently, discovering a more rational understanding of our fundamental humanity that may help us to become healthier individuals – and importantly, to improve our childrearing strategies.

There is a core in us of love. A powerful desire to help others, to develop and share our best as individuals with the world. I have found it at the deepest levels of my psyche and I know that I'm not alone in this construction of my basic nature. Rational Faith is intended as a new way of living that can help to tap and free this core.

But that's not possible as long as we're afflicted with Identity Failure. When our immediate fear and anger smother our far stronger if buried love, when everyday living is all about "me" each day and all day, then we cannot hope to see this core much less express it.

And we can't change the omnipresence of Identity Failure until we view ourselves more honestly, without sentiment or romanticism. This is why I've devoted so many words to such detailed observations about the root problem as I see it. The philosophy of Rational Faith is founded entirely on these observations.

Just as at the café table peopled by so many different identities, our world is crowded with rigid irrational self-images that massively damage others and ourselves. We each suffer needlessly from these senseless notions about who we should be. I still suffer at times but much less so now than earlier in my life. In all likelihood, you suffer as well and so does everyone you've ever met.

We are victims of a disease we don't even know we have.

Identity Failure.

And as with all illness, the cure can only be administered following an accurate diagnosis.

Chapter 9: The Why Within You

"A question that sometimes drives me hazy: am I or are the others crazy?"
                    Albert Einstein

Personality Plus

Who are you?

Right now, which you are you?

Or rather, which identities among the many possibilities make you feel most valuable at this moment?

Since you are reading a challenging book, perhaps you are (insert your name)-the-intellectual. Or maybe

(   )-the-openminded-person. You could be feeling like the-spiritual-seeker or the-philosopher or the-voracious-reader. You might find yourself gravitating toward the-restless-learner or the-humanist, the-psychologically-curious or the-moral-explorer. Or if you're wading through this book because you happen to know me, you might just be feeling like (   )-the-devoted-friend. Should that be the case, dear person, please feel free to stop. I appreciate the effort but you've done enough.

Assuming that we don't know each other, however, I can't speculate any further on which specific identities you may have adopted right now as representing the real you. Only that you've selected some automatically, in all likelihood without any awareness that it happened. And that more than one identity is active in your mind. And that reading this book in some way is helping you manage what I've named the Fundamental Law of Mind: interpreting experience to create the weakest possible emotional resistance to the strongest possible feelings that your existence is valuable to you at this moment in this world.

Everything you do is governed by that psychological law. You can't behave otherwise.

Those identities that your mind has chosen during this session with my book are your psyche's effort to satisfy that demanding law in what seems to you the best way right now. With some identities stronger than others, some more important than others, exactly as detailed during that fictional-but-real café meeting in the last chapter. This is what's happening inside your head.

And that means you are under the enormous influence of something else as well.

Identity Failure.

Unpuzzling The Pieces

The problem isn't the Fundamental Law of Mind. It's how you've learned to cope with it. The same way nearly all of us have learned to cope with it: by forming identities based on personality types you've learned, then seeking outside confirmation that those identities truly are you.

As I've explored Identity Failure within me and to the extent possible in others, I've recognized that this affliction comes in many forms. Identity Failure can appear very different in you than in me. But I believe that it shapes our lives profoundly, whatever the variation. Identity Failure cripples us, whether through the severe wounds inflicted or through the severe limitations imposed. And one way or the other, I.F. makes us self-centered and unfulfilled.

Rational Faith is an antidote, as I'll ultimately explain in some detail. Identity Failure creates an urgent need for this new philosophy, with the Fundamental Law as the driving force. To fully understand Rational Faith's significance, though, we first must fully understand both the Fundamental Law of Mind and Identity Failure.

In this chapter my goal is to convince you that you're a fellow I.F. sufferer. Your worst problems are the problems of Identity Failure. In Chapter 10 we'll examine why I believe the same is true of our society, past and present.

All of which may very legitimately lead you to wonder at this juncture, "OK, how do I have Identity Failure?"

It may reveal itself in what you do. Or in what you don't do. In the choices you make or in the choices you avoid. It may cause you to feel or think or say things you don't understand. Or it may prevent you from feeling or thinking or saying things that otherwise might benefit you and others. I.F. can drive you to talk endlessly or to talk as little as possible. It can make you obsess about something or run away from something, lose sleep or sleep too much, quit jobs you should keep or keep jobs you should quit. Identity Failure can cause anxiety or depression – or both at the same time. Or it can make you feel nothing at all. I am utterly convinced I.F. causes physical illness as well, as I'll discuss in Chapter 12.

Identity Failure's varieties look to be endless.

I also have discovered that Identity Failure seems to vary in strength, person to person. As far as I can tell, some people are profoundly infected, others less so. The variables appear centered around the extent that we require outside confirmation to feel our individual existence is valuable.

As I began this portion of my book in 2016, I only recently had realized something that fascinated me. For all the unspeakable misery I've endured throughout my life as the clearly identifiable results of I.F., I am highly self-reliant psychologically. I don't really need that much outside confirmation and appreciation to function.

That's why I've been able to write this book and create this philosophy without any exterior sources cheering me on. It's why I was able to pursue other important goals in my life such as becoming an investigative journalist or playwright or composer with little to no outside support. I've now estimated that, for as far back as recollection allows, I had been roughly 80% reliant on my own deep belief in me, seeking only an additional 20% from others to boost my confidence to maximum levels. I reckon that my psychological self-reliance in later years has been even greater – 85% with a need for 15% from other people and the world at large. Of course as with most psychological states, my self-trust has been variable. My best guess is that it may sometimes have fallen as low as 60% and risen as high as 95%. But on average, I believe, around 85% would have been my norm before fully implementing Rational Faith. That philosophy significantly strengthened my self-trust, reducing my need for outside validation to levels that are negligible if detectable at all.

If those figures are accurate this means my massive anxiety and other torments throughout my lifetime, both psychic and physical, stemmed from lacking a relatively small amount of outside confirmation. Small, perhaps, but intensely important to me. I recognize now that I'd learned from my parents and siblings, from friends and from my culture that I could trust myself to a great degree but not totally. Somehow I formed the notion that others had to confirm what I already believed about myself. Otherwise, it might not really be true. Looking back, I understand the process felt something like being a scientist whose laboratory findings must be verified by independent experiments: I believed my results but couldn't place full confidence in them without external confirmation. This was my almost constant condition – someone else had to independently validate my observations about me. All my self-confusion and self-doubts, all my huge insecurities and my feelings that something might be wrong with me … all of it came from lacking just this final 15-to-20 percent quantity of self-trust.

It's not difficult to imagine Identity Failure's life-altering impact on the person who hovers at 70% self-trust – or 60% or 50%. They surely would be paralyzed to a significant extent without enormous and unwavering encouragement from the world, something that's denied even to many widely popular cultural figures. Daily living would be a continual struggle against consuming self-doubt. On the other hand someone who averaged, say, a 90% or 95% level of self-trust probably would appear greatly confident in most situations. But not in all situations. This individual still would suffer psychological soft spots, specific areas of their life that would be vulnerable to Identity Failure. These might revolve around large themes in their psyche such as masculinity or femininity, intellect or creativity, material success or sexual attractiveness or compassion for the feelings of others. Themes they would do their best to avoid confronting. The profound insecurities, the self-confusion, would be there somewhere beneath the surface for the most part, the sensitive nerves waiting to react to the wrong touch at the wrong time by the wrong person.

I have long known both these sorts of folks, the people I would imagine in the 90-95% range as well as others who would seem perhaps closer to the 60% level or less in daily life. And of course many other individuals whose self-confidence likely falls somewhere between those relative extremes. Obviously I can't peer into their psyches. But having peered so deeply into my own, I can develop well-informed speculations about their Identity Failure based on decades of closely observing their behavior and the overall arc of their lives – supplemented by questions I've put to them and conversations we've had.

Clearly these are close friends of one kind or another. Just as clearly I would not want to write something that might hurt them in any way. For this reason, I'm going to change irrelevant details here as needed. But the facts otherwise will be as accurate as I can make them when exploring Identity Failure inside other people's heads.

Familiar Faces

Maybe you're something like my friend, Delia, whose strong fear of Identity Failure appears to have enormously limited her confidence and so also her choices, experiences, assertiveness, willingness to take risks and even her daily personality in key ways. She doesn't know it's Identity Failure, naturally, but this is the source of feelings that so often seem to terrify her.

For Delia, being human demands being small. A perpetual wan smile, an eagerness to be helpful no matter the personal inconvenience, the reserved manner that fades into the wallpaper within a group … She holds strong, intelligent opinions on many things, often well thought-out and sometimes fairly non-traditional. She likes to laugh and has a charming sense of humor. Delia can be very good company. But most people wouldn't know this side of her.

I believe that Delia suffers intense I.F. nearly any time she tries to break out of the conventional mold that she's allowed to shape her life. That is, to free herself from very limited and very conventional identity poses.

Delia works as an insurance agent but longs to become a nurse – yet she refuses to do what's needed to make that happen because her husband objects. The change could be risky afterall. In this and many areas of her existence, she goes along and gets along and drifts through everyday living with the goal of sidestepping any potential conflict. Conflict with Delia. As best I can determine, Delia avoids anything that would require viewing herself as somehow more important than she feels now. Society sees her as a very small cog in a very big wheel. So does she. Adopting any identity pose beyond this comfortable model evidently seizes Delia with anxiety. She can't envision herself in a larger, more challenging role in this world. Identity Failure has made her what she is by preventing her from becoming all that she might be. Or so I have observed anyway, over and over and over and over.

*****

Or perhaps you more closely resemble my longtime friend, Giorgio, who seems to have everything going for him. Except self-confidence.

Giorgio is unusually good-looking, extremely sensitive, insightful to a rare degree and almost incapable of reaching firm conclusions about things, whether the grand or the mundane. If it's a personal decision, he asks everybody he knows – and still can't decide. Move to a different city or stay where he is? Start a promising romantic relationship or tell the new man to go away? Take a vacation to Hong Kong or rent a cabin in Florida? Who knows? Because he might choose badly. He could be wrong. If it's a joint decision involving Giorgio, whatever you want is best. Steak or pasta for dinner? Action movie or comedy? Turn up the heat or turn it down? Sure, either's just fine.

Despite all that indecision, his feelings are very easily hurt and often for no sensible reason. He needs to be treated gently at almost all times, with great attention and frequent encouragement. But Giorgio also is wonderfully warm and fun-loving with an appealing chuckle he shares often. He makes a delightful friend.

After watching him up close for many years, I've reached the unexpected conclusion that Giorgio likely has formed pretty definitive concepts about who he is. At some private level, he firmly regards specific identity poses as being the genuine Giorgio, a quite remarkable chap. But he can't understand why no one else can grasp these truths about him. As with most of us, the world doesn't treat Giorgio as Giorgio feels he merits. No one truly gets him. And lacking outside confirmation for his deeper self, Giorgio lives in the perpetual grip of a fierce Identity Failure. Who is Giorgio, really? Is he the amazing person he recognizes from within or something else entirely? Giorgio feels there's no way to be sure about that.

Or anything else.

I.F. has seized control of Giorgio.

*****

Or you might feel a kinship with two other gay men, a married couple. Coleman and Simon. To me they have always appeared remarkably alike in one very important way: their huge amount of surface confidence and the reasons for it.

Both are highly social, personable and gregarious people, seemingly comfortable in any group whether strangers or friends. Coleman is a successful entrepreneur and largely supports their household while Simon pursues poetry as a profession. Simon struggles, of course. Coleman salts away investments for their retirement as he provides them an upscale lifestyle. Sadly, to my eye at least, Simon isn't really much of a poet. But he writes on year after year, evidently with a firm conviction that he's a brilliant if undiscovered bard. It's taken me well over a decade to figure out how Simon maintains this self-assurance in the face of almost unrelenting rejection. And also to understand how both he and Coleman can appear so consistently even-keeled, neither one easily ruffled by much of anything including the opinions of others about them.

Where is their Identity Failure – or are they the rare exception? No, they are not.

Over the years, I've come to realize both Coleman and Simon are terrified of intense emotion. They don't understand it, don't know how to handle it … and do their best to avoid it. They accomplish this by intellectualizing everything in their lives and wearing very thick blinders night and day that block out frightening truths. Coleman and Simon see only what they want to see, which includes just what agrees with their prefabricated view of anything or anyone. Especially themselves. They hold I.F. at bay much of the time through a near-absolute refusal to perceive themselves in any other way, meaning in any other way that may feel uncomfortable or unsettling. I've detected the soft spots in each of them, those sensitive nerves that can be set off by the wrong touch at the wrong time by the wrong person. But I have only seen these nerves touched on a few occasions in all the years, and even then only barely and briefly. Each instance seemed a mere glimpse of some underlying vulnerability that was quickly covered up again.

For a long while I wondered if their kind of unwaveringly upbeat approach to life might be healthy. And I think it would be healthy if their self-images were realistic, complex and flexible, taking into account their irrational emotions. But that's not the case.

Instead Coleman and Simon cling to their own rigid irrational identities no matter the consequences. I've observed the process firsthand: They consistently sugarcoat their perceptions of themselves and their relationship. Everything's fine, always. Those attitudes have severely restricted their emotional bonding with each other and anyone else. Because they so fear strong emotions, they can seem charming but cool to those who care about them.

I also believe Coleman and Simon have lived significantly diminished lives, never realizing their fullest individual potential. Both could do and be much more than they are, I feel certain. They are very talented and very smart in myriad areas that might have made a larger difference in the lives of other people. But the dread fear of really challenging their core self-concepts constrains this couple. In that sense, they're similar to Delia but have learned to function at a more dynamic level.

Still, Identity Failure has exacted its steep cost for Coleman and Simon. Individual fulfillment and intimacy with others require the willingness to feel things, even deeply unpleasant things as we confront difficult realities. These two men can't do this – or won't. Though admirable in many respects, Coleman and Simon have denied themselves greater fulfillment as well as true intimacy in their efforts to avoid the horrors of Identity Failure.

*****

Perhaps you'll find you have more in common with my longtime friend, Noelle. She is the CEO of a major corporation, a classic achiever. And what she most often achieves in life is to possess precisely what everyone else seems to want. Wealth, title, social status for both her and her family. That is Noelle's constant drive, that is her purpose: to appear important.

During social interactions, Noelle's identity plainly is bound up in the desire to impress others. That so many others are so easily impressed by such superficial achievements makes daily living feel easier to Noelle. She's attained the dream, at least in the popular mind. To my mind, however, Noelle only has attained a slew of shallow identities that demand constant outside validation. As long as this validation continues, she can avoid the worst effects of Identity Failure. Her ego feels relatively safe. But if she should lose the wealth, the title, the social status, God help her. Noelle would come unglued.

I've known Noelle long enough to remember a time before that wealth, title and status. The person she was then remains inside her, somewhere. I've caught sightings in recent years. And I adore that woman. Quick and witty, loving, sensitive. But now more often Noelle seems anxious and uncomfortable, unable to sit still for long. Doing one thing, she must try to do others at the same time: the computer, the cellphone, television or music or even conversation are each accompanied by one or sometimes two other activities. Distraction is needed at all times.

Despite appearances, Noelle's is not a happy life. It is not fulfilled. And even when the focus falls on her twin boys, it's really all about her. Their achievements have become her achievements. She is self-obsessed to the maximum. Left to drift in the wake of her worldly successes are Noelle's deeper talents, genuine concern for others, love of adventure and especially travel. Those qualities have been smothered by Noelle's efforts to outrun Identity Failure.

*****

I'll offer one final example here. Ivan is 51-years-old and floundering still to find himself. We have been close friends for a long time now – the kind of friends who have talked at enormous length on many occasions about his struggles. Ivan is one of the most kindhearted people I know, in part because he suffers huge self-doubts when he's any other way. I know this because Ivan has told me how much he agonizes over that and similar demands on himself. It's one of the things that attracted us to each other as close buddies. Both of us have wrestled with an unyielding necessity to be good and nice and generous and caring. At all times.

Without knowing for sure, obviously, I suspect Ivan often feels a greater need for outside confirmation than I do. He can come across as uncertain about his words and beliefs, his actions and opinions. I get the sense he's always waiting for the response of others to anything he says or does, feeling comfortable or uncomfortable depending on their reaction. I know what that's like too. I've been there.

I regard Ivan as among the brightest, deepest, most talented people I know. We have great conversations for hours at a time. But Ivan bounces from job to job, all of them far below his abilities. He has tried to focus on more valuable and challenging work, but always falters in the end – from lack of self-confidence, it appears. His failed persistence really is failed self-trust.

To me, Ivan seems a man in search of an identity, one that feels like a good fit. But his search is limited to the identity poses he finds around him in the world. Is he Ivan-the-teacher or maybe Ivan-the-athlete? Is he Ivan-the-filmmaker or possibly Ivan-the-entrepreneur? No identity pose works for Ivan, no matter how many he tests out. I often think that Ivan simply may be too smart and self-knowledgeable ever to comfortably adopt a readymade persona as the real Ivan. I hope in time he finds the truly gifted and complex individual within himself. He can offer the world a lot.

But for now, Ivan trundles and tumbles along an aimless path constructed for him by Identity Failure.

*****

How can I know any of this? As I've readily admitted, I obviously can't peer into their psyches. The honest answer is that I can't know some of the things I have just written about my good friends. Not with great certainty, that is. No doubt some of the conclusions I reached about them may be mistaken – misinterpretations based on limited information or on misleading influences drawn from my own experience.

But I'm reasonably sure that at least I am correct about the broader outlines of their Identity Failure. Each friend is someone I've known so intimately that we have shared many secrets. I have observed their behavior and beliefs with enormous interest for a long long time. And as I understood more and more about my own I.F., I seemed to have an increasingly clear insight into their personalities. You'll notice that I did not venture here into the more uncertain region of which specific identity poses they may be protecting, though privately I have some guesses. Perhaps one friend highly values feeling like the-team-player, another the-caregiver, another the-reliable-person and so on. But perhaps not.

As we consider these five friends, it's important to keep in mind a psychologically accurate definition of Identity Failure: I.F. results from significant emotional resistance to a self-image that contributes significantly to an individual's feelings that their existence is valuable to them at this moment in this world. That is, Identity Failure happens when an identity pose you highly value feels threatened with being exposed to your mind as a fraud. The world isn't confirming that you're a nice guy, therefore you might not be a nice guy. Or gal. This means that each of my friends suffers from protecting those most prized identity poses at the expense of other identity poses they value less. They're trying to feel their lives are worth living because they more or less maintain being a team player or a reliable person or whatever the identity. In the process, they give up on many other qualities they also possess – and abandon the many ways those qualities could help others and themselves. Like nearly all of us, they become limited by their most valued self-images and obsessed with trying to validate them.

I hope those short capsule descriptions may capture the essential flavor of their affliction. To the best of my ability, I've recounted their experiences to give you a very small sampling of Identity Failure's sweeping variations. Perhaps one of these variations even rings a familiar chime when you examine your own experiences. Perhaps one of my friends is much like you.

Same But Different

Or maybe they aren't.

Maybe none of those five examples seems anything like you. Entirely possible, of course. They're only brief samples, as I've noted, not a complete catalogue of Identity Failure. I don't believe that could be assembled because the variables and combinations are limitless.

But all forms of Identity Failure have many things in common. Including your form of Identity Failure.

For one, you can hear the sounds it makes.

Shhhhh …

Pause for a moment and listen to the voices inside your mind. Can you hear them? They are the voices of your Identity Failure, whispering to you. And sometimes shouting.

These are the words of self-doubt that come at you with the emotional force of words spoken by others. They are words of self-criticism, self-contempt, self-abuse. They are the voices of confusion about yourself, who you are and what you say and what you do. They remind you of all your failings. They question your abilities. They question your experience. At times they even may question your sanity.

Those are among the expressions of pose-weakeners, as I've called them – your mind's efforts to attack some of your identity poses in order to protect other more vulnerable identity poses that you value highly.

The voices in your mind also can resound in huzzahs of great praise for you. They may sing of your achievements, your brilliance, your sexual athleticism or your intellectual insight. They may obsess over someone's compliment or offer choruses of self-congratulation for what others surely will say about you. Whatever the specifics, those are among the pose-strengtheners in your psyche – your mind's attempts to compensate for your perceived flaws by emphasizing the virtues of some other highly valued identity poses.

The voices in your head are very different from other types of psychological experiences. Of course thoughts can be deliberate and rational, particularly when you engage in critical thinking. These may seem similar to listening to your own voice speaking as you think. There also is, in Emerson's words, "that gleam of light which flashes across (your) mind from within," a sudden and clear insight. Emerson referred to this as instinct, often arriving for me as an unusually powerful and clear sense of understanding, a feeling of truth. Other varieties of positive inner messages occasionally come to me too, maybe some words of encouragement or a supportive pronouncement of some sort. These can feel something like sensing the commands of God: "Start writing your book!" "Move to Vermont!" "You need to get a divorce!" They pop automatically to mind from somewhere within. I have experienced these many times.

Our heads are filled with all manner of assertions, questions, decisions and more. But they're very different from those voices of Identity Failure. To my knowledge, there is nothing else that's like Identity Failure's internal monologue. Friends and colleagues have shared similar tales, even recounting how they sometimes cover their ears and shout at the voices, "Shut up!" Just as I on occasion also have done.

The voices of I.F. land in our psyche very like real voices. They can feel disturbing or they can feel intoxicating. Either way, they are the chatterings of a mind coping as best it can with the outside world.

I would imagine that if your own level of self-trust is high, you hear these voices infrequently. If rather low, you likely hear the voices often. Or if the world's treating you pretty well, giving you important appreciation, you may not much detect the voices for a while. Or if the world's being hard on you, the voices may come fierce and fast. Most probably this varies – sometimes they're quite silent, sometimes vocal indeed.

Being You

Maybe you're still doubtful.

You might buy the idea that, yes, I have this illness that I've named Identity Failure. Perhaps others have it too. But you don't. Your mindvoices, your insecurities, your need for appreciation in some form or many forms … it's all just normal human stuff. That's simply how you were made.

So let's take a closer look – at you. Answer some questions for me, if you would. Honestly. Not the things you believe you should say but what you really feel is true. I'd suggest writing down your responses, if only so you can see them all in front of you at the end. But don't think too long or hard about these, please. Just pick the answers that feel most right to you at the time. Focus on those feelings more than on deliberate thoughts, trusting gut impressions more than intellectual analysis.

OK, then. For starters, please choose the one quality you most value in yourself. This should be an inner quality, not something purely physical. Which aspect of being you feels most meaningful, the single trait you would hate to lose more than any others?

How did you first know that you possessed this trait? Write down one key way you learned this trait was an important part of who you are.

All right, now name the three people still living in the world who are most important in your life?

Of those three other people, pick the one person whose opinion of you is most important to you, please. Whose judgment of you means more than that of anyone else?

Almost done. Just a few more to go.

On a 1 to 10 scale, rate the importance of that person's judgment of you? For this question, 10 is the greatest possible importance and 1 the least possible importance.

Next, some imagination is needed to complete this short quiz: No matter how unlikely, imagine that the person you just named has suddenly and permanently changed their mind about that single most important trait of yours. For reasons of their own, this key person in your life has concluded you aren't nice or smart, not hard-working or not witty. And they make their deep disappointment unmistakably clear. You try hard repeatedly but simply cannot reverse their feelings. Their new opinion is set in concrete.

Briefly write down how you would react to this change. What would you say or do as a result? More importantly, what would you think and feel privately at the deepest levels within you? Remember it's impossible to alter their new attitude about you. What does that new attitude do to you emotionally?

On a 1 to 10 scale, rate the level of emotional pain this person's new attitude causes you. Again, 10 is the greatest possible and 1 is the least possible.

Got all your answers recorded now? Good.

Because here I will venture an informed guess: You did not react well to your most-important-person's change of heart. Not well at all. Their rejection of your best trait felt far more than merely annoying or frustrating or even sad. This new attitude toward you felt darkly wounding. The numbers on those two scales likely make clear the degree of wounding to you. Assuming you summoned enough imagination to conjure the situation in realistic detail, you should better see how profoundly you depend on this person for some form of emotional support. And how very deeply troubling it would be to completely lose their emotional support in this way.

Their psychological support.

Their psychological confirmation of your most important trait.

That, my friend, is Identity Failure.

Fixed Opinions

If you were able to honestly offer quick and simple answers to those questions, you almost surely suffer from Identity Failure.

Why?

Back to those starters, for starters. How did you describe your most important single trait? In one or two words, perhaps? "being nice" or "I'm smart" maybe? Or simply "kindness" or "intelligence" or something else such as "good sense of humor" or possibly "an original creativity"? If so, this suggests your tendency to define yourself through collections of simplistic and irrational identities. Identity poses, one of the prerequisites for Identity Failure. If you expressed your most valuable trait in a more nuanced sentence, good for you. But sorry, it doesn't let you off the hook yet.

The following step takes you outside yourself. By naming one key way you first recognized your most important trait, you may have revealed that at least some of your important sources of self-value came from without, not within. If you're like many of us, you likely wrote down something such as "from my parents" or just "teachers" or "friends." Or maybe "through family members" or "at my elementary school." Or perhaps the names of someone in your youth such as a specific parent or grandparent, sibling or teacher or friend.

The next question is intended to connect you with others actively part of your life today, with the follow-up question then pinpointing a single person whose judgment of you feels vital.

Now come the most telling questions.

Because if any other person's opinion of you feels profoundly important, then you suffer from Identity Failure. This isn't asking how much you care about that person – whether you love them entirely or respect them more than anybody who ever has lived. It asks whose opinion of you is most important. "Whose judgment of you means more than that of anyone else?" The number you attached to this person's feeling about you should say a lot.

Your answers reflect more than your affection. If that number is large, it suggests that you psychologically need another human being's appreciation or approval, respect or validation, their confirmation of your value as an individual. And that you very strongly require this confirmation. This wouldn't happen unless you depended on that person in some form to ease your I.F., your uncertainty about who you are and the value of your existence.

The final questions make this point unmistakable. I hadn't asked whether that person believed in your single most important trait. But if you so much care about their opinion of you, it's highly probable that they are one major source of reinforcement for your belief in that trait. If they are so significant in this way, then removing that person's confirmation from your psyche totally and irrevocably would feel bitter indeed.

Indeed. It might be devastating.

What did you write down in reaction to this imagined loss? Were you angry, perhaps furious? Maybe depressed? Did you cut yourself off from them, ending your relationship somehow or changing the way you normally interacted with them? Did you think less of them? Did you think less of yourself?

One friend who sampled my quiz when I was first writing this chapter told me she would have felt "embarrassed and ashamed." She explained this was true because her respect for that one person was so great. If that person had changed their mind irrevocably, my friend would have felt that the fault must be her own. She'd have doubted herself deeply as soon as a significant outside source of her confidence doubted her.

Now look at that last number, the amount of your pain over losing a key external source of psychological strength. On a 1-to-10 scale, that's a lot of pain in all likelihood.

As with most quizzes of this type, the psychological test isn't foolproof. Failure to answer honestly or imagine fully will skew the results. And some readers may interpret my questions differently than I intended. But I suspect the I.F. quiz will be revealing enough for most of you. Even though it's entirely fiction. Fortunately. Your most-important-person still feels the same about you. Yet if you could muster the imagination to truthfully and vividly inhabit that scenario, you almost surely came away from your answers with a fresh perspective.

Your honesty and your imagination allowed you to peer down through layers of your psyche for a first glimpse of an unfamiliar sight.

The sight of your Identity Failure.

Unless ...

Unless you are that rarest of human specimens, the person who has managed to either avoid or defeat Identity Failure. Among all the people I have known well for more than six decades, I can't think of a single one who would fall into that category. But I have little doubt that such people exist, somewhere. Devout Buddhists might qualify, for example, as an outgrowth of their strenuous psychological training.

I may have met individuals who lived free of I.F. but I didn't know them well enough to get any clear insight into this. Still, after all my travels I've not walked in any land whose people seemed unafflicted by Identity Failure. I have so far visited 53 nations on six continents and talked with folks from a wide variety of cultures. In a Papua New Guinea village where they communicated with drums and killed bats with slingshots for food. In the High Andes of Peru where indigenous people had mingled their DNA and their customs with the descendants of European conquerors. In a riverside tribal settlement in Borneo, in the rustic Water Village of Brunei, in death-obsessed Torajaland on Indonesia's remote Sulawesi Island. The residents of China and

Australia and Jordan, of Italy and Estonia and Romania, of Egypt and Malaysia and Turkey and Argentina and Thailand. As well as people throughout the United States, whose citizens are widely regarded around the world as exuding confidence if not arrogance.

In each place, I looked for any indication that someone appeared entirely indifferent to outside praise or outside criticism.

I haven't found that person yet.

Unfixed Opinions

How would that person have responded to my quiz? How would you if you didn't have Identity Failure?

Very differently than you did. Or so I imagine anyway without looking over your shoulder at the answers.

You might, for instance, have tussled with your choice of a single trait you most value in yourself. The question could have seemed shallow or misleading. And you probably wouldn't have responded with the kind of answers I mentioned above such as "being nice" or "I'm smart" or "good sense of humor." More likely you would think of yourself in nuanced phrases – maybe expressing a key quality with a short sentence: "that I care very deeply about the well-being of other people." Or some such.

The manner in which you first learned about that personal trait may be somewhat telling, another indication that you acquired significant information about your personality from others rather than yourself. Or it may not show this, even if you have Identity Failure. The specifics can vary broadly here.

Yes, you could have named the three most important people in your life as a measurement of how much you care about them. Probably that wasn't the emotional yardstick you used, though it's possible. But by the time we get to the person whose judgment of you means more than that of anyone else, the reader without I.F. might well feel puzzled again. Your affections would be strong, you would hope for the same in return to maintain the most significant of these three relationships. You might even attach a number to that hope if you were bending backwards to cooperate with the quiz. A strict interpretation of those two questions, though, may lead the person without Identity

Failure toward frustration: "What does all this mean? I really don't see things in that way!"

As they were phrased, the final two questions probably would have appeared even more confusing to you – if you weren't afflicted with Identity Failure. You would react much more rationally to this important person's change of heart, with a greater sense of equanimity and much reduced feelings of loss. This self-reliant attitude would be reflected in your responses, assuming you felt it was sensible to respond at all. Perhaps you would have decided to talk with the person simply to gain some explanation for their altered opinion, some closure. Or perhaps not. And the level of your emotional pain almost certainly would be relatively small compared with the misery experienced in such a situation by someone who suffers from I.F. day in and day out.

With Identity Failure greatly diminished or eliminated from your mind, you would see humanity differently. Your humanity and the humanity of others.

Both you and they would appear unique, each thoroughly original rather than a walking set of resemblances to other people. They would not be mere types. Nor would you.

Instead you would emerge to yourself as you are from within, complex and shaded, strengthening and weakening, a human stew flavored by undesirable qualities mixed among those personality strains you prefer. You would understand that everyone else is made the same way. You would be unlikely to judge them or yourself quickly, harshly.

If a friend or family member suddenly rejected you, you would react as a self-confident but caring human being would respond to the troubling shift by someone you love strongly: You would feel hurt and sad, but you would push on and soon recover. You'd have lost a very close friend, in essence, but not a fundamental pillar of your psyche.

Most of all, you would profoundly feel that you are OK and so is everyone else. There's nothing wrong with you. There's nothing wrong with them – except the many problems stemming from their great fear that something is wrong with them.

That's your life as it could be and can be. Without Identity Failure.

Missed Understanding

But it's not how your life is. That's my guess.

I.F. isolates us, focusing our attention on our own immediate emotional needs. We can see this everywhere in the society of my era, here in 20th and 21st Century America. We all know the husband or wife who begins an affair because their spouse "doesn't understand me." Or the employee who quits a good job because the boss doesn't appreciate hard work. Or we watch the highly paid professional athlete who complains that the public doesn't recognize his real contributions to the team. The list is long. The famous singer who feels personally insulted after losing a prestigious music award, the university scientist who feels personally angered by colleague indifference to her finest work, the commercially successful artist who feels personally embittered because his truly original paintings never sell.

Each example hearkens back to that same great quote by William James: "The deepest principle in human nature is the craving to be appreciated." And to my own notion that it's not the deepest principle on display here but merely misguided attempts to cope with the deepest principle: the Fundamental Law of Mind.

The only thing missing from the lives of these people is appreciation, a deeper understanding by others of who they are, whether personally or professionally.

Why? Why do these people care what others think?

Why do you?

We're all much like that unhappily philandering husband, whose impatience seethes while waiting for his wife to stop talking so he can complain about his tough day at the office. Waiting, without listening to a word she says. This husband already is aware of every detail he's so eager to share. He knows the pace was hectic, the supervisor unreasonable, the co-worker incompetent. He won't gain a grain of information from the exchange. Yet venting about the trials he endured all day is the only thing that will help him feel better tonight.

Until his wife's inattention demonstrates again that she's no more interested in his day than he is interested in hers. When his wife won't provide the appreciation he craves, the husband soon finds it elsewhere. And on this goes ... Misunderstanding, self-obsession, damaged relationships – and the desperate search for someone who can deeply know "me." Me, me and more me, just as I've experienced it.

And as you have too.

Ask yourself why you feel such a throbbing need to talk about insignificant details you already know. What could you possibly gain? Other than someone's understanding, which is to say confirmation that you are right. Yes, your workdays really are as crazy as you think and, yes, you really are forced to cope with much distress to pay the family's bills. Remember that you observe this struggle firsthand daily. You know from direct experience the emotional and physical toll of your job. The reality should not be in doubt. But somehow you're not quite certain about the difficulties you must overcome at work until some other person agrees with you. It's neither sympathy nor empathy you really seek – it's validation.

You are battling your Identity Failure.

I've long observed in myself and others that talking is among the major forms of identity validation for many of us. We speak to elicit affirming comments or grunts, gestures or expressions – or at the least, silence that we can interpret as agreement. For the desperate talker, lack of argument can qualify as a form of appreciation when necessary.

Those unwelcome folks who talk incessantly have learned to rely on this emotional tool heavily, ironically forcing nearly everyone within earshot to tune them out much of the time. The many silences of agreement they hear instead are merely silences of absolute boredom.

Conversely, some people rarely talk at all. And oddly, it's for the same reason: to manage the Fundamental Law of Mind's demand for feelings of self-value in a person afflicted with Identity Failure. These individuals aren't looking to share anything with most people, whether insignificant details or significant insights. Why are they so reluctant to discuss things they deeply believe? To contribute, to offer experiences and opinions and ideas?

And if you're like this, why are you?

It's a style of ego-protection, that's why. Again, I've seen this in myself at times and in other people many times. When I have something valuable to say but don't say it, that's because I'm afraid of the reaction in some way. I believe in advance they won't understand or won't agree or won't see me in a flattering light after I utter the words. And why do I care about that? Because their lack of appreciation for my comments would make me doubt myself. It would strengthen my Identity Failure.

Those people greatly lacking self-confidence often appear shy for this reason, it seems to me. They are like my friend, Delia, who tries to live so small. As I wrote about Delia, "Identity Failure has made her what she is by preventing her from becoming all that she might be." So too for the other quiet ones morbidly afraid to open their mouths.

I.F. also accounts for our strong preference to chat with like-minded people. Most everyone is like this, with the exception of some professors, scientists, artists and others who gain feelings of self-value from lively intellectual engagement. Debate is part of their culture and a source of validation.

Again, examine this so-common, so-natural preference for affirmation during conversation. Why are we like this? Why are you?

Simple. It's because we're all so uncertain of ourselves due to Identity Failure.

If you weren't looking for outside confirmation of your identity poses, you might well feel inclined to seek out conversationalists with views very unlike your own. What do we learn from talking to people who parrot our ideas and harbor our values? How is this stimulating? How can it bring us growth, intellectually and emotionally?

It can't, at least not when we're in total agreement.

But it can make us feel darned good. For a few brief brief brief moments, mutual appreciation through conversation can quiet the voices in our mind, muffling I.F. among our friendly chatter with agreeable folks.

Fundamentally How

I believe you and I and just about everybody else are sick, literally ill.

The why is Identity Failure. But what about the how?

How does this illness settle upon the minds of human beings almost universally? How did I catch the I.F. virus?

How did you?

Just think about the way you were raised. Whatever the specifics of your upbringing, or mine or anyone else's, similar lessons were taught to almost all of us. And learned absolutely, taken deeply to heart without our awareness.

From the beginning, for instance, you learned your own judgment is untrustworthy. Particularly your judgment about yourself. Everyone knew better than you at the very start. Not only did they know what you should do, what you should say, what you should eat, what you should think. They knew what you should or shouldn't touch, how you should or shouldn't play, when you should or shouldn't sleep. And much more. What's good about you and what's bad. What kinds of people on this planet are worthy and what kinds aren't – and how to be like the worthy ones, whatever that meant in the specific. Your parents and siblings and friends may have encouraged you to be kindly. Or they may have urged you to be a bully. Outgoing and dynamic, reserved and isolated, humorous or serious or intellectual or athletic or … We learn many of our most valued types early on, the identity poses we will assume as we grow up.

And as we do grow up, we absorb many other lessons that worsen the Identity Failure infection.

As a child or teenager, you probably felt good about yourself from time to time in some comfortable situation. Protected by this sense of relaxation, you may have said or done something spontaneously in your buoyant enthusiasm – only to find that another person made you feel it somehow was wrong to say or do this. Or bad. Shameful or embarrassing or stupid or crude or whatever the fault. If that person was very important to you, such as a parent, their reaction especially may have cut well into the bone. You apparently were being too much somehow in that moment, or perhaps not enough in some other way. So you began to further lose trust in yourself: "They know more about me than I know." That was the feeling, the impression left on your psyche.

It's easy to spot the adult spillover from these unsettling lessons. This happens all the time. A woman or man abandons their continual self-censorship in a public expression of the spontaneous and real. Hearty laughter, a loud comment, an unorthodox opinion – followed immediately by self-censorship reimposed. They may glance around the room, cover their mouth, blush or even apologize. And you can almost hear them thinking, "Was I too loud?" "Did I sound stupid?" "I hope that wasn't offensive!"

Was I too much or too little? And did people notice?

It's all one of the very common faces of Identity Failure.

Later in your youth and on into adulthood, you probably gathered much additional evidence for the unreliability of your opinions about you. This process takes place at deep levels in nearly all of us, I believe, experience interpreted and stored as vericepts that then form into large powerful nexes with huge amounts of emotion.

For example, you probably recognized that other people sometimes really had understood meaningful things about you that you'd missed. Or that you had intentionally ignored. It's another lesson that reasonably mature persons typically acquire. Maybe a friend noted that your comment to a mutual acquaintance was hurtful. But you hadn't known how harsh your words sounded to others until ... Ah yes, you could see your rudeness now – you had been caught up in the discussion's momentary heat. Or maybe a high school teacher realized your richest talents might best carry you toward industrial chemistry rather than a professional football career. Ah yes, you could perceive the truth of your teacher's insight now – you had been misled by your passion for sport. Or maybe your parents warned that your new romantic partner would not make a good spouse. Ah yes, you could acknowledge the disastrous marriage as divorce neared now – you had mistaken a sexual attraction for a perfect lifelong match.

You sense my drift, no doubt. Swept along everyday life among currents of intense emotion and vast ignorance, we all make judgments about ourselves, our lives and others that are simply wrong. Sometimes people around us can see our errors before we do. And I think this contributes to an overall feeling of mistrust in our judgments, particularly judgments about "me." Actually, though, I believe these mistakes are most always situational on our part, much like those few examples just offered. And the information possessed by another person about us is extremely limited. Our specific misjudgments don't mean others know more about us than we know about ourselves, not in deeper and more significant ways. Only you can know the truth of you, knowledge accessible from within not without. But the conclusions you've drawn from these misjudgments reinforced your sense of an unreliable self-understanding. Someone knew more about you than you did. And this contributed to your need for external confirmation of your individual value. It strengthened your Identity Failure.

Similarly, I believe we almost all come to feel that outside opinion is needed to keep us in line, morally. After so many years of worrying about other people's judgment of us, we develop the conviction that their praise and blame are required to prevent our running amok. By then we've experienced this form of inner guidance countless times, instant ethical judgments that censor our thoughts or emotions, demanding that we avoid some comments and actions, make other comments or take other actions – because of what someone would think otherwise. When this happened to you, you interpreted these experiences automatically through vericepts that joined powerful nexes. And those vericepts in essence told you, "The opinion of others is my moral enforcer. Without it, who knows what I might think or feel or say or do!"

You live constantly with the same sense I had endured for most of my life: Left to my desires alone, I could possibly think or feel or say or do terrible terrible things. I may break the law. I may harm someone or even harm myself. Anything was possible. Thoughts about such terrible terrible undeniably terrible things had flitted through my mind so often that those notions eventually frightened me. I sometimes felt so angry I wanted to grab and hit someone. I sometimes felt so attracted I wanted to grab and kiss someone. I had been tempted to run the endless red traffic light because I'd grown impatient or to cancel an important meeting because I wanted to go swimming. Etcetera … And each time this happened, my ultimate decision to do the responsible thing included strong worry about the judgment of others. So I formed the belief that outside opinion about me is necessary to keep these irrational impulses in check.

But it's not. I've learned this too is a serious error. I don't need a fear of other people's judgments about me to live as a moral and responsible human being. And you don't either. Not at all. A lifetime's learning to the contrary, though, is one more important "how" of I.F.

You also may well never have learned the distinction in your mind between wishful thoughts and reliable judgments. This can seem trivial at first glance but it's decidedly not trivial. Confusion about that difference contributes to Identity Failure.

As with most of us, the clutter of your conscious psyche includes fantasies that may revolve around unlikely achievements or longshot relationships or the plan for world peace that just popped to mind. Whatever it might be. You alone may be the star of your imagination or the spotlight could extend to friends or colleagues or lovers at your side. Or perhaps even focus on a close family member such as a child whose glory you would share. These fantasies might be about today's accomplishment or tomorrow's legacy. Future scenarios that you'd like fulfilled or past scenarios that you'd like relived. Everybody has these, the daydreams of our personal Walter Mitty. It's part of the charm and the excitement of human imagination.

But this becomes a problem when we don't distinguish between our pleasant fantasies of what-could-be and our profound feelings of what-is. For me it is a highly significant distinction that I had to teach myself over many years.

Perhaps it was for you as well. Or perhaps you've not yet recognized it.

Because all those pleasant fantasies about good things you would merely like to happen can appear very much like all those profound feelings about who you are and what you could accomplish in the world. How can you tell the difference? And if you can't tell the difference, how do you judge whether your notion is only wishful thinking? Outside confirmation of course. That's what you've learned over time. Someone else must validate your judgments about yourself and your abilities, what you have achieved and what you feel sure you yet could do. Otherwise it might be just a daydream. You have swallowed another lesson that you can't trust the things you believe about you. The amount of that distrust correlates with the severity of your Identity Failure.

It can seem a tricky business at the start. The fantasies and the feelings all are part of your inner world, both experiences typically grand and enjoyable in their way.

Which is which?

One moment you feel utterly convinced that you could write that novel you've conceived over the past two years, the next moment you feel certain that your nation's highest leader would want to be your close friend if once you met. But examine these two experiences more closely. If the novelist desire is based in reality, it is persistent. You've been aware of that same feeling many times during those two years, over and over. Without doubt, you can write. You feel this intensely. And without doubt, you can write this novel. Recalling those words of Ralph Waldo Emerson, your feeling is like "that gleam of light which flashes across (your) mind from within." A sudden and clear insight, something deep and powerful. But your compatibility fantasy about a famous politician is another thing entirely. If you can dissect that sensation in your mind, the feeling is shallow and insubstantial, not deep and powerful. On a host of levels, it seems to you like what it is. Wishful thinking. But your aspiration to write a book, this feels rich, this feels whole, this feels real. It is an outgrowth of the complex evolving human being who's the genuine you.

I suspect that many of us never grasp this subtle psychological distinction. And the misunderstanding leads to more deep confusion about who we are and what we should do, what we want and what we value. We ignore our independent judgments, casting about outside us for the big answers in our lives. We've learned not to have faith in our own mind.

Others know more about you than you know – and only others can help you discern what's real and what's unreal in your psyche, what's good and what's bad. The result is greater dependence on exterior confirmation of your value, more strengthening of the I.F. virus in you.

Our learned self-mistrust appears to lead many people to suffer from a related problem, easily morphing into a terror that we might be insane. I've experienced this personally more times than I'd prefer to confess: Among my deepest horrors is an abject fear of losing my mind. And looking back, I have struggled with it most directly and miserably during periods of my life when Identity Failure has been at its worst. The more unsure of myself generally, the more unsure of my general sanity.

This came upon me as a persistent series of intense uncertainties. At these times I couldn't escape the feeling that my moment-to-moment judgments were so unreliable that I shouldn't place any trust in my otherwise strong sense of sanity. Yeah I felt sane, but who could tell for sure?

I mention it in this context because I've picked up clues over the decades, many strong indications that insanity is a nightmarish terror for lots of people. Yeah they feel sane, but who can tell for sure? I believe one root of this is our self-mistrust: Others know more about us as individuals than we know and only others can help us each discern what's real and what's unreal in our psyche. The good and the bad.

Once you buy into this idea, feeling crazy isn't a long stretch for most of us. Who are you to imagine you could write a novel? It's ridiculous! You've only tinkered with a few short stories, all unpublished. Nobody has paid any attention to your writing. Even your family seems bored when they read your work. Without outside confirmation, you feel like any decision to launch into page one of your novel would be nuts. Everyone will think you're mad, especially you.

That's the sort of uncertainty I'm talking about. And once again, it only fuels more Identity Failure. To avoid this feeling, you may give up on your novel-writing entirely. Or you may become increasingly desperate for someone to validate your perception of yourself as a novelist. Lacking that, you might become seriously depressed or angry, deeply bitter or resigned or who knows what. You may even start to wonder if you're truly going mad.

But you aren't.

You're engulfed by a spiraling downforce of Identity Failure. You wonder more each day what's wrong with you. Why are you like this suddenly? Why can't you get your feelings under control?

As that all happens, another portion of your psyche becomes stronger as well, almost certainly without any knowledge this is happening to you.

There is some part of you that wants to die.

Will To Die

I watched it happen to both parents the last few years of their lives.

And horrifyingly, I watched it in me… for a few years.

In my mind and, I believe, in the minds of my parents before their deaths, life began to feel less and less livable. Competing against the innate will to live, a will to die was building.

For me the feeling was, yes, horrifying. Based on all I could glean, I think it was for them too.

After lengthy observation and reflection, I've reached the conclusion that this will to die is a byproduct of Identity Failure. Whether entirely or in large part, I can't say for sure. Within my own mind, at least, I.F. seems the most significant cause.

And I feel sufficiently certain about this phenomenon that I couldn't escape the need to include it here. I believe recognizing our will to die offers one more urgent reason for each of us to accept the reality of Identity Failure. And to find ways to overcome it.

The self-centered perspective on our lives contributes to I.F. and in turn feeds a will to die.

During the roughly five years immediately before I began to effectively practice Rational Faith, I was troubled for some good chunk of most days by a sense that I might be dying. I didn't understand what this was really all about for a long time. I knew only that I often felt overwhelmed by anxiety and a welter of physical symptoms accompanied by a terrible fear of impending death – and I recognized that the cause of all this was psychological. My conflict again concerned the world's response to my independent creative work. That much I knew. But I couldn't put my finger on a still-deeper emotional cause that I suspected.

I began to understand this deeper cause very clearly on one of those unending black nights I wrote about earlier in the book. As my heart raced and fluttered uncontrollably for hours and swells of anxiety pulsed through me, I genuinely felt that I was on the precipice of imminent death. Any moment I might die. I cried and I prayed and I repeated the words: "I want to live!"

But I was struck later by those words. Why would I say them? Who had ever suggested I didn't want to live? Yet there were those same four words, an urgent nightcall again and again on my lips.

I suffered through several similar nights before this misery was done, teetering along that same precipice for hours among tears and prayers. "I want to live!" More than anything else I wanted to complete this book and create this philosophy but I prayed to live for many years more as well. Live for as long as possible, at least assuming I could recover my health and continue to work productively. I did want to live.

Afterwards teasing apart the complexities of these black nights, I started to recognize that something was going on far far below the surface that I'd earlier refused to face. Something so deep and so painful and so, yes, horrifying that I'd tried my best to keep it from my awareness.

Some part of me now wanted to die. A will to die as a counterpoint to my will to live.

The main cause? Identity Failure. My I.F. had grown so fiercely powerful and pervasive that everyday living had become a trial at best, a torment at worst.

By this time two decades of incidents over my creative work had piled up inside my head, one adding to the next, incidents of indifference or misunderstanding or rejection. Incidents when I had felt underestimated and humiliated and painfully unsure about my proper place in the literary world. During the latter portion of that same time, I was struggling to give birth to a hopeful philosophy of living and an inspiring organization to carry these ideas to adults and kids, the creation of Rational Faith and founding of the Humanity Project. Of course this paradox only heightened my pain. One part of me felt more openly caring and loving than ever just as another part was awash in an acidic rage. I could sense half of me flowering as the other half withered.

I hadn't known about identity poses for much of that 20 years. And so I had felt an intense need for outside confirmation of my most valuable identities as I viewed them, validation for all the Bobs that I knew would be required one day to write this book. Bob-the-writer, Bob-the-artist, Bob-the-genius among others. Yet I wasn't getting that validation. I did press on with my work anyway, but only by isolating myself as a buffer to prevent the world from shattering my confidence. Whether it was 15% or 20% or some other amount of external confirmation that I still required by then, I quite apparently still required it. Badly. Over the days and the years, over the months and the decades of this accumulating psychological pain, my will to die expanded into a greater emotional force unbeknownst to me. A force so great that at last I couldn't ignore it.

During the blackest minutes of those black black nights, I finally had to remind myself that I overwhelmingly wanted to live. Because by then some frighteningly large portion of me really didn't want to live at all.

Will Versus Will

This clash between my natural will to live and my acquired will to die had its origins in the Fundamental Law of Mind. I believe this basic law determines much about all our lives. Why we do what we do, how we go about doing it.

The Fundamental Law of Mind: "Individuals interpret experience to create the weakest possible emotional resistance to the strongest possible feelings that their existence is valuable to them at this moment in this world." It's what makes us each tick at the most fundamental level of our psyche. We are in a perpetual struggle to feel that our own existence is valuable to us in the here and now.

But it's possible to steam that law down to an even simpler essence. An existential question recurring continuously in our minds, something that I've named the Fundamental Question.

"Is my life worth living?"

That's really what it's all about for us as human beings, I believe. Our efforts to answer "yes" to this question can account for much of our creativity and our destructiveness, our health and our sickness, our glories and our tragedies. The inspiring Parthenon and the savage Colosseum, a beloved Lincoln and a hated Hitler, the birth of democracy and the institution of slavery, the uplifting and the depraved and a great deal of what was in-between too. We have found our answers in wealth and in power, in poverty and humility. In war and in peace. In art and science and industry, in garish ostentation and in deliberate ignorance and in selfish commercialism. Our reactions to that deep question are as individual as each of us.

"Is my life worth living?"

We may or may not ever think these words to ourselves. That's not what I mean. The question underlies our lives at every moment as the necessary result of the Fundamental Law of Mind. The Fundamental Question simply comes to us as the essential consequence of our mind's deepest workings. It is the subtext to all we think or feel or say or do.

I've asked myself whether I'm wrong about this, just as I've challenged all my ideas and theories repeatedly. Could this Fundamental Question merely reflect my own sufferings? Maybe my ferocious personal crisis thrust this question on me, but others living with less emotional turbulence aren't troubled by that doubt. I don't think so. Upon careful thought, I feel that my extended inner troubles allowed me to scrape through so many layers of my psyche that at last I hit the bedrock bottom of it all. This Fundamental Question squares with the rest of my experience too, experiences with my personal and professional life as well as experiences with other people. And not only my parents. Since I was in my 30s anyway, I've often repeated the common observation that "everyone needs a reason to get out of bed." I still believe that's true. And to me, it hints at this core question.

In my view, the will to die does not exist as some intrinsic part of our humanity. I believe it's there only as the end product of massive accumulations of psychological and physical pain. Unlike the will to live, which I believe is the automatic product of the Fundamental Law of Mind. We naturally search for valuable reasons to exist. We want to reply affirmatively to the Fundamental Question: "Is my life worth living?"

In my vocabulary, we deepwant to live. Until we don't.

Again, I can't emphasize enough that I think the will to die usually is interred underneath countless layers of mind. Without any way for me to confirm this just now, I would imagine most people possess little if any sense of that emotional force until their later years. Like my parents, we become aware of a growing fatigue. My father especially little by little lost interest in things he'd cared about, activities he'd enjoyed. Watching him the last half decade of his long life reminded me of looking at an old black-and-white photograph gradually fading out to white. Much of my dad slowly vanished. I don't think that was a purely physical process. I think it was overwhelmingly psychological.

Despite the hidden nature of our will to die among most of us, you nonetheless may have made its acquaintance from rare time to time. Ask yourself if you've experienced moments when something happened that made you briefly think your life was pointless. Ever felt like just giving up completely? Entertained the strong feeling that death would seem a relief?

If so, you have sampled the will to die, tasted some of its essential flavors.

It is a bitter mouthful.

You, You And More You

Before this chapter, I've necessarily been writing mostly about me. Me, me and more me, as I've said. I believed that only a concrete-solid foundation of empirical personal experience would qualify me in your mind to offer credible observations about you. And about all of us.

As the Emerson quote at the top of Chapter 8 noted, "He then learns that in going down into the secrets of his own mind he has descended into the secrets of all minds."

As hard as I had tried for so many years, I could never shake my absolute conviction that this was what I'd done. For at least the first 20 of those years, I had no intention whatever of sharing this experience – because I thought no one would believe a word of it. How could anybody else know about my uncountable hours of painstaking self-observation and all the meticulous theorizing and testing and confirmation, something I've now carried out for more than 45 years? Why would anyone accept this is what I've actually done with my life? I have only the slightest formal training in psychology and philosophy, without any university degree to show for it. Who would give credence to so many unconventional ideas offered by an unknown source?

That's why I also tried to be painstaking and meticulous in laying out the key psychological details as best I could for you. I hoped a fair, openminded reading of my experiences and ideas would convince you that I might just be on to something valuable here. Valuable for me, valuable for you. And valuable for others too, perhaps.

To the extent possible, I have tried to make this chapter about you, you and more you – and after that, the book will be about us.

All of us, each of us.

As I suffer from Identity Failure, so do you. And so do they. We each grapple with the Fundamental Law of Mind much more miserably than necessary because we look outside us for confirmation of our identity poses.

You believe this type of person is you and that type of person is you and the other type of person is you as well, Poses X and Y and Z, all fixed and simple identities. If I agree with your belief and tell you so, you feel pretty good. For a while, for a while. Until someone else disagrees or someone else agrees but doesn't tell you. Then you don't feel so good.

And then your contest with I.F. likely takes a similar course to mine. Without knowing it, you grow more and more desperate for someone or something to make you feel your life is worth living. Not only other people but outside events take on emotional significance. That's a losing game for sure. The more you connect the value of your existence to anything beyond yourself, the more tortured you are sure to feel. When everything becomes all about your personal wants and personal needs, you will endure great pain in this life because … well, think about it. For you as for any of us, so much of the world isn't what you want it to be so much of the time.

Your increasing awareness of dissatisfaction with others and the world-in-general provides fuel for your will to die. Things over which you have no control at all help determine how strongly you want to live.

They become part of your answer to the repeated question: "Is my life worth living?"

An attitude of psychological self-reliance and a commitment to helping others can eliminate much of this pressure. Learning to have faith in your own experience, sharing that experience unconditionally, recognizing the great value you gain from this shared approach to daily living – these are among the core goals of Rational Faith, as you will soon see.

I've labored to build the philosophy atop a granite groundwork of the Fundamental Law of Mind and Fundamental Question specifically to help cure Identity Failure. The philosophy flows as a necessary and logical consequence of the psychology. Without firmly grasping the foundational concepts, you can't understand Rational Faith. Like learning the basic mechanics of a car before ever starting the motor, as I wrote earlier, Rational Faith requires learning the deeper mechanics of mind.

Your Good Life – Or Not

Let's try a short and simple thought experiment. This may help me to make a point.

Imagine you live in a world where every other human being is homeless. Not like today's homeless population whose sad condition at least may include a shopping cart of belongings. Every other person you see is primitive, wandering for food and sleeping on the open ground.

But you have a home. A mud hut. To your knowledge, you are the only person who possesses shelter from the elements. Your mud hut offers enough room to stand, to walk several paces, to sleep comfortably, to build fires for cooking and warmth. Your food supply is reliable and ample. Compared to every other single member of humanity, you live like an emperor.

How would you feel? Does your life seem worth living?

Now. Imagine a quite different scenario.

Every other human being on the planet earth owns a lovely modern home. You? You still live in a mud hut.

As far as you can know, you are the lone person who resides in a dirty miniscule dwelling exposed on one side to wind and rain and snow. You see all around you the luxurious conditions of your neighbors. They have air conditioning and heat, swimming pools and patios, fully equipped kitchens stocked with food, bedrooms with thick mattresses and silk sheets. Everybody appears to live like royalty – except you.

How would you feel? Does your life seem as worth living as before?

Reflect for a few moments on your reactions to those two situations. Nothing about your own life had changed from one to the other. Only the relative poverty or wealth of all the other people around you.

Why would you feel so differently? Why was life so good in your mud hut ... and then so bad?

You are viewing these scenarios through the windowframe of your life as it is now. Your contrasting responses to these hypotheticals suggest how much you judge the value of your existence based on the outside world.

Your status, your power, your possessions, the attitude of others about you all play into your assessment of your life's worth. As the mud hut owner in Scenario 1, you sensed that you'd feel special. Important. Envied and respected and appreciated by your fellows. You would live as You-the-rich-person, an identity pose reinforced by the surrounding society a hundred times daily. As the mud hut owner in Scenario 2, you'd feel just the opposite. Remarkably unspecial and unimportant. And surely much unenvied. Living in a hovel among opulence, you would find yourself tirelessly reminded that you're nowhere as valuable as you know yourself to be. You deserved better, didn't you? Life was being unfair to you. Some of your most important identity poses would find no confirmation whatever from the world.

The mud hut was no less comfortable when everyone else lived with electricity and running water and their many other conveniences. Whether comparably elevated or comparably lowly, your lifestyle was exactly the same.

But you almost certainly didn't see it that way. Hardly anyone would.

And that's important to understand.

You were able to recognize that life as the mud-dweller in a wealthy world wouldn't feel much like living to you. The thought experiment helped you once more to connect with your Identity Failure.

Final Questions

I've asked you a lot of questions in this chapter. Questions that I hoped you would take time to answer seriously and truthfully. So let me conclude this chapter all about you with several more questions. Not a quiz, but an analysis I'd like to suggest.

I would like you simply to compare your own experiences with mine.

Consider what I'd detailed in the first eight chapters, particularly my feelings and my reactions, the things I had believed necessary to living a good life. Recall how I placed so much vital importance on everyone's opinion of me – and the ways even the smallest outside frustrations could loom inside my head. Red lights and baseball scores and news stories often acquired a personal significance far beyond anything sensibly justified. I warmed immediately to any hint of appreciation, chilled to suggestions of criticism. And whatever seemed annoying to me right now soon created the strong urge to escape. Even a mildly unpleasant picnic with a good friend.

My existence was outside in. The quality of my moment-to-moment inner life was inextricably connected to outside people and external events, both small and large. Remember some of my stories, if you would.

Then ask yourself this question: Does your experience resemble my experience in important ways? True, the details probably differ. Red lights may not irritate you. Or fly-filled picnics. You may require less praise and appreciation and confirmation than I had needed for most of my life.

But are the broad outlines of our lives similar? Is your existence outside in too?

And this question: Do my experiences and explanations make sense to you?

Are you prone to self-doubt as well as episodes of inexplicable fear and anger? And are the folks you know intimately also prone to these feelings? Do you have psychological buttons others can push, areas of emotional vulnerability that people or happenings sometimes trigger to make you feel bad? Do your friends and family have buttons of their own?

Are you and most people you know basically insecure in some manner? Whatever the specifics may be … Do others seem easily offended, easily hurt, responding quickly and unpleasantly to perceived slights? Do you?

When you had read the Einstein quote at the beginning of this chapter, did you smile the smile of recognition, immediately sensing both its charm and its wisdom? As the good professor wrote long ago, "A question that sometimes drives me hazy: am I or are the others crazy?" Why does that seem so true?

What quality in human beings feels both so intrinsic to our character and so utterly mad? Does Identity Failure seem to account for this quality?

I'm expecting you, by now my loyal reader, to examine your life through the microscope of my experiences. As honestly as possible, do you detect an underlying commonality among the more superficial contrasts between us?

Then ask yourself these questions, please, from an intellectual standpoint: Do my theories offer a more detailed, integrated, coherent and sensible explanation of your life than other ideas you've come across? Your life and the lives of people you know, your feelings and your thoughts and your motivations? And theirs?

And does the hidden structure of human nature as I've described it look something like the structure of all nature as you understand it? The construction from small things to large things, for instance, and the fundamental simplicity among the outer complexity: vericepts collecting into nexes, with nexes combining into larger and larger units that emit energy in the form of emotions – and the stronger force of emotion winning the conflict. Identity poses and pose-weakeners and pose-strengtheners and the rest, but in the end all of it governed by the simplicity of a Fundamental Law of Mind and a Fundamental

Question.

Is that how life functions at a profound level?

Do my ideas feel to you like wild-eyed fantasy or carefully observed science? Does what you've read now appear to be crazy ... or insightful?

And just a few questions more, please:

Have you ever sensed yourself being driven uncontrollably toward a state of being that you hoped intensely to avoid, unable to escape your own irrational behavior or some destructive pattern of thoughts or feelings? If so, you've experienced psychogravity, just as I described.

Have you ever noticed how much you wanted something that seemed very important, only to learn later you had really wanted something else entirely all along? If so, you've experienced deepwanting as I explained it.

Have you ever enjoyed a buoyant sense of vigor-renewed after a prolonged period of emotional turmoil, an enthusiasm for daily life that seemed to fill you again like a strong zephyr that billows a sail? If so, you've experienced the will to live as I've detailed this.

I believe these experiences are crucial for our species to understand more fully than we have because only this kind of self-knowledge can help to free us. To liberate humanity from our slavish obsession with outside opinion and events, from the damaging affliction of Identity Failure. Up to now, I don't think we've quite put our collective finger on the basic problem. If we had, why does it continue?

And it does continue. All around every one of us, all day and every day.

As Identity Failure has shaped my life and yours, it also has molded the past and present of our human race in ways that have yet to be widely perceived. It has severely limited our potential and seriously damaged our relationships, individually and as a society. It has generated con artists and murderers, powergrabbers and warmongers, sadists and racists, masochists and invalids.

No single force alone is responsible for crime or for war, of course, or for anything else in our lives, in my judgment. Everything happens as the result of a complex of causes. But some forces are more important than others. Some forces are dominant, exerting a fundamental influence on events.

I think Identity Failure is one of those, the desperate search for outside validation to make us individually feel our life is worth living.

Whether manifested as the Colosseum or Hitler or the institution of slavery, Identity Failure has served a formative function in our destructiveness. Then as now, "the craving to be appreciated" observed by William James explains a large portion of our history as it does a large portion of our everyday lives.

As an article of my faith, my Rational Faith, I believe absolutely that this can change. Individuals are capable of learning to become more psychologically self-reliant, more rational, more self-trusting, more helpful to others. I've seen it in myself and others. I know it is possible.

But humanity hasn't yet escaped the massive power that Identity Failure exerts on us. Not yet.

Not by a long shot.

Chapter 10: A World Of Me

> "Let us consider that we are all partially insane. It will explain us to each other; it will unriddle many riddles; it will make clear and simple many things which are involved in haunting and harassing difficulties and obscurities now."
>
> Mark Twain

"Don't think money does everything or you are going to end up doing everything for money." Voltaire

What explains the lust for money?

Most of us have never given this a thought. Why does money seem so profoundly important to nearly everyone? Not the rational need for money, I mean, but the obsessive need that at its most intense can rival any addictive craving for another pill or one more cocktail.

In our society money is a necessity that allows us to live decently and healthfully, to raise children constructively, to enjoy a self-reliant existence. Yes, the balanced sensible desire for sufficient money to achieve fulfillment of our best qualities and highest goals is part of a life that also is balanced and sensible. We require money.

But the question is, Why do so many people so often crave so much money? Money beyond our needs, money beyond our wants, money beyond the spending of many lifetimes. Most folks don't dream of enough money, we fantasize about excessive money. And in my experience, those who already possess excessive money want nothing more than to possess it in greater excess. Much greater excess.

Today and throughout recorded history, some human beings have proven they will do anything for money, anything at all. Murder for money is common in our species. Cheating, lying, deceiving for money is the stuff of the everyday right up to this moment. Homo sapiens launches wars for money. Enslaves cultures for money. Betrays spouses and parents and siblings and friends, risks prolonged imprisonment, turns traitor to its homelands, all for money. In my time, corporate leaders frequently have valued profit over the lives of those who use their products and services, allowing known dangers to pollute the marketplace.

Why?

What explains the lust for money?

No doubt the warmongers and slaveowners, the murderers and thieves and traitors, and perhaps even the corporate leaders, can offer their explanations, their justifications. Haven't they always? They were extracting resources for their people or sustaining a vital economic system, they were making revenge on someone who had unfairly wronged them, they were honoring a responsibility to company stockholders. But in the end their justifications annoy like the clink of a cracked wine goblet. There is something unsound about the sound.

And I believe that's because all their justifications are specious. They're phony. As so often, Mark Twain approached much closer to the truth than most when he observed that "we are all partially insane."

The cause of that insanity is Identity Failure.

"Too many people spend money they haven't earned, to buy things they don't want, to impress people that they don't like." Will Rogers

That lust for money is among the more obvious expressions of I.F.

During my years as an investigative reporter I learned to look for two main influences whenever probing someone who apparently had succumbed to corruption: money and sex. Sometimes, of course, these two are both in evidence and in any case the first can easily buy the second of them. Those are the twin forces strong enough to entice some people irresistibly to abandon their most important principles and values, promises and vows. The amount of money may be staggering or insignificant, the sexual rewards bacchanalian or modest. But at the time it all felt sufficiently powerful to lure responsible adults toward their doom.

And that is because both money and sex offer us such immense feelings of individual value. Cash and caresses are sought-after commodities in this world precisely because they temporarily can counteract our self-confusion, the terror that our lives may not be worth living. A sizable balance in the bank and a sinful partner in the bed can make existence appear pretty indeed ... for a while.

Since the next chapter will focus solely on the role of Identity Failure in romance and sex, let me stick here to money as an entry point for my discussion of I.F.'s disastrous effects on our society.

Money is a pose-strengthener.

Or more accurately, the irrational craving for money is a quest for one of our most effective pose-strengtheners: the feeling of having abundant money. Naturally, some of us don't suffer from this appetite for cash. I've already written about my own irrational relationship with money, the exact opposite problem: a fear of money. I am afraid money will corrupt me too, just as it has so many others. As a result I've quite skillfully if mostly unconsciously managed to avoid having very much of it. I've deepwanted just enough money to get by.

But clearly that's not the norm. Certainly it's not what I see around me all the time.

I see too many people spending money they haven't earned to buy things they don't want to impress people they don't like, just as Will Rogers noted. I've even done this myself now and then, despite my suspicion of the almighty dollar. I watch individuals I know well who gladly devote two hours of their lives to travel significant distances in order to save $1.73 on toothpaste or some such thing. And it's always a $1.73 that they don't need to save. I've witnessed excruciating cheapness of a variety I hadn't imagined possible, every bit of it distinctly crazy. I befriended an elderly multi-millionaire who delighted in buying her glassware at the dollar store, then re-used her tea bags in those glasses. I've observed owners of significant property who nonetheless feared impoverished old age, squeezing every dime so tightly they could have wrung juice from it. I've often witnessed financially comfortable folks eating cheaply made food they didn't want because it was a great bargain. And I once stayed as an invited guest at a friend's home overseas for more than a week without ever being offered a single morsel of food that I didn't buy myself.

Over the years I've developed a great distaste for cheapness of this sort. For cheapness of any sort, really, except when demanded by economic circumstances. The misers not only lose many opportunities to help others, they become limited by an emotional shallowness and a warped value system that accompany an overfondness for money. I admire the generous among us, especially generosity by those of modest means. I take it as a genuine sign of character.

On a much broader scale, I see profitable companies constantly weakening the value of their goods. What was sturdy metal now is flimsy plastic. What was rich leather now is an unconvincing imitation. The ounces of food in a container keep shrinking as the price inches up. This kind of thing is everywhere in my society. Even more broadly, vast segments of that same society are treated unequally. And badly. The profit motive underlies racial disadvantages that permeate my culture, whether in job opportunities, health care, legal protection, political representation, media coverage or nearly anything else you can name of wide significance. Complex systems remain in place in the United States that discriminate against blacks, Hispanics and other people of color, systems established by white men long ago to benefit their pocketbooks.

What is it about Identity Failure that makes people eager to do so many destructive things for money, whether destructive to others or in some fashion self-destructive?

It is the relatively simple equation that dominates their lives: Money = lifevalue. This isn't the value of things but rather the value of a feeling. Year by year, vericept by vericept, these people have formed powerful nexes that push them toward feeling that money makes their days worth living. As always, the specifics vary person to person. For some, accumulated money represents a major measurement of their life's value though not the only one. For others, money overwhelms any alternative means of finding value in their existence. To be rich is to live a valuable life.

"If you want to know what God thinks of money, just look at the people he gave it to." Dorothy Parker

The confusion of money with personal worth is an understandable error for anyone to make in our world. Money is a tangible, measurable unit of value that everyone wants. We all agree it's valuable. And money is a form of value that's easily compared among us – it's usually not difficult to tell which people have more money than other people. Quite naturally, having more money makes the wealthy feel they're better than those other people, whether better human beings or merely better at business or perhaps only better at being lucky somehow. It would be challenging to live in a penthouse overlooking New York's Central Park, ferried around in your personal limousine to the most exclusive galas and expensive restaurants without harboring some sense of superiority. Money becomes a concrete symbol of your life's value. And almost everybody agrees with you. They think you're better too.

But money only symbolizes the value of your life if you suffer from Identity Failure. If you need identity poses of social status to compensate for more personal and significant identity poses that feel in doubt, you can latch on to money as an accepted measure of your worth. The greater the amount of money, the easier the latching on. Maybe you're not a nice guy or girl. Maybe you're not as creative as you'd believed. Maybe you're really not all that bright. Still you must have something going for you, right? Just look at that bank account and all the symbols of your wealth that surround you continually – and continually impress other people. As a rich person, you enjoy an endless stream of outside appreciation.

The irrational craving for money is one common consequence of Identity Failure. Money has been transformed into an end in itself, a simplistic way for individuals to assess the value of their existence at any given moment. The pursuit of a life worth living turns into the pursuit of money.

This may be more true for the wealthy than the rest of us. I can't say for sure. But I suspect for most people in contemporary societies, to some larger or lesser extent, money evolves into a symbol of their individual value – and also offers them greater insulation from a disheartening world. Their feelings of self-worth are better defended against outside assault. Money seems to provide security, safety, comfort, respect, friendship, protection. Money seems to buy happiness. In his great tale, A Christmas Carol, Charles Dickens crafted thoughts that I find especially insightful about this very thing, uttered to Ebenezer Scrooge by his fiancée, Belle: "You fear the world too much … All your other hopes have merged into the hope of being beyond the chance of its sordid reproach." For Scrooge, money served as his barrier against life's pain, especially disapproval of him as a human being by fellow human beings.

And of course for many real life people, money also equals achievement. As a successful businessman once told me, "Money is a way of keeping score."

Score of what?

Who's better, that's what. Which individual is more important to society, more appreciated, more validated than the others. Whose life is more worth living.

For weighing human worth, money provides us with a more comprehensible scale than subjective judgments about messy things such as values, ideas, relationships, feelings, contributions to the well-being of others. Money is clearcut. My pile is higher than yours, I'm better than you.

Remember how you felt during our mud hut thought experiment in the last chapter? You had a sense of an increased value to your existence when you were the only person on earth with a permanent dwelling and ample food. That's the feeling money gives people in our society.

And this only happens because nearly every single one of us suffers from Identity Failure, the nagging terror that something may be deeply wrong with "me," that my life may not be worth living afterall. I feel myself the very core of the universe but the universe won't revolve around me as it should. What's the problem here anyway?

Our economic system enables money to look like an escape from this confusion.

With enough money, anyone can feel like Anyone-the-tycoon. Or Anyone-the-powerbroker. Or Anyone-the-fiscal-genius. He can fancy himself He-the-dealmaker or He-the-billionaire or He-the-playboy. She can imagine herself She-the-entrepreneur or She-the-philanthropist or She-the-trophywife. Whatever identity poses propel his or her ego away from the psychogravitational push of Identity Failure, the many many identities they deeply value in themselves but fear they may not possess.

Money is a forceful pose-strengthener for the rich and the unrich alike. That's a reality evident throughout modern society once you look for it.

To most folks, money appears to even up their psychological profit and loss statements. Money can seem to reimburse human beings for losing something vastly more valuable than any sum of cash: a portion of their deepest humanity.

"Power tends to corrupt, and absolute power corrupts absolutely." Lord Acton

In both personal affairs and the systems of society, money often is about power. Power to control lives, influence to shape events. Wealth both symbolizes and creates advantage over others.

And typically, power is about ego.

And ego is about Identity Failure. A person driven by ego is focused on the seeking and the finding of pose-strengtheners that inflate some identity poses to counterbalance more highly valued identity poses they question in themselves. They feel there's something profoundly wrong with them. They're trying to prove to themselves that there isn't. Ego gathers evidence of their worth. That's as true of the ego in public life as in private.

Money confers power of many types. For the monied individual, wealth bestows the power to forge personal connections with other people who hold important positions in society. And to get what you want from those people. To significantly influence politicians and policies, or become a successful politician in your own right. To treat your fellow humans pretty much as you like in private life, kindly or shabbily, without fear of serious repercussions. To help individuals or to hurt them in meaningful ways. To have the best of whatever you need or want, from medical care to cars and clothing, from food and beverage to homes with live-in staff and hotel suites with personal butler service.

Money gives the wealthy a much more effective tool than most of us possess for making the world what they want it to be. All about "me." That is a real power.

Society can seem a greatly more appreciative place to a rich individual, with the power of money bending their reality around them to conform to the whims of wealth. This doesn't cure Identity Failure – it would tend to strengthen I.F. by reinforcing psychological dependence on outside validation. Profoundly important identity poses still would remain in deep doubt, among the rich no less than the rest of us. Most wealthy people would feel there may be something terribly wrong with them, just as you and I do. Perhaps even more so in some instances. But daily life would present many opportunities to push aside those doubts through the compliments and congratulations and companionship of all those who want something from rich persons. And this feeds the ego of the wealthy, offering the illusion of personal accomplishment when the accomplishment mostly results from owning a very large stack of cash.

But that personal power can only go so far. The wealth of institutions provides individuals a far greater power over the destiny of human beings, giving some the authority to determine the fate of many. And in the process, rewarding the ego of the select some.

Even in the more democratic countries, this type of power evidently is an intoxicant. It is sought after much more often than it is willingly given up. As a journalist in the United States, I never covered a politician at the local, state or national level who didn't possess an obvious ego. A strong need for outside appreciation clearly played at least some role in motivating their career choice. And their official failings seemed more or less directly related to the degree that ego gratification was their main concern. Strong feelings that holding political office was all about "me" weakened the chances this politician would do much for anyone else. Their focus was on gaining a sense of personal importance through public service.

That's often as much the case inside wealthy corporations and even wealthy nonprofit groups. The bank accounts of these organizations frequently contribute to personal wealth for those in charge along with connections to many powerful people – and a huge influence over everyday men and women. Influence over employees, influence over customers and clients, influence over needy populations. Those who wield this influence more to bolster their egos than to help others often discover that Identity Failure becomes a corrupting force. Top officials focus on their salary and their bonus when in power and their payout when moving on. They preserve the status quo out of self-interest rather than pushing for innovation out of interest in society's betterment. They may snatch up ever more power to heighten their prestige, enlarge their investments, broaden their sexual conquests.

It is a common problem among the powerful, CEOs and political leaders alike. Power tends to corrupt because power brings with it temptation. Bigtime temptation. And when you scrape down through the psychological layers, you generally find that power's most enticing temptations are the things that make people feel more important. Especially status, money, sex. These pose-strengtheners emit currents forceful enough to inflate the egos of powerful persons and carry many leaders toward corruption.

The corruptions of power are the consequences of Identity Failure. Power allows people to strengthen their egos, diluting the feeling there's something wrong with them. They can't escape the sense of being deeply flawed, but power helps hide them from this more often.

Too many are not strong enough to resist. If the world hands you chance after chance to lessen your overwhelming self-confusion, to diminish your terror that something may be seriously wrong with you, you will want to seize those opportunities. Even if those opportunities may be unethical or illegal. If your position can bring an immediate sense that your existence is valuable to you, you may well experience a psychogravitational push toward those feelings no matter what's needed to gain them. The temptations of power help individuals answer firmly yes to the Fundamental Question: Is my life worth living?

For the moment, anyway, yes it is worth living. And few think beyond that moment.

The cure for this intoxication is integrity. As protection from the many corrupting forces around them, genuine leaders summon the integrity of their values, their faith in a goal or a mission or a purpose that fuels a strong desire to do something meaningful for others. Just as there is a distinction between the rational need and the irrational craving for money, so there is a distinction between the rational quest for leadership and the irrational lust for power. Leaders who are worthy of the name may savor the benefits of pose-strengtheners among their rewards, enjoying boosts of ego-building confidence that come naturally through their position. But ego is not their primary motive. They believe in their ability to forge positive change in the world somehow. Leaders want to guide their fellows toward a vision that's focused not on the leadership but on the purpose. This is the effort that makes their lives feel more worth living.

When I visited the Solomon Islands in 2008, I stopped by their National Parliament. It was a simple small building with a sign over the door that read, "To lead is to serve." That struck me then and has stayed with me since. Leadership wisely practiced is about service, not self-aggrandizement. No matter how impressive the egos of those leaders also may be.

But for the lusty powercravers, leadership is something else entirely. Ego inflation is their primary purpose, often their overwhelming purpose. They cope with the Fundamental Law of Mind by attempting to smother doubts about themselves, both their own fears and any outside doubters. In this process they obsess over attracting appreciation wherever they can find it. Self-serving leaders answer the Fundamental Question throughout each day by way of validation from others. For them, "Is my life worth living?" becomes only another way of asking, "Am I proving my superiority to someone else?" Pose-weakeners will still run through their psyche, mounting assaults on some identity poses to insulate other more significant and more vulnerable identity poses. They may worry frequently about their speaking ability to guard against insecurities about their intellect. But they will seek out pose-strengtheners constantly to pump up those identities that help justify their existence to themselves, with a craving for appreciation that wildly exceeds the norm. They must hear how important, how powerful, how extraordinary they are. Like hospital patients who need medicine from an IV, these leaders require a constant drip of external confirmation.

As a result, Identity Failure thoroughly molds their leadership style. Their goal and their mission are to escape the terrors of I.F. by transforming the world around them, whether that means as the dominating boss of a local bookstore, the headline-grabbing commissioner of a police department or the backroom powerbroker of a legislative body. Our planet is permeated with ego-fueled leaders who damage our societies in service of self-interest. Heads of vast nations and heads of tiny committees, planners of sweeping military campaigns and planners of modest charitable events. Teachers and principals, editors and publishers, ship captains and football coaches and hotel concierges.

To them, self-service is the only service that matters, a leadership that diminishes others to engorge their own identity. Humanity weakens through their irrational ego-strengthening. We are the victims of these victims of Identity Failure.

A 2011 article by Harvard Business School Senior Fellow, William W. George, noted that many in authority end up ruled by the money and the attention and the other perks of leadership. "This creates a deep desire to keep it going, often driven by desires to overcome narcissistic wounds from childhood. Many times, this desire is so strong that leaders breach the ethical standards that previously governed their conduct," he wrote. "When leaders focus on external gratification instead of inner satisfaction, they lose their grounding."

Sometimes leaders lose their grounding so completely that almost nothing remains underfoot for support.

Nothing but a shifting topsoil of ego.

"Unexpressed emotions will never die. They are buried alive and will come forth later in uglier ways." Sigmund Freud

Identity Failure's unexpressed emotions reveal themselves predictably. The specifics vary greatly. But the psychological outlines of this powerful illness are identifiable from the outside, typically with these among the symptoms:

Struggling with an irrational relationship to praise from other people, ranging on a scale from obsessive need to dread avoidance. Applying shallow, simplistic descriptions to fellow human beings. Applying shallow, simplistic descriptions to yourself. Suffering extreme sensitivity to criticism, whether about a limited area of identity or about many areas.

There are other predictable indicators as well.

An unwillingness or inability to see yourself realistically. An unwillingness or inability to see others realistically. An unwillingness or inability to see society at large realistically. Emotional or physical symptoms that surface suddenly and worsen without clear cause. Excessive anger that materializes abruptly, whether infrequently in private or commonly in public or something in between. An inexplicable attraction to some people. An inexplicable dislike for other people. Those, among other basic signs of an I.F. victim.

Now take that psychological blueprint and lay it over the identity of Adolph Hitler.

You will find that the outlines of Identity Failure and the known outlines of Hitler's personality align perfectly.

Yes, I am really saying that Hitler was Hitler because of Identity Failure. Not as any kind of excuse, obviously, but as an explanation and as a warning. I believe I.F. explains Hitler's behavior more fully and rationally than any other account I know. And the behavior of countless tyrants and despots and dictators of the past, present or future. Many pages of human history bear the blotches of Identity Failure.

I claim no special expertise about the specifics of Hitler's life or the life of anyone else in the public realm, now or earlier. What details I've picked up were learned from teachers, books, documentaries, films and the like as well as my travels and my conversations with folks who lived through historical events. But during some six decades of unrelieved curiosity about history, I have detected patterns. I have sought out information about both current and past figures that seemed relevant to my intense interest in people, in the human mind. And just as an understanding of my I.F. allowed me insight into individuals I knew personally, the same appeared true of these public persons. To draw again on Emerson's observation, "He then learns that in going down into the secrets of his own mind he has descended into the secrets of all minds."

I believe that's as accurate on the grand social scale as on the small personal one. People are people and the underlying functions of the mind apply to all. If I deeply and genuinely explore my psyche, my discoveries must hold for every psyche.

Even Hitler's.

For this reason I'm convinced utterly that Identity Failure is an indispensable concept for correctly analyzing the violence, the brutalities, the excesses, the inhumanity of human beings toward each other. At the macro level of Hitler or Stalin or Pol Pot, at the micro level of Capone or Manson or Bundy. Oswald and Booth, Caligula and Vlad the Impaler. I can find no alternative to the firm belief that, in different forms, each of these men was driven to their worst acts in large part by Identity Failure.

Like me, like you, they were attempting to cope with the Fundamental Law of Mind as best they could. Every mad one of them in essence was trying to answer the Fundamental Question somehow in the affirmative. My answer to that question and yours have been found in smiles and compliments, hugs and handshakes. The men I just named, and the untallied psychopaths I didn't name, found their answer in blood.

To reach this sweeping conclusion, I don't need to know every detail of every life. I need only extrapolate what I know for certain about the functions of my mind and then transfer that knowledge to what I witness of criminals large and small, whether my information about them is gleaned from history books or the daily newspaper.

In my time, Hitler remains the symbol of human evil. I don't believe in evil – never have, really, as an adult. To me, the idea seems romanticized and simplistic. It's another example of notions that offer black-and-white easily digestible answers to complex issues. They may not be true but at least they make us feel better about the world. The concept allows most of us to feel superior and provides an absolute division within humanity: Good. Evil.

Evil doesn't exist. We are all the children of nature's workings, each individual fashioned by an unique assemblage of genes and vericepts to be launched on our pathway through a lifetime, every human a massive mechanism of wildly complicated cause and effect. Whether we like it or not, our lives are determined – Hitler's as much as my own.

But disease does exist. It lurks among all living things, corrupting the healthy and the constructive. In my view, then, for us to recognize the causes of humanity's willful horrors we first must thoroughly grasp the disease or diseases that cause such catastrophic effects.

And an extraordinarily important cause is the disease I've named Identity Failure.

" ...Violence, whether spiritual or physical, is a quest for identity and the meaningful. The less identity, the more violence." Marshall McLuhan

From my perspective, Adolph Hitler was not evil but instead was profoundly diseased. As with any disease, I.F. sickens people in degrees of affliction. You can have a mild or severe case of pneumonia, a mild or severe case of Identity Failure. Quite clearly, Hitler stands as a terrifying example of someone who suffered at the far end of severe. His I.F. became overwhelming – to him and to the world.

Let's go back to that short, incomplete list of obvious symptoms. Historians and contemporaries both documented his irrational struggle for outside praise, his obsessive need to prove himself significant. Even the slimmest knowledge of Hitler reveals his insanely shallow and simplistic descriptions of other human beings, Jews tragically included. And of course his equally crazy descriptions of himself, with monumental delusions about his qualities and abilities and achievements. It's also apparent that the Fuhrer endured an extreme sensitivity to criticism over many areas of his identity. Evidently the merest suggestion of disagreement with his views could ignite arm-flailing rages.

Hitler obviously was unwilling or unable to see himself, others or society at large with any semblance of rationality. History also knows much about his emotional and physical symptoms of all sorts, which swept the German dictator to dependence on a broad array of powerful drugs. Excessive anger that materialized abruptly, in private and public, has become so identified with Hitler that it's now virtually a caricature. And he appears to have been powerfully drawn toward some people and repelled by other people for reasons unclear to us today.

But seen through a lens of Identity Failure, the reasons for these and other personality traits grow clearer. Hitler was all about ego. Ego is all about Identity Failure. Identity Failure is all about a soulterror that one's life may not be worth living, that you might not really be the person you feel you must be. Those others may be right about your inadequacies. In Identity Failure's most extreme manifestations, people destroy fellow human beings to gain various types of validation. These deeply troubled minds construct self-value out of identity poses that require more than appreciation from others. They thrive also on the misery of others. For them misery is a measure of their superiority – and so, of their human value.

During World War Two, the United States covert agency at the time assembled a lengthy report on Hitler to understand and predict his behavior. American psychologist Henry Murray headed up the evaluation, which found that the German ruler suffered from a massive inferiority among many other mental problems. The report said Hitler coped with these feelings through his passions for "brute strength, physical force, ruthless domination, and military conquest." The Fuhrer was judged an impotent masochist with "exorbitant cravings for superiority," a narcissist who demanded total agreement from those around him, a suicidal paranoid schizophrenic beset by "hypersensitivity, panics of anxiety, irrational jealousy, delusions of persecution, and messiah-ship."

The report correctly predicted a last-minute highly dramatic suicide among the possible ends for Adolph Hitler. And it noted, "He has nightmares from a bad conscience, and he has long spells when energy, confidence, and the power of decision abandon him." For Hitler, the report said, "his irreal world has become real, insanity is sanity."

All this is Identity Failure pressed to its limit.

"Cravings for superiority … hypersensitivity … panics of anxiety … messiah-ship." And "insanity." The partial madness nearly everyone exhibits from I.F. had so bloated in Hitler that he remains one of history's fullest expressions of a madman.

I feel sure Identity Failure more closely approximates the underlying realities of Hitler's mind than other theories, just as it does with the partial insanity each of us endures. It is the best truth available now. We can never create a full and complete picture of anything in nature, of course, and all our theories will be replaced in time with something better. That's called science. We discover fuller and more complete images of reality in an unending series of humanity's best available approximations, through the centuries refining our understanding of the complex simplicity of nature.

We'll never understand anything perfectly. This is the human condition. But we can understand a lot through the diligent application of science, logic, critical thinking and experience. In the end we can believe in the empirical, we can have faith in experience. Especially our own experience.

My experience with both humanity and I.F., collected from the inside as an individual and the outside observing other individuals, tells me Hitler was consumed by Identity Failure. The great dictator's mind had constructed self-images over many years that made his life feel worth living – self-images constantly threatened by significant emotional resistance from an array of sources, psychological and worldly. Who knows what his identity poses may have been as a youth: Perhaps Adolph-the-masculine-male or Adolph-the-artist. As some of these poses floundered within him, he found other identity poses to make his existence feel valuable. Eventually Hitler needed to view himself as Adolph-the-visionary, Adolph-the-conqueror, Adolph-the-genius. These clearly were among the identity poses he coveted. But like all identity poses, Hitler's self-images were irrational and unsustainable. He required outside validation to prove to himself they were real. His need to validate those identity poses, his response to the world's frustrating reactions to him – these made Hitler into Hitler. It all happened within that middle shaded area of the overlapping circles, the intersection of the person and the world.

For a time Adolph Hitler could get by on Adolph-the-unrecognized-visionary, Adolph-the-unrecognized-conqueror, Adolph-the-unrecognized-genius as he attracted admirers and sympathizers, as he struggled toward fulfillment of his identities. For a time later on Adolph Hitler could relish an unqualified Adolph-the-visionary, Adolph-the-conqueror, Adolph-the-genius and myriad other identity poses, with Germany bestowing its mass appreciation. Adulation and conquest became confirmation of his self-concepts.

Even Hitler, though, couldn't keep it going for long. As his ego ballooned further and further, he gave the world too many chances to prove him wrong. When it did, over and over and over, he collapsed more deeply into his peculiar variety of madness in efforts to sustain those identity poses, to continue seeing himself as the visionary and the conqueror and the genius. Finally, he couldn't believe in them. The world around Hitler had made these identity poses untenable – and the finale predicted by the secret government report came to pass with a cyanide capsule and a bullet.

"We don't see things as they are, we see them as we are." Anais Nin

I believe Adolph Hitler can represent all mad tyrants here. The line of them stretches out to the crack of doom, to twist Shakespeare's phrase, and no doubt will lengthen in the decades ahead. Examine the backgrounds of any others you choose. I'd mentioned Stalin and Pol Pot earlier, Caligula and Vlad the Impaler. Look into Mussolini if you like, or Mao.

Or perhaps Saddam Hussein, the executed ruler of Iraq. A 1990 Central Intelligence Agency report to Congress describes Hussein as obsessed with dreams of glory from his childhood onward. It notes that an examination of his life and career reveals a pattern played out through Hussein's lifetime: "All actions are justified if they are in the service of furthering Saddam Hussein's needs and ambitions." The report explains Hussein was "surrounded by sycophants, who are cowed by Saddam's well founded reputation for brutality and are afraid to contradict him. He has ruthlessly eliminated perceived threats to his power and equates criticism with disloyalty." And a bit farther in, the report says this: "In pursuit of his messianic dreams, there is no evidence he is constrained by conscience; his only loyalty is to Saddam Hussein."

The details differ. The story's the same, Hussein or Hitler or any of them.

The real villain is Identity Failure.

So too for less ambitious killers. I believe that murder is always an attempt to achieve psychological equilibrium in some way, to satisfy the demands of the Fundamental Law of Mind and the Fundamental Question. And I think it's as true for the spouse slayer or the mob boss as for the serial killer or the terrorist.

Within about three months of the September 11, 2001 terrorist attack on the United States, I'd completed a poem about the tragedy. As I write this chapter of my book today, my poem remains posted in the Artists Registry at the National September 11 Memorial & Museum in New York City, where the World Trade Center collapsed into ashes that day. The work was my effort to explain the murders of nearly 3,000 innocent people:

September 11, 2001

Why?

They shattered our glass sky,
and three thousand human shards
tumbled through holes made in
jetcraft silhouettes.

Did you see them disappear?
Did you ask the question?

Not for Jesus or Abraham this time.
Not for the swastika, the rising sun
or even the crescent moon.
You may not like the answer.
But if you would look,
turn inward.

Find the hovel where all
your secret rage demands explanations.
Find the streetcorner where all
your hidden self-contempt begs for revenge.
Find the cave where all
your private fears grovel for redemption.

Try then, if you can, to imagine
this cacophony of desperation
without respite or reprieve,
listening always to those morning prayers
and evening exhortations,
a permanent dissonance
with all silence, all peace denied,
long denied,

too long denied.

Until now.

In essence, this is how I view every human being who willfully destroys other human beings without rational cause. The killers among us. They are responding to those prayers and exhortations in their head. Painful noise unyielding, the voices that remind these people who they aren't but should be. Or who they are but shouldn't be.

Until they find a way to quiet the din, if perhaps just briefly, by proving who they can be. They kill to gain validation, a sense of identity that makes their existence feel valuable to them at some moment in this world. At least for an instant and possibly much longer, their life seems more worth living through murder. This doesn't mean they're seeking direct outside appreciation necessarily though killing can bring approval for some, including terrorists and mobsters. The world's confirmations can come in many forms, sometimes through the widespread fear created or the excessive media attention garnered, or perhaps through the responses of the killer's victims or even simply an awareness now of the way others will react later to the atrocities. Imagined future fame can be a strong incentive to kill.

The Fundamental Law of Mind and Fundamental Question drive each of us, whatever we do, the constructive as well as the destructive. But the destructive side of people in our societies is shaped greatly by the psychological illness that those fundamentals have spawned: Identity Failure. That reality is all around us.

I understand this by way of the prolonged and detailed explorations of my psyche, true, as well as the application of my investigative strengths discussed in Chapter 2. But perhaps I should briefly point out another tool that I bring to this analysis of the outside world: I'm able to imagine someone else's inner life and inhabit it, looking around at things through their eyes, feeling what they would feel in this situation or that. It's something writers have done for centuries and I seem to possess the ability as well. Fine actors do it too. For my part, I've always thought this resulted partially from my self-knowledge and partially from my very strong sense of empathy. I feel what others are feeling, often painfully so, a reality confirmed all my life in conversations with family, friends and strangers alike. They've told me that I somehow understand their emotions. This also means I'm capable of sensing what might motivate me if I were a different human being, existing with a largely altered set of personal characteristics and external circumstances. In this way I can explore the psyche of others, fictional or real. And I believe that has allowed me to more or less skillfully imagine some portion of the things a person such as Hitler must have felt.

Still, it takes no grand imagination to detect the obvious Identity Failure in a murderer like John Gotti, the famed mob boss. A New York Magazine article written after Gotti's arrest notes the gangster was "in love with himself and equated his ego with all of La Cosa Nostra." The piece noted that Gotti was reminiscent of earlier narcissist mobsters including Al Capone, who was "addicted to publicity." As for Capone himself, his courtship of celebrity was the stuff of newspaper headlines during the Prohibition era. The Chicago killer went so far as to hire the writer Damon Runyon as personal press agent. The well-known addiction to outside appreciation by these notorious underworld figures offers evidence that they are two more examples of Identity Failure as a force for bad in our society. We would discover the same disease within nearly anyone involved in organized crime, no matter how unlike Gotti or Capone in other ways. These people find their individual value in society through living outside society's norms. Criminal success becomes their reason for being.

The serial killer Ted Bundy represents another type of psychopath. Among those quotes reliably attributed to him is this admission: "I'm the most cold-hearted son of a bitch you'll ever meet." I believe that Bundy found value in existence through his many murders of young women, forging special identities for himself in the process. Another Bundy comment suggests as much. Bill Hagmaier was an FBI expert on serial killers who knew Ted Bundy in prison, quoting the murderer's description of looking into victims' eyes during their final breath: "A person in that situation is God," Bundy said.

What is that feeling of omnipotence through murder? It is a grandiose sense of personal power perverted into sadistic ego. And here as ever, ego is Identity Failure: the struggle for substitute identity poses that compensate for other identity poses that have failed. At some earlier time Bundy felt an urgent need to be Ted-the-this and Ted-the-that. Whatever those conflicted identities might have been during his young life. When he couldn't view himself in these ways, he created other serviceable identities that included Ted-the-coldheartedsonofabitch and Ted-the-God. These identity poses made his life feel worth living.

I can't resist one last telling tidbit to bolster my case here, more support for my brash contention that I.F. is the most pervasive and most severe illness to plague humanity.

Charles Manson was a cult leader who conspired with his followers on several infamous murders – but he was a songwriter as well. It is no coincidence that one of his songs is titled, Ego. Read its ending lyrics in a new way now, illuminated here by an awareness of Identity Failure:

"Old ego is a too much thing
Old ego is a too much thing
He'll make you fool yourself
You'll think you're somebody else
They got the whole subway train
Makes you want to jump on up there an' fight
And you can't stand left to your right

He'll make you lie
Make you cheat
Jus' so you won't be beat
He'll make you get on outta sight
You get afraid you gonna, act like a clown
And you get mad when somebody puts you down

Your heart's a-pumpin' and you pan-heart's a-jumpin'
Look out ego is a too much thing
When everything seems goin' so fine
Old ego puts itself on a bind
Your certainty turns to doubt
Then you start flippin' out

Then you ease on out of your mind"

Identity Failure is why Charles Manson eased on out of his mind.

"What white people have to do is try and find out in their own hearts why it was necessary to have a nigger in the first place." James Baldwin

Humanity's violence, of course, assumes many forms. Whether Hitler's genocide or Manson's killings, murder is merely one method of acquiring individual feelings of value by vanquishing other individuals. Our species has been particularly creative in this endeavor.

Slavery is among our creations.

In slavery we see a monstrous personal power over other human beings, a total domination that comes from the confluence of several ego-driven forces: wealth, status, violence. America's long experience with slavery offers a clear example of the way this ancient institution ripples through history as another reflection of our Identity Failure.

That is the answer to James Baldwin's call for the questioning of white conscience.

I.F. is the reason it was necessary to have a nigger in the first place.

We can't explain slavery as the outcome of mainly economic need. That's a very shallow analysis of a fundamentally ego-centered system. Because ultimately slavery wasn't and isn't truly about money, except to the extent money buys a sense of self-value. More than anything else, slavery has always been about identity.

We are better than them. They are less than human.

We are elevated. They are lowly.

Our lives are worth living. Theirs? Not so much.

We are the superiors among a world of inferiors. And we know their place in the cosmic order, a knowledge that surely must benefit them as much as us: Their proper place is to serve ... us.

To serve me.

I can believe I'm a better me simply because I'm not them.

If you doubt this interpretation, take a look back at the writings of American slaveholders. They can tell us a lot. One good source is a pamphlet written by a South Carolina cotton plantation owner named John Townsend. In 1860, he warned about the consequences of an Abraham Lincoln presidency:

"The color of the white man is now, in the South, a title of nobility in his relations as to the negro," Townsend explained. "In the Southern slaveholding States, where menial and degrading offices are turned over to be performed exclusively by the Negro slave, the status and color of the black race becomes the badge of inferiority, and the poorest non-slaveholder may rejoice with the richest of his brethren of the white race, in the distinction of his color. He may be poor, it is true; but there is no point upon which he is so justly proud and sensitive as his privilege of caste; and there is nothing which he would resent with more fierce indignation than the attempt of the Abolitionist to emancipate the slaves and elevate the Negroes to an equality with himself and his family."

I believe this honest confession of psychological benefit does more to reveal slavery's true appeal than all the economic and sociological justifications combined. By its very nature slavery is about superiority. The money only makes it easier to feel superior in many ways. "I'm smarter. I'm healthier. I'm more moral. I am selected by God for this role in society. And yes, all that superiority finds daily expression through my large house, my fine clothes, my abundant food, my personal appearance, my beautiful wife and children, my status in the community. I am better than them."

How comfortable this must have felt.

Imagine yourself in the place of any large slaveholder in the Confederacy. Look at the world for a moment through his privileged eyes.

You awaken and, if you like, are served breakfast by an attractive young female slave. The same slave you rape in the barn now and then whenever the urge strikes. Her behavior each morning may seem frightened, at least deferential. How does this make you feel about yourself as you begin a new day? You feel special, of course, a much better creature than the slave and all those other half-humans you own.

You are powerful. You are superior. Whatever the deep lingering uncertainties about yourself, this anointed place in the world order helps you push many of those feelings aside. To a significant extent, you can dismiss your perceived inadequacies for long stretches throughout most days: "Look at the life I lead! Truly, how could anything be wrong with me?"

As you dress to begin the working hours, your wife and your children also may be deferential – respectful of your primary position in the family. You are uniquely empowered everywhere on your plantation and among the most distinguished personages for many miles around. Your orders cannot be disobeyed, your intelligence cannot be questioned, your status cannot be diminished. How would you feel?

At the intersection of the world and you, in that shaded space, your existence probably feels highly valuable at most moments. You can offer a resounding "yes" to the Fundamental Question. Living is worthwhile indeed.

The pestering doubts from low in your psyche still will pester. But you and your culture have carved identity poses for you that command constant validation from nearly everyone. Clearly, you are exactly who and what you conceive yourself to be. Society says so. You view yourself as the-chosen-one, perhaps, or the-brilliant-businessman, the-land-baron or the-manly-dominator. And your world agrees. How are you feeling about this?

The severity of those persistent doubts, of your self-confusion, will greatly determine how much outside confirmation you require to maintain your identity poses. And how you find that confirmation. You will treat your family more lovingly or more harshly based on the degree of your psychological uncertainty. The intensity of your Identity Failure. Your slaves too will suffer less or suffer more from your state of mind. Do you feel better about yourself without the whip or with it?

You and I and most of us in the world of today struggle to get what we want and be who we think we should be. It is a continual battle for our identity. To prove to ourselves that our life is worth living. Consider, then, the existence of the slaveholder as I've described it – or the more common small slaveholder who completely possesses one or two human beings as his own. Or even the many non-slaveholders among Southern whites before the Civil War. As John Townsend pointed out so well, "… there is no point upon which he is so justly proud and sensitive as his privilege of caste."

Why was this true? Why was it necessary to have a nigger in the first place? As James Baldwin continued in the same interview that I quoted above, "…because I'm not a nigger, I'm a man, but if you think I'm a nigger, it means you need it."

Southern whites, slaveowners or no, needed a nigger in 1860 to feel handpicked by God for a privileged life. How could slavery at its deepest levels have flowered from any other soil of the human soul? Whatever the economic or sociological realities, slavery is domination. Domination is power. Power is ego.

Ego is Identity Failure.

And this must be true whether in Ancient Egypt or Ancient Greece or the Roman Empire, whether in Great Britain or the Ottoman Empire or the United States. Or among modern day human traffickers. In psychological function, human beings remain human beings then and now. And human beings own other human beings for the same basic reason.

To feel better about themselves.

"No one is born hating another person because of the color of his skin, or his background, or his religion. People must learn to hate." Nelson Mandela

Nelson Mandela was right. People must learn to hate. Love comes naturally – hate is acquired through the world's lessons.

And the great teacher of hate is Identity Failure.

When you feel there's something fundamentally wrong with you as a human being, you automatically will try to find anything to water down that feeling. Money, sex, status, power, war. Violence, domination.

Or racism, the root of slavery.

As I write this in early 21st Century America, racism still nestles at the core of our national life. Racism has been a basic trait since long before our founding as a country. It may yet contribute to our undoing as a leader of nations.

But unfortunately, the United States of America is far from the only region on earth afflicted with some visceral form of racism. It seems every peopled continent has deep veins of belief that some humans are better than others purely because of their race. Of course scientists now argue that race isn't a physical reality but rather a social construct, an imagined truth. Yet most of the world remains well insulated against the influence of empirical evidence on the issue.

As with slaveholders, racists of all stripes cling to their prejudice for personal reasons. Meaning, for psychological reasons. And the psychological reasons are the same – an effort to bolster identity poses they hold especially dear. No matter their shortcomings, their flaws, their deficiencies, they are imbued with superiority by race alone. They may beat their children, lose job after job, flounder through marriages awash in alcohol. Yet they have something many don't. They have white skin. Or whatever the preferred color in their part of the world. Many racists are more subtle, less obvious than the virulent bigot of popular culture. They may be the boss who harbors deep concerns about hiring a black man or the waitress who crosses the street when she sees an African American heading toward her on the sidewalk. The police officer who pulls over black motorists without good cause or the patient who prefers a white doctor, thank you.

I have seen racism in my overseas travels. I have read about or watched video footage of many other racist incidents in various nations. But I am an American, for better or worse. Probably both. So let me focus on racism in this country as an expression of Identity Failure – and an example that is representative of the world at large.

I grew up among racism of the more subtle variety. My father was born in 1914, my mother in 1917. Their parents were raised in 19th Century America, not too long after slavery was abolished. How could my white parents have been anything but racist at some level? During the turbulent 1960s, I often heard comments around the dinner table about black persons, not tirades but quiet remarks mixed with a measure of disgust. "Those people …" was one phrase that often began such sentences. "Why can't they …" or "They shouldn't be allowed ..." were among the others. To my parents, Dr. Martin Luther King Jr. was a "rabble rouser." Protesters calling for equality were "troublemakers." This was the common stuff of suburban life during that time and in that place. Not only my parents but most parents I knew held similar views, as well as my teachers and my playmates and just about everyone else in my field of vision. Racism in this era was overt. That terrible word, "nigger," still was uttered openly in polite conversation among educated people in the north no less than the south.

In part because of this background, I understand racism. I have struggled to eliminate it from my thinking, from my perception of the world. Naturally, I can't do that entirely. I heard what I heard, saw what I saw, learned what I learned as a child. The memories are embedded. Despite my best efforts, they sometimes briefly bubble up unwanted in some new form. And when a racist thought materializes, I've found that it is from Identity Failure. Just as it was for my parents. Racism is an easy and comfortable way to dismiss the confounding behavior of others who don't look like me, which instantly allows me to feel better about myself. "They" often are bad drivers. "They" often don't have good manners. "They" often don't care about quality education. Whoever "they" happen to be at the moment. That's the sort of feeling that can come over me momentarily and infrequently during my most stressful days. I know these notions are nonsense but my psyche now and then gravitates toward them when I'm under emotional pressure before I push these stupidities away again.

Racism in this nation is not the exclusive affliction of white people. As near as I can see, it infects almost every American somehow. I have many times been on the receiving end of racism toward whites by blacks and Hispanics, even Asians living in the United States. Attitudes, facial expressions, comments, behavior. A group of hostile young Latinos in San Francisco stole a wineskin from me one day in 1974, daring me to fight them for its return. I wisely declined and walked on my way.

Racism at bottom is a means of pose-strengthening. It helps the racist feel special, important, valuable. For a moment or two, we feel superior to at least some other human being. Racism is a technique our minds learn to drive off Identity Failure's uncertainties about ourselves. It is readily available in our culture. And it makes the racist feel like somebody.

And conversely, it makes the target of racism feel like nobody.

Martin Luther King understood this well. During a television interview, Dr. King was asked about the civil rights movement's main achievement for black Americans. He answered that it had "given the Negro a new sense of identity. A new sense of somebodyness. And this is maybe the greatest victory that we have won." And in a justly famous 1968 Sunday church sermon, King focused on something he called the "drum major instinct" that results in "pushing others down in order to push yourself up." He spoke also about "a need that some people have to feel that they are first, and to feel that their white skin ordained them to be first." Then King continued, "And think of what has happened in history as a result of this perverted use of the drum major instinct. It has led to the most tragic prejudice, the most tragic expressions of man's inhumanity to man."

Long long before I ever named this disease, Dr. King recognized facets of Identity Failure. He knew there was an illness within the human heart – within some human hearts anyway. Now 50 years later, I.F. still inspires racists, both the subtle and the virulent. In very recent years at this writing, a young Southern American man loaded up a weapon, visited a historic black church in Charleston, South Carolina during a Bible study and opened fire on the people who had welcomed him to their worship. He killed nine African Americans. After his arrest, the gunman told authorities he'd hoped these murders would bring back racial segregation or possibly spark a war between races. At his trial, the shooter told jurors that he "felt like I had to do it."

I have little doubt about that. No detailed psychological examination of this individual is necessary to offer an accurate diagnosis. Whatever the specifics of his life, the young killer needed to feel his white skin ordained him to be first. White skin was his value in this world. White skin permitted him to feel his life was worth living. Profound confusion about some highly significant identities found satisfaction through violent racism, forging new meaningful identities for him. In his imagination he had become the-racial-defender and the-white-warrior, the-visionary-agitator and the-justified-murderer. He was the champion of the good, the decent, the white. History would look on him kindly.

But history won't. This young man and the many others like him, before and now and after, merely will be lumped together as racism's killers. Each a victim of Identity Failure, each a perpetrator driven by a need for some personal identity they felt acceptable to them. Me-first through group superiority.

Though he'd never heard of Identity Failure, Dr. King knew this psychological need – and saw that the irrational behavior it often motivated was the cause of damages far beyond individual racism. He realized that a lot of destructive me-firsts could come together to form an even more destructive us-first.

"This is why we are drifting," King said during that same sermon. "And we are drifting there because nations are caught up with the drum major instinct. 'I must be first.' 'I must be supreme.' 'Our nation must rule the world.' And I am sad to say that the nation in which we live is the supreme culprit." He went on by explaining, "God didn't call America to engage in a senseless, unjust war as the war in Vietnam. And we are criminals in that war ... and we won't stop it because of our pride and arrogance."

Dr. King called this the drum major instinct. I call it Identity Failure.

"Each nation feels superior to other nations. That breeds patriotism – and wars." Dale Carnegie

I've never cared much for patriotism. Never. When even our enlightened U.S. presidents have talked about encouraging the greatness of our country, I couldn't help but recoil a little. Why not encourage the greatness of every human being, the greatness of humanity? It makes no sense to me. We need to think bigger. We need to recognize the whole picture. That's not the American family posed in the image. It's the human family.

Instead it's still us vs. them, which is only another formulation of me vs. them. For most people, I believe, the world is all about me much of the time ... until the issues are outside individual control. Financial markets, war and peace, trade negotiations, immigration and so forth. Then of necessity the concept of me opens just enough for their psyche to include fellow countrymen and countrywomen as part of looking out for Number One. Because, hey, we're all in this together – as long as the interests of my countrymen and countrywomen align with my needs.

And for many this sense of belonging to one special nation becomes an important element of their identity. Joe-the-salesman elevates the value of his existence through his new identities as Joe-the-patriot, Joe-the-flagwaver, Joe-the-freedomlover. His life as "me" feels like much more through clutching tightly to the patriotic "us." He is Joe-the-American!

Or Pablo-the-Spaniard! Or Ming-the-Chinese! Or Ahmed-the-Saudi! Maybe Luiz-the-Brazilian! Or Adika-the-Ghanaian! Or Martin-the-Australian!

Or whatever.

The individual feels like more through membership in a club they view as exclusive. Nevermind that this club may include hundreds of millions of others. To them, it seems an extraordinary privilege awarded by God.

Call it the drum major instinct or Identity Failure, the psychological processes here are much the same as with racism. "I am better than you because I live in the greatest country in the world." It's not about skin color or hair texture or facial features. This version of superiority is solely about geography.

As George Bernard Shaw observed, "Patriotism is, fundamentally, a conviction that a particular country is the best in the world because you were born in it …"

I hear it all the time in my society: "America is the greatest country in the world!" It's a cliché among politicians but also a core value for millions of our citizens. Some Americans embrace that conviction so jealously that they have slandered or attacked or even murdered other Americans perceived as less than patriotic. Many many in this country consider burning an American flag more offensive than personal insults. And many wish to punish the flagburners. Really? Our flag is simply material easily replaced, ignited as some form of protest. I admit that flagburning makes no sense to me either but I'm not personally offended by it. This is because I don't link my identity to my country to any significant degree. I identify with humanity. But for those whose identity has become thoroughly enmeshed with their nationality, every attack on the flag or on their country appears an assault on that patriotic "us." Meaning, "me." It seems a personal affront.

As with racism, America is not alone in this. Far far from it.

To a great extent, things still are just as Dale Carnegie said many years ago. "Each nation feels superior to other nations."

At the United Nations, member countries maneuver for strategic and economic advantage over each other. At the Olympics, athletes compete as national patriots rather than as individuals. Country Z pollutes the water and air of Country X because Z makes more money doing it, no matter the longterm contamination of the planet we all inhabit. Country Y demands territory from Country W, though the landmass is small and worthless. The ego of national leaders and the egos of their people intertwine with the issues of the day, problems grand and problems small. "I must be first." "I must be supreme." "Our nation must rule the world."

And wherever you find patriotic ego, you also find I.F. as the underlying force: I need to feel better about my life by proving it's superior to your life.

This is nothing new. History is a dumping ground of patriotic egos that flourished and failed.

The egos of Ancient Egypt and Ancient Greece and Imperial Rome, among too too too many others. The egos of Nazi Germany and Fascist Italy and Imperial Japan. The egos of the French and Spanish and British colonialists. The egos of the Soviets. Perhaps eventually the egos of the Americans too, each in turn emptied of status by history's pitiless hourglass.

Like all identity poses, any rigid patriotic identity is irrational. It represents imagination, nothing more. It is wishful thinking. And in the end, reality imposes disturbing truth on the patriots – those, at least, who remain toward the finish of a nation's reign: A particular country is not the best in the world because you were born in it.

"The greatest fear in the world is of the opinions of others." Osho

Patriotism and its counterpart, nationalism, frequently do breed war. Carnegie was right about that as well. And during this modern era anyway, wars are fought by individuals who would rather die than face Identity Failure. The fear of feeling I.F. is greater than their fear of combat.

I can't say what may have motivated the soldiers of Sparta or Rome, even the militiamen of our Revolutionary War. At rock bottom level, I'd guess, the motivation wasn't patriotism. Something deeper psychologically must have been going on – the need to prove individual bravery, strength, superiority, to gain promotion or reward, or possibly to help establish the value of your own race or your own country in battle. Some such thing. That's my conjecture. But I have learned that it is very distinctly a fear of Identity Failure that in more modern times pushes infantrymen out of airplanes and landing craft into fusillades of enemy fire.

During my years as a daily journalist, I was fortunate to interview dozens of men who had endured desperate fights on the battlefield. Especially World War Two veterans who had survived the Japanese attack on Pearl Harbor and the invasion of France on D-Day. I even spoke through a translator by phone with two Japanese pilots who had bombed Pearl Harbor and I covered the 50th anniversary ceremonies of Pearl Harbor and D-Day in Hawaii and France, respectively. I learned many lessons in those prolonged discussions with aged veterans. I never spoke to a single vet who felt he was a hero, however dramatic his experiences. Over the years I came to realize this wasn't modesty. It was the truth. They weren't heroes and they knew it – no one is. Heroism, to me, is another of those romanticized ideas that so many folks cherish. I suspect a belief in heroism may help people explain to themselves why they don't attempt these dangerous things done by others, whether soldiers or spies or police or firefighters. Or the local Good Samaritan who saves a life. This guy is a hero, that's why he did it. I'm not, that's why I don't do it.

In any case, modern military training in the United States focuses on building a sense of brotherhood among the troops. The men, and now also women, in your unit depend on you. On your actions, your judgment, your courage, your buddy-to-buddy commitment. That explains the military ethic to never leave behind fellow soldiers in combat. Training is fashioned specifically to emphasize this I-have-your-back, you-have-mine mentality. My favorite film director, Stanley Kubrick, demonstrates that process in an insightful if stylized movie called Full Metal Jacket. For the recruit, individuality is stripped away in the film and in real life. It's us vs. them again, but this time the us is your combat unit. Bonding within that unit is the ultimate morality. Our troops are taught to prize their relationship with comrades above all.

Now put yourself in the place of a recruit on D-Day after months of indoctrination in this value system. He's learned that the only thing that really matters is being there for his buddy, who stands beside him waiting to wade into the cold Atlantic Ocean on June 6, 1944. If this recruit collapses in panic, if he refuses to attack, he is worse than a coward. The military has created new identity poses for this soldier. He will risk the possibility of death in that chaotic beach assault rather than endure the certainty of extreme Identity Failure by seeking to escape.

For most of those who go through military training, this is their reality. And it's not heroism, just as the old veterans understand. The soldier's psyche will not allow him another choice. He attacks because the alternative would be emotionally unbearable – and even death feels preferable.

"The relation of male to female is by nature a relation of superior to inferior and ruler to ruled." Aristotle

As I write this in 2019, American women finally have been allowed into combat with male soldiers. They may die equally with the men but can't yet live in our society as equals, another consequence of Identity Failure.

I find it astonishing that so many men in so many parts of this modern world, so called, still feel superior to women. To be perfectly blunt, I've often viewed this issue in the reverse: If anything, women often seem superior to me, though I know this is foolish too. No gender can lay claim to natural advantage over the other – and that's also true for those with more complicated sexual identities such as transgender people. Again, human beings are human beings and no race or nationality, no gender or anything else justifies feelings of superiority.

But in my travels around the world, I've experienced many cultures that openly treat women as inferiors, sometimes as virtual slaves. John Lennon wrote a controversial song about this, Woman Is The Nigger Of The World. Controversial or not, the great songwriter was correct then and now. In First World societies such as the U.S. and Europe, women are very often harassed and hassled sexually and otherwise, paid less than men for the same work, expected to earn money and raise a family and manage a household at once. In many less developed nations, women are abused verbally and physically, forced to obey the demands of men whether these are fathers or brothers, husbands or employers. The courageous struggle to educate girls in some of these places has triggered violent attacks. Genital mutilation and honor killings go on to this day, incredibly. At my desk is a relatively recent newspaper clipping I saved for this book. The digest article reads, "Police in Pakistan have arrested a mother suspected of killing her pregnant daughter for marrying against the wishes of her family in a so-called honor killing. Police say the mother and her son slit the throat of Muqadas Tofeeq, 22, in the village of Butrawala. Tofeeq was the mother of a 10-month-old infant."

In these cultures, even women find ways to feel superior to women.

Once more, this is nothing new for our species. The quote from Aristotle only helps to make the point. Despite exceptions, including the disputed possibility of truly matriarchal societies, women throughout history have been both repressed and oppressed. They have been coerced into laborious lives of drudgery. They have been ignored and discouraged. They have been lawfully required to bear children they didn't want. They have been insulted, belittled, manhandled, raped, forced into prostitution, sold into marriage and much much more.

Male superiority remains a cosmic truth among billions of human beings, men and women alike. It is enshrined in great religious texts and in societies around the globe.

Sexism's cause is the same as with any other brand of human superiority. Even between men and women, someone must suffer diminishment to elevate someone else. To again quote MLK, this human instinct has us "pushing others down in order to push yourself up." Much like the slaveowner, the racist or the patriot, the sexist feels better about his individual existence by regarding something about himself as better, inherently and permanently. His maleness is better than her femaleness. Period.

And so we have abandoned too much of humanity's potential – lesser not quite by half, of course, because women sometimes do transcend their circumstances. But by some large percentage of our population, unique talents are smothered still and unique experiences dismissed. Over the centuries, women have come and gone unnoticed who surely could have left a great wake of achievement behind them.

It is our loss, all of us. To our detriment, the fragile male ego for now has prevailed.

"Every normal person, in fact, is only normal on the average. His ego approximates to that of the psychotic in some part or other and to a greater or lesser extent." Sigmund Freud

Everything I've been describing in this chapter is viewed by most people as a regrettable reality of our existence. It's simply the way things are, the way we are. Human nature, you know. Nothing to be done.

But the behavior we call "human nature," isn't.

The insanity that Freud and Twain and Einstein and many others have noted everywhere around indeed is a form of madness in some meaningful sense. It is Identity Failure – and like any madness, it is an illness. There's nothing innate, nothing immutable, nothing natural about a lust for money or power, about despotism and violence, slavery and racism and patriotic egotism. Nothing necessary about sexism or anything else that diminishes the human race.

We can change all of it. The problem is just that not enough of us know this ... and believe it so deeply that we search for solutions. Our psychological evolution as a species remains stymied in very early stages.

Look at the detailed evidence I offered earlier in this book, all drawn from my direct experience. Explanations of the motivations that have so damaged my life, creating so many mad moments of my own, causing me so much intense misery. My identity poses and pose-weakeners and pose-strengtheners in response to I.F. and the Fundamental Law of Mind, the Fundamental Question. What I thought I wanted and what I deepwanted. Recall my responses to my profound self-confusion, to my "insecurities." Psychogravity pushing me toward behavior I knew to be destructive to myself and others as the emotional force of nexes swept me beyond my better judgment. My almost continual need for outside approval in pursuit of that final 15% or 20% external validation to live comfortably with my conceptions of Bob. My reactions to even minor annoyances that seemed to symbolize the injustices of the world toward me.

And remember too the previous chapter's linking of these I.F. symptoms with your life, a rational explanation of your irrational feelings, your own mad behavior.

Now look at the utter madness outlined in this chapter in view of these same psychological forces. The world's lust for money and power, our tendencies toward despotism and violence, slavery and racism, patriotic egotism and sexism. It's not human nature at all. It's human nature perverted by disease. By Identity Failure.

And let me offer even more proof. If it was merely human nature, then ego-driven insanity would be absolute and universal. Without exception, every single person would behave in self-obsessed, me-first, irrational and egocentric fashion, though likely to varying extent. But we know of people who overcame their egos, people who weren't "normal" in the sense suggested by Freud. If it's all just human nature, how do you explain Buddha? How do you account for the self-reliance of Emerson? What about the many Buddhists and other spiritualists who apparently have successfully cast off their me-centered desires? As with any evidence outside my personal experience, I can't claim with complete confidence that these disciplined minds had fully escaped Identity Failure. But their writings and quotes and testimonies lead me to believe they well may have. As I wrote previously, I've no doubt that some human beings have existed without Identity Failure's afflictions – but I suspect they have been only a relative handful.

We also have many examples of famous folks who may still have craved outside appreciation in some form for their work but were highly enlightened to the point of a deep and genuine altruism.

Mohandas Gandhi and Martin Luther King Jr. would seem to qualify. So would Albert Einstein and Albert Schweitzer and Marie Curie among the long list of great human beings. At the least they prove that our insanity can be largely controlled and channeled into grand constructive outlets.

And in my private experience too, I have learned that I.F. is a corruption of me, not the essential me. It's a sickness.

Rational Faith has helped me find a more profound layer of myself unencumbered by Identity Failure. There is a me that's so much me I become more when I uncover it. The details of that process are what I explain broadly in the last chapter of Beyond Me, with hopes that I may complete a fuller analysis in a second book. For now, let me say only that I have witnessed direct proof that I.F. isn't part of my humanity. With as much certainty as is possible for any human being, I know that I have lived at times without this horrific disease of the mind – and even at an advanced age have enormously reduced its influence on my thoughts, feelings and behavior. I consider myself living evidence that Identity Failure is a sickness, not an intrinsic element of our humanity.

The crazy things I've been talking about in our society, past and present, are crazy because they feed our egos. Our very crazy egos. These insanities make some of us feel our individual existence is valuable, our lives worth living. That's it. That's all there is to it, basically.

We each feel there's something wrong with us when there isn't. We believe outside appreciation and validation are absolutely needed to prove to ourselves that we're OK. When we don't get that validation as required, we go nuts. We flail around for it wildly. And destructively.

I listed above some of the typical key symptoms of Identity Failure, signals that aligned quite nicely with personality traits of Adolf Hitler among other crazies. But I left out the most telling of all I.F. symptoms, and the simplest to recognize: Anyone who relies on any outside source to feel better about who or what they are unquestionably suffers from Identity Failure.

I'm not referring to mild feelings of gratification or accomplishment, a sense that someone somehow benefited from something we said or did. Let's say that I help an old man change his automobile's flat tire and he thanks me. I may experience pleasant feelings that aren't Identity Failure, rational feelings, some minor emotional response that's here and gone quickly. I'm glad I was able to help, but I don't feel better about myself as a human being. His thank you isn't a big deal to me. I react to it in the sensible context of my overall existence. A healthy rational mind draws feelings of living a valuable life from within, not without. Exterior appreciation is nice enough but unneeded.

No, I mean something else by "anyone who relies on any outside source to feel better about who or what they are." I'm talking about the readily discernable emotional boost that comes to one individual by way of another person. Or often even by way of some external event. It may be someone's comment or someone's action, some situation or some circumstance.

When this happens to any of us, our emotional response will vary from one time to the next. The comment, action, situation or circumstance may seem of negligible significance or of greatest meaning. It may feel fleeting or may return to lift our spirits intermittently all our life. But whatever its lasting import, the comment or action or situation or circumstance feels like some validation for our existence. Our lives appear at least a little more worth living because of it.

With practice you can learn to detect these psychological validations reliably, as I have. I can easily sense now when I'm absorbing into my psyche something outside me as a source of appreciation, approval, validation for my own existence. In other words, when I'm relying on the world in some way to make my life feel more worth living. Each time that happens, I'm suffering from Identity Failure. Each time I allow that to happen unchallenged, I'm again letting the disease take hold of my life.

Now using just this standard alone, look back once more at all those crazy things. Lust for money or power, despotism, violence, etcetera. Quite obviously, each is some variation on this need for external validation. Each indisputably relies on comments, actions, situations and circumstances in the world outside, not the world inside. Without more money than others, the wealthy person doesn't feel so valuable to himself. Without more power than others, the CEO doesn't feel so valuable to herself. What is Hitler without his fanatical followers? What is Capone without his mob? A slaveowner absent his slaves? A racist without her targets? And so on and so on and on and on … In every instance, these people feel their existence validated by something beyond their own hearts and minds, beyond their own values and their own private experience. They need something outside them to feel life is worth living.

That is Identity Failure. And in any variation, public or private, slight or severe, it is an illness that causes problems for the victim and those around the victim.

Over the years I've decided that most people in my culture become psychologically arrested at about the middle school level. Every adult around me really is about 12-years-old. Permanently. They may or may not grow beyond this intellectually. But emotionally, we are most all still adolescent children worrying constantly how others see us, taking offense at nothing, backstabbing and gossiping eagerly about both our friends and our rivals. I've learned you can't go too far wrong in treating most adults as if they are very smart pre-teens. Perhaps even more so here in America: Be careful to offer at least three comments of praise for every one slight suggestion of criticism. Keep in mind always their insecurity and oversensitivity to the outside world. Confirm agreement with their opinions and actions often.

Believe me, I mean this without condescension. I don't see others as lesser human beings in any way. This middle school analogy merely offers me an easily remembered rule of thumb, a reminder of the bottomless uncertainty about self that troubles nearly everybody. No matter how accomplished, how lauded, how awarded, how anointed, how titled, how monied, how affirmed, how appreciated, just about every person alive is unsure of themselves to some significant degree. You may be king or president or emperor, you may have won multiple Oscars or the Nobel Peace Prize, but deep down somewhere you feel something may be fundamentally wrong with you.

Some portion of you feels like a worm.

For no good reason.

When this feeling gets strong enough, humans find their own methods to hide from it. Some of these methods have been devastating for millions, whether Hitler's Nazi Germany or Stalin's Soviet Union.

Other methods cause more limited destruction.

"If our condition were truly happy we should not need to divert ourselves from thinking about it." Blaise Pascal

I am convinced that most of our widespread social ills stem from this same problem. Looking outside ourselves to find our value. Identity Failure.

What is alcoholism but another attempt to quiet the noisy inner voices of I.F.? What is drug addiction? Or an addiction to gambling or sex or food or you name it? These have in common an effort by the individual to latch on to something outside the self to feel better about life. "I think of myself as human pondscum but there is one thing that makes me feel better …" Nobody who finds their value from within becomes an addict. Addiction is the province of the profoundly uncertain.

I am equally convinced that physical and mental illness are fueled by I.F., as explained in an upcoming chapter. Identity Failure generates the intense and prolonged destructive feelings that we bury inside ourselves, repressed emotions that emerge over time as sick bodies or sick minds. I've suffered this personally all my life and become keenly aware of it since 2000, when Dr. John Sarno's work helped me gain much more control of the process.

Take a glance also at some of our society's other serious and seriously common problems. Domestic abuse, sexual abuse, self-abuse. At bottom all are ways of easing the pain caused by Identity Failure. They are compromises of the psyche, an exchange of one psychological misery for another that feels slightly less miserable. Each is destructive behavior that temporarily satisfies a person's rage at the world for its lack of identity validation.

Let's imagine that an acquaintance named Thomas strongly feels that he needs to be Thomas-the-good-provider, the classic father figure. It's the way he was raised by his parents. But for whatever reasons, the world doesn't see Thomas that way. Everyone in and out of his family makes Thomas feel there's something wrong with him for struggling with his career. So by doing that or this destructive thing Thomas compensates for Thomas-the-good-provider, giving himself new self-images that feel like the best available right now. Doing that or this destructive thing can mean wife beating, sexual activity with a child, addictions of one sort or another. Or any of a broad range of destructive behavior.

The forms of I.F. that I'm addressing now are more personal, affecting only a few people directly in cases of abuse against others. Affecting only one directly in instances of self-abuse. There is broader social damage with any of these. That's especially true of domestic or sexual abuse, whether by causing damage to family or friends, to the school or the community. Physically beaten children may become bullies and often rack up criminal records later in life, for example. Sexually abused people are likely to endure enormous pain from the incidents as long as they're alive, affecting their children and marriages.

Physical self-harm harms others too. Even leaving out its extreme form, suicide, we know that self-harm can tear yawning holes within families, rip up marriages, leave tattered friendships. But at quick blush, viewed out of context, self-harm is puzzling. It appears to violate the Fundamental Law of Mind, to answer the Fundamental Question with a no. How could doing damage to yourself increase feelings that your existence is valuable to you at this moment in this world? How can it make life feel more worth living? A much closer look, though, reveals that self-harm can do precisely that, strengthening a wide range of identity poses. It's only necessary to understand the state of mind before the self-harm to understand the state of mind during it.

I have experienced this personally. I can speak directly from my life, sadly. To be honest with you, this is the one part of the book I've dreaded writing. I have known from the start that it would be a necessary explanation, a necessary confession if you will. I'm committed to telling this story as accurately as I possibly can, without pretense and without ego protection. And I would be untruthful by omission if I left this out. But despite all my other deeply personal admissions in these pages, this is to me the most unsettling.

Here it is, unprettied. I have since my early 20s engaged in self-harm – off and on, yes, and mostly off. I've stopped it altogether now, permanently I hope, thanks to Rational Faith. But during the most prolonged periods of my most deep-felt emotional conflicts, I have sometimes hit myself. Almost always my tight right fist into my right thigh, sometimes without great force once or twice, sometimes very hard several times in a row. I even wrote a scene portraying this in my play, In Mordant Whispers, with a character pounding his leg in furious frustration. That has been me at my worst, my most extreme expression of Identity Failure.

The fundamental psychophysics are the same with self-harm as with Identity Failure of any type. But of course the specifics differ greatly type to type, from the money-mad to the power-crazed to the dictators and mobsters and slaveholders and on through all of them. Because I have experienced self-harm up close, and because I'm so practiced at detailed self-analysis, I've been able to rather fully explore this behavior. And I am quite sure my understanding creates a window into other kinds of self-harm, from cutting to burning to bulimia to anorexia.

My version of self-harm feels to me less serious and less destructive than any of those. The worst it's ever caused me physically was some minor bruising on my thigh. Yet it is self-harm nonetheless, nothing to take lightly. And I don't. Whenever it's happened to me, I've felt stunned by my attack. Sometimes it's overtaken me suddenly and without warning in response to some situation that feels intensely frustrating, something grossly unfair to me and insoluble. Other times I've deliberately let loose a volley of punches in a desperate bid to ease relentless anxiety or persistent physical symptoms caused by these hopeless situations. Two straight days of anxious heart palpitations or some such thing. But immediately after each episode I recognized that no other behavior appeared possible for me at that moment. I had to let it out through self-harm.

Odd as this may sound, self-harm is the product of a horribly frustrated but loving mind. I've hurt myself because I couldn't bear to hurt anyone else – though I often knew at the time I was enraged at others. My values wouldn't allow violence against someone else, my self-concept could never accept it. Even verbally attacking other people would run counter to some of my most significant identity poses including Bob-the-good-person and Bob-the-nice-guy. I believe that same dynamic holds true for self-harmers right up through suicides. As a young character in a fictional short story framed this notion, explaining his attempted suicide to a friend: "Who else was I going to kill?" That sums it up. We're enraged at someone else but take it out on ourselves. The exception to this loving mind dynamic, obviously, would be self-harming criminals in prison and others who may be dangerous to society but now have no outlet for their rage except their own bodies.

My self-harm began during that period of hellfire I described in Chapter 2: As I remember it, the terror of losing my mind and the waves of anxiety that washed through me built at times to an almost unendurable level. I don't recall hitting myself often during those several agonized years but I know that I did every now and then as I felt the emotional necessity. That's when it began. My mind gravitated toward this behavior automatically as a form of emotional release, a satisfaction of my intensely conflicted emotions. I may have punched my leg a few widely scattered times in mid-adulthood but truthfully don't recall with certainty – other than during a long Pacific Ocean cruise in 2004 through South America. My father died during this voyage and I reacted one or two times with enraged punches of frustration to my leg.

The worst of my self-harming took hold during the years immediately before I began to understand and implement Rational Faith more completely. From about mid-2013 well into 2018. That was an horrendous period for me, as I've explained elsewhere, a purgatory of searing self-confusion. I've learned this had many deep emotional causes, several distinct and powerful elements of my personality that collided at once, touched off in large part by the world's indifference to my most original creative work as I saw it. Which intensified my isolated struggles for the confidence to write this book. Without getting into all those complex specifics just now, I have finally recognized that these psychological conflicts pushed me toward a deeply terrifying feeling. That I hated my life. As I wrote earlier, my psyche's constant battles were constructing my will to die. My self-confusion about the value of my existence had caused in turn a terror and then a rage – rage at the world, or "world-rage"; rage at myself, or "self-rage"; rage at life, or "life-rage." And so my will to die swelled day by day. To cope, I hit myself more often now. Dozens of instances over those five-plus years, some with repeated and very forceful punches to my thigh.

In my defense, I must say that I always understood I was doing all this as the least destructive form of self-harm I could conceive. I never wanted to truly damage myself. I rarely bruised from my hits and when I did, I felt disturbed by it. And the hitting was very occasional. But I can empathize with those people who regularly hurt themselves from Identity Failure, whether teens who cut their skin with razor blades or fashion models who eat almost nothing. I think I felt much the same sense as they must experience, my emotions expanding within me like a teapot of steam until they finally whistled out as something harmful to me. Except for a couple of instances around Lydia in San Francisco and once with Jill during the South American cruise, I was always alone when I unleashed on my leg. I felt shocked by it each time. Often I would cry right after.

I offer all this as direct experience of I. F. heightened to an intensity most people will never know. And to explain why even self-abuse in essence is only a psychological reaction caused by Identity Failure. My self-harm was a symptom created by a disease. The same happens with domestic or sexual abuse or the addictions. The destructive behavior is an individual's effort to create some acceptably significant compromise identity poses.

Which raises the question at last. How did my self-punching make my life feel more worthwhile?

In many ways. Among them:

- Often I hit myself when I was experiencing a fierce barrage of physical symptoms or anxiety. Self-harm felt so extreme to me that it nearly always stopped those physical or emotional symptoms instantly. My life without those symptoms felt more worthwhile than with them, despite the self-violence needed to knock them from my system.
- Just before hitting myself I was aware of a massive frustration mixed with rage. At some automatic emotional level, I feared this could boil over into violence against others. Of course I knew differently, but I felt afraid of this. I was too uncomfortable with so much frustrated rage. Harming myself

reinforced my self-image as someone who would never physically hurt others, no matter what I'd do to me.
- When I was reacting to the world's rejection of my writing or other creative work, self-harm strengthened the Bob-the-tortured-genius identity pose. I may be tortured but I'm also a damned genius. I felt better about myself because the emotional conflicts, the physical and emotional symptoms and the self-hurting all could be explained as part of something important in my life, something worth terrible sufferings to fulfill.
- Self-harm also strengthened other identity poses, including Bob-the-victim – which helped relieve me of responsibility for my conflicts, symptoms and behavior. It wasn't my fault, it was their fault.
- Self-harm was much easier for me to accept than the rage and hatred I often felt toward my mother, who I loved much more than hated. I was acutely aware of the psychological damage she did by making me feel flawed as a human being. For several years after my mother's death in 2012 especially, I found it necessary to hide from the furious hate I harbored toward her as a result of this deep self-confusion. Hating myself was easier for me to accept than hating her. Hitting myself satisfied some of that hateful rage.
- Self-harm eased the emotional pressure in other ways as well, making life feel more livable. These included stirring a sense of self-pity and self-compassion, a feeling that I'd now suffered enough for a while. "Man, you've just pounded your own leg with a fist! How much more punishment do you need in order to give yourself a break?" That feeling offered some temporary relief.
- All this gave me a sense of greater control over my life, a feeling of at least some empowerment. And that also increased feelings of my life's value. I may be a victim but I still had something left to force positive change if needed. I could always hit myself.

This is a very incomplete list but, I hope, gives you the general idea. No matter who's doing it or how, self-harm is just one more consequence of Identity Failure – simply another symptom of humanity's most destructive virus.

Through self-harm Joanna the cutting victim may strengthen her Joanna-the-angstridden-teen identity pose, with its connotations of precocious intelligence and a deeper if darker insight into life. Frederick the alcoholic may strengthen his Frederick-the-decent-person identity pose, relying on bourbon to prevent outbursts of rage toward his family. Meagan the anorexic may strengthen her Meagan-the-gorgeous-woman identity pose, every hunger pain a reminder of her thinning beauty.

I.F. makes individuals angry at the world, very very very angry. That rage is a response to terror, which itself is a response to our self-confusion. We're confused because the world has caused us to feel that something may be wrong with us. By believing those feelings could reflect reality, they begin to reflect reality. Suddenly there is something wrong with us: We doubt ourselves. And it damages both others and ourselves. We are terrified by it, then enraged by it. And we are, almost all of us, infected. Only the symptoms differ significantly.

For some, though, Identity Failure's worst problems are always self-inflicted. I've learned this too well.

"Look into the depths of your own soul and learn first to know yourself, then you will understand why this illness was bound to come upon you ..." Sigmund Freud

Can there really be just a single cause for all this misery in our world? As I've noted before, no. I don't think anything of significance in our universe happens from a single cause, the physical universe or the human universe.

Everything I've been talking about resulted from a combination of causes that together created effects. That's as true of my self-harm as it is of Hitler's death camps. Identity Failure was not the only cause. Instead Identity Failure was one profoundly significant, if unrecognized, cause. In some cases, it was *the* profoundly significant cause.

In nearly all human lives, I.F. is a massively influential force, pervasive yet unseen. And without its presence in our psyches, we would react differently to the other causes. The results wouldn't be as dire lacking our constant need for the outside world to show us we're OK.

Our learned psychological requirement for external validation does us in.

In my life I wouldn't react to the world's professional rejections as I have, descending into emotional and physical violence against myself – not if I had been 100% confident of my work's quality. My need for that final 15% outside confirmation has been my problem. Rather I would have responded to all the other causes in more constructive ways, the pressure from other internal and external forces that included my strong need to help people and my intense creative drive and modern theater's preference for conventional plays that seem likely to make money. These and many other causes combined with Identity Failure to create my inner torment. But Identity Failure was the essential spark.

The same is true in society. The racist young man who killed those nine black churchgoers in Charleston wouldn't have committed his crime without Identity Failure. Whatever the many other causes, he'd have stumbled toward a different way to cope somehow or other. I'm not inside his head. But I'm sure his urgent need to prove his white superiority forced him to pull the trigger, to establish heroic identity poses for himself, to transcend his troubled existence by transforming his self-image into the-racial-defender and the-white-warrior. The same is true on the wider scale. Yes, an agricultural labor-intensive economy was among the causes of American slavery in the 1800s. But without the slaveholder's desire to feel better than other people, without the unrelenting psychological pressures of Identity Failure throughout that society, slavery could not have flourished. Plantation owners would have created another system.

Imagine an entirely unrelated problem in the world, having nothing to do with Identity Failure. A rabid raccoon bites a child's hand. Is rabies the only cause? Of course not. Many causes created this effect. Among them: the raccoon got into a fight with a rabid dog; the raccoon was hungry and looking for something to eat; the child's ill mother was lackadaisical in supervising her children; the child recently enjoyed an illustrated raccoon in his storybook; the child was eating lunch alone in the kitchen when he spotted the raccoon outside; the unlocked back door allowed the child to leave the house holding a sandwich. Etcetera, etcetera, etcetera. Lots of causes. But rabies was the worst of them, the match that ignited the fumes. Rabies turned a bad situation into a life-threatening crisis.

So it is with human beings. Identity Failure isn't the only cause of our insanity. It's a key cause.

And this is true because of the foundational significance in our lives of the Fundamental Law of Mind and the Fundamental Question. Our perpetual moment-to-moment need to feel that our individual existence is valuable in this world, to feel that our life is worth living. This deepest reality of the human psyche plus our learned need for outside validation – together these are primary causes of the illness I call Identity Failure. All my tortures and troubles that you've read about earlier, your own worst miseries and those of our society, none would exist as they do now without Identity Failure.

But just as nothing significant in our universe has a single cause, nothing is all good or all bad either. This includes Identity Failure.

Does I.F. contribute to some positive results in our lives, then? Yes.

Is I.F. necessary to produce those results? No.

Let me explain. And again let me here use my own example. My need to write, to create, is among the most powerful drives in me. I couldn't be me without this. There's no question that Identity Failure has added great force to these drives, pushing me to improve and achieve. I wanted to establish myself in the world as Bob-the-writer, Bob-the-journalist, Bob-the-novelist, Bob-the-playwright, Bob-the-genius. I felt that by proving these identity poses to others I would prove the value of my existence to myself. When things went well with these efforts, when the world reacted as I hoped, I felt good about me and good about life. And when things went badly, I felt badly. I've realized, though, that I.F. was not a necessary motivation – and actually limited my growth. My throbbing drive to write and create doesn't come from Identity Failure. It's a wonderfully positive force in my psyche, something much deeper than merely a reaction to insecurities about Bob. When I free myself of Identity Failure, I shed identity poses that locked me into the mature writing styles I'd adopted later in my career. I believe they were good writing styles, true enough, highly creative writing styles that I had worked hard to develop over many years. But I have learned I can advance farther, faster without I.F. than with it. By its nature, Identity Failure is limiting. I am trying to feel valuable through identity poses A and B and C. As a result Identity Failure presses me into literary corners, demanding that Bob's work must possess qualities in some way consistent with A and B and C. Without Identity Failure, I can more easily explore new creative territories, escorting my writing through fresh places.

In addition, of course, Identity Failure brings me all its horrible problems, emotional and physical and otherwise. At times in my life, I've accepted the feeling that those problems might be necessary to my creativity. This is the artist's age-old misconception, a sense that the soul's dark edges produce creative greatness.

It's not true. Whatever positive motivation I.F. produces, a real artist is driven forward by something much deeper and better. So is the real scientist, the real philosopher, the real educator, the real anything of value in this world. We only need to recognize this, shedding Identity Failure so we can freely tap the true source of creative originality.

We don't need Identity Failure to make anything better. But to make many things better, we need to cure ourselves of Identity Failure.

"The mass of men lead lives of quiet desperation." Henry David Thoreau

Identity Failure is our society in a nutshell.

We all know we're far too hard on ourselves. We each struggle for feelings of importance, of personal value. I've never had a single man or woman disagree with me when I've shared these observations over the years – or seem remotely puzzled by the statements. Even kids acknowledge this is true.

We also all recognize that everyone else is crazy … and that we can be crazy too. Again, general agreement it seems.

We feel confused by much of our behavior. We feel very confused by much behavior of others, especially their most destructive behavior. So we resort to concepts such as evil to explain Hitler and Capone and

Manson. Or the spousekiller who was just arrested down the street.

As I've noted, I don't believe in evil. I do believe in Identity Failure. In a sense, so do most people for the reasons just mentioned: Everyone is familiar with its symptoms. We're all hard on ourselves, we're all crazy, we don't understand ourselves or others. We accept the truth of these tendencies. The problem is that most people don't view them as symptoms of an illness that can be prevented or cured but as something that simply is. Human beings are this way and that's all there is to it.

Others may not yet agree with me that this side of "human nature" is really a disease. But many others have known it is our species' greatest weakness.

I especially was fascinated by a comment made in recent years by former President Bill Clinton during a late night talk show interview. The talk show host began by expressing deep frustration with most everything happening just then in the world. He asked Mr. Clinton to explain the bottom line cause: What exactly created all these troubles? An insightful man, Clinton did not hesitate: "Identity," he replied firmly. I didn't record his comments but I recall that the former president elaborated briefly, saying the basic problem was our human tendency to insist I'm-better-than-you, I'm-bigger-than-you and so forth.

He had described the contagion of Identity Failure. My uncertainty spreads like a plague: Because I feel bad about me, I make you feel bad about yourself – and I view this as proof that I'm somehow better than you. Then to make yourself feel better, you do the same to someone else. And on it goes.

This may be the most insidious side of Identity Failure. The subtle everyday damage it does to us as we infect each other with ever-stronger strains of the disease. Little by little, vericept by vericept, germ by germ of self-doubt, we all grow sicker individually and as a society. People who are judgmental about themselves are judgmental about others. People who are hypercritical of their behavior are hypercritical of their children's behavior. People who feel cheated by life cheat in daily life. People who feel others don't care about them in turn don't care about others. Kids who are bullied bully other kids.

The targets of this judgment, criticism, cheating, uncaring and bullying come away more convinced there truly is something wrong with them. Or else why would anyone treat them so badly?

In other ways too, I.F. does its great harms. You don't need millions of dollars to obsess about money as a measurement of your life's value: People who haven't enough money to feed their families buy dozens of lottery tickets weekly, holding on to the hope they may become wealthy after Sunday's lotto drawing. And you don't need to be Al Capone or Charles Manson to commit violence in some form against our society: Too many troubled parents and troubled teachers routinely do their violence to the minds of children.

Children who grow up to perpetuate Identity Failure in the next generation.

Not all manifestations of I.F. are extreme – wars and holocausts, slavery and serial killers. They are everywhere about, in our own minds and in our own families. Just look around you.

Martin Luther King Jr.'s sermon, the Drum Major Instinct, offers still more insight into Identity Failure. His comments that Sunday to the congregation strongly suggest that Dr. King didn't only view the drum major instinct as something that some people cope with. He saw it as something all people must cope with. He had recognized Identity Failure:

"But now the problem is, it is the drum major instinct. And you know, you see people over and over again with the drum major instinct taking them over. And they just live their lives trying to outdo the Joneses. They got to get this coat because this particular coat is a little better and a little better-looking than Mary's coat. And I got to drive this car because it's something about this car that makes my car a little better than my neighbor's car. I know a man who used to live in a thirty-five-thousand-dollar house. And other people started building thirty-five-thousand-dollar houses, so he built a seventy-five-thousand-dollar house. And then somebody else built a seventy-five-thousand-dollar house, and he built a hundred-thousand-dollar house. And I don't know where he's going to end up if he's going to live his life trying to keep up with the Joneses. There comes a time that the drum major instinct can become destructive. And that's where I want to move now. I want to move to the point of saying that if this instinct is not harnessed, it becomes a very dangerous, pernicious instinct. For instance, if it isn't harnessed, it causes one's personality to become distorted. I guess that's the most damaging aspect of it: what it does to the personality. If it isn't harnessed, you will end up day in and day out trying to deal with your ego problem by boasting. Have you ever heard people that – you know, and I'm sure you've met them – that really become sickening because they just sit up all the time talking about themselves. And they just boast and boast and boast, and that's the person who has not harnessed the drum major instinct. And then it does other things to the personality. It causes you to lie about who you know sometimes. There are some people who are influence peddlers. And in their attempt to deal with the drum major instinct, they have to try to identify with the so-called big-name people. And if you're not careful, they will make you think they know somebody that they don't really know. They know them well, they sip tea with them, and they this-and-that. That happens to people. And the other thing is that it causes one to engage ultimately in activities that are merely used to get attention. Criminologists tell us that some people are driven to crime because of this drum major instinct. They don't feel that they are getting enough attention through the normal channels of social behavior, and so they turn to anti-social behavior in order to get attention, in order to feel important. And so they get that gun, and before they know it they robbed a bank in a quest for recognition, in a quest for importance."

He went on but these remarks seem clear enough. To say the drum major instinct takes people over, must be harnessed, must be dealt with … this implies the drum major instinct lives in people who are seen as good as well as people seen as bad. The good ones harness it. The bad ones don't.

As best I can determine, Dr. King believed the drum major instinct is universal. Much as William James believed "the deepest principle in human nature is the craving to be appreciated." And much as President Clinton understood that identity conflicts are the central force shaping our society. Others too have realized the underlying destructive force within us, long before Rational Faith.

Identity Failure has given us lives of quiet desperation. Unquiet desperation as well. And to escape I.F.'s painful influence even briefly, human beings will do almost anything.

Anything that might make us feel better about ourselves.

"A trifle consoles us because a trifle upsets us." Blaise Pascal

Take a careful look at some of the most common diversions here in our youthful 21st Century – or perhaps in your own later time. The Internet is a prime example just now. In 2019 the Internet remains swaddled but, like all toddlers, commands the attention of everyone nearby. Intelligent women and men and old people and kids, the invalid and the athlete, the anonymous and the famous, everyone coos into the Internet's charming face. In particular, most folks in my era are obsessed with social media, the first opportunity given humans to share our most personal thoughts and feelings and experiences with the entire planet at once. Or so it seems we're doing anyway. Actually this scrambled welter of cybercommunications buries almost everything posted online far from the view of all but a few family and friends. Yet social media makes us feel good. We've said our piece.

The attraction to social media appears by and large an attraction to talking about "me." I think it has taken our self-obsession to new lengths, encouraging folks to share photos of their unappealing breakfast muffin, their unremarkable new shoes, their tipsy cocktail toast with a friend. "Wow, look at me!" That's what it's all about.

I know people who appear addicted to social media. Truly addicted. Almost any time of the day or night I can expect an immediate response from them to something I post on the Internet. They will follow, like, friend me online, they will offer retorts and arguments, they will share my photos or join my groups at noon or midnight, 3 p.m. or 3 a.m. It's scary to me, truthfully. Their virtual life has taken the place of their real life.

As it is now the Internet, and social media particularly, create the illusion of friendship, of connection with others when social media mostly prevent us from building meaningful face-to-face relationships. People obsess about their social media pages because they feel a kind of validation from this for some identity poses they cherish. Feedback from friends tells them how smart, how beautiful, how lucky they are. The Internet is an extraordinary leap forward for humanity, launching a revolution of a scope and swiftness never experienced before. It can help us accomplish many important things that may include a greater sense of oneness on Planet Earth. The Internet already is shrinking our vision of the world. But the Internet's more important contributions will come in time ... For now, the cyberworld is still a toy for most people, another expression of me.

Other communication innovations also have fed modern society's Identity Failure. One is the cellphone, so omnipresent that you find these devices even in the remotest and poorest nations. Really a portable computer now, the cellphone is another techie toy that gives people a feeling of individual value, a confirmation of their importance. For some, this comes through incessant conversation with their family or friends – these constant talkers appear never to remove the phone from their ear. For others it is email or text messages. But no matter the preferred communication method, cellphones used to this extent are one more reflection of Identity Failure. They distract our minds, they provide an outlet for emotions, they attract validation of me.

Still another outcropping of I.F. comes to us in the form of the super-serious sports fan. Fan for fanatic, literally the word's origin. And with good reason. Remember my description of feeling personally depressed when my Detroit Tigers lost some important game? I had linked my value as an individual to that of my team – and their loss became my failure. When they had a great season, my ego was inflated. Everyone around me knew I was a longtime Tiger rooter and so my team's winning ways allowed me to boastfully tease fans of other teams. Note what I called the Tigers just now: "my team." That's what all bigtime sports fans say in our society and it reveals something about such fanatics.

This strong ego-connection is why some fans can react so violently, either to losses or wins. The guy who paints his face in team colors before the game, who always wears a team jersey or hat, whose automobile bumper stickers blare his sports allegiances – this person is likely to take it hard indeed when his team doesn't succeed. The bigger the game, the bigger the personal sense of disappointment and anger ... or personal elation and joy if his team pulls out a victory. Again, sports for this individual is a diversion, an emotional outlet and a validation of his value. No matter how messy his everyday life, no matter how horrible his problems, he can feel like a winner in this world sometimes. He just has to root for the right team. Go Tigers.

I don't mean to suggest that sports or any other diversions are unhealthy in themselves. Certainly not. But rabid sports fans are so prevalent in our society that they're another good example of I.F.-driven escapism. Internet or social media, cellphones or sports teams or what have you – the diversions and distractions, the endless forms of emotional release and identity validation have a common thread when taken to extremes. They are attempts to free ourselves from the pain of Identity Failure.

We try again and again, day in and day out, to cope with feeling so terrible about ourselves.

Eventually our Identity Failure becomes exhausting.

"Life is one long process of getting tired." Samuel Butler

We require a very strong reason to fight this battle.

Life.

Human beings need to feel emotionally engaged with living, especially to feel useful to others. That's part of the reason we tend to flourish when we connect our existence with something larger that helps people. And it's part of what Rational Faith can achieve for people.

Without something like this, our individual life can appear to lose meaning over time. As has often been said, we need to feel needed. Living must seem necessary in some way – even truer when we're pitted in a daily psychological combat. Identity Failure wears most of us down.

When that happens, our will to die strengthens. At some point, it may overtake our will to live.

But first we feel the fatigue. A weariness with our existence. It turns out that the German language offers two intriguing words related to our will to die. One is "lebensmude." It means "life-tired." As I understand it, lebensmude denotes an exhaustion with living so strong that we'd like to just give up. Then there's the word, "weltschmerz."

It means, "world weariness." My understanding is that the term suggests a powerful fatigue with the world as it is rather than as it should be.

Because of Identity Failure, we've spent much of our lives knowing full well what it should be. The world should be about me. It should appreciate me, recognize me, understand me fully. The world should give me its confirmations, its validation for the person I know myself to be.

But it doesn't.

Rather, it offers us precisely the opposite. And because of Identity Failure, the opposite torments us to varying degrees depending on the severity of our illness. The world seems to fight against us as if in a colossal conspiracy to humiliate, defeat, frustrate, terrify, infuriate. And to exhaust.

If I must slay the world to establish meaningful identities within my psyche, I am likely to lose. And I may be inclined to experience my private variations on lebensmude and weltschmerz.

Unless …

Unless I've got you under my skin.

Unless I'm all for you body and soul, day and night, night and day.

Unless, that is, I find love.

Romantic, intoxicating, irresistible, soul-filling love. The world's preferred drug, healer of men and women and children. The soulmate love of maturity, the puppy love of youth. Whatever the variety, it makes life feel "very much like walkin' on a cloud," to quote another love song lyric. I've experienced it many times. I know.

And I know something else now too.

I know romantic love is a product of Identity Failure. Romantic love is profoundly irrational, as most folks probably would concede. That's the point, isn't it? We "fall" in love – and who knows why? Poets have tried to explain it. And novelists and composers. And as we've just seen, lyricists. But I don't think they've explained it at all. I think they've swallowed the romantic fallacies because romance made them feel good. For a little while. Just as it makes all of us feel good. For a little while.

I recognize this may not come as welcome news. Forgive me. Even if you've not felt irritated by my efforts to analyze other misconceptions as I see them, you may feel irritated by this one. I do understand, truly. Romantic love is so deeply threaded into our culture that it's difficult to imagine any other type of love between partners – romantic love and its natural companion, romantic sex.

Romantic love is the ideal.

But like many ideals, it's built on fantasy. We expect one other person to complete us, fulfill us, be our one and only and be our everything. It's impossible. Hence all the misery of relationships, all the fights and breakups, all the resentments and misunderstandings, all the lies and infidelities, all the divorce, all the violence and even murder. Nothing can make relatively sensible people quite as abruptly ridiculous as romantic love and its inevitable troubling aftermath.

As I'll try my best to explain in the next chapter, romantic love is simply another insanity of Identity Failure. It's one more attempt to escape feeling bad about who we are.

But a more rational love for our partners is possible. I've experienced that too. As an element of my philosophy, Rational Faith will argue for this post-romantic view of our significant others. The new concept doesn't make us less as human beings. It makes us more – and makes our love more balanced, more real.

No, I'm not insisting that you give up romantic love to practice Rational Faith. Not really, though it can help us to live the philosophy more completely. Just keep reading, please. See for yourself if my dissection of romantic love makes sense based on everything else you've read up to now. I think you'll find it does.

The madness we call romantic love is really the madness of Identity Failure.

Chapter 11: The Other Half

"We are never so defenseless against suffering as when we love, never so forlornly unhappy as when we have lost our love object or its love."
                    Sigmund Freud

All, All Alone

Have you ever pondered why tough, violent men crumble in solitary confinement?

Why would simple untortured isolation in prison quickly become an exquisitely painful form of torture? What makes it so hard for human beings to be alone with ourselves?

For those incarcerated men, and women as well, the problem isn't the prison. It's the separation from others. Reliable reports show that people can utterly lose their minds during prolonged stints of solitary. Pulling out their own hair, beating their heads against concrete walls, suicide. The agony is so severe that prison reform advocates have called for an end to solitary confinement as a cruel and unusual punishment.

But why is it so bad?

To me, the chaos of prison life with its sexual predators and racist gangs would seem much worse than residing alone in a cell apart from all the hatred. On the surface. Digging down farther into myself, I can imagine that solitary's safety in time would be overwhelmed by solitary's insanity. Of course there's the lack of company and conversation, the absence of activity, the cascade of unexpressed thoughts. I believe it goes deeper, though.

And here's why. Like nearly everyone else, I have tied my grip on reality to outside opinion – or I did before Rational Faith anyway. Sometimes I still lapse, despite my best efforts. Whenever it happens, I rely on validation from other people to feel connected with my sense of myself and the world. This is who I am, this is who they are, this is how things around us are. I have my own notions but can't believe them completely without someone's agreement. So what do you do when there's no one to agree? You watch yourself slipping loose of all hold on the real. You begin to see yourself losing your mind.

There's no diversion. No distraction. Nothing else to fill the psychological void. Nothing except your own doubts and fears accompanied by a building rage. This is the kind of all-me-all-the-time that no one wants. And it greatly exacerbates that tendency in many of us to wonder whether we're mad, a common fear I discussed in Chapter 9:

"Our learned self-mistrust appears to lead many people to suffer from a related problem, easily morphing into a terror that we might be insane. I've experienced this personally more times than I'd prefer to confess: Among my deepest horrors is an abject fear of losing my mind. And looking back, I have struggled with it most directly and miserably during periods of my life when Identity Failure has been at its worst. The more unsure of myself generally, the more unsure of my general sanity. This came upon me as a persistent series of intense uncertainties. At these times, I couldn't escape the feeling that my moment-to-moment judgments were so unreliable that I shouldn't place any trust in my otherwise strong sense of sanity. Yeah I felt sane, but who could tell for sure? I mention it in this context because I've picked up clues over the decades, many strong indications that insanity is a nightmarish terror for lots of folks. Yeah they feel sane, but who can tell for sure? I believe one root of this is our self-mistrust: Others know more about us as individuals than we know and only others can help us each discern what's real and what's unreal in our psyche. The good and the bad. Once you buy into this idea, feeling crazy isn't a long stretch for most of us."

Now consider again this human psyche locked up with itself alone for weeks or months or years. I should think only an extraordinarily strong and focused mind could endure that way of being for any length – or perhaps a mind that's exceptionally diseased and uncurious. I'm not certain about that. But for most people, the isolation would feel unendurable. Nobody to confirm that the food is awful, the guard is a sadist, the warden is a fool. Nobody to confirm that you are you. Identity Failure would surge because you wouldn't have any method to validate your identity poses, the self-images that seem to give your existence its value.

You would come unhinged.

Here once more I can speak with some confidence based on personal experience. Very very fortunately, this didn't come to me in prison. Imprisonment has been another of my most intense lifetime fears and I hope never to confront it. No, I've endured another type of imprisonment, a different form of solitary confinement. It went on for many years, starting as romance and then engulfing me through marriage and home ownership and divorce.

As I complete the final rewrite of this chapter in Winter 2019, my sense of a vast psychological isolation at last is slowly fading from my life. That's some 24 years of solitary for me.

The period honestly felt like a type of torture in some ways, infrequently at first, then more and more often. It ultimately triggered irrational but profound uncertainties about my sanity. And it whipped up in me a yearning for the one thing that I'd believed might end my mind's isolation.

A new love. A new consuming and enveloping romantic love.

All You Need ...

Our culture loves love.

As far as I can figure, the whole world loves love – if in many variations. That's my guess. Just about everybody appears to crave the special relationship, the exclusive connection with another human being. Or sometimes with more than one human being at the same time. In my experience as traveler and observer, love is a nearly universal obsession whatever the local form of romance.

In the West, our contemporary society was shaped by 19th Century Romanticism to a frightening extent. Great minds and great artists, great ideas and great works came from this time, as we all know. Much of my favorite music emerged from that era, including the revolutionary canon of Ludwig van Beethoven. I hugely admire these creators. As I see it, the problem is that some of the movement's concepts have lingered far too long. In Europe and the Americas our notions of love and sex and marriage and childbearing, of families and childrearing all are fogged by a cloud of Romanticism. And this romantic ideal seems to have influenced many other regions of the planet as Western songs and books and films have dominated popular culture, especially songs and books and films from the United States. Whether they love us or hate us as a nation, people worldwide sing to the American melody.

In music on both radio and the Internet, in the nightclub and the Broadway theater and the opera house, you can't escape a romantic love story. In plays too, no matter comedy or tragedy. In literature, popular and serious. In movies of all stripes. It is the rare offering that doesn't include romance in some way, as main theme or subplot, its pleasures or miseries, its beginnings or endings. Our culture loves love, a consuming and enveloping romantic love.

So do I.

But I'm learning.

I confess this has been very hard for me. I say that without pride or ego, rather with a measure of embarrassment. Intellectually, I've been well aware of the dangers of romantic or sentimental perspectives on daily life since my mid-20s. But I managed to forget these dangers after meeting Jill, who would become my second wife. Actually, I consciously chose to ignore what I'd known for some 15 years by then. Once my youthful and highly romantic experiences with Lydia turned moldy, I had devoted much thought and observation and curious conversation with friends to the topic of relationships. Love, I told them, seemed more about ourselves than anyone else. We love someone because we need them – more specifically, we need to take something they can give us. Some of my more perceptive married friends agreed.

During my 10-year relationship with Susan, including five married years, I allowed myself to enjoy a highly romantic love for her. We had some good years, some hard years, some bad years and I loved her through them all. Susan is a strong individual and a cherished friend to this day. But in this context there's not much more I need to say about our relationship. And that's for a good reason: Throughout our time together, I maintained a relatively rational connection with my earlier thinking, never abandoning my logic entirely for sentiment.

This changed completely after I met Jill, soon after my separation from Susan. In Jill I found a remarkably creative and remarkably emotional woman who quickly decided to leave her marriage for me. Just as quickly I was right there with her – deeply in love. We savored an intense romance that lasted for some ten years, though chip by chip our foundation of devoted mutual affection slowly broke apart. Our coupledom lasted about 12 years in total, a decade of these married. Other than my work, I gave myself over almost entirely to romance during this time, drifting into Jill's preferred lifestyle of isolated togetherness. Soon we didn't want to see much of anyone or do much of anything except be with each other, sipping our martini or kamikaze cocktails in chilled glassware each evening before sliding eagerly into bed. We both were highly sexed and uniquely turned on by each other – and we made the most of this intoxicating combination. Often we joked about being broke financially but hitting "the love lotto." Even more often, others commented with envy on our obvious romantic love for one another, a love that was fired intensely far beyond any romance either of us had known before.

Truly, this was a consuming and enveloping romantic love. As my perceptive brother-in-law, Jack Lucas, told me the day Jill and I announced our plans to divorce, "But you have what everyone wants." To which I immediately answered, "Yes. But it doesn't work."

And it doesn't. And it doesn't because it's rooted in Identity Failure.

Jill and I created the kind of relationship in reality that I wasn't sure was possible in reality. The kind depicted in those films, the kind envisioned in those songs and plays and books. We would have done anything for each other. We genuinely adored each other. And we felt this way because we'd found a partner who was both equally giving and equally needy as ourselves, someone capable of a wildly romantic imagination and hopeful of living out those fantasies in everyday life. Someone who wanted the world to feel like a better place than we'd experienced, somewhere fair and caring and encouraging. So we constructed a place of our own, just as they do in those films and songs and plays and books.

For a long time, longer than you might imagine, our relationship seemed to us a very beautiful sanctuary.

Yet ours was an existence of great isolation. And ultimately very great pain for us both because our private sanctuary had been erected on a highly unstable soil. As in many romantic relationships, the reality wasn't what it appeared to be. Even to us.

She became the primary source of outside validation for my most significant identity poses – Bob the good person, the nice guy, the journalist, the writer, the musician, the artist, the genius. And I filled the same purpose in her life, whatever her deeper identity poses really may have been. I had a strong sense of who Jill envisioned Jill to be, I think. We served as mirrors that reflected the images of each other we wanted to see, precisely as I'd imagined great romantic partners should do. She confirmed the value of my existence and I confirmed hers. Jill and I spoke frequently of "staying connected" emotionally, cultivating a deep sense of mutual understanding and trust and love. Yes, isn't this precisely the way a great love is portrayed in all those movies? It happened for us in real life.

But over the years, we couldn't maintain this one-and-only-person illusion. I learned that no one can fill all the needs of anyone. We had thought precisely-the-right-someone could. And because we kept trying to live this romantic lifestyle, year after year, I eventually began to resent my relationship with Jill. I felt more and more alone. Heightening the isolation for me, I had left my newspaper job less than two years after meeting her, working as a stay-at-home freelancer. The newsroom collegiality was gone, something I miss to this day. And then even worse, we had bought a single-family home that I'd not really wanted but she seemed to badly need. That home became my prison. Most weekdays I worked alone, largely confined to this modest house in a quiet neighborhood without many folks out and about on the streets. I had lost even the limited human interaction that was pleasant in my first years as a freelance writer at a canalside condominium complex in Fort Lauderdale, a spot with quirky sociable neighbors to spare.

Looking back, I recognize that my dissatisfaction already was percolating during the most satisfying early years of my relationship with Jill. I recall sensing that something was wrong somehow in our romantic arrangement. We would obsess with dread for days about the misery of separation during some upcoming out-of-town writing assignment I'd landed – even if my absence would only be overnight. The intensity of our love reached absurd extremes. I knew this at the time. And eventually I knew that our marriage felt to me like a very strange form of solitary confinement. I was imprisoned all day long and most of the night, an aloneness interrupted for a few hours by the same visitor evening after evening. Then on weeknights she went to sleep early, I stayed up late.

My loneliness bloated month by month. An especially painful sort of loneliness, I think, the type that comes alongside someone who no longer meets your most important needs. I've found loneliness when living alone much less troubling than loneliness when living with the wrong person. I knew I still loved Jill. Finally I also knew I couldn't stay with her and asked for a divorce. By that time our relationship had become unpleasant for us both, at best. We even tried an open marriage toward the end. It didn't work either.

We parted amicably, as Susan and I had done, but I felt isolated still. I had known a grandly fulfilling romantic love. Now I wanted it again. I'd long realized that my romantic sensibilities as well as my tendency toward sentimentality are strong characteristics of my personality. I imagine that Lydia, Susan and Jill would acknowledge that I often was much more the romantic than they during our lives together. After my second divorce, I suffered from the absence of a sweeping romance. The heartache was constant.

From that time to today, I have slowly developed a deep love for someone else. Gwendolyn has become my best friend, my lover, my confidant, my travel companion during my occasional cruise writing assignments all over the world from 2007 on. But as I see things, ours is a very different, more balanced and rational love than I'd ever found before. We are not dependent on one another for outside validation in the way Jill and I were. We live in our own condos, each with our own friends and separate lives. Gwen's a beautiful caring person and I do know she loves me. But we have no desire to live together or become more wrapped up in a relationship than we are. We've talked of this many times. To me it seems a grownup love, a love mature.

Oddly, that variety of love, so drastically altered from my earlier experience, has required many years for me to fully appreciate. I knew it was a much healthier attitude of course, but emotionally I still craved the obsessive romantic love I'd once had. And I continued to feel horribly isolated, not by a possessive relationship now but by its absence. I needed someone who would validate those identity poses again. I needed the same extreme connection with another human being. I needed someone who was fully and unquestionably on my side as I tackled the work ahead for me. This unfulfilled passion contributed to one of the most agonizing periods of my life as I've already described, enormously exacerbating my wounded writer's sense of indifferent rejection by the world. I felt misunderstood by everyone, including Gwen. I felt unappreciated by everyone too. And I felt my confidence wavering as I worked to build the Humanity Project and aimed toward writing this book. How could I manage all this alone? Entirely, absolutely alone.

And so came the anxiety, the symptoms, the self-harm.

The deepening isolation.

Without any conscious awareness of it, I now isolated myself psychologically to defend my writing against self-doubt. I became isolated also by my deepening fury at the world's failure to recognize what I viewed as my best creative work. Remaining separate physically and emotionally from people to the extent possible offered a barrier to an Identity Failure that threatened to destroy my determination to create this book and this philosophy of Rational Faith. I understood that I would have to summon the guts to begin writing my big book at last – and to continue through to the end. I can say with no arrogance that some considerable magnitude of confidence is needed for the task. Reflect on the audacious assertions and theories you've read so far. Imagine that you are the only human who believes many of these expansive new ideas, to your knowledge. And that you want to share the ideas with as many other humans as possible in an effort to help them. It's a challenge. This daunting prospect greatly increased my sense of isolation from others, those folks who would think my beliefs insane if offered in casual discussion. No one would ever truly understand my work without reading this book – the entire book, cover to cover. Unfortunately, it wasn't yet written.

That awareness made me feel intensely alone. Intellectually, I was wholly confident of my concepts. Emotionally, I felt isolated and afraid. Maybe I was crazy afterall. Who could tell for sure? At the same time, I craved more than ever another great romance with someone who would take Jill's place. This missing romantic partner combined with all the rest of my problems to confine me in a perpetual loneliness. For some 24 years from start to finish, from the isolating relationship to the isolating work. Not the solitary confinement of a prison cell, obviously, but a prolonged isolation of the mind.

To free me from my terrible isolation, I felt desperate to savor once more a consuming and enveloping romantic love.

And for similar reasons, just about everyone else desperately wants love to consume and envelope them too.

Locked Within

Each of us endures a solitary confinement.

No matter how we pretend otherwise, everyone is locked up with our private thoughts and feelings, our pleasures and pains, our perceptions and sensations and judgments. We each live alone. That's the way nature designed us.

If we are psychologically self-reliant individuals, this isolation poses far fewer troubles. We are confident from within, not from without. We're sure of our thoughts and feelings and pleasures and pains and perceptions and sensations and judgments. Naturally, we still require the society of our fellows. To share with them, to help them, to let them help us, to collaborate and to plan, to exchange experiences, to converse and laugh and learn. Every human is a "social solitary," in the phrase of Dr. Jacob Bronowski. Homo sapiens is a species whose members need both solitude and society.

I believe one of art's deepest purposes is to make us less alone. The novel, the drama, the symphony, the painting or sculpture or photograph or film or digital creation – they express someone's experience as a human being. How could we know otherwise what another person feels when they hate or love, how could we understand sacrifice and courage and perseverance without art? Creations by true artists reassure us that we feel and want and need much the same things that everybody feels and wants and needs. Art connects individuals in a common humanity.

But most of us are not psychologically self-reliant and most of us forget art's great lessons among the stresses of daily life. Instead we wrestle all day with varying strengths of Identity Failure, perpetually searching for somebody or something to confirm that we're OK, that our lives are still worth living. We're incarcerated inside our heads, besieged by all those thoughts and feelings and pleasures and pains and perceptions and sensations and judgments. We are isolated. And we feel isolated – misunderstood, unappreciated, confidence forever wavering. And very afraid.

Isolation intensifies Identity Failure, for you and me no less than for the solitary inmate. It's a matter only of degree. And like the prisoner, we will find that isolation can become its own form of torture, even an isolation of the more ordinary kind. I know this from experience. Typically we feel pretty much alone in our battle to gain the world's appreciation and approval. Friends and family somewhat ease this feeling for us. But if we become more deeply isolated as I did, the struggle for outside validation of our self-images, our identity poses, grows more difficult exponentially. It's not just me against the world, with a little help from my friends. It's me alone against the world entire.

Romantic love changes this instantly. It dilutes our Identity Failure with a permanent and reliable source of external appreciation rather than the usual string of temporary and tenuous approvals served up grudgingly by the world. That's how it feels anyway while the romance remains. We have someone who always will help us feel important, always understand us, always make the world seem like that better place. Romantic love gives us a way to confirm our cherished identity poses and also to greatly diminish our perpetual sense of isolation. That's why it is so fiercely addictive. If we are already hooked on outside approval to feel good about ourselves, romance appears to hand us a lifetime supply. At the same time, we no longer shoot up our drug of choice all alone. We have company now. There's nothing else quite like that shared romantic high, as the love stories all remind us constantly.

As a recovering love addict, I know the sensation well.

At its best, romantic love gives us a feeling of profound connection with a fellow person that can't be experienced any other way. For a time your perpetual sense of isolation evaporates. And your Identity Failure is much less troubling. You and your significant-other suddenly make up a team of two, deliriously apart from the rest of the pack, a highly exclusive mutual admiration society where even faults and peccadillos become charming. You can do no wrong. Neither can he or she, your partner. Life is good.

Or rather, romantic love offers the illusion of this profound spiritual partnership until it doesn't. As long as that illusion lasts, we are reprieved from our solitary confinement. When the illusion collapses, we are locked up again feeling more alone than ever. And yes, I've learned of couples who seemingly never lost their great romantic love, those people who were married for 58 years and died a day apart or whatever. But I don't for a second believe such relationships are what they appear. In my estimation, the path to this kind of loving longevity is for one person to give up everything for the other – and to not resent it. To willingly subsume your most significant personal preferences and interests as well as your personality within those of your partner. In my time, U.S. President Ronald Reagan and his wife, Nancy, seemed this sort of marriage. She looked adoringly at him no matter how mundane the president's speech might be. Accounts of their marriage strongly suggest her devotion was no act. Nancy evidently was fiercely protective of Ronald behind the scenes and cared for him over many years of Alzheimer's Disease before his death. Quite clearly, he loved her too. I don't know any of this for sure. I wasn't with them. But from the outside anyway, theirs appeared a relationship built on a joint agreement that one spouse was caregiver and the other cared-for. President Reagan even called her "Mommy."

As long as a couple views their relationship in the romantic mold, I believe, one partner must do most of the compromising for their relationship to endure the decades. My parents were married for more than 60 years before my father's death in 2004. My mother gave up much to maintain their lives together, moving when she didn't want to, abandoning important travel plans that didn't suit Dad, turning away from the kind of career that I feel she would have liked, and more. Mom loved Dad to the end and Dad still loved Mom in his way. But I feel certain she resented being ever the giver to his taker.

Probably anyone with a strong personality eventually would resent acceding constantly to the expectations, desires and demands of another person.

They should. That's not what love is, in my view.

But it's the situation romantic love tends to create for many once the mutual intoxication subsides. One partner is generally dominant, the other submissive. One partner enjoys the sense of being in control, the other partner endures the sense of being controlled. One flourishes, the other withers. In this way, a relationship is maintained over time.

To many of the submissive partners it feels like the easier path, preferable to splitting up. Though individuals crave appreciation from society, we crave romantic appreciation from one member of society much more. And once we have that, we don't want to let it go. Divorce requires courage, whether legal divorce or just packing boxes and moving out. As an old pop song noted, breaking up is hard to do. So the submissive partner often will make whatever compromises are needed to avoid a breakup – and the dominant partner knows it. In our culture, most people are terrified of being alone, of returning to the isolated struggle, no matter how bad life is within the relationship.

And even when we do finally muster the gumption to escape one romance, many of us immediately want another. Rebound relationships are commonplace, bouncing into a new romantic partnership right after extracting yourself from an unsatisfying entanglement. Look at my reaction after the divorce from Jill. I still needed the heady love affair with someone entirely smitten by me, something not available in my healthy relationship with Gwen. She didn't want the job. I suffered a long time before letting go of this quest to play out the film version of love again.

Many individuals live that drama repeatedly all their lives, one searing tragedy of romance after another. Romantic love is the ideal. And personal evidence to the contrary notwithstanding, most people continue to believe in it, ache for it, seek after it … and fall topsy-turvy for the illusion over and over. Such is its fearsome appeal.

Unforgettable

It's not only our concept of romantic love that is illusory.

So is our concept of the beloved.

This is one of the keys to understanding the deeper nature of romance, fueled by our desire to escape the miseries of Identity Failure.

Just think back for a moment on one of your own more poignant romances. You'll see what I mean.

Remember how you felt about that person in the beginning. How incredibly beautiful or sexy. Or smart or wise. Or funny or charming. Or what have you – those qualities that delighted you, intrigued you, pushed you almost instantly into fantasies of great sex, perhaps, or even a great marriage with great kids. You quickly wondered whether you at last had discovered your soulmate.

You hadn't.

Remember how this image of your lover shifted over time. Yeah, she was beautiful but had crooked teeth you'd overlooked before. Yeah, he was sexy but very tense and uncomfortable when physically touched. She wasn't as smart as she'd seemed, he wasn't wise at all. The funny or the charming faded quickly into a recognition that this person really was kind of a jerk. It's happened to us all – and if you're anything like me, it's happened many many many times. Again and again I hyperventilated over people I hardly knew because I wanted to believe the romantic illusion.

I can barely begin to tell you how keyed up with nervous anticipation I usually felt on the day of a first date with a lovely woman. Those romantic and sentimental tendencies of mine kicked in, full power. And let me give you one especially ridiculous example, a true incident I turned into fiction through the main character in my first novel, Hard News. I wrote the book immediately after leaving my fulltime newspaper job – an entertaining though fact-based tale of investigative journalism's value to society along with an indictment of the money-mad media. But the first-date catastrophe detailed there was unadorned truth.

Living in a one room efficiency in Burlington, Vermont, I was preparing to take out a woman I'd recently met at my bank. A gorgeous teller, as I remember. I must have been in my late 20s. Dressed up for the evening, I was only minutes away from heading out the door to pick her up when I decided to drink a quick swig of soda pop first. I pulled from the fridge a large unopened bottle of Pepsi Cola but, in my nervous haste, dropped it. The glass exploded like a hand grenade. Sticky bottle shrapnel landed everywhere. I glanced at my watch, then grabbed a cloth to begin hurriedly cleaning up when I soon noticed another problem. I was bleeding. Bleeding rather a lot from my hand. I picked my way around the shattered glass to the tiny bathroom, checked out the time once more and quickly cleansed the gash. A bandage or two later, I was back at the sticky glass-shard cleanup, racing to finish so I could make my date promptly. I've always hated being late for anything. Finally my linoleum floor seemed reasonably clean and I scooted through the door for my wonderful evening ahead. By now it was dark. Another time check – I had only a few minutes left. So I started to run, sprinting down the sidewalk when I spotted a convenient shortcut over someone's lawn. Someone's lawn with a booby trap. A thin dark metal wire had been stretched just above the grass, perhaps to anchor some new-planted tree. I couldn't see the wire, of course. Not until I was sprawled all over the lawn after tripping, now with grass stains and a hole in my good slacks. I may be sugarcoating the memory but it seems to me I laughed at the total absurdity of it all. One memory I know for sure: This date turned out to be uninspiring and I never saw her after that night. I don't even remember anything about the woman except that she was pretty.

So much for wonderful evenings.

Without any remotely rational reasons, I had felt this date on this night with this gorgeous bank teller might be important. We might hit it off. We might have sex. We might start a real relationship. Maybe she was the one.

This was among my more colorful incidents of romantic self-abuse but far from the lone example. Why did I keep doing things like this to myself? Why do any of us put ourselves through it? Why do we so easily imagine another person to possess a broad assortment of desirable qualities they almost certainly don't have?

Because doing this makes us feel good. Very good.

Keep in mind that we secretly doubt ourselves. We feel there's something wrong, deeply flawed, about us as individuals. That's what we've learned over our lifetime, that's been the world's message to us each. I accept that I should be Bob-the-good-person every minute but feel that I only rarely live up to that highly significant identity pose. I try to compensate for this perceived shortcoming by validating other important identity poses but even that doesn't work very well. Society's appreciation comes to me hit or miss. I am wracked repeatedly by I.F.

Now, though, I'm infatuated with this extraordinary creation, someone who seems some kind of ideal. My psyche has distorted the reality of my love interest out of all recognition. Why? Because this drastically changes the way I see myself. I'm suddenly a guy who is desired in return by this same extraordinary creation. The more amazing my lover, the more amazing I must be.

In broad terms, this is the psychological process I've observed in myself and others for decades. We exaggerate our partner's best qualities to feel this person is more than they could possibly be. And then we bask in their reflected aura.

If you don't believe me, turn to the source of much trustworthy insight into our collective notions about romantic love. Popular songs. To me, one of the most telling is a lovely tune recorded by the fine singer, Nat King Cole. It's called, Unforgettable, and these are among the lyrics:

"Unforgettable in every way
And forever more, that's how you'll stay
That's why, darling, it's incredible
That someone so unforgettable
Thinks that I am unforgettable too"

This about sums it up.

As sung by Cole, the man feels it's incredible that a woman who's eternally "unforgettable in every way" could bring herself to find him worthy. She finds him unforgettable, in fact. And if such an unforgettable lover recognizes so much good about him, then it must be true.

That's exactly how we feel in our lover's company. Romance transforms a nearly continuous awareness of our own serious flaws into a recognition of something wonderful about us. To our eyes, we're instantly improved. Love makes us new.

Naturally, our perfect other half doesn't feel so perfect. In all likelihood, the unforgettable woman crooned over by Cole also would view herself as severely flawed. And her psyche would warp his image into a reflection of wishful imagination just as his mind distorted perceptions of her. She really would find him unforgettable. This creates that mutual admiration society I mentioned, where even unpleasant qualities can seem delightful. Within romantic love's delirium, the bad stuff is ignored or excused. Or enjoyed as good stuff.

That psychological process is one thing when it happens during the relatively harmless early period of romance. It's much more serious when we are suckered into marriage and children based on delusions. But this happens all the time. That bad stuff isn't so bad, we tell ourselves. And if it is bad, we'll just change our spouse into something better. No problem.

Most of us learn that's not true. The bad stuff is a problem and it will stay a problem. Troubled people rarely change by way of a transformative relationship. So the marriage is a constant shout-fest or worse and the children grow up terrified and angry. And very confused about their value as human beings.

Still, romantic love beckons and we go. Because it offers us even more than an end to our individual isolation, more than a fountain of external confirmation to strengthen feelings of our life's value, all flowing from our beloved. Love also provides lots of additional appreciation from others. Most of us know how it feels to exist as a kind of social outcast without a partner. Couples are discomforted by our company as a single. Strangers, colleagues, even friends and family often question our unattached status – and convey an impression they think there's something wrong with us. We can almost hear their doubts: "Maybe you're a misanthrope. Maybe you're difficult to live with. Maybe you have some strange sexuality. Maybe you're weird." But all this uncertainty melts the moment we "have" a steady partner, especially a spouse. The couples relax and everyone from strangers to family regards us as normal.

Including us.

You and I and most everybody else feel we fit into society much more comfortably as individuals in a romantic partnership with other individuals. This arrangement seems to answer many of those pesky questions people otherwise would have about us. Folks find less reason to doubt our value. Which means we find less reason to doubt our value. Our self-image is burnished by a fixed intimate connection to someone else, regardless of how unsatisfying this connection is in daily living. Alone, it's easy to share the same type of concerns about ourselves as others harbor: "Maybe I'm a misanthrope. Maybe I'm difficult to live with. Maybe I have some strange sexuality. Maybe I'm weird." In a relationship, we feel some measure of our worth confirmed purely through coupling up.

Even after the delirious romance has long passed. And even if the relationship has become more appearance than substance, more pretense than truth. No matter the emotional gulf that yawns between you and your partner, outsiders still imagine a romance. If that partner brings obvious attributes such as great looks, wealth or social status, you will share in all the appreciation through association. Since people think he or she is something special, they'll think you must be something special. Simply holding your partner's hand publicly can serve as a pose-strengthener, briefly easing your Identity Failure.

Trophy wives and trophy husbands often stay around for more than just the money. For them, the marriage itself can seem a trophy envied by everyone in their orbit.

Love Mainlined

By now researchers have discovered something fascinating about love: It is a true addiction.

I'm looking at a newspaper clipping from February 12, 2009 that says, "Love works chemically in the brain like a drug addiction." The brief piece includes this quote from a scientist who studied the physical dynamics of romance. "Romantic love is an addiction; a wonderful addiction when it is going well, a horrible one when it is going poorly," the researcher noted. Under the article scotch-taped into my notebook on that date I jotted this comment: "I wrote exactly this same thing years ago in one of my notebooks! Nice to know science is confirming it!"

I've long believed we are literally addicted to romantic love. And I now am convinced we are addicted also to outside appreciation, praise, approval. Validation of our worth by others. It only happens that romantic love is the ultimate outside appreciation.

Hardly surprising, then, for scientists to identify chemical responses to romance like those of drug addiction. We all know what it's like to feel hooked on a love affair, unable to focus on anything else. There's even a phrase for this. We call it being "love sick." Once again, the lyricists brilliantly express our experiences.

"I'm as restless as a willow in a windstorm
I'm as jumpy as a puppet on a string
I'd say that I had spring fever
But I know it isn't spring"
Oscar Hammerstein II

"I've got you under my skin
I've got you deep in the heart of me
So deep in the heart you're really a part of me
I've got you under my skin"
Cole Porter

"Old black magic has me in its spell
Old black magic that you weave so well
Those icy fingers up and down my spine
The same old witch craft when your eyes meet mine"
Johnny Mercer

"Maybe I'm amazed at the way you love me all the time
Maybe I'm afraid of the way I love you
Maybe I'm amazed at the way you pulled me out of time
And hung me on a line
Maybe I'm amazed at the way I really need you"
Paul McCartney

"You give me fever when you kiss me
Fever when you hold me tight
Fever in the mornin'
Fever all through the night."
Eddie Cooley and Otis Blackwell

The examples are endless. And if the songs aren't about the dizzying rush of romantic love, they're about the agonizing withdrawal when romance ends.

"You know I can't sleep, I can't stop my brain
You know it's three weeks, I'm going insane
You know I'd give you everything I've got
For a little peace of mind."
John Lennon

"What'll I do with just a photograph
To tell my troubles to?
When I'm alone
With only dreams of you
That won't come true
What'll I do?"
Irving Berlin

I've written love songs of my own. But now I hunger for songs that celebrate something deeper and more inspiring than commonplace romance. Why not songs of universal respect? Songs of unconditional self-value? Songs that enshrine human diversity, human sacrifice, human achievement? They can be written.

But in the early 21st Century anyway, few people would want to listen.

Sexual Healing

There is, of course, that related addiction of ours.

Sex.

For many of us romance and sex are intertwined almost as one, experiences that seem coupled as firmly as first-time lovers. Separating the two is difficult.

Unless age or infirmity are issues, romance without sex appears devoid of passion. An asexual romantic relationship feels empty somehow, as though something central is missing. Often sexual problems are an early indicator of darker conflicts afflicting romantic partners.

Sex without romance, on the other hand … well, that's different for lots of folks including me. My sexuality does not require romance or sentiment, which quite frankly often seemed only to get in the way.

For most of my life I've viewed sex as an activity separate from romantic love, though nearly always enjoyed with a woman I loved greatly. It's just that during sex I tend to emphasize the visual and the fantasy more than the deeper emotion. That's merely my particular turn-on in general, though not always. I've also had my one-night stands – and one afternoon stands. I've explored sex in some adventurous variations that have brought me for sensuous massages, ménage a trois experiments, even several occasions of swapping lovers for an hour or two, always by mutual agreement and always with respect among all involved. And since you're probably curious, let me tell you something more. The massages typically were delightful, the ménage a trois moments were with two women and the lover-swapping mostly was disappointing, with some notable exceptions. Interesting, surely, all of these explorations. I regret none of them.

As I explained a bit earlier, I'm a highly sexed man. Always have been. In the past my sexual desires sometimes have seemed to me borderline obsessive, with my libido forever scouting for some fresh encounter. These days as I try to live the tenets of Rational Faith, I see things differently. Still highly sexed, I regard sex as a healthy lifeforce, a wellspring of energy that increases my will to live. But I'm much more likely to be interested in making love with a whole person, not just a gorgeous face and pair of shapely legs in stockings. In choosing a lover, I don't focus mostly on the looks but instead mostly on the person within the appearance.

Before now, not so much. Whenever I traveled from my teen years on, I was always looking. On the plane, in the train, at the hotel. In daily life too. At work, around the neighborhood, when visiting friends or family. I was determined to meet someone when I could, if only to flirt a while. I wanted that high. Usually I didn't meet anyone, predictably enough, although rarely for lacking effort. Even male friends and colleagues teased me about my sex drive, which they found much more insistent than their own.

Curiously for all this sexuality, I recognized that sex confounded me. For most of my life I've never really understood what it's all about. Why did sex seem such a big deal? Why was it any better to have intercourse than to masturbate? The release was the same. What was going on here?

I can't tell you the number of hours that I've spent puzzling over this grand mystery. I could sense a quality in sexuality that felt excessively irrational, a frightening emotional force that seemed capable of controlling my behavior. I didn't want to be swept off by it all, doing something that would hurt me or jail me or make me ill. And some portion of me, left over from upbringing, deemed sex as a rather lowly activity that I should strive to rise above. Sex could appear to me almost bestial at a time when I aspired to human elevation. Why did I so obsess over it?

Even after several decades of reflection I won't pretend to understand all about my sexuality. Far from it. I believe human sex drives are extraordinarily complex, pulling together many facets of our lives. But this is what I have learned so far, in summary.

- Sex is without question one of our most favored pose-strengtheners. We desire sex as a key method of proving positive things about ourselves to ourselves. A session in bed with a partner reinforces some of our important identity poses, our self-images. When another human being consents to share our most physically intimate activity, we experience an intense variety of outside validation. Sex gives us one of life's great, if temporary, escapes from Identity Failure. For most people, sex makes our lives feel more worth living.
- Our individual sexuality expresses our prevailing self-concept at the time. As with every other thing we do, think or feel, our sexual activity focuses on whatever our psyche views as the best compromise to satisfy the Fundamental Law of Mind: Individuals interpret experience to create the weakest possible emotional resistance to the strongest possible feelings that their existence is valuable to them at this moment in this world. That means our sexual preference gravitates toward whatever behavior best minimizes our emotional conflicts and maximizes our sense of self-value. Right now. We're aroused by things that help us feel the world accepts us as we see ourselves at very deep levels. Our partner is the world's stand in. I think this phenomenon at least partially explains why one person wants only intercourse in the missionary position and

another craves a hard spanking with a wooden paddle, why this man wants to wear diapers and that woman needs many different lovers. Our sexual desires spring directly from the way we see ourselves as individuals. They express whatever we most want the world to accept about us. Right now.

- My own sexual desires express my deep love for other human beings, generally shared in bed more tenderly than roughly with some playful exceptions now and then. I love sex in part because I love people. I also think my sexual preferences reflect my need to feel I'm not forcing anyone to do something they don't want to do. I'm strongly attracted to women who also are highly sexed and my fantasies often conjure my lover with another man. I interpret this to mean partially that I require strong belief that she chooses to have sex with me: Because she needs sex with many men, I'm clearly not seducing her against her true wishes. I also suspect there's some element of psychological detachment here. As a portion of me still feels sex is a base activity for human beings to bother with, my mind blocks some of my deeper emotions about that concern through attention to my partner's passionate sex drive and alternative lovers. This keeps me from scraping too deeply into my psyche during sex, focusing instead on less morally complex matters.
- I can feel that a great many things are happening at once with my sexuality. It's fulfilling a range of psychological needs all at roughly the same time. And I'm sure many remain unknown to me.
- As has been long established by researchers, I've also learned that sexuality is fundamentally set at a very young age. For me, one of the most erotic features on women is their legs, especially if dressed in nylons and high heels. I clearly recall this same attraction when I was no more than eight or nine. I also remember feeling the intense appeal of girls when I was perhaps five-years-old or so. No one decides their sexuality. Like everything else, it is caused – and caused early on.
- Sex feels so good physically because it's so satisfying emotionally in so many ways. Without the attached emotions, the purely physical side of sex to me feels pointless. I don't mean emotions of love necessarily, as I've explained. But

feelings of liking someone anyway, of sharing excitement and passion, the exchange of intimacy, enjoying their pleasure in your touch and more. For most people, these feelings include a strong sense of self-image validation. As has often been said by others, the most important sex organ is between our ears.

Like humanity's obsession with romance, our fixation on sex is significantly motivated by our wish to avoid feelings of Identity Failure. Just think back to what I wrote in the last chapter about "the most telling of all I.F. symptoms, and the simplest to recognize: Anyone who relies on any outside source to feel better about who or what they are unquestionably suffers from Identity Failure." Romance or sex or both together, that's precisely what we're all doing with each other. We're using our partners as outside sources to feel better about who or what we are.

Listen to those romantic songs again, watch the romantic films, read the romance novels either pulp or classics. Romance and sex and romantic sex have this in common – we need another person to make our life worth living. That's always the message.

Society's attitudes about romance and sex serve as powerful examples of our attempts to escape Identity Failure.

Unfortunately, they fail in this effort. Romance and romantic sex only make Identity Failure worse.

From Me To You

Both our romances and our sexual liaisons are highly irrational. We accept this as another one of those human realities. Oh well, just the ways things are …We fall in love, we fall into bed. And we enjoy it while it lasts. Then we fall out of love, fall into bed with someone else and the cycle continues.

But once more, it's not just the way things are – as in, determined by human nature. It's just the way things are now.

I know that a much more balanced and rational approach to love and sex is attainable, as I'll explain. But first it's necessary to understand some of the other consequences of our romanticism. We need to recognize the very large role played by I.F. in almost every romantic relationship.

I believe Identity Failure helps explain the typical sexual roles of men and women in heterosexual relationships. In my time these roles have started to change. A bit. Generally, though, it's still the case that men are the pursuers and women the pursued, as the situation has been for centuries. Romeo appeared at Juliet's balcony, not the other way around.

Most of us are trying to live up to identity poses we've learned from parents, siblings, friends, media and the rest. The masculine, the feminine. As a young boy I accepted that my proper place in the cosmic order was as the more aggressive to her more passive during earliest courting. As a teen I had to risk looking foolish by walking across the room to request a dance. Later I had to make the beginning move at a bar or a party, pleading for a phone number. Quite honestly, I hated this ... and I felt it was unfair. Why was it always up to us as the guys, always up to me not her? But it was.

So I did the predictable thing partly to reinforce my Bob-the-masculine-guy identity pose among others – I made that move. And she waited for me, partly to reinforce a She-the-sought-after-lover identity pose. Or whatever the real identity pose for whoever She was at the moment. If I chickened out halfway across the room and never asked the girl to dance, my masculine-guy and other identity poses met sudden emotional resistance. I felt wimpy. Likewise if she accepted a dance invitation from someone she felt not up to her standards. Even a quick dancefloor spin with the wrong man could threaten her sense of self-value. We each upheld our self-images by restricting our behavior to society's defined masculine and feminine roles.

But I.F. shapes our masculine and feminine lives in a way I find more intriguing than who asks who first. I believe Identity Failure importantly accounts for the sexual dynamics of conventional male-female relationships as they've long played out in our culture. In these, the married man often wants to conquer new sexual challenges. The married woman often wants to keep the existing arrangement firmly in place. Of course this is a broad generalization, open to many exceptions in every direction. Yet it remains the more common condition even today among heterosexual couples.

I have asked myself why. I can't answer for any genetic influences.

Perhaps we're hard-wired in this manner. But I don't think so. And even if genetics is part of the cause, I believe something else is at work.

Identity Failure.

In our society, men and women are cemented into those roles just described. He pursues, she's pursued. This means that men ordinarily are in frequent search of someone to have sex with them, at least until they're committed to one woman. Early in our lives men learn to acquire feelings of self-worth by romantic and sexual conquest. In the way cats love to hunt even when they have a stable food supply, males often feel good about themselves by gaining a new lover even when they're married. That's the mindset many men were encouraged to prize.

Not for women. Just the opposite, actually. As the pursued, women often are required to rebuff potential suitors. For especially beautiful women, this can seem an all-day everyday process of rejecting romantic and sexual advances by the streamload. Most women know they can have sex with a man pretty much any time they like. It's not hard for females to plunk themselves down in a dark bar at 1 a.m., ending up naked and sweaty by 3 a.m. If that's what she wants. But in our culture, women often get their feelings of self-worth by romantic and sexual stability. Once happily married, the trick is to stay happily married. Western females feel good about themselves by holding on to a lover. That's the mindset many women were encouraged to prize.

I think this basic conflict in our modern world has created uncountable arguments and rifts and misunderstandings, and countless divorces. Marriages have collapsed, children upended and troubled for a lifetime, by this clash of identity poses. To feel like a man, very many men seek sexual variety. To feel like a woman, very many women seek sexual constancy.

Both needs are fueled by underlying struggles with I.F.

As individuals we already accept that there's something deeply wrong with us. We feel profoundly inadequate, trying to compensate by confirming other key identities. And for millions of people in 21st Century societies, traditional masculine and feminine identities still assume exaggerated importance. They are key identity poses indeed.

Feeling less-than-masculine or less-than-feminine can appear unbearable on top of our other perceived character inadequacies.

Which frequently creates another problem that plagues human relationships.

Jealousy.

Hold Me Tight

For years I've believed firmly that jealousy is as close to true madness as most of us will ever come. There's a reason for the phrase, "insanely jealous." This too I've experienced.

Intermittently in my past, I found myself prone to jealousy. Usually this snatched me very early in a relationship that I cared about. My imagination would take me over and abruptly I saw things that weren't there. She's flirting with this other man. She wants this other man. She's meeting this other man for secret trysts. I've accused women I loved of things that seem absolutely nuts to me as I look back.

Fortunately, these illogical seizures were shortlived. And even more luckily, I've long since overcome this occasional insanity. I despise jealousy.

But I can recognize Identity Failure's fingerprint all over my past jealousy. I felt deeply threatened by a scenario entirely concocted through my overactive fantasy life. As much as anything, I also felt intellectually insulted. You know, like: "How could she believe I wouldn't be smart enough to figure out her lies?" That was the sort of feeling that would wash through me.

But below this intellectual masculine swagger, I was reacting to a psychic nerve touched by my newborn love affair. For a while I'd felt fairly wonderful about myself because my unforgettable partner thought I was unforgettable too. Now it suddenly appeared she'd changed her mind – or worse, had been fooling me all along. She didn't find me unforgettable at all. Maybe never did. And on top of it, she instead was drawn irresistibly to someone else. All of this then combined with my existing insecurities.

That was enough on several memorable occasions to froth my psyche into a foaming case of jealousy. In truth, an acute attack of Identity

Failure. Reflecting on this now, I understand that I actually believed my suspicions could be real no matter how absurdly improbable they were. I just knew that she might be ... well, maybe, OK probably ... yes, she really was meeting that guy behind my back, exactly as I suspected. I had to know the truth.

Now that's crazy.

Shakespeare famously labeled jealousy the "green-eyed monster." I'm not so sure about the eye color but a monster it is no doubt.

As we know, jealousy often causes irreparable arguments, causes separations and divorces, causes domestic violence and murders. It twists weirdly our passion for passion, our obsession with our romances and our sexual partners. Jealousy warns us that highly significant psychological needs met by our beloved are immediately threatened. Without our lover, we may end up feeling very unspecial. We may have to admit we were never unforgettable.

We fear losing our partner too dreadfully because we value the relationship with our partner too intensely. Maintaining a relationship can feel more important than life itself – just look at the murder-suicides as evidence.

Our delusions have combined with our profound self-confusion, making romantic love appear life's greatest gift.

And making lost romantic love seem life's worst cruelty.

Tough Love

Romance and sex are challenging enough for those of us in the majority. Heterosexuals.

For folks who love in other ways, the burdens are worse.

Through my work at the Humanity Project, I've become well acquainted with the LGBTQ community here in South Florida where I live. Lesbian Gay Bisexual Transgender Questioning. They support our antibullying programs because LGBTQ kids are disproportionately bullied, leaving these children with scars that last throughout adulthood.

As a result I've learned much more about the difficulties of growing up in love with the wrong people. "Wrong," of course, in the view of too many citizens who still cannot grasp that sexuality is set at a very young age. And "wrong" because too many of those same citizens are threatened personally by sex outside the conventional male-female roles.

Once more, I.F. is significantly to blame.

As explained in the last chapter, human beings diminish others to elevate themselves. The drum major instinct, as Dr. King called it. Add to this tendency the emotional charge that accompanies issues of romance and sex for most people – these subjects are important to our self-concept. We think about romance and sex a lot and we react to them viscerally. Now mix in a great dose of ignorance, not only about human sexuality but also nearly complete ignorance of any deeper realities of the mind. I'm forever stunned by the commonness of paper-thin psychological insight. Most people know almost nothing of themselves, therefore almost nothing about anyone else. Such folks easily may feel unsure about their sexuality. Some may sense their own attractions to fellow men or women, fearing they'll somehow be enticed into gay sex. Others fall back on religious objections.

Faced with a lesbian or gay man or a bisexual or transgender or questioning person, a great many of us just can't comprehend. Why aren't LGBTQ people "normal"? Why do some dress or act differently than the straight population? What man in his right mind would find other men attractive, what sane woman would be drawn into bed exclusively with others of her own sex? They are living a lifestyle of sin. Lack of understanding about such issues often splits families apart, with fathers and mothers and siblings piling on hostility. People in the street, on the job, in restaurants and clubs commonly sneer, ridicule, sometimes even physically assault those who love someone of the same sex. Or who identify with a gender other than the one given them at birth. Heterosexuals feel superior to a person who would check the L or G or B or T or Q box in a survey. Clearly there's something wrong with them that isn't wrong with me.

In this period of human history, the LGBTQ community struggles for acceptance. Some parts of the world still execute anyone who engages in gay sex. And gay relationships remain illegal in many places. By the time you're reading these words, I hope, the prejudice may have dissolved.

But that won't happen any time soon.

Our irrational obsessions with romance and sex have commingled with our Identity Failure to torture people who simply want the opportunity to date and love and make love and marry like anyone else.

And like anyone else, LGBTQ people also are obsessed with romance and sex. Their relationships no less than heterosexual relationships are driven by the fierce desire to escape human isolation and diminish feelings of I.F., to water down a powerful sense that they're flawed.

For most of us, gay or straight or something other, our lives are enveloped in a romantic haze.

But romantic delusion, it turns out, obscures more than just romance.

Heroes & Warriors

I find it ironic.

We live in a supposed age of science. But few apply logic or reason, critical thinking or empirical evidence to their daily existence. Science has become the domain of men and women in lab coats holding clipboards full of numbers. When I look around at the people I know and the people I meet, I see little indeed of science reflected in their beliefs. Theirs is a lifestyle of tradition, convention, accepted ideas – and romance.

The smog of romanticism obscures experience.

I suspect this too is a ripple effect from the 19th Century Romantic movement. We don't only see our lovers and spouses in soft focus. Almost everything else is understood in romantic terms.

Our police and firefighters and soldiers, anyone in uniform – they're all heroes. I hear this constantly, even on television network newscasts. And those same soldiers are warriors too, every one of them. Nevermind that this makes no sense whatever. Police and firefighters and soldiers are individuals, like each of us. Some are competent, some aren't. Some are corrupt or bloodthirsty, some are honest and responsible. Some barely managed to pass their training, some are remarkable public servants. Heroes and warriors they're not, in my view anyway. Besides, you'll recall I don't believe in heroism.

But the romantic interpretation of life encompasses much more than our uniformed protectors.

We see children unrealistically, both having children and raising children. Conventional wisdom insists that children strengthen marriages when the opposite often is true. And that children are pure blessing when any honest parent will admit childrearing usually includes much that's bad with much that's good, an exhausting if potentially rewarding commitment. I rarely hear people talking about kids sensibly – or offering sensible cautions to couples thinking of starting their own family. In our culture, everyone simply knows that kids make life great even if they often don't.

Of course every child on the planet is a darling. Instead of looking at children as complicated organisms that require wise nurturing, we romanticize them into simple creatures, each oh-so charming and cute. And we view our parents and grandparents through layers of sentiment as well. Naturally we recognize there are sometimes terrible exceptions but most parents and grandparents are warm loving people who gave us their best. In return they deserve our undying affection and gratitude. My experience suggests otherwise and I think it's much healthier to see all parents and grandparents as what they are. People. People who raised their kids and helped their grandkids for reasons of their own, all aimed at making their lives feel more worth living. By recognizing the deeper unromantic humanity of these relatives, we better grasp their strengths and weaknesses as caregivers, as educators – and we understand ourselves more clearly.

Our romantic delusions include people with socially significant jobs such as lawyers and doctors. Conventional wisdom holds that lawyers are very smart, doctors profoundly insightful. These people attend universities for long years and we can trust them always. They make a lot of money. And they should, fulfilling vital functions in our complex arenas of litigation and infirmity. Experience has shown me these stereotypes frequently conflict with the facts. As with society's members in uniform, our lawyers and doctors are individuals. Some are smart, some aren't, some are insightful, some aren't. Some can be trusted. Some can't. But this isn't the way most people see things. And missing the deeper truth, they can end up in serious trouble by unequivocally trusting the wrong lawyer or wrong doctor.

Billionaires are brilliant dealmaking tycoons. Farmers are hardworking salt-of-the-earth folks. Artists are emotional and slightly mad, scientists are unemotional and logical. We always can trust banks with our money, schools with our children, legislatures with our best interests, although experience proves repeatedly these notions aren't universally true. And the genuine goal of large pharmaceutical companies is to heal our ills, even when it isn't: For many, their aim is nothing but money as they pawn off unneeded drugs at reprehensible prices.

We believe that major car manufacturers care about our safety when they've shown themselves for decades to care mostly about bottom line profit margins. The corpses of motorists who died unnecessarily through carmaker greed could fill vast graveyards.

Over and over, our direct personal experience counts for nothing in our perspective on the world.

Many of us believe there are good people and bad people. Period. And some bad people are so bad that they're evil people. Our popular films and books portray the entire universe like this, a battle between good and evil, the light side and the dark side, heroes and villains. How convenient for us, how comforting.

We view life as two-toned, black and white mostly. Few people explore the grayshaded areas that make up reality.

Romanticism rules.

Our favorite television personalities are genuine, exactly what they seem when talking to huge broadcast audiences in exchange for massive paychecks. Characters in our shows and movies are believable, behaving just like real humans would in those situations. Reality TV programs show us reality. Here too, we can trust what seems.

Our friends and family understand us at deep levels. And they love us for who we truly are.

Awards and honors go only to the worthy. Promotions at work are given to the deserving. If a book is really good it will be published and widely read, if a play is quality it will be produced and acclaimed. Symphony or song, the best get noticed. If you're a singer who's got it, an actor who has that special something, a dancer whose moves delight, you'll make it big out in the world if you really try. Guaranteed.

Ability is rewarded in the end. Genius is recognized. And hard work and perseverance always pay off.

Society is fair.

Examine any of these claims critically and you'll find they don't stand up to scrutiny. But it doesn't matter.

They just feel like they feel good to believe. The ideas are simplistic and they make us simplistic by accepting them into our heads as expressions of reality. They help form our identity poses and they feed our belief in the importance of maintaining identity poses, absurdish one-dimensional self-images all. And this perpetuates Identity Failure. Our continual efforts to validate these identity poses from the outside world have made our individuals sick with desperately needy egos.

Nonetheless most people cling to our endless romantic fallacies as truth. Those misconceptions are the underpinning of contemporary life among even the best educated populations. At some level of our psyches, each member of our society is a romantic.

Of course the people of less educated regions often are influenced most by religious teaching or superstitions.

And so collectively, as a species, we are held in the past. Humanity remains mired in ignorance. Our technology may seem advanced, but our people do not.

Not intellectually, not morally.

I believe a massively significant cause of our lingering struggles is Identity Failure. As I've been trying to point out now for many thousands of words, I.F. is a fundamental and unrecognized contributor to much human misery. It is a disease of the mind, a disease of the soul, and it infects almost all of us.

There is, though, a cure for Identity Failure. I'm certain of that much.

And I believe it waits for humanity, concealed in plain view as our individual experience.

Primary Emotions

We can replace the art of love with the science of love. And I feel deeply that we should.

To my thinking, this is only one among many great shifts of perspective that can benefit humanity by helping to break Identity Failure's pernicious hold on our thoughts and feelings and actions, the destructive influence of the me-centered ego in contemporary society. Rational Faith will offer a full-blown method aimed at doing exactly that.

I believe this must include recognizing some fundamentals about the emotion of love, basic ideas that contradict the conventional attitudes on romantic love and the romantic view of life. Our applied science will require us to fan away the haze that has blinded humanity in this realm for so long. Not to diminish our relationships or our daily existence, but to enrich these with a deeper understanding of the realities that govern human beings.

Our connections with family and friends, with lovers and partners and spouses, all can hugely improve with a vision much more clear-eyed than we've experienced before. If we begin to understand what love is and why it is, we aid the elimination of unrealistic expectations and demands on ourselves as well as on them. We see that all our relationships are grounded in the Fundamental Law of Mind, and so in the Fundamental Question. Is my life worth living? We love people because we deeply need people and they love us back because they deeply need us.

I'm not talking here of the irrational need for outside validation that pushes us toward obsessions with romance and sex, which in turn encourage those romantic ideas about most everything around us. It's not Identity Failure or the urge to escape it. I'm speaking of something more basic to our humanity, as I experience it. When I remove my notions of love from all the romantic mists that surrounded these ideas for most of my life, I regard what remains of love as something innate. It's intrinsic to my existence, not for someone else's benefit but for mine.

That's not a cold and sterile concept, it's freeing. It doesn't make our love less. I think it makes it more.

Let me explain. I believe love is best viewed as one of three primary emotions. I wasn't sure about this for a long while. It's difficult to tease out all the psychological elements involved to separately examine each empirically. But the more I look, the more I dig through my mind's layers, the more I'm convinced that this is a sensible way to conceive of human love.

As I see this, we innately possess love, fear and anger as primary emotions, which can be compared to the primary colors of blue, red and yellow. Just as all other colors are combinations of those three colors, all our complex nuanced feelings start as combinations of love, fear and anger.

You'll recall that I have largely avoided studying modern psychological theories since college, mainly so that I would discover whatever I discovered on my own, without undue outside influences. But after deciding on my primary emotion model independently in recent years, I became curious to learn how psychologists categorized emotions. I found many different theories and categories but was intrigued to learn about the work of John B. Watson, who established behaviorism as a school of psychological theory. It turns out that Watson also believed in three innate emotions: love, fear, rage, as he termed them. I took this as encouraging news. Long ago he had seen what I've now also seen for myself.

In the end I believe this question is a matter of interpretation more than anything else, mostly dependent on what we define as emotions. But based on my experience, I would argue for the primary emotions model.

For one thing, I never was able to identify any experience that involved emotions beyond those three basics. What else is there, fundamentally? We love: the emotion of attraction toward something. We fear: the emotion of avoiding something. We anger: the emotion of eliminating something. Love makes us want to embrace, fear makes us want to run, anger makes us want to destroy. I couldn't recognize anything beyond those three at the root level.

Obviously, we have an extraordinary range of feelings. Watch the eyes of a great actor in closeup and you can spot several of these feelings within seconds. And I've long been fascinated to notice my own eyes in the mirror from time to time – with one eye conveying some mix, say, of a frightened misery with sorrow, but the other eye expressing perhaps some latent hope and even joy. Fix your spontaneous expression at a given moment, find a mirror and separately explore each of your eyes carefully. If you try this when you feel something strongly, you'll likely observe that blend of emotions. There's a lot going on in our brains at the same instant.

I distinguish, then, between emotion and feeling: Emotion is one of our fundamental psychic materials. It is intrinsic. Feeling is that inner sense of our psychological reaction to situations. Emotion is energy in human form. Feeling is the presence of this energy combined in many ways. Every emotional experience we know as mature human beings appears to us as feeling, I suspect. Hope, bitterness, anxiety, courage, adoration, sacrifice, hate, revulsion, compassion, satisfaction, pride, embarrassment, disappointment, admiration, joy, an endless litany of our humanity. But I believe they're all powered by just the three primary emotions blended in staggering variety.

Of course we know that humans experience many different kinds of love, fear and anger. I think each begins in some fashion as fundamental units of these emotions. And this is where I must confess a fair degree of ignorance. What's the nature of those basic units? When love, fear or anger first form in our mind, what do they look like? I think of them as units of energy, literally, something like calories. But are they each the same? Possibly every unit of love is formed and stored in my mind with its own distinct level of intensity, some stronger than others. Maybe there's some quality of this instant's love unlike that next instant's love beyond just strength at the fundamental building block level. I'm not sure, honestly.

But I believe only three types of emotion exist, basically psychological fuel: Love. Fear. Anger.

Take the example of anxiety, an experience I know all too well. I understand anxiety as a specific blend of love, fear and anger together. When I'm anxious, I care about doing something, accomplishing something, giving something. Maybe I want to help students or regain my health or learn to drive a race car well. I want to be effective, to make it good. That is all caused by love, as I define the word. At the same time, I'm fearful I may not be able to do or accomplish or give that something. I know from my past that I sometimes can suffer tendencies toward arrogance or maybe complacency or even laziness, feelings that may well interfere with making my best contributions. I also know about the many ways outside elements can conspire against accomplishing whatever I feel so important to do. That's fear. And I'm angry from my memories of those past inner and outer experiences that contributed to failures – an anger, often a repressed rage at the world and myself and life as I've discussed in earlier chapters. Our society can seem an impossible place to offer up our highest talents. Combine all those emotions, along with the more nuanced feelings they generate, and I endure anxiety. It's like a chemical formula: a quantity of love, a helping of fear and a portion of anger.

Every individual's feelings, I think, are built step by step in a complex manner from emotions of love, fear and anger that become connected to our expcricnces, beginning at birth. Perhaps even before. We want this, we want to avoid this other and we want to make that go away.

You'll remember that emotion combines with our interpretations of experience in discrete units that I call vericepts, the emotion and concept balled together as one thing. Concepts and emotions are inextricably linked in our psyche, with emotion making the ideas stick to memory. As our memories begin to fill with more interpretations and more emotions, they organize into nexes – collections of concepts arranged by topic. New interpretations with their emotion will activate, and connect with, existing interpretations and their emotion, creating more complex and more nuanced understandings of reality as nexes expand. I speculate that when many experiences connect and combine forces, they somehow generate feelings. This may happen through the interactions of increasingly sophisticated interpretations with increasingly mixed emotions as we grow up. Clearly our feelings become ever more complicated as we mature. Exactly how these feelings come about, more precisely, I won't guess. Possibly the difference only is the number of units of emotion activated at a given moment, with variations in my feelings caused by the specific amounts of love, fear and anger that are combined in specific ways.

Possibly not.

But these technical questions aside, I am sure of this from direct experience: It is concept and emotion together that help give us feelings. Feelings actually include our interpretations of reality, though most people think of feelings as just another word for emotions. I have seen for myself that they are not. Feelings carry with them information and emotion both. It's why we talk naturally about our feelings as if they're thoughts. "I just feel I need to change jobs." "I have a strong feeling we should visit Greece this year." "I feel like we should get married."

The union of interpretations and emotions builds over time to give us feelings about ourselves, others and the world. The feelings can be based on rational interpretations of experience as well as irrational interpretations.

Which brings us back to love.

For centuries, we've based our thoughts and feelings and actions about love on the irrational. Romantic love comes over us, consumes us, addicts us. As the researcher pointed out, it's "a wonderful addiction when it is going well, a horrible one when it is going poorly." But we don't have a clue what love is.

As romance and sex feel incomprehensible, so love of any kind usually feels outside clear explanation. Feelings of love for parents, siblings, pets, friends, maybe for colleagues or even teachers or mentors – all of it seems to defy our understanding. Yes, we can mutter something about how kind these people were, how helpful, how caring, how much they gave us in one way or another. We even may identify a few specific qualities we like about them. But we can't truly say what we love and why.

We just love. And as we've accepted this irrational view of love, we've permitted many concepts of our world to feel equally fuzzy. Obviously cops and soldiers are heroes and obviously our doctors know all they need to cure us. Obviously people are good or bad and just as obviously evil exists. The Romantic perspective on life diminishes us as individuals and as a species. Our muddled concepts inevitably lead us to muddled thoughts and feelings and misguided actions, in the public sphere as much as in our private lives.

Romanticism feels good. Sometimes.

But it doesn't work.

From Romantic To Rational

So what is love, really?

For many years I've looked for a universal love, an emotion each of us enjoys as a birthright of being human. And I wondered if a love for humanity is innate. Do individuals feel an instinctive attraction to others of our species? Sometimes it has seemed so to me. There appears some quality in every person that wants to reach out to our fellows. To connect, to share, to experience together. Even killers like company. What is all this if not a kind of automatic love for each other?

I'd like to believe we are born with an intrinsic love of that sort. But a more persistent exploration of the issue suggests that's probably not the case. Instead I recognize something equally heartening in its way, offering us a richer, healthier understanding of our loving relationships.

In my judgment, there is only the innate love I discussed above, one of three primary emotions along with fear and anger. That's it. And this innate love flows naturally from the Fundamental Law of Mind, as does all other human psychological experience. Its purpose is to increase our will to live, to create the strongest possible feelings that our existence is valuable at this moment in this world. It helps us feel life is worth living.

And this innate love is the desire to be.

To exist.

Nothing more and nothing less than that. We simply want to be. In this world, at this moment. To express, to create, to do, to think and to feel and to act as seems most natural to us right now. That's what I was getting at in my earlier definition of love as a primary emotion. "We love: the emotion of attraction toward something." We're attracted to things that allow us to be as we like. I love music, for instance. By all accounts I've been musical since earliest childhood, knocking rhythmically on my crib with wooden sticks of some type. I had my first drum set not very long after I began to walk. As I look at music from this vantage point, I see it has always allowed me to be. Even as that young boy, I discovered that music let me express creativity, emotion, thoughts, helped me connect with other people. These days I couldn't live without music. I need it – and love it completely. I'm drawn toward music as one of my deepest loves because it permits me to be in many ways that are highly significant to me.

As I see it, love is the desire to be, just as fear is the desire to escape and anger the desire to demolish. Those desires materialize as energy streams from within, our innate emotions. But love requires an outlet, an avenue of expression, as fear and anger require something to flee or eliminate. Love is the force driving me outward toward existence if unthwarted by the desire to escape or demolish something. It's not that music stimulates my desire to be, it's that my desire to be finds important fulfillment through music.

By our nature, we all want to be.

If I'm right about this, the play Hamlet takes on an even deeper profundity than already long believed – a drama that revolves around a to-be-or-not-to-be dilemma. The young prince's quandary may explore more than a practical problem of action that also troubles our unroyal lives. It focuses our attention on a central issue of the human psyche.

I think our innate love helps explain more meaningfully why humanity fell in love with falling in love.

We're each in a perpetual struggle every instant of every day to be, to exist. More specifically, to want to exist, to find value in our own lives. "Is my life worth living?" Our intrinsic desire to be is an innate passion for existence. Until we encounter the world's slings and arrows, to borrow again from Mr. Shakespeare. Society makes us question our individual value constantly because we constantly seek its validation.

I believe we've developed the romantic concept of love as a response to all this.

If we're innately drawn toward being, then we're naturally drawn to people who help make that process easier. Just as I'm drawn toward music. People too can serve as outlets for our need to exist. Some of them may become friends, some may be our family. And we may feel love for these people.

But romantic love is reserved for someone who seems to make being in this world easier for us in many respects. Through intimacy and frequent validation of our self-images, we feel an intense bond with a person who appreciates us at last – and gives us permission to better express ourselves. In the company of our beloved, our humor and tastes are welcomed. So is our appearance, our clothes, our smile and our body. As noted, even our faults and peccadillos seem charming. We are freed to be in ways that were impossible before. We can exist more completely. We can relax. We have one human being to make love with, to hold hands with, to attend movies and play cards and go dancing and take trips with. They help us feel better when life is hard. They take care of us when we're sick. And as a consequence we develop an extraordinary appreciation for this person, a great sense of gratitude, a deep feeling of need for somebody who allows us to be more of who we want to be.

I believe the concept of romantic love is partly an expression of our dynamic psychological drive – our need to be. Romantic love is that sense of gratitude and comfort and pleasure and need for a person who allows us to be ourselves, all those feelings and our innate love mingled together into a single idea. Romantic love is an outlet we've created for our innate love. So is every other form of love. And so is sex. Human sexuality has become much more than a physical act to procreate. Sex allows us to be in ways we find deeply satisfying. Combine these elements with our desire to avoid isolation and our need to attract outside validation for our identities ... and there you have it.

The romantic love we know so well.

But what if we untangle the fantasy and the fallacy of human love – and sex for that matter ... What if we tweeze out the romantic and sentimental threads that have cheapened the fabric, leaving only the stronger more substantial fibers?

What if we replace the art of love with the science of love?

In the popular mind, this would be unthinkable. To view love as an innate drive-to-exist in search of effective release would seem clinical. It's hard to feel unforgettable if you see yourself as one element in a physics problem, merely a space sufficient to vent a force of human energy.

What the popular mind might think unthinkable, though, my mind thinks wondrous.

Once we unsmudge love's canvas, removing the yellow tarnish of ages past, only the original colors remain. The science is revealed as art of another kind.

This recognition follows our deeper perspective on who we really are.

I fail to find anything clinical about a force as life-affirming as an unyielding passion to exist. Every one of us is dynamic, generating love from within as our sun generates helium. A human being is energy. Our relentless desire is to make fullest use of that energy, with time and opportunity to exist in a way unique to each of us.

I want to be Bob. You want to be you.

Identity Failure has held most of us back from this fulfillment. We are hampered, we are restrained by our fear and our anger, especially fear and anger over our treatment by people. To be, we feel that we need others to appreciate, approve, confirm, validate.

But we really don't.

As you will soon read, Rational Faith is a philosophy aimed at freeing us each from these constraints through trying to free others from the same psychological knots. When I am entirely me, totally and utterly Bob, I allow myself to be in ways that transcend me. I become so much me that I become more. I need to help people – and helping them helps me to be me.

That's what Rational Faith is really about. And our innate love is at its core.

As a social solitary, I've learned that my innate love requires both solitude and society. I need to be alone sometimes in order to be me. But not all the time. Because I also need to be with other people sometimes in order to be me. I cannot fulfill my drive to exist in isolation.

For me this is one elegant facet of love seen from a rational perspective. By understanding that my intrinsic human need to exist demands satisfaction partially through relations with others, I connect with the rest of humanity at an essential level. Not an innate love for humanity as I'd once thought but an innate love that necessitates humanity's presence. And you will find that this is where the philosophy of Rational Faith is taking us.

To my mind, how much more breathtaking to see that our deepest nature commands us to commune with our own kind, not to take from them but to share with them. To exist, to be who we are with them and through them. To create and procreate. To examine and explore. To aid and empower and enjoy.

To live.

We require each other for this, but not in the way commonly believed.

The Romantic conception is needy and self-absorbed. I must have someone to make me feel less alone, less frightened, less angry, less confused, less flawed. It's all about me. Romantic love and the sexuality that flows from it focus on one thing: Taking. And taking and taking some more. I give sometimes too but mostly so I can continue to take. When my beloved gets tired of giving, I just find somebody else to take from – or I go mad with jealousy.

Rational Faith's conception of love is very different.

We need others so that we can give to them, not so that we can receive. Love doesn't ask us to take something. Love asks us to share something.

It's about the knowledge of a higher self-interest, a love that requires my robust existence as an individual among individuals. I don't need to romanticize them or me. My unique humanity demands expression in the world and so does the uniqueness of everyone else. Rational love's beauty lies in this complex interplay among independent components, much as we discern beauty in the scope and complexity of nature's intricate choreography. There's poetry in the dance, whether the gravitational motions of the galaxies or the seasonal arrival of red leaves in the Green Mountains of Vermont. And there is poetry to be found in a realistic assessment of love. I share myself with people because I must and you do the same and so do billions of other human beings.

That's the science of love in action, stripped of sentimentality.

And yes, I find it wondrous.

The old romantic notions no longer feel necessary to my life. One by one, I cast them off, replaced with something deeper and truer. I still enjoy candlelight and soft jazz and a good bottle of wine, particularly when shared with someone else. I still like to hold hands, still love to kiss as I always have and still eagerly step into the bedroom. But to me, these pleasures are all enhanced by understanding my relationship to this person more sanely. Not as my savior, not as an ideal, not as an escape from isolation. Not as an appreciator or validator of my value. Not as completion. Not as someone who gives me fever or even someone who thinks I'm unforgettable.

Instead I see her as a friend. By regarding her as a human being of a vast complexity who struggles and suffers and hopes and needs as I do, I no longer feel pressured in any way to win her over. If she doesn't laugh at my puns, fine. If she doesn't always listen to my rambling tales, no worries. And if she has something else to do this weekend, I'll look for other ways to entertain myself.

Things that before would have upset me, don't anymore. My ego isn't on the line over her every reaction. Or over any reaction at all.

I see us as individuals sharing experience – and it's not my job or hers to confirm my value as part of that experience. It's the job of us each simply to be … To exist as feels healthy and natural and comfortable with one another for whatever time we both choose to spend together. Many of the old expectations and demands disappear. Sexuality evolves into something healthy and natural and comfortable too. I view sex as a matchless method of bonding between two people in constructive ways that strengthen our individual existence rather than romanticized ways that strengthen our Identity Failure. Expressed freely and openly and without possessiveness or other romantic delusions, sex brings us together in shared vulnerability. We allow ourselves to be something we can't be otherwise, opening up our sensual preferences and fantasies and quirks in the hope they'll also please our partner. It is an act of trust. And if that act goes even reasonably well both lovers uncouple their bodies with a rewarding sense of existence, of being by way of a temporary intimacy with another person. Sex also offers us a more lasting sense of trust in this person that may extend to other human beings we encounter.

As you'd expect at my age, this more rational approach to relationships is imperfect in execution. I'm still sometimes seized by Identity Failure. And so I'm still sometimes troubled by a desire for outside validation and a romantic bonding that might eliminate my isolation. But not often anymore, not often.

I'm also letting go of as many other sentimental beliefs and romantic perspectives on daily life as I can. One by one. I strive to perceive myself and my fellow humans and the world in general as rationally as possible. By which I mean, in a manner that reflects my experience most fully and sensibly. This too is part of the practice of Rational Faith. My experience stands up to critical scrutiny. It hangs together with enormous integrity. I possess a highly powerful awareness of the sum of those experiences that reflects reality as I know it. I can feel the truth if I let myself. So can all of us, I believe. It's the instinct identified by great writers such as Emerson and Thoreau. With Rational Faith, I'm setting about to free up more of that reliable instinct and to abandon as many romantic distortions as I can.

I strongly believe that our society would function much more effectively by embracing ideas such as these – and so would our individuals. Post-romanticism will move us a step or two toward more constructive relationships and more rational behavior.

For now, though, Identity Failure keeps our minds and bodies in a romantic past. As we hold one another we worry, afflicted by fragile frightened egos.

And afflicted too by a terrifying raft of illnesses, the physical and the psychological – illnesses caused by Identity Failure to an extent much greater than you may care to believe.

Chapter 12: A Bitter Pill

"When the heart is at ease, the body is healthy"
Chinese Proverb

Chapter 12 is dedicated with deep appreciation
to Dr. John E. Sarno and his pioneering research

Mindbody

This is the chapter that almost wasn't.

Without a lifetime's brilliant work by another man, surely, I would have written it much differently if at all. Dr. John E. Sarno's startling discoveries sadly remain on the margins of medicine here in 2019. But I know from many personal experiences that his medical theories are much more than mere anecdote. They are demonstrably true. On what must easily be thousands of occasions by now, I have watched them play out in my life and the lives of others close to me – and I have read firsthand testimonials as well as statistics relating similar successes among throngs of people I don't know.

Dr. Sarno's probing insights into physical illness saved me from debilitating sufferings that reduced my existence to semi-invalidism from about 1998 until early 2000, when I stumbled across his books. Before reading Sarno's explanations, I'd endured daily living constrained by the demands of excruciating chronic back pain. Regular physical therapy, frequent hot baths and stretching exercises, pain medications, limited sexual positions. I even took one terrifying trip to the hospital emergency room when I was able to move only by way of an agonized crawl. After that episode, a highly trained orthopedic surgeon strongly recommended surgery. By all appearances, I was settling into a life of medical treatment and misery.

Dr. Sarno's work changed that prognosis within days of buying his book, accomplished exactly as promised on the cover: without drugs, surgery or exercise. That is a fact. And that story is a key piece of this chapter's story. And it's also part of the reason this chapter indeed almost wasn't. Sarno's books clearly and thoroughly describe the profound psychological involvement in many of humanity's physical maladies, including but not restricted to back and other muscular pains. More importantly, his extraordinary therapeutic cure is spelled out for readers. Though I'm among his many cured admirers, he doesn't need me to repeat those explanations.

In addition I also recognize that in some ways this chapter's tale may challenge my own readers more than any other. Most people in our society have accepted traditional medicine's prescription for health all their lives. Patients have been wholly trained to believe what doctors have been wholly trained to believe: the body and mind are separate entities. The mind may sometimes influence the body, some physicians concede. But the body is treated like a mechanical unit, as if an automobile. Just patch the radiator, add fresh coolant and you're good for another 10,000 miles.

Dr. Sarno is among the pioneers of mindbody medicine – the recognition that the mind and body are one functioning organism and not separate things at all. There is no division between them.

Mindbody.

This is a tough concept for many in our culture to swallow. For lots of reasons. It requires a much more penetrating perspective on the psyche than most folks are prepared to attempt. The average man and woman flee from self-knowledge, one of the great challenges I face in spreading the ideas underlying Rational Faith. Mindbody medicine also empowers the individual enormously but necessitates accepting personal responsibility for our own health. People tend to dislike that idea. It's much easier to simply let the doctor handle everything for us. And mindbody notions even can seem to suggest that patients are to blame for our illnesses. As I'll explain further in this chapter, that's a mistake. But again, how much more reassuring in some sense to feel illness simply befalls us without any connection to our emotions. Responsibility can be a tough sell when complete victimhood is the comforting conventional wisdom.

I was fortunate enough to briefly interview Dr. Sarno by phone sometime in 2000 for an article I wrote on his work. This was only a few months after I had eliminated my back pain entirely through following the recommendations in one of his books, Healing Back Pain. We had a stimulating conversation that I enjoyed – and I thanked him profusely for helping me recover a normal life. But I'll never forget something he told me then: "At least eight or nine out of every 10 people won't believe my ideas." I was surprised but have come to recognize that he's right. Over the years since, I've tried repeatedly to introduce Sarno's theories to sufferers of all sorts, some of them my family members. Only rarely has anyone followed my advice, bothering to buy one of the books to try out for themselves. Among those friends who made a genuine effort to apply Sarno's method, the program worked for them too. They were healed. But for most, mindbody concepts were too much. And so those patients just returned to their doctors.

I mention all this with a purpose. I am loathe to undercut whatever credibility I've established in your mind with a digression into the psychological underpinnings of disease. I believe it's essential that you understand the psyche's realities in detail as I've described them in order to see why they lead inescapably to the philosophy of Rational Faith. The psychology is the philosophy. In my thinking, one absolutely determines the other.

Knowing the intense controversies over mindbody medicine, then, I was reluctant to go there in this book. I don't want to lose you now.

Ultimately, though, I couldn't escape an awareness that this chapter isn't a digression at all. My discussion of mindbody is part and parcel of Identity Failure's untold story, which is sweeping us along toward the resolutions of Rational Faith.

With illness as with so many other aspects of human life, Identity Failure's influence is key.

TMS

Let's start at the start. The work of Dr. John E. Sarno.

The good doctor is a professor of Rehabilitation Medicine at the New York University School of Medicine, a bestselling author and a practicing physician since 1950 – two years before I was born. By detecting similarities and patterns over many years among his patients, he began to slowly recognize that purely physical explanations could not account for their symptoms, including complaints such as back and neck pain. Something else clearly was going on.

Something psychological. Their minds were greatly influencing their bodies.

He named the disorder TMS, or Tension Myositis Syndrome. Basically, tension in inflamed muscle tissue.

Through direct experience with great numbers of his patients, Dr. Sarno devised a method to cure them without surgery, drugs or physical therapy. Hard as it may be for many of you to believe, he instead created a psychological therapy where knowledge and self-acceptance become the healers. It works, believe me. It truly does work. And not only with back or neck pain and related ailments. Again, I know this from the personal application of Sarno's ideas during more than 19 years.

Dr. Sarno of course also understood that the same psychological dynamic creates many physical conditions and so coined the term "Tension Myositis Syndrome Equivalent" for those other maladies caused fully or partially in his view by emotional factors. He has written that these conditions can involve the cardiovascular or gastrointestinal systems among others and may contribute to heart conditions, cancer, migraine headaches, skin problems, allergies, autoimmune disorders and a wide range of physical miseries. Even conventional research is verifying some of these notions such as the connection between anger and heart attacks.

Untrained in psychology, Sarno turned to colleagues for help in analyzing the mind's mechanisms beneath the infirmities. What was going on – and what would eliminate the physical symptoms? As a result, he settled on Freudian explanations with special attention to repressed emotion. In the end Dr. Sarno concluded that repressed emotions, particularly repressed rage, cause all these physical and sometimes psychological problems as well, everything from ulcers to anxiety, from hypertension to depression.

Sarno's books give the details of his medical theories, psychological interpretations and therapy. I strongly urge you to read them to grasp the great importance of his ideas. He has done brilliant work. For our purposes, though, I can briefly summarize a few other key points needed as a basis for my own mindbody story and its connection to Identity Failure.

Dr. Sarno has written that repressed rage and other emotions are generated in the unconscious, as Freud defined it. Those repressed emotions are the problem. In essence, our minds often respond to this repression by distracting our attention away from the unpleasant emotions with symptoms. Our pain or other conditions are defense mechanisms that prevent us from confronting the disturbing emotions deeply buried in our psyche. Dr. Sarno's therapeutic approach involves teaching patients an intense awareness of this reality – learning to accept that we have these powerful emotions even though we don't feel their presence and likely would insist they don't exist. The symptoms are proof they do exist.

And exist they surely do.

I can't imagine that anyone who understands much about their mind would dispute this. Quite obviously, Sigmund Freud was right about repression. I have never doubted this since learning about the concept in a college psychology course. But only Dr. Sarno revealed to me repression's devastating impact on my health.

Repressed emotion, especially repressed rage, makes me sick. Once I sincerely admit this, I get well. Dr. Sarno's therapy works, over and over and over. But what sounds simple, isn't. The acceptance process is challenging at best, sometimes infuriatingly difficult. That struggle only causes more repressed rage until the accepting is accomplished. As you might expect by now, I've explored the psychological dynamics of my maladies in great depth over those 19 years since my fortunate encounter with Dr. Sarno's work. And I have reached my own conclusions about them, all grounded in those decades of extensive research into my own psyche.

In the broadest terms at this point, here are my two main realizations:

- Repressed emotion is a major cause of human illness, just as Dr. Sarno explains.
- And Identity Failure is a major cause of that repressed emotion.

Which is to say that Identity Failure is often what really makes us sick.

RET

Before I'd ever heard of Dr. John E. Sarno, I was already well primed to understand his work. Think back to Chapter 5, where I quoted from my notebook entry of summer 1998 about a cold I had managed to avoid. Here are some excerpts as a reminder:

"I have been fascinated for more than 20 years by the interaction between mind & body & how this influences our illnesses ... I know that the most important thing I did was to consciously remind myself why I didn't want to get sick. I long ago realized that people often bring on or at least allow illnesses that they could prevent. They very rarely do this consciously. But at an emotional level, they see things about the illness as a way of finding some emotional relief, a 'satisfaction' of emotional needs ... For example, I understood that I 'wanted' to get sick at some level for several reasons ... Illness is often used as a cure. It is not a cure for anything – it causes its own problems &, though it can satisfy some emotional needs, there are more constructive ways to accomplish the same emotional goals, without suffering through illness & without making yourself into a person who increasingly sees illness as a solution to trouble & stress."

So I clearly recognized a mindbody connection some two years before reading Dr. Sarno's books. But even much much earlier, back into my late teens, I recall a strong awareness that my mind greatly influenced my physical health. Whatever knowledge I possessed was minimal and unsophisticated, of course, but I was engaged by thoughts about the issue decades before learning about TMS and its equivalents.

I note this personal background into mindbody healing as a way of pointing out something I find especially remarkable about Dr. Sarno's teachings – to me, the true greatness of his work. Sarno tells his patients and readers that there's no need to change anything about our lives to stop symptoms caused by repression, only to accept that repression is the cause. We don't have to dig out the root of the repressed rage in most cases. We don't have to learn to generate less stress, quit our job, get a divorce or alter our personality. We simply must believe that we harbor repressed rage and that it causes the illness. Period.

That's an extraordinary insight. And it's something I never would have discovered on my own, no matter how many years I explored the mindbody. I know myself and I know how I think. My natural tendency is to examine problems and address them directly. Head on, "untying the knots" as I suggested in an earlier chapter. This means I had always assumed that if Problem A and Problem B were causing emotional distress and emotional distress was causing my ailment, I would need to work through Problems A and B completely before I could be well. Even my 1998 notebook entry reveals this approach. Troubles in my daily life were making me want to escape through illness, which I tackled directly by understanding that I didn't really want to be sick despite those troubles.

Dr. Sarno's therapy doesn't require this. Change your life if you like but it's not necessary to be well. Only the acceptance of your repressed emotion, particularly the pool of repressed rage that sloshes around inside nearly all of us. He teaches the afflicted to shift our awareness from the physical symptoms to the repressed emotion again and again until we believe the diagnosis totally. As he wrote in The Mindbody Prescription, "In essence it is a contest for conscious attention."

For this profound discovery I am eternally grateful to Dr. Sarno. It transformed my existence from a semi-invalidism riddled with doctors and pills and therapy of all kinds into a life of renewed vigor. As importantly for me, Dr. Sarno's work handed me a lifelong tool to prevent or heal my ills, or at least diminish them, body and mind. Without his work my most intensely isolated years of psychological suffering would have been unbearable. Sarno's writings allowed me to more fully understand what was happening to me physically during this purgatorial period, to minimize my symptoms much more effectively than I could have otherwise – and to believe I would in time make the maladies go away.

And so I have in large part. And so I thank Dr. Sarno for his grand labors.

Although I accept the validity of his therapeutic prescription, however, my personal journey has led me in directions quite different from the psychological explanations in Sarno's books. With the greatest respect, I must disagree with him on these matters. During our telephone interview, I actually told Dr. Sarno about one of the differences with his theories I already had found early on. The repressed rage was more than rage at the world, I could sense within me – it was rage at myself too. Sarno listened for a minute or so before politely changing the topic.

All these years later I still feel sure I'm correct on that point. And I have developed a psychological theory of my own that draws on all the observations and ideas I've laid out in this book up to now, an understanding of mindbody dynamics based on repeated and carefully examined personal experiences since my first reading of Healing Back Pain in 2000. At its core are the Fundamental Law of Mind and Fundamental Question and Identity Failure. As I see it, these are among the central forces that have helped to create a vast amount of human illness.

Together they have made illness feel as if a necessity to cope with our existence, much as I'd felt a cold was necessary to cope with my confluence of daily troubles in 1998. The basic psychological mechanics are the same.

To express my ideas on mindbody illness, I've invented a new word. Honestly, I never much liked Tension Myositis Syndrome Equivalent to cover such a wide range of ailments. Dr. Sarno has written in a later book about his discontent with the term but concluded he was by then stuck with it. I suggest another name, first jotted in my notebook in February 2002: Repressed Emotion Transfer, or RET. Taking into account both Sarno's medical theories and my own psychological observations, this seems a good phrase for what's happening in our heads to generate sickness. That process is the literal transfer within the mindbody of repressed emotion. RET is the psychological energy of emotion as I've described it, sealed up and finding an outlet somewhere as a physical expression.

Its purpose in my view is far more than as a mere distraction. Illness is another form of psychological compromise, an individual's automatic response to the demands of the Fundamental Law of Mind. At superficial glance this may be hard to comprehend. But yes, I believe we deepwant our maladies, physical or mental, because at the time they appear the best available satisfaction for our emotions.

At a heavily concealed level of our psyche under immediate difficult circumstances, we actually feel as if sickness will make our life more worth living.

Exhibit A

I'm always vaguely mystified whenever folks resist all notion of the mind's influence over the body. We've seen it happen with our own eyes many times.

Everyone has observed some fairly dramatic examples, whether experienced in ourselves or witnessed in others. Who hasn't watched tension create sweat in an uncomfortable situation? Or seen a face change color from embarrassment? Nervous performers sometimes vomit before taking stage. We learn how stress can cause a headache. And as mentioned in the previous chapter, the role of our minds in sexuality is widely accepted. It's much more the emotional than the physical that makes our penis hard … or soft. Or makes a vagina wet or dry. Most men have watched the mindbody in action hundreds of times in unmistakable ways during masturbation. What else is happening when we pant over an enticing photograph, penis already erect before the first touch? Or when stuck with a boring partner we simply give up, roll over and fall asleep? The emotional response determines the physical response.

Still, a wide majority of people insist on believing the conventional explanation. The body as machine, the mind as separate computer. But as the Chinese proverb suggests, that simplistic concept simply isn't true: "When the heart is at ease, the body is healthy" is an accurate if poetic expression of physical well-being in humans.

And this age-old knowledge has not been limited to nameless Asians.

"The wish for healing has ever been the half of health."
Lucius Annaeus Seneca, 4 B.C – 65 A.D.

"Patience and tranquility of mind contribute more to cure our distempers as the whole art of medicine."
Wolfgang Amadeus Mozart, 1756 – 1791

"Worry affects the circulation, the heart, the glands, the whole nervous system, and profoundly affects heart action."
Dr. Charles Mayo, 1865 – 1939

Encouragingly, there is much new research by forward-thinking scientists and physicians on the mindbody connection. And some fascinating stories that suggest our psyche's power over physical health.

I have a thick file of news accounts and other descriptions of many medical studies reported since 1998. They include research that shows the effectiveness of the placebo effect, with biologically useless medicines producing impressive results. In one University of Michigan study, patients who believed a placebo would relieve pain instead released natural painkillers within their brains. Another report concluded that Parkinson's disease sufferers improved on a sham drug, with brain scans revealing that their bodies produced a greater amount of a muscle-controlling chemical than people given genuine medication. A University of Chicago study linked high blood pressure with loneliness. And of special interest to me, a British epidemiologist named Sir Michael Marmot assembled 25 years of research to demonstrate that social status is a massively significant factor in our health – not even genetics or lifestyle habits compared. Marmot's findings strongly suggest a connection with the Fundamental Law of Mind and Identity Failure, our unyielding requirement for feelings of individual value and the psychological consequences when we're unable to believe in that value.

At the University of California Berkeley, scientists discovered that exposure to profoundly inspiring works of art or natural wonders can strengthen the immune system by reducing chemicals that cause inflammation. And then there is the long-term study of convent nuns that includes an autopsy analysis of their brains, research that's ongoing as I write this book. It found some of the deceased nuns had fullblown Alzheimer's disease without showing any external symptoms. Nuns who were interviewed for the study made clear their emotional engagement with life: their faith, daily masses, helping others. Again, I believe this indicates the importance of feeling personally valuable. Our lives must seem worth living – and when they do, we tend to stay much healthier.

The research and the undeniable facts are piling up. So are the insightful observations offered by professionals in medicine, some wise thoughts on physical illness.

A 2006 Chicago Tribune article quotes Dr. Michael Jones, who was a director at a major Chicago area hospital: "We have all the bells and whistles, and none of it really does anything (if chronic stress is involved). But when you talk to people and put their problem in the context of their lives and look at the big picture, they start to get better."

And a 2002 book by Michael Gearin-Tosh, A Medical Mutiny, quotes an especially frank assessment made to him by Sir David Weatherall of the Weatherall Institute of Molecular Medicine at the University of Oxford: "What you must understand, Mr. Gearin-Tosh, is that we know so little about how the body works."

I find this the most genuine admission I've read by an expert in the field. We just don't know very much yet. In my judgment based on personal experience, I believe this is because the mind's role is underappreciated if acknowledged at all by many physicians and researchers.

As Dr. Sarno discovered, something else is going on in our bodies that purely physical diagnoses can't fully explain.

With his invaluable assistance, I've learned that's certainly true in my body.

Physical Rage

I wish I could convey how confident I am of this idea. A confidence that's as near total as possible without lapsing into dogmatic certainty.

I've been acutely in touch with both my body and mind since boyhood, no doubt often too much so for my own good. I can feel, isolate and analyze many elements of them minutely and accurately, it seems. On the question of mindbody, I feel sure I've never been ill in my lifetime without repressed emotion as the underlying cause. Repressed rage in particular, exactly as Dr. Sarno writes.

Illness in me is the physical expression of a swelling rage I don't even know I have. That's been my consistent experience since reading Sarno's research and, looking back, I believe the same was true in my past.

This is an incomplete list of illnesses, ailments and symptoms that I have confidently traced to Repressed Emotion Transfer, in my phrase:

- Skin conditions including rashes, seborrhea, red skin, scaly skin
- Allergies
- Colds, flu, respiratory viruses
- Pneumonia
- Chronic ringing in the ears (tinnitus)
- Stomach disorders including nausea, pain, vomiting
- Headaches
- Chronic and acute back pain
- Neck pain
- Various pains in limbs, hands and feet
- Bodily weakness and tingling
- Eye twitching
- Toothache
- Cold sores
- Sneezing attacks
- Persistent coughing
- Heart palpitations, rapid heartbeat, irregular heartbeat
- Squeezing of the chest and back muscles
- Difficulty breathing
- Muscle spasms
- Uncontrollable trembling of the head, limbs or torso
- Infections including skin, eye, kidney, sinus
- Diarrhea
- Constipation
- Hernia
- Hiccups
- Fatigue
- Insomnia
- Weight gain and loss
- Anxiety
- Depression
- Phobias

The vast majority of these conditions came and passed relatively quickly, a list to which I also should add impotence in the way nearly all men have experienced it – infrequently but sometimes at inopportune moments. These are only the problems I can think of just now, an incomplete list as I said. But I hope it makes the point.

My mind and body are a singular organism. Mindbody. I find that my existence is psychologically based, meaning my beliefs and emotions are the key to living healthfully and productively and dynamically and joyfully. I often think of myself as being "all mind" – like some science fiction creature from another world who inhabits the universe solely as a mental presence. The role of my psyche feels that sweeping to me.

I have many times experienced intense symptoms only to observe as they vanished instantly by applying Dr. Sarno's therapeutic method. Crippling back pain, coughing and congestion, palpitations and similar heart irregularities, skin problems, aches and throbbing of many varieties in different parts of my body, among other problems. Gone. Instantly …

Perhaps you can see why I hesitated to write this chapter. If you've not experienced that relief for yourself, it's almost impossible to believe. It smacks of some old-time grifter promising his elixir as a quick cure for every malady known to humankind. But it's the truth, believe me or not. And I can't avoid writing about it in this book because I've come to understand Identity Failure's significant part in creating the repressed emotions that in turn create my ailments. And, I suspect, your ailments too.

Even to me, Sarno's method still can seem miraculous when I do it right. With practice, some symptoms disappear as if flipping a lightswitch. But doing it right – ah, that's the hard part, summoning the energy and courage to refocus my attention away from the physical over to the psychological during attacks of bodily distress. Despite my past success with Sarno's technique, I often find that eliminating a new symptom with his method is challenging for many reasons I'll explain a bit later. The good news is that determined repetition breaks through my resistance. Eventually the symptom vanishes.

When my chronic back pain was diagnosed as sciatica, I was given the usual tests including an MRI. The testing conclusively proved I had a herniated disc, scoliosis or curvature of the spine, and spinal stenosis or narrowing of the spinal canal. I possess the medical reports and images to this day as proof – just ask, as I'll be glad to share the evidence with you. Now the traditional therapies began, including stretching two or three times daily, a long hot bath each day, regular physical therapy that included special exercises and massages, frequent doctor visits for checkups, pain medications that sometimes carried unpleasant side effects. None of it did much good. I lived in near constant radiating pain that made everyday life a torture. There were periods when I wasn't sure how much more I could stand. My whole existence seemed focused on back pain. Just as Dr. Sarno writes, my pain was usually the last thing I thought about before going to sleep and the first thing that popped to mind in the morning.

During these nearly two years, I noticed oddities from time to time. When I became emotionally engaged in some pleasant activity, like a card game or film, I lost all awareness of the pain. It was as if the symptoms went away. On the other hand, some less-than-joyous occasions made the pain much more severe: a fight with my wife, a rejection by a publisher, money troubles, a visit from my mother-in-law, unexpected major home repairs and the like.

There seemed some connection between my mind and my back. But given the diagnosis supported by laboratory results, I didn't know what to make of it. So I continued to accept the advice of my doctors. And I continued to feel miserable, physically and emotionally.

I discovered the work of Dr. Sarno online. As I recall, this came through an Internet recommendation by Dr. Andrew Weil, the alternative medicine advocate. Even before I had Healing Back Pain in hand, I felt optimistic. The little I'd already read by then about Sarno's work made sense to me. When I began to pour over the pages of the book, I soon decided Dr. Sarno's methods could be effective. I remember experiencing some relief from my back pain almost immediately after finishing the first chapters. Within two weeks, my back pain was gone.

The herniated disc, scoliosis and spinal stenosis were still there. But exactly as Dr. Sarno predicted, they were not the cause of my pain.

The pain was generated by my emotions.

The Knife's Edge

Here's the moment in my story when Dr. Sarno and I part company. And it's the reason for this chapter, a new version of the psychology beneath the physiology. Ultimately, I believe, these ideas will help to strengthen the case for Sarno's medical discoveries.

As a therapeutic method, Sarno's borrowed psychological model works very effectively. He believes the symptoms are created by our mind for the sole purpose of distracting our attention from the terrifying repressed emotions. This necessitates a therapy whose central task is to shift the patient's awareness from those symptoms to the repressed rage. It sets up a contest for conscious attention, as he points out.

No question, conscious attention devoted completely to the repressed rage rather than the physical symptoms dissolves the problem. Once the mind fully accepts the emotional cause, symptoms stop. But just because the therapy works doesn't mean the theory is correct. I'm not suggesting a placebo effect. I simply don't believe that Dr. Sarno's psychological explanations account for the vast complexity of our psyches as they involve illness. To me there seems something else going on in our mind, much as he first detected something beyond the conventional physical diagnoses.

For starters, the repressed emotion itself. I have examined this question over and over since 2000. Hundreds of times at least, surely. And each time I reach the same conclusion no matter how different the starting place for my thought process: Identity Failure generates a deep terror that in turn generates an intense rage over time. These emotions are repressed. The repressed rage provides the psychological energy that's transferred elsewhere in the mindbody, creating an ailment as a source of emotional satisfaction. Essentially the illness offers a way to replace those terrifying repressed emotions with more acceptable emotions that accompany the illness. I can't say for certain, but I strongly suspect that only Identity Failure can create repressed rage sufficient to necessitate physical symptoms.

The repressed rage seems to fall into three categories, as I've described in earlier chapters. World-rage first, a fury at people or events or situations or whatever it may be – the things that enrage me in daily life. Eventually this produces self-rage, a fury at myself for not being smart enough and strong enough to better cope with the world or for some other perceived fault. This shift diminishes the rage directed at others. And in time this self-rage produces life-rage, a fury at life itself, at the universe, at god for things being as they are. World-rage becomes frightening to me when I start to feel as if I might do something irrational as a result, no matter how unlikely in reality: Without being aware of this, I sense I'm so enraged that I could hit someone or scream at people or some such madness. The same with self-rage: Below my awareness, the rage becomes so intense that at some level I fear self-harm or even suicide. So my mind turns its increasing rage to the unfairness of the cosmos. As best I can tell, self-rage and life-rage don't completely replace world-rage. They appear to exist in fluid, oft-changing combinations. My mind's goal is to focus a large portion of the building repressed rage where it feels most comfortable given all the circumstances in the present moment. When my mind senses the rage is excessive for me to point outward at the world, I turn it in on myself. When that too begins to feel excessive, a significant amount of the rage hones in on life in general – as if shaking my fist at the universe for its hardships.

I've found it very helpful therapeutically to recognize these differing levels and targets of my repressed rage. By understanding what I hate so much and why at the time, I can more easily accept Sarno's diagnosis just then. It makes more sense to me.

As my above list of maladies shows, I agree with Dr. Sarno that repressed emotion causes emotional and mental symptoms as well as physical symptoms. But for clarity's sake here let me talk only about the physical symptoms created by RET, with the word "illness" representing a wide range of ailments, from minor symptoms to major disease.

These are the psychological mechanics as I see them in myself, the realities that I must assume apply to other mindbodies as well.

I view illness as an idle knife. It is sharp and it is dangerous. But it's also harmless until I decide to pick up the knife and use it as a weapon – against myself. So with illness. My mind seems to latch on automatically to whatever illness is available to me in whatever way feels necessary at this moment. Options are many. We know that humans harbor within our bodies an array of viruses and potential illnesses that do no harm. I learned years ago from a blood test that, like lots of us, I carry the Epstein-Barr virus. And like most carriers, I've never had any illness from it. That's often the case with viruses. Only about 20% of those infected with the Zika virus become sick. The latest research I could find shows about 25% of people infected with the dengue virus suffer any symptoms.

I know too that my body has weak points. I imagine we all do, those places susceptible to dysfunction without obvious cause. I've always had skin that could become flaky, itchy, red, for instance. My stomach gave me many troubles in my 30s and 40s, from indigestion to sharp pains. My heart is another area, with palpitations and various abnormalities striking me intermittently since boyhood. And there are other vulnerable spots as well. My mind has these at the ready any time one or more are needed. The hidden knives, waiting for my psyche to select the appropriate level of suffering it feels needed at the moment.

This really does seem the process. The greater the strength of my repressed rage and other repressed emotions, the greater the severity of physical symptoms required for me to cope. My mind selects the symptoms as it deems necessary, often more than one at a time. If the rage is profound and prolonged and entirely hidden from all awareness, I may even become very ill as I did with pneumonia soon after a stressful transition from Vermont to Florida, from small city broadcast journalism to large city print journalism. I have no doubt that potential illnesses of many kinds lurk inside my mindbody, the possibilities available to my psyche if they appear needed by my life circumstances.

The trick is to consciously make sure I don't need them – and don't want them.

Just Cause

I believe illness in human beings evolved to serve a psychological purpose.

Unquestionably illness performs this function for me. I've always detested being sick, right from childhood on. I don't even like thinking about illness – or writing about it. But I recognize now that when I'm ill, my symptoms are an effort to reach what feels like the optimal psychological compromise at the moment.

Illness is my psyche's attempt to steer the best available path through my life given the present situation. Sickness is trying to help me, not hurt me.

That seems an astonishing assertion. But I've found it's true.

And it makes sense when seen through the lens of the Fundamental Law of Mind and the Fundamental Question. We're always trying to interpret experience in a way that weakens emotional resistance to the strongest obtainable feelings that our individual lives are valuable to us right now. We want something that helps us answer yes to the question, "Is my life worth living?"

Unfortunately, we look outside ourselves for the answer. We're perpetually seeking exterior approval and appreciation, the validation of others for our identity poses – those identities we most value as representing who we are. And unfortunately also, we often don't get the validation we need. This confuses us deeply, then terrifies and finally enrages us. Deeply, very deeply. But these forceful feelings don't fit with the identities we're striving to confirm with the world. So we repress them. Bob-the-journalist mustn't admit he's afraid of failing at his new job and furious about experiencing any such fear. I can't view myself this way. My response? I repress the terror and accompanying rage that come from my uncertainty about succeeding as a South Florida reporter. And naturally Bob-the-nice-guy can't acknowledge he's furious at his wife. Or at himself or at life, for that matter. Those intense emotions are submerged within the psyche. They are repressed: still active within me but not easily accessible to my awareness. I don't want to know anything about these emotions. I pretend they don't exist.

But they do.

How can the mind handle this uncomfortable situation? What compromise will best fulfill the demands of the Fundamental Law of Mind?

Illness often works very nicely, thank you.

My self-image as Bob-the-journalist can feel relatively unchallenged as long as an appropriate illness satisfies the repressed emotion. Bob-the-nice-guy can exist with much less emotional resistance as well despite the rage I feel at my wife or at myself or at life – if I can successfully avoid awareness of that rage by allowing illness to consume my thoughts and feelings.

When circumstances challenge my ability to maintain key identity poses, my psyche often summons illness. These days it's mostly a series or combination of symptoms, which I eventually confront with Dr. Sarno's method. The more I feel a victim of circumstances whether exterior or interior, whether coming from the world or emanating from emotions, the more likely I will suffer these symptoms. A feeling of powerlessness easily creates a need for physical distress, no matter if I'm stuck briefly at Cynthia's unpleasant picnic or mired in lingering financial hardship. At the picnic I might start to grow nauseous, for example, giving me an excuse to cut short the outing. Among the mounting money troubles, I may start to endure increasing bouts of back pain – which indeed is what happened before my back pain became chronic. In retrospect, my fiscal situation helped create my physical situation.

Identity Failure strengthens victimhood. Once I give other people a large influence over my feelings about who I am, I'm in trouble. Once I allow outside opinions and events to determine how valuable my existence seems to me, I'm setting myself up for illness. If those people underestimate or misjudge me, if those opinions and events turn against my favor, I soon enough feel helpless. And illness is a common response.

Key identity poses feel threatened. I irrationally question whether I am who I need to be. This generates a deep uncertainty about the value of my existence. Identity Failure. In turn, this creates a powerful terror about whether my life really is worth living followed by a rage that tries to counteract the terror. Anger can outshout fear, keeping me from falling apart emotionally. I continue to function for a time. But the uncertainty and the terror and the rage are only repressed, driven well below my awareness. And if my Identity Failure persists or worsens, the repressed rage builds. I feel the world is treating me most unfairly. Then it seems mostly my fault. Then life in general is to blame the most. The universe, god. These reactions also mean I am a victim, I am helpless, I am powerless. That's the feeling overwhelming me now. I attempt to carry on as best I can, probably acting in irrational ways, surely thinking and feeling things that make no sense. The repressed uncertainty and terror and rage further intensify, all far beneath my surface thoughts and feelings. I have no idea what's really going on in my head. And when all this repressed emotion reaches a critical mass, something has to give.

My psyche's compromise is illness. It permits me to maintain some meaningful pretense that I am the person I need to be. I can avoid facing up to the Identity Failure. I'm still Bob-the-nice-guy – but now I'm Bob-the-nice-guy-who's-sick.

This is among the many reasons why we must overcome our natural tendency to feel like victims of the world, why we need to take responsibility for our thoughts and our lives as if free will were real. Even though it's not. The Free Will Paradox that I outlined in Chapter 5 says that determinism is the way of everything including human life. All things are caused, each reality determined. In daily practice, though, we must look at present and past events as caused but see future outcomes as subject to free will. In effect this allows us to cause a better effect. And that's very true for our health.

A sense of responsibility for our thoughts and our life is a great antidote to illness – and an effective act of preventive medicine.

Inflamed By Rage

After a lifetime of closely observing illness in me and others, and decades of thinking about the mindbody processes involved, I've come to a straightforward conclusion: Illness is a physical over-reaction to an emotional over-reaction. It is our mindbody's response to the intense emotions that flow from irrational interpretations of our experience. Or so it seems to me.

We over-react to the buffets of the world and the insults of fellow human beings. And we over-react so severely due to Identity Failure. As outlined above, this emotional over-reaction ultimately causes a physical over-reaction, the mindbody working as a unified organism to make our life feel worth living to the fullest extent that appears possible in the moment.

I've been most interested to read in recent years that some researchers have put forward the theory that inflammation is the cause of all illness. I can't argue for or against the notion. But from the outside at a serious glance, I instinctively feel they may be on to something. If their idea turns out to be true, I hope these researchers will look at the influence of emotions on this process. My summation about illness would fit with their model: Illness is a physical over-reaction to an emotional over-reaction.

Human beings fundamentally are irrational. All of us much of the time, including me. In the everyday, we rarely stop to put things in sensible context, no matter how minor they may be if examined critically. I want to feel better now, I want to relieve the emotional pressure now, I want to believe my life is worth living ... now. Even if I'm only grimacing through Cynthia's picnic I can become trapped. I am afflicted with the sense that I'm powerless to take control of the situation without violating my feelings of self-worth, which are built from my important identities such as the-nice-guy. This helps explain why people turn to illness so readily. We're not thinking rationally about how the illness will make us feel tomorrow or a week from now – or a year from now. We're not thinking at all. Our mind automatically selects the solution to our troublesome circumstance, whatever seems to best preserve feelings of our life's value. Right now.

If we become aware of this tendency to lapse into illness as a solution to life's dilemmas, we make a significant advance toward defending ourselves against sickness. Dr. Sarno's work can give us another extremely useful tool to strive toward health. But it takes much effort and energy.

As I understand things, we must make certain we never want to be ill. Not for any reason or in any situation. Again to quote from my 1998 notebook, people "at an emotional level ... see things about the illness as a way of finding some emotional relief, a 'satisfaction' of emotional needs." That's what happens when we feel cornered by life. The more threatening the attack, the more we want to escape. So we actually want illness.

We deepwant it, in my terminology.

I view this as a critical point. Remember that deepwanting causes us to do what we deeply want to do at an emotional level, always. And we can do nothing else until we change what we deeply want. As I explained in Chapter 5, "Deepwanting is the insistent overall craving for something that feels profoundly significant to me, my truest and deepest desire underlying all the other desires about that thing. In a meaningful sense, deepwanting is the sum of my psyche's parts at a given moment. It demands that I hold fiercely on to those values that I feel make me me – and to keep holding on no matter what. In life, there's what I claim to want and there's what I deepwant."

Of course I claim to want health. Everyone does. But in reality, I easily can deepwant illness. Suffering some physical ailment often preserves my self-image, my feelings about the value of my existence at this moment in this world. Physical maladies give me a simple out. I'm also well aware that sickness is a generally accepted excuse in nearly any situation, something nobody else feels they can question. Probably most of us have fallen ill as a highly effective shield. I can't confess to my boss that I'm seriously anxious about a big presentation – I may not even admit it to myself. She'll order me to give the talk anyway and I'll just feel more nervous than ever. But if I call the office on presentation day to report that I'm home with a high fever, the boss will tell me to stay there.

So yes, unwelcome as this analysis likely will be, it's my very careful and honest assessment. I believe that we want our symptoms, sufferings, miseries, illnesses at a profound level of mind. But we don't know we want them. We don't beforehand critically examine this deepwanting to consider what the illness will mean for us. Unintended consequences will emerge soon enough. In the moment, our mind explores possible solutions to our difficult situation. Illness is one option often presented automatically without our awareness. It is the psyche's subtle suggestion. If we allow ourselves to accept that suggestion because we feel a need for its short-term emotional benefits, we will get sick.

I believe that Sarno's method cures because it alters what the patient deepwants. He teaches us to overcome our fear of both the symptoms and the repressed emotion. Until that happens, we remain afflicted.

He also teaches us to cast off our old belief system about conventional medicine, in essence exchanging the traditional theories for his theories. Until that happens, we remain afflicted. Those old fears and those old beliefs create barriers that at deep levels confuse us about what's real. Our doubt means we can't truly want Sarno's treatment to work yet. We're not sure it's in our best interest. But once we thoroughly believe in Sarno's method, overcoming enough of our fears and doubts, we begin to deepwant his cure. His system has guided us through the overcoming process, little by little.

It all happens mostly under the psychic radar, the illness and the cure both. I recall that my second wife, Jill, lived through my embrace of Dr. Sarno's work – and learned to apply his method to improve her own health. One day Jill pointed out how important it was to "catch a thought" about any symptom or illness when first it crossed her mind, consciously rejecting that ailment. And I believe she was right. I've found the same thing. Staying on guard against thoughts of maladies is very helpful in preventing illness.

Catch a sick thought. Then throw it away as unhealthy, unnecessary. And unwanted.

Unblaming The Victim

I know in advance that some people will see my mindbody theory as victim blaming.

They will be mistaken.

Reflect on my views about determinism once more. All that happens is cause and effect. This means there is no wiggle room over blame. Illness is the necessary result of the patient's total inner and outer experiences. Given everything in their life, nothing else can happen. Sickness is an effect caused.

The victim of illness is not to blame.

But the victim can assume responsibility for healing – a forward-facing responsibility for their own health. Through understanding the mindbody dynamics of illness, the patient becomes empowered. Through exploring a remedy such as Dr. Sarno's method, the patient may turn that power into recovery as I did. Through recognizing our tendency to deepwant illness, the former patient may fend off much future distress.

I find this greatly hopeful, not disturbing. It is a burden as all responsibility is a burden. To seize control of our health is to work hard at staying generally symptom-free. When an ailment begins we must immediately react by fiercely applying our knowledge and our desire to be healthy, eliminating the symptoms as quickly as possible. We must tap into that powerful innate need to be, to exist, our love as one dynamic wellspring of motivation in this effort. We must labor at wanting to be healthy.

It is not easy.

In his writings Dr. Sarno describes many of the mind's shell games designed to distract our attention from the repressed emotions, perpetuating the illness. Shifting symptoms to new locations in the body is one. Intensifying the symptoms is another. I view these as more than distractions just as I regard the initial symptoms as more than distractions. Confronted with Identity Failure, the mind uses illness to satisfy the demands of the Fundamental Law of Mind.

Preserving this psychological relationship seems the purpose of another mental distortion I've observed within me, a distortion not mentioned in any of Sarno's work that I have read. But I believe it is a significant impediment to the application of his therapeutic technique. When I first try to focus on my repressed emotions as Sarno teaches, I have noted again and again that my mind presents me with a warped interpretation of both my immediate emotional and physical problems. My psyche automatically has magnified the scope of my emotional troubles – and has minimized the consequences of illness. That is, my mind gives me a strong feeling: "You suffer from a huge emotional conflict. Avoid facing it. And really those physical symptoms aren't too bad afterall. You're better off with them than with all that awful emotion."

Essentially, that's the message I receive repeatedly at an emotional level. My mind doesn't put this into words but that is the general feeling I get. This isn't merely the repression at work but rather a specific mechanism designed to perpetuate the repression. It's a clever system to maintain the psychological status quo.

And it works. Too well.

For me to apply the Sarno technique, I must overcome this distortion. I have to understand that the amount of repressed rage and other repressed emotions is not what it appears. I can handle it, fairly easily once I deeply acknowledge the repression. I also need to accept that the physical symptoms are serious problems that require elimination. It seems surprising that this would be an issue, but it is. Humans adapt to our lives. We grow strangely comfortable with things as they are, no matter how terrible. That applies to illness as well. We're often so intensely afraid of facing the realities of our mind that something like horrible back pain can feel preferable to confronting those deeper emotions. So our mind obliges us, preserving the situation we deepwant by distorting our sense of the situation: bloating the rational significance of our psychological conflicts, shriveling the rational significance of illnesses that will try to replace those conflicts.

This distortion phenomenon reminds me of looking at my emotion through binoculars, then turning them around to peer through the wrong end as I view my physical symptoms. The psychological problem is enlarged out of all proportion, the physical problem is similarly diminished. I suspect many of Dr. Sarno's patients have contended with this same issue without knowing it because his method eventually overcomes the distortions when applied diligently. Bit by bit the patient loses fear of the emotions and accepts that the physical symptoms are unnecessary. But again, this takes work.

I've observed other but related fears at play as well when employing the Sarno technique. Among them is an underlying sense that I must have some horrible psychological conflict to produce such extreme repressed emotions. Naturally, I'm terrified to look this conflict in the eyes. Along with that sense, I often experience a strong worry that if I stop one symptom I'll be stricken with a worse condition in its place. Best to live with the devil I know ... Together these fears make it much harder for me to face the repression.

I have learned that all the fears are unfounded. The repressed rage isn't nearly so strong as I'd imagined. I'm not torn by some horrific emotional conflict that I can't solve. And I won't suffer a worse condition, though as Sarno notes the mind frequently does try out different symptoms for a time before they all disappear. It's part of the psychic effort to create some new physical outlet that satisfies the repressed emotions. The very moment I fully accept that my repressed emotions cause my physical distress, all the symptoms evaporate. It's an astonishing thing to experience.

At that same moment I can comfortably accept the repression as much less significant to me than I'd imagined. It feels now merely like one of many elements within my mind, which is the truth. It's not a big deal. I also recognize how unpleasant were my physical symptoms. And I don't want them back. When this all happens to me, I often feel puzzled over my earlier attitude about the repressed rage. Why on earth didn't I just accept it immediately? Why did I pretend it didn't exist? It's just not that scary.

No, but it seemed scary. It felt scary.

And that scary feeling helped my mind rediscover a psychologically effective process. Repressed Emotion Transfer again offered illness as a way to ease my Identity Failure.

Confidence Levels

Dr. Sarno believes that repressed rage is universal. It's an inherent part of being human in this stressful period of our history.

I see things differently. I believe repressed rage is nearly universal because Identity Failure is nearly universal. The prevalence of symptoms, illness, disease in our world is another indication of Identity Failure's prevalence. I.F. generates the repressed emotions that often seem to necessitate illness.

That's how it looks to me. Once more, I do recognize how controversial are such notions. And I'm well aware of natural agents of disease that include parasites, worms and the like. I know newborns can come into the world with illness. I've given some prolonged thought to these questions – and I have reached some tentative suspicions about what may be happening in those cases. But frankly they seem too speculative to share here. I'm not a medical researcher in the conventional sense. I am an explorer of my mind who believes the firsthand experiences are accurate and insightful and original enough that they must have some value for other human minds. And mindbodies. My psychological observations seem to lend a fresh perspective to the groundbreaking work of Dr. John E. Sarno, pointing toward a new model that may help account for all that repressed emotion and the illness it clearly causes.

Can I say with certainty that all illness is caused by Repressed Emotion Transfer? No, I can't. Of course not. Can I claim with great confidence that Identity Failure generates repressed emotion and this repressed emotion causes at least some significant amount of illness? Yes, I think so.

As always in this book, I can only report honestly what I have personally experienced including my direct observations of other people, then draw conclusions, formulate theories and test them as thoroughly as possible for me to do. To my eye, that's science. And so I'm outlining my individual pain and sickness and suffering of body and mind, my mindbody, and the healing too. I am drawing heavily on the brilliant work of Dr. Sarno, recommending it strongly to those unfamiliar with his method and adding my understanding of what actually happened to me when using his technique. I can't and don't advise that anyone ignore their physician's counsel or change their medical routine based solely on my thoughts. That's a decision only the reader should make. I do suggest that folks explore for themselves Dr. Sarno's books, then strain his ideas through their memories of sickness and health. See if you think it makes sense.

I have decided that it does make sense. Sarno's discoveries to me help reveal our illnesses as another serious consequence of Identity Failure – and one more significant reason to recognize this psychological disease so that we can defeat it. The drum major instinct of Dr. King marches humanity forward into profound troubles of many kinds, with physical sicknesses among them.

I.F. is an unrecognized illness that causes illnesses we all can recognize too easily.

Drifting Toward Illness

Most people in contemporary society view good health as our natural state. Humans are healthy without effort required except perhaps some exercise and dieting. Basically, though, the majority of people in modern nations possess health as a birthright. During relatively rare periods of illness, an individual's goal is to recover that innate health.

I think this could be true but is not. Humans would be naturally healthy if not for Identity Failure. I.F.'s presence ensures a tendency to drift naturally over time toward illness.

As long as we look to the outside world for validation and appreciation, as long as the value of our individual existence is linked to external conditions, we will gravitate toward infirmity. Look carefully around at that oh-so-contemporary society of ours, at our ultra-modern nations. If you scratch below the surface, sickness not wellness is the norm. Your colleagues may not seem ill but more than likely they each go home and suffer silently with some malady you know nothing about. Depression or anxiety, perhaps, insomnia or back pain or severe allergies. Or maybe constant colds and infections, or eating disorders or alcoholism or a dependency on pain pills. What person do you know intimately who doesn't endure some form of chronic misery or at minimum an ailment of great frequency? You almost have to live with someone to know for sure. Digestive troubles, heart troubles, muscular troubles, reproductive troubles, respiratory troubles, headaches or joint aches or aching arches. The terrible options are endless for us to take out rage on ourselves.

Identity Failure is the cause of that rage.

Until we recognize and address I.F. widely, I believe, we should admit the obvious fact: Humans tend to become ill, more so with each passing year. I don't see this so much as a necessary consequence of aging as it is the predictable result of our battles with Identity Failure. Our rage at the world increases through experience with the world – and so do our illnesses. As we get older we get angrier and sicker.

The general exception to this is children, I think. Many parents say their kids are sick constantly. I attribute much of that illness to a child's lack of control, with a welter of intense emotions that are confusing, frustrating and ignored. Kids repress their emotions, just like adults, and have even less experience at coping with them.

Young person or old, repressed emotions often satisfy themselves through illness. I suffered skin maladies and heart palpitations from middle school right up through my time with Lydia. I know now what I recall suspecting even back then: These problems were psychosomatic, my reaction to bullying and later to a romantic relationship I began too young. Moving through my 20s I gained a greater sense of power over my life with improved health resulting, though I still was forced many times to fight off some or other affliction.

Since then the severity and frequency of my infirmities has varied widely, depending on my circumstances. One of the healthiest periods for me was the two years or so after first implementing Dr. Sarno's method, when I practiced his technique regularly and rigorously. I rarely suffered any physical complaint for more than a day. One of the sickest periods for me was the five years or so immediately before I could learn to apply Rational Faith effectively, when I was continually beset by several symptoms at once. I've recently recognized a major difference between these two: In the good period I consciously worked at staying healthy but in the bad period I only worked at recovering from symptoms. In the first I focused on avoiding a natural tendency to become ill, in the second I assumed good health was a norm I needed merely to re-discover. The preventive approach was better than the recovery model. Significantly so. Nonetheless I feel certain that my health at all times since first reading Sarno's books in 2000 would have been much worse without an understanding of his work. I don't know how I'd have managed without him. My profound emotional and intellectual conflicts prevented me from thoroughly incorporating his ideas in my early to mid 60s but Sarno's work also kept me out of the doctor's office and out of the hospital. Dr. Sarno allowed me to get by.

So much for me. Now reflect for a moment on your own health over time. When have you ever been perfectly healthy for long, without some ailment or other troubling you? Without some unpleasantness you didn't really understand, pains-and-aches or colds-and-allergies or indigestion-and-nausea or what-have-you …

Looking back, I consider myself relatively healthy for most of my life compared to many others. But a closer examination shows I was completely symptom-free for more than a few days at a time only infrequently. Tension stomach cramps and tension headaches came and went, soon enough replaced by sniffles or a rash or muscle pains or a fullbown flu. This procession of infirmities seemed normal. Everyone around me was like this, more or less. No person I knew well ever savored good health uninterrupted.

I am convinced we don't have to live this way. Mark Twain commented, "I have seldom been sick since I was 15; I am 69 now." I believe him. But for most people, the affliction of I.F. regularly brings us other afflictions of the mindbody. This perspective on our lives can lead us to take active steps that may prevent many illnesses, or at least more quickly end them. Drawn naturally to sickness for now, we can do much to strengthen our desire for health.

If we can learn to deepwant wellness, we're a lot more likely to get it.

Om

In my own efforts to stay healthy, I've now found that daily meditation is greatly helpful. In combination with Sarno's method especially, meditation can work fine things in the mindbody.

Much scientific research and personal anecdote already exist on meditation's benefits. I don't see sensible reason for me to offer more on the topic here except to note my experience with its highly significant results. The Sarno technique of repressed emotion awareness includes a daily period of reflection to reinforce his ideas. I began this religiously when I first read Healing Back Pain in 2000 and do it still each day, though during those brutal years in my 60s I practiced with less commitment than earlier. And with less dramatic healing. But on New Year's Eve 2014 I also added a traditional meditation of mindfulness every morning. This too has become my unfailing routine and I can't say enough about its value. Eastern meditation has aided my acceptance of all emotion and helped me flow more easily with difficult situations in everyday living. I recommend it to you – and I genuinely believe every human being can benefit from dedicated meditative practice.

My experience with meditation taught me something else: Dr. Sarno's method actually is a form of mindfulness. The difference is that traditional meditation teaches us to focus on what's most apparent moment to moment. Sarno's cure asks us to focus on what is most hidden. But the two techniques bear many similarities. With Sarno as with mindful meditation we bring our attention over and over and over back to something – repressed rage in Sarno's methodology, often the breath or a mantra in Eastern traditions. In each case we must learn to be more present, more conscious of what's happening right now.

That's interesting to me from the standpoint of the Fundamental Law of Mind and the Fundamental Question. At the deepest level, our psyches naturally target the present moment. The human mind wants to feel life is worth living … right now. Meditation opens our experience to this right-now and shows us that even the most frightening elements of the present moment aren't nearly as bad as we've imagined. We can face them. We can accept them. We can handle them. We are still breathing and life goes on, in a better right-now than before our mindful interlude.

Beyond The Frustration

In a real sense, I think illness is frustrated energy. Think about love as I describe it, that desire to be. To exist. This is our innate love, a human being's need to express, to flow from within toward the outside, interacting with the world in a manner that feels natural to us. Bob being Bob, you being you. When the world interferes with our desire to be for too long, the intense frustration eventually can become a terror and then a rage that turn our natural outflowing energy into something else. For many people, illness is one convenient outlet. It is our physical over-reaction to an emotional over-reaction, irrational feelings as an effervescence bottled but bubbling out around the cap. Frustrated energy.

I sometimes speculate whether illness in other living beings may happen in much the same way. A caged wild tiger, a hunting dog confined to a small apartment, even a tree or plant without sufficient space often become sickened. Why? I can't know for sure, obviously. But yes, I do wonder. Possibly the tiger and the dog and the tree and the plant in their fashion are re-directing frustrated energy. It's an engaging notion, with one simple dynamic accounting for illness in all things alive.

I do know from carefully examined direct experience that this holds true for my illness, which also tends to take on a life of its own after grabbing hold of me. That's an important point. My sickness runs away with me.

I've seen many times that illness generates much additional rage, mostly repressed, which then only creates new or stronger symptoms, which then generate more rage and on it goes. Basically, I'm angry at the world and then at myself and then at life for being sick, which creates more anger and more sickness. Once Sarno's method absorbs fully into my consciousness, a significant pool of repressed rage seems to dry up like an evaporating reservoir. Repressed though it is, I've learned to have some sense of its power in me, of its insistent gravitational push toward symptoms. I can feel when it's stronger or weaker. Whenever my symptoms go away, a lot of repressed emotion goes with them. I've also noticed repeatedly that illness begins a cycle of psychological events that sustain my misery. My fear and rage are major factors in this process working in combination with a variety of other psychological components that include conditioning, expectation and deepwanting. They coalesce to heighten symptoms, prolonging and intensifying the ailment far beyond anything commensurate with the irrational emotions that first triggered it. They lock in my illness. After I'm really and truly sick, I require a great deal more energy to reverse the symptoms on my own than if I'd employed Sarno's method early on. As has long been said about human disease, an ounce of prevention is worth a pound of cure.

In my past, a doctor's confident diagnosis along with a shot or some pills – these could break that sickness cycle when my mind was ready. They helped me believe I was being cured. And to truly want to be cured. Today, I try to do this myself whenever possible. I've learned that I have a vast capacity for self-healing, a lesson gained thanks in great part to Dr. Sarno. I should think all people have that same capacity.

In his towering essay, Self-Reliance, Ralph Waldo Emerson recounts travelers' tales about the recovery powers of native warriors: " … Strike the savage with a broad-axe and in a day or two the flesh shall unite and heal as if you struck the blow into soft pitch, and the same blow shall send the white to his grave." As with Mark Twain's claim of health, I believe there's truth to the story. Again I speculate here and I admit it. But I can't escape the conviction that human beings possess much untapped ability to make ourselves well. I have personally experienced some remarkable instances of self-healing. In time, I feel sure, this will be the everyday norm for our species.

Humanity will keep itself healthy more with mind than with medicine.

But from my vantage point, that time looks distant. A recognition of Identity Failure as a disease-causing disease can bring us closer. When collectively we can agree that almost all people to varying extent suffer this soul-sickness, that our obsession with outside validation is unnatural and unhealthy, we then can find ways to diminish I.F.'s power over our lives. And to eliminate it altogether. I believe that's do-able – in time.

My psychological theories of the mindbody dovetail nicely with Dr. Sarno's great medical discoveries. As I've been trying to show throughout this chapter, my insights reinforce his. They offer a more thorough reinforcement, I think, than the borrowed psychological ideas that had sufficed for his therapeutic purpose.

I even recognize many unintended glimmers of agreement with me in his books.

One of the most striking examples comes by way of his colleague who contributed a chapter to Sarno's superb book, The Divided Mind. Andrea Leonard-Segal, M.D., is an internist and rheumatologist who worked at George Washington University Medical Center to relieve chronic pain. She's among several physicians who chronicled their experience with patients as supporting evidence for Sarno's theory about Tension Myositis Syndrome and its equivalents. TMS, or Repressed Emotion Transfer in my phrase. This is a short excerpt from Dr. Leonard-Segal's chapter: "Getting better from TMS is learning how to extract yourself from needing recognition from others and learning how to fill that need yourself. It is about learning to parent yourself in perhaps a kinder, gentler and more benevolent way than one may have actually experienced during childhood." The paragraph continues with a succession of similar observations that include the value of lowered expectations for yourself and others as well as the need to take care of yourself psychologically. To me, this advice directly addresses Identity Failure as a cause of illness. To extract yourself from needing recognition from others is to overcome I.F.

In his books, Dr. Sarno and his colleagues write about self-worth as a key issue in the infirmities they heal through mindbody medicine. In The Mindbody Prescription, Sarno notes the following: "Deeply repressed feelings of inadequacy foster the development of personality traits that are almost universal in people with TMS." And just a bit later in this book Sarno continues, "Deeply repressed feelings of inadequacy and self-doubt appear to be our common lot," suggesting this is one significant source of human rage.

The human rage that can turn into human illness.

Experience As Science

I believe in science.

All my life I've believed passionately in science, a word of course that comes from the Latin for knowledge.

The work of Dr. Jacob Bronowski in his extraordinary series of essays, The Ascent of Man, first helped me to understand that science is forever incomplete. It's an unending exploration of reality, never finished and for this reason never perfected. In some sense, science is always wrong. Today's theory will be replaced by tomorrow's more insightful description of nature, whether this insight is entirely different or simply a refinement.

I do believe in science.

So I believe also that mindbody theories of medicine including Dr. Sarno's work will be proven correct through experimentation. In his books he expresses frustration with researchers who simply say his ideas can't be proven, that the evidence is anecdotal. To me this is a failure not of Sarno's theories but of those researchers who give up before they try. As I see it, Dr. Sarno's discoveries are based on direct well-documented experience over decades with huge numbers of patients. Surely it's possible to do controlled studies that can point to the validity of his method. I suspect it's possible to conduct experiments as well, something in the lab that eliminates enough variables to verify key aspects of his medical writings.

How can a scientist honestly sense that a theory may reflect some deep truth about nature without exploring every conceivable avenue of confirmation? At some point, it seems, science can become less about the sincere pursuit of genuine knowledge than about the superficial validation of specious observation. Simply because it's easier to prove doesn't make it real.

But I believe in science. And I do feel confident that the weight of direct experience about mindbody theory will grow so great that researchers equal to that greatness will confirm it. There must be ways. Science is founded on the notion that the truth is the truth – and humanity should invent methods to prove this truth.

We now understand it's only the best available truth. And I believe mindbody theory is a better available truth than the conventional model of a mind and body as things separate and apart.

As you might expect from my optimism about science, I am equally confident that in time my own theories may be taken seriously, studied and established as a better available truth. I know that Identity Failure can be proven as a reality of the human mind and therefore recognized as a disease both pervasive and malicious. A disease that causes other disease by way of Repressed Emotion Transfer. I am certain related ideas I've put forward in Beyond Me also are worth the time, money and hard work to examine for scientific validity – and just as certain they can be proven accurate. The Fundamental Law of Mind and accompanying Fundamental Question, deepwanting, vericepts, psychogravity and more ...

I believe a critical but open-minded analysis of the empirical evidence laid out in these chapters will lead the perceptive reader to an overall feeling that my explanations make sense. You wouldn't still be reading my book if you didn't feel this at some level. My ideas can help clarify direct personal experience with your passions, your conflicts, your needs, all those observations of your own behavior and your own mind that always left you so confused.

Perhaps you're a bit less confused about them now. They make more sense just as my detailed theories make some sense to you. And this should tell us something. The ideas make sense when viewed through your experience because they are true.

As importantly, these accurate psychological descriptions are profoundly hopeful for us all. If I am right about my mechanisms of mind, or even partly right about even some of them, they show us up as a species far more remarkable than generally appreciated. As a humanity whose love is innate and unquenchable, requiring connection and caring among individuals. Requiring. They're not merely nice optionals. Rational Faith is a natural extension of our psyche's fundamental functions, revealing that human beings can only achieve fulfillment through a deeper knowledge of self-interest that necessitates helping others. The love, the connection, the helping are built into our nature.

It's who we are.

That's what I'm attempting to prove with my psychological theories: What seems like an unfortunate aspect of human nature isn't human nature at all. It's Identity Failure. It's learned – and correctable. We're not irretrievably self-obsessed, selfish, greedy, violent, diseased, insecure, terrified and enraged. We are emotional and we are irrational, no question, but our true human nature can lead us straight toward ways of living that are far more respectful and cooperative, enriching and fulfilling for many individuals.

And this benefits society as a whole.

Humanity can be more. It's already inside each person, much more, waiting for us to see it and free it.

But I believe only a profound self-knowledge can realize this vision. To make the next great leap forward, we must understand the human individual deeply and accurately. It's time.

As it happens I've been trying all my life to understand myself, deeply and accurately. That's who I am. Nothing heroic about it, no credit deserved. Nor blame if I'm mistaken. I'm doing what I have to do.

But since I'm utterly convinced that I'm not mistaken about my empirically based conclusions, I have to do something else too. I have to share them with you – and trust that you may take me seriously.

Read on, dear reader, my friend unknown to me. Read on …

Chapter 13: Physics Of The Mind

"Nothing is too wonderful to be true, if it be consistent with the laws of nature; and in such things as these, experiment is the best test of such consistency."
Michael Faraday

Knowledge From Nowhere

Insight appears in unexpected ways.

It propelled the wings constructed by bicyclemakers in a small Ohio town.

It warped the geometry of the universe and extended the length of time through the musings of a clerk in a Swiss patent office.

It pitted species against species before the eyes of two Victorian adventurers hiking in virgin rainforests.

Insight explored the solitary life beside a small New England pond in pre-Civil War America. Insight painted the secretive smile of a young woman during the Italian Renaissance. Insight inspired self-knowledge among Athenians on the streets of Ancient Greece.

All these insights emerged from the needs of their period. But none was derivative, none was borrowed. Their true source was inside individuals who observed and decided for themselves, intellectually independent of conventional wisdom. They emanated from original minds. As the American author Eudora Welty noted: "Insight comes … from nowhere but within."

To their societies, such insights seemed to materialize as if dropped whole from the clouds. The painstaking efforts that produced these new ideas typically took place well away from public view. For a time they were each a private knowledge, innovation wrapped in anonymity.

I sometimes wonder if our modern world has choked off the insights of some imaginative thinkers. Education and specialization can bring the world great benefits. But so can independent knowledge acquired through individual experience. Michael Faraday is regarded as among history's greatest scientists – and was self-taught. As was one of music's most influential composers, Richard Wagner, whose scant youthful training in composition seems irrelevant beside his grand artistic breakthroughs. Autodidacts have sprinkled the centuries with significant accomplishments. But achievement without formal training today somehow feels suspect. Perhaps our society will rediscover its merits following important contributions in our time by people such as Bill Gates and Steve Jobs, both college dropouts. Not all wisdom is handed down. And insight never can be – just as Welty understood, it must come from within the individual.

That's why knowledge of this type appears to arrive from nowhere. No one can follow its progress, sit in on the staff meetings, watch the PowerPoint presentations, read the incremental findings step after step toward the final success. The meetings all take place for a party of one inside a mind. Even collaborations such as the Wright Brothers require inspirations that bubble out of a single psyche at a time, offered up to the team and usually known among very few. But for me it's the discoveries of the lone innovator that I admire most, whether Einstein or Darwin or Wallace, Thoreau or Leonardo or Socrates, the people who had little but faith in their private experience to guide them forward. My list of such courageous thinkers is long, including Emerson, Shakespeare, Joyce, Beethoven, Bruckner, Mahler and in my own time insightful theorists such as Sarno and Bronowski. Not all of them self-taught, surely, but each taking their ideas far beyond anything learned from books or teachers.

I won't call them heroes of mine as I've already explained that I don't believe in heroism. Our behavior is determined by everything that went before it. We do what we have to do. But I regard these and others like them, women and men both, as great sources of personal inspiration for me. On my desk sit busts of Leonardo, Shakespeare and Socrates, Homer and Aristotle. Over my desk are photos of Gandhi, Thoreau and Emerson. I have framed quotations from Emerson and Martin Luther King, Jr. on my office walls as well. They remind me of a lesson I somehow began to understand from an early age: Human beings must each think for ourselves. I must, just as these people did. And the older I get, the stronger this truth becomes for me.

As a species we should seek change, not repetition. Humanity doesn't need more of the same thing. It's not working very well, as you may have noticed. Our society requires independent observation and unconventional thought, grounded in the rational, in the direct experience of individuals. That's what can carry us forward best at this moment in our history. We have more than enough meetings and presentations, plenty of groupthought to water down every solution to every problem. We lack the insightful perspectives of individuals outside the mainstream, concepts created far away from the consensus beliefs of our society.

We should encourage the freethinkers among us, those who can assemble their ideas into detailed coherent form. We should welcome and seriously reflect on the new notions these innovators offer. In all fields, not only science and art but also education, childrearing, sexuality, health, safety, government, law and nearly every other area of meaningful inquiry. They just may have a thought or two worth hearing out. Our inflexible insistence on weighty titles, degrees and affiliations as the sole source of knowledge is holding us back.

Of course I also must note in fairness that my views on the topic are somewhat self-serving if also completely sincere. This entire book is an individual's call from relative anonymity for a new way of thinking about humanity based mainly on personal experience. Without my own weighty titles, degrees and affiliations, why should anyone believe me? I've asked myself that question for decades. Perhaps the true answer is that no one will.

But I have hope.

When prosecutors judge the veracity of a potential witness, one measure they use is the person's track record. What has this witness done before now? Is there reason to believe the individual? I like to think my life has earned me some credibility by this standard anyway. Nearly everything I've done of any significance was largely or completely self-taught. Writing, reporting, investigative journalism, broadcast journalism, public speaking, composing music, playing several instruments (though I had a few drum lessons as a child), creating educational and safety programs from scratch, founding and maintaining an accomplished nonprofit organization, among other efforts. I've put together music videos including storyboards and dance choreography, though I had no training. My own mother, never a woman for idle compliments, once told me, "Whatever you've got, you've gotten all by yourself. No one helped you." Naturally that's an exaggeration. I don't claim to have done it all by myself without lots of guidance and support at various times. But aside from a basic education at mediocre schools and a year and half of college at Eastern Michigan University, I've received almost no formal training. And financially my family was never in a position to give me a boost in any way at all. When both my parents were gone, each of the three kids in the Knotts clan got something like $200 as I recall.

I don't offer this explanation with any arrogant or boastful intent, honestly. It's simply that I feel right down to the soles of my feet that my ideas have some merit – and may be able to help others. That includes my psychological theories. I'm not comparing myself to Einstein or Darwin or Leonardo or anybody else. I am who I am. Robert Spencer Knotts – Bob to my family and friends. I was born in Detroit, Michigan at Mt. Carmel Hospital on December 9, 1952. My parents were Bill and Jeanette Knotts. I've been a Detroit Tigers fan all my life. My favorite breakfast is cold leftover pizza. And I've explored in very great detail for a very long time many of the intricate complexities of my own mind.

And now I believe that I just may have a thought or two worth hearing out.

Mindful Vision

And so this is the chapter I have waited more than 40 years to write. If Chapter 12 emerged grudgingly as the section that almost wasn't, the passages you're reading now were the first envisioned by me long ago for some possible future book. Putting it down on paper at last feels surreal.

I was unprepared wholly to write about the physics of the mind back then. My knowledge was shallow and my literary abilities undeveloped. Only today, as I begin, do I finally sense that I'm ready to address the topic in carefully observed detail.

In scientific detail.

Those three words come hard for me: in scientific detail. They stake a claim that I regard simply as a fact, yes, an accurate assessment of the arguments I've been making up to now in Beyond Me. I've said as much earlier in different ways many times. But the moment has arrived in this lengthy project when I can no longer avoid clarifying that point without equivocation: I believe the major concepts presented in my previous chapters are scientifically valid – and can be proven by independent studies and experiments. My goal throughout has been to create a solid scientific foundation for a new philosophy that can prevent and cure Identity Failure, which I view as a fundamental undiscovered problem of humanity. This philosophy, Rational Faith, flows directly and necessarily from this science. The human psyche's composition determines the most effective antidote to I.F.'s poison.

Yet not one human being thinks of me as a scientist. Nor do I, being mindful to avoid new identity poses that strengthen and perpetuate my Identity Failure. Bob-the-scientist is no more sensible than Bob-the-writer. I do recognize, though, that I have an innate strong scientific bent, as I've noted elsewhere in this book. Meticulous, even tedious and repetitious and often obsessive investigative inquiry is a forceful need of my personality. Always has been, which is why I made a good investigative journalist. I have discovered over the years my own methods of observing, examining, theorizing, testing and re-testing in prolonged efforts to unearth what seemed deep truths about myself, other people and life in general. Looking back, I can see that this task has always felt like my real work, some sort of guiding mission more important than any other labors.

In this sense, then, I do consider theoretical psychology among my passions. And my talents. I may not "be" a scientist but I do science.

Yet we live in an age far different from the era of the Victorian gentlemen scientists, whose findings were taken seriously by that society. Here in the early 21st Century, scientists are specialists with letters after their names, the women and men in lab coats at universities, foundations and corporations. They analyze long numbers gained with the aid of elaborate equipment. They examine nature from the outside-in through studies and experiments constructed to reveal its disguised realities. They often require large sums to carry out these investigations.

I admire every committed scientist who explores their subject with insight and integrity. We need them, the good ones. Their efforts are highly valuable to all of us, of course.

Of course.

But I am different from these folks, an anachronism of sorts. I probably have more in common with the Victorian naturalists than with most contemporary scientists. I simply observe and think, then find ways to test before I observe and think again. And for me the observing and the thinking and the testing have been focused primarily within, my attempt to examine human nature from the inside-out. All my life I've been trying to understand my own mind and the minds of my fellow human beings. With the greatest humility in the presence of such complexity, I genuinely believe I've made significant progress toward that goal. And now I simply have to trust that at least some people will judge my theories on the evidence alone, not on my titles or degrees or affiliations.

These open-minded people will take my ideas seriously enough to read them over carefully, more than once. And to ask themselves, "Do these claims make sense? Do they square with my personal experience? Can they be tested?"

I think a fair-minded reader will find the answer is yes. I believe they offer a new and valuable vision of the human mind – and of our humanity.

So this chapter is a pause in the storyline of Identity Failure and Rational Faith that I've been laying out piece by piece until now. Instead I will attempt to collect the theoretical fibers that tie that story together, assembling them into a single fabric.

They all fit neatly as one unified theory, one integrated psychological system.

I call it psychophysics.

The physics of the mind.

Intentional Ignorance

You'll remember I noted earlier that since leaving college in 1973 I have avoided nearly all reading or research into contemporary theory about either psychology or philosophy. I've mentioned a few exceptions to this. But for the most part, that's how I've gone about my own work ... for good reason.

I worried about being swayed unduly by the findings of others. No matter how independent my thinking, I was likely to be influenced by widely accepted ideas once exposed to them. Quite possibly without even knowing it. I can offer a very recent example of the value I've found in this intentional ignorance. Only several weeks before writing this chapter's first draft, I discovered that my previous understanding of vericepts was wrong in some significant ways, obviously all now corrected. But at first and for some long period I had conflated two psychological processes, balling them up as one thing: I hadn't yet recognized quancepts as something separate and apart from vericepts. They appeared to me as if a single mechanism of mind. Suppose then I had read something in the psychological literature about an eminent theorist who had identified the presence of vericepts as I originally conceived them, whatever she or he happened to name these mini-concepts. This would have validated my own incorrect ideas – and probably locked me into them permanently. But lacking that confirmation, I was free to keep exploring the subject.

My ignorance of prevailing theories by others helps me to strengthen my own theories based on continuing unprejudiced direct observation.

In college, I gained a very basic knowledge of very basic psychology, just as I did with some fundamental ideas of philosophy. I learned about things like the unconscious, repression, projection, about conditioning and experiments with babies and animals. That was it. So what follows now as my theory of psychophysics is drawn almost entirely from direct experience explored as fully as I am able. I don't know if some of these ideas may parrot similar concepts already in the journals and books. I've always felt that, even if that's the case, surely my observations would provide some valuable verification. They come from the source itself. They come from watching the workings of my psyche.

I also have long believed that some of my theories could only be formed by others through this same kind of introspection, which I've named intrasentience as a more apt description. There's no method I can imagine to discover many of these psychological functions from the outside, through observation of one person by another person. They must be witnessed by the mind's eye, usually repeatedly over lengthy periods.

Perhaps someone else has done this ahead of me, for all the decades and in much the same scrupulous manner as I've conducted research into psychophysics.

Perhaps.

But I'm skeptical. For one thing, if my theories already had been described and widely disseminated I would hope such information by now might have influenced mainstream thought both within and outside the practice of psychology. During a few discussions with psychologists when researching magazine articles some years ago, I tried to feel out these university professors to learn whether any of my main ideas had been explored by their colleagues. My strong sense was that no, they had not. Professional psychologists were not thinking in the same ways I was thinking.

Even if psychophysics should eventually prove largely in error, I believe laying out a new system in great detail will in itself be worthwhile. Folks would know that one whole line of theoretical inquiry had been tried and failed. And even if that's so, this would not negate my philosophy of Rational Faith because the main psychological points are beyond sensible dispute. We all recognize the problems of ego within us and almost everyone else. We all know that we depend on outside validation to feel good about ourselves. We all can see how much of our existence is focused on ourselves, on "me." And we all accept that it's not a very healthy way to live – but we don't understand how to change it. That's what Rational Faith will try to offer. A way out of the ego-driven life. The Fundamental Law of Mind and Fundamental Question, deepwanting and vericepts and the rest, they provide a specific and powerful scientific foundation for these broader everyday observations. But even without the scientific specifics, the basic argument holds.

Call it Identity Failure or call it something else. Call it a disease or call it human nature.

The end conclusion is the same. Human beings continue to live self-obsessed, frightened lives that thwart the fulfillment of individuals and of society.

Psychophysics can help explain why.

Psychophysics 101

Psychophysics is the theory that the human mind functions with discoverable precise laws and principles and forces like any other entity in the universe. Emotional forces are at the core of psychophysics, the relative strength of combined and competing emotions. These emotional forces are quantifiable, with the stronger forces prevailing over the weaker. Such relationships can be expressed mathematically, just as in physics.

In psychophysics, all forces are governed by a central mechanism: the Fundamental Law of Mind, which states that individuals interpret experience to create the weakest possible emotional resistance to the strongest possible feelings that their existence is valuable to them at this moment in this world. This law may be simplified into a Fundamental Question that every mind perpetually is attempting to answer: Is my life worth living? The perceived value of individual existence at this moment in this world is central to psychological function and vital to biological function. Human beings experience the strongest emotional force in favor of whatever feels most necessary at this moment according to the Fundamental Law of Mind. The underlying principle is not survival of the fittest but dominance of the necessary.

This automatic attraction to whatever feels emotionally necessary causes the mind to deepwant that thing, often in opposition to something the individual claims to desire. There's what we say we want and there's what we really want. Deepwanting reflects our deepest values, which are expressed by the individual through various means during daily life – often as irrational identities as well as goals, beliefs, feelings, actions and more. These all are efforts to satisfy the demands of the Fundamental Law of Mind.

Deepwanting contributes to a related force called psychogravity that in effect warps the psychological universe as gravity warps the universe outside us. As we deepwant those specific things that express our profound values, our mind automatically intensifies our desire for those specific things through accumulating new concepts and activating related existing concepts. The need for immediate emotional satisfaction demanded by the Fundamental Law of Mind creates a push within the individual toward the perceived source of that satisfaction, a psychological force typically exerted outside the individual's awareness. We can feel ourselves being propelled to something but don't know why. Maybe an old relationship or a new car, maybe alcohol or drugs or cigarettes. Maybe we feel an increasing need for some outburst of anger or for a withdrawal into complete silence. Perhaps we want to compete in triathlons – or write an ambitious book. Whatever appears to us right now as the most effective way to replace our current feelings with new ones that best satisfy the demands of the Fundamental Law of Mind.

At the core of our quest for feelings of life's value is one of three primary emotions: love. As defined by psychophysics, love is the innate human need to be, to exist, to express our feelings in the world. The other two primary emotions are fear, the desire to escape, and anger, the desire to eliminate. These three primary emotions combine in highly complex ways and attach to our interpretations of ourselves, the world and our place in the world. Our perceived feelings are made of these bundles of emotion and interpretation, all combined in great variations and combinations to produce the breadth of human feeling.

In psychophysics, the bundles of emotion and interpretation at the basic level are called vericepts – "truth concepts" that join our psyche as discrete interpretations of experience in conformance with the Fundamental Law of Mind. Those vericepts join one or more larger units of interpretation called nexes, which are made of many vericepts, vary greatly in size and carry both our interpretations of experience and the emotions attached to those interpretations. Nexes are arranged in the mind by subject.

The new theory describes a "chain of consciousness" that drives every human mind, unlike the conception of consciousness as a stream or flow. Psychophysics explains that the mind works in segments, each thought or action preceded by a series of reactions, one causing the next akin to an atomic chain reaction. Vericepts and nexes are integral elements within this chain of consciousness but so is another new psychological component called "quancepts" for "quantum concepts"

– automatic minute analyses of experience based on prevailing feeling and situation.

Psychophysics says that some psychological processes are manifest to the individual, others are mostly or entirely hidden from awareness. The theory proposes two new words as replacements for the conventional terms taken from Freudian psychology, the "conscious" and "unconscious" minds. Instead the "deliberate" and "automatic" minds may be more accurate, both because they are free of erroneous connotations carried over from past theories and because they describe the psyche's nature in ways that express our real world experience. Our minds possess functions that can be used deliberately, with intent. And they also have functions that are mostly or entirely automatic, happening without our intention. Some automatic processes can become deliberate, just as I have directly felt repressed emotion that is normally considered part of the unconscious mind. Other automatic processes occur completely apart from deliberate observation.

Psychophysics recognizes the key role of conditioning and coincidence within the mind at the same time that it accounts for the psyche's hidden processes and the crucial relationship of human emotions, feelings and thoughts to our lives. In some real sense, then, psychophysics may be viewed as a synthesis of Freudian, behavioral and cognitive theories, fusing together some of their central tenets into a new theory with emotional strength and individual value as fundamental forces of mind.

Psychophysics describes the causes of an unrecognized disease that afflicts nearly every human being and profoundly influences humanity. Identity Failure. The theory explains why and how this illness takes hold of individuals, essentially as the result of irrational ideas conveyed to most children by family, friends and society during upbringing. Key among these irrational concepts is the need to seek outside validation for individual value. Because this belief is held in various ways almost universally by human beings, we have developed identity poses that are rigid and irrational self-images for which we perpetually seek approval by other people. Identity poses are bolstered by pose-weakeners and pose-strengtheners, mechanisms intended to preserve the most important self-images.

Psychophysics says that Identity Failure is a preventable and curable disease.

The theory states that individuals find feelings of value, a sense that life is worth living, through the process of being – the honest expression of genuine values, feelings, thoughts, needs and desires in the world. That is, through the expression of their love. Fear and anger conflict with love in a clash of emotional forces, with the strongest taking precedence moment to moment.

The will to live is innate in human beings. This innate will gains strength from an individual's feelings of their life's value. Those feelings of life's value strengthen when love, or the desire to be, is stronger than fear, or the desire to escape. Anger is a reaction to fear and automatically weakens or strengthens relative to the levels of fear. It is fear that fundamentally opposes love within the human mind.

These concepts can be expressed as a simple equation, according to psychophysics:

$V = L > F$, with V for value, L for love and F representing fear.

Value comes to human beings when love is greater than fear.

Natural Laws

So much for a broad overview of psychophysics. Let me tease out the specifics for you.

I've long considered the human mind, the entire human being actually, as neither more nor less than a part of nature. Quite literally, another element in the universe alongside stars and planets, lakes and trees, butterflies and whales. The human entity is alive and unique but governed still by natural laws. Some of those laws apply to all living things in the universe to our knowledge, including a cycle of birth and existence and demise. Other laws are human only, such as the Fundamental Law of Mind. The point is that psychophysics requires us to view the psyche's mechanics with the same neutral attitude we would adopt in studying fusion or supernovas. Or butterflies or whales.

We must begin by recognizing ourselves as neither more nor less than a part of nature. How we got to be a part of nature is another issue altogether.

Psychophysics also insists that these human laws, including those of the mind, can be identified, studied and verified. We do not need to content ourselves with mapping the brain from the outside. We can observe directly the psyche's workings from within, examine them and make sense of them. We can understand not merely the brain but the mind as well – consciousness as we experience it.

Psychophysics explains important elements of this experience, from the familiar to the unusual. It tells us why we can love and hate the same person at the same time or why we want badly to quit our job and desperately want to keep it too. As we've seen in earlier chapters, psychophysics offers insight into romance and health, violence against others and self-destructive behavior, war and slavery, boasting and greed and even gangsters. The previous lengthy discussions about Identity Failure, identity poses, pose-weakeners and pose-strengtheners are central to grasping the underlying dynamics of these realities of human life. But psychophysics also takes us deeper.

We can love and hate the same person at the same time, for instance, or both want to leave and retain our job for a simple reason that is a central concept of psychophysics: Our mind automatically creates countless independent interpretations of our experience based on the Fundamental Law of Mind. Many of these interpretations are not linked but instead often conflict with each other. They exist in our psyche separately.

As I enjoy a new female friend, I form ideas about who this person is. Pleasant ideas. But these are more than ideas, more than interpretations of my experience with her – they also include emotions that are part of those experiences, perhaps powerful emotions that involve my innate love as described in Chapter 11 on romance. It's the emotions that make our interpretations of experience stick to memory. I find that in my friend's company, I can be myself in some ways that seem important. My existence feels more valuable to me around her. Because I am afflicted with Identity Failure, many of my reactions to this person will be irrational. Maybe she makes me feel strong and masculine, smart or talented. She helps to validate some key identity poses such as Bob-the-writer.

Later as this same friend inevitably disappoints or hurts me, I form entirely different ideas about who she is. Unpleasant ideas with powerful emotions of fear and anger attached as I experience her changed behavior. Her new attitude threatens some of my important identity poses such as making me feel like less than Bob-the-nice-guy. My mind doesn't take into account the earlier pleasant ideas. It just begins to store the unpleasant ideas as if the pleasant ideas don't exist, trying to satisfy the demands of the Fundamental Law of Mind right now. Troubled by fear and anger around my friend, I can't be myself with her in some ways that seem important. My existence feels less valuable to me around her. And now the love I sometimes genuinely feel around my friend enters a contest for supremacy with the fear and anger I sometimes feel as well. The pleasant ideas about my friend's character and their accompanying emotions exist independently of the unpleasant ones. They clash in an emotional battle.

If my relationship to this woman is like most in our society, my experience will swing back and forth for me between pleasure in my friend's company and displeasure. The pleasant and unpleasant interpretations and emotions evolve into more and more complex feelings, in ways I'll describe later in this chapter. Not just the basics such as, "I really like this girl" and "I really don't like this girl." Also feelings such as frustration, disgust, admiration, sexual desire and more. And if the friendship should gain greater importance in my life, perhaps turning into a serious romance, I'm likely to continue creating many more ideas about my newly beloved, both pleasant and unpleasant. In time I may begin to love her deeply based on some of those interpretations and hate her just as deeply based on different interpretations. I've collected huge numbers of pleasant and unpleasant ideas, in essence. Probably most or all of these are irrational on both sides of the psychic equation.

"She is so sweet and loving!"

"She can be such a self-centered jerk!"

Unless I deliberately sort through those shallow concepts to reconcile them and look for a more realistic middle ground between the pleasant and unpleasant ideas about this lover, my mind will hold on to them as competing concepts. The pleasant and unpleasant, the good stuff about her and the bad stuff. She makes my existence more valuable, she makes my existence less valuable. It all depends on the situation.

My irrational psyche doesn't try to make sense of the confusion. It simply emits energy in the form of emotion attached to the concepts on both sides. This emotion can be quantified through self-reporting if by no other means available at present. Using the earlier 1 – 1,000 scale of emotional force, I might decide that my love for her is 850 and my hate for her 925. If that's the case for long, I probably will break off the romance eventually. But the point here is to demonstrate that my emotions cast energy into my mind and body, real forces of nature no less than starbursts. For me, for every human being, emotion is energy. Energy is emotion. This is why I'm confident that psychophysics can be expressed in mathematical terms. At bottom our psychological processes involve the creation, conflict and release of energy – emotions that attach themselves to the interpretations of our experience. And those processes follow natural laws.

Surely a gifted mathematician could absorb a deep understanding of such concepts and express them through elegant equations. I sense strongly that this is possible in psychophysics just as in physics. I simply am not a mathematician, gifted or otherwise.

Bob-the-mathematician has never been among my delusions.

Battery Powered

One way to think about these separate collections of pleasant and unpleasant ideas of my friend is this: Imagine they're powered by batteries that illuminate the ideas in my mind, like battery-powered lights.

Here are the pleasant ideas powered by love. Battery A.

Here are the unpleasant ideas powered by fear. Battery B.

Here are more unpleasant ideas powered by anger. Battery C.

I have lunch with my friend. She asks lots of questions about me at first and Battery A is activated. Love.

After a while, she begins to make me feel unattractive and Battery B is activated. Fear.

Soon she implies my opinions about an important social issue are foolish and Battery C is activated. Anger.

What happens next will depend on the relative force of each battery. If Battery A can overpower the other two batteries, we may well end the lunch without any serious argument. If Battery B takes precedence, I probably will stop talking for the most part and wait anxiously for a chance to leave. If Battery C is strongest, that harsh argument becomes more likely.

But of course this is a highly simplified example of the mind's reality.

As my friend and I eat lunch, each of the three batteries surely will gain strength at some moments and lose strength at other moments. One or more of them sometimes may turn off completely before snapping back alive. There will be a constant interplay inside me among these emotional forces. But if all three batteries should emit roughly equal force for any length of time, I will feel thoroughly confused – and I will react in whatever ways I've learned over the years to cope with similar confusion. Life has switched on all three batteries without any concern about the contradictory ideas they power within my psyche. Each exists independently of the other two. I feel a mishmash of intense love, fear and anger when eating that meal with my friend.

Yet in real life, the batteries will be many more than three. In this situation or any situation.

Let's make the analogy a bit more realistic. At our lunch, I will feel the influence of great numbers of interpretations acquired through my experience, many many ideas about the world, about me and about the way the world and I fit together. The grand trio, as I called it earlier, the three major categories of human thought. Each of those interpretations, or ideas, also is attached to a battery powered by love, fear or anger.

Now I no longer merely feel the effects of Battery A, B or C. My lunchtime battery array extends far far beyond the 26 letters of the alphabet, drawing the force of emotion from uncountable sources of power.

One small battery may light up my ideas about having a hamburger for lunch. Love.

A larger battery may illuminate my thoughts about noisy restaurants. Anger.

A much larger battery may send strong currents of emotion to make shine my notions about hurting a friend's feelings. Fear.

Except it's not really quite like this either. The explanation remains crude.

Because all the batteries mentioned so far, including A B and C, in truth are themselves fueled by still other batteries. Even the hamburger-for-lunch ideas draw power from lots of sources that collectively join forces to create my feelings about this tasty meal. During my early youth, I had experiences with hamburger that joined my psyche with emotions attached. Mostly these experiences were good ones. It's as if each time I took a bite through the bun and meat and ketchup and mustard, my mind created a small new idea about hamburgers and a miniscule battery to power it. A very small pleasant idea with a very small amount of emotion. A vericept, as I have named this phenomenon. Over the years all these small ideas and small amounts of emotion combined forces with many other interpretation-and-emotion bundles about all kinds of things – meat and bread and food in general, backyard barbecues and family get-togethers and my mother's cooking, fun outings with friends and fast food joints and pleasant meals while traveling by car. And much much much more. Together they help create my positive feelings about hamburgers.

To return to the battery example, even simple concepts like a fondness for hamburgers are powered by vast battery packs rather than one small, medium or large battery. Not every battery in the pack will be switched on every time I eat a hamburger. Some will, some won't. Some will give off more force than others for a while, then some number of the others will gain strength for a while longer. The power levels are continually changing. Emotions and the ideas they light up are activated, gain and lose force, are overpowered by different emotions and ideas. Then they are activated again.

And even this is vastly oversimplified.

Within that hamburger battery pack just described, some of the supporting batteries will be attached to many other separate battery packs, helping to power them too at times. Or drawing power from them. My love for hamburgers is connected to memories of my mother's cooking, which itself is fueled by a large battery pack of its own – and also is attached to many related battery packs including some just mentioned such as backyard barbecues and family get-togethers. The power, the emotion, flows back and forth among them.

And that battery-like flow of emotion affects my everyday life.

Let's stay with my mother's hamburgers. I liked my mom's cooking. Unfancy, tasty and wholesome meals in our home. Some of my memories about those meals involve hamburgers, many don't. Those that do will sometimes serve to strengthen my feelings about hamburgers. I may feel something like this: "I don't know why but a big hamburger sounds like good comfort food right now after a hard day." The mom's-cooking battery pack provides energy for the hamburger battery pack. I feel more like eating a burger because of my pleasant memories about eating her burgers.

On occasion it's the other way around. I may feel something such as this: "That was a great juicy fresh hamburger I devoured for lunch. Just the kind of burgers that Mom used to make for the family." The hamburger battery pack provides additional energy for the mom's-cooking battery pack.

To put it simply ...

But there's more, of course.

Poised For Poses

Of course there's more. And the more is important to understand as a foundation for grasping the intricacies of psychophysics. The astronomical number of independent ideas in our heads, each powered by its own battery that feeds other batteries and draws from other batteries too, all lighting up in sweeping psychological combinations as determined by the Fundamental Law of Mind ... These concepts are essential to my theory.

To help in this effort, think back to the complex shifting energies you read about during the fictional café scene earlier in the book – Chapter 8 with its awakening, strengthening, conflicting, dissipating identity poses motivating me as I met with my old colleague, Gary, and his friends Karen and Allison. You may even want to pause for a quick peek back at the "Rewind" sections later in that chapter, which spelled out in some detail what was happening in my head.

If so, go right ahead. I'll wait ... I'll even mark your place so it's easier to find when you come back.

***** ***** ***** ***** *****

OK, then, welcome back! To resume ... During that unfolding dinnertime scenario, my psyche automatically struggled to draw on a variety of important identity poses to satisfy the Fundamental Law of Mind as seemed best in the moment. Now Bob-the-nice guy, then Bob-the-writer, then Bob-the-artist and so on. Often many at once. It was a continual effort at psychological compromise. And as it took place, the emotions attached to these identity poses swelled, flowed and ebbed.

Each identity pose comes alive as needed to maintain my emotional equilibrium, to make my life feel more worth living, powered by huge numbers of interpretation-and-emotion bundles. Ideas and batteries in my analogy. Each identity pose in my psyche developed independently, each an attempt to make my life feel valuable to me at those moments when my mind created that rigid self-concept.

So what does any of this have to do with eating a hamburger?

Plenty.

Here's why: All those battery-powered ideas activated during my burger meal become illuminated largely to reinforce my identity poses in some way or another. Not only for that purpose but to a significant extent.

They are pose-strengtheners, my mind's automatic efforts to increase the emotional force of important identity poses to compensate for even more significant identity poses that feel threatened. Or they are pose-weakeners, my mind's automatic efforts to attack less important or less threatened identity poses in order to protect more significant identity poses that feel threatened.

It works like this. We'll stay with the very simple hamburger-at-lunch example to show how even such an apparently meaningless event connects with my feelings about me.

My decision to eat a hamburger may well be influenced by what my friend is eating – and what she might think of my choice. Is she a vegetarian who will feel revolted at my meal? Bob-the-nice-guy likely would insist I dine on something else. Am I feeling fat? If Bob-the-sexual-stud was in the room, I also might forego the burger. On the other hand if Bob-the-unpretentious-person felt highly important for some reason in the moment, he might push me toward ordering a hamburger to reinforce that identity pose. Other motivations behind my hamburger lunch could include rekindling feelings about my mother's cooking to strengthen Bob-the-good-person in some way. Etcetera, etcetera.

This is the critical point I'm laboring so hard to make here: My interpretations of experience each form moment to moment to create the weakest possible emotional resistance to the strongest possible feelings that my existence is valuable to me at this moment in this world. The Fundamental Law of Mind. My psyche is always working to answer the Fundamental Question – Is my life worth living? This continual drive shapes what I accept as the truth about everything, instant to instant. My interpretation of my experience often is distorted as a result, it is twisted irrationally to fit the psychological needs of the moment. That's why I, why each of us, so often accept nonsense as if it were reality. We see what we want to see. Hear what we want to hear. Believe what we feel we need to believe, all accomplished automatically as part of the psyche's obedience to the Fundamental Law of Mind. I absorb this information into my head in my best attempt to cope with that law right now, independent of much other information already there. Each of those new interpretations then sticks in my mind permanently because of the emotion attached to it: love, fear or anger in some form. In my battery analogy, these interpretations and emotions are the ideas and batteries.

Each interpretation-and-emotion is called a vericept and each new one connects with many existing others that the mind sees as related somehow. Basically like a battery and its idea plugging into other batteries and ideas to provide power and to draw power as needed. Together they form those battery packs, which I've named nexes as part of my theory of psychophysics. Nexes are bundles, or collections, of vericepts and they vary in size from the micronexus to the supernexus. Larger nexes have much more energy and therefore much more emotion. And much more influence on my life.

All these vericepts and nexes came into existence willy-nilly to answer the Fundamental Question in what appeared to me the best way possible at the time. Irvericepts are irrational vericepts, ravericepts are rational vericepts. Mostly vericepts are irrational, though, and many of them directly conflict with many others. Taken as a whole, they make no sense. No, they simply have gathered themselves together as if windblown debris, pushed into piles by the prevailing emotional gusts. As much as I love hamburgers, I also have vericepts and nexes from experiences when a hamburger disgusted me for some reason. My brain contains conflicting information about almost everything and almost everyone. And now all those vericepts and nexes remain stuck in my head. For good. And they're all available whenever my psyche feels the need to switch them on, to click open the flow of power from their batteries and light up their ideas as seems required moment to moment by the Fundamental Law of Mind's stringent demands.

For most people, afflicted with Identity Failure, this process involves continual attempts to strengthen or weaken a welter of their identity poses: the types of individuals they feel they need to be as represented by rigid self-images. As part of their mind's effort to protect the identity poses that appear most important right now, huge numbers of conflicting nexes frequently are activated. Bob-the-unpretentious-person badly wants a burger, Bob-the-nice-guy wants to avoid eating a burger in front of his vegetarian friend. Bob-the-rebel wants it, Bob-the-concerned-friend doesn't. And so forth. It then depends on the strength of the emotional forces generated by the nexes on both sides of the equation, the power of the battery packs switched on in this situation by the pro-burger and anti-burger identity poses. The strongest emotional force will win the psychological tussle.

The interaction of those independently created vericepts and nexes according to the Fundamental Law of Mind determines the character and quality of my life.

As I wrote in Chapter 8: *"... In Bob's mind, in any mind, energy is emotion.*

Like the pirouette ballet of stars and planets, then, like the valleyed warping of spacetime, the movements of mind obey the natural laws established within their own human universe – the universe within.

And the universe within functions with a fundamental goal. To create the weakest possible emotional resistance to the strongest possible feelings that one's existence is valuable at this moment in this world. At the deepest psychological levels, this is what is happening moment to moment, every moment of every day.

So now at the café, as during every now of his life, Bob was propelled automatically and irresistibly toward vericepts and thoughts and feelings, toward words and actions that felt best able to satisfy this constant need. And he was pushed away from those that didn't. Together this created a profound effect that shaped Bob's life at the moment, as during all moments of Bob's life – it decided what he deepwanted right then.

All these inner realities had combined themselves in a way that determined how Bob reacted ... "

What's Wanted Here

All those vericepts and nexes that strengthen and weaken in massive numbers release the emotional forces that motivate us at every level, including the deepest. The nexes with the strongest emotional forces feel most important to us. They represent the things we want in life more than anything else.

The things we deepwant.

Psychophysics holds that deepwanting is the dominant motivator in every human life.

We feel it, we think it, we do it because we want it. And we want it because it feels best able right now to satisfy the Fundamental Law of Mind. That psychological law establishes the profound human need, deepwanting tries to fill this need for us each in what seems the best available way. Deepwanting focuses our desire, aims our attention and effort, a direct immediate expression of those strongest emotional forces.

Each mind automatically makes a priority of serving those nexes that are emotionally strongest and therefore feel most important. These are our deepest values. Often the nexes are built from irrational interpretations – highly significant goals and beliefs acquired over the years without reflection. Sometimes those highly significant goals and beliefs may be rational, gained through knowledge critically examined. Either way, they exert great energy. They are huge emotional forces that push us toward action. Essentially, deepwanting makes an individual care more about this than about that. And we act in accordance with the caring, in thought and emotion and feeling and word and deed. Simply put, we deepwant what we most care about in life, the things that make our existence feel most worth living. The things that we feel best meet the demands of the Fundamental Law of Mind.

Deepwanting is covered in some detail back in Chapter 5, of course. There seems little need to repeat all that information. But to refresh the topic in the context of presenting psychophysics, let me offer this reminder taken from that section of the book:

"Deepwanting is the insistent overall craving for something that feels profoundly significant to me, my truest and deepest desire underlying all the other desires about that thing. In a meaningful sense, deepwanting is the sum of my psyche's parts at a given moment. It demands that I hold fiercely on to those values that I feel make me me – and to keep holding on no matter what. In life, there's what I claim to want and there's what I deepwant."

You'll recall some of my own dramatic experiences with deepwanting illness, financial struggles, even romantic relationships that seemed to offer escape from life's harsher realities.

It's very important to remember the enormous distinction between our superficial wanting of things and what takes place below the surface during our deepwanting. I've learned that deepwanting is mostly concealed and automatic. I believe deepwanting helps account for human behavior of every kind in ways that other psychological theories with which I'm familiar do not explain. Deepwanting is not a mere strengthening of the everyday variety of desire. It describes a complex psychological mechanism that is a potent and, to my knowledge, an unrecognized force in all our lives. It results from the interaction of those independently created vericepts and nexes according to the Fundamental Law of Mind, as described just above. The urgent demands of that psychic law mean we're always trying to answer the Fundamental Question with a yes as best we can, instant by instant: "Is my life worth living?" We deepwant whatever vericepts, feelings, thoughts and actions appear to offer the moment's best available yes to that question. Illness, financial struggles, romance, anything it may be right now.

Let me further clarify. What we genuinely deepwant, in essence deeply deepwant, are the underlying values that we cherish more than any others. Our most powerful nexes. They seem to best enable us to cope with the Fundamental Law of Mind, to answer yes to the Fundamental Question. We then end up deepwanting moment to moment whatever appears to best serve those most powerful nexes. We deepwant the small everyday things we do as a direct result of deepwanting the profound things of greatest significance to us. In our mind, the small things offer the best available compromise at this moment to live in harmony with the profound things. No matter how dissonant the actual outcome.

Among those profoundly significant things, you may have somehow learned to deepwant safety and security, which you now pursue by accumulating great wealth. It's extremely important to see yourself as (You)-the-business-tycoon to feel comfortable in a threatening world. But because of your upbringing you also may deepwant to help people, to be (You)-the-generous-person. You are aware that every human being is important, with many requiring a hand to transcend their struggles. For illustration purposes let's say those are the two strongest forces in your psyche. And that each is based almost entirely on irrational concepts automatically formed throughout your life. You have not thought through these two ideas rationally to recognize that wealth acquired ethically also can allow you to help people in meaningful ways. You could be a tycoon who's generous to others. But lacking this insight, you are likely to find yourself struggling with two values and two key identity poses that frequently conflict intensely with each other – often working at cross-purposes within you. You will view them as mutually exclusive. Either you want to make money for yourself or you want to give it away to others. And whichever desire dominates at this moment will shape the way you interpret things, feel about things, think about things and do things. At this moment. Perhaps today you closed a lucrative business deal, activating more of your tycoon nexes. Because your wealth-deepwanting is stronger, you may coldly pass the homeless person asking for money as your mind automatically labels him lazy. Your cash will be wasted on a bum. Or maybe you met with several inspiring nonprofit CEOs this morning about feeding hungry kids. If your generous-deepwanting emits more energy just now, you may feel compassion on the street and gladly hand over $10 to the homeless person. Your money might help this poor man buy a meal.

That process is unending. In an effort to meet the demands of the Fundamental Law of Mind, deepwanting drives us continually. To repeat this point for emphasis: The fundamental law establishes the profound human need, deepwanting tries to fill this need. Deepwanting focuses our desire, aims our attention and effort.

Engaging in self-harm, driving a car dangerously, spouting racist ideas, hitting someone who insults us. Writing books, playing baseball, curing cancer, climbing mountains. Falling in love, getting married, having an affair, getting divorced. Talking too much, not talking at all. Being cheap, being a spendthrift, killing for money, killing for pleasure. Leading great social movements and walking on the moon and donating to charities and negotiating peace treaties. Starting a war. Parachuting into battle. All these things and all the other things humanity does only occur because at least one person deepwants them. For that individual, they appear to offer the best available method to cope with the Fundamental Law of Mind in their present situation.

We feel it, we think it, we do it because we want it. More than anything else.

I don't know how we can understand the human mind without recognizing this hugely influential force. Deepwanting is a necessary psychological mechanism. It is created from the mind's basic components and it is caused by the need to continually maintain feelings of our life's value.

I believe it is one key to more fully mapping what Freud and others have called the unconscious. Deepwanting is the result of a comprehensible process that makes sense at many levels. We're not yanked around in life by our id or any other entity of the sort. Our mind forms interpretations by the thousands daily, which adhere to memory by virtue of the emotion they carry. These interpretations are categorized in an elaborately detailed system, referenced and cross-referenced countless times. They collect in larger bundles by subject matter, each interpretation still holding energy in the form of emotion. When these bundles are activated in the course of living our lives, the interpretations they possess and the emotion they hold are released. Typically other conflicting interpretations and emotions also are active at the same moment, competing bundles that often present the psyche with many mutually exclusive concepts simultaneously. The bundles that collectively emit the strongest force of emotion in favor of some action will win out over the weaker bundles. This action represents our deepest desires in some way. It reflects our most profound values.

It is what we deepwant right now.

In that brief explanation, the interpretations are more accurately called vericepts. And the bundles are nexes. And the entire process unfolds according to the Fundamental Law of Mind. The vericepts come into our head via that law. They collect into nexes via that law. The nexes are activated moment to moment via that law. And that law determines which nexes are strongest right now, pushing us to an action. The action, of course, can be anything we believe, think, feel, do or don't do, an action deepwanted.

I wrote earlier that our minds don't attempt to reconcile the competing bundles of interpretation-and-emotion, the endless assortment of vericepts and nexes. And this is true – each is created independently by way of meeting the immediate needs of the Fundamental Law of Mind. But deepwanting is the mechanism that attempts to manage those competing bundles, trying to juggle the conflicting nexes and their emotions as effectively as possible. It takes stock of the nexes that feel important to me at this moment in this world, then looks for the best available compromise to satisfy the Fundamental Law of Mind right now. That compromise is what I deepwant. Right now.

I may even deepwant it over a lengthy period of many right nows.

I can offer an example from my own life. I've identified at least four major forces of this type, four foundational values that have made me who I am to a significant degree. One is the desire to help people. Another is the desire to fulfill my talents and contribute to humanity as much as possible. Another is a desire to achieve true greatness in my work. And finally, there's my experiential desire, the need to live a fun and adventurous life filled with many experiences – friends and parties and sex and travel, fine food and fine cocktails and fine conversation. What many in our society might call the good life. I viewed that insistent drive as an effort to live my days to the fullest outside my work. And it's why I've savored many chances to travel in extravagant luxury as part of my writing career.

In my mind, these four needs typically were represented by a broad variety of identity poses. But at a glance, there's a problem here. It took me a long time to realize how significant that problem was. My deepwanting to help and contribute conflicted directly with the experiential deepwanting and, to some extent, even with the greatness deepwanting. The first two desires were focused outward on others, the second two were focused inward on me. On my wants, what I deserved.

Over the years, I found it possible to reconcile these four internal forces by feeling that fame could meet all these major needs. Satisfy all my deepest deepwants. I would use my fame to help and contribute, to achieve greatness ... and to have a very good time while doing it. This seemed like a workable plan, though I didn't understand it in this way. I knew mostly that I just needed to be famous to gain all I wanted in life. As a result, fame is something I deepwanted intensely. Except fame didn't come to me. Nonetheless, I held fiercely on to the need for fame as the only route through the maze of my four deepest needs. How else could I be the man I clearly was destined to become? For decades, that's how I felt. Time after time I seemed to approach fame as a writer only to find it denied me time after time. Eventually my psyche created a catalogue of grievances, a bitter list of things that had prevented me from my rightful place in this world: our society's obsession with commercial success as an indication of value (my work was not commercial); our inability to recognize genuine innovative quality (to be understood, my work often required psychological insight); the rampant me-first attitude by cultural gatekeepers who block off talented outsiders (they appeared more worried about keeping their jobs than discovering original work); literary agents and theater managers who seemed impossibly shallow (career self-preservation and ignorance were common traits); specific editors and artistic directors and educators who failed to grasp my work's merits (a raft of "we like it but ..." rejections already were yellowing in my closet's cardboard boxes). Along with many more targets of my indignant fury. At the same time, I was creating Rational Faith and the Humanity Project as expressions of my desire to help people, fulfill my talents and contribute to humanity. And so I suffered as my mounting rage bashed up against an ever-more expansive sense of my own compassion and love. My profoundly opposed deepwants had made life a daily misery. For many years, I couldn't understand why I felt so bad. Or how to change it.

It turns out that Rational Faith offered me the answer to this dilemma. I had to let go of my desire to regain the experiential side of my life, which crescendoed to its hedonistic loudest during my marriage to Jill. I also had to move beyond my self-centered desire for greatness.

These difficult attitude changes eventually aided my efforts to resolve the very deep, very powerful emotional conflict in me. Without fame. Now my focus necessarily centered on my relentless needs to help others, fulfill my talents, contribute to humanity. I learned to deepwant this way of living – above all else. The discard of my self-obsession helped reveal a genuine if challenging pathway toward a kind of psychological salvation.

That same type of soulful conflict is all too common among my fellow humans. When massive components of our personality collect around opposing fundamental life values, we are tortured. Grand psychic forces are unleashed at one another in a desperate combat. We deepwant this, we deepwant that, we deepwant the other. Perhaps we deepwant several things. But often we can't have them all and so we rage over the agonizing void. Because of near universal Identity Failure, the vast majority of us deepwant to validate, or at least protect, those identity poses we cherish most as representing our profound values. That process was dramatized in Chapter 8's café scene. For almost everybody on our planet, these inflexible self-images seem to express who we each should be. At the deepest strata of mind, they make our lives worth living.

Or so it seems anyway.

Chain Of Consciousness

The mechanisms of the automatic mind create deepwanting.

But how do these mechanisms function at the micro level, in the moment to moment formation of our interpretations of experience? These are the atomic and subatomic machinations of mind much as in physics. They are the minute processes that cause the more obvious processes.

I call these micro processes the chain of consciousness. (Though I created the phrase independently, later research showed me that the term had been coined by the English philosopher Shadworth Hodgson, if with a different meaning.)

As described in the summary above, psychophysics views consciousness as a series of reactions, each caused by the one before it. Consciousness isn't really a stream, despite the brilliant writings of

James Joyce. It is a chain. Our minds function in discrete segments.

Among all the explorations of my own psyche, the chain of consciousness in some ways has proven the hardest to crack. Despite my best efforts over much time, I can't seem to break into the direct observation of all the segments that comprise this chain. Most, as far as I can tell. But not all. And this makes me very uncomfortable. I believe one significant virtue of psychophysics is that it's based on intrasentience, the firsthand observation of my mind's workings. The theory results from years and decades of looking within, feeling my way through confusing thickets of concept and emotion, of feeling and need. With the chain of consciousness, I can't do that entirely. This portion of psychophysics has required me to make a couple of educated guesses where my mind seems impenetrable to direct observation.

I have tried repeatedly to feel my way there too as best I can – until I finally keep hitting a blank spot. It seems something important is missing. At that point, I've been forced to draw on my experience and on my instinct to explain the gap.

For that reason, I will divide my theory into three categories of confidence within this section of the book:

1. High confidence portions of the theory: things I've observed directly and believe with a significant degree of certainty.

2. Medium confidence portions of the theory: things I've observed directly but with less clarity than those high confidence observations. Likely true but possibly erroneous in some ways.

3. Lower confidence portions of the theory: things I suspect are true based on other evidence but not observed directly. Likely have some validity but could easily be erroneous in key ways.

One area of high confidence for me also makes a good starting point in exploring the complex chain of consciousness. Feelings.

You've already seen that I view feelings and emotions as different psychological elements. I think this is a significant separation in grasping the essence of consciousness. Humans have three primary emotions: love, fear and anger. In some form these emotions attach to our vericepts, allowing them to adhere permanently to the mind. The emotions permit the interpretations to form part of our memory. Emotion is the psyche's glue.

Feelings are something else.

Feelings are thoughts.

I've not expressed the idea quite this clearly before now. But I believe it's quite clearly true. Feeling is really just another method of thinking.

Many others have recognized this in some fashion for themselves. The great film director Stanley Kubrick among them in saying, "The truth of a thing is the feel of it, not the think of it." Another, predictably, was the great Ralph Waldo Emerson who wrote: "Trust the instinct to the end, though you can render no reason." That quote is framed above my desk.

What could either of those sentences mean unless feeling, or "instinct," were a form of thought? My guess is that you too already know this.

You may feel that you should buy a new pair of shoes. You may feel that you spent too much money on those shoes. You may feel you look good wearing those shoes. You may feel those shoes now require a new belt to go with them.

Everyone talks this way. We feel ideas: We shouldn't take the job offer. We should take a vacation to Bali. We shouldn't flirt with our sibling's spouse. We should visit our grandmother more often. And we often express these notions by saying we "feel" them. These aren't emotions, though each concept is attached to many powerful emotions. Instead they are beliefs – our interpretations of the world, ourselves and the interaction between the world and ourselves. We've confused feelings with emotions because feelings offer us a very different form of human thought, because feelings include emotions and because more complex feelings aren't easily put into words.

And because feelings themselves aren't all the same. This makes them hard to understand. Some feelings come over us in a great irrational wave: I'm suddenly overcome by the need to impulsively kiss the person I just met at the party. That's a feeling, but not one grounded in my deeper experience and values. It's likely to get me into trouble if I act on it. Other feelings are persistent and profound, whispering relentlessly into our ears. These are the feelings Emerson describes in his essay, Self-Reliance, "that gleam of light which flashes across (our) mind from within." They can give us insight into the grand issues of our lives. Our work, our relationships, our health, our values. They may guide us beyond smaller confusions about some task at hand or some response to a thoughtless comment or some choice from the wine menu. I relied on a feeling just moments ago when I decided to split the first sentence of this paragraph away from the paragraph above, where I'd initially written it. Why? It could work either way. But to me I was starting a new but related idea with the sentence, "And because feelings themselves aren't all the same." I also understood the new idea was likely to involve explanation that might make the preceding paragraph too long at this point in the story.

But until now I didn't think about any of this analytically. I just felt my way through it based on all my experience as a writer. I've learned feelings of this type are vital to good writing as one important step in the long and complicated process. Again to quote that same majestic essay by Emerson, "Trust thyself: every heart vibrates to that iron string."

Emotion and feeling are two different things.

As I noted in Chapter 11: "Emotion is one of our fundamental psychic materials. It is intrinsic. Feeling is that inner sense of our psychological reaction to situations. Emotion is energy in human form. Feeling is the presence of this energy combined in many ways. Every emotional experience we know as mature human beings appears to us as feeling, I suspect. Hope, bitterness, anxiety, courage, adoration, sacrifice, hate, revulsion, compassion, satisfaction, pride, embarrassment, disappointment, admiration, joy, an endless litany of our humanity. But I believe they're all powered by just the three primary emotions blended in staggering variety."

In my judgment, the individual's growing accumulation of interpretations linked with varieties of love, fear and anger over time create our feelings. We know our feelings become more nuanced, more sophisticated, more complex as we mature. Many require long years to appear because only long years of experience allow them to evolve. I sense that my feelings are a synthesis of existing interpretations that my mind deems relevant in a situation. The process requires a kind of opening up within me, a little like widening my field of vision to take in the peripheral sights as I look straight ahead. There's a relaxation required by it. I must stop analyzing, trust myself and feel for an answer without forcing in anyway. Whenever I do this, my psyche usually gives me what I need.

That understanding of feeling as thought is essential to comprehending the atomic and subatomic mechanisms of psychophysics. But in this theory, feeling is even more than just an important method of human thought.

It forms the central element of the chain of consciousness.

Now. And Then...

I have directly watched this portion of the chain of consciousness for most of my life, well before I understood much about it. I regard my conclusions about feelings with a high level of confidence.

Our feelings tend to set up whatever comes next within our psyche. And our life. That is, our prevailing set of feelings at this moment necessarily determines the next reaction in that chain. Just as with the simplified example of deepwanting above: the most active feelings at the time, need for wealth or need for generosity, decided the ultimate reaction to the homeless person.

Let me offer another hypothetical example that I think will ring true with nearly everyone.

A young man awakens in an unfamiliar hotel room far from home. It is 4 a.m. He visits the bathroom, sips some water but can't get back to sleep immediately. The man hears a peculiar but distinct noise coming from the hallway somewhere near his hotel room door. How will he react? What will he think and what will he do?

It all depends on his prevailing feelings. I'll offer just three possibilities for simplicity: A) The young man is feeling very anxious about an important business meeting tomorrow but generally feels stable about most other things right now; B) he's feeling excited to be on vacation in a new exotic place, which he'll explore with friends in the morning; C) he's feeling terrified because his trip was arranged for a life-threatening surgery by out-of-town specialists who will cut him open in a few hours. In Scenario A, he's worried but feels in control. In Scenario B, he's close to feelings of elation. In Scenario C, he's almost in a panic.

All other things being equal in these scenarios, the ambitious young man in A easily could react to the hallway noise by wondering if someone was trying to break into his hotel room. His anxiety has set him up to worry about anything else that suggests some potential problem for him. But the otherwise stable sense of well-being helps him not to greatly over-react.

The lucky man visiting an exciting destination in Scenario B more than likely will ignore the sound unless it's repeated. His good feelings make the whole world look beautiful just now. So he easily dismisses the noise as having no importance – why would anyone want to break into his room afterall?

The unhealthy gentleman in Scenario C views everything just the opposite from this. The world is a deeply threatening place. His very life will be in jeopardy only hours from now. To him, the worst thing imaginable might happen. He could die soon. So this young man over-reacts drastically. Hearing that peculiar nearby noise, he immediately assumes that someone truly is breaking into his hotel room. He feels sure of it. What happens next depends on his values and other experience. He might yell at the intruder behind the door. He might hide in the bathroom. He might even grab a knife or a gun. Under exactly the wrong set of circumstances along with continued galloping fear, the young man conceivably even could fire a bullet at the door. Such things have been known to happen, especially in a gun-mad society such as the United States.

Obviously these are simplified for-instances. Each of the young men would be aswirl with many feelings of many sorts. And each could react in a variety of other ways if we impose some of the many possible variables on their situation. But the example is valid if we assume that the general feelings described are dominant at the time of the hotel disturbance. Put yourself in the place of these youthful fellows. Might not you also react somewhat as they did given the circumstances? If we're stressed about life, we tend to worry a lot about lots of things. If we're happy about life, we tend to see everything else as pretty good – or at least no big problem. But if we're terrified for some reason, the universe appears menacing. As when a film character explores an abandoned tumbledown house at midnight, our senses magnify experience to the point of distortion. All things around are trying to get us.

This happens because the mind views as true our prevailing feelings – the interpretations and emotions most active right now. The psyche believes them. It automatically assumes the interpretations and their accompanying emotions are valid, a solid foundation on which to base the next judgment.

Of this much my confidence is high because I've experienced and observed it happening in me many hundreds of times, I would estimate. My feelings build on each other in fairly predictable ways – unless something takes place that jolts my mind into a new set of feelings. I'm crying but unexpectedly notice a Laurel and Hardy short playing on television. Which inspires a joyful response that may quickly coax me into letting go of whatever misery caused my tears. Without question human beings can jump from one set of feelings to an entirely different set of feelings if just the right stimulus activates just the right nexes. That's why we can switch mindsets so instantly. I'm crying. Now I'm laughing. To me this suggests a possible therapeutic method, a kind of psychological wormhole created by the therapist to transport a suffering soul immediately into an encouraging inner realm. Having the patient recognize that such a place still exists within them should be helpful in itself, I would think. Reassuring if nothing else. But perhaps strategies can be discovered to enable the patient to visit that better interior world more often.

In any case, our prevailing feelings provide the jumping off point in any examination of the chain of consciousness.

And this is where things get trickier.

Quancepts

Let me return to one of my new concepts and the new word to go with it.

Quancepts. For "quantum concepts."

As mentioned in Chapter 3, I minted that term to point out the invisible, fleeting and microscopic nature of this psychological mechanism. As also mentioned then, for those very reasons quancepts have proven extraordinarily hard to study.

I'd noted that I can't seem to observe quancepts directly, quite different from the vericepts that I have eventually learned to detect just after they are absorbed into my mind. And so some portions of this discussion come with high or medium degrees of confidence, others with lower confidence levels. I'll specify which are which as necessary while going along.

With high confidence I know that feelings are thoughts, as explained, and that the mind is in constant dialogue with those feelings. With high confidence I know this dialogue activates nexes that release both interpretations and emotions, creating a shift in our feelings – and that from these feelings, vericepts materialize to continue interpreting our experience in the moment. Each new interpretation then causes more feelings and an action of some kind, whether simply the formation of additional vericepts or the more apparent reactions such as thoughts, words, deeds or intentional inaction.

The missing component in this chain of consciousness is the quancept. I believe my understanding of how this psychological element works within us is reasonably accurate. But I'm willing only to award it a lower degree of confidence: The quancept is something I suspect is true based on other evidence but not observed directly. The concept likely has some validity but could easily be erroneous in key ways.

I believe quancepts are incredibly brief self-observations made with enormous frequency by the automatic mind. They instantly observe our immediate prevailing feelings along with other relevant aspects of our immediate situation. A quancept appears to pause the flow of feelings for a fractional instant to assess which among the many active feelings are most important at this moment, that is the feelings most strongly engaged and emitting the most forceful emotions. It processes the feelings, in essence awarding priority to the most immediately powerful. At that same semi-instant the mind assesses a vast amount of other information also available just then about the individual and the world. The psyche seeks out key relevant details that can be exploited to satisfy the Fundamental Law of Mind. And they can be anything at hand that seems to fill this need. Perhaps automatically scouting for some of the individual's physical or emotional weaknesses, which often can be used to relieve the pressure of psychological conflicts as we've seen. Perhaps sorting through external conditions such as our surroundings, people we're with, sensory input, the weather, the traffic conditions or just about anything else. They might even include information gleaned by the mind during an especially unpleasant summertime picnic with a dear friend named Cynthia.

As best I can determine, the psyche then selects which parts of all this other information will be most useful to meet the demands of the Fundamental Law of Mind given the immediate prevailing feelings. It finds the best fit at that moment. And somehow presents this information for consideration, everything done in a moment far less lengthy than the flash of a camera. That subliminal assessment, so remarkably minute, is the quancept.

In Chapter 3, I pointed out that the quancept's precise nature remains a mystery to me: "It could be an unknown variety of concept as the word suggests, some strange collection of observations rolled together in the mind's equivalent of a subatomic particle. Or it really may be more a filtering or sorting process of some kind. I just can't tell with any of my methods. And what happens after the quancept's appearance is only an educated guess. Educated, I emphasize, but still a guess. I suspect that quancepts trigger nexes. The mind activates nexes related to this moment's most useful information, giving these topics more psychological significance. More immediate emotional force, thereby creating a new feeling. This is the point when another vericept forms, cementing to my memory a fresh interpretation of this moment in this world."

It will be a permanent part of my mind unless I deliberately challenge the new vericept to recognize that it's irrational. And unless I deliberately challenge it, the vericept will help shape my behavior.

I'm saying, then, that even at the most basic psychological level a human psyche automatically searches for the best way to satisfy the Fundamental Law of Mind. To continuously answer the Fundamental Question as affirmatively as possible. This automatic search requires the mind to process enormous amounts of information about the individual and the outside world and their interaction almost instantly – in a fraction of a fraction of a second. The information often involves things our deliberate mind doesn't yet acknowledge. It knows the complexity of our feelings at any given moment, that weird blend of conflicting ideas and hopes, of love and fear and anger in many forms. It knows too what can best help us maintain some sense of emotional equilibrium right now, coping with our feelings to preserve a belief that our existence still is valuable. Anything the mind finds both handy and appropriate for the purpose can be exploited, unpleasant or pleasant. Just as long as the compromise seems to work. Our quancepts are aware of that slight pressure in the left ankle that can become a sharp pain if needed to satisfy repressed rage. Our quancepts are aware of the song heard two hours ago that can be recalled to uplift a sour mood. Our quancepts notice the housefly escaping through the open kitchen window, automatically offering this observation to other parts of the mind as a coping mechanism: perhaps finding the insect's freedom a source of hopefulness for our own future. Or sadness that we too can't simply fly away.

In the Chapter 3 initial discussion of quancepts, I reminded us that science has recognized the power of subliminal suggestions for many decades. And that Dr. Sarno's mindbody research supports the notion that our mind must detect many physical and emotional conditions that merely rest harmless outside our awareness until we need them. Our automatic mind knows we have a herniated disk in our back many weeks before the doctor tells us – and our psyche eventually exploits the weakness by creating chronic back pain to help us endure an unhappy marriage. I believe these observations reinforce my argument for the quancept.

As does the tiny pause in my chain of consciousness I'd noted earlier as well, something I regard with a medium level of confidence. It's like a stutter in my flow of feelings, followed by a different feeling. This sensation started my original pursuit of vericepts. As I wrote, I repeatedly experienced "some powerful sense that my mind was stopping for mini-assessments of my changing situation moment after moment. Something akin to mental snapshots, the wandering psyche halting repeatedly for photo ops." My mind was recording the instant and sending me each new image: "Here's how things are right now." My mind's reaction to that information then altered my feelings.

Even based on our common experience, quancepts seem to make sense. Everyone knows we can be feeling one thing at this moment, something entirely different in the next. Maybe there's an obvious stimulus for that shift, like my Laurel and Hardy short film. Very often, though, nothing is obvious. It just happens. I was feeling this, now I'm feeling that.

Why?

The quancept may be part of the answer.

It absorbs the grand trio in a micro-fractional moment by assessing me, the world and how I am fitting into that world based on my prevailing feelings about those things. Right now. It then reacts in a way appropriate to that assessment. And my feelings change. And the chain of consciousness, reaction after reaction, continues on according to the Fundamental Law of Mind: Individuals interpret experience to create the weakest possible emotional resistance to the strongest possible feelings that their existence is valuable to them at this moment in this world.

My mind is striving to answer yes to the Fundamental Question yet again.

Is my life worth living?

Quanceptual Questions

This conceptual overview of quancepts leaves many questions.

Among these, what happens more specifically during the chain of consciousness? How does this series of psychological reactions cause our behavior?

My explanation of the specific reactions within that chain carry overall a high confidence level. That is, I am confident that such a chain takes place, causes our behavior and is based on prevailing feelings. I am as certain about these elements of my theory as I can be given their difficult nature anyway. I'm equally confident about the existence of vericepts, those barely noticeable absorptions of information and emotion bundled as one unit, inhaled as automatically as our breath. And as just explained, I have both medium and lower confidence levels about quancepts. Medium confidence in the mental pause, the stutter – something is taking place. Lower confidence in the details about quancept function.

I would attach a medium degree of confidence to my analysis of the chain of consciousness' exact sequence: I'm quite sure that I am basically correct but could be off on some specifics. As I've said now repeatedly, this portion of psychophysics is deeply concealed and profoundly subtle. But here is my best understanding of the process.

Because the chain of consciousness is a continuing series of psychological events, one reaction after another, our starting point is arbitrary. But we can most easily break into that chain with a set of prevailing feelings. I believe this prevailing feeling typically is complex with many interpretations and emotions combining and conflicting at any moment. The mind can accommodate them all – and all at once. I'm feeling angry at Cynthia for taking me on this miserable picnic, yes, but I'm also sexually attracted to her and don't want to lose her as a friend. I want to preserve my identity pose as a nice guy and so I am suppressing a strong urge to vent my anger. I'm feeling miserably hot and tormented by flies. Etcetera and so forth. At this moment, my interpretations and emotions have been activated to create these and other feelings.

Now the quancept. I suspect that it assesses a broad range of my prevailing feelings in the instant as it searches out the most active of them, the strongest emotional force. At this particular moment, it may decide the most important feelings are my need to be seen as a nice guy along with my sexual attraction and desire to retain Cynthia's friendship. And my misery in the South Florida heat.

The quancept also takes stock of the world and my interaction with it. And it decides which aspects of these circumstances can be most useful to satisfy the Fundamental Law of Mind right now. Perhaps it focuses on the intense heat as the best way to create the weakest possible emotional resistance to the strongest possible feelings that my existence is valuable to me at this moment in this world. It recognizes the possibilities for suitable psychological compromise here. No one can be faulted fairly for feeling discomfort in extreme heat. The quancept also grasps the opportunities to express this discomfort while maintaining an amiable attitude, perhaps even to make a pretense of disregarding the heat out of loyal friendship. These are the kinds of assessments collected by that instant's quancept.

In that fraction of a fractional second, the quancept gathers together all these and likely many additional assessments of this particular instant with Cynthia at an unhappy picnic. That collection of information causes the stutter, the mind's scarcely detectable pause. The quancept sends to another part of the brain this new assessment of my strongest prevailing feelings and how to best manage them to satisfy the Fundamental Law of Mind.

I believe this quancept then activates relevant nexes about sunshine, heat, South Florida, heatstroke, dehydration and many related topics as well as about my nice-guy identity pose, my feelings for Cynthia, friendship, sexuality and a range of other issues of significance at this moment. These nexes create a new set of prevailing feelings about my intensifying discomfort in the heat: the temperature is getting hotter, I'm feeling much warmer than before, I may pass out if I don't drink more water, people die of heatstroke, I'm a nice guy to put up with this even for Cynthia, my friendship might land me in the hospital today, I'm angrier now than before but still can mask it as physical discomfort. And more.

These strong feelings generate my next vericept, which will enter my mind with the attached emotions and stay there. This will be one moment's interpretation of experience as I've lived it. To me, it will be truth. The emotions of love, fear and anger will be there in a specific combination. So will many complicated feelings, perhaps of anxiety and lust, frustration and affection, resentment and a general concern for my friends. And more. Together they automatically will create an overall judgment about this instant's reality, an irrational judgment. An irvericept. Its purpose is to help me cope with the world according to the Fundamental Law of Mind.

At this moment the vericept assembles all this interpretation and emotion to say, essentially: "I'm getting so hot I may get sick." That's the ultimate idea I inhale without knowing it, one new concept created from the materials of many previous concepts.

This vericept activates additional nexes or additional portions of active nexes, likely about my general physical health and stamina, experiences with dehydration, previous sufferings that involved over-exertion in some way and many more subjects that to my mind seem related. These could include additional nexes on sunshine, heatstroke, nice-guy identity pose, feelings for Cynthia and so on. Then in reaction to all my active nexes, my mind generates a fresh set of feelings. Basically, I'm feeling more miserable than ever.

Now I react to these new feelings, often in some more apparent way. The feelings cause a response. It might be only another vericept. But in this example, a thought, a comment, an action or a deliberate inaction is needed to deal with my situation.

And so at the picnic, my mindbody's response creates an obvious sudden sweat. My face and arms almost instantly break into big beads that drizzle down my skin like ice cream dripping from a cone.

That unmistakable distress allows me to briefly share my overheated condition with Cynthia, directing at her a passing expression of uncomfortable surprise as I wipe my brow and force a smile. I also will make comments delivered as humor but not intended for laughs. I'll guzzle some water as if I'd just emerged from a sandstorm, I'll uncomfortably moan once or twice under my breath. And I will play out an occasional brief martyr scene for her: "No, don't worry about me. I'm sure I'll be fine ... It's just so nice to see you!"

I do all this as I protect my nice guy identity pose and preserve a relationship with Cynthia.

To my psyche, it's the best available compromise at this moment to answer the Fundamental Question with a yes. I'm getting as much of what I deepwant as seems possible right now. The chain of consciousness will roll forward relentlessly within me, perhaps generating several more vericepts in the next five to ten seconds. Without my awareness, the chain's rapid series of reactions for the duration of our picnic will intensify my emotional and physical miseries repeatedly – and my resentment toward Cynthia.

This resentment will last much longer than my discomfort.

As a result of my irrational reactions to our outing, I'm likely to stay angry with her for a long time. And no matter how hard I try to disguise my feelings, they will show through. Unless I muster the gumption to discuss my feelings honestly with Cynthia, my festering anger will damage a friendship I care about greatly.

That will happen feeling by feeling, quancept by quancept, vericept by vericept. Reaction by reaction. Until Cynthia inevitably is hurt by me.

The chain of consciousness will help cause it all.

A Chained Reaction

It's one more highly significant mechanism of mind, another key to understand why we do what we do.

The chain of consciousness.

A prevailing feeling causes a quancept, which activates nexes and causes more feelings that generate a vericept, which activates more nexes that generate more feelings and, finally, a response.

The chain of consciousness can be illustrated in this way:

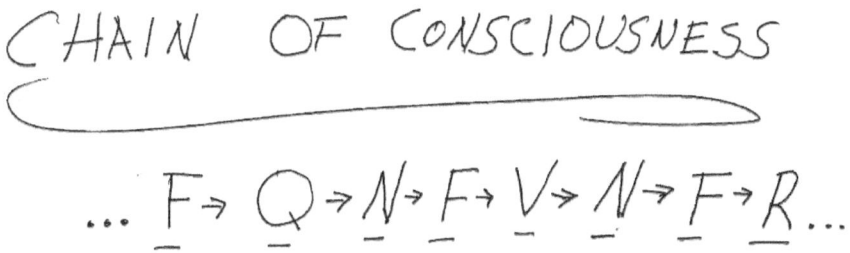

F = feeling. Q = quancept. N = nexes. V = vericept. R = response.

I see the above lengthy analysis of the chain of consciousness as a simplified but reasonably accurate explanation, noting that my use of words such as "decide" and "recognizes" in that context are more literary than literal. I'm describing a highly complex and subtle psychological mechanism as I understand it. Such words help to make my point.

My best sense is that the entire process takes one-half to three-quarters of a second as a general rule. From first prevailing feelings until final response. I base this on personal experience more than anything as well as observations of other people and a variety of tidbits about the mind I've picked up through the years from readings and documentaries. Looking recently through some scientific studies on reaction times, I discovered much disparity among them. I found research that reported college athlete reaction times of about a quarter-second or less. But studies on driver reactions turned up slower times, more in the 2-3 second range. The complexity of the task appears to be one variable in these tests. I would imagine another variable is the extent to which your mind has prepared by envisioning the response in advance. A college track runner knows precisely what the sound of the gun means. An everyday driver who must avoid a sudden obstruction is forced to make many unexpected judgments very quickly.

But there's no need to get bogged down in fractional specifics here. As I've reminded you repeatedly throughout this book, I'm well aware that I'm not inside anyone else's head. Perhaps some people have much more frequent, or less frequent, vericepts than I do. I have no way to know without conducting experiments or studies. So for purposes of rough estimates, I'll use my half-to-three-quarter-second figure to roughly calculate the number of vericepts that each day become part of an individual's understanding of life. My personal observations suggest these interpretations happen at irregular but very frequent intervals. Sometimes perhaps three vericepts in 1.5 seconds or so when I'm pressed, sometimes much slower when I'm relaxed. Maybe one vericept every three seconds or more at the unhurried end of the scale.

Let's assume, then, that on average many people absorb a new vericept into their brain at this rate: one vericept every second-and-a-half to two seconds, depending on the person. There are 86,400 seconds in a day. At the faster rate of one vericept every second-and-a-half, this would come to 57,600 new vericepts daily. At the slower rate of one vericept every two seconds, the total would be 43,200 vericepts daily.

Now I'll split the difference. For ease of calculation, I'm going to say that the average person has 50,000 new vericepts every day, year in and year out for a lifetime. This means 350,000 a week. And each month 1.4 million. In a year, we absorb 16.8 million new bundles of information and emotion. By the time we're 10-years-old, that's 168 million vericepts. By age 40, we've collected 672 million separate beliefs about ourselves, the world and our place in the world. And at 80, we have floating around our minds more than 1.3 billion vericepts.

Remember please that I'm talking here about vericepts specifically. Not total information held by the brain. As explained in Chapter 3, each vericept carries varying amounts of information along with emotion, sometimes quite a lot of information. It is a small but complex unit of overall interpretation of the moment, taken in and stored whole. A vericept crystallizes that information into a single concept about the now. How much information the brain may accumulate by other means, and how that may happen, I don't know. It does seem possible to me, though, that all of it comes in by way of the vericept, building up the mind one tiny piece at a time. Obviously, this is pure speculation.

Nor do I think it's pertinent to an understanding of psychophysics as I'm outlining the theory in this chapter. We are dealing here with psychological energy in the form of emotion attached to interpretations. The volume of those vericepts is relevant.

And if I'm even vaguely correct in my supposition about the totals, as well as the chain of consciousness as I've explained it, this means there should have been the same number of quancepts. The mind's equivalent of the subatomic particle in my analogy. The quancept offers the mind's instant analysis, the vericept makes the mind's instant decision: "I'm getting so hot I may get sick."

All these millions of vericepts have organized themselves into nexes by subject and related subject, with vast interconnections. Some nexes have great amounts of emotion – psychological energy. Some much less. Nexes store our beliefs about everything of any importance to us as human beings and the emotions attached to these beliefs. Collectively they form our feelings over the years, our thoughts that come to us as an overall sense of things we know. As mentioned, I view feelings as a synthesis of information held by our psyche, a source generally more reliable than analysis.

And more useful. And more creative.

And sometimes necessary to save our lives.

Reactions Unchained

With all this as background, I now want to put the chain of consciousness into a real world context. Just how does it help make us do what we do? Think what we think?

Another thought experiment may illustrate, followed by an example from my life. First, our imaginary scenario.

Put yourself in the place of a stock broker who works among the lovely skyline of downtown Chicago, a city I happen to love. He's left his office for the day late as usual, walking to his condominium along the same five blocks he covers at least twice daily. The man is well accustomed to city life. Its flow, its rhythms, its sensory assaults. And its dangers. He stands now with other pedestrians on a busy streetcorner waiting to cross. Though he's not thinking deliberately about his surroundings, the man is acutely aware of Chicago's chaotic traffic. As a light signals the corner safe for walkers to cross, he steps off the curb before anyone else. But a metro bus whose distracted driver spotted the traffic light too late can't brake in time to avoid the crosswalk. Luckily, the stock broker spots the barreling bus from the corner of his eye and reacts in about a half second, leaping back to the curb just before the bus would have killed him.

Now put yourself in the place of a highly respected scientist, a researcher doing groundbreaking work in some important field. Let's say he's a physicist – why not? This academic man is in Chicago for his first visit, where a major university has interviewed him for a faculty position with little teaching and much time for research – and all the funding he'd require for several years. At exactly the same time the next day, the physicist approaches exactly the same busy streetcorner as the stock broker. But there are two significant differences between the situation of the stock broker and the physicist. The physicist lives in rural Vermont, commuting to his University of Vermont job in relatively quiet Burlington. And the physicist a moment ago had received a phone call from the Chicago university: He got the job! Of course the physicist is elated after finishing the phone conversation. And completely preoccupied by the thrilling news when he stops at the streetcorner. As the light signals the all-clear for pedestrians, he also steps off the curb first. Incredibly, the same bus driver makes exactly the same mistake as yesterday, unable to brake before the crosswalk. The physicist eventually notices the approaching bus from his peripheral vision, but too late for him to react. For the briefest instant he stands frozen, gaping at the speeding bus as it careens into him. (I am, though, glad to report the physicist was made of sterner stuff than the stock broker. The physicist was not killed as the financier would have been – and after a prolonged recovery his important research continued.)

What accounts for the outcome in these two hypothetical but entirely believable incidents? Why did things turn out so differently for the two men? The chain of consciousness is one key reason. Setting aside other variables between the stock broker and the physicist, I think it's fair to focus on one aspect of their situations. Their prevailing feelings.

The stock broker's mind is more or less focused on his present circumstance. He knows the risks of city life and takes care to minimize them. When he steps off the curb, his mind is alert to unexpected danger. His experience and his emotions are properly engaged in the task at hand. At this moment, he satisfies the Fundamental Law of Mind by deepwanting to get home in one piece. His existence feels important – and in potential danger. With the first glimpse of an uncontrolled bus, his psyche processes the life-threatening problem and immediately pumps him full of powerful emotion attached to a vericept that essentially amounts to one command: "Jump back!" His value as a human being right now is connected with his safety.

It's very different for the physicist. Surely a college professor must have experienced city traffic many times. But it's not the daily norm for him these days. In Burlington, the cars are far fewer and create much less havoc. Even more importantly now, his scientific mind is almost totally absorbed in reflections about the new university appointment and what it means. He is basking in the aura of his success. The physicist's psyche isn't merely distracted by the phone call just ended – it is consumed by that most welcome news. He satisfies the Fundamental Law of Mind by dwelling on the Chicago faculty position, his life's value at this moment appearing centered around the exciting research opportunities. The physicist basically deepwants to call his wife, sell their Vermont house and begin work in Chicago. Yesterday if possible. And so his mind is not engaged by the task at hand. All those prevailing feelings will require time to shift drastically, his mind letting go of a subject that seems so immediately important to the physicist. Too much time is needed. More than a second longer than the stock broker. When the physicist finally recognizes his pressing peril, he can't react quickly enough to jump.

Just like examples I've offered in previous chapters, I ask you to inhabit these scenarios with as much imagination as possible. Feel yourself inside these two characters. I believe you'll understand my point if it's not already clear to you. No doubt we've all experienced much the same things, if in less dramatic situations. Scenario 1: We're present, we're attuned to immediate needs, our prevailing feelings allow our mind to react to something almost instantly. Scenario 2: We're distracted, we're preoccupied with something either past or future, our prevailing feelings prevent our mind from reacting quickly to something else. If any of us were that physicist, with the same background and same circumstances, we'd also fail to respond in time to avoid the bus. Our mind would have been busy telling us all that mattered in the here-and-now was our new job and the important work ahead. Like the physicist, the value of our existence just then would have been bound tightly to our newfound academic status.

The true example from my daily life illustrates some other aspects of the chain of consciousness and its role in the workings of the mind. I wrote down the details on September 26, 2017. To me, the experience of that day revealed something of the chain's influence on creativity but also on what we commonly regard as stray irrelevant, even bizarre, moments of our inner lives. Our crazy thoughts.

I've always enjoyed celebrating holidays. Almost any holiday that catches my interest, not only the standard American festive periods. Chinese New Year is among them. So is Oktoberfest. With Oktoberfest in full swing again, I had for some days in late September been listening to traditional oompah music. I even had visited a real German deli to take home bratwurst, German bologna and German potato salad. On this autumn morning, the German music was booming almost non-stop in my head, all simply imagined by me as a collection of tunes in that classic folk style. During non-working hours, this is often a constant in my life. Mental music of some kind, sometimes composed by others and remembered by me, sometimes improvised by me on the spot. I actually can listen to imagined music almost as though it was playing on my stereo, with melodies, harmonies and rhythms all sounding together somewhere between my ears. Anyone else in the room would hear only silence.

So to me in recent days, German music and the Oktoberfest celebrations had been feeling a welcome diversion, an outlet for injecting some fun back into my life. But on this morning it also happened that I was greatly out of sorts. I was not yet fully free of my years-long funk that I've described throughout the book, despite noticeable improvements by then that resulted from Rational Faith. I had not slept well, stalking around my apartment in the middle of the night. At the moment, German music or no German music, I was feeling groggy, unproductive, frustrated and angry about the direction this day was taking. A prolonged heart palpitation added to the unpleasantness.

Then an unexpected thought materialized, one word that appeared and left me in an instant: "Heiligenstadt." How strange. It's the sort of thing we usually dismiss. Silly nonsense, whatever, who cares?

But this time I didn't ignore it. I explored the meaning of that odd random thought. And fairly soon I realized what had happened.

The famous Heiligenstadt Testament was written by Beethoven in October 1802 as an expression of his agony from deafness and isolation – a desperation nearly to the point of suicide, he confesses to the document. But the great composer writes that an intense desire to fulfill his musical gifts held back his hand from self-destruction. I've always found the letter at once tragic and inspiring.

So why had it popped into my head right then?

Because my automatic mind exploited the chain of consciousness to satisfy a variety of conflicting feelings in me at that instant. Reflecting on it, I understood the single word was intended to offer some emotional equilibrium by drawing on my immediate fascination with all things German, expressing my own intense sense of desperation and frustration in a way that at the same time offered hope. With upbeat tubas tooting in my imagination, "Heiligenstadt" connected my life with the life of someone I admire enormously. I've long romanticized Beethoven in spite of myself, a sentiment that made my emotional struggles at this moment feel more heroic too. And more endurable. We were fellow sufferers striving toward fulfillment. Besides, Beethoven didn't kill himself. This encouraging awareness now eased the persistent worries about my own occasional suicidal ruminations in recent past years. My mind's selection of a German word to manage the clashing feelings also functioned as a reminder about Oktoberfest and the joys it had been serving up to me.

All of this, and likely more, was accomplished with one foreign word that disappeared from my thoughts almost before I could notice it.

I believe that the incident shows how my automatic mind seized the materials at hand to satisfy the Fundamental Law of Mind, striking what it deemed the best available compromise to minimize emotional resistance and maximize feelings that my existence was valuable to me. And that it did this through the chain of consciousness as I've described it, a quancept sending an array of information that activated relevant nexes and feelings and a vericept, ending in a sudden thought. "Heiligenstadt." My psyche grabbed disparate elements of my situation, combined them creatively in an instant and helped me struggle through another short stretch of my difficult day.

In my experience, this is how it goes no matter the particulars. Whether I'm feeling good or bad or some curious mix of both. The automatic mind is perpetually engaged on my behalf, coping with the strict demands of the Fundamental Law of Mind.

As I've noted many times in my book, this process often makes our lives at the surface level feel more painful rather than less. The mind protects our most valued identity poses by ruthlessly attacking other identity poses we hold only slightly less dear. It sabotages our attempts to achieve something we badly want in order to preserve something we deepwant even more. It makes us sick rather than admit troubling feelings.

And it often heightens our unhappiness in upsetting situations, link by link by link in the chain of consciousness.

I've observed for decades that when I'm under great stress my emotions feel as if they ratchet upwards in bursts of intensifying pain. Perhaps you've experienced the same. This too is the chain of consciousness in action. Maybe it was some moment in my youth when I felt especially jealous about a new girlfriend. The thoughts and the emotions washed into me as waves of strengthening feeling: I sensed my attraction to her and doubted her attraction to me. I remembered she cancelled our recent date. For no good reason, I decided. And now I recalled the way she talked with such admiration last week about an attractive male college classmate. I wondered what she was doing at this instant. I phoned repeatedly but she didn't answer – and so then I imagined her in bed with the classmate. Suddenly, I felt that I had to see her. Now. We had to talk so I could put a stop to all this. I wanted her very badly.

Etcetera. Etcetera. Etcetera. I had connected this new relationship to a sense of my own value in absurdly exaggerated ways. My mind concluded that I had to hold on to this girl. Now. For the moment, nothing seemed more important to my feelings about me.

The level of emotion jumped in abrupt leaps during this cascade of idiocy. Using my 1 – 1,000 scale of emotional force to measure only the jealousy, this feeling might have started at 350 or so. Bounced up to 425 as the next thought came to me. The college classmate knocked it up suddenly to 630. On it went, until peaking at something in the wild 925 range as I understood the need to put a stop to all this. Like a ratchet, it clicks forward only with no clear method to release the tension.

Wise people with hard life experience behind them sometimes learn we must "control our thoughts," as the idea usually is expressed. And it works. Taking responsibility for thoughts that pass in and out of the mind allows us to grip our psyche's steering wheel much more skillfully. But I've come to understand that when we control our thoughts, we're actually controlling our chain of consciousness. By sincerely challenging whether some strange thought is rational, we alter the chain reaction. We can force our mind to reject the latest irvericept – we now recognize it's untrue. This knowledge immediately activates different sets of nexes and shifts our prevailing feelings in many ways. We feel saner. We feel powerful. We feel more in control of our lives, which makes our existence feel more valuable to us. Now the quancepts feed off these positive prevailing feelings and the chain of psychological reactions brings us happier results.

With practice, the human mind can work for us as well as against us.

Logic Of The Mind

One psychological reality that seems to work both ways, for and against, is something I've long noticed. The mind has its own kind of logic. Concepts are necessarily connected to each other, linked so that activating one also activates others that the mind considers inextricably related. Once connected they can't be separated without deliberate rational reflection to sort them out.

The logic of the mind.

This is nothing like the rational logic of philosophy. It is part of the mind's architecture.

I stumbled across this reality as I have so many others that led me toward a deeper understanding of my mind: It caused problems in my everyday life. So I investigated why. I'd noticed that I sometimes couldn't shed notions that I viewed as unhelpful, irrational or even ridiculous. Something prevented me from accepting that these nonsensical beliefs were nonsense. I knew it but was unable to accept it emotionally, to feel the ideas were absurd and not just think that. This problem puzzled me for many years.

It turns out that the connections among our vast assortment of nexes create systems of a kind. Psychological systems that I simply call psychosystems. Again, I imagine most of us have experienced the results of psychosystems without knowing it. The mind's logic creates these systems as it builds nexes out of the continual stream of vericepts. Stronger, more important nexes are supported by weaker, less important nexes within each psychosystem. Just like the big batteries in my earlier example relied on smaller batteries for power. Basically, those bigger concepts rely on many smaller concepts to function effectively. So they become an interconnected unit as it were. A take-one-take-them-all collection.

Let me give an example pulled from my experience. During the dreadful years when my Bob-the-tortured-genius identity pose had swollen to peak emotional force, related identity poses gained strength with it. Necessarily. Bob-the-artist was one. Bob-the-writer was another, along with Bob-the-deep-thinker and Bob-the-misunderstood-loner among others. Irrational ideas also grew more powerful in tandem with Bob-the-tortured-genius. Romantic beliefs

I'd started to form in childhood about great artists, tortured geniuses throughout history, the heroic value of art, the need for people to suffer to achieve important things and on and on. All, and lots more, were connected within my mind in various ways. And when Bob-the-tortured-genius eventually came most fully into being, these many related identity poses and beliefs came fully attached to him.

Necessarily.

That is, Bob-the-tortured-genius depended on the system of related concepts I'd constructed by then. Bob-the-tortured-genius couldn't exist without Bob-the-writer. As I experienced the identity, Bob-the-tortured-genius couldn't exist without Bob-the-misunderstood-loner either and all the other distorted notions of romantic grandness and grandly romantic sufferings. That means an attempt by me to chip away at any one part of the system would threaten the entire structure. If I had seriously questioned whether Bob-the-misunderstood-loner was a healthy and sensible idea for me to believe, my mind automatically would have rejected the challenge. The mind's logic wouldn't allow it.

That's how it works. The interpretations fit together over time into one tightly constructed mental puzzle. All the pieces feel important. And the larger concept is built atop the smaller concepts.

Often this can cause trouble. I realized at some point that my Bob-the-tortured-genius identity pose was contributing to my ill health – even though I also had a Bob-the-healthy-man identity pose that had been very important to me throughout my adulthood. But Bob-the-tortured-genius carried much more emotional force at this time in my life, as I struggled with feelings of artistic rejection and a deep sense that I could no longer fit comfortably into the world as the type of creative individual I had become. Bob-the-tortured-genius drew strength, gathered emotional energy, from all those other identity poses and irrational beliefs connected to it. These made the identity a powerful presence in my psyche. Bob-the-healthy-man couldn't compete successfully because it would have created emotional resistance to Bob-the-tortured-genius, energy pushing back against energy. They were in direct conflict.

It was pure psychophysics: Bob-the-tortured-genius emitted much greater force than Bob-the-healthy-man. The stronger force prevailed, as in the physical world. This happened because Bob-the-tortured-genius felt more important to my sense of personal value. It best satisfied the Fundamental Law of Mind. Once again, the dominance of the necessary. I deepwanted Bob-the-tortured-genius, in spite of my misery.

At first glimpse, psychosystems may confuse you a bit. It may seem difficult in the beginning to comprehend their distinct qualities among other psychological mechanisms such as psychogravity and deepwanting. Even tigertails as I described them in Chapter 4: "…This is what I call a tigertail: A past experience that feels so significant to me that I refuse to let go of it emotionally, though my insistence on holding fast only damages me now. This might happen in the turbulent wake following a serious loss, disappointment, failure, illness, misery of one kind or another. Or it could focus on a previous period of life that felt glorious, heroic – like being the long-ago star of a championship college hockey team. As with so many other psychological forces, tigertails come in varying strengths. It just depends how much emotion is attached to the specific nexes activated by the tigertail. A small example from my experience would be individual rejections I've received as a writer from editors and publishers. In some cases, I viewed these for many years as personal affronts – and I remained angry about them. A major example from my life would be something I alluded to earlier: a feeling that my best creative work remains largely unknown and unappreciated. I required decades of effort, and a deeper understanding of myself as explained in this book, to overcome that bitterness and that rage. I would not let go of those feelings, adding poison to my daily existence for a long time."

So yes, tigertails as above. And deepwanting, psychogravity and psychosystems – each psychological component is different from all the others. But they are very closely related, working together to help drive our behavior as demanded by the Fundamental Law of Mind:

- Deepwanting reflects our most meaningful values, shaping our identities and actions in pursuit of those things. It tries to focus our lives on what feels most important to us, deeply deeply important. I may think I want more money but as an artist I

- deepwant to protect myself from money's corrupting influence – and so find ways to avoid added income. Deepwanting is a state of mind, what I most deeply desire.
- Psychogravity is that pull we feel toward some attitude, feeling or action resulting from a connected set of interpretations that is gaining strength right now. This results from the accumulation of new vericepts and nexes and the activation of existing vericepts and nexes in service to deepwanting. As I dwell on my need for more money, my mind forms new irrational interpretations and frees existing irrational interpretations about money's corrupting influence, supporting what I deepwant in this situation: to avoid added income. I can sense myself being pushed relentlessly toward refusing a lucrative new writing assignment for no sensible reason. But I can't seem to stop that drift. Psychogravity is a process, the strengthening push.
- Psychosystem is the mind's logic, the attachment of concept to concept because we view them as inextricably connected within our understanding of things. To believe money necessarily and always corrupts the artist I first must believe romantic concepts about the creative process and commercialism in the arts and the intellectual purity of a true artist. The notions become linked in my thinking, like a solar system of the psyche that revolves around an important idea. Psychosystem is a structure, an architecture of the mind.

As with everything else in the psychological universe, these mechanisms are governed by the Fundamental Law of Mind. They try to help us answer the Fundamental Question in the affirmative.

Because I discovered the logic of the mind from the problems it caused me, I haven't had the same need to explore positive aspects of psychosystems. Clearly the mind orders itself around subjects, with related vericepts forming nexes and related nexes linking together. Some of the interpretations in these nexes are rational, many aren't. I think the more rational nexes organize themselves into psychosystems as well, an architecture where Concept One is necessarily supported by Concept Two and Concept Three – beams of belief firmly joined. The difference may be that because One, Two and Three are rational, I can at any point examine them rationally. If I find a serious flaw in

Concept Two, true, this may require me to re-examine Concept One and perhaps Concept Three also. But I probably won't resist re-ordering the psychosystem in the same way I do when the beliefs are irrational and emotionally charged.

To question sensible ideas is easier than to challenge irrational feelings. The emotional power of my irrational psychosystems may bind them together with a much greater force than psychosystems held together with rational thought.

Coincidentally Enough

Chance joins the other forces prominent in psychophysics. It has an enormous impact on our vericepts, emotions, feelings, thoughts and actions.

Especially chance in the form of coincidence in the form of conditioning. I'll explain what I mean.

I learned about psychological conditioning during my first semester at Eastern Michigan University. My professor was a charming man named Zakhour Youssef, so naturally funny that he referred to himself as "the Bob Hope of psychology professors." Like most Psych 101 students, I was introduced to conditioning through Pavlov and his hungry dogs. The bell rings, the dogs salivate. With or without food. OK, I get the idea.

A bit later I discovered B.F. Skinner and the behaviorists. And I was intrigued. Hey, there's something to this conditioning thing, for humans as well as dogs.

Over the many years since my college days, I've continued a fascination with conditioning. I have recognized that it's a very distinct force in my everyday existence. Dr. Sarno buttressed this interest by helping me understand that my chronic back pain in part happened from conditioning. For instance, there was a period when I found that sitting seemed to make my pain much worse. Sarno's great book, Healing Back Pain, explained that this had resulted from some moment when my back began to spasm coincidentally just as I sat down. I had connected the two unrelated events, then worried about this apparent connection and soon found that sitting indeed caused more back pain. Once I saw the situation for what it was, I was able to separate those two events. And to stop feeling pain when seated.

In similar ways, I have seen conditioning at work in other areas of my health and my life. And I now regard the process as an important part of psychophysics.

As best I can determine, the strength of emotion in any situation determines the extent to which I'm conditioned, if at all. The intense pain of sitting as my back went into spasm immediately linked the two unrelated events in my mind because of my accompanying strong fear and anger. If I'd been able to brush off the coincidence as meaningless, I wouldn't have been conditioned. Continued worrying set me up to reinforce the conditioning, ensuring I would feel pain from sitting.

Or imagine an extreme incident. I'm dining in a lovely café, sipping red wine during my meal with a lifelong friend. Then, chaos. A gunman runs through the café front door and randomly opens fire, the type of terrorist incident that in my era has become increasingly common in America and Europe. My friend is hit by a stray bullet and killed. My red wine had nothing to do with the gunman, the bullet or the death. But I may very well be conditioned by the trauma, never touching an ounce of red wine again. The intensity of emotion fuses the unrelated things together in my memory.

I think this kind of irrational connection happens all the time. To me and to each of us.

It is chance as coincidence. And sometimes the coincidence adheres to the mind.

Conditioning.

I hate gin because of conditioning. I once got violently sick on it as an experimenting teenager. Only vodka martinis for me today, thank you – straight up, extra dry with olives.

I enjoy coffee because of conditioning. When I analyze this affinity, I actually like coffee's smell better than its taste much of the time. But over many years coffee became associated in my mind with fancy dinners and relaxed mornings, European cafes and overseas travel. Now I start each day with coffee. I'm drinking more coffee in mid-afternoon as I first write this chapter.

I suspect many of our tastes and preferences take shape in similar fashion. Of course these tastes and preferences influence the interpretations we absorb through vericepts, which turn into nexes that affect our emotions, feelings, thoughts and actions. Our conditioned predisposition toward or away from things usually helps form the way we continue to view them as well as the way we perceive other things that seem related somehow.

But conditioning cuts much deeper in the psyche. Conditioned responses to both praise and criticism, for instance, clearly contribute to the development of our identity poses. To make this point briefly in simplified examples: If I'm lauded as a child by my parents for honesty, my mind may begin to create Bob-the-honest-person. Indeed this is among my identity poses – in part for this reason. My gratification from their approval conditioned me to seek more of the same through continued honesty. But if my parents criticize me after I mistreat a neighborhood playmate, I could begin to doubt my value in their eyes … and my own eyes. And in response I may conceive Bob-the-good-person as an ideal I must strive toward, irrational and unattainable though it is. My pain from their disapproval conditioned me to avoid being mean. Obviously the psychological process is much more complex than outlined here, but it suggests conditioning's role. And conditioning's important effect on the chain of consciousness. That chain transforms these budding identities into fullblown identity poses.

I also see coincidence itself as a key element in my psychological life and yours. Not only through the conditioning process but simply through the randomness of simultaneous events. These too are significant to the chain of consciousness.

Think about quancepts as I described them, one central reaction within the chain. "Quancepts are incredibly brief self-observations made with enormous frequency by the automatic mind. They instantly observe our immediate prevailing feelings along with other relevant aspects of our immediate situation … (The quancept) decides which aspects of these circumstances can be most useful to satisfy the Fundamental Law of Mind right now."

This means the mind relies on the materials at hand to manage life. It automatically draws coping options from my surroundings: where I happen to be at this moment, who I happen to be with, what happens to be going on around me. Then it decides which among all that information is most relevant, most helpful, and this causes the next events in the chain of consciousness ultimately resulting in action.

In one sense that explanation is all too obvious – we react differently in different circumstances. Of course we do. Everyone knows this. I will respond to problems that cause me similar amounts of stress according to my situation. In one way during a vacation cruise. In quite another manner during an unpleasant picnic. And in another manner still during a workday at the office.

The causes for this everyday reality are less obvious.

Quancepts and coincidence are among those causes.

Some Summary

Let me now tie together the main strands of psychophysics. I have separated those threads to tell the story effectively, highlighting the key details as I understand them.

But at this juncture, a straightforward overview without the jargon may be most helpful. So I'll give it a go.

Psychophysics, streamlined and bulleted:

- The mind automatically creates an individual's basic understanding of himself, his world and his interaction with that world. (Or her world ...)
- It accomplishes this through a complex psychological chain reaction that uses experiences to form interpretations of those three major elements: himself, his world and his interaction with that world.
- Emotions automatically become linked with these interpretations in greatly varying strengths.
- These interpretations cluster around subject areas, connecting various subject areas that seem related in some way.
- Those subject areas exist within the mind in greatly varying strengths of emotion. Much more emotion is attached to some than others – and this emotion is freed to influence the mind as various subject areas are needed by the individual's

circumstances.
- Vast numbers of subject areas are active within the mind at any moment in a continual contest for supremacy. It is a psychological war of conflicting interpretation and competing emotion.
- An individual will accept the validity of interpretations held by those subject areas that emit the strongest emotions.
- Within the mind, the stronger emotional force always prevails over the weaker emotional force.

*****

- Only three primary emotions exist: love, fear, anger.
- Love is the desire to be. Fear the desire to escape. Anger the desire to eliminate.
- Feelings are different than emotions. Feelings are thoughts, a combination of interpretations and emotions.
- An individual's emotions, feelings, thoughts and actions are governed by a fundamental law.
- So is the process by which an individual forms interpretations and the subject areas they create in the mind.
- This fundamental law requires each mind to create the best available psychological pathway to feelings that an individual's life is valuable to him in the here-and-now.
- Essentially, the mind is always trying to answer yes to one question: "Is my life worth living?"
- Everything the mind does serves that purpose in some way.
- The will to live is innate.

*****

- This relentless fundamental law determines an individual's deepest values.
- At a profound psychological level, an individual wants to express those deepest values.
- An individual's desire to express those deepest values greatly influences his everyday behavior.
- This desire along with an individual's upbringing automatically help create many distinct self-concepts within his mind.

- An individual views each self-concept as important to widely varying extents.
- An individual's mind automatically protects those self-concepts that emit the strongest emotion and therefore feel most important to the value of his life.
- The mind accomplishes this by attacking less important self-concepts to preserve more important self-concepts that feel threatened.
- The mind also accomplishes this by inflating less important self-concepts to compensate for more important self-concepts that feel threatened.

*****

- Because of our upbringing, nearly every individual attempts to verify the accuracy of those self-concepts by seeking favorable opinions of other people as well as favorable events in daily life.
- This sets up a constant competition among most people for attention, appreciation and reward.
- This competition makes most individuals ill to widely varying extents.
- This illness causes most individuals to behave in ways that are destructive to themselves, other people and society as a whole.
- This illness is preventable and curable.

*****

- An individual gains feelings of the value of his life through being: the honest expression of genuine values, emotions, feelings, thoughts, needs and desires in the world.
- This is the expression of love.
- Fear and anger are emotions that oppose the expression of love.
- Anger is a reaction to fear and automatically weakens or strengthens relative to the levels of fear.
- When love is stronger than fear, an individual's innate will to live gains strength.
- This concept can be expressed as an equation: $V = L > F$. Value comes to an individual when Love is greater than Fear.
- The major concepts of psychophysics can be verified,

quantified and expressed in mathematical terms.
- Psychophysics establishes a solid rational foundation for a new philosophy based entirely on profound psychological realities.
- This new philosophy is called Rational Faith, pointing the way toward a belief system that offers greater human fulfillment as well as faith based in rational individual experience.

Confirm Or Deny

When I was a journalist, I worked often with the need to confirm information. "Can you confirm or deny" was a question I asked many sources.

As I've tried to make clear throughout this book, I take accuracy seriously. Very very seriously. There's a good reason I had to print only one minor correction in my reporting career after writing hundreds of complicated stories, including many highly detailed investigative pieces. I'm proud of that record. I always review my writing obsessively: Have I made assumptions? Have I left unfilled holes? Have I checked and re-checked the facts?

And I have taken the same kind of care with every word in this book.

No, that's not quite true. I've taken much much greater care in this book. I regard it as the culmination of my life's work: to try to comprehend myself and other human beings at the deepest levels, then use this information to decide how I and others can live healthier, more productive lives that benefit humanity. The deepest psychological realities determine the most fulfilling way of living – without sentiment, without romanticism, without misconception.

This has always been my personal humanity project.

The last thing I would want to do is put forward a mass of new complicated ideas that turn out to be misleading. As mentioned very early in this chapter, I know with certainty that the broadest concepts explained in Beyond Me are correct – and therefore in themselves build a reliable foundation for Rational Faith.

As I wrote above, "Even if psychophysics should eventually prove largely in error, I believe laying out a new system in great detail will in itself be worthwhile. Folks would know that one whole line of theoretical inquiry had been tried and failed. And even if that's so, this would not negate my philosophy of Rational Faith because the main psychological points are beyond sensible dispute. We all recognize the problems of ego within us and almost everyone else. We all know that we depend on outside validation to feel good about ourselves. We all can see how much of our existence is focused on ourselves, on 'me.' And we all accept that it's not a very healthy way to live – but we don't understand how to change it. That's what Rational Faith will try to offer. A way out of the ego-driven life. The Fundamental Law of Mind and Fundamental Question, deepwanting and vericepts and the rest, they provide a specific and powerful scientific foundation for these broader everyday observations. But even without the scientific specifics, the basic argument holds. Call it Identity Failure or call it something else. Call it a disease or call it human nature. The end conclusion is the same. Human beings continue to live self-obsessed, frightened lives that thwart the fulfillment of individuals and of society."

And as I also noted above, psychophysics can help explain why. I believe this deeply.

If I were a scientist with a well-funded academic institution's laboratory behind me, I would conduct experiments and studies in an effort to prove the main points of psychophysics. I feel certain they can be confirmed independently. But lacking those resources, I'm afraid I shall have to leave this work for others.

I hope someone will rise to my challenge. Were I doing this research, I probably would begin by looking at the Fundamental Law of Mind or perhaps deepwanting. These two concepts are key to psychophysics and should be demonstrably true. There must be ways to prove, or at minimum strongly indicate, that individuals interpret experience to create the weakest possible emotional resistance to the strongest possible feelings that their existence is valuable to them at this moment in this world. A perpetual quest to answer yes to the Fundamental Question: Is my life worth living? Similarly, deepwanting is such a powerful force in our lives that it must be subject somehow to verification. An innovative researcher should be able to establish the difference between wanting something and deepwanting something.

Or I might even begin the experiments and studies with Identity Failure, which surely can be confirmed. As explained over the expanse of many chapters, we already know it exists. What's needed is to recognize this phenomenon of mind for what it is: a disease. And then to act accordingly in the way we live our lives and raise our children.

Vericepts too could be confirmed through experiment, I believe. These just-under-the-radar interpretations shape our existence without our knowledge. Many of us wonder, "Why?" Why do we keep feeling so insecure, so anxious, so depressed, so angry? We're forever sliding back to emotional places we hope to escape. Vericepts help explain this common experience: In effect we inhale new bursts of insecurity, anxiety, depression, anger at frequent intervals. Over and over and over as our vericepts struggle to make sense of our lives. It's not our thoughts, as many people believe. The problem happens well before any conscious thought pops to mind. Irrational vericepts, or irvericepts, cause our troubles. Understanding those instant interpretations for what they are can help us each guide our chain of consciousness more effectively.

Obviously I have laid out in this book a complex theory with many components. Identity poses, pose-weakeners, pose-strengtheners. Quancepts. Feelings as thoughts. The significance of prevailing feelings within the chain of consciousness. The dominance of the necessary, with the stronger force of emotion always defeating the weaker force. Primary emotions and love as the desire to be. Among others ... To my mind, each is worthy of independent study.

As touched on before, I also believe that psychophysics is a kind of synthesis of Freudian, cognitive and behavioral theories. Not in every detail, of course, but in the overall reach of my theory, drawing together three major earlier theories that focus respectively on unconscious activity, the central role of thought and emotion, the importance of conditioning. Psychophysics offers a fourth approach that may help account for significant ideas in those previous theories.

As I've committed the central concepts of psychophysics to my computer, and ultimately to paper, I have tried to cultivate two different but compatible attitudes about my work. Confidence in the face of existing theory – I feel that I'm correct with as much certainty as I deem sensible. And humility in the face of nature – I know that no matter how accurate my theories, they are incorrect in some important ways. Or at best they are incomplete. The work of Dr. Jacob Bronowski helped lead me toward a deeper understanding of human knowledge and its limitations. No theory can ever explain nature fully and every theory eventually will be replaced with something better. Even should psychophysics prove as accurate as I believe in some or even many basic concepts, my theory can only provide a crude approximation of the human mind as it truly exists.

Like the great painter, anyone whose ideas aspire to truth creates an individual version of reality. Not reality itself.

So yes, I am well aware that psychophysics is only a rough rendering of the mind's landscape. If I've been lucky enough to stumble into some new vistas along my meandering journey there, I have tried to share them to the best of my abilities here.

Please, then, experiment with my theory. Study it. Show where I am right and where I am wrong. I welcome the testing. But please also take great care to construct experiments and studies that will accurately examine psychophysics, with the same passion for truth that I felt when exploring, forming and confirming these concepts within my own mind.

It may be that, in some cases, others will need to go where I have gone to see for themselves. To rely for verification on what I call intrasentience, the undeniable human ability to observe many of our psyche's workings from the inside. To the man or woman who advances toward that bewildering region, I advise patience and persistence as you search out the most hidden places. And courage. You will need all those qualities to find what you're looking for. Good luck to you.

Over the past four decades, I've become convinced many of the mind's most profound facets can only be seen from within, not without. If so, other explorers will have to follow the same interior pathway. Their independent observations can help provide the confirmation of psychophysics in many significant particulars. And lead toward the development of valid experiments and studies to provide further proof. These intrasentient researchers can look for deepwanting and Identity Failure, vericepts and the Fundamental Law of Mind. And then report back what they find. I believe they well may be amazed.

And one more point worth making about the accuracy of psychophysics if you still possess strong doubts about my conclusions. I am living these ideas in my own life, day to day, instant to instant. Think of what this means.

Knowing my background of careful analysis and complicated journalistic investigations, you must realize by now that I rarely believe things easily and quickly – and never if those things are important, complex or unconventional. So my ideas, especially key large concepts, have been tested and re-tested uncountable times before incorporating them into my daily existence. Before you cast much doubt on my theories, then, look at my work from this angle. Would anyone adopt these beliefs as a lifestyle without making sure they are accurate, especially someone so committed to pursuing truth all his life? Why would I put myself through such extreme painful changes if I wasn't certain they will work? The answer is that I wouldn't ... and you wouldn't either. I would never gamble with my life unless I knew that I was correct. My intellect, my integrity, my emotional and physical well-being have been at stake throughout my own personal experiments in psychology. This level of confidence by me should offer some confidence to others that I may be on to something valuable here.

In the end, you will find that I am.

It's called psychophysics.

A Way Forward

Let me make one last argument in favor of verifying key details of psychophysics. If accurate, this theory is buoyant and optimistic. It offers a very hopeful new perspective on humanity.

Naturally, I'm not saying this provides any reason to adopt the theory. I'm saying it provides more good reason to attempt proving it.

If Identity Failure can be regarded as the disease it is, we then can take steps as a species to defeat it. Instead of writing off the everyday hostility and violence, the self-obsession and fear and anger as human nature, we can begin to understand these things much more clearly. We can explore cures for adults, including Rational Faith. And we can find new strategies for raising our children, an area that greatly interests me. I hope in time to create pre-natal parenting classes that would help future mothers and fathers better grasp the dynamics and needs of their child's psyche. I know that children can be taught to be more fully human, without Identity Failure.

Psychophysics also contributes significantly to a more rational, understandable knowledge of human behavior, both large scale and small. From war and slavery to boastfulness and money worship. The parts of this theory all hang together as a whole. And they make sense – one unified, highly detailed explanation of who we really are. In a world where most of us often feel baffled about our own actions and those of others, psychophysics affords more clarity.

In addition, my theory helps account much more sensibly for some of the mysteries of love as generally understood, romantic love and other varieties too. Stripped of sentimentality, psychophysics sees our most powerful relationships in terms of ego satisfaction as a direct result of Identity Failure. This perspective can aid us in important ways as we learn to build our relationships on less shifting soils.

The theory of psychophysics is encouraging for improved physical health as well. Rooted in the great work of Dr. John Sarno and his colleagues, psychophysics lends even more weight to his pioneering efforts by constructing a new psychological framework around Sarno's ideas. I believe his concepts about the emotional source of much illness become more digestible when they rely on Identity Failure as an explanation for the repressed rage that he regards as universal in our society. This may mean that more lay people and more medical professionals in time will apply Dr. Sarno's prescription for better health.

I think psychophysics points the way toward transforming psychology from a so-called soft science to a hard science based on verifiable concepts that can be expressed through math. By viewing the mind as a natural entity that functions by the creation, clash and release of energy in the form of emotion, psychologists may be able to delve further into the psyche's processes by way of numbers and equations, as in physics.

And how optimistic to realize that everything we do as individuals is aimed at creating a sense of our life's value. That we are motivated continually by a profound need to feel our existence is worth something. Along with an innate will to live, such concepts are deeply life-affirming.

Whatever we may sense at more superficial levels, our most forceful psychological necessity is to gain feelings of individual value.

I need to feel that I matter as me. You need to feel that you matter as you.

This need is fundamentally human, something shared by all.

When Love Conquers

Then there is that psychological reality closely related to the Fundamental Law of Mind.

Love.

Not the sentimental or romantic love mentioned just above. Rather it is love as psychophysics defines it: the need to be, to exist.

Love, without the sentiment, without the romance. And a love thereby rendered much more beautiful, as I see it.

As explained in Chapter 11 this love is an innate emotion that drives us to extract our deeper and better values, freeing our truer self from within and releasing it out into society. It is a natural energy that fuels our most genuine feelings, thoughts, needs and desires. This energy is the emotion of love.

It is who we are as a species. By nature, human beings feel love.

Love strives to meet the demands of the Fundamental Law of Mind, pushing us toward stronger feelings that our existence is individually valuable at this moment in this world. When other individuals, activities, events allow us to express this outflowing energy, we love them. People love anything that helps them to be. We think we love the thing. Actually we love the opportunity to exist around that thing as we feel the need to be.

Few of us, very few, seem to free many of those genuine feelings, thoughts, needs and desires. We try but are met with resistance in the world. We find little outside validation for our better instincts. So we compromise as best we can, struggling to express some part of the deeply concealed person we know inside. We pick from a menu of pre-fab identities that we hope represent portions of our personality. But they don't. And they don't work. We search for a soulmate who will see us for who we truly are. But they can't. And so this doesn't work either.

Psychophysics leads directly to a different way of being because it explains each individual's profound need to live out those deeper and better values. And it encourages the individual to express them, trust them without external validation. To have faith in them.

The best within each person won't lead away from a good life. It directly clears the pathway toward a good life. I call this new philosophy Rational Faith, founded entirely on psychological realities.

Rational Faith calls on every individual to believe in their innate love and give voice to it among their fellows, especially in ways that help others.

Based in psychophysics, Rational Faith also demonstrates that fear cannot be allowed to overwhelm this love. Fear is an integral part of being human. Fear and its ally, anger. But sound psychological science now proves the necessity for us to learn courage and bravery. Courage as the refusal to be governed by fear – action in the face of fear. And my definition of bravery as a refusal to permit fear – an unfearing action in the face of risk.

Each man, woman and child requires such virtues to feel individually valuable.

$V = L > F$

Every individual psyche gains feelings of value when love is stronger than fear.

What if we could prove this to be a valid equation? What if science can demonstrate the central importance of faith in our better instincts as individual human beings, the psychological requirement to believe in our deeper selves despite our fears and angers? What if this principle were viewed by millions of people as scientific fact, not mere philosophical conjecture?

Wouldn't this alone bring significant improvement to the lives of individuals and the life of our society?

Wouldn't many of the concepts of psychophysics?

I believe they would.

And I hope they will.

PreScript

"The notion that science and spirituality are somehow mutually exclusive does a disservice to both."
Carl Sagan

A Deeper Vision

We each must find more of the best things we already possess.

Intelligence and wisdom. Compassion and courage. Strength and resilience and perseverance and confidence.

Love and a profound self-value, these two above all else. Everything is within us already, struggling for ways to emerge and exist among our fellow beings. We want to free our finest qualities. With them and through them we want to be.

But we are afraid.

And in this fear, our struggles of becoming often falter and fail.

We could have been, yes, and still we could. But we are not.

Still.

Not as individuals, not as tribes or groups or societies, not as a species. Instead we accept the sad void that separates the potential from the reality, the human of fulfillment from the human of stagnation. In most of us, the dynamic has withered inactive.

But this is just how things are, we say and shrug. It is human nature and the human condition, a necessary consequence of our natural self-doubt. Nothing to be done.

I disagree.

Throughout this book, I have endeavored to demonstrate that quite the opposite is true. Our relentless self-confusion is not instilled by nature. It is learned.

And like all things learned, it can be unlearned. And untaught, replaced with better methods of parenting and educating and motivating our children. People do not innately suffer psychological dependence on outside approval, outside validation. The need is acquired over time.

We believe we need appreciation, so we do.

To recognize this, though, we require a much clearer vision of who we truly are, of what most deeply makes a human human. I believe psychophysics offers this clarity.

The theory is precise, detailed to a significant degree. Without sentiment or romanticism, it helps explain both everyday experience and a broader sweep of history. Psychophysics is empirically based. This means it can be tested, it can be verified.

Psychophysics also is remarkably hopeful for the human race.

Understood fully, this theory of mind makes a powerful case that what most ails humanity is not somehow built-in to our genes. It is an illness that we have the power to cure. As individuals, as societies, as a species.

Identity Failure can be eliminated.

As a first step, we must accept that I.F. is very real. Only then can we discover its remedies.

Which leads to yet another hopeful recognition: Psychophysics itself provides a formula for one such cure.

Just as thorough knowledge of an automobile teaches us how to best exploit its distinctive features, so a more thorough grasp of our humanity points toward more skillful ways to tap into our best characteristics. That is where I have been going with all these details and discussions from the beginning. It is the entire point of this book.

Psychophysics constructs the foundation for Rational Faith.

A Prescriptive Postscript

More conventionally, I would have called this chapter a postscript. But this is far from a conventional book and I like to think I'm something other than a strictly conventional man.

And so I have used the term "PreScript" here because it gives readers both a postscript to the preceding pages and a hint of what's to come in the second of two volumes that will make up the complete Beyond Me narrative. Until that final book is finished, this brief section outlines a broad prescription of sorts, something intended to suggest the type of cure I have in mind for Identity Failure. Possibly it may even bring relief to some people before all the details become available.

I hope so.

Because to me, the science is the philosophy. And the philosophy is the cure. Once the key concepts of psychophysics are accepted, the key concepts of Rational Faith naturally follow. They are inextricably entwined. For this reason I appreciate the comment of the great physicist Max Born: "I am now convinced that theoretical physics is actual philosophy." Just as he detected in subatomic realities some new understanding of our humanity, I perceive within the physics of the mind some fresh approaches to living.

If my psyche of necessity does this, I necessarily must respond by doing that. The one determines the other.

And the absolute need for feelings that my existence is valuable to me sits at the heart of it all.

Fundamental Value

As psychophysics describes a Fundamental Law of Mind and an accompanying Fundamental Question, so Rational Faith posits a Fundamental Value. That value is based on that law.

And the Fundamental Value of Rational Faith is this: unconditional self-value. That is entirely different from self-esteem or outward confidence or arrogance in any form. Unconditional self-value is an individual's profound feeling that their existence is valuable to them at this moment in this world. It's a deep and genuine self-confidence that "I matter." Looked at another way, unconditional self-value is a person's unwavering conviction that their life is worth living as long as there is any hope of being human in some meaningful manner. There will come a moment for us all when the time to die arrives, when lack of function makes us profoundly and permanently crippled as an individual without any route to worthwhile self-expression. We must cease to exist gracefully when any genuine existence is no longer possible. But short of terminal dysfunction, we believe completely in the value of our own being.

Unconditional self-value says that an individual must recognize their unique importance in the world, the one-of-a-kind combination of characteristics that renders them an original. A human being who truly enjoys unconditional self-value believes that nature never can duplicate them. And therefore what they offer humanity is both valuable and meaningful. A human being in full must fully feel their unique value.

I believe that the more traditional values flow automatically from unconditional self-value – including those mentioned above. They are natural by-products. Intelligence and wisdom, compassion and courage. Strength and resilience and perseverance and confidence. And love. Unconditional self-value can only exist when love is much greater than fear, freeing an individual's deep desire to exist, to be.

And so Rational Faith teaches that we must encourage self-value in others as a primary goal of all our interactions. And we must nurture unconditional self-value in ourselves. It is our highest aim.

Ah, all so easily said of course. But how?

Rational Faith provides its followers with a clear and simple method to accomplish both ends. The method is simple, the underlying philosophy is not. Before presenting this method, then, I first must make an important point: All the principles described in this PreScript are necessarily broad summaries only, offered without most of the psychological underpinnings that will give them much greater heft in the second volume of this work. For that reason, certain aspects of Rational Faith may appear less grounded in psychophysics than they are. Please keep this in mind. Some doubters may dispute the major ideas of psychophysics but I don't believe any fairminded reader would consider those concepts less than thoroughly reasoned. In Volume Two, you will find the same is true of Rational Faith.

With this caveat, I do believe it's important here to give the method for encouraging self-value in others and nurturing it within ourselves. That much shouldn't wait for the next book. At the most basic level, I as a practitioner of Rational Faith adopt a single specific aim as a guide for daily life: to show individuals I feel they each are uniquely valuable as they are at this moment. Because at this moment I represent the world to them, or an important part of it at least. I have some measure of influence on how they will see themselves right now, perhaps a large influence, perhaps a small one, often something in between. Whatever secondary purposes I may have in dealing with other people, this high value must take precedence. In private, I work toward doing whatever will best help me realize this value. It's a motivation to find more of what I already possess. In public, I work to live out this value in the everyday.

The psychological reasons behind these efforts will be explained thoroughly in Volume Two. They are greatly detailed, as you might imagine. But in essence they revolve around the need to counteract not just the Identity Failure of others, but also our own. Especially our own.

To me, this is the essence of Rational Faith's significance.

As I help others in this way, I more than anything else help me. And by helping me in this way, more than anything else I help society. Let me back up a bit to clarify.

I've learned that direct assaults on my own I.F. are only partially fruitful. I can remind myself a thousand times daily about the importance of unconditional self-value without truly incorporating that value into my feelings and my life. But a committed focus on inspiring unconditional self-value in others shortcircuits my resistance to feelings of my self-value. It seems nearly impossible to view everyone else in the world as uniquely valuable individuals without finally being forced to accept that I must be uniquely valuable too. One concept is linked to the other in my mind. This is a psychosystem that works in my favor.

In that way, I acquire stronger and stronger feelings of my self-value as I do what's possible to encourage such feelings in others. Little by little by little, I edge through the back door toward my unconditional self-value. For the committed follower of Rational Faith, the determined effort to inspire self-value in others automatically instills self-value within.

And it does something else too.

It creates for that person a greater purpose, a profound reason for being.

Moving Beyond Me

The title of this book has many meanings.

The undeniable need for individuals to discover a larger purpose for their lives is among them. We each must expand our attention to include something beyond merely "me," something of depth and significance outside ourselves to believe in.

Recent research indicates strongly that people become happier through purposeful engagement. That's not new. The 19th Century English novelist Mary Shelley put it this way: "Nothing contributes so much to tranquilize the mind as a steady purpose – a point on which the soul may fix its intellectual eye."

Rational Faith offers its followers not only the specific practical focus just mentioned but also a steady overarching purpose for it all: to help humanity be fully human.

Despite its wildly ambitious, almost quixotic, sound, that purpose is attainable under the tenets of Rational Faith. The philosophy provides both a sensible explanation of the goal and methods for the individual to accomplish it in a meaningful way, everything constructed from our commitment to the Fundamental Value.

For this PreScript, I will briefly explain the approach.

We start with the observation that the world's problems are the problems of individuals magnified by the billions. We have analyzed the underlying cause of many of these individual problems, labeling it an undiscovered disease of epidemic scale: Identity Failure. Though individuals continually seek feelings of their own value according to the Fundamental Law of Mind, we know that Identity Failure robs most people of such feelings to an alarming extent. Those people react to its absence badly. And one person by one person, the world becomes a mess.

As a consequence, practitioners of Rational Faith make it their business to inspire a sense of unique value within every individual. As explained above, we want each person to feel they are special, they are important. We learn that our focus on the value of every individual works, here and now, in the real world. It strengthens self-value within other individuals. Yet more than anything else, it transforms our own humanity. It takes the target off "me," shifting my attention outward toward helping others. Which is what helps me most of all. The practitioner becomes more fully human. One by one, more and more practitioners spread the transformation.

Recalling the words of Marie Curie, "You cannot hope to build a better world without improving the individuals. To that end each of us must work for his own improvement, and at the same time share a general responsibility for all humanity, our particular duty being to aid those to whom we think we can be most useful." In light of the Fundamental Law of Mind, what could be more useful for others than to consistently reflect their unique individual value back to them, holding up a clear-polished mirror to encourage a healthier self-image? For some of those individuals, the reflection may afford only a momentary escape from an intense case of Identity Failure. For some individuals, it may connect with previous experiences that together open fresh vistas of self-value and its possibilities.

But for the Rational Faith practitioner, it is a transformation. The philosophy requires a radical shift in perspective: from seeing a world that should help meet my needs to seeing a world where I meet my needs best by helping others.

My life is no longer about me. It's about us.

And this is the true intent of Rational Faith. This is the vision. To transform each practitioner from the inside out and thereby add one being, fully healthy and fully human, to the population. That's the reason for the detailed theories of psychophysics. By understanding more accurately who we are as natural organisms, we can more rationally find how to become increasingly advanced natural organisms.

Our humanity fulfilled.

Each sincere practitioner of Rational Faith furthers this grand cause. Through science applied as philosophy, every follower becomes a genuine part of a much larger purpose: to help humanity be fully human. Their commitment to the goal automatically brings the goal that much closer, by one at least. Our sense of a personal power and responsibility combined with knowledge allow us to cause a better effect. To some extent in others, to a large extent in ourselves. We can transform our own humanity and further the humanity of others. We can create social change, individual by individual as envisioned by Rational Faith.

If we profoundly embrace our purpose under Rational Faith, if we steady our focus to deepwant a more fully human humanity, we begin to make it happen.

Fundamentally Equal

Equal value among every individual is another logical philosophical consequence of psychophysics. The science says this isn't simply a nice idea. It's essential in the world as it is now. And it's a truism in the world as it could become.

Every human being continually seeks the strongest possible feelings of his or her individual value in this world right now. It is a constant quest. Because of Identity Failure, nearly all of those individuals accomplish this in varying degrees through outside validation. Everyone seeks the approval of everyone else. That's one effect caused by I.F.

Leaving aside those rare individuals who feel a potent self-value without exterior confirmation, the rest of us are in perpetual competition with each other for the world's approval.

"I'm more important!"

"No, I'm more important!"

And as we've seen from vast experience past and present, this tussle doesn't work. In the end, everybody's unhappy.

But that competition dissolves once each individual honestly accepts the equal value of every other individual. This acceptance comes not from sentiment, not based on romantic misconceptions, but from understanding the realities of psychophysics: Feelings of your individual value are more important to you than anything, feelings of my individual value are more important to me than anything. In a world afflicted with almost universal Identity Failure, most of us will do whatever seems needed to gain those feelings from others.

This presses me to accept the obvious. Our society, our species, function more effectively if I simply acknowledge that you are more important to you and I'm more important to me by agreeing we are both equally valuable. We are different, we are unique individuals, each having precisely equivalent value to humanity. Every individual's self-obsessed perspective requires us to remove the competition from our interactions by admitting, OK sure, we all have the same value.

In a world dominated by Identity Failure, that indeed is essential.

In a world mostly liberated of I.F., no such bargain is necessary. Unconditional self-value creates an automatic recognition of equal value among all human beings. Once we know our own value isn't threatened, we're free to perceive the same intrinsic value in every person.

Either way, a deep belief in equal value among all people emerges from Rational Faith.

The psychology is the philosophy.

The philosophy is the cure.

A Case For Compassion

Rational Faith relies on compassion as a necessary lubricant.

Compassion helps us replace the anger and rage that accumulate so readily, allowing our intrinsic love to slide back within our grasp. To the practitioner of Rational Faith, this is vital.

For several reasons.

When still held under Identity Failure's sick influence, an individual is highly susceptible to rage, as explained in earlier chapters.

Anger and rage that you allow, anger and rage that you suppress, rage that you repress entirely. You still feel fiercely drawn toward outside validation from other people and from the world in general. You want to collect compliments and savor rewards, you want your sports teams to win and your traffic lights all to be green. The universe should treat you properly. But it doesn't.

Why not?

This worry creates intense fear. Perhaps there's something wrong with you. Perhaps you're not the person you feel yourself to be. Perhaps you really are crazy. And in time this fear becomes anger, rage, bitterness. At the world first, then at yourself, then at life.

Those feelings make it very difficult to believe each human being possesses equal value. Or to show individuals you feel they're uniquely, if equally, valuable at this moment. You're focused only on your own needs and your own value. Your fear and rage push away your love, which is overwhelmed by the more active and thus more powerful emotions of the moment. Dominance of the necessary. With this set of prevailing feelings, you can't transcend Identity Failure.

To accomplish that, you must first find ways to weaken your forceful fears and rages. For this, compassion is needed.

I have created my own definition of compassion as part of Rational Faith. I think it may capture the essence of compassionate feelings better than other definitions I've come across.

To the practitioner of Rational Faith, compassion is the appreciation by one individual of the difficulties of being a different individual.

This is distinct from empathy, which I regard as one individual's sense that they can share the feelings of another individual. Empathy is an overall sensation of emotional unity with someone else. You're joyful and I share your particular brand of joy. You're sad and I share your special variety of sadness. Empathy comes from sensitivity.

Compassion is something else. It is based on experience and the wisdom this experience has taught.

Most of us drift through our self-centered days observing everyone through the narrow lens of our own life. Why doesn't the homeless man just go out and get a job, as I would do in that situation? Why can't the drug addict simply summon the kind of willpower I have? Why is my spouse too thickheaded to comprehend Shakespeare when I love every line?

The answers, of course, are all the same. As the answer to such questions is always the same: Because these people aren't me. The trajectory of their experience is entirely different and entirely unique, starting at birth. Each was born in a place I wasn't, to parents I didn't have, among siblings unlike my own in at least some important ways. Each grew up among different peers, likely in a different place with different customs. And each was shaped by the unique combination of these and every other experience in their individual lives, including their genetic makeup. They had different teachers and different educations, struggled with their personal collection of limitations and embraced their personal strengths. This man suffered an undiagnosed learning disability. That woman endured an abusive father. The other man was overcome with anxiety any time he walked into a classroom – but also discovered he was a natural athlete. The woman with the abusive father carved out her escape from intimidation as a girl through ballet classes. And the man with the learning disability exulted as a youth in his instinctive gift for music.

In this way, nature sculpts every individual with chiselstrokes that can never be repeated blow for blow. Each finished artwork is one of a kind.

Compassion allows us to see this. We recognize the uniqueness of individual experience, the many formative differences among the great weight of commonality that exists from one person to the next. Experience teaches me that those creative details that made you into you are unlike my own in key particulars. And for the most part they will remain hidden from me. I accept them as real by trusting my experience.

So yes, I believe compassion is best understood as the appreciation by one individual of the difficulties of being a different individual. I must acknowledge that it's as hard for you to be you as it is for me to be me. And that our struggles are not the same.

As Buddhism and other spiritual teachings have long long understood, compassion dissolves anger. The instant I perceive that your personal battles are every bit as daunting as mine, I can't as firmly hold on to my grievances against you. And when I also must admit that your combat is waged against enemies I've not encountered, my psyche is forced to greet your behavior with broad tolerance. I cut you slack because I view us as fellow warriors.

This new compassionate attitude permits me to free much more of my intrinsic love, my desire to be. I can more easily accept the equal value of every human. I can work toward advancing the tenets of Rational Faith, viewing unconditional self-value as humanity's Fundamental Value and encouraging individuals to recognize their unique importance. I truly can strive to fulfill humanity's humanity.

Compassion for others also tends to morph into compassion for myself. To do this, I view myself with detachment as if I were another individual. Much like my focus on the special value of each person, my awareness of their unique struggles influences my understanding of me. People are hard on others because they're even harder on themselves, but the polar opposite is true too. When we cut slack for others, we soon will cut slack for our own behavior. Once again, the concepts are connected in our minds.

The compassion we feel for others and ourselves diminishes our Identity Failure. All that extra psychological slack-cutting causes less rigid identity poses among our array of self-images as well as lowered expectations for everyone else. Compassion adds value to our life by diminishing feelings of fear and its accompanying anger, at the same time increasing feelings of love: $V = L > F$. We value our existence when our love is greater than our fear.

Which means that compassion greatly aids our efforts to manage the Fundamental Law of Mind, to answer yes to the Fundamental Question.

Rational Faith practitioners quickly will discover that compassion is necessary to a healthy perspective on the everyday lives of human beings, their own lives included. Compassion washes away our dustpile of harsh judgments about humanity, exposing the clean deep reality beneath.

Beyond Romanticism

Rational Faith removes something else too. It scrapes off the age-ambered veneer of the sentimental and the romantic from human life. These notions are long since outdated and worse than useless in our societies – they are damaging. Romantic love is another force that prevents us from finding more of the best things we already possess.

Romantic love strengthens Identity Failure, our reliance on outside validation.

As explained in earlier pages, Rational Faith allows us to recognize instead a genuine intrinsic love of existence that motivates each person's heart. It is a love in direct opposition to fear, and fear's anger. It is a love that impels us to be, a love that constantly seeks an outlet in the world.

To emphasize the point from Chapter 13, " ... This love is an innate emotion that drives us to extract our deeper and better values, freeing our truer self from within and releasing it out into society. It is a natural energy that fuels our most genuine feelings, thoughts, needs and desires ... Love strives to meet the demands of the Fundamental Law of Mind, pushing us toward stronger feelings that our existence is individually valuable at this moment in this world. When other individuals, activities, events allow us to express this outflowing energy, we love them. People love anything that helps them to be. We think we love the thing. Actually we love the opportunity to exist around that thing as we feel the need to be."

The clearer understanding of this emotion's profound psychological nature leads directly to an awareness that love's primary outlet must be helping other people. Freed of the quest for outside validation from a parent or sibling, a spouse or colleague or friend, we can focus on the meaningful expression of our love in one direction only. From the inside out, absent any expectation of mutual admiration. This automatically brings us a much stronger sense of bonding with others because our love for them is no longer conditional, based on reciprocity. It is a one-way unconditional sharing, the centerpiece of shared value as a major tenet of Rational Faith. We share our finest qualities with humanity to aid individuals, especially by showing individuals we feel they're each uniquely valuable as they are right now. That overriding goal of daily life is continually available to any of us. It is an undying source of satisfaction for our innate love.

If we express love in self-centered ways, our desire to be is frustrated more often than not. When being loved is more important than loving, we bang into the usual conflicts with the immediate self-interests of others. We're back in that constant competition for recognition and reward. Not so with unconditional sharing as love's main outlet. We want to help people; people want our help. Seen in this light, stripped of sentimentality, love works. More than that, love is necessary, the force that creates feelings of our individual value.

Love makes our life worth living.

This type of love not only requires compassion. It needs courage and bravery as well, fostering these virtues as we learn to extend our caring hands to others unconditionally, without awaiting permission or expecting gratitude. That effort takes some moxie. And much intelligence and wisdom, strength and resilience and perseverance and confidence. And a profound self-value, among other virtues that flow naturally from Rational Faith. These ideas will be explored fully in Volume Two.

As will the many other benefits of Rational Faith, which include so-called "practical" things. Though what could be more practical than the strongest possible feelings our lives are worth living? But I have in mind here life's necessaries such as sincere friendships and adequate income. Oddly enough, these also may come more readily to the practitioner of Rational Faith. To follow the philosophy with commitment is to strengthen other people's feelings about us, although this is never the intent. We know, however, that most folks are drawn toward anyone who expresses genuine interest in their experiences, in their hopes and struggles. Because every Rational Faith practitioner must do this to inspire greater self-value in others, each practitioner more easily forges friendships, partnerships, collaborations that benefit all.

By overcoming our self-centered attitude, we view the world differently and the world views us differently too.

Responsibility Without Blame

Rational Faith changes the world for each of us by changing each of us who practice Rational Faith.

The world beyond us is mostly the same. Our perception of it is not.

Our world looks different not only due to our altered attitude toward others, not only from our inside-out unconditional sharing. That removed veneer of sentimentality and romanticism allows a more rational, more scientific vantage point on everything else as well.

This fresh perspective follows directly from psychophysics.

The psychological theory already has edged into philosophy by showing us that the mind's functions are entirely determined, which means all that we think, feel, say or do is caused. Nothing else could have happened. But the theory also posits that human beings have the ability to cause a better effect by embracing free will as though it applied to the future only. A firm belief in our responsibility to make changes that help others and ourselves gives us a far greater power to bring about those changes.

I call it the Free Will Paradox.

In daily living this means adopting a peculiar but effective, and highly rational, attitude: that the present and past have been caused but the future can be improved. The Free Will Paradox works because it reflects the reality of humanity's existence. What happens happens as a result of the things that happened before – our chain of consciousness is one example. It makes no sense to assign blame to ourselves or anyone else for the determined outcome. But knowledge and experience provide access to useful new information that can help shape the future. Once aware of that resource, we can assume responsibility for future change through nurturing a strong sense of our own power to influence events. Though not technically free will as described in other philosophies, the experience feels the same. We exert effort that creates something intentionally good. A belief in free will of this kind empowers the mind and increases feelings that our existence is valuable to us.

Under Rational Faith, an individual is responsible for future improvement, without blame for present or past problems. Free will is prospective, determinism is retrospective. The Free Will Paradox.

That also means an individual must accept that they're entirely without credit for past and present achievements.

Rational Faith encourages in the practitioner a neutral view of human life. We each are a unique force of nature whose behavior is determined by the creation, interaction and release of energy in the form of emotion. We are psychological organisms, essentially. And our functions are driven by the Fundamental Law of Mind. Absent the sentimental romance of commonplace conceptions, the human being is endowed with a refreshed beauty. We regard ourselves as the most inspiring expression of the natural world. The mechanisms that produce the starburst or black hole, the drifting of ocean currents and the grinding of earth's tectonic plates – each seems simple when contrasted with the wonders at work within Homo sapiens.

As Shakespeare wrote, we are the beauty of the world, the paragon of animals.

This new attitude isn't cold, isn't harsh. It is newly fulfilling as Rational Faith followers find an awe inspired by themselves and all others, akin to gazing down at the Grand Canyon or up at the Northern Lights.

Only more so, a wonderment at our individual humanity.

Picture Of Health

By revealing Identity Failure as a major source of an individual's fear and rage, psychophysics also aims the Rational Faith practitioner toward better health.

The new physics of mind theory dovetails precisely with the groundbreaking work of Dr. John Sarno into mindbody medicine, with his brilliant method for healing through a recognition that repressed rage fuels illness. As Chapter 12 described in detail, psychophysics arguably provides a more solid psychological explanation for Sarno's medical insights. Repressed rage is a significant cause of our maladies, Identity Failure is a significant cause of our repressed rage.

You'll recall that I have coined a new term for the process by which the mind's destructive emotional energy infects the body: Repressed Emotion Transfer, or RET.

The wise follower of Rational Faith will read and thoroughly comprehend Dr. Sarno's explanations about the physical responses caused by repressed rage – and study his prescription for improved health by way of this knowledge. And the same follower will look to psychophysics to better understand the underlying dynamics at play in the psyche.

She or he will regard good health as a duty of sorts, a responsibility that comes with the committed practice of Rational Faith. For we can't help others effectively when we are ill. By its nature, sickness is all about me. My pains, my sufferings, my needs. I believe that's the point of getting sick, really. Think back to the incident recounted in my notebook when I had deepwanted a cold to avoid financial and other problems in my South Florida house so long ago. In the same way, each of us deepwants our ailments in a misguided attempt to cope with life. This is no one's fault, of course. It is caused, determined like everything else. But as with almost every other area of our lives, knowledge allows us to cause a much more desirable effect on our health. And so the Rational Faith follower employs Sarno's theory and psychophysics to work toward healthfulness.

Rational Faith itself eases this effort. Our embrace of the Fundamental Value and equal value; our outward focus on showing others their unique importance; our powerful purpose and genuine compassion; our recognition of I.F. as a profound destructive influence on our lives – all of it diminishes repressed rage, which in turn brings us far fewer symptoms.

Through its insights, Rational Faith helps practitioners to live healthier, fuller lives today.

And helps others live healthier and fuller lives in years yet to come.

Rearing Ahead

The philosophy of daily living that emerges from psychophysics includes a new philosophy of childrearing.

Parenting. Grandparenting. Teaching. The behavior of siblings, of friends. All of this needs much clearheaded rethinking, according to Rational Faith.

And Rational Faith details a plan.

Obviously, psychophysics shows us plainly that we must raise our children to live without any dependence on outside validation. Kids are capable of learning that the truth already is within them – and to embrace complete faith in this wellspring of thought and feeling and action. To tap into and express their love, to understand fear and anger and accept these as frequent companions, to recognize the value of their persistent instinctive feelings, to resist simplistic identities imposed on them by others. It is possible to raise children in this way, without identity poses, without Identity Failure.

But of course the parent or other caregiver will immediately confront confusing problems. How can we convey these ideas to infants? How can we keep our kids safe from the world's many dangers without their unquestioning reliance on parental warnings? How can we guide their knowledge and their behavior without simply imposing our own experience on them? There's a reason that the old-fashioned parental response to the balky child still remains common: "Because I said so!" I heard it more than a few times myself when growing up.

But Rational Faith insists there are much better alternatives.

Some of us may know the rare adult who remembers feeling unconditional love from both their parents – and who now enjoys a sizable reserve of unconditional self-value. There have been exceptional parents for centuries before Rational Faith came along. This alone suggests that more elevated childrearing techniques are known to certain parents, methods that produce far more desirable results.

Rational Faith says such ideas as well as many new notions can be explained and widely adopted based on the observations of psychophysics. Surely there are rational conclusions about parenting that must follow if we know children's minds continually create the weakest possible emotional resistance to the strongest possible feelings that their existence is valuable to them at this moment in this world. This knowledge should tell us a lot about how to raise our kids. So should the necessity to avoid contaminating them with the world's Identity Failure. They must learn about deepwanting and the science behind human love early on, then later about the chain of consciousness and quancepts and vericepts and nexes. Simpler explanations at first that become more nuanced and complex as the child matures. The psychological origins of illness. Compassion, the Free Will Paradox, the Fundamental Value. And more. It can be taught and learned, absorbed incrementally piece by piece by kids as they grow up.

And it all can and must inform the decisions reached moment to moment by parents, by teachers, by brothers and sisters ... By anyone who presumes to influence the psyche of any child.

In Volume Two, Rational Faith will make that case forcefully and at some length.

This philosophy argues that, yes, the world's problems are the problems of individuals magnified by the billions. Improved childrearing methods broadly disseminated and generally accepted around the globe in time can rid individuals of those problems, by the billions.

A Sensible Faith

I have for some time recognized my need for faith. Our need for faith.

A very human need for faith.

As an atheist in my early adulthood, as an agnostic now, this has been a frequent source of puzzlement and discontent and sometimes misery. I need faith – but faith in what?

I realize that only faith can reassure me against the fangs of a future that awaits coiled and concealed. Faith alone can counteract the fears that accumulate in my consciousness year by year by year. Faith and nothing else but faith can tell me, "Believe. The time ahead is welcoming. You will be OK."

The future without faith is terror. It is the imagination unrestrained, bounding through fantasies of humiliating failures and insufferable losses and all the miseries of life's worst. When anything can happen, anything can happen to me. No wonder so many of us in the modern world are plagued by anxiety.

I have pondered this problem nearly all my life. I have often wished that I could believe, like the others, in a prefabricated vision of safety and salvation. In Jesus. In Abraham. In Muhammad. In Krishna. In Buddha. In the old philosophies or in the New Age.

But I couldn't. I could not intellectually accept a total faith in something so utterly outside my own experience, without any test in reality. Something that can't stand up to a vigorous critical thinking. A child's game proves a line of five people can't whisper the same simple phrase to each other accurately. How am I to believe that words uttered in passing two millennia ago were really said at all, much less correctly written down and handed from person to person in the ancient world?

How could I base my thoughts and feelings and actions on such ideas, especially when they may conflict with my own judgment about a healthy, constructive way to live my life? It made no sense to me.

But still the feeling chewed at me over and over. I need faith.

Faith in what?

I regard faith and trust as quite different, if related, psychological states. For me, trust means I possess knowledge that allows me to accept that something desired is likely to happen. It is a cerebral function: Everything I know reassures me that I can trust my wife, my friend, my doctor, my car mechanic. I can harbor doubts but still trust. If that trust is betrayed, though, I probably will never give it to that same person again, at least not to an equal degree. Faith is something else. Faith for me means to believe in something so profoundly that I dismiss doubts about it. I have examined the subject in sufficient depth that I've formed unshakable conclusions about it despite possible room for doubts.

This isn't to suggest dogma. I can't ignore incontrovertible evidence to the contrary of my faith. Science believes in testing truth and so does Rational Faith. That's what makes it rational, as you will see. But every idea, any concept or belief or experience can be doubted, often for very convincing reasons. That's the art of a fine debater, to adopt a position on either side of an argument and make it sound plausible. Rational Faith recognizes this reality of human knowledge. We can never know anything with the certainty of a god.

I have a rational faith in something only when a great weight of my direct experience has proven to me its rare value, over and over in unmistakable ways. No matter that I may see its shortcomings too. No matter any possible confusing information that could weaken my faith. Both trust and faith are grounded in my experience. But trust can vanish in an instant. Not so with faith. And so Rational Faith is a fierce emotional commitment built out of knowledge, out of experience ... and out of something else. My decision that this emotional commitment is justified permanently.

At some point that decision simply transcends the possible doubt.

Because experience proves to me the need for faith, I decide to decide that a few key beliefs are worth sticking with, period. Come what may. My faith is reserved only for something I can embrace desperately during the blackest hour of the blackest night of my life.

Through psychophysics, Rational Faith will make a persuasive case for this kind of profound intellectual and emotional commitment to a series of demonstrably rational beliefs. And for a deep trust in the knowledge that logically emerges from those core beliefs. Like some other forms of faith, Rational Faith offers practitioners a set of fundamental concepts that establish a firm foundation for daily living. As well as many other ideas that follow from these fundamental concepts. For example Christians accept Christ's divinity and resurrection as core beliefs, with baptism and sainthood among ideas that don't carry that same indisputable weight within their system. Some practicing Christians are baptized late in life if at all and others may not believe in saints.

Similarly all the beliefs of Rational Faith outlined above are highly important ideas within this philosophy, as baptism and sainthood are for Christians: the Fundamental Value, for instance, or equal value among individuals, our purpose of helping humanity to become fully human or the method for carrying out this purpose each day. But even these do not qualify as the foundational articles of Rational Faith. Instead they may be regarded among the knowledge that justifies our profound trust, key concepts streaming from our philosophy's core beliefs. In Volume Two of Beyond Me, I'll try to show that these secondary ideas are logically valid in the strict philosophical sense. If you accept the premises, you must admit the truth of the conclusion. For example: If you accept that Identity Failure as I've explained it is real, and if you accept that every human more than anything seeks feelings of their individual value, then you must accept the ideas that logically follow.

This will be among the ambitious tasks of my next book.

Humanity As A Faith

It has taken me the better part of 65 years to figure out an answer to my question. Faith in what? Over the years and the troubled decades of my life, I realized that one source of faith did make sense.

Experience.

My own genuine experience acquired by living as Bob Knotts. I could believe what I saw with my own eyes, heard with my own ears, smelled and tasted and touched. And I could believe as well in ideas that materialized from this experience – or that first came to me from others but proved themselves over time through my experience with them. I can have trust in my experience. And sometimes faith in it too.

I've not experienced natural selection directly but I trust that the theory offers our best available understanding of nature's variety, at least for now. In some ways, it jibes with my experience. Still, I do not hold a faith in natural selection. I hold no faith in any theory, not even the whole of psychophysics. As I've noted elsewhere, some details, some assumptions, some conclusions of psychophysics in the end will be shown wrong. It is the fate of all theories that aspire to truth. There's always something a bit better to account for the facts, or something more to discover. Darwin and Wallace at some point will suffer such revisions, no doubt. Perhaps after many years so even will Einstein. Believing this, I certainly can't remotely imagine that my theory will stand up to prolonged scrutiny unblemished.

I trust that my conclusions in psychophysics are accurate. Of course. But no, that's far from faith as I mean the term.

I do feel a faith in some components of psychophysics that seem to float like a layer of cream atop the milk of my psychological theory. These elements bubble up from several major concepts of psychophysics, which taken together help form central beliefs that I regard as unassailable. On these and other points, my convictions are more than merely firm. This is the intersection, the turning point, where psychophysics becomes Rational Faith.

Primary among these: Faith in humanity.

Humanity overall, as a species, and more specifically a faith in the ascent of humanity to paraphrase Dr. Jacob Bronowski. I have a deep, abiding and unshakable faith that humanity has advanced, continues to advance and will continue to advance, a physical and psychological, cultural and moral evolution. This faith is based on everything I've experienced throughout my life, including much knowledge acquired from outside writings and documentaries, from art and science and a broad swath of human achievement as well as the credible personal experiences of other people. History backs up this claim in undeniable ways. So do many facts and statistics.

So does psychophysics.

The psychological theory speaks to an innate love that drives every human being out into the world to gain feelings of their individual value. And the need to connect with other people to gather these feelings, best accomplished by helping them in meaningful ways. It identifies an underlying cause for much unnecessary human suffering, an illness that can be cured by knowledge. Psychophysics demonstrates that Homo sapiens fundamentally is an outward-focused, positive and dynamic species. We are not hostile and violent by nature. We are not born afraid of life. We are creatures fueled by a love that is inherent and hopeful.

I believe my faith in humanity is beyond sensible dispute even should any of those important details somehow prove mistaken. No thinking person can reasonably question our persistence and resilience, our adaptability and our innovation, our personal quest to establish feelings that our lives matter. Who can intelligently argue against the notion that most people clearly care about others despite superficial evidence to the contrary?

Even with our destructive self-obsessed pursuit of validation still lingering, there's much cause for hope. In spite of our egos, we mostly cooperate, collaborate, create the things needed for us to march forward century after century. We live together, work together, play together. We govern alongside our fellows, from the United Nations to the City Hall to the local society of stamp collectors. Bronowski noted that humanity's progress is uneven at best, halting and uncertain and continually threatened. But in the end, we advance. We collectively take the next step ahead. Psychophysics and the experiences that led me to its theories have greatly strengthened my longstanding belief in Dr. Bronowski's Ascent of Man. Faith in the future of humanity is among the core beliefs of Rational Faith. This brief PreScript can't explain why with any justice. For that, I will need the time and breadth of Volume Two.

My Humanity As A Faith

If history, facts and statistics, human achievement and my own experiences created my faith in humanity as a species, they also have established my bedrock-solid faith in our individual humanity. My individual humanity. And yours.

Again, psychophysics is an important part of this faith. And again most of the explanations must wait for the following book. But for now, let me summarize a few of the major points. These articles of Rational Faith to me appear beyond any reasonable attacks by even the most skeptical mind. I can't imagine incontrovertible proof to the contrary about any of them – and only such evidence could undermine my faith. As with a faith in humanity, the below concepts rationally justify not merely a deep trust but faith in the true sense.

- Rational Faith states that our experience inarguably shows that the human individual possesses a unique ability to learn and change and to create solutions to problems if solutions are possible. Each person is heir to those same qualities that define our species: persistence and resilience, adaptability and innovation, a quest for feelings of value, concern for the welfare of other people. These and other shared characteristics are always available if we learn to exploit them effectively. They will never leave any of us unless we simply forget they're forever within our grasp. We need only deepwant to use them. For this reason, it is entirely rational to believe unquestioningly in our individual capacity for learning, changing, improving whatever needs improving. I am the inheritor of our humanity. So are you. In that, we can have a rational faith.
- Rational Faith states that one of our universal characteristics should be singled out for great attention ... and great faith: The individual human being often best approaches truth through feeling it, not thinking it. This is one of the profound lessons found in the writings of Ralph Waldo Emerson, who said: "Trust the instinct to the end, though you can render no reason." Psychophysics maintains that this instinct actually is a form of thought that comes to us as feeling, as discussed at some length in the previous chapter. And that it is

overwhelmingly the most reliable and creative form of thought. It is a synthesis of our relevant experience that can be accessed at any moment – if we learn to free it and have faith in it. I call it Experience Synthesis or E.S. Of course humans also can accurately analyze things, as I hope this book demonstrates. The ability to learn and teach by parsing out particular detailed truths is something I've named Experience Analysis or E.A. I need both synthesis and analysis to function effectively. Every human being does. But this new philosophy spotlights our inborn ability to form the most accurate judgments in partnership with our emotions rather than through detached intellect alone. That very human gift should be elevated to a rational article of faith.

- Rational Faith demonstrates why we do not need outside validation to enjoy our fullest feelings of individual value. And why faith in our own deepest judgments about our value is justified. Psychophysics explains the damage done to our lives and the lives of others through the irrational search for external confirmation of our worth. The disease called Identity Failure. The science further shows the irrational psychological process that creates this illness – and the individual human capacity for dependable judgment just described above. Rational Faith takes all this as a starting point to teach us that no one ever can understand anyone else fully, that by nature we each dwell alone within our individual psychological experience and therefore that only our genuine assessments of ourselves are meaningful. Nobody can know me better than I know myself. It's impossible. And so at all times I must cling to a rational faith in the human being I truly understand myself to be. Put more simply, self-confidence is necessary to function fully, self-confidence is rationally justified, self-confidence must be maintained through faith.

- Rational Faith states that this self-confidence cannot be fully exploited by an individual who cares about their own needs-and-wants above all else. The human innate love of existence that is explained by psychophysics requires reliable outlet. Rational Faith contends the only reliable outlet sufficiently significant to satisfy this continually surging love is helping other human beings. Obviously most people trundle through their lives with a largely self-centered approach. They get by – survival isn't the issue. But they cannot be fulfilled, not deeply. An absolute necessity for fulfillment through helping others is imposed by the realities of the psyche as well as the realities of living with that psyche in our society. The Fundamental Law of Mind and Fundamental Question, love as the desire to be and other elements of human psychology otherwise collide with a complex, diverse and competitive world, especially when nearly every person suffers a raging compulsion for outside validation. Society renders individual fulfillment impossible through a me-first attitude: Confidence-sapping conflict is constant. Without attention focused first and foremost on helping others in some meaningful way, no one can be fully human – fulfilled psychologically and physically. It is another article of our Rational Faith.

- Rational Faith asks something else of us as we work to aid others: to believe that our sincere efforts to help actually do help, regardless of the immediate reaction. And this too becomes an article of our faith. Volume Two of Beyond Me will draw on psychophysics to demonstrate why so many of us struggle to acknowledge our strong influence on fellow human beings. This seems a strange thing. We vibrate with a massive power to uplift or discourage other people. In our wake we each trail an unseen residue of smiles and tears. But most of us refuse to believe it. Yet our own private experience proves that it's true – we know firsthand the dramatic effects that the people we encounter daily have on our thoughts and feelings and actions, effects rarely obvious to those who cause them. In no small part this reflects our continuing affliction with Identity Failure. A slight gesture, a passing expression, a few words by someone can send us reeling backwards. Or propel us energetically and enthusiastically forward. It needn't be so, and shouldn't be. The practice of Rational Faith can diminish or eliminate such reactions. But for the time being at least, almost every person we meet will look toward us for validation of their existence. It's a potent responsibility and a grand opportunity. This philosophy will explain why only infrequently will we see how our behavior helps others ... and why we must hold a forceful faith that it does.

Experience As God

For me, for the future practitioners of Rational Faith, experience is god.

Experience is a rational, personally observed god that is within us always. As will be explained in the next book, this belief does not negate the possible existence of a more conventional God or gods of some kind. Or of some natural phenomena that may influence our lives without our awareness. Rational Faith simply says, "There is no way to know. It's not rational to accept the existence of such forces, nor is it rational to deny their existence. It is rational to say that this is knowledge beyond the human mind."

Not too many years after I attended a lecture and press conference by the Dalai Lama in 2010, I was interested to read a comment by him about morality: "We need an approach to ethics which makes no recourse to religion and can be equally acceptable to those with faith and those without."

I completely agree, naturally. And I offer Rational Faith as one such approach to ethics. This philosophy does not argue against faith in a religion or in a God. It is grounded in a scientific and logical understanding of our deeper humanity, which surely is compatible with any religion worthy of the name. Rational Faith tells people, "There is a sound basis for genuine faith that's rooted in our direct experience. This experience can guide our behavior and our beliefs, helping to fulfill our humanity as individuals and as a species. If your experience also necessitates a faith in something beyond the strictly rational, you are welcome to those other beliefs, my friend."

It's critically important to understand that Rational Faith is just that: faith in its fullest sense, but only applied to personal experience. Only to what can be rationally accepted as valid. There is utterly nothing in Rational Faith that smacks of the New Age approach – including this philosophy's emphasis on Experience Synthesis, which we can more informally call "instinct" after Emerson. Such instinct is provably real, testable by any individual with the desire to learn about it. More than anything else in my life, this instinct to me is the silent voice of god. It pulls together all I know and offers me highly reliable guidance that I must learn to follow by way of feeling, not thinking. Such feeling is a universal human trait and a vitally significant one. It is experience, distilled. That's why it is one core concept of Rational Faith.

Its existence is rational. Its past reliability is rational. The proof comes from our experience.

But its future reliability is faith – rational faith.

In that way, the philosophy really is a logical extension of something most of us do routinely. We weigh the odds with a clear understanding that the outcome isn't absolutely guaranteed. Rather, our oddsmaking offers us the best possible method to decide what to do about the future.

Each movement during our daily life is a gamble. Getting in the shower, driving a car, walking through a parking lot, eating in a restaurant: Every year some folks slip and die in the shower. Every day hundreds are killed in auto crashes. Pedestrians are sometimes mowed down by inattentive drivers in parking lots, diners often are sickened or worse by poorly cooked restaurant meals. We all know these facts. But overwhelmingly our odds of safety are very good. We make calculated judgments as we go about everyday life, lots of potentially significant decisions without thinking about them. And when we do, we're just playing the odds. We trust that our experience is the most reliable guide to the future – and we shower, drive, walk, shop. Most of the time, it all turns out fine. The system works.

Rational Faith urges us to extend much farther this wise approach to living. It draws on psychophysics to identify fundamental realities of the human psyche, then constructs from them several rational articles of faith along with related ideas that all are logically defensible. In the end, though, the process is the same as with our little acts of daily trust. We depend on what we've experienced in the past to form sensible judgments about the present and the future. The main differences are in the significance of the judgments made by Rational Faith, centering on the deep substance of our humanity – and in the degree of trust given those judgments, with core beliefs accorded a faith unassailable by any but the most indisputable contradictory evidence.

In Rational Faith, experience becomes more than common sense.

Experience is god.

A Faith Beyond Me

Oh yes, our need for a faith of some kind is very human. Especially for a faith in ourselves.

As with so many other aspects of the mind, William James understood this: "There is but one cause of human failure. And that is man's lack of faith in his true Self." If not the sole cause, perhaps, feelings about ourselves greatly determine our individual contributions to humanity.

Sadly, we vastly underestimate our potential in most ways.

To get the best from ourselves, to fulfill our talents and our best traits, faith can lift us beyond those self-doubts. Think about it. You may feel insignificant but your complete faith in Jesus or Muhammad or the Norse Gods or Pink-nosed Fairies automatically forges a new relationship between you and the world – you love Pink-nosed Fairies and, more importantly, they love you. This makes you personally valuable. Less insignificant anyway. And so also less vulnerable to self-doubt, less afraid of the world. More prepared to do something that may be useful to other people.

At bottom all faith is a system that makes possible a consistent belief in ourselves, a faith in the true self of William James. It is an antidote to Identity Failure, a buffer against future uncertainties. That's a big part of faith's function for human beings. Rational Faith accomplishes this without the supernatural, the superstitious, the sentimental, the romanticized.

Rational Faith also pushes us beyond another psychological barrier that hinders individual fulfillment. A fear that we don't deserve good things. This grating sense of unworthiness is far more common than widely recognized, so embedded in our chain of consciousness that most of us rarely notice. But it's there within nearly everyone – and it severely interferes with a fuller expression of our innate love. We hold back our boldest thoughts, our strongest feelings. We're quickly and easily discomforted by our insights that others don't see, by our achievements that others can't match, by our vitality that others won't summon. We fail to commit fully to our inspirations and so never fully create anything inspiring. Everything is half done. Such feelings carry us toward a daily mediocrity: Who am I to deserve more friends, better health, meaningful accomplishment? What allows me to believe that my everyday life should transcend the ordinary all around me? What qualities, what experiences do I possess that actually would benefit anyone?

These worries congeal from the drippings of Identity Failure.

Our identity poses lock us into self-images that feel most comfortable at this moment in this world. They are psychological compromises negotiated among our love, our fear and our anger. We believe these identity poses represent who we are – or should be. This means most attempts to think, feel or act outside those rigid self-concepts will frighten us. The effort to be more seems dangerous somehow. We feel as if we're stepping beyond our life's proper limits. And so we pull back, abandoning our progress while doing whatever we can to maintain our existing identities.

But a sincere faith in humanity and in our own humanity, a genuine belief that we can help our species to become fully human by specific everyday actions – these raise our lives to heights unexplored. They force me to confront my fears of unworthiness and to overcome them for a loftier purpose than me alone. Afflicted with Identity Failure, I will never tap into the finest veins of my humanity. By my self-obsession, the barriers inevitably appear.

Rational Faith carries me beyond me. And in looking constantly beyond me, I find me.

I transcend Identity Failure. I am liberated by working to liberate others.

This new science-based philosophy says most of us don't know our true self-interest as we endlessly pursue immediate gain in this or that self-centered way. We want what we want. Right now. It will make us feel better. Rational Faith presents an alternative that lifts our chin and shifts our gaze upward toward a more rational vision of self-interest. A genuine self-interest showing us that individuals get most when we have the courage to give most, fully and unconditionally, to inspire our fellow beings. By deepwanting to help them, by caring more than anything about living our purpose, we transform ourselves into full human beings.

And humanity adds one more name to the expanding list of the fulfilled, the productive, the helpful.

Rationally Irrational

In my time, a brilliant website was launched successfully by the philosopher Alain de Botton, whose work aims to bring the great concepts of philosophy to the everyday person. Called the Book of Life, the online site published an unsigned essay in March 2015 that included these lines: "Today – unlike any other period in history – the major impediments (to economic progress, better politics and more flourishing lives) are all psychological. It's mainly the flaws in our emotional capacities that ruin existence. But we've not yet really concentrated on addressing how to make ourselves more mature. It's been left to the hazards of individual experience."

As you'd expect, I entirely agree.

All my life I've believed fiercely that there must be a better way to live than I was living. Sometimes I could feel myself transported to a place that I seemed only to visit as a tourist, walking through avenues lined with a robust self-confidence and a vigorous health, populated not by threatening strangers but by others much like me. Everything around me appeared beautiful because I'd connected with more of the beauty hidden inside me. This place seemed a paradise of sorts. An attainable human form of paradiso – and a land where I wanted not to sightsee but to dwell.

Why was my time there always so limited? Why did I descend after each trip so quickly back to the gray struggles with myself, to those searing self-confusions that pulled me to the lower portions of my humanity? I had seen with my own eyes somewhere much more elevated. But I could never figure out how to stay there.

This quest was the genesis of Beyond Me, first broadly envisioned now well over four decades ago. The book is drawn almost completely from my personal experience – composed without any outlines, written with virtually no notes other than some number of sketchy observations jotted down randomly here and there over those decades. The pages of Beyond Me were pulled from my head as I sat alone at my desk. For the most part I was writing what I had lived and already integrated into a complex theory, or reflecting on those experiences to more fully understand and explain them. That's the irony I've seen from the beginning of this project. Beyond Me is all me in one sense, all Bob Knotts. But I would never have assembled my life into a book of this kind merely to leave behind some record of my unique brand of Bobness. I have suffered mightily to write it, to piece together the pieces, to relive and reveal so much of my intimate interior life. I could not add up all the tears or estimate the dark unslept hours. I've gained 15 unhelpful pounds, endured frequent episodes of daylong heart palpitations for years along with a constant fusillade of other miserable symptoms that included an almost continuous ear ringing and bouts of body tremors. And no one ever will truly know of the protracted pitched encounters among my opposing emotions as I struggled to replace the romantic with the rational, to exchange my softheaded sentiments for a rational love as my way of being. To understand and live Rational Faith. So much fear, so much disappointment, so much rage marched beside me throughout the first draft of my book.

Every bit of it contending with that even stronger love. My intrinsic human need to be, to exist, to express, to help. The conflicts seemed unending. But if I suffered during the writing of Beyond Me, I would have endured far greater pain from keeping it inside unwritten.

To my core, I believe in the experiences, theories and ideas here offered. And to my core, I believe they can help other people to better understand themselves, to become more as a result and to aid the process of humanity's fulfillment thereby. This is the reason I wrote Beyond Me.

I hope and I pray for the opportunity to expand on this PreScript by completing Volume Two of my work. There is so much more to say, the full development of a faith that is grounded in rational personal experience. Look toward the re-definition of love in psychophysics as a good example of how the psychological observations profoundly mold the philosophical conclusions of Rational Faith. Understanding the true nature of love at a deep level reveals to me at a deep level how I should love – not outside-in by seeking a soulmate to save me but inside-out by seeking people I can help in daily life. The experience determines the science, the science determines the philosophy, the philosophy determines how to be most fully human.

It's important to note again that this doesn't suggest some cold cerebral approach to life. Precisely the opposite. As I've pointed out repeatedly about myself and everybody else, we are basically an irrational species. We operate on emotion more than anything. And so Rational Faith more than anything is about emotion. We can't live more sanely, more wisely, more logically without accounting for our emotional nature, beginning with the Fundamental Law of Mind. A grasp of our basic psychological mechanism is needed to inform better ways of being human.

And how can humanity move forward morally without recognizing Identity Failure? Or identity poses? How can we manage our thoughts and feelings and emotions without knowing about vericepts and nexes and the dominance of the necessary? How can we more skillfully guide our destinies without understanding the Free Will Paradox or the central significance of deepwanting?

To me, these are the necessary starting points. They are the pathstones laid down for a future journey by the species Homo sapiens, leading not to a new place without but a new place within. There is no perfection in this paradiso of the soul. It will always be a region of continual conflict among competing emotions, competing needs, competing desires. In a world populated by competing people. This is the human condition. But a deeper knowledge of who we are can help individuals better cope with our many conflicts along the uneven avenues ahead. One by one, our humanity fulfilled.

To do this, we each must find more of the best things we already possess.

Intelligence and wisdom. Compassion and courage. Strength and resilience and perseverance and confidence.

Love and a profound self-value, these two above all else. Everything is within us already, struggling for ways to emerge and exist among our fellow beings.

Built atop the bedrock foundation of psychophysics, Rational Faith can help to set it all free.

Glossary

Automatic mind: Psychological activities that take place without deliberation and typically without any awareness by the individual. Conventionally called "the unconscious mind."

Chain of consciousness: In psychophysics, each psychological event is preceded by a series of reactions, one causing the next akin to an atomic chain reaction. The theory explains that the mind works not as a continuous flow but rather in a continuing series of separate segments.

Compassion: As defined by Rational Faith, the appreciation by one individual of the difficulties of being a different individual.

Deepwanting: A state of mind that automatically reinforces an individual's most emotionally forceful values, an insistent overall craving for something that feels profoundly significant. Normally concealed from awareness, deepwanting is an individual's truest and deepest desire beneath the more obvious and superficial desires.

Deliberate mind: Psychological activities that take place with at least some deliberation and awareness by the individual. Conventionally called "the conscious mind."

Experience Analysis, or E.A.: One key form of thought that uses an individual's ability to learn by deliberately examining specific details. E.A. is the analytical thinking popularly regarded as the only form of thought.

Experience Synthesis, or E.S.: One key form of thought that comes to individuals as feeling. The most reliable and creative form of thought, E.S. is a synthesis of an individual's relevant experience accessed through feelings.

Free Will Paradox: Living daily life as if all present and past events have been caused but future events can be improved by deliberate effort. This principle states that everything in human life is governed by cause and effect but that this paradoxical mindset causes better effects for human beings than viewing future events as determined.

An individual is blameless (and without credit) for the past and present, but responsible for the future. It is the intentional acceptance of paradox as a more rational and effective tool for living.

Fundamental Law of Mind: A natural law that governs all psychological functions: Individuals interpret experience to create the weakest possible emotional resistance to the strongest possible feelings that their existence is valuable to them at this moment in this world.

Fundamental Question: A restatement of the Fundamental Law of Mind, reduced to one essential question that the mind in effect continually attempts to answer in the affirmative: "Is my life worth living?"

Fundamental Value: Unconditional self-value – an individual's profound feeling that their existence is valuable to them at this moment in this world. It is a deep and genuine self-confidence in one's own equal value among all human beings.

Grand trio: The three basic categories of information as perceived and stored in the mind – an individual's interpretations of the world, interpretations of oneself, interpretations of the way the world and oneself fit together.

Identity Failure, or I.F.: An unrecognized but nearly universal psychological disease of sweeping destructive effect on humanity. Identity Failure happens when an individual values a rigid irrational self-image that the world appears to doubt, which in turn creates self-doubt about that identity. More specifically, it is a psychological illness that results from significant emotional resistance to a self-image that contributes significantly to an individual's feelings that their existence is valuable to them at this moment in this world.

Identity pose: An individual's irrational inflexible self-image, a distorted concept regarded by that person with varying degrees of significance as one aspect of their personality. Typically, individuals possess dozens of diverse identity poses. Two other key concepts of psychophysics are closely related.

- **Pose-strengtheners**: The strengthening of specific significant identity poses to compensate for even more significant identity poses that feel threatened with failure through lack of outside

validation.
- **Pose-weakeners**: The weakening of specific significant identity poses to protect even more significant identity poses that feel threatened with failure through lack of outside validation.

Intrasentience: Inner perception, the detailed observation of psychological events within an individual's own mind based to a significant extent on feeling. Distinct from conventional introspection, which psychophysics regards as reflection upon important issues of daily life.

Nexus: A cluster of stored interpretations and emotion arranged by topic within the mind, the combination of many discrete units of experience into larger units of experience that vary greatly in size and stength. Nexes are divided into five categories:

- Micronexus: A fundamental clump of interpreted experience with very little emotion attached to it.
- Mininexus: A small grouping of information without any strong emotion attached.
- Midnexus: A complex collection of information and emotion that doesn't include topics connected with deeply powerful values, beliefs and the like.
- Macronexus: A greatly significant cluster of interpreted experience, with vast amounts of information and vast amounts of emotion.
- Supernexus: The largest, strongest clusters of interpreted experience and emotion, including the deepest values, most powerful beliefs, most meaningful attachments to others.

Primary emotions: Human beings innately possess love, fear and anger as primary emotions, which can be compared to the primary colors of blue, red and yellow. As other colors are combinations of those three colors, an individual's complex feelings start as combinations of love, fear and anger.

Psychogravity: The increasing emotional strength of a connected set of interpretations that advance an individual toward something deepwanted in any situation. Psychogravity is a process, the strengthening emotional pressure that automatically pushes an individual toward a profoundly desired outcome.

Psychophysics: The theory that the human mind functions with discoverable precise laws, principles and forces like any other entity in the universe. Emotional forces are at the core of psychophysics, the relative strength of combined and competing emotions. These emotional forces are quantifiable, with the stronger forces prevailing over the weaker. In psychophysics, all psychological forces are governed by a central mechanism: the Fundamental Law of Mind, which states that the perceived value of one's existence at this moment in this world is central to that individual's psychological function and vital to biological function. Human beings experience the strongest emotional force in favor of whatever feels most necessary at this moment according to the Fundamental Law of Mind. The underlying principle is not survival of the fittest but dominance of the necessary.

Psychosystem: The mind's logic, the automatic attachment of concept to concept because an individual views them as inextricably connected. Psychosystem is a psychological structure, an architecture of the mind.

Quancept: An extremely brief automatic observation by the mind of an instant's most prevalent feelings along with details about an individual's immediate situation, created in frequent succession to provide relevant information for the formation of vericepts.

Rational Faith: Based on the concepts of psychophysics, this philosophy states that psychological realities provide a firm rational basis for constructive daily living. This includes a Fundamental Value that reflects the constant psychological demands of the Fundamental Law of Mind and the Fundamental Question. Rational Faith explains the psychological need for concepts such as compassion, equal human value and self-value. And the philosophy establishes Seven Articles of Rational Faith that include a deep abiding faith in personal experience and in the continuing ascent of humanity.

Repressed rage, three types in order as formed in the mind:
- **World-rage**: An individual's rage directed at other people or at some portion of society or both – blaming others for causing problems.
- **Self-rage**: An individual's rage at herself or himself – blaming

oneself for causing problems.
- **Life-rage**: An individual's rage at some power beyond oneself – blaming life, the universe or god for causing problems.

Tigertail: An individual's intense irrational desire to satisfy some deepwanted values that feel profoundly threatened by circumstances. The fear of violating these values fuels self-destructive repetition such as obsessive thoughts and feelings or compulsive behavior.

Vericept: The mind's automatic conversion of interpreted experience into accepted reality, created and stored as discrete units that include both information and emotion. Vericepts combine to form nexes. Vericepts are divided into two categories:

- **Irvericept**: An irrational interpretation of experience based on distorted values and beliefs, superficial preferences, emotional judgments, ignorance, etc. Irvericepts will not withstand critical scrutiny.
- **Ravericepts**: A rational interpretation of experience based on deep values and beliefs, genuine preferences, clear judgments, knowledge, etc. Ravericepts will withstand critical scrutiny.

About The Author

Robert Spencer Knotts is the author of 24 previous published books, most of these for young readers and written under the name Bob Knotts or a pseudonym. He also has written five plays, numerous poems, fables, blogs, lyrics and other literary works. In addition, Knotts is a lifelong musician who has composed more than 100 compositions including "A Symphony of Some Humanity - Symphony #1 for Strings and Choir" and "All, In Joyful Song - A Carol In Three Movements."

In 2005, he founded the 501(c)3 nonprofit organization, the Humanity Project, and still serves as the group's president and primary program creator. Based in South Florida, the Humanity Project teaches respect for the unconditional equal value of every human being. Three core concepts form the foundation of every Humanity Project program: respect for all, the importance of diversity and the need for self-worth. www.thehumanityproject.com

Knotts is among fewer than 50,000 Americans whose biography is included in the Marquis "Who's Who In America" and "Who's Who in the World," the standard biographical references.

www.rsknotts.com

www.ingramcontent.com/pod-product-compliance
Lightning Source LLC
Chambersburg PA
CBHW020348080526
44584CB00014B/927